Spahn, Sain, and Teddy Ballgame

BOSTON'S (almost) PERFECT BASEBALL SUMMER OF 1948

Edited by Bill Nowlin

ASSOCIATE EDITORS
Mark Armour, Bob Brady, Len Levin, and Saul Wisnia

an imprint of
Rounder Records Corp.
One Rounder Way
Burlington, MA 01803

ISBN-13: 978-1-57940-160-3
ISBN-10: 1-57940-160-0

Edited by Bill Nowlin.
Associate editors: Mark Armour, Bob Brady, Len Levin, Saul Wisnia

Spahn, Sain, and Teddy Ballgame: Boston's (almost) Perfect Baseball Summer of 1948
1. Boston Red Sox (baseball team) 2. Boston Braves (baseball team) 3. 1948 baseball season 4. Biography
I. Nowlin, Bill.

First edition

Library of Congress Control Number: 2008928975
796.357'092

Interior design and composition by Jane Tenenbaum
Cover design by Rachael Sullivan

Contents

Acknowledgments

Boston was blessed to have two great teams in the summer of 1948. Only one loss prevented the Red Sox and Braves from facing off against each other in that year's World Series. As events unfolded, neither team ended up with the championship but both teams had very good seasons.

This book about the summer of '48 grew out of a project of the Boston chapter of the Society for American Baseball Research (SABR). Chapter member David Southwick conceived of a publication to honor the 30th anniversary of the 1975 Boston Red Sox team that won the American League pennant and took the quest for a world championship to the seventh game of the 1975 World Series. That work was published by Rounder Books as '75: The Red Sox Team That Saved Baseball. It was edited by Bill Nowlin and Cecilia Tan. In 2007, Rounder published The 1967 Impossible Dream Red Sox: Pandemonium on the Field (edited by Bill Nowlin and Dan Desrochers), a book that drew on the collective efforts of more than 60 members of SABR, as well as contributions of photography from the Boston Herald and the Boston Red Sox and numerous others. And earlier in 2008, we published When Boston Still Had the Babe: The 1918 World Series Champion Red Sox, the work of an even 30 SABR members who contributed a biography or editing work, as well as many other SABR members who helped out in one way or another.

This book includes biographies of every player on the 1948 Boston Braves and every player on the 1948 Boston Red Sox.

Future volumes in the series are in production, with the next intended to be a book on the 1939 Red Sox.

Additional thanks are due to the Boston Red Sox for the use of numerous photographs throughout the book, and to Bob Brady for access to his extensive collection of Braves photographs and memorabilia.

All Braves images, and the image of Jim Britt, are courtesy of Bob Brady, except the photograph of Marv Rickert on page 109, which is courtesy of Jonathan Fine.

All Red Sox images are courtesy of the Boston Red Sox, except as noted.

Trolley photographs on page 15 and page 189 are by an unknown photographer, courtesy John F Bromley Archives.

Special thanks to:
Mary Brace of George Brace Photos
Bob Brady
John F. Bromley
Warren Corbett
Denise Holman
Sean Holtz and baseball-almanac.com
Mike Ivins, Boston Red Sox
Terry Kitchen
John Klima
Luke Kraemer
Debbie Matson, Boston Red Sox
Ray Nemec
Steve Netsky

The Greatest Summer

—Mark Armour

Although it might come as a surprise to more casual fans, the city of Boston has a long history of baseball success, starting with the very early days of the national pastime. The Boston Red Stockings, who later became the Braves, won 13 championships in 30 years in the 19th century. With the coming of the American League in 1901, the two Boston teams won six of the first 15 World Series. By 1948 it had been 30 years since a title flag was raised in Boston, but a big part of each club's fan base likely remembered their team winning a championship.

As the 1948 baseball season dawned, the fans of Boston had every reason to be optimistic about the year ahead. Both teams had finished in third place in 1947 but had substantially fortified themselves in the offseason. The Braves, whose third place showing was their best since 1916, added slugger Jeff Heath and All-Star second baseman Eddie Stanky to their lineup. The Red Sox, whose 1947 was a disappointment after taking the World Series to the final game in 1946, brought in standouts Vern Stephens, Stan Spence, Jack Kramer, and Ellis Kinder to a team already filled with stars. Both teams were not shy about outspending their rivals to get the best players.

Baseball was experiencing a renaissance of popularity after the Second World War, and nowhere more so than in Boston. Both local clubs set all-time team attendance records in 1946, and each club broke those marks in 1947, and again in 1948. Although the 1910s were the glory days of Boston baseball on the field, with each team winning championships, the late 1940s represent the heyday of the game as a central experience in people's lives. The first time the Red Sox and Braves combined to draw 1,000,000 fans to their games was in 1942. In 1948, just six years later, slightly more than 3,000,000 fans saw major league baseball in Boston. (This record has never been broken, though recent increases in the capacity of Fenway Park make it likely that it will be soon.) These 3,000,000 fans spent their afternoons at two classic ballparks that were located about 1¼ miles apart, just a 20-minute walk down Commonwealth and Brookline.

These fans saw a lot of great baseball—the brilliant pitching of Johnny Sain and Warren Spahn at Braves Field, and the slugging of Ted Williams and Vern Stephens at Fenway Park. You could take the trolley to see Dom DiMaggio and Bobby Doerr on Sunday, and then go back on Wednesday to see Alvin Dark and Eddie Stanky. All these great players, managed by the two most respected managers in the game—Joe McCarthy and Billy Southworth, both Hall of Famers—nearly every single day of the summer. To say nothing of seeing all of the visiting players—the best players in each league just a short subway ride away.

The Braves led the league all summer, held off a big Dodgers charge in early September and then pulled away to win by 6½. The Red Sox started terribly, did not reach .500 until late June, but got to first place a month later. They then took part in the greatest three-team pennant race in league history, three outstanding teams going to the final weekend, the Red Sox beating the Yankees twice to force a playoff game with the Indians. The Indians beat the Red Sox in the playoff, and the Braves in the World Series, two annoyances that could not erase what was otherwise a wonderful season in the Hub.

Sadly, it did not last. The Braves could almost equal the Red Sox attendance when they were winning the pennant, but could not really compete otherwise. Internal conflicts and dissension contributed to their fall from contention the next season, and fans soon began staying away. By 1953, the Braves were in Milwaukee.

But let us not dwell on that here.

This book is a celebration of the 1948 season, when the fans of Boston saw more great baseball games than any other city in America. The bulk of the book tells the stories of the men who played on these two great teams. In these pages you can relive, or learn for the first time, about Earl Torgeson, and Mel Parnell, and Sibby Sisti, of Junior, and Spahnie, and The Greatest Hitter Who Ever Lived.

So, pull up a chair, grab a 'Gansett, and relive Boston's greatest baseball summer.

Boston's 1948 Opening Days

by Bob Brady

Boston's baseball citizenry eagerly anticipated the start of the 1948 season. Dedicated followers of the National League Braves and the American League Red Sox were excited by the distinct possibility that the two teams would, for the first time, win their respective circuits and settle old scores in an all-Hub World Series. There had been same-city fall classic matchups between AL and NL teams in Chicago, New York, and St. Louis, but never in the "Athens of America." The city was primed and optimistic.

The Braves had finished third in 1947, going 86–68 under manager Billy Southworth and attracting a club-record 1,277,361 fans to cavernous Braves Field. The last time that the Tribe had reached so lofty a perch in the standings was way back in 1916. Since Southworth's reign began in 1946, the Tribe had been creeping up in the Senior Circuit's first division. The time appeared ripe for a run at the pennant, which had eluded Boston's NL fans since the "Miracle Braves" went from last place in July to a World Series championship in 1914.

In contrast, the Red Sox had disappointed their followers in 1947, dropping from the previous season's 104–50 first-place finish and near-miss World Series down to third, reflecting a 21-game slide in the win column. Still, they continued their supremacy at the turnstile, similarly setting an attendance record by drawing 1,427,315 folks into the cozy confines of Fenway Park. Fan interest for '48 was piqued by changes made during the offseason. Manager Joe Cronin ended his 13-year tenure at the helm of the club, moving upstairs into the front office. However, his chosen replacement was a proven winner. "Marse Joe" McCarthy, ex-Cubs and Yankees skipper, came to Boston with a managerial portfolio that included nine first-place finishes and seven world championships. Folks were hopeful that he'd bring his Midas touch with him to Fenway Park. He certainly had plenty of material to work with; when the impoverished St. Louis Browns held a late-fall 1947 fire sale, Sox owner Tom Yawkey replenished the Bosox ranks with the likes of Vern Stephens, Jack Kramer, and Ellis Kinder, stoking further feelings of euphoria.

Prognosticators supported fandom's feelings. Pre-season odds-makers required a six-dollar wager to win five dollars for a first-place Red Sox or Yankees finish. In comparison, Cleveland was regarded as a 20:1 shot. Over in the National League, the Cardinals were favored by gamblers at 8:5 with the Braves following at 2:1. A poll of the membership of the Baseball Writers' Association of America by *The Sporting News* envisioned a Braves-Yankees World Series in 1948.[1] The 238 members that voted predicted two-team races in each circuit. The Tribe received an unexpectedly strong showing of support, with 43% of the scribes placing the club first on their ballots and only 32% voting in support of the Cards. Exactly 50% of those polled forecast a repeat pennant for the Yankees, while 45% prophesized a return to the top by the Red Sox. Even a non-baseball periodical got into the act. The April 26, 1948 issue of *Newsweek* featured front cover color photos of Joe McCarthy and Billy Southworth with an accompanying story on the high expectations for Boston's home teams.

The road to Opening Day began in Florida. The Braves returned that February to their pre-war Sunshine State residence in Bradenton, after a two-year stint in Ft. Lauderdale. The Red Sox, meanwhile, encamped in Sarasota, their spring training home since 1933 with the exception of a wartime-driven relocation to northern locales in 1943–45. While the Red Sox had grabbed the Hot Stove headlines with their offseason player transactions, the Braves drew their own fair share of media attention after a March 6 deal with the Dodgers for second baseman/sparkplug Eddie Stanky.

Boston baseball scribes were quick to notice the dramatically differing training regimens established by the respective clubs' high-salaried skippers. Veteran writer Harold Kaese of the *Boston Globe* even had a title for each: Southworth's "Metronomic" system versus McCarthy's "Magic-Eye" system. According to Kaese, "whereas Southworth uses a stop watch and slide rule, McCarthy relies on instinct and judgment."[2] The Braves were broken up into squads that followed a timed practice schedule that formally commenced in the early morning hours and lasted until 4 p.m. Southworth observed his squads with a chart in hand to record pertinent data. An 11:30 p.m. curfew, a half-hour earlier than the regular season, was also instituted. According to Southworth, "[Bradenton] is a quiet town and there's no reason for anybody to be out any later."[3]

Joe McCarthy, in steep contrast, assembled his club at 11 AM and usually wrapped up practice by one o'clock. Unlike Southworth, Marse Joe casually roamed his facilities as his men practiced, leaving the players to individually meet his expectations. Ted Williams was a strong supporter of McCarthy's system. "For the first time in my career I haven't been handicapped by sore legs and a sore throwing arm. The way Joe plans our different chores, you don't have to overdo anything to the extent you pull up lame or have a sore arm. I feel so good I can't help but think I'm in for a big season."[4]

Back in Boston, Hall of Famer Ty Cobb was taken ill on a train while en route to the Hub from California. At New England Baptist Hospital on March 23, the Georgia Peach, who was keeping close tabs on spring training happenings, couldn't resist offering advice to the Splendid Splinter. "Learn to hit to left field," one baseball legend counseled the other. In reflecting on the "Williams shift" in which teams placed all four infielders near or to the right of second base, Cobb opined, "If they ever insulted me in that fashion, I'd switch from the left to the right side of the batters' box, get away from the plate and push the enemy back into their natural fielding stations."[5] From Sarasota Williams responded by predicting that Cleveland manager Lou Boudreau's strategy was on its last legs, as he intended to hit more often to left field in 1948 and break up the concentration of defense on the right side of the diamond.[6]

Baseball's emerging labor-management strife also reared its head in Boston while the teams were down South preparing for the regular season. Acting on behalf of unnamed players, local labor activist and union organizer Robert Murphy presented a bill to the Massachusetts legislature proposing the banning of the reserve clause that bound a player by contract to one club until said club traded or released him. A committee on labor and industry effectively killed the proposal, reporting it out negatively on March 23 after taking testimony, purportedly on behalf of the players, from the likes of Red Sox coach Johnny Murphy, who contended that the subject provision was a "protection for the game."[7]

After a one-year hiatus from playing each other, the Braves and Red Sox squared off twice in Florida. The 1948 rivalry commenced in Bradenton on March 31, with the Tribe defeating the Crimson Hose, 4–1. The Red Sox reciprocated on April 4 in Sarasota, handing the Braves a 3–1 defeat. After completing their southern stay, both clubs headed north and wrapped up their pre-season with a traditional "City Series" set of exhibition games at their respective ballparks.

Baseball in Boston "opened" on April 16 at the Wigwam before 12,630 spectators. The home-team Braves were routed by the potent line-up of their neighbors, 19–6, with the visiting Red Sox tallying in every inning but the sixth. Last season's 21-game winner, Johnny Sain, was driven from the mound in less than two innings by a relentless Bosox barrage that would ultimately result in 24 Red Sox hits, good for 35 total bases. The Braves humiliation was compounded by poor play on the field that resulted in five errors. There was plenty of excitement for a one-sided contest, however. Fans were treated to Ted Williams' first pre-season homer for the visitors, a 420-foot drive over the wall in dead center field. Last

season's Triple Crown king, Williams had only appeared in 10 of his team's 30 exhibitions due to an appendicitis scare. The game was also enlivened by a fourth-inning donnybrook between the Tribe's fiery first baseman Earl Torgeson and Red Sox utilityman Billy Hitchcock. Renewing a feud that had begun in Sarasota, the two tangled in a botched play at first as Hitchcock was running out a hit. Fists flew, and both benches cleared. Once calm was restored, the respective combatants were banished from the scene.

The City Series resumed at Fenway Park for two more games over the next couple of days. Despite the smaller locale, 16,341 showed up to view another chapter of the rivalry on April 17. While the Red Sox continued their mastery over the Braves in this contest, the 2–1 result more accurately reflected the competitive balance between the Hub's Junior and Senior Circuit entries. The game wasn't decided until the last of the ninth when Johnny Pesky clubbed a long drive to right with the bases loaded to plate the victorious run. Although the Red Sox had thus clinched the three-game City Series, even more fans turned out for the pre-season finale the following day—26,663 individuals passing through Fenway's portals to witness a Tribe 3–2 victory. All runs were scored in the third inning, and future Hall of Famer Warren Spahn recorded a complete game win. After the game, the Red Sox commenced to ready Fenway Park for the official season inaugural while the Braves left for Philadelphia and an opener with the Phillies.

Later in the season, a bit of doggerel would immortalize the down-the-stretch performances of Braves' pitchers Warren Spahn and Johnny Sain and include a plea for precipitation. However, even before the first pitch of the season was thrown, both clubs were greeted by an almost prophetic verse appearing within a newspaper advertisement by The First National Bank of Boston (since consumed by the Bank of America behemoth).

> *Here's to the Sox*
> *And here's to the Braves,*
> *An April wish that's hearty,*
> *Good luck along the pennant trail*
> *To Southworth and McCarthy!*
> *And when September rolls around,*
> *Imagine this…Oh brother!*
> *One pennant flies at Fenway Park.*
> *Above Braves Field, the other!*

The Kenmore Square station of the Metropolitan Transit Authority was very busy on April 19. Not only was it disgorging passengers on their way to the Bosox home opener at Fenway, but also those coming to view the 52nd running of the Boston Marathon, annually held on the anniversary of the Revolutionary War battles of Lexington and Concord. The huge "Cities Service" sign, constructed by a gasoline company in 1940 and sitting atop an adjacent building, caught the eye of those emerging from the subterranean subway stop. The iconic billboard now reflects the change in the company's name to CITGO and has attained registered historic landmark status.

Over 56,000 fans poured into Fenway Park for the season's inaugural festivities. No, the Red Sox didn't egregiously violate the city's fire laws in housing such a crowd in their bandbox of a ballpark. Back then, the Hub traditionally celebrated Patriots' Day with a baseball doubleheader designed to accommodate those interested in the National Pastime as well as marathon running. Morning and afternoon contests at Fenway were built around the famed road race—which passed down Beacon Street just a block from the ballpark enroute to its finish about a mile away.[8] Those unable to attend the baseball portion of these festivities could listen to broadcaster Jim Britt's description of the games over the radio on WHDH-AM, "850 on your dial."

Early arriving fans to the first game were entertained by Jimmy Coughlin's Band, a combo that furnished music at such revelries in prior years. New Sox skipper Joe McCarthy shared the media spotlight with 85-year-old Hall of Famer Connie Mack, beginning his 48th year managing the Athletics. McCarthy thought highly of Mack and had an inscribed photograph of "Mr. Mack" hanging in the trophy room of his home. The Grand Old Man of Baseball was easy to spot—as always, he wore his trademark suit and hat rather than a uniform—and received a very cordial reception from the spectators in the stands. Five minutes before the 10:15 AM starting time, two bands and a squad of Marines marched to the left-center-field corner flagpole for the raising of Old Glory as both the Red Sox and A's stood at attention on the first and third base foul lines. Robert F. Bradford, the 59th governor of the Commonwealth of Massachusetts, was given the honor of throwing out the first pitch. The single-term Republican, accompanied by his young sons attired in Red Sox caps, threw the ball to Sox catcher Birdie Tebbetts as the band played the theme song of the Royal Rooters, "Tessie," in the background.

The Red Sox got off to an auspicious start in the second inning when Stan Spence, Vern Stephens, and Bobby Doerr clouted successive bases-empty home runs off of Philly starter Phil Marchildon. It was the 22nd time in major league history that the three-in-a-row feat had been accomplished. It hadn't taken long for the Bosox to exhibit the potency of their lineup, which had drawn so much preseason newspaper ink. Unfortunately, Sox bats went cold for the next eight innings, while Marchildon hit his stride—pitching 10 scoreless frames while his teammates clawed back to tie Boston and send the game into extra innings. Marchildon, who hailed from Penetanguishine, Ontario, was used to coming back from adversity, having been shot down on his 26th mission while serving as a gunner on a Halifax bomber with the Royal Canadian Air Force and enduring maltreatment in a Nazi POW camp for nearly a year. He ultimately garnered a complete game win when the Athletics scored two runs off of Red Sox reliever Joe Dobson in the top of the 11th, and Dobson's mates were only able to scrape up one run in the bottom half of the inning. It was Marchildon's second straight season opener triumph. The 22,409 in attendance witnessed the 5–4 affair over the course of two hours and 51 minutes.

Ironically, another Canadian claimed the spotlight during the recess in baseball action. Gérard Côté, a 34-year-old Quebec special policeman, finished the 26 mile, 385 yard marathon route from Hopkinton in two hours, thirty-one minutes, and two seconds. He crossed the finish line at Exeter Street in the Back Bay, 250 yards ahead of his nearest competition. It was the fourth time since 1940 that the French-Canadian led the pack;[9] when Côté crossed the finish line, he gestured to a bystanding bartender employed at his hotel to get him a beer and later lit up a victory cigar. An estimated 500,000 spectators had lined the course from start to finish.

Attendance for the day's second game at Fenway Park swelled to 33,875. Before the 3:15 p.m. start, Vaughn Monroe's "Moon Maids" serenaded the crowd from atop the Red Sox dugout. The female vocal group was named after the big band leader and baritone crooner's 1941 signature hit, "Racing with the Moon."[10] The pre-game pleasantries were disturbed by the roar of a jet plane that buzzed the field and startled many in attendance.

Apropos of the Patriots' Day theme, another of Connie Mack's war hero hurlers was featured in the afternoon tilt. Portsider Lou Brissie had nearly lost his left leg after being hit with shrapnel from an artillery shell that killed his Fifth Army squad of comrades in Italy. Twenty-three operations were required to repair the leg, and Brissie needed to use a steel brace and shin guard when pitching. McCarthy countered with Denny Galehouse; Marse Joe's questionable selection of this same hurler at the conclusion of the season would secure a spot for both in Red Sox infamy.

Brissie, achieving his first big league victory, held the powerful Bosox to four hits and two runs in a 4–2 win. However, the last of the hits, a sixth-inning line drive by Ted Williams that smashed off of Brissie's bad leg into right field, stunned the crowd into silence. The valiant pitcher collapsed in agony on the mound. Fellow WWII veteran Williams kicked the first base bag in disgust at what he'd done as Brissie writhed in pain. After several minutes of treatment, Brissie gamely retook the hill to finish what he'd started. In the ninth, the crowd waited with baited breath as Williams returned to face Brissie. This time, Teddy Ballgame went down—swinging futilely at a Brissie curveball for strike three. All told Brissie faced 11 batters after the blow to his leg and retired 10 of them, yielding only a base on balls to Dom DiMaggio.

After the game, Brissie was sent to Faulkner Hospital

for X-rays, but fortunately the encounter resulted only in a severe bruise. Years later, the pitcher recounted the incident. "After Ted got to first base, he came over to the mound and expressed concern. I said, 'Ted, why don't you learn to pull the ball?' Later in the season he hit a home run off me in Philadelphia. As he was rounding the bases he yelled, 'Did I pull that one far enough?'"[11] At the end of a long and emotional day, Connie Mack congratulated rookie Brissie on his courageous performance. Mack related, "My eyes were moist. I could not help myself."[12]

The weather of the day was symbolic of the feelings of Red Sox fans. It began with bright sunshine but ended in a drizzle. After being swept by the Athletics, the Sox wouldn't garner their first win until venturing to Yankee Stadium and defeating the New Yorkers 4–0 on April 23 before Babe Ruth and a crowd of 44,619 at the Bronx Bombers' inaugural. In Philadelphia, the Braves weren't doing much better. The Phillies took the first two games of the season with the Tribe salvaging the road trip with a 10–4 triumph on April 22 before returning to Boston and their belated home opener.

The Braves joined a number of other clubs that had debuted on the road and that were conducting a "secondary" round of home openers on April 23. Braves Field was decked out in red, white, and blue bunting to greet the 11,553 hardy fans who entered on this chilly spring day. Many were delivered to the festivities via orange and cream colored MTA trolleys, dubbed "cattle cars" by the ridership, that turned off Commonwealth Avenue onto a spur that led directly into the ballpark. The Wigwam's groomed field presented a fine appearance despite adverse weather conditions. The attention of many patrons was drawn to the new Tribal "Sky View" seats, constructed on top of the grandstand roof. Hank Gowdy, former Braves catching great and a member of the club's last pennant winner in 1914, returned to the scene of past glories as a member of the visiting Giants coaching staff.

Unlike those of their Red Sox neighbors, the Braves' opening ceremonies were relatively simple. The Pat Sands Orchestra provided a musical interlude, competing with the infamous Troubadours, or the "Three Little Earaches" as they were affectionately known. This trio of mirthmakers would play ditties that related to some aspect of a particular Brave or visiting player. Foes often would be on the receiving end of tunes conveying a not-too-subtle sarcastic message. The Troubadours had been chastised in the past for occasionally crossing the line of good taste. Their most notorious incident occurred when the group played "Three Blind Mice" as an umpiring crew took the field. The Troubadours' special treat for this day was a rendition of "Happy Birthday" to Braves starter Warren Spahn, who was turning 27.

As starting time approached, a band of Marines marched to right-center field for the traditional flag raising ceremony. Reinforcing the perception of their lesser status in Boston, the Braves were provided with a "pinch heaver" for Governor Bradford. Lieutenant Governor Arthur W. Coolidge, also a one-term Republican, stepped in to deliver the ceremonial first pitch while club president Lou Perini looked on.

Boston's victory-famished populace wouldn't be satisfied today. The Giants scored all the runs they would need in the first inning against last season's 21-game winning ace. Uncharacteristically, Spahnie set up the opposition's two-run inning through walks that were followed by base hits. New York finished its scoring with a single tally via a Sid Gordon homer to left in the third, and Braves bats remained cold until the bottom of the sixth when Danny Litwhiler drove home Earl Torgeson. Giants starter and complete game winner Ray Poat snuffed out a potential rally in the ninth to claim his initial victory of the '48 campaign. This allowed New York to match its 1947 victory total against Spahn, when the Ottmen had only been able to beat the star lefty once in six attempts. The Braves were not alone in disappointing their fans, however; every other major league team making a belated home opening on April 23 went down in defeat.

The Giants wound up sweeping the three-game series, outscoring the Braves overall, 31–12. Hub fandom would not witness a win on home turf by either of its teams until April 26, when the Tribe whitewashed the Dodgers, 5–0. The Red Sox's Fenway Park victory drought would end on May 1, when they triumphed over the archrival Yankees 8–6.

In contrast to the discomfort endured by the chilly crowd at Braves Field, several hundred Hub baseball followers had been invited to partake of the Red Sox—Yankees contest while comfortably seated in a room at the Parker House hotel. The site was chosen for the first local television presentation of a ballgame in Boston. This event was sponsored by the Atlantic Television Corporation and was provided through a relay from New York television station WABD (named after Albert B. DuMont, founder of the DuMont Television Network). In attendance were Sox owners Tom and Jean Yawkey, along with team general manager Joe Cronin. Both the Red Sox and the Braves had been studying the possibility of granting television broadcasting rights to home games, and had to be impressed with this display. Reception proved to be very clear, and the spectators were able to follow the batted ball and the game's goings-on. Although regular broadcasts were still a year or two away, further experimentation would take place during the post season when a number of television sets were set up on Boston Common for fan World Series viewing.

The first blush of the 1948 season failed to meet lofty expectations held for either club. Their performances were nearly identical in their futility—the Red Sox winning only one of their first six games while the Braves tallied but a single victory out of their initial seven contests.

Early despair would evaporate, however, and optimism would be restored as both teams shortly commenced to play up to expectations and rise up the standings. The Braves would eventually post 91 victories to capture the National League flag for the first time in 34 years. But despite accumulating five more wins than their hometown National League counterparts, the Red Sox would come to regret their early season missteps as those losses helped set the stage for a full-season tie with the Cleveland Indians and a disastrous one-game playoff that would forever slam the door on an all-Boston World Series.

Notes

1. *The Sporting News*, April 21, 1948, p. 1.
2. *The Sporting News*, March 17, 1948, p.7
3. *Ibid.*
4. *Ibid.* at p.22.
5. *The Sporting News*, March 31, 1948, p.26.
6. *The Sporting News*, April 7, 1948, p. 29.
7. *The Sporting News*, March 31, 1948, p. 25.
8. Boston was truly the hub of the sports universe on April 19. In addition to the crowds attracted to the ballgame and the Marathon, nearly 38,000 individuals made their way to the opening of the horseracing season at Suffolk Downs, constituting the largest throng to ever attend that event.
9. He also won in 1943 and 1944.
10. Monroe has another link to the Red Sox. On his "opening" date with his future wife Emily, Dom DiMaggio took her to a local dinner-dance club where Vaughn Monroe was performing. Dom and Emily were dancing to "Racing with the Moon" when Monroe spotted The Little Professor and promptly switched to "Take Me Out to the Ball Game." When Emily asked if such things frequently happened to him, DiMaggio modestly nodded in the affirmative. The two married on October 11, 1948. Halberstam, *The Teammates*, p. 133.
11. Marazzi and Fiorito, *Baseball Players of the 1950s*, p. 46.
12. *The Sporting News*, April 28, 1948, p. 14.

The 1948 Boston Braves

JOHNNY ANTONELLI *by Alex Edelman*

G	ERA	W	L	SV	GS	GF	CG	SHO	IP	H	R	ER	BB	SO	HR	HBP	WP	BFP
4	2.25	0	0	1	0	4	0	0	4	2	1	1	3	0	0	0	0	17

G	AB	R	H	2B	3B	HR	RBI	BB	SO	BA	OBP	SLG	SB	HBP
0	0	0	0	0	0	0	0	0	0	0	0	0	0	0

Johnny Antonelli, somewhat unfairly, is remembered by the incidents he was part of, instead of as an individual who had an impressive pitching career. Labels abound and, of the memories attached to them, controversies.

He was, in the minds of many, a "bonus baby" who never paid his dues in the minors. A player on a National League championship club who was not voted a World Series share by his Braves teammates. A rarely used pitcher for Boston who had the gall to make more money than Warren Spahn. A relative unknown who was traded for October heroes and former batting champs. A malcontent, who at a certain point was one of the most despised players in San Francisco Giants history. A southpaw who, rather than play for an expansion team, chose to retire from baseball for good.

It would be wrong, however, to remember Antonelli in this fashion. He was a good southpaw whose pitching was masterful when he was healthy and brilliant when he was at ease. He wasn't perfect, but the decisions he and his family made—especially the decision to take a boatload of Lou Perini's money—are no different than those most any teenager with big league dreams and strong self-confidence would have undertaken.

John August "Johnny" Antonelli was born on April 12, 1930, in Rochester, New York, to Augustino "Gus" Antonelli and Josephina Messore. From Johnny's first year at Rochester's Jefferson High School, where he was a three-sport star (basketball, football, and baseball), he attracted major-league publicity and major-league scouts. Johnny's father, Gus, a railroad construction contractor who had immigrated to the United States from Abruzzi, Italy, in 1913, was actively involved in nurturing and promoting his son's baseball career. Johnny remembers that his father would "go down to spring training every year, and bring along my scrapbook and brag about me."[1] The scrapbook Johnny refers to was a bulging tome, filled with newspaper clippings and pictures of the young Antonelli from his high school years. Occasionally, great ballplayers like Joe Cronin, Bobby Feller, and Leo Durocher were invited by the elder Antonelli to come to Rochester to take a look at both the scrapbook[2] and the loping curve that Johnny had developed in the semipro Vermont Hotel League in 1947.[3]

During those high school years, Johnny played baseball under coach Charley O'Brien, who converted him from a freshman first baseman to a pitcher (despite the teenager's protests). Watching his son develop rapidly as a sophomore and junior hurler and fearing he might hurt his arm, Johnny's father made him quit football and focus on baseball full time.[4] The teenager threw three no-hitters and drew praise from scouts like Hall of Famer Carl Hubbell, who said that Antonelli had the best all-around stuff he had ever seen.

Gus began to see that his son might be a major leaguer in the making and eventually began taking him to spring training, where Johnny "talked and observed, but mostly…listened and absorbed all he could about talent and procedure."[5] After Johnny graduated from high school in 1949, Gus wrote to a number of ballclubs and then rented out Silver Stadium, home of the International League Rochester Red Wings, to showcase Johnny to the scouts. Nine scouts and 7,000 fans came, and the youngster did not disappoint, as Antonelli struck out 17 batters against a "strong semipro club" on his way to a no-hitter.[6]

Scouts were enthralled. The Braves, Red Sox, Yankees, Giants, Indians, Tigers, Cardinals, Pirates, and Reds were all interested. Braves scout Jeff Jones called Lou Perini, the club president, to come as quickly as possible. "He's by far the best big-league prospect I've ever seen," exclaimed the excited Jones. "He has the poise of a major league pitcher right now and has a curve and fastball to back it up. I think so much of this kid's chances that if I had to pay out the money myself, I wouldn't hesitate to do it—if I had the money."[7] Jones didn't have that kind of money, but Perini did, and he got the youngster under contract on June 2, 1948, by giving him an amount reported in excess of $50,000, the largest bonus in baseball history at the time. Johnny has never stated the figure, but indicates that the figures reported in the press were often inflated.

Everyone knew that Gus Antonelli was involved and interested in his son's future. With the ever-expanding scrapbook, the handwritten letters to scouts, and the staged exhibition games, one could argue that Gus was a bit of an overbearing father, one of those hard-driving Little League dads whom we might click our tongue at today. But the younger Antonelli had aspired to be a major-league player since he was 12 years old and eagerly and dutifully took his father's counsel. It paid off with the huge bonus, which under the rules required the Braves to put Antonelli on their major league roster, immediately fulfilling the youngster's dream.

Was there resentment from other Braves players? Almost certainly. Johnny Sain, the team's gentlemanly, mild-mannered ace, made $21,000—considerably less than Antonelli's bonus—and was so upset about the discrepancy between him (a 20-game winner) and Antonelli (with nary a big league appearance) that he threatened to walk out on his contract. "I meant it," Sain said later on, "I was going to walk away from the whole thing."[8] The club soothed the anger of its star pitcher by giving him a new contract worth $30,000 just before the All-Star break. Antonelli insists today that there wasn't as much tension with his teammates as the press would have had one believe—that it was actually a good thing for the other players, who used his high paycheck as leverage in salary disputes with Perini.

But the Braves were in the middle of a pennant race and, according to major league rules, the size of Antonelli's bonus required them to keep him on the major-league roster for at least two years. Consequently, Antonelli sat on the bench for months, an untried teenager with no experience under pressure, simply taking up valuable space on a club that was clawing its way in pursuit of its first National League pennant in 34 years.

The circumstances of his presence on the club sent shock waves throughout the league, and players, writers, and managers weighed in with opinions and speculation. Walker Cooper of the Giants said Antonelli should "...take the 75 gees and call it a career right now." Jeff Heath, one of Antonelli's teammates, reminisced about the days when his roommate, Bob Feller, was given a few thousand dollars so Feller's father could put an addition on the barn—and it was a big deal![9] Mel Ott, the Giants' Hall of Famer, recalled that for his signing bonus, he received $400 from John McGraw, but was kind enough to say that a "dollar went further" back then. But kind and supportive remarks were few and far between. Whatever the sentiments, Antonelli would battle against the "bonus baby" tag for years to come.

Johnny pitched only four innings during Boston's historic 1948 sprint to the championship. He finished the season with a 2.25 ERA and a 0–0 record, although he got plenty of pregame activity. While manager Billy Southworth wasn't willing to risk Antonelli giving away any ballgames, he wasn't opposed to getting a little out of his bonus baby. So five days a week, Southworth put him to work throwing batting practice for half an hour each day.

Looking back, Antonelli says he bore a lot of disrespect

Teenage bonus baby Johnny Antonelli strikes a pitching pose on a penny arcade Exhibit Card.

from his bosses and colleagues. Johnny should have been eligible for the World Series, but his spot was instead given to first baseman Ray Sanders, technically ineligible but allowed to play by the league and team anyway out of respect for an injury he had recovered from. When the players divided World Series shares, Antonelli didn't get a dime (while the batboys each made $380.89). That slight did steam up Antonelli, who said that though he understood Southworth's decision not to use him during the stretch run, the fact that he had pitched batting practice each day without complaint should have warranted at least a little of the World Series money. The situation was eventually remedied by the league and Commissioner Happy Chandler, who stepped in and conferred upon him one-eighth of a share, about $571.34.

In the winter of 1948, though ineligible for collegiate baseball, Johnny enrolled at Bowling Green University, following his brother Anthony, a junior quarterback for the school. He majored in voice and was active in the choir, causing Oscar Ruhl of *The Sporting News* to remark that Antonelli would be the second "songbird" on the Braves, joining teammate Red Barrett.

The next season, 1949, was a bit better for Antonelli, but more difficult for the Braves. While Johnny pitched 96 innings with a 3–7 record and a 3.56 ERA, the Braves slipped to fourth place. In one of those wins, a 4–2 win over the Giants on May 1, Antonelli pitched excellently, showing his true potential and startling both teammates and opponents. Even umpire Artie Gore said there was something different about the way Antonelli presented himself on the mound; he marveled at Antonelli's remarkable confidence in his pitching prowess, and the fact that he was self-assured enough to throw curves "when some pitchers wouldn't dare."[10]

But it was to be the one of the last flashes of brilliance Antonelli had the chance to exhibit with the Braves. In 1950 aces Vern Bickford, Johnny Sain, and Warren Spahn kept the team competitive until late August, and when the season was over those three had accounted for 60 of the team's 86 wins. Antonelli himself only pitched 58 innings, going 2–3 while his ERA rose to 5.93. The youngster started only six games, and shared the role of fourth starting pitcher with several other players.

In March of 1951, with little fanfare in the Boston sports pages, Antonelli began an active-duty stint of two years with the Army. He spent his time at Fort Myer,

Virginia, where he was once again able to flourish. Antonelli had never spent time in the minor leagues (he is one of only 17 people to have completed his major league career without spending a single day in the minors), but at Fort Myer, pitching for his Army team during 1951 and 1952, Johnny went 42–2. The Fort Myer stint resurrected his career and showed the league what he could do with regular starts. In essence, the Army team was like minor league service for Antonelli, who also found relief in the Army from allergies that had previously not been diagnosed or treated.[11]

By the time Antonelli was discharged in 1953, the Braves had moved from Boston. He found himself a Milwaukee Brave, and when the All-Star Game rolled around, he already had a 9–3 record. Despite his large signing bonus, his salary was only $5,500. After Antonelli became a starter in 1953, general manager John Quinn had given him a raise to $9,000. The young hurler contracted pneumonia, however, and as his strength waned a bit, his record flipped over—turning from a 9–3 first half to a 3–9 second half. Despite Antonelli's relatively strong showing (his 3.18 ERA was good for fifth best in the league), Warren Spahn suggested that three left-handers (himself, Antonelli, and Chet Nichols, a solid young pitcher returning from the Army) would be too many, and that he preferred Nichols over Antonelli. The club listened to its ace. On February 1, 1954, Antonelli was shipped to the New York Giants in a six-player deal along with pitcher Don Liddle, catcher Ebba St. Claire, infielder Billy Klaus, and $50,000 for outfielder Bobby Thomson and catcher Sammy Calderone. It would be, as Antonelli later called it, "the best break of my career."[12]

Bobby Thomson was a hero. On October 3, 1951, he had delivered Giants fans the pennant with his famous "Shot Heard Round the World," a ninth-inning walk-off home run off Ralph Branca of the Brooklyn Dodgers in the deciding game of a three-game playoff series. Though the Giants lost the World Series to the Yankees in six games, Thomson was forever embedded in Giants lore, and losing him to the Braves shocked and dismayed fans. Antonelli, naturally, was less than a fan favorite as the year got underway, but despite that obstacle he had his best year in 1954.

After leading off the season with a decent 5–2 record, Johnny reeled off eight victories in a row before the All-Star Game, to which he was elected for the first time.[13] On May 16, Antonelli faced off with the Braves for the

Even early in his career, Antonelli had a stylish presence on the mound.

first time since his departure from the Milwaukee club. The Giants were quick and plentiful with their run support against their young southpaw's former teammates, beating them soundly, 9–2. On June 9, Johnny had another shot at revenge, facing off against Warren Spahn in Milwaukee. Antonelli drove in one of the runs off Spahn and spun a complete game shutout in a 4–0 victory. The next day's New York Times wrote that "30,018 disconsolate fans looked on in silence."

By October, Antonelli was the number one starter on the team. All season long, he had been relatively consistent in his dominant pitching. He was vitally important to the Giants, and when the team began to falter in late August, losing seven of nine games, Antonelli stood tall with New York's only two victories during that dismal streak. Behind his clutch hurling and offensive support from the likes of Willie Mays, Monte Irvin, and Alvin Dark, the Giants advanced to the World Series against the Cleveland Indians.

In Game One, which Antonelli witnessed from the bench, one of the most memorable plays in World Series history took place. With the score tied at 2–2 and two men on base, Cleveland first baseman Vic Wertz hit a fly ball to the deepest part of the cavernous Polo Grounds centerfield. Antonelli, watching from the dugout, recalls centerfielder Mays pounding his glove, sprinting with his back towards home plate, reaching up, and snaring the ball as it streaked over his shoulder. It would come to be known simply as: "The Catch."

In Game Two, Antonelli started against future Hall of Famer Early Wynn. Johnny had a rocky beginning, giving up a home run to Al Smith on the first pitch of the game, but didn't allow a run the rest of the game. "The Good Lord was on my side that game," Antonelli said years later. "I don't think I had my best stuff that day."[14] But it was good enough to hold the Indians the rest of the way, and give him a win in his first World Series appearance.

After losing Game Three, the Indians, who had gone 111–43 during the regular season, were once again humbled by Antonelli in the fourth contest. Before the game, Leo Durocher, the manager of the Giants, was told by his captain, Alvin Dark, that it was hard for hitters to pick up the ball against lefties because of sun glare off the scoreboard.[15] So when Durocher noticed that reliever Hoyt Wilhelm was faltering in the eighth inning, with the Giants one win away from a World Series championship, the manager turned to his best lefty to close it out—and, dutifully, Antonelli did so, getting the last five outs of the World Series on three strikeouts and two popups. When Indians pinch hitter Dale Mitchell popped out in foul territory, Johnny could celebrate both a World Series victory and the completion of a year that transformed him from a question-mark prospect to a successful pitcher, All-Star, and valuable member of a championship team.[16] He had led the league in shutouts (6), ERA (2.30), and win-loss percentage (.750). His regular season record was 21–7. Meanwhile, back in Milwaukee, Chet Nichols went 9–11.

After the World Series, Antonelli returned to Rochester, where he was given a hero's welcome by his hometown fans—made even sweeter since he had received *The Sporting News'* Pitcher of the Year award (this being two years before the establishment of the Cy Young). He was honored with a parade and spoke at an assembly at his alma mater, Jefferson High School.[17] He was even given a Buick by the local Italian-American Businessmen's Association.

In Boston he had met and married a young lady named Rosemarie Carbone. They had made their home in Lexington, Massachusetts, during the years that Antonelli played for Boston, but after the 1954 season he went into business as a Firestone/Michelin tire distributor in Rochester and the family relocated there. He sold the business 40 years later, in 1994.

When Antonelli received a contract offer from the Giants before the '55 season it was for the same amount as his prior deal, despite his being arguably the best pitcher in the league. Al Dark advised him to send it back to the ownership and general manager Chub Feeney, asking for double or more. He did so, receiving $28,000.

But Johnny had a tough year in 1955, and the Giants sagged as well, finishing 18 games behind the first-place Dodgers. Antonelli went 14–16, and was suspended by manager Durocher in early September when he refused to leave the mound leading 3–2 in a game against Philadelphia. In 1956, Antonelli rebounded magnificently, getting elected to his second All-Star Game and winning 20 games for the second time in three years. The Giants, however, did not recover quite as well as their ace and wound up in seventh place.

Antonelli does not keep many physical remembrances of his baseball career in his home, but one that he does keep is a three-foot-high trophy given to him by a group

Antonelli caught in action by a photographer during a rare rookie season game appearance.

of diehard Giants fans who sat in Section Five at the old Polo Grounds. Those fans voted him the team's most valuable player in 1956, something that he says means a lot to him even today.[18]

The 1957 season, the Giants' last in New York, brought Antonelli another All-Star spot, even though he wasn't dominant at all during the year, which he ended with a 12–18 record. The next year, 1958, was better in that he finished 16–13, but he failed to throw a shutout for the first time since his rookie year and gave up a league-leading 31 home runs—a career high. Then, after a 19–10 record and yet another All-Star appearance in 1959,[19] Antonelli imploded.

In '59, rumors of Antonelli's dissatisfaction with the Giants, the media, and San Francisco in general had surfaced, and a year later those rumors proved to be solid fact. After a strong start to the 1960 season, Antonelli's performance suffered. He was booed mercilessly by Giants fans as tension mounted in early June, and then manager Bill Rigney shocked everyone by ditching the team—with the Giants only four games behind the league-leading Pirates. When the year ended, with the Giants in fourth place and Antonelli just 6–7 and no longer even in the starting rotation, new manager Tom Sheehan proclaimed that the "controversial left-hander" would be dealt soon enough. In the offseason, Sheehan was fired, and replaced with Antonelli's old teammate, Alvin Dark. Dark, who seemed to truly believe Antonelli was a great pitcher, promised to do all he could to keep "the stylish southpaw."[20] But shortly after, Johnny and Willie Kirkland were traded to the Cleveland Indians for Harvey Kuenn.

For Antonelli, these later years with San Francisco bear certain similarities to his early career with the Boston Braves. Playing outside his home state, in a setting that was unfamiliar to him, Antonelli had found himself in a new environment where he had trouble adjusting. Thousands of miles from his hometown, he began to reach the end of his rope, and the Cleveland Indians became convinced that the only thing wrong was his unhappiness with San Francisco. His dissatisfaction with that west coast city was a sentiment that had been shared by his teammates in the Bay Area,[21] and the tension in the clubhouse was compounded by the fact that Johnny had been moved to the bullpen for the first time since his rookie year. Expectations were high for Antonelli, and when he started to fail to meet them, the media was quick to pounce on him as a primary cause for the Giants' failures.[22] Antonelli, for his part, drew the "undying wrath of fans when he grumbled about the wind [in San

Francisco]."[23] Even today, his strong feelings of discomfort are noted and remembered in the Bay Area:

> The Giants played at Seals Stadium for two seasons, now fondly remembered by everybody but Johnny Antonelli, the San Francisco pitcher who disliked the place, said so and was roundly booed, a New Yorker on the wrong coast.[24]

In any case, manager Bob Kennedy of the Indians, who had taken a keen interest in Antonelli and brokered the trade, was left with the assumption that the left-hander's discomfort in San Francisco was the only reason he had faltered the year before. Kennedy was confident Antonelli would return to form as soon as given a chance to do so in a place where he could feel comfortable. But the high hopes at the start of 1961 turned to disappointment when Johnny entered May with a 0–4 record. He was soon dealt to the Milwaukee Braves, where he was, at 31, one of his old team's oldest players. His impact on the Braves was minimal, and he played in just nine games winning once. In October, Antonelli was sold to the expansion New York Mets, but rather than play for a team that promised to be one of the worst in major league history, Antonelli famously decided to retire from baseball for good. "I quit baseball because I didn't like traveling," Johnny said in 2007. "Not for any other reason. I had no injuries or anything. I'd had my fill of traveling. I had a business to fall back on or else I would have played longer, I'm sure."[25]

After retirement, Antonelli worked at his tire distributorship back home in Rochester. He was never again involved in organized baseball, though some have confused him with another John Antonelli, an infielder who played in 1944–45 for the Cardinals and Phillies and later managed in the International League. For a time, pitcher Johnny did serve on the board of directors of the Rochester Red Wings, and the two Antonellis met once at an IL game in the city. Neither a fisherman nor a hunter, Johnny enjoyed an active game of golf and is a longtime member of Rochester's noted Oak Hill Country Club.

The Antonellis had three daughters and one son. Their daughters were a schoolteacher/homemaker, a vascular nurse, and a homemaker, and their son (after working for the family business) became an executive with Starbucks who helped open stores in Europe and the Far East. As of October 2007, Johnny has 11 grandchildren and one on the way and one great-grandchild with another on the way.

Rosemarie Antonelli died in 2002. Johnny remarried in 2006 and he and his wife, Gail, have enjoyed traveling together. "…I enjoy it, but when you play ball, you stay in a hotel or you go to the ballpark and you never see much of the sights because you're playing ball. Now I'm seeing sights," he says.

Notes

1. Interview with Johnny Antonelli by Alex Edelman on March 11, 2007. Additional information in this biography comes from a brief interview by Bill Nowlin on October 24, 2007.
2. *Sport Pix*, June 1949.
3. *Total Baseball, The Biographical Encyclopedia of Baseball*
4. Letarte, Richard H. *That One Glorious Season*. (Portsmouth NH: Peter Randell Publishers, 2006).
5. Letarte, op. cit.
6. *Christian Science Monitor*, June 30, 1948.
7. *The Sporting News*, July 7, 1948, p. 6.
8. *Total Baseball*.
9. Cooper, Heath remarks in *The Sporting News*, 7/14/48, p. 13. Heath's Feller reference is ironic, because in the aforementioned SportsPix article, Gus Antonelli referred to his son as "a left-handed Feller."
10. *The Sporting News*, 5/11/49, p.11. Birtwell, Roger. "Braves Try Out Bonus Kid and Get Man-Sized Hill Job."
11. *The Sporting News*, 3/4/53, p. 24. Antonelli was allergic to feathers in pillows, apparently something that had previously caused him to miss a start with the Braves.
12. Pitoniak, "Reluctant legend Antonelli being honored," *Rochester Democrat and Gazette*, January 25, 2004.
13. In the All-Star Game, Antonelli pitched in relief, giving up three runs in an NL loss.
14. Marazzi, *Baseball Players of the 1950s*.
15. Boston Braves Historical Association Newsletter (2004 Annual Reunion edition), p. 5. The Pitoniak article also describes this point.
16. It is one of the greatest curiosities in baseball history…How did the Giants (89 wins) beat the mighty Indians (110 wins) in such a dominant fashion? Many attribute it to the brilliant catch of Willie Mays in Game One. A little-known fact, mentioned by Antonelli in an interview with the Boston Braves Historical Association and its members, is that the Indians and Giants, who trained near each other in Arizona, played together *18 times* during Spring Training—with the Giants usually coming out on top. Thus, many Giants pitchers were well acquainted with their AL opponents. (Antonelli interview with BBHA, 10/10/2004).
17. Pitoniak.
18. Author interview with Antonelli.
19. Actually, in 1959, baseball held two All-Star Games. Antonelli was elected to both.
20. *The Sporting News*, "Dark Tosses Cold Water on Rumors of Antonelli Swap", Jack McDonald, August 1, 1960. It is worth noting that Dark was kind to Antonelli during the uproar surrounding his large bonus. In *The Sporting News* article chronicling the reactions of players to the bonus, Dark's was one of the few kind comments. He said he hoped Antonelli would "get more."
21. *The Sporting News*. "All Giants Want To Be Traded, Says Long" by Young, Dick. August 31, 1960.
22. *Los Angeles Mirror-News*, by Charlie Park, August 17, 1960.
23. "Notes: Bochy sticks by Benitez." MLB.com. Chris Haft, 5/30/2007.
24. *San Francisco Chronicle*, "Baseball Has Been Big-Time in S.F. Since the '30s," Carl Nolte, April 11, 2000. The *Chronicle* comment isn't entirely true, Antonelli's dislike for Seals Stadium was minimal; it was the ballpark the Giants moved to in 1960, Candlestick, and the wind in the Bay Area that agitated him so much.
25. Interview with Johnny Antonelli, October 24, 2007.

CHARLES HENRY "RED" BARRETT *by Sidney L. Davis*

G	ERA	W	L	SV	GS	GF	CG	SHO	IP	H	R	ER	BB	SO	HR	HBP	WP	BFP
34	3.65	7	8	0	13	8	3	0	128⅓	132	56	52	26	40	9	0	0	527

G	AB	R	H	2B	3B	HR	RBI	BB	SO	BA	OBP	SLG	SB	HBP
34	39	0	7	0	0	0	3	0	11	.179	.179	.179	0	0

Red Barrett made a solid contribution to the 1948 Braves pitching staff, as both a spot starter and reliever. He appeared in 34 games with a 7–8 record and an impressive ERA of 3.65, besting both ace hurler Warren Spahn's earned run average of 3.73 and the league average of 3.84. Overall, Charles Henry "Red" Barrett's major league career spanned 12 years, starting in 1937 with the Cincinnati Reds and finishing with the Braves in 1949.

While his lifetime record was an even 69–69, he earned a page in the record books when he threw only 58 pitches for the Braves in a complete game. It was a 2–0 win over Bucky Walters and the Cincinnati Reds in a one hour, 15 minute affair the evening of August 10, 1944, at Cincinnati's Crosley Field. During the historic outing Barrett's pitching included 13 groundouts, five fly balls, three popups in fair territory, four foul pop outs, and two line-drive outs. Barrett threw an average of two offerings per batter faced, giving up singles to Gee Walker and Eddie Miller. Known for his fast pace on the mound, the redhead faced only 29 batters and neither walked nor struck out a man. According to his son Bob Barrett, when Red was asked how it was that this game went so fast, "He would always answer that the other pitcher was working just as fast, and without him the record would never have been set."[1]

A lesser-known fact about the fun-loving and vocally gifted Barrett is that just two pitches nine months apart may have separated him from a plaque in Cooperstown. Twice he came within a single toss of a perfect game. On September 2, 1945, in a game Barrett pitched for the St. Louis Cardinals, Lennie Merullo of the Cubs made the only hit, in the third inning, and was the only baserunner. Merullo was caught stealing; the final score was 4–0, and it was the redhead's 20th victory of the season. The following June 6, the Phillies' Del Ennis celebrated his 21st birthday by singling in the eighth inning off Red, and no other batter reached first base. Barrett had retired 22 batters in a row before the Ennis hit. The 7–0 victory was Barrett's first win of the 1946 season.

Red Barrett could perform with equal ease on a major league mound and a nightclub stage.

Red Barrett was born February 14, 1915, in Santa Barbara, California, one of four children of Joe Barrett, a rancher, and Josephine Barrett. At an early age, Red excelled in track and field as well as baseball. Simi High School had only 69 students and, he told a sportswriter years later, there was no football team. "The school would not let us play football because there weren't enough able-bodied boys," Barrett said. "The farmers were afraid the boys would get hurt and they would have to do the chores themselves instead of their sons; consequently we played baseball."[2]

After graduating, Barrett played semipro ball for a team in Reseda, California, and then competed in a tryout camp with 500 players for 17 spots on the Los Angeles Angels' Western Association Class C team in Ponca City, Oklahoma. He made the cut, and in 1935 signed with Ponca City and registered a 15–12 record.

The next year, however, he dropped to 5–12 and was released by manager Mike Gazella, who thought "Red was too screwy."[3] Barrett wired Joe Magota, president and owner of the Muskogee Reds, a Cincinnati farm team in the same Western Association, and promised him that if signed he would help the team win the pennant. Muskogee did win the pennant in 1937, with Barrett recording 24 victories plus two more in the playoffs, chalking up 213 strikeouts against just 49 walks, and posting a 2.85 ERA. During that season, he faced Ponca City seven times and won six of the games. Barrett later commented, "It was a lucky day for me when I got away from the (Ponca City) Angels, and a lucky day for Cincinnati when it got me, because if ever there was a major league pitcher it's Red Barrett."[4] In 1937 he was with Waterloo of the Class A Western League when his contract was purchased by Cincinnati. Late that season, he made his major league debut, appearing in the second game of a September 15 doubleheader against Brooklyn. He pitched 6⅓ innings, allowing five hits and just one earned run.

In 1938, the Reds optioned Barrett to their Syracuse team in the International League, where he won 16 games with only three losses and a league-leading ERA of 2.34. His moundmates ranked second, third, and fourth in ERA. Near season's end, the big-league club brought him up again, and on August 31 he defeated Brooklyn, 9–3, allowing three runs and eight hits under the lights at Crosley Field. He followed that first victory with another complete game win, a seven-hitter over St. Louis.

Red started the '39 season with Cincinnati, but after appearing in only one game he was sent to Indianapolis of the American Association, where he recorded a 16–12 record and an ERA of 3.41. The next year, 1940, was another year in the minors with a short stint in Cincinnati, where he pitched a total of three innings in three games and chalked up one victory without a defeat. During the four-year period 1937–1940, Barrett pitched 44 innings in the big leagues and won three games without a loss. From all indications, Barrett was not the most popular player with his managers; this may have led to fewer opportunities.

Barrett outlined his view on pitching to *Los Angeles Times* sportswriter Bob Ray in a 1938 interview: "I'm no strike-outer. These strikeout pitchers are chumps in my book. Me, I try to make them hit that first ball. After all, those other guys out there are supposed to work too. If everybody in business was like me there wouldn't be so many people out of jobs. My idea is to throw as few pitches as possible. Even when you strike out a batter it generally takes four to seven, and sometimes even more pitches. I'd rather get that batter out on one pitch and save my arm. I am a control, and if you don't mind my saying it, smart pitcher."[5]

Red's off-field work during his minor league career included a job as a guard at a Cincinnati roller skating rink and another as a salesman in a sporting goods store. He was also quick with a song, and when he appeared at Cincinnati's Moonlight Gardens in September 1938, he was spotted in the audience by famed bandleader Tommy Dorsey, who called the right-hander up to sing "Please Be Kind" and "The One Rose" to an appreciative crowd of 3,000. The 1939 *National League Green Book* described Barrett as the "Sorrel thrush of the pitching mound, sweet singer in lighter moments, tough man on the twirling tee."

Barrett's 5–13 record in 1940 with Indianapolis was the poorest of his career, but in 1941, hurling for Birmingham of the Southern Association, he rebounded with 20 wins—tops in the Southern Association (he lost 16). On August 17, he pitched in a twin bill against Knoxville, winning both games, 9–1 and 5–2. Barrett did not reach the majors in either 1941 or 1942, even after, in 1942, duplicating his 1941 total with a league-leading 20-win season at Syracuse, this time with just 12 defeats. His 20th victory was a one-hitter over Jersey City. Pitching his best ball to date, Red had an ERA of 2.05 in 1942, also leading the league in starts (34); shutouts (7); complete games

(25); innings pitched (268); strikeouts (114); and longest winning streak (7). Not surprisingly, he was named the International League's Most Valuable Player, the first Syracuse Chief to win the honor. Forty-six years later, on July 25, 1998, Charles Henry Barrett was posthumously voted in as a member of the first class in the Syracuse Chiefs' Wall of Fame.

It must have been a relief to Barrett when the Boston Braves purchased his contract from the Reds on September 30, 1942. Boston gave him the shot Cincinnati never did. In 1943, at the age of 28, Barrett finally played his first full season in the majors. He pitched in 38 games with a record of 12–18 and a respectable earned run average of 3.18. The Braves finished that season in sixth place with a 68–85 record. Barrett won his first game on April 29 against the New York Giants—he gave up six singles in a 5–2, complete-game victory at the Polo Grounds. His own single aided in the win, driving in two eighth-inning runs. During the season he also bested Cincinnati ace Bucky Walters three times.

Barrett's first year in Boston, 1943, was manager Casey Stengel's last season at the helm of the Braves. Stengel once related a story of how he counseled Barrett on pitching to slugger Stan Musial. "Feed the eager kid a slow pitch," Stengel instructed his right-hander. Barrett followed orders and Musial hit the pitch out of sight. An angry Barrett snarled at Casey, "You don't know how to pitch to him." Stengel thought a moment and then retorted, "Lemme tell you somethin'. We still don't know how to pitch to him."[6]

Barrett finished 1944 with a 9–16 tally, appearing in 42 games and pitching 230⅓ innings during another sixth-place season. Despite the dismal record and a 4.06 ERA, he did have two very unique experiences on the mound that year. One, of course, was the 58-pitch win over the Reds. The other came on July 12, when, before 12,000 spectators at Braves Field, Barrett pitched to both Ted Williams and Babe Ruth during Boston Mayor Maurice J. Tobin's annual charity field day. Ruth led a military service All-Star team that faced the Braves. Before the game, won by Ruth's All-Stars 9–8, Ruth and Williams attempted to put on a long-range batting duel for the fans, with Barrett serving up batting practice lobs. Williams sent three balls into the right-field stands, while the 48-ish Bambino, hampered by an old knee injury, was unable to clout a ball out of the playing confines.

Barrett continued to pursue his off-field singing career while with the Braves, winning first prize in Kay Kyser's Kollege of Musical Knowledge contest with his song "So You Want to Lead a Band."[7] He followed this with a two-week engagement in Boston singing with the Sammy Kaye Orchestra.

The right-hander seemed headed for another losing year in 1945—with a 2–3 record and lofty 4.74 ERA in mid-May—when he was traded to the St. Louis Cardinals in a "throw-in" deal, with the Braves paying $60,000 and Barrett for disgruntled Cardinals pitching ace Mort Cooper. Cooper and owner Sam Breadon had a long-festering salary dispute and the St. Louis owner was happy to exchange the high-priced Cooper for the Boston journeyman. One columnist commented on the sale, "There was nothing to do but get rid of the troublemaker, even if the Cardinals received nobody more impressive than the 30-year-old Barrett."[8] Barrett himself quipped, "The Cardinals should have thrown in Kurowski," a reference to the Cardinals' slugging third baseman Whitey Kurowski.[9]

The self-confident hurler's shift to St. Louis proved to be a career-saving move for the redhead. He won 21 games and lost nine for the Cards, and directed them to a second-place finish with a 95–59 record behind the Chicago Cubs. He led the league in complete games (24); victories (23); and innings pitched (284$\frac{2}{3}$). Dan Daniel, a columnist for the *New York World Telegram*, wrote, "Barrett is not endowed with a lot of stuff. He isn't fast, his curve ball is not especially baffling. He has no particularly elusive delivery but he jitters the hitter into a state of agitation." Barrett explained his newfound success by saying, "The difference between the Cardinals and the Braves is that the Cards are fast enough to catch line drives hit off me."[10] Obviously not superstitious, Barrett chose the number 13 for his uniform when he joined the Cardinals in 1945, the same number he would later wear with the pennant-winning Braves in '48.

Barrett defeated every club in the National League at least twice in 1945, including a 4–0 record over the New York Giants. The light-hitting pitcher's bat also came to life when he slapped a two-bagger against the left-field wall in Boston good for two RBIs to help him beat his old teammates, 8–4, on August 21. He was named to the All-Star Team and was third in the MVP voting, trailing the Cubs' Phil Cavaretta and Boston's Tommy Holmes. Barrett was philosophical about his All-Star status, recalling, "I made the All-Star team in 1945, the only time the All-Star team never played a game because wartime gas rationing prevented travel."[11] Adding to his workload, after the season, he toured with a group of National Leaguers to play before 225,000 troops on a USO tour of islands in the South Pacific. Among the players on the 22-game journey were future 1948 Braves teammates Frank McCormick, Jim Russell, Bill Voiselle, and Ed Wright. Barrett pitched in Honolulu, Guam, and the Philippines, throwing 39 innings and striking out 23 while walking just four. He posted a 3–1 record and batted .285 at the plate, usually playing in the infield or outfield while not pitching. He didn't hesitate to sing a few songs from the USO stage, either.

Barrett had continued his singing career while with the Cards, appearing with Dick Slack's All Star band. They were on the radio at 5:30 a.m., "before the birds even got up," he commented.[12] For several years during the winter

season, the "amiable thrush" (*The Sporting News*) earned extra money by singing country music on the radio. Son Bob recalls, "Dad used to sing in nightclubs and speak at dinners. He could tell a joke better than most comedians, with a great range of dialects and had a wonderful Irish tenor voice."[13]

The singing redhead's fame spread beyond the diamond when the April 1, 1946, issue of *Life* magazine featured the 23-game winner on its cover. A newspaper in St. Petersburg, where the Cardinals held spring training, reported, "Newsstands around Central Avenue were understandably bare of copies of *Life* magazine shortly after the issue hit the streets. Pitcher Red Barrett…took ample precautions to see that each of his mates would receive a copy of the publication. The redhead was up at sunrise to buy every available copy in St. Petersburg. He explained, 'Just getting them to sell to the other Cardinals so they'll be sure to have one.'" Prophetically, the caption describing *Life's* cover stated, "The 31-year-old Barrett is working hard on his tricky pitching and change of pace to meet this year's younger and stiffer competition."

There was a little confusion in Beantown during this time. In 1944 and 1945, both the Braves and the Red Sox had right-handed pitchers named "Red" Barrett. The Red Sox' "Barrett" was christened Francis and served as a reliever. Adding to the confusion, Francis "Red" Barrett was picked up by the Braves in 1946 during Charles "Red" Barrett's exile to the Cardinals. That same season, the Tribe also briefly employed an outfielder named Johnny Barrett.

Red (Charles, that is) turned up a week early for 1946 spring training, raring to go for new Cardinals manager Eddie Dyer. But although it was a great year for the Redbirds, climaxing in a thrilling seven-game World Series victory over the Boston Red Sox, Barrett's role was relegated to 23 appearances, a total of 67 innings, and a disappointing 3–2 record (though one of them was that near-perfect game against the Phillies). Dyer had replaced Billy Southworth, who left to join the Braves for what at the time was a record-breaking contract of $50,000 a year for five years. Dyer was blessed with a young pitching staff of strong-armed hurlers led by Harry Brecheen, Murry Dickson, and Howie Pollet, diminishing Barrett's importance to the staff. The manager told *The Sporting News* in April that Barrett had been "hit hard most of the spring." Giving up 18 runs in 32 innings, he demoted himself to low man in the rotation. In midseason, sportswriter Fred Lieb wrote that Barrett "seems to have lost his touch." The only complete game he won during the year was a masterful 7–0 one-hitter against Philadelphia, a near-perfect game on June 8, broken up by a Del Ennis single with one out in the eighth.

Barrett's transformation from *Life* cover boy to afterthought in 1946 may have been related to a perception held by manager Dyer. "He's essentially a control pitcher but control isn't enough this season. A pitcher has to have more than that. I was talking about him to Mel Ott last winter and remarked that Barrett had twirled some low-hit games against the Giants. However, Ottie stopped me cold. 'I know that,' he said, 'but the park still was full of line drives.'"[14]

The Cards used only seven pitchers during their seven-game World Series victory over the Red Sox, and Barrett did not make an appearance. The autumn classic was not a total washout for the Barrett family. Red's wife, Margaret, was chosen as the "most chic World Series wife" and was presented with a hat valued at $1,000. Dyer, who piloted the club to a 98–56 record in his first year, was named National League Manager of the Year.

In a reversal of fortune after the season, Barrett was sold back to his old team, the Boston Braves, joining his former manager, Billy Southworth, and Mort Cooper, the pitcher he was traded for two years previously. Southworth was "hopeful that the loquacious flinger will be able to regain some of the winning form he displayed in St. Louis in 1945."[15] Boston Globe cartoonist Bob Coyne heralded the return with a drawing headlined "Back With Billy!" and a compilation of small sketches with the following captions, "Arrived in camp with a well developed front porch wearing a ten gallon hat, boots and chaps!"; "Served as a professional entertainer singing hillbilly songs during the winter months"; and "The guy has more color than a crazy quilt."

During the 1947 season, Barrett was the third starter in Boston's four-man rotation and the club's third leading winner with an 11–12 record. Fellow pitchers Warren Spahn and Johnny Sain each registered 21 wins. Barrett appeared in 36 games and pitched 210 innings. Never considered a strikeout hurler, he issued 53 walks and struck out 53. He recorded three shutouts, twice defeating the Cubs' Hank Borowy, by scores of 1–0 and 2–0, and the Dodgers' Vic Lombardi, by 3–0. Barrett hit just .118, but five of his eight hits were doubles—including two in a 6–2 victory over the Pirates on June 13. The Braves finished in third place with an 86–68 record.

Barrett's tendency toward braggadocio proved somewhat embarrassing toward the end of the '47 season. The Pirates' Ralph Kiner went on a home run tear in September, and on September 11 in Pittsburgh hit four homers in a doubleheader against the Braves. His circuit clout string stood at six in three straight games, and scheduled to face the slugger the next day, Barrett predicted that Kiner wouldn't hit one off of him. Barrett was only partially correct. In a 4–3 victory over the Tribe on the 12th, Kiner lashed out *two* homers, besting the old record of seven in four consecutive games, set by Tony Lazzeri of the Yankees in 1936.

At the opening of the 1948 season, Red changed his uniform number to 13, the lucky numeral that produced 23 wins for him that year. The Braves were primed for

a big year with the league's highest paid manager, two 20-game winners and a shortstop, Alvin Dark from Louisiana State University, who was given a $50,000 signing bonus to join the Tribe. To induce fan attendance, the team offered a special night-game package that included tickets, a room at the nearby Somerset Hotel, and dinner for $4.50.[16] Barrett became a sometime starter, replaced in the regular rotation by Vern Bickford. While he, Nelson Potter, Bobby Hogue, and Clyde Shoun shared the bulk of the bullpen work, Red did have several key wins as a starter. He threw a complete game six-hitter against the Dodgers on April 27, winning 3–2. This was followed by a 3–2 victory over Cincinnati on May 8. Another big win over the Reds was on August 31, 3–1, to get the Braves within two percentage points of the first-place Dodgers And on September 5, with Boston now in first, Barrett defeated the Phillies, 5–1, allowing only five hits and retiring 15 in a row. Del Ennis, the outfielder who spoiled Barrett's perfect game bid in 1946, broke the spell with a harmless two-out single in the ninth.

During the season, Barrett also had the dubious distinction of losing both ends of a twin-bill against Cincinnati on June 12, as a starter in the first game and in relief in the second. Reds' pitcher Johnny Vander Meer (who'd been Barrett's teammate with Indianapolis in 1940) hit the only home run of his career off Red in the first game. Ultimately the Braves finished in first place with a 91–62 record, and also won at the gate by drawing a franchise-record 1,445,437 fans. Barrett had just a 7–8 record, but his big wins, versatility, and solid 3.65 ERA outshined his record. In the World Series against the Indians he appeared in Games Two and Three, pitching a total of $3\frac{2}{3}$ innings of shutout ball, but the Braves lost in six.

The *New York Times* recapped the Braves offseason plans after the '48 season:

> The Braves most vociferous off-season planner was right hand pitcher Charles (Red) Barrett, proud thrower of the game's only "mushball."
>
> "As usual," Barrett said without being asked, "I will resume my musical career as soon as possible. That means as soon as anybody offers me money to sing. I'll admit I'm not one of the world's topflight vocalists. But I do sing loud and I've been able to make more money with my voice during the cold winter months than I could driving a truck.
>
> "I'll let you know as soon as one of the more astute Boston night club owners comes through with a professional engagement," Barrett continued despite many raucous interruptions. "Be sure to come up and see me and bring all your friends. But be prepared to pick up the check."[17]

While in the minors, Red Barrett had married Helen Margaret Knutsen on April 5, 1936. A son, Bob, was born in August 1937, followed by daughter Kathleen in January

1940. Bob recalls his family's stay in the Boston area: "We lived in a big house in the Auburndale section of Newton and had a French couple living with us, serving as a maid and butler. Dad had a lot of friends on the club but was closest to Sibby Sisti, Earl Torgeson, and Bob Elliott. I remember when Bob Elliott was voted the league MVP and I took a picture of him holding his trophy. Basically everyone liked my dad except the management. He was kind of a rabble-rouser and got into trouble a few times. And although he did not drink, he sure knew how to party. He had great control and was probably the first pitcher to throw a slider, although he called it a nickel curve."[18]

After the pennant season, 1949 was not a good year for either the Braves or Barrett as dissension wracked the club. Spring training started with a closed-door meeting in which players confronted manager Southworth, who throughout his managerial career had been a hard disciplinarian. Barrett was a Southworth supporter. He suggested taking a vote of confidence among the players but was rebuked by Eddie Stanky, who declared, "If Southworth wants a vote of confidence, let him ask for it himself."[19] Southworth, who had long struggled with alcoholism, was rumored to be drinking heavily and near nervous collapse. In August, he was persuaded by owner Lou Perini to take a leave of absence and was replaced by coach Johnny Cooney.

Despite the return of All-Stars Sain and Spahn, however, the Braves fell to a lackluster 75–79 record and a fourth-place finish in '49. Their attendance slumped to just over 1 million, and the cross-town rival Red Sox—led by superstar Ted Williams—captured the headlines with a photo-finish finale that climaxed in their losing to the rival Yankees on the last day of the season. The 34-year-old Barrett was now used exclusively in relief, compiling a 1–1 record in 23 games and a total of $44\frac{1}{3}$ innings. He played his final game in a Boston uniform on September 29, 1949, hurling one shutout inning in a 9–2 loss to the pennant-bound Dodgers. It was also his final game in the majors. Evidently he didn't feature in the Braves' plans for 1950, and no other big league team picked him up.

Barrett remained in organized baseball for four more years with minor league teams in Los Angeles, Nashville, Buffalo, Toronto, and Tampa, and ended up in Texas with the Paris Indians of the Big State League in 1953, where, at the age of 38, he had a record of 6–4 in 15 appearances. Barrett's playing odyssey had taken him to 11 minor league cities and three major league cities. He appeared in 253 major-league games, 149 of which he started.

Life after baseball saw a move to North Carolina and a job with Sealtest Ice Cream. He was divorced in 1951 and while managing a plant for the ice cream company in New Bern met his second wife, Libby, whom he married in 1957. Red and Libby had one son, Rick, who remains in the North Carolina area. Red never lost his love of sports, and "officiated just about every sport—baseball, softball,

basketball, and football at midget through college levels." He worked for the North Carolina High School Athletic Association and for the U.S. Slo-Pitch Softball Association, where he also served as a director. Barrett commented on officiating to a local reporter, "Officials receive a lot of kidding and criticism. Ninety-nine per cent of calls are judgment calls—the call was right, but maybe my judgment was bad."[20]

Barrett eventually settled in Wilson, North Carolina, where he became active in the Wilson Hot Stove League, bringing many major league players to meetings, including former teammates Stan Musial and Enos Slaughter. In 1971, he went to St. Louis to participate in a replay of the 1946 World Series between the Cardinals and the Red Sox. Another trip, in 1987, took him to an old-timers game, an event he described as a "bunch of old veterans getting together to play five innings of baseball."[21] His retirement also improved his golf game, and he received two hole-in-one awards from the local Willow Springs Country Club.

Under the auspices of the New England Sports Museum, Barrett returned to Boston one last time in August of 1988 to celebrate the 40th anniversary of the 1948 NL championship. At an onstage question-and-answer session held in an auditorium on the Boston University campus, which contains the remnants of old Braves Field, Barrett was cajoled by former Tribe publicity director Billy Sullivan to demonstrate his vocal talents and croon a tune.

Around this same time Barrett was diagnosed with cancer, and after a prolonged illness died at the age of 75 on July 28, 1990. He was buried at Evergreen Memorial Gardens in Wilson. The following year the Wilson Hot Stove League dedicated their banquet to the fun-loving redhead. Among the remembrances in the program:

- He played the quickest round of golf of anyone in the United States of America.
- He officiated every conceivable athletic contest that was ever played.
- He, year after year, led the Hot Stove League in singing "Take Me Out to The Ballgame." In tune or out of tune made no difference.
- He was a great philosopher fond of saying, "Be careful of the words you say—keep them warm and sweet—because you never know from day to day which ones you'll have to eat! And never complain of *not getting everything you want—just pray to God you don't get all you deserve.*

Numerous photos and memorabilia from Barrett's career are displayed at the legendary Dick's Hot Dog Stand in Wilson, owned by Barrett's good friend and fellow Hot Stove Leaguer Lee Gliarmis.

After Red died, son Rick, president of CityScape Builders, decided to honor his father, and in appreciation of the care he received during his illness, established the

Charles "Red" Barrett Memorial golf tournament. The event has raised thousands of dollars for a local hospice.

Notes

1. Interview with Bob Barrett, May 13, 2007.
2. McCrory, Rosellen. Interview with Red Barrett sent to author.
3. Ray, Bob The Sports X-Ray, *Los Angeles Times*, November 9, 1938.
4. *Ibid.* Bob Brady located a story by Arthur Daley in the March 31, 1943 *New York Times* that tells how teammate Albert "Dutch" Mele led the Association in batting average (.354) and homers (30). Mele beat out "Mad Russian" Lou Novikoff of Ponca City for the batting title in the final game of the season. Red Barrett took the mound that game and told Mele, "You'll win the title if you get a loud foul today, because I intend to take care of Novikoff myself." He held Novikoff hitless while Mele went 4-for-4.
5. Ray, *ibid.*
6. Daley, Arthur, *New York Times*, August 16, 1962, p. 19.
7. McCrory, Rosellen, *Wilson North Carolina Daily Times*, June 18, 1990.
8. Drebinger, John, *New York Times*, December 8, 1946.
9. Kaese, Harold, *The Boston Braves*, p. 259.
10. *Ibid.*
11. McCrory, Rosellen, *Wilson North Carolina Daily Times*, June 18, 1990.
12. McCrory, Rosellen. Interview with Red Barrett. Barrett also told Rosellen McCrory that he "dated" Betty Grable while on a USO tour and that the two double-dated with Jane Wyman and Ronald Reagan.
13. Interview with Bob Barrett, May 13, 2007.
14. Daley, Arthur Daley, *New York Times*, September 21, 1946, p. 21.
15. Drebinger, John, *The New York Times*, December 8, 1946.
16. Pietrusza, David, "Boston Braves Finale" at http://www.davidpietrusza.com/Boston_Braves_Finale.html
17. *New York Times*, October 13, 1948.
18. Interview with Bob Barrett.
19. Kaese, *The Boston Braves*, p. 279.
20. McCrory, Rosellen, *Wilson North Carolina Daily Times*, June 18, 1990.
21. *Ibid.*

JOHNNY BEAZLEY *by John C. Fuqua*

G	ERA	W	L	SV	GS	GF	CG	SHO	IP	H	R	ER	BB	SO	HR	HBP	WP	BFP
3	4.50	0	1	0	2	1	0	0	16	19	13	8	7	4	2	0	1	75

G	AB	R	H	2B	3B	HR	RBI	BB	SO	BA	OBP	SLG	SB	HBP
3	4	0	0	0	0	0	0	0	1	.000	.000	.000	0	0

For most of pro baseball's first century, when a "sore arm" sidelined a pitcher for an extended period, it began a descent in skill too often resulting in an untimely exit from the game. Frequently, these players were victims of whisper campaigns, having their courage and valor called into question. Surgeons were unable to repair their defects, and they faded quickly from the scene, ultimately to appear on lists of hurlers who had great seasons but brief careers.

As a result of the era in which he pitched, John Andrew Beazley, Jr. would not benefit from the progress in medical therapies and surgical procedures for his injured arm. As a rookie in 1942, "Beaze" had pitched brilliantly for the St. Louis Cardinals during the regular season and World Series, posting two victories over a supreme New York Yankees ball club and rightly earning the nickname of "Yankee Killer" as St. Louis

Ex-Redbird ace Johnny Beazley was unable to overcome arm woes to pitch effectively in 1948.

captured the Series. He answered the call of war shortly thereafter, and when he returned, his arm and career were on a downward trend. His lifetime 31–12 record is a most impressive one, but also leaves one wondering what could have been.

Johnny Beazley was born on May 25, 1918, in Nashville, Tennessee, the son of John Andrew and Mattie Sue Robertson Beazley, known as Sue. From 1925 to 1932, young Johnny attended the Barker School in Birmingham, Alabama. Returning to Nashville, he enrolled at Cohn Junior High in West Nashville. While he was still young, his father died.

By the age of 16, Johnny was passionate about boxing. An article by Dick Farrington in *The Sporting News* explained that Beazley had a friend who was a Golden Gloves champion, and Johnny frequently worked out with him. His buddy eventually won the Southern Amateur Light

Heavyweight Championship, and Beazley served as his cornerman whenever he boxed. It was Johnny's ambition to become a fighter too, but when he told his mother of these intentions, she put her foot down. "I don't want you going around with your nose on the back of your head," she told her young son. Earlier, Johnny's younger brother, Felix, had died because of an injury suffered during a football game at Nashville's Cohn High School, so her objections to "rougher" sports were understandable. Mom had her way, and when Johnny heeded her plea and forsook boxing for baseball, she had no objections.[1]

Johnny did not play much baseball before high school. He always took jobs during the summer months—as a delivery boy for a local drugstore, delivering orders to customers on his bicycle, or clerking in a grocery store six days a week. It was out of necessity, as he had to find work and earn income for his mother. She had now been a widow for several years, and Johnny, her only living child, had to help provide for her.[2]

There was time for athletics in high school, though. At Nashville's Hume-Fogg High, baseball coach Fred "Ox" McKibbon listened to some of Johnny's teammates who saw a boy with pitching talent and moved him from the outfield to the mound. Beazley quickly became the team's number one hurler, and recorded a 9–0 shutout over Franklin High in his first start. He took to other sports as well, and finished at Hume-Fogg as a four-letter man.

Upon graduation, Beazley went to a baseball school conducted at Nashville's historic Sulphur Dell ballyard. Jimmy Hamilton, a scout for the Cincinnati Reds, managed the business office for the school ("tuition" was $25, but it was waived for Nashville residents); while the instructors, all current or former big-leaguers, were Tom Sheehan, George Kelly, Charlie Dressen, Gilly Campbell, Hub Walker, and Paul Derringer. Hamilton's job was also to sign any decent prospects for the Reds. Of the 40 or so who attended the school, Johnny was the only player signed. He was inked to a contract with the Nashville Vols of the Southern Association in the fall of 1936, when he had just turned 17 years old. Cincinnati had a working relationship with Nashville. Beazley was sent the following spring to the Leesburg Gondoliers of the Class D Florida State League.[3]

Leesburg was managed by former Pirates pitcher Lee Meadows. Johnny was a mediocre 4–3 for Leesburg with a 3.96 ERA, and in midseason, he was moved to Tallahassee in the Georgia-Florida League in the hopes that he might prosper under manager Dutch Hoffman. His performance there was worse (1–7, 4.50 ERA) but Hamilton still believed in his potential and moved him to Lexington, Tennessee, in the Kitty League. Playing for his third ballclub of the year, Johnny won a couple more games but still had a mediocre record (2–5, 4.50 ERA). All told, the rookie was a disappointing 7–15 for the '37 season.

In 1938 Beazley began the year at Greenville in the Class C Cotton States League. Reds scout Hamilton thought he looked great in exhibition games this time, but Johnny hit a roadblock when the regular season got under way. He began 2–4 with a 7.63 ERA, and not long after the season started was declared a free agent because of a technicality over his transfer from Lexington to Greenville. Disgusted with his pitching, Beazley decided to go home to Nashville. In July, he accepted a $250 bonus to sign with Abbeville in the Class D Evangeline League, but he had a hard time getting going there as well and returned home a second time. Only at the urging of Abbeville manager Jess Petty, the former Brooklyn pitcher known as "The Silver Fox," did Johnny return and finish the season. His skipper's confidence must have helped, as Beazley won several games and put up a better earned run average (6–8, 3.27 ERA) down the stretch.

Still more challenges were to come. After the '38 season, Beazley's contract was sold to the New Orleans Pelicans (scout Bob Dowie was instrumental in his acquisition) of the Class A1 Southern Association, a considerable jump in caliber.

At the end of his first month with New Orleans, Beazley injured his elbow. He had pitched just 25 innings in 10 appearances for the Pelicans, with a woeful 1–3 record and a 9.36 ERA. He walked 13 batters and allowed 27 runs on 39 hits during this brief stint, and was thus sent packing again—this time to Montgomery in the Class B Southeastern League. There he pitched only one game before being sent home yet again to rest his arm. Apparently only a fierce determination and encouragement from his coaches along the way kept Johnny in the game. Sue Beazley, his mother, also cited Vanderbilt coach Bill Schwartz, who had Johnny pitch batting practice each spring and offered a number of tips.[4]

Reporting back to New Orleans in 1940, Johnny was now a St. Louis Cardinals farmhand because the Pelicans had signed a working agreement with the Cards. After allowing 13 runs in nine innings over four games for the Pelicans with no decisions, he was moved back to B ball and hurled only moderately more successfully for the Sally League's Columbus Red Birds (5–3, 5.17 ERA). While with Columbus, he injured his back and returned home to Nashville to recover. Still struggling to gain his earlier promise, he was sent to the Montgomery Rebels in the Southeastern League and finally showed some real improvement—going 4–2 with a 2.04 ERA in eight games. Beazley's rebound during his final Class B stop of the year foreshadowed his return to New Orleans and his development into a major league quality pitcher during 1941.

The '41 season was a pivotal year for Beazley. While in New Orleans, he finally learned how to truly pitch under Pelicans manager Ray Blades. Previously, Johnny said later, he had only tried to "fog the ball past the batters. It didn't work, but I thought I knew it all." Blades convinced the still-young Beazley that "there was more to pitching than just throwing the ball" and taught him to pitch to locations and change speeds.[5] He got a lot of work, pitching in 44 games (including 31 starts). Injury-free at last, Beazley went an impressive 16–12 with a 3.61 ERA over 217 innings.

When the Cardinals expanded their roster in September, he was called up to "The Show." The Cardinals were were battling the Brooklyn Dodgers for the National League pennant, but surrendered the flag to the Bums during the final week. Beazley, now 23, made his major-league debut on the meaningless last day of the regular season, starting against the Chicago Cubs. His mound opponent was another late-season rookie call-up, Russ "Babe" Meers, also making his initial big-league appearance. Meers and Beazley had battled each other during the 1941 Southern Association season, and here they battled again. Meers lasted eight innings, allowing only five hits, but Beazley scattered 10 hits while pitching a complete game and securing his first major league win, 3–1. "I was lucky I had a manager who was so patient," he later said in appreciation of Blades. "Otherwise I wouldn't be up here winning in the National League."

The Gas House Gang of the 1930s was gone, and Beazley joined a young and hungry Cardinals ballclub in 1942 spring training. Manager Billy Southworth remembered Johnny's performance the previous year and gave him an opportunity to make the parent club. Beazley earned a spot on the Cardinals' big league roster and later claimed a slot in the starting rotation after early success in relief.

Just two years after almost bombing out of the minors, Johnny was the top rookie pitcher in the major leagues—and one of the top pitchers, period—during the '42 season. Compiling an impressive 21–6 record with a 2.13 ERA in 215⅓ innings, he helped the Cardinals storm past archrival Brooklyn and win the National League pennant during the final days of the season. Beazley's pitching repertoire included a whistling fastball and a snapping curve; his changeup was mostly off the fastball with an occasional slow curve. He recorded the second-best winning percentage in the league, along with the second-most wins. His 2.13 ERA was also second in the senior circuit; behind teammate Mort Cooper's leading 1.77. Beazley thanked Southworth for giving him confidence and the chance to pitch, and he credited coach Mike Gonzalez for his turnaround. Apparently Gonzalez had taken a personal interest in the hard-nosed rookie.

Beazley was part of an unflattering incident during the 1942 season. The night before he was to pitch in a key game against the Phillies, he got into an argument with a porter at the train station. Beazley did not want the redcap to carry his travel bag; the porter was African-American, and Beazley reportedly did not like blacks. This was not uncommon, but Johnny's prejudice may have been less controllable because of the fact that he was commonly known as "Nig" around Nashville after his grandfather stuck him with the nickname when he was about 3 months old. A squabble ensued at the train station, and the porter cursed him. Beazley responded by throwing the bag at him, after which the porter pulled a knife and slashed Beazley on his right thumb. Beazley raised his arm in self-defense, resulting in a deep (but not serious) cut. His Cardinals teammates didn't know how he would be able to pitch the next day, but Johnny did pitch and carried a 1–0 lead into the ninth before Philadelphia rallied for a 2–1 victory. His teammates knew he was a cocky, hard-nosed player with a terrible temper, and, the temper did not always serve him well.[6]

Led by Beazley and Cooper on the mound and future Hall of Famers Stan Musial and Enos "Country" Slaughter at the plate, the '42 Cardinals had an extraordinary 106–48 record for the 1942 season, setting a franchise record for wins that still stands today. In the World Series, Southworth's Cardinals were matched against the New York Yankees of Joe McCarthy, defending Series champs and winners of five of the previous six fall classics. The Yankees took the opener at St. Louis, and Beazley was dubbed by the Cards to try to even things up at home in Game Two. Before the contest, Johnny satisfied a promise he had made to three of his former Hume-Fogg High baseball teammates. The self-assured hurler had signed a note back in school promising the trio tickets to his first World Series game, and sure enough, the three were at Sportsman's Park to see his start.

His guests and the rest of the 34,255 on hand had plenty to cheer about most of the day, as the Cardinals spotted Beazley a two-run lead in the first and added another tally in the seventh. Johnny, meanwhile, held the Yankees scoreless until the top of the eighth, but then New York outfielder Charlie Keller tied the score with a three-run homer off the right-field roof. In the bottom of the frame, Slaughter hit a two-out double and Musial singled him home for a 4–3 lead. Despite surrendering a couple of singles in the top of the ninth, Johnny retired the side and Cardinals fans joyously tossed thousands of seat cushions onto the playing field at game's end. Afterward, Beazley pulled a lucky brown rabbit's foot out of his pocket and told gathered reporters that a female fan had given it to him.

A *Time* magazine writer noted of Beazley after the victory: "He grips the ball so hard his hand quivers for a half hour after each game. But the 'Beaze' has plenty on the ball. When Manager Billy Southworth chose the 'Beaze' for the second game of the series, even his staunchest admirers feared he would blow up with World Series jitters. The kid was walloped for ten hits, got into one jam after another, but at the last out he was still on the mound, the first rookie to win a Series game since Paul Dean trimmed the Detroit Tigers for St. Louis in 1934."[7]

Games Three and Four went to St. Louis, too, as

their pitching and hitting dominated the mighty Yankees. They held a three-games-to-one advantage over the Bronx Bombers, and with the title within reach, Southworth gave the ball to Beazley again for Game Five at Yankee Stadium. Leadoff batter Phil Rizzuto homered for New York in the first, but Slaughter tied the score with a homer of his own in the top of the fourth. The Yankees pushed another run across against Beazley in the bottom of the inning, but St. Louis tied it again it in the top of the sixth.

Both Johnny and the Yankees' Red Ruffing were pitching well, but in the top of the ninth, with Walker Cooper on base, Whitey Kurowski crushed a line-drive home run into Yankee Stadium's left-field bleachers. St. Louis had a 4–2 lead and New York was down to its final three outs. The first two Yankees up in the ninth reached base on a single and an error, but Joe Gordon was picked off second base by Cards catcher Cooper, and Beazley got the next two on a popup and a groundout to win his second game and clinch the Series.

In the victorious Cardinals' locker room, Johnny was surrounded by reporters as well as a special guest. Babe Ruth burst into the proceedings and exclaimed, "Where's that guy that whooped my Yankees?" Shaking the great Bambino's hand was a cherished Beazley memory that lasted a lifetime.

The World Series hero returned to his native Nashville, where his achievements were celebrated and acknowledged by Mayor Tom Cummings and throngs of fans. They lavished him with gifts and awards; when asked by a reporter what he would do with his $6,100 Series share, the devoted son said he would give it to his mother. For his performance in 1942, the Chicago Chapter of the Baseball Writers Association of America named Beazley the most valuable rookie of the year. (The "official" Rookie of the Year Award would not be given until 1947.) *The Sporting News* named him to the All Star Freshman Team along with Stan Musial and Johnny Pesky.

By the time of these honors, Johnny had become Corporal Beazley. In the midst of his whirlwind 1942 season, he had faithfully committed to military service, now that the U.S. was embroiled in World War II. The Army Air Force was waiting for him as the World Series concluded; and after graduating from Officer Candidate School, he was commissioned a second lieutenant in March of 1943.

Lieutenant Beazley was assigned to a morale-boosting unit, and spent much of his time traveling to military bases and playing baseball for the troops. The frequent service games caused an enormous strain on Beazley's arm. He eventually injured it, which effectively ruined his baseball career.

Beazley's oldest son, Terry, said his dad would go to a base, pitch two or three innings, then get on a bus and travel 40 miles to the next base without being able to cool down his arm. Cardinals teammate Marty Marion told author Peter Golenbock: "Beazley was in the Army, and we played his Army team in an exhibition game in Memphis. Ol' Beazley hurt his arm pitching against us. He tried to beat us, I guess. He babied it for a couple of years, and it never did come back."[8]

Shortly before he died in 2002, Enos Slaughter shared some reflections on his old teammate. "Johnny Beazley was an excellent pitcher for the Cardinals in his first season," Slaughter recalled. "He was easy to get along with. He went out and did his job when he was supposed to."

Still, initial expectations for Beazley were that he could regain his 1942 form when he returned to civilian life and the Cardinals organization after the war. It wasn't to be. Concerns about his arm and lost velocity first arose early in spring training of 1946, and were justified when the regular season got under way. While he recorded a decent 7–5 record during the year, he made just 18 starts, and his 4.46 earned run average made it clear that the mastery he enjoyed during the '42 season was history. That magical summer would remain his only great season, and in September Beazley actually announced his intentions to retire at the age of 28. "My arm is all right now, I think," he told reporters, "but I feel weak and tired and just don't have any strength anymore, so I'm quitting when the season's over. I'd quit now, but I don't want to let [Cards manager Eddie] Dyer down." Dyer insisted that Johnny stay with the team down the stretch, and although he didn't pitch again in the regular season, Beazley did appear briefly in the '46 World Series against the Boston Red Sox—pitching one scoreless frame in Game Five after the Sox had taken a 6–1 lead after seven innings.

St. Louis won the series in seven games, and Dyer got Beazley to change his mind about retiring. He reported to spring training with the Cards in 1947 with new hope that he could regain his prior form, and had a few encouraging, headline-producing outings during the exhibition season. Most experts remained skeptical, but one man who still believed in Johnny was watching with interest. Former Cardinals manager Billy Southworth had moved to the Boston Braves in 1946 after presiding over a dominant St. Louis squad from 1940 to 1945, and immediately led the Boston club to its best season (third place) in nearly 30 years. Beazley had pitched brilliantly for Billy during the '42 season, and Southworth—ever loyal, perhaps to a fault, to his old players—expected that Johnny would return to his prewar brilliance. He encouraged Braves owner Lou Perini to acquire Beazley, and Perini, anxious to put his own rising club into pennant contention, complied. On April 19, just as the 1947 regular season was getting under way, the Braves purchased the erstwhile ace for an undisclosed sum.

A few weeks later, on May 8, "Beaz" won his first start with the Braves—going the distance in a 12–5 victory over the Pirates that gave Boston a share of first place with the Dodgers. Southworth called Johnny's possible revival a key to the team's pennant hopes, but the enthusiasm was short-lived. Beazley won and completed his next start, against Cincinnati a month later, but his arm woes never really subsided. He wound up throwing just 28⅔ innings the whole '47 season (2–0, 4.40) and even less in 1948 (0–1, 4.50 in 16 innings of work). Johnny did get to play on his third pennant-winning club in four years when the Braves copped the NL flag in '48, and no doubt appreciated the bonus money, but it was likely a minor consolation. He appeared in just one game in 1949, retiring all six batters he faced in finishing a game, but his career was over. Southworth's long comeback chance for his old ace officially ended on May 12, when Beazley was optioned to the minor leagues.

Beazley's major-league statistics consisted of a six-year record of 31–12 in 76 appearances; along with 147 strikeouts, he finished with a career 3.01 ERA. He attempted to revive his career in 1949 by playing with his hometown Southern Association Nashville Vols, but was unable to overcome his arm injury. Meekly, he recorded a 1–3 record in five games in a Nashville uniform. In 1950, he attempted a comeback by playing for the Dallas Eagles in the Texas League finishing with a 2–2 record. In 1951, he played for the Oklahoma City Indians of the Texas League and finished with a 6–6 record. Finally, he walked off the mound for the last time and retired from baseball. In 1943, Johnny Beazley had married Carolyn Jo Frey of Springfield, Tennessee, in Fort Lauderdale, Florida, and he now had plenty of time for his hobbies of hunting, fishing, and golf. His post-baseball business career began with the Falstaff Brewing Company of St. Louis, for whom he was general manager of his hometown Nashville branch beginning in 1950. He later purchased the distributorship and ran the company until 1972. His wife died in 1974, but he kept busy by serving on the Metropolitan Nashville Council and as a councilman from 1974 to 1976. He also found a new bride, marrying Jacqueline Spurlock Ezell in Montgomery, Alabama, in 1975. They enjoyed 15 years together until, after being diagnosed with cancer, John Andrew Beazley, Jr. died at his home in Nashville on April 21, 1990. He was 71 years old, and was buried in the Mt. Olivet Cemetery in Nashville.

He was inducted into the Tennessee Sports Hall of Fame in 1977, and in 2005 was elected to the Metropolitan Nashville Public Schools Sports Hall of Fame. And while the big one, in Cooperstown, will not be opening its doors for him, there are few men there who showed more promise in their rookie years than the hard-nosed Yankee slayer from the Volunteer State.

Notes

1. Farrington, Dick. "Beazley, Cards' Flashy Freshman," *The Sporting News*, September 3, 1942.
2. *Ibid.*
3. O'Donnell, Red. "It Comes Out—Beazley Was Nashville High 'Blue Devil,'" *The Sporting News*, October 15, 1942.
4. *Ibid.*
5. Farrington, op.cit.
6. Rains, Rob. *The St. Louis Cardinals: The 100th Anniversary History* (New York: St. Martin's, 1993), p. 96. A contemporary report is found in the September 13, 1942, *New York Times* on page S3. Peter Golenbock asked Marty Marion about the incident and was told, "The porter wanted to carry his bag, and Beazley didn't want him to. Beazley was that sort of guy. [Translation: he didn't like blacks. All the porters were black.] He was a hard-nosed pitcher. He would knock you down." Golenbock provided the translation, making Marion's meaning clear.
7. *Time*, October 12, 1942.
8. Golenbock, Peter. *The Spirit of St. Louis* (New York: Harper, 2001), p. 351.

Sources

The John Andrew Beazley Papers (1916–1990) Manuscript Section, State of Tennessee Library, Nashville.

Nashville sports historian Bill Traughber (including his interview with Terry Beazley)

Golenbock, Peter. *The Spirit of St. Louis* (New York: Harper, 2001)

Rains, Rob. *The St. Louis Cardinals: The 100th Anniversary History* (New York: St. Martin's, 1993)

Websites:
baseball-almanac.com, baseballhistorian.com, baseball-reference.com, cardinalshistory.com, findagrave.com, mlb.com

Nashville Tennessean Archives

New York Times Archives

Time Magazine Archives

The Sporting News

1947 Boston Braves Sketchbook

1948 Boston Braves Media Guide

Assorted Associated Press stories, 1942–1947

Thanks to Bob Brady, Bill Francis, and Ray Nemec, and for research assistance from the Baseball Hall of Fame in Cooperstown, New York.

VERN BICKFORD *by Les Masterson*

G	ERA	W	L	SV	GS	GF	CG	SHO	IP	H	R	ER	BB	SO	HR	HBP	WP	BFP
33	3.27	11	5	1	22	5	10	1	146	125	59	53	63	60	9	3	0	625

G	AB	R	H	2B	3B	HR	RBI	BB	SO	BA	OBP	SLG	SB	HBP
33	49	3	10	2	0	0	7	2	12	.204	.235	.245	0	0

Baseball fans know the stories of superstars like Ted Williams and Bob Feller who lost some valuable years of baseball during World War II. But one pitcher actually gained from those years in the service.

Before being drafted into the U.S. Army in 1942, Vern Bickford scuffled for the Class D Welch Miners in the Mountain State League. He returned to baseball three years later after receiving sage advice from a host of major leaguers. "If it wasn't for the war, I'd still be pitching in Welch, West Virginia," Bickford told *The Sporting News* in 1948.

Vernon Edgell Bickford was born on August 17, 1920, in Hellier, Kentucky, on the same day that Cleveland Indians shortstop Ray Chapman died after being hit by a Carl Mays pitch. Hellier is in the coalfield country of the Cumberland Mountains near the borders of Virginia and West Virginia. Known as the location of the Hatfield-McCoy feud in the 19th century, the region was growing in population when Bickford was born, having ballooned by more than 50 percent in 10 years.

Bickford grew up with six siblings (Estil, Raymond, Robert, James, Inez, and Irma). His father was a coal miner in Kentucky who for a short time owned a general store in a mining district until a strike by miners put him out of business.

While Vern was a child, the Bickfords moved to New Canton, Virginia, 60 miles northwest of Richmond in Central Virginia, where Bickford captained the local high school baseball, football, and basketball teams. After high school, Bickford played semipro ball for a briquette plant in Berwind, West Virginia, which is where Welch Miners manager "Sad Sam" Gray, a 20-game winner in 1928 who pitched in the majors for 10 seasons, heard about the scrawny right-hander. Bickford signed with Gray's team in 1939, and pitched in 10 games, winning five and striking out 47 in 62 innings.

"I still didn't know anything about pitching. I was a thrower—strictly. I could throw them by the Class D boys

A flip of a coin brought Vern Bickford to Boston.

pretty well, but that was all I was good for," Bickford said.

Bickford struggled with his control during his four years with the Welch Miners before being drafted into the Army. He started in the Air Corps, and ultimately was transferred to the infantry. The first bit of good fortune during the war years was when Bickford met his future wife, Jean Margaret Froyne, while he was stationed at March Field in Riverside, California. They married on November 4, 1944.

During the early years of the war, Bickford spent little time playing baseball. It was later, while stationed in the Philippines, that he picked up the horsehide again, playing for the Leyte All-Stars and the Manila Dodgers. In Manila, he threw alongside Brooklyn Dodger Kirby Higbe and Jim Hearn, and the pitching was so strong that supposedly future Hall-of-Famer Early Wynn played shortstop. Higbe talked positively about Bickford's ability.

"'Fifty percent of them don't have any more stuff than you have,' Higbe reportedly told Bickford. "But what you need is another pitch—a pitch you can throw for strikes."

Bickford spent the closing days of the war developing a slider and controlling his changeup while getting pointers from major leaguers Roy Partee, Max Macon, and Al Milnar.

Bickford told the *Boston Globe* in 1950: "While I was in the low minors, we always put big-leaguers on a pedestal. But when I played with them in the service, I learned a lot…and I said to myself, 'If those guys can play in the major leagues, so can I.'"

Bickford returned to the States after the war as the property of the Boston Braves. He threw one game for Hartford in the Eastern League before joining the Jackson team in the Southeastern League. He won 10 games that year, and was third in strikeouts and tied for first in the league with four shutouts He later recalled that it was in the middle of that 1946 season that he finally gained control.

The following year, he went to Indianapolis, where a coin flip brought him to the attention of Braves owner Lou Perini. The owner of the Indianapolis team, Frank McKinney (also a Braves stockholder), led a group, which included entertainer Bing Crosby, that bought the Pirates for $2.5 million. Faced with the question of who in fact owned the Indianapolis players, McKinney or Perini, Organized Baseball asked them to divide the squad.

They agreed upon all but eight of the players. They held a draft for the eight in the Hotel Floridian in Miami Beach, and Perini won the first pick with the coin flip.

Perini acknowledged later that he was unfamiliar with minor-league players' names. He scanned the list of players and the name Bickford stuck out because during the war Brooklyn's Branch Rickey tried to acquire the pitcher. He knew that if Rickey wanted Bickford, he must have been a good pitcher.

Perini selected Bickford with his first choice, and sent the righty to the Braves' farm club in Milwaukee. Bickford did not impress over the first two months in relief, but a string of doubleheaders forced the Milwaukee club to start him. He shut out St. Paul on two hits, and over two weeks he threw four complete games and allowed only one run.

Recalling his year with the Milwaukee Brewers, Bickford said, "By that time, I was married and had a youngster to support. I had come to the conclusion that if I didn't make good with Milwaukee and show myself a pretty good chance of moving up, I'd have to quit baseball and try to find something else to do for a living." So 1947 was a turning point for Bickford.

"Bickford has everything—speed, a dandy change of pace, and his sidearm sailer," said Brewers catcher Norm Schlueter. "He's easy to catch, too, because all I have to do is put my glove where I want him to pitch the ball and he hits the bull's-eye. He is going to be a big leaguer, that's sure."

On September 5, 1947, Bickford hurled eight hitless innings against Minneapolis before giving up a single to pinch-hitter Andy Gilbert to lead off the ninth. "With his curve, speed, and his great change of pace, Bickford is definitely a fine prospect," said Brewers president Jake Flowers. The Braves agreed and five days later they brought Bickford to Boston.

Bickford achieved an American boy's dream on May 19, 1948. Nine years after signing his first professional contract, he started for the Boston Braves against Rip Sewell and the Pittsburgh Pirates after scheduled starter Red Barrett complained of a sore throat.

The 27-year-old rookie was "considered little more than a relief hurler," according to *Boston Globe* reporter Clif Keane. After a rough first inning, when he loaded the bases, Bickford shut down the Pirates, 4-1, handing Sewell his first loss of the year and making Barrett look like 1948's version of Wally Pipp.

Despite fighting a sore arm, Bickford impressed not only the Braves fans; his bosses gave him a raise at the All-Star break.

Bickford won 11 games in 22 starts in 1948 and none was more important than the September 26 game against the Giants before 31,172 fans at Braves Field when Bickford won a 3-2 game to secure the franchise's first pennant since 1914. Bickford's 11-5 record, his team-leading winning percentage of .688, and his 3.27 ERA were a big factor in the Braves' success.

Bickford started Game Three in the World Series for the Braves after his team's top twirlers, Warren Spahn and Johnny Sain, split the first two games. After two scoreless innings, the Indians scored an unearned run off Bickford in the third. He gave up three hits and a walk in the fourth before manager Billy Southworth replaced him with Bill Voiselle. The Indians went on to a 2-0 win behind Gene Bearden.

That was the end of Bickford's year as Southworth decided to start Voiselle in Game Six, which the Indians won, 4-3, and took the Series.

In 1949 Bickford had 16 wins and 11 losses, though his ERA rose by almost a full run, to 4.25. He added an All Star Game appearance to his résumé as well. Braves ownership was still pleased with his performance; for the second straight year, the Braves gave Bickford a raise during the season. Then, in 1950, Bickford went from a reliable number three pitcher to one of the finest right-handers in the league. By August, baseball writers foresaw the possibility that the Braves trio of Spahn, Sain, and Bickford might win 20 games apiece. *The Sporting News* called Bickford "an aggressive, mean-eyed employee on the mound, but quite gentlemanly off the field."

The difference for Bickford in 1950, according to his manager, was control. "Control is what has made Bickford better than ever before. He's putting that ball where he wants it to go," said Southworth despite the fact that Bickford was among the league-leaders in bases on balls for the second straight year.

"I've worked a lot with Bob Keely, our bullpen catcher, and I've just kept throwing and throwing. As a result, the hitters can't 'take' on me the way they used to. For the pitches are going where I want them—for strikes," said Bickford that year.

Along with his 10 wins by the middle of July, he was leading the league with 15 complete games. After 22 games, Bickford had accumulated 169 innings.

"Bickford thrives on work," said Southworth. "He's the type that retains his good stuff even when he gets a little tired."

After Bickford took a ball off his elbow during batting practice, he entered his August 11 start against the Dodgers surrounded by questions.

"It is a crucial spot for the Braves because two questions need quick answering. One, Bickford's elbow, hurt

As a 27-year-old rookie, Vern Bickford became a key member of the Braves starting rotation.

last Monday by a batting practice pitch. Two, when are the Braves going to start banging out wins in bunches?" wondered the *Boston Globe* prior to Bickford's start.

Before more than 29,000 fans, Bickford answered the first question by no-hitting a Brooklyn Dodgers lineup that featured Jackie Robinson, Duke Snider, Roy Campanella, and Pee Wee Reese. With an assortment of curves, sliders, fastballs, and changeups, and "the precision of a master craftsman," Bickford kept the Dodgers off-balance for his 14th win of the year. The nighttime no-hitter was saved by a defensive gem when Willard Marshall caught a fly ball in short right-center field after colliding with Sam Jethroe and Roy Hartsfield.

Twirling the franchise's seventh no-hitter, Bickford faced 30 batters and didn't allow a runner to reach second until the ninth.

In that inning, with two men on base and one out, Bickford snapped off a curve to Snider, who bounced a grounder up the middle, where Buddy Kerr grabbed the ball, stepped on second, and threw to first baseman Earl Torgeson for the double play.

"All I wanted was the game. That was all. No, I didn't think anything about it for eight innings. But, truthfully, I did in that ninth. Especially when I walked those two hitters," Bickford said.

The no-hitter gained Bickford a certain level of celebrity, but he settled down and won five more games over the next month. Stuck on 19 wins, though, Bickford failed six times to win number 20, finishing the season at 19–14 (Spahn won 21; Sain won 20). Bickford led the league with 27 complete games, 39 starts, 1,325 batters faced, and 311 2/3 innings pitched, and posted a 3.47 ERA. He even received MVP consideration, garnering four points in the balloting.

Bickford spent his winter hunting, fishing, and working around the house in Virginia, and answering questions about his no-hitter.

"I've heard some talk that maybe I gave out too much for the no-hitter. A couple of fellows, Ed Head and Rex Barney, never did much after their no-hitters. But I know I was pitching better after that big night. I'll be satisfied to take up where I left off, not losing, of course, but with the same stuff and strength. There's no reason I won't," said Bickford.

Though he was the only one of the top three Braves hurlers who didn't win 20 in 1950, Bickford got the ball for the season opener against the Giants in 1951— the first Braves pitcher not named Spahn or Sain to get an Opening Day start since the war.

The year 1951 looked bright for Spahn, Sain, and Bickford after they combined for 60 wins, but only Spahn maintained that level of mastery. The Braves lost 4–0 in the opener. On May 6, Bickford watched as Pirates pitcher Cliff Chambers no-hit the Braves. After the game, the reporters surrounded Bickford for some words of wisdom.

His comment: "Cliff will have to remember that this game won't win his next start. It's just like any other game you win. Yesterday's no-hitter never wins tomorrow's game for you, just as yesterday's victory never wins your next start. No-hitters don't happen very often. After they happen, they don't mean a darn to you."

During that same month, Bickford tangled in a classic pitchers' duel with another no-hit club member, Ewell Blackwell of the Reds. Bickford kept the Reds to two hits, but one of them was a home run by catcher Johnny Pramesa, giving Blackwell, who allowed just one hit, a 1–0 win.

After becoming the first NL pitcher to win six games by the middle of May, Bickford struggled and was injured on July 5 on the same day the Braves lost their other top righty, Sain, to injury. Bickford pulled a muscle in his right shoulder and left after the fourth inning against the Phillies.

After more than two weeks off, Bickford returned and was shelled for six runs by the Pirates, but won the game 11–6 to pick up his 10th win. He followed with a handful of inconsistent starts, and then lost nearly two months after breaking his right ring finger during a game of pepper at Wrigley Field. He threw one more time in 1951, going three innings in relief in a September 23 game against the Giants. Bickford gave up four hits and two runs.

Bickford said he was pleased with his performance, and explained why he wanted to return to the Braves that year. "Now I know I won't be worrying all winter about this hand of mine," said Bickford, who finished the year at 11–9 with a 3.12 ERA, which was eighth best in the NL.

Bickford's 1952 campaign was plagued with inconsistency, injury, and strife. At the beginning of the year, he took part in the new medium of television. With Tommy Holmes, Spahn, and Bucky Walters, Bickford was part of the Braves' *Baseball in Your Living Room* on a Boston TV station, WNAC-TV, which provided baseball tips from the pros.

Bickford may have wondered if television was a safer bet after starting his 1952 season. Umpires tossed him from two games within three months—and he didn't pitch in either. During an April 24 game against the

Giants, umpire Art Gore threw out Bickford, who argued from the dugout after a hidden ball play in which Torgeson tagged Max Lanier. Gore told the Braves that he had stopped play before Torgeson tagged Lanier, which wiped out the hidden ball trick.

"Some of the umpires are too complacent. They've got these jobs for life and they know they can't lose them unless they break a leg. So they don't hustle," Bickford said after the game.

Bickford was tossed out of another game on July 2 after Torgeson punched Giants catcher Sal Yvars. Bickford argued that the umpires should have ejected both Yvars and Torgeson.

Bickford's year didn't get any better. He finished the 1952 campaign in August after a Willie Jones liner struck his pitching hand. Not realizing the extent of the injury, Bickford pitched another $2\frac{1}{3}$ innings before leaving the game. X-rays showed he suffered a broken middle finger. He'd finished the year 7–12 (3.74).

Stormy weather continued to follow Bickford during the offseason. While hunting in Medford, Maine, he was part of a deer hunting party that ended in a fatality. Phil Page, former pitcher and coach of the Reds, was part of the group of baseball-playing hunters. The trip ended when Page and his guide, Carlton Bragg, reportedly mistook an 18-year-old Howland, Maine, resident for a deer. They fired at the brush and fatally wounded the teen.

The strange circumstances surrounding Bickford continued. Shortly before spring training, his friend Torgeson was traded to the Phillies as part of a four-team deal. Torgeson planned to fly to spring training in New Orleans, but he borrowed Bickford's car instead. The Torgesons made it safely to New Orleans, though the plane in which he planned to fly crashed into the Gulf of Mexico, killing 46 people.

Bickford followed his disappointing 1952 season with another tough year, winning only two games while pitching mostly in relief for the Braves, now relocated in Milwaukee. But it wasn't his pitching that made news in 1953. While the nation celebrated the end of the Korean War, there was another battle brewing in New York City. Bickford and fiery teammate Johnny Logan came to blows at a Midtown Manhattan restaurant. The cause of the fight was reportedly baseball-related.

"It was a case of a couple of tempers flaring up for a couple of minutes, but it was all over in a hurry. We swung a couple of punches and then shook hands....We were both sorry...Johnny's a good guy and we're still friends," said Bickford.

"It was a one-punch scrap. We got into an argument over something that happened in the game. We shook hands and it's all forgotten. We're buddies now," said Logan.

Though Bickford called the fight a "silly little argument," those who saw the skirmish reported otherwise.

Spectators told reporters about a battle that stretched into the street.

"The fight was a beaut while it lasted," reported Bill Mathias of the *New York Daily News*. "Names were called. Logan waited for Bickford to land the first punch, and they were off. But it lasted no more than a minute. I did what I could to break it up. Bickford came out of it with a slight mouse over one eye. Logan hurt his hand."

Newspapers had some fun at the players' expense, including one Chicago sportswriter who reportedly asked Braves manager Charlie Grimm, "Is it true that the only pitcher Logan can hit is Bickford?" Grimm did not find the aftermath amusing, saying it was a "tempest in a teapot." Bickford reported to Ebbets Field the next day with a black eye and cuts to his face.

After a difficult season, the Braves granted Bickford's trade request and dealt him to the new Baltimore Orioles for $10,000 and catcher Charles White Jr., who was with the Orioles' San Antonio farm team.

Bickford impressed during the early days of spring training, outrunning Orioles rookies in wind sprints and chasing fly balls for hours. He was hopeful for a new start.

"I think I'll have a better opportunity to show my appreciation to the fans of Baltimore," he said. "Milwaukee had lots of pitchers and I guess Charlie Grimm wanted to use his younger men ahead of me. I pitched only 58 innings and won only two while losing five. I'm the type of fellow who needs a lot of work, and with Baltimore a little short of pitchers, I think I'll get it. I know I'll be a winner for the Orioles."

Bickford was given his only start on April 24, hurling four innings in a 14–4 loss to the White Sox. After the start, Bickford complained of elbow stiffness. He was released two weeks later.

After having an elbow spur removed in the summer of 1954, Bickford gave it one more shot. He tried a comeback in 1955 with the nearby Richmond Virginians of the International League. It didn't work out; he posted a 1–0 record but with an ERA of 8.49 over just 35 innings of work, and retired from baseball.

With his baseball career behind him, Bickford spent his remaining years as a car dealer, traveling salesman, and carpenter.

Still not yet 40 and with three boys at home (Michael, Kenneth, and Vernon Jr.), Bickford's life came to a premature end on May 6, 1960, at McGuire Veterans Hospital in Richmond. From his hospital bed, Bickford, stricken with cancer and down to 120 pounds, spoke optimistically just days before his death about the future and possibly returning to baseball.

"The doctors tell me I'll walk again, and that's just what I intend to do. I believe that because of my experience I could get a coaching job. At least, I could teach my three boys something about pitching," said Bickford.

Bickford was buried in Zion Baptist Church Cemetery in Albemarle County, Virginia.

The saying of "Spahn and Sain and Pray for Rain" is a popular refrain when baseball fans think back to the late-1940s Braves. But from 1948 through 1950, Vern Bickford was a strong number three hurler, accumulating 46 wins, throwing a no-hitter, and leading the league in innings pitched one year. Finding a word that rhymes with Bickford would prove a difficult task, but baseball fans should know that for those three years Bickford rivaled his more famous mound mates in the eyes of his teammates and competition.

Sources

The Boston Globe
The Sporting News
The New York Times
Coberly, Rich. *The No-Hit Hall of Fame: No-Hitters of the 20th Century* (Triple Play Publications, 1985)
Wikipedia.com
City-data.com

PAUL BURRIS *by Jay Hurd*

G	AB	R	H	2B	3B	HR	RBI	BB	SO	BA	OBP	SLG	SB	HBP
2	4	0	2	0	0	0	0	0	0	.500	.500	.500	0	0

Paul Robert Burris was born on July 21, 1923, in the small town of Hickory, North Carolina, population at the time approximately 6,000. At the age of one, he moved with his family to Charlotte, 50 miles southeast of Hickory. He grew up in Charlotte, and graduated from high school in 1941, having attended both Derita High School and Central High School.

In 1942, Burris returned to Hickory and worked in a sandwich shop for 10 months. During this time, he placed a telephone call to the manager of the Hickory Rebels and, as a result of the call, was invited to try out for the team. After a three-day trial, Burris earned the job as backup catcher. He signed his first professional contract with the Hickory Rebels of the Class D North Carolina State League. He soon earned the role of first-string catcher.

A "burly" catcher, he weighed in at 190 pounds—a weight he maintained throughout his career—and was an even 6 feet tall; he batted right and threw right. Burris played 75 games

Rookie Paul Burris was a late season call-up, appearing in the Tribe's final two 1948 regular season contests.

with the Rebels in 1942 and, in 223 at-bats, averaged .176. That same year, while playing with the Rebels, Burris attracted the attention of a scout for the Brooklyn Dodgers. The Dodgers ultimately signed him as a free agent and sent him to Durham of the Class B Piedmont League. However, due to the strong competition posed by catchers Ferrell Anderson and Bruce Edwards, Burris' playing time with Durham was limited to fewer than 10 games.

Both Anderson and Edwards would go on to the major leagues: Anderson with the Dodgers (1946) and the Cardinals (1953), and Edwards with the Dodgers where he yielded his starter's role to Roy Campanella. Edwards would play 10 seasons and two World Series with the Dodgers.

The outbreak and escalation of World War II interrupted Burris's career in baseball when he was drafted into the Army. In his 31 months of service, Burris "saw plenty of action" on the Pacific Front, in Guadalcanal and the Philippines. He received an honorable discharge, having achieved the rank of sergeant, in 1946.

Also in 1946, the Class D North Carolina State League resumed baseball after having suspended play during the war. Now 23 years old, Burris began playing again, in the North Carolina State League, with the High-Point-Thomasville (Hi-Toms) Dodgers. He caught 74 games and batted .198. During the 1947 season he saw action with the Class B Danville Dodgers of the Three-I League, where he played 117 games and raised his batting average to .287. At Danville, Burris caught Carl Erskine, who that season was 19–9 with a 2.94 ERA. After the season, Burris was drafted from the Dodgers farm system by the Milwaukee Brewers of the American Association, a Braves affiliate. Reportedly, Bob Coleman, manager of the Evansville Bees, a Braves affiliate in the Three-I League, recommended selection of Burris to the Braves front office. Coleman himself was a former major league catcher and had managed the Braves in 1943–45.

In 1948, despite his 21 errors in 100 games (league high for catchers in the American Association) Burris was called up to the Boston Braves, who had already clinched the National League pennant. Burris made his major league debut on October 2, 1948, at the age of 25. Wearing number 11, he caught Warren Spahn in the first game of the day's doubleheader against the Giants, going 1-for-1 at the plate. The following day's game was the final game of the season, and Burris caught again, going 1-for-3. These games were the first two of his 69 career major league games, all played with the Braves. Although he was not eligible for the World Series, he did receive a one-eighth share ($571.34, the same amount received by Johnny Antonelli, who appeared in four games) from the Braves' Series receipts.

For 1949, Burris was initially penciled in as third catcher on the Braves' staff. However, Del Crandall, Bill Salkeld, and Phil Masi wound up sharing the backstop duties. Burris was returned to the Brewers and played with them for the entire 1949 season. He continued his steady play behind the plate while hitting for a .263 average.

The Braves again called on Burris in 1950, keeping him with the team throughout the season, and playing him in 10 games as the backup catcher to Walker Cooper and Del Crandall.

Although his batting average in 1950 was only .220, Burris continued what would be a streak of errorless games—by the end of his major league career, in 69 games, he had a 1.000 fielding average, handling 271 chances without an error. Burris was known to have a strong arm (Nick Cullop, the Brewers' manager said his throws "travel down to second base with the speed of a rifle shot"), but his weak hitting and relative lack of power limited his playing time and kept him in the role of bullpen catcher for most of his career. The Braves had hopes for Burris. Cullop said he would be a regular in the major leagues if he could learn to hit the curveball. "All he needs is to hit around .275 and he'll stay in the Big Show for a long time," Cullop said. "He's a conscientious player, the type Billy Southworth prefers." Cullop said Burris "was sent to us with orders that he work regularly. Billy Southworth is figuring on him to be a full-time receiver for the Braves next season. One more full campaign in the American Association will prepare him for such purposes."

Following an offseason operating a soda shop near Charlotte, Burris began his third stint with the Milwaukee Brewers in 1951, where he was the backup catcher to Al Unser, who caught 115 games, batting .293 with 17 home runs. Unser, in organized baseball since 1933, and with major league experience (Tigers and the Reds) appeared in 122 games overall that season, which limited Burris to 48 games. Burris was called up to Boston on

September 4, but didn't get into any games. This season, however, prepared him for 1952, when he would have his most productive major league season. In that season, he played in 55 games for the Braves, with two of his 37 hits representing his entire major league career home run production. His first, a solo shot in the fifth inning of the second game of a doubleheader, came off Carl Erskine, his old Three-I League batterymate, on May 30, 1952, at Ebbets Field. The homer was the only hit Erskine gave up in seven innings of relief. Burris's second home run, a two-run blast, came on June 12. and was part of Burris's biggest day in baseball—he was 4-for-5 with a home run, a double, two singles, and six RBIs.

Burris also saw 1952 as an important year personally as he married Bette Burgess. He and Bette had their first daughter, Paula, in 1953.

Burris was in the Braves' spring training camp when, on March 18, 1953, the franchise was transferred to Milwaukee. Notably, in a hastily taken team photograph, Burris is seen between Billy Bruton and Lew Burdette wearing a Milwaukee cap while others sport their old "B" hats. Many years later a collector would issue a black and white "Boston/Milwaukee" team set of baseball cards made up of pre-move player shots, with Burris receiving his own pasteboard after having retired.

On June 22, 1953, Burris broke his left elbow in a collision at home plate during an exhibition game with the Braves' Class C farm club in Eau Claire, Wisconsin. Up to then, he had played in only two games, with just one at-bat. He was placed on the disabled list on July 3 and remained on the DL until September 18. On December 2, 1953, Burris was assigned outright to Toledo of the American Association but Baseball Commissioner Ford Frick ordered that the Braves give him another trial. If he was not retained, the Braves would need to obtain waivers on him before sending him to the minor leagues. Ultimately, Burris was optioned to Toledo of the American Association (the Milwaukee Brewers had moved there after the Braves moved to Milwaukee) and assigned outright on September 20, 1954. He had played his final major league game in Milwaukee on June 4, 1953. He was 30 years old.

Burris played well at Toledo in 1954. In 108 games, he batted .265. His playing time, however, began to decrease. Through 1955 and 1956, he saw action with a number of other teams, including: the Jacksonville Braves of the South Atlantic League, the Columbus Clippers of the American Association, the Atlanta Crackers of the Southern Association, the Austin Senators of the Texas League, and the Louisville Colonels of the American Association. At Austin, where he played 13 games, his manager was a 1948 Braves teammate, Connie Ryan.

Although the life of a professional baseball player was challenging for Burris's young family, they had been looking forward to his continued play with the Braves in 1954.

His broken elbow and his assignment to Toledo had, unfortunately, affected his career plans. He did stay in the game until 1956 but as he was being used less frequently, he must have recognized that his professional career was coming to a close. He and his family returned to North Carolina to Huntersville, about 10 miles from Charlotte. There he was employed by the Douglas Aircraft Co. and the Duff Norton Co. until his retirement in 1985.

Paul Burris died in Huntersville on October 3, 1999, at the age of 76. His obituary in the *Charlotte Observer* said he "will especially be remembered for his dedication to his family and great love of seeing his grandchildren [Erin and Paul Taylor, Katie and Phillip Carter] play ball." The obituary also noted that he had once "thrown out Mickey Mantle at second base," without explaining when that happened. A lifelong member of the Presbyterian Church, Burris was laid to rest in Williams Memorial Presbyterian Church Cemetery in Charlotte on October 6, 1999.

Bibliography/Sources

Johnson, Richard A. *Boston Braves (Images of America: Massachusetts)*. Charleston, S.C.: Arcadia Publishing, 2001.

Kaese, Harold. *Boston Braves 1871–1953*. Boston: Northeastern University Press, 2004.

Peeler, Tim and Brian McLawhorn. *Baseball in Catawba County*. Charleston, S.C.: Arcadia Publishing, 2004.

Podoll, Brian A. *The Minor League Milwaukee Braves 1859–1952*. Jefferson, N.C.: McFarland & Company, 2003.

A. Bartlett Giamatti Research Library. National Baseball Hall of Fame. Cooperstown, N.Y. http://www.baseballhalloffame.org/library/research.htm

Baseball Almanac. http://www.baseball-almanac.com/players/player.php?p=burripa01

Catawba County Historical Association. Newton, N.C. http://www.catawbahistory.org/contact.org/contact_the_ccha.php

Charlotte/Mecklenberg Public Library http://www.plcmc.org

Hickory Public Library. Hickory, N.C. http://www.hickorygov.com/library

Milwaukee Braves Historical Association. http://webpages.charter.net/milwaukeebravesha/mbha_001.htm

Reference and Information Services. Widener Library. Harvard University. Cambridge, MA. http://hcl.harvard.edu/research/at_hcl/#widener

University of North Carolina. The North Carolina Collection. Chapel Hill, N.C. http://www.lib.unc.edu/ncc/index.html

State Library of North Carolina. Information Services Branch. http://statelibrary.dcr.state.nc.us/

Wisconsin Historical Society. http://www.wisconhistory.org/museum/exhibits/braves.asp

CLINT CONATSER *by Saul Wisnia*

G	AB	R	H	2B	3B	HR	RBI	BB	SO	BA	OBP	SLG	SB	HBP
90	224	30	62	9	3	3	23	32	27	.277	.370	.384	0	1

Clint Conatser's career was given a boost by a strong endorsement from childhood neighbor, Bobby Doerr.

A few more feet was all Clint Conatser needed. His hard shot to center with the bases loaded and the Braves trailing 4-1 in the eighth inning of Game Six of the 1948 World Series was caught by Cleveland's Thurman Tucker against the outfield fence; had the ball hit or cleared the wall just above Tucker's glove, there is a good chance the Braves might have rallied to capture the game and set up a winner-take-all finale at the ballpark the next afternoon. Ace Johnny Sain, who had allowed just seven hits and two runs over 17 stellar series innings, was already set to start the seventh game for Boston.

Conatser, however, didn't get those extra feet. His pinch-hit smash off Indians hurler Gene Bearden wound up as a helpful but inglorious sacrifice fly that scored Tommy Holmes from third and cut the score to 4–2. Phil Masi followed with a pinch-double to bring Boston one run closer, but Bearden stopped the rally there. After he shut down the Braves in the ninth as well, the victory and the championship went to Cleveland. Bearden (who also pitched a shutout in Game Three) was the hero, and Conatser merely a footnote in the box score—long forgotten to history.

The easygoing Californian has always pondered what could have been. "[Cleveland manager Lou] Boudreau had taken Larry Doby out and put Thurman Tucker in center field," said Conatser. "If you look at the reports, it says I hit a long fly. Well, I hit a SHOT, on 3-and-2, that Tucker made a hell of a play on in left-center. I think Dark, who was halfway, was able to go back to first, tag up, and advance to second. Tucker hit the fence—it was just a great play. Doby played everybody shallow and never would have made the catch. Boudreau said that was the determining play of the World Series right there. If that ball goes in, we win, and come back with Sain the next day."

Incredibly, as he recalled in another interview, Conatser didn't even see where the ball went after leaving his bat. He's heard the radio reports that "it was a well-hit ball, a line shot that was really kissed hard. But I didn't see it because I had my head down. A ballplayer should never look at the ball until he rounds first base, at which time you can see the play in front of you." As frustrating as it may be to speculate on the possibilities, however, the veteran who played just 143 big-league games has always maintained a sense of humor about the whole thing. "I always say, if it had been Musial batting, the ball would have gone in. But with rinky-dinks like me, somebody always makes the play."

From Manchester to the minors

Being close to glory was nothing new to Clinton Astor Conatser. Growing up in Los Angeles, where he was born on July 24, 1921, he lived within shouting distance of a local legend who made it all the way to Boston's other team—the Red Sox—and the Hall of Fame: Bobby Doerr. "He lived on 85th street, I lived on 84th, and I could walk over to his house maybe 300–400 feet away," recalled Conatser. "I went to school with his sister and his brother Hal, who was a heck of a ballplayer. His sister played football and softball, and Hal caught in the Pacific Coast League and was an outstanding ballplayer. He just didn't hit enough to make it to the big leagues."

Conatser's dad and Doerr's father were fishing buddies, but Bobby was more an idol to Clint than a friend. "Bobby was my hero as a kid; that's why I started out as a second baseman," said Conatser. "He was never recognized for being as great as he was until after he was through, but what a credit he was to the game. If he had played in New York, they would never have heard of Flash Gordon. Joe Gordon was a good ballplayer, but Bobby Doerr was a great ballplayer. He made everything look easy, just quietly going along."

As strong a player as Doerr was, however, Conatser says he wasn't even the best in the neighborhood. "On our American Legion team we had [George] Catfish Metkovich, who played first and the outfield for the Red Sox and other teams; Dick Conger, who pitched for the Tigers, Phillies, and Reds; and Merrill Combs, a third baseman for the Red Sox. We were representing John C. Fremont High School, where Doerr and George McDonald had gone before us. McDonald was the big star, and hit great in the Pacific Coast League, but he never made it in the majors."

Fremont's opposition in those days was equally impressive. Rival George Washington High School had a Legion team that included Eddie Malone, who later caught for the White Sox; Louis Stringer, a future second baseman for the Cubs and Red Sox; Jerry Priddy, a second baseman for years in the American League; and Brian Stephens, a Coast League star. Conatser says a catcher named Al Montgomery might well have been the best of them all, but he was killed in World War II while stationed in the Philippines. "The last of the bunch to come out of Fremont High was Gene Mauch, who came up with the Dodgers and later played with the Braves." [Mauch, also a Red Sox, would eventually achieve greater fame as a longtime big-league manager.]

It was a terrific environment for a young athlete to grow up in. Although his father had been a semipro ballplayer for the L.A. Creamers, it was with and against his peers that right-handed Conatser honed his skills. "We all played over at the Manchester Playground—all year round, nothing but baseball. We had no coaches or organized teams until we got to Legion ball, but we had a playground director named Bill DeVernet who would make out lists of 'teams' like the Cardinals, Braves, and Yankees. Then we'd just go out and play. We watched the older pro players when they came back home and practiced. Kids are pretty good mimics." Among the guys they imitated were Dodgers catcher Mickey Owen, Reds third baseman Steve Mesner, and Red Sox star Doerr.

A 1948 article would later confirm that 73 players who graced the four diamonds at Manchester Playground had gone on to play professionally over the previous 20 years—including 28 in the majors—so it goes without saying that scouts came around regularly. After the "big-shot" representatives for clubs like the Yankees and Tigers had made their signings, "all of us little guys were left running around," Conatser recalled. "There was a guy named Johnny Angel who scouted for Cleveland and signed guys that nobody else wanted. One of them was Bob Lemon, one of them was Cliff Mapes, and one of them was myself. Lemon got $500 to sign, Mapes got $200, but I only got $100—plus $75 a month salary. Angel just signed guys who he saw had potential, and was probably the most successful scout back then for judging talent."

Tough transitions

Conatser, fast with a strong arm, was 16 when Angel started scouting him and 17 when he signed. He quit high school and in 1939 reported to spring training in Springfield, Ohio, of the Middle Atlantic League—Class C ball. "I walk out on the field the first day," he remembered, "and here's who they've got on the roster: Jim Hegan catching, Jim Conway at shortstop, Bob Lemon at shortstop where he had played the year before, Billy Southworth, Jr. in center field, and a guy named Andy Spruskie in right field. Here's the pitching: Red Embry, Pete Sutter, Allie Reynolds, and a guy named Ray Benson—who could throw harder than Feller. I can remember standing at home plate watching him throw, and thinking, 'Jeez, if Feller throws harder than this guy, I'm in trouble.' I'd stand there and the ball would just go whoosh right past me. I thought, 'What am I doing here?'"

It was a formidable roster indeed; Lemon (a future

Hall of Famer) would star in the majors, as would Hegan and Reynolds. Edwards and Embry were also future big-leaguers, and with such talent to choose from, 18-year-old Conatser, a 5-foot-11 outfielder and second baseman, was sent down to Class D Fargo-Morehead in the Northern League when the season started. Before the year was out he would play for Class D Logan (in the Mountain State League) and Johnstown (in the Pennsylvania State Association) as well, and all told he hit .261 with nine homers and 57 RBIs in 107 games. The next spring he was rewarded for this solid debut with a $10 raise to $850 per month and a spot with Class C Flint in the Michigan State League. By this point he had been converted to a full-time outfielder.

Freshman Clint Conatser was a part of Billy Southworth's righty-lefty outfield platooning strategy.

"I believe the hardest transition is going from high school to professional ball," Conatser said of those days. "Instead of playing 10 or 12 games a year, you're playing every day. You have to play sick, and you're just a kid. You're staying in fleabag motels, getting $2 for meal money, and eating in grease joints. You play doubleheaders on holidays in one town, keep your uniform on, and go on to the next town. If you have a long trip, you try to sleep—and those were old, old buses that shook an awful lot. I remember in the Northern League, we went from Fargo to Warsaw, an all-night trip, and we slept sitting up. It was tough, but when you're a kid it's fun. You're playing ball."

After hitting .327 for Flint with excellent power (10 homers and 44 RBIs in 54 games), Conatser was sent back to Fargo-Morehead midway through 1940 and fell off to .236 the remainder of the year. This kept him at the Class C level in '41, predominantly at Charleston of the Middle Atlantic League, where in addition to the outfield he also saw time at shortstop and third base but hit .248 with just three homers. Although he remembers some scouts from other big-league clubs showing interest, Clint decided to put himself on the voluntary retired list and enlist in the Coast Guard after Pearl Harbor. He would eventually serve his country from 1942–45, including a stint in the South Pacific.

"After the war, it would have cost Cleveland $150 to pick up my option, but they figured I had retired and didn't bother," explained Conatser. "So I became a free agent while I was still over in the Philippines. I started getting letters from teams in South Carolina, Georgia, everywhere. I was keeping myself in shape by pumping iron. I was probably one of the first ballplayers to be really into weightlifting. I came out of the service weighing 185; when I went in, I had weighed 165. I was pretty strong."

Deciding to give pro baseball one more shot, Clint went home to Los Angeles and tapped the skills of Bobby Doerr—by then one of the American League's top stars with the Red Sox. "I started working out with Bobby, and he was telling me, 'Boy, you can really hit,'" Conatser remembered. "And I really could. I was whacking it pretty good. Bobby told this Tigers scout named Dan Crowley about me, but the scout who had signed me for Cleveland seven years before—Johnny Angel—was all upset because now all of a sudden I was gaining people's interest. I had a better than average arm, better than average speed, and better than average power."

Scout Dan Crowley, at Doerr's recommendation, signed Conatser to the Tigers for a $3,000 bonus. No doubt rejuvenated, Clint went out and hit .280 for Dallas of the Texas League in 1946 with 30 doubles, 13 homers, 70 RBIs and 20 steals. He recalled also performing well with Detroit in big-league training camp the next spring, but manager Fred Hutchinson still sent him down to Buffalo of the International League. "I had three options left in the minor leagues before they had to decide whether to keep me or leave me open for the draft. That's how they saved money when they had extra ballplayers. So they optioned me to Buffalo, then on to Seattle [of the highly competitive Pacific Coast League]."

Clint had a strong year in 1947 split almost equally between the two coasts, batting .287 with 14 homers in 120 games (.279 with Buffalo, .298 with Seattle). He figured he had earned another invite to Tigers training camp, but now out of options, he was left on the Buffalo roster—and promptly plucked up by the Boston Braves organization in November of '47. This time he was determined to stick on a big-league club come spring, and prepared accordingly.

On to Boston

"I had a good spring in 1948, because after I heard I had been signed, I spent a month and a half getting in shape. When I got there, brother was I ready. I stood out. The first day of spring training, I was out there hitting, and the other guys were just worried about losing weight. I was a rookie, and I wasn't supposed to make the team. Danny Litwhiler was kind of a fixture there, but [manager] Billy Southworth liked me. That's the way Billy did things—he had judgments on what was good for the team, and he went with them. I think Billy had a special touch. Of course, the players didn't like him, because you could never make any money platooning. They didn't pay you unless they played you."

With an overflow of outfielders in camp, Conatser was a long-shot to make the club. In addition to Southworth, however, he had another big backer: old pal Bobby Doerr. In a March 30, 1948 article appearing in the *Christian Science Monitor* under the headline "Rookie Clint Conatser May Make Grade in NL," the Red Sox All-Star second baseman recounted winters spent tossing the ball around in LA with his friend and neighbor. "He has good wrists and gets around pretty good in the outfield," Doerr told the *Monitor*'s Ed Rumill. "He has a good arm, too. I'd sure like to see him make it. He's a nice fellow."

In addition to his strong showing in exhibition play—which included a home run to help defeat the Red Sox—Conatser was involved in an incident of a near-calamitous nature as the Braves were barnstorming north through Virginia. During warm-ups before an April 12 game with the Richmond Colts, he hit a "savage line drive" that struck teammate Warren Spahn in his left (pitching) shoulder. Spahn quickly recovered, however, and Conatser made the club.

The Braves traded off Litwhiler to the Reds on May 11, but this didn't make Conatser a regular starter. Although Tommy Holmes was a fixture in right, Southworth kept his other four outfielders shuttling in and out of the lineup based on the opposing pitcher. Only Holmes played more than 110 games, with Conatser, Jeff Heath, Frank McCormick, and Jim Russell all getting into 75 or more. Right-handed Clint hit primarily against lefties; so insistent was Southworth in his righty-lefty swaps that he had Conatser regularly switching with his left-handed roommate, Heath, even though one could make a good case that Heath—who hit .319 with 20 home runs and 76 RBIs in just 364 at-bats—deserved to be in the lineup every day as the team's best power threat.

Making his mark

Conatser hit .277 with just three homers and 23 RBIs himself in his first big-league season, but he made several key contributions to the Braves' pennant-winning campaign. He went into the starting lineup for a stretch when Jeff Russell got hurt, and hit all three of his home runs in a one-month span as Boston battled for the top spot in the National League. His first homer, one of three hits Clint had vs. the Pirates on July 27, helped pace the club to a 5–1 win before 29,031 at Braves Field. On Aug. 17 he had a single, triple, and homer as Boston beat the Giants at the Polo Grounds, and five days later he delivered his biggest long ball of all—a two-run, eighth-inning blast off Erv Palica into the left-field stands at Ebbets Field that provided the winning runs in a 4–3 win that moved the Braves two games in front of the second-place Brooklyn Dodgers.

"The Dodgers were making their move that night—they stole eight bases on us—but I hit that one off Palica, and that took the wind out of their sails," recalled Conatser, looking at a wire service photo of him crossing the plate after the shot. "We were only ahead by a game at the time, but after that we widened the gap."

Clint haunted the Dodgers with more than homers in August. The day before his clutch shot off Palica, he had collected a key fifth-inning RBI double as the Braves won 2-1 to gain a split of a doubleheader at Ebbets Field and stay one game ahead of the Bums. And in a 4-3 win at Braves Field a week before that, he had kept a three-run, ninth inning rally against Brooklyn alive with a bunt hit down the third-base line, then finished it by scoring the winning run on a sacrifice fly. Once the Cardinals moved into second place, Conatser helped beat them as well—going 4-for-9 with a pair of doubles in back-to-back road wins on August 24 and 25.

Such performances earned Clint respect from teammates on the veteran-laden club, and likely spared him some of the usual rookie hazing. "The veterans were very good to me. I was 27, not like an 18-year-old rookie. They had some fun with me, but nothing malicious. I remember Bob Elliott helping me with my hitting, and I appreciated it. Tommy Holmes, Phil Masi, Jeff Heath—they were all good guys. They all really tried to make me feel at home and tried to help me. There was no jealousy or anything among ballplayers, not even the old timers."

And although many Braves players reportedly grumbled about Southworth's platooning, Conatser—who benefited from the system as much as anyone—had nothing but praise for his manager. "I'll tell you, Southworth had a lot of respect from the ballplayers. I think there was some talk that he grabbed all the headlines, but I think the papers did that. The sportswriters worshiped him, and called him the 'Little General.' He was outstanding as a manager, and he did outstanding things.

"Tommy Holmes had told me what I could expect from Southworth when I joined the club. He said, 'Clint, you're going to see something this year that you've never seen before. This man is uncanny. He'll pull things that are against all logic, and they'll work for him.' And he did. He'd get up on top of that batting cage, and he'd look for something in a guy's timing or whatever. Then he'd make a move. Tommy was right. Once he pulled Bobby Sturgeon off the bench when there were three or four other guys on the bench doing a better job, and Sturgeon hit a triple down the line that won the ballgame."

Conatser had strong memories of his teammates as well, but was not shy to tell it as he saw it. "They talk about Spahn and Sain and two days of rain. I always get a kick out of that, because Spahnie won 15 games that year—one of the few times he didn't win 20. It was one of his worst years, but he did lose some tough games. It seemed like every game I played in was a one-run game, or something like 3-1, and Spahnie was in a lot of those games coming up on the short end.

"Spahnie was a good hitter, too. He started as a first baseman, and he could hit it out of the ballpark. Sain was not a power hitter, but Spahn could jerk it out of there. He hit one out in Philadelphia—beat the hell out of it—using my bat. Back then, so many players played so many positions before they found where they belonged. Generally, as a kid, the pitcher is the best athlete. He pitches, and maybe plays shortstop. They lose their focus on hitting later on, because pitching takes a special focus where you need to blank every thing else out. But both Spahn and Sain could hit. Sain would just wait all day for a curve ball, and poke it to right field. [For the record, Sain hit .245 lifetime, Spahn .194 with 35 homers.]

"All our pitchers came through. We don't win it without Nellie Potter and that screwball. All the managers then were into platooning no matter what — and you don't put a left-handed hitter up against a right-handed screwball pitcher. He'd strike them out or get them to hit the ground ball, and he'd do it time after time after time. I got to thinking—this is stupid! Why not hit a right-hander against a screwball pitcher? They just wouldn't do it. But he did a hell of a job for us, even though nobody gave him much credit."

Conatser's biggest admiration, however, was reserved for his roommate. "Jeff Heath was quite a guy. On those hot nights when we couldn't get to sleep, we'd stay up until three or four on the morning, just talking. He'd tell me about how they had blamed him for all that stuff in Cleveland—some of the things they pulled on him. [When Heath was with the Indians in 1940, he and other star players were blamed for costing manager Ossie Vitt his job by complaining about him to ownership, and were lambasted as the "Crybaby Indians" in the newspapers.] We would have won the World Series against the Indians if he didn't break his ankle at the end of the year. I think he would have set a record for everything in that Series, he wanted to beat Cleveland so much."

Almost the hero

Clint helped Heath get through some of the early pain from his late September injury by sneaking over two bottles of pennant-clinching champagne to his roommate's Brooklyn hospital bed. Heath's absence left Conatser as the natural man to take over in center field fulltime for the World Series, but the Braves instead received special permission from the National League to bring up veteran left-handed batter Marv Rickert—who that year had 27 homers and 117 RBIs for minor league Milwaukee and had also played in the majors. Rickert went in to left field, Mike McCormick moved to center, and Conatser stayed on the bench. "After he got hurt, Jeff said it was up to me,"

Conatser recalled, "and I would have loved to play more in the Series. But then the Braves brought Rickert up, and I only played in two games—hitting against [Gene] Bearden when he started and relieved." [Rickert, meanwhile, would go 4-for-19 with a home run.]

The results of Conatser's limited series appearances were mixed. Playing center in place of Rickert during the third game, he went 0-for-3 against Bearden in the fellow rookie's 2-0 shutout victory for the Indians at Cleveland's Municipal Stadium. Clint didn't get in again until the fateful eighth inning of the sixth and final game back at Braves Field, when he hit his near-grand slam/sac fly. "We thought we were going to win the Series; we felt we had a better ballclub," he reflected. "There were just a few dumb plays here and there. My kids gave me a videotape of about 30 minutes of Series highlights, and you can see watching it the mistakes we made. Sisti popped that ball up and they got a double play out of it, Torgie made a few bad plays. It just wasn't typical of us; we didn't play that way all year."

There was some consolation to go with the postseason setback—a record loser's share of about $4,600 thanks to the crowds of 80,000-plus in Cleveland. "I took my money and paid cash for a house in Gardenia [California], which cost me $6,500," said Conatser. "My mother raised me that you didn't charge anything and you don't owe anybody, so I bought a little house. Trouble was, we didn't get the money until December, so I came back and went right to work at Santa Anita racetrack as an usher and ticket-taker with Bob Dillinger [of the St. Louis Browns]." An amusing Associated Press photo ran nationwide on February 13, 1949 that showed the pair in their "other" caps and uniforms and played up the fact Dillinger had sent back his latest Browns contract unsigned. The caption read:

Bob Dillinger, bespectacled third baseman of the St. Louis Browns, is shown discussing his baseball salary problems with Clint Conatser, Boston Braves outfielder, at Santa Anita Park, where both are clubhouse attendants.

With Heath's availability for the 1949 season up in the air, Conatser was expected to compete for a starting job in spring training. But on March 27, facing rookie Frank Fanovich of the Reds in an exhibition game, Clint was hit in the back of the head and taken from the field on a stretcher. "We didn't have helmets, and I was in the hospital for three days," he recalled. "I came out the fourth day, and Southworth put me right back in—like a guy falling off a horse."

Up, down, and out

Conatser recovered quickly to make the club, and was a starter in left field for many of the season's early games. The Braves started slow, but took over first in May and were still in the top spot when they headed to Philadelphia at month's end. Boston won two of three, and Clint was on fire—going 8-for-10 including three doubles, two home runs, and eight RBIs. Despite this output, part of a 10-day stretch on the road in which Clint hit .486 (18-for-37), Southworth amazingly had him platooning again with Russell when the team returned home June 1. Clint fell cold at the plate, and his average, once comfortably above .300, dropped well below this mark during the next month.

Ironically, it was the return of his old roommate that signaled the end of Clint Conatser's big league career. On July 8 newspapers reported that Heath would be ready to resume playing within two weeks after a 10-month recovery from his broken ankle; his return to the roster would give the Braves one too many outfielders, and shortly after the All-Star break, on July 15, Clint was sent to minor league Milwaukee. He was hitting .263 with three home runs at the time, and his last hit in the majors had not even counted—a homer slugged over the left-field wall at Fenway Park in a mid-season exhibition game with the Red Sox on July 11 to benefit charity.

His departure from the Braves was unceremonious. "I was the only player who had any options left, so they optioned me out," Conatser recalled. "I was 29 years old at the time, and I just said to myself, 'Hey, you gave it your best shot. Just get out of it.' So I quit." The player recalled by Boston to replace him on the roster was none other than Heath, who after an unsuccessful comeback would be gone from the majors himself by year's end.

Clint figured he was done with baseball, but it wasn't quite done with him. "That fall, the Dodgers bought me in the Sam Jethroe trade, because I had hit well against Brooklyn. Supposedly the Braves gave them $100,000 and me for Jethroe. [Newspaper accounts don't mention Conatser as part of the deal, but it did occur around the same time.] The Dodgers had tried to get me the year before, but Boston had traded them Mike McCormick instead. I was working on a ranch down in Texas, and [Dodgers GM] Branch Rickey came down there and asked me to play again. So I came out here and played with Hollywood a couple of years."

Back in the Pacific Coast League after a three-year hiatus, Conatser could not duplicate his 1947 PCL success at Seattle. He hit .231 with Hollywood in both 1950 and '51, appearing in fewer than 100 games both seasons and peaking at nine home runs for manager Fred Haney (who would later distinguish himself as pilot of the 1957 World Champion Braves). It was during this period that Stars management tried to boost sagging attendance by having its players wear shorts, a novelty that made for intriguing photo ops but also plenty of cut-up legs. In 1952, then with the Portland Beavers, Clint was doing much better (a .268 average playing every day) when he surprised the team by quitting abruptly on July 6. He was still just 30 years old.

"There was just no financial incentive. I gave it my best shot, but eventually I figured I just had to go make some money," said Conatser. "It's wonderful to be a ballplayer, but you've got to make a living. My father made me learn a trade when I was 14—sheet metal. I took shop 14 hours a day for two years. I didn't learn much, but it was all I knew how to do. He had an air conditioning business, so I got into it too. The years I played in Hollywood really opened the doors for me. That was in '52, when all the building out here [in Los Angeles] was just getting started. I was very, very lucky. I met people that ended up getting me business all over the country. I think people believe that ballplayers are basically honest, and I think that carries over after you retire. You learn to speak to people, and it helps you become a successful salesman."

The only time Conatser's name popped up in the sports pages after this was when he would join other former ballplayers living on the West Coast at fishing derbies and golf tournaments (he was among the best of the old-timers at both pursuits). His air conditioning business prospered, and he later spent more than 30 years buying and breeding race horses—often partnering with another old Brave, Joe Adcock, who raised Clint's mares on his Louisiana farm. As the decades passed, Conatser's alma mater, Fremont High, continued turning out big leaguers like Bob Watson, George Hendrick, and Chet Lemon.

By the 1990s photos of horses shared space with old baseball pictures on the walls of Clint's comfortable condo, located just off Route 5, 30 minutes from Anaheim Stadium. He stayed ruggedly handsome into his 80s, and came back to Boston a few times for Braves reunions. By the summer of 2007 he was one of the last living players from the 1948 NL champions, and when his daughters gave him a copy of the '48 World Series on videocassette, he enjoyed playing back his Game Six at-bat in slow motion and adding his own commentary with a sly grin.

"If that ball had just been an inch or two more inside, I'd of put it out!"

Sources

Author interviews with Clint Conatser, 1991 and 2004.

Mort Bloomberg interview with Clint Conatser, 2007.

"Manchester 'Alma Mater' of Many Stars," by John De La Vega, *Los Angeles Times*, Feb. 19, 1948.

"Rookie Clint Conatser May Make Grade in NL," by Ed Rumill, *Christian Science Monitor*, March 30, 1948.

Other assorted *Boston Globe, Chicago Tribune, Christian Science Monitor, Hartford Courant, Los Angeles Times, New York Times,* Associated Press, and United Press International articles, 1946-1984.

"Looking Back at a Few Diamond Memories," by Mort Bloomberg, Boston Braves Historical Association Newsletter, summer 2007.

Retrosheet.org

Baseball-reference.com

ALVIN DARK *by Eric Aron*

G	AB	R	H	2B	3B	HR	RBI	BB	SO	BA	OBP	SLG	SB	HBP
137	543	85	175	39	6	3	48	24	36	.322	.353	.433	4	2

President John F. Kennedy was said to have correctly answered a trivia question that had been floating around for years: Who is the only man to ever hit a home run off Sandy Koufax and catch a pass from Y.A. Tittle? The guess was always Alvin Dark. "It's not quite accurate, however," says Dark. "Tittle played at LSU after I did."[1]

That JFK's answer was presumed true said it all about Dark—a terrific three-sport athlete at Louisiana State University who in baseball excelled at each phase of the game. Joe DiMaggio called Dark the "Red Rolfe type of hitter," meaning that he was ideal for the No. 2 spot, the type of batter who could "bunt or drag, hit behind the runner, or push the ball to the opposite field."[2]

One of the best shortstops in Giants history, Dark played in 14 major league seasons with the Boston Braves, the New York Giants, the St. Louis Cardinals, the Chicago Cubs, and the Philadelphia Phillies, before returning to the Braves, then in Milwaukee, to finish his career. A three-time All-Star, he started at shortstop for the senior circuit in both the 1951 and '54 contests. He was 24 years old when he broke into the big leagues on July 14, 1946, with the Braves, but was already nationally known for his collegiate exploits on the diamond and gridiron. A lifetime .289 hitter with 126 homers and 757 RBIs, the "Swamp Fox" played on league pennant winners with the '48 Braves and '51 Giants, and also helped win a World Series title for New York in 1954. He won Rookie of the Year honors in 1948 and was captain of the strong Giants teams of the 1950s.

Dark also had a successful managing career. He won a National League pennant with the 1962 San Francisco Giants just after his playing days, a world championship with the Oakland A's in 1974, and a divisional flag for the A's in 1975. Accordingly, he became the first man to manage All-Star teams for both leagues: the National League in 1963 and the American League in 1975. It was not quite a Hall of Fame career either on the field or in the dugout, but he was still one of the few men to reach the top of the heap in both roles.

1948 Rookie of the Year Al "Blackie" Dark lettered in baseball, basketball and football at LSU and was drafted by the NFL Philadelphia Eagles.

Born on January 7, 1922, in Comanche, Oklahoma, Alvin Ralph Dark was the third of four children born to Ralph and Cordia Dark. Ralph was a drilling supervisor for the Magnolia Oil Company who also worked as a part-time barber. An amateur baseball star, he declined an opportunity to play in the Texas League to marry Cordia, who was just 15 at the time. Work brought the family, which also included son Lanier and daughters Margaret and Juanita, to Lake Charles, Louisiana.

Young Alvin battled malaria and diphtheria as a child, rendering him unable to attend school until the age of 7. Although he did not play any sport in elementary school, his athletic career blossomed at Lake Charles High School. As a teenager he made all-state and all-Southern football teams as a football tailback, and his skills as a basketball guard were superlative enough to earn him the team captaincy. Lake Charles High lacked a baseball team, and Alvin played American Legion ball during his teenage years.

Dark reconsidered a basketball scholarship from Texas A&M University to accept a free ride in football from Louisiana State in 1940. Playing halfback as a sophomore for the Tigers in 1942, he carried 60 times for 433 yards and a fantastic a 7.2-yard rushing average. He also played basketball and baseball for LSU that year, lettering in all three sports.

With World War II raging, Dark in 1943 joined the Marine Corps' V-12 program, which allowed him to continue his education for another year. The Marines sent him to the Southwestern Louisiana Institute in Lafayette, where he played for the greatest football team in the school's history. Undefeated at 4-0-1 (most Southern schools did not play a full schedule during the war), SLI beat Arkansas A&M University 24–7 to capture the inaugural Oil Bowl. In that game, played in Houston, Dark ran for a touchdown, passed for another from his tailback slot, and kicked three extra points and a field goal.[3]

In addition to playing football in the 1943–44 school year, Dark was a member of SLI's track, basketball, baseball, and even golf teams. His Marine V-12 obligations prevented him from playing in his entire baseball season, but he made the most of his limited at-bats—going 12-for-26 for an impressive .462 average. When the Marines selected his number, Dark was assigned to the Pacific Theater for combat action. After completing his basic training at Parris Island and Camp Lejeune, Dark was commissioned at Quantico in January 1945. As he awaited orders at Pearl Harbor, he tried out for the Marine Corps baseball team, earning a berth on the lower-division squad.

In the end Dark never saw combat, but he still faced a pretty dicey situation. After the declaration of an Allied victory in the summer of '45, he was sent to China that December to support the Nationalists against the Communists. He was dispatched to an outpost south of Peking (now Beijing) to guard the railroad and help transfer supplies to another station. Although his platoon did not know it, they had to pass through a Communist-controlled town to complete their mission. "Our group ran the supply line for four months before being relieved," said Dark. "A month after I got back to the United States, I received word that the Marines who took our place were ambushed in the Communist town and massacred."[4]

When he returned home to Lake Charles, Dark learned that he had been drafted to play pro football for the NFL's Philadelphia Eagles. His first love was baseball, however, and Ted McGrew, a scout for the Boston Braves, had been watching Dark play in college. McGrew, who had helped engineer the trade of Pee Wee Reese from the Red Sox to the Dodgers, admired young Dark for his tenacity and competitive spirit in all sports. Spurning reported interest from several clubs, Dark signed with the Braves as an amateur free agent for $50,000: a $45,000 bonus, and $5,000 to complete the season with Boston. The date was July 4, 1946.

Dark's obligations to the Marines prevented him from joining the Braves until July 14. That day, in the second game of a doubleheader against the Pittsburgh Pirates at Forbes Field, he pinch-ran for catcher Don Padgett in the ninth inning of a 5–2 loss. A month later, on August 8, Dark got his first hit—a double off Phillies' pitcher Blix Donnelly at Philadelphia. Once again, the Braves were defeated, as the Phillies triumphed, 9–8.

Dark played a total of 15 games for the fourth-place Braves in 1946. Although he had just three hits in 13 at-bats for a .231 average, all of them were doubles—a nice harbinger of things to come (he wound up hitting 358 big league two-baggers). At spring training in 1947, Dark pleaded with manager Billy Southworth to retain him as a regular player. Southworth preferred to keep veteran Sisti as his starting shortstop, however, and consequently optioned Dark to Milwaukee.

That summer, his only season in the minors, Dark hit .303 with 10 home runs, 7 triples, 49 doubles, 186 hits,

and 66 RBIs. He earned American Association honors as All-Star shortstop and Rookie of the Year, and finished third in the Most Valuable Player balloting. Playing for manager Nick Cullop, Dark led the Association in at-bats, runs, putouts, assists, and, dubiously, errors. His fielding, however, was considered solid; while not the flashiest of shortstops, he had good range and would become a good double-play man.

After the '47 season, Dark returned to Southwest Louisiana Institute to complete his degree in physical education. Although he wanted to compete in collegiate athletics, his request was denied because he had signed a professional contract. He did, however, serve briefly as the football coach's athletic assistant.

Dark made the Opening Day varsity for the Braves in 1948, but was relegated to the bench as veteran Sibby Sisti continued as the regular shortstop. Nevertheless, Dark persevered. His contributions as a reserve player eventually won him the starting job, and he wound up fourth in the National League in batting with a .322 average. He also contributed three home runs, 39 doubles (third in the NL), and 48 RBIs from his No. 2 spot in the order, while fielding his position strongly (a .963 fielding mark, well above the league average). Initially, his tenure in 1946 disqualified him from the Rookie of the Year ballot. However, the Baseball Writers Association of America ruled that year that players with 25 games or less in previous seasons would qualify for the ballot. This allowed Dark to win Rookie of the Year honors for 1948, the last season both leagues combined to acknowledge one freshman player. He also finished third in the race for NL Most Valuable Player, but was a letdown in his first World Series by batting a paltry .167 with one double in 24 at-bats. The Braves as a team were equally disappointing at the plate, compiling a cumulative .230 mark in losing the series to the Cleveland Indians in six games.

Dark's outstanding rookie campaign was augmented by the exploits of his keystone partner, second baseman Eddie Stanky. Known as "The Brat," Stanky was traded to the Braves by the Dodgers during spring training. Not only were Dark and Stanky a great double-play combination for years to come, but the tandem also became close friends and roommates. Dark considers Stanky and Danny Murtaugh as his greatest mentors; as Dark remarked in his autobiography, "Stanky knew so much more about the game than anybody else. If there were ten possible percentage plays to make, most guys would know four or five. Stanky would know ten."[5]

Their strong double-play duo notwithstanding, the Braves had a disappointing 1949. The defending league champions fell to 75 wins against 79 losses, good for just fourth place in the NL. Despite three home runs and 53 RBIs, a slight improvement, Dark's batting average fell as well—to .276.

Just behind the Braves in the '49 standings were the

New York Giants, who finished a pedestrian fifth place at 73–81. New York manager Leo Durocher and president Horace Stoneham attributed the shortcoming to inadequate speed and defense. To improve in these areas, the Giants traded outfielders Willard Marshall and Sid Gordon, shortstop Buddy Kerr, and pitcher Sam Webb to the Braves on December 14 for Dark and Stanky. The blockbuster deal was panned in Gotham, as the trade cost the Giants power hitters Marshall and Gordon—the latter a particularly strong fan favorite as one of the league's foremost Jewish sluggers. Fans at the Polo Grounds were also initially lukewarm to accepting Stanky, as he had previously played for the archrival Dodgers.

Dark, however, came with no such baggage, and "Leo the Lip" immediately took to his new shortstop. As Dark later reported, "Leo stuck by me in the early part of 1950, when I first came to the Giants and couldn't seem to get started...yet Durocher stood by and kept telling me not to worry, that I would seem to come out of it."[6]

Durocher surprised Dark once again that first season by declaring the shortstop his team captain. Most sportswriters assumed that Stanky, not Dark, would get the nod. After all, it was the extroverted Stanky who emulated Durocher, in speaking his mind to the press and in the clubhouse. Yet "The Lip" chose Dark, speculating that the position could easily build confidence in the mild-mannered infielder and help him emerge as a team leader.

"In my first year [as captain], all I did was take the lineup to home plate. After the success we had in 1951, I began taking on some responsibilities—automatic things, like consoling a guy after a bad day. After a while some of the younger players came around, and some of them, like (Willie) Mays, still call me 'Cap.'"[7]

In 1950, the Giants improved in the standings to third place with a record of 86–58. Playing in all 154 games, Dark batted .279 with 16 homers and 67 RBIs—by far his best power numbers to that point. It was in that season that the Giants made history.

Early in the '51 campaign, the Giants promoted rookie outfielder Willie Mays from Minneapolis, and he was soon dazzling the league with his graceful catches and power. The Giants also boasted clutch-hitting outfielder Monte Irvin, who had 121 RBIs that year, 32-homer man Bobby Thomson in the third outfield slot, and pitchers Sal Maglie and Larry Jansen, each a 23-game winner. Dark,

Dark's .322 average was the fourth best in the National League in 1948.

for his part, had a terrific year—hitting .303 with a career-high 196 hits, a league-best 41 doubles, 114 runs scored, and 14 homers. Defensively he led the league with 45 errors at shortstop, but he also was tops in assists (465) and double plays (114) in making his first All-Star team. Still, the Giants trailed the Dodgers by 13½ games as late as August 11. How was anyone to guess that they were about to complete one of the greatest pennant races in baseball history? The Giants won 37 of their last 44 games to tie the Dodgers at the end of the season, thereby forcing a three-game playoff.

In the third and final game, Brooklyn had a 4–1 lead going into the bottom of the ninth. With Dodgers' ace Don Newcombe on the mound, Dark led off the inning with a single off the glove of first baseman Gil Hodges. "I must have fouled off six or seven pitches with two strikes before getting that hit," Dark recalled.[8] Four batters later, after Dark had scored, Bobby Thomson hit his legendary three-run homer to cap the "Miracle at Coogan's Bluff" and win the pennant, 5–4. Dark hit .417 with three doubles, a home run, and four RBIs in the subway World Series that followed, but the Yankees reigned supreme, winning in six games.

After the 1951 season, Dark's friend and teammate Eddie Stanky was traded to the St. Louis Cardinals. Without this sparkplug, and with Willie Mays gone to the Army most of the year, the Giants finished 1952 in second place, 4½ games behind the Dodgers. Meanwhile, Durocher had become impressed with farmhand Daryl Spencer, who dazzled at shortstop while playing for Minneapolis. "The Lip" wanted to play Spencer at short and move Dark to second or third base. Dark expressed his displeasure by intruding on a press conference orchestrated by Durocher. Things smoothed over, however, and Spencer departed the Giants for military service following the 1953 season. After his greatest season at the plate in '53, batting .300 with 23 home runs and 88 RBIs, Dark emerged as the undisputed shortstop for the New York Giants.

Perhaps the resolution of this conflict helped the club. After a disastrous 1953 season, in which the Giants finished fifth, the team went on a roll the next spring. The press began referring to Durocher's '54 squad as "Happy Heroes, Inc.," because they would always find a way to beat you, whether it was a pinch-hit home run or solid pitching.[9] Dark was reunited with erstwhile Braves teammate

Johnny Antonelli, and the starting pitcher won 21 games after the Giants acquired him in a trade for Bobby Thomson. Center fielder Mays returned from the Army and emerged as a superstar, leading the National League with a .345 average while slugging 41 home runs and driving in 110 runs. The Giants finished five games ahead of the Dodgers, winning the pennant with a record of 97–57.

This time, the Giants faced the Cleveland Indians, winners of 111 regular season games, in the World Series. After hitting a solid .293 with 20 home runs and 70 RBIs during the year, Dark had another outstanding post-season with a .412 batting average and seven hits and a walk in 18 plate appearances. Boosted by Alvin's output and the incredible pinch-hitting of Dusty Rhodes (two homers, seven RBIs), the Giants surprised all experts by sweeping the Indians for the world title. While Mays was the runaway choice as league MVP, Dark finished fifth in the balloting and even got one first-place vote.

An injury-plagued 1955 campaign was Dark's last full season as a Giant. After fracturing his rib in a game against Cincinnati on August 7, he separated his right shoulder against the Phillies on September 2. Dark's injuries limited him to 115 games, and he ended the year hitting .282 with 9 homers and 45 RBIs. New York finished 18½ games behind the Dodgers, in third place.

The next season started off dismally for the club, and by early June the Giants were settled into sixth place with a record well under .500. A shakeup was in order, and in an eight-player deal on June 14, 1956, the Giants sent Dark, along with Ray Katt, Don Liddle, and Whitey Lockman to the St. Louis Cardinals for Dick Littlefield, Jackie Brandt, Red Schoendienst, and Bill Sarni. New York wanted a second baseman in Schoendienst, and the Cardinals wanted a shortstop in Dark. It was initially a good move for Al; the 1957 season, his last as a regular shortstop, was also his final pennant race as a player. He hit .290 as the Cardinals finished in second place, eight games behind the Milwaukee Braves.

Dark now became a third baseman—and a "traveling man." On May 20, 1958, the Cardinals traded him to the Chicago Cubs for pitcher Jim Brosnan; in his two seasons in Chicago, he hit .295 and .264 while playing alongside another standout shortstop—Ernie Banks. On January 11, 1960, Dark was swapped again, along with pitcher John Buzhardt and infielder Jim Woods, to the dismal Philadelphia Phillies for outfielder Richie Ashburn. Al's first hit of the season in Philadelphia's home opener against the Braves on April 14 of '60 was the 2,000th of his major-league career. He played 53 games at third base (hitting .242) before a June 23 trade for infielder Joe Morgan (later the Red Sox' manager) sent him to the Milwaukee Braves. Now 38, he was used primarily as a utility infielder, pinch-hitter, and occasional outfielder. Appearing in 50 games for the second-place Braves, Dark upped his productivity—batting .298 with one homer and 18 RBIs.

Still, it wasn't long before he was sent packing again. On October 31, 1960, Dark was traded for the sixth and last time when the Braves dealt him to the now-San Francisco Giants for infielder Andre Rodgers. With his future uncertain, Dark accepted a sales position with the Magabar Mud Company in Louisiana. He did not peddle mud for long, however, as he was named to replace Tom Sheehan as the Giants manager for 1961.

In his first press conference as skipper, Dark was asked if he retained any memento from the 1951 Miracle at Coogan's Bluff. "Yeah," the manager replied humorously. "Willie Mays!"[10] He demonstrated very quickly his ability and fortitude to make bold moves with his roster and in game situations, thereby emulating his mentor Leo Durocher. He intended to eliminate any racial cliques by reassigning lockers, thereby integrating whites with blacks in the clubhouse. "We're all together and fighting for the same cause. This way we'll all get to know each other better" he said.[11] Dark also moved the Giants' bullpen across the field to better monitor pitchers who might not be focused on the game.

Although Dark earned a reputation for avoiding controversy as a player, he embraced it as a manager. Despite his strong religious views as a Baptist fundamentalist, Al was prone to temper tantrums. To ventilate his anger after a 1–0 loss to Philadelphia on June 26, 1961, for instance, he flung a metal stool against the wall. In the process, he lost the tip of his little finger, requiring hospitalization for its repair. "I made up my mind two weeks ago not to take out my anger out on the players. So, I guess I took it out on myself tonight," he said in jest.[12]

In his first season as manager, Dark guided the Giants to a third-place finish at 85–69, eight games behind pennant-winning Cincinnati. The next season, 1962, he led the Giants to a sparkling 103–62 record and their first National League championship in San Francisco. Mays, Felipe Alou, Orlando Cepeda, and Willie McCovey combined to hit 140 homers, and Jack Sanford led the pitching rotation with 24 wins.

The Giants' 1962 campaign was not without its controversy. Even as West Coast transplants, they retained their rivalry with the now-Los Angeles Dodgers. LA shortstop Maury Wills was en route to swiping a then-record 104 bases, and according to the Dodgers, the Giants were trying to slow him down. At one point during a three-game series at San Francisco's Candlestick Park in August, the infield was soaking wet around first base. The umpires had no choice but to douse the wet surface with sand, thereby preventing baserunners from stealing. For his alleged role in the situation, Dark earned the nickname "Swamp Fox." To this day, Dark responds to the incident with a "Who, me?" attitude. As he remarked to *Baseball Digest* some 40 years later, "I just remember that one day they had trouble with a hose that broke."[13]

Just as in 1951, the '62 NL pennant race came down to

a tie finish and a three-game playoff with the Dodgers to decide a champion. The Giants triumphed again, and in another '51 rematch, they faced the Yankees in the World Series. The M&M Boys, Mickey Mantle and Roger Maris, sparked the Bronx Bombers' offense, complementing a rotation led by Whitey Ford and Ralph Terry. San Francisco took New York to the limit, but fell 1–0 in Game Seven at Candlestick Park. After this near miss, the Giants returned to third place under Dark in 1963, posting an 88–74 record to finish 11 games behind Los Angeles.

On June 7, 1964, during the last of a three-game series with the Phillies at Connie Mack Stadium Dark exemplified why the Bay Area had dubbed him the "Mad Genius" when he used four pitchers in the first inning alone![14] He sent starter Bob Henley to the showers for surrendering two runs without retiring a batter, and when reliever Bob Bolin walked one man, he, too, was replaced, by Ken MacKenzie. The Yale alumnus retired a pinch-hitter before Gaylord Perry was summoned to record the final two outs of the frame. The craziness worked; 10 innings later, the Giants beat the Phillies 4–3.

Dark's Giants completed the 1964 season with a fine 90–72 record and a fourth-place finish. However, his role at the center of a controversial article numbered his days in San Francisco. Midway through the season, Stan Isaacs of *Long Island Newsday* asked about the Giants' performance in an interview with Dark. The manager responded by accusing his players of making recent "dumb" plays.[15] Although he later insisted that his comments were specific to baserunning mistakes by Orlando Cepeda and Jesus Alou, it was already too late; because his team was made up primarily of African-American, Puerto Rican, and Dominican superstars, Dark was unfairly painted as a racist.

On August 4, 1964, Dark called a press conference at Shea Stadium in New York to explain that the newspapers had misinterpreted him, but it mattered not; Horace Stoneham fired him at the end of the season. Several high-ranking baseball officials declared their support for Dark, including Commissioner Ford Frick. Perhaps most significantly, former Dodgers great Jackie Robinson quickly rushed to Dark's defense. The two had been friends since their playing days, and Robinson told the *New York Times* that he had "known Dark for many years, and my relationships with him have always been exceptional. I have found him to be a gentleman, and above all, unbiased. Our relationship has not only been on the baseball field but off it. We played golf together."[16]

Surely boosted by this vote of confidence, Dark moved beyond the Giants and was subsequently hired as third-base coach for the Chicago Cubs. Then, at the end of the 1965 season, Charlie Finley hired him to manage the Kansas City Athletics. Dark was already the sixth manager hired by the maverick Finley in the six years he had owned the team. The A's boasted an unknown young club

with Jim "Catfish" Hunter, John "Blue Moon" Odom, and Lew Krausse in the starting rotation. After losing 103 games in '65, the A's went 74–86 in 1966 during Dark's first season as skipper.

Despite considerable talent, lackluster baseball and personality issues caused the A's to fall back into the cellar in 1967. After an incident that alleged player rowdiness on an airline flight, Dark had the distinction of being fired, rehired, and fired again on August 20. Not even Hall of Famer Luke Appling could resurrect the A's as Dark's replacement. With two All-Star shortstops at the helm, the A's finished with a record of 62–99.

After the '67 season, the Cleveland Indians hired Dark as manager and general manager. He led the Tribe to its best record in nine years in 1968, with 86 wins against 75 losses. But in '69, the Indians finished last, at 62–99. Without a substantial budget, they improved a bit in 1970 but returned to last place in '71. Posting a record of 42–61 on July 30, Dark was fired as manager and general manager—completing his four years at the Cleveland helm with a lackluster .453 winning percentage (in San Francisco, he had won at a .569 clip).

For the next two years, Al lived in Miami, where he excelled as a regular golfer by winning local club tournaments. He supplemented his savings as an after-dinner speaker at churches, lecturing on baseball and the Bible. By 1974, however, Dark missed managing. As spring training dawned on February 20, he accepted old pal Charlie Finley's offer to return to the A's, by now in Oakland, as their skipper.

Dark faced enormous pressure assuming the reins of baseball's most combative and successful team. Under Dick Williams, the A's had won the World Series in 1972 and 1973. Although one year remained on Williams' contract, personal differences with Finley led him to resign as manager. Dark accepted a one-year, $50,000 contract as Williams's successor, complete with incentive bonuses if he won the pennant or World Series. An Oakland reporter heralded Dark's arrival by defining "the only thing worse than being hired by Charlie Finley [is] being hired by him a second time."[17]

Al claimed that he was a changed man due to his renewed faith in Christianity. No longer would he berate his players or belittle them publicly. He also vowed to accept Finley's suggestions, avoiding a renewal of their feud. Certain players, like Reggie Jackson, accepted Dark's new personality, while others, such as Vida Blue, were rather critical. A fellow Louisianan, Blue "knew Alvin Dark was a religious man, but he's worshipping the wrong god—Charles O. Finley."[18]

The Oakland team Dark assumed in 1974 had few weak spots. Jim "Catfish" Hunter posted a record of 25–12, led the league with a 2.49 ERA, and won the American League Cy Young Award. Powered by a lineup featuring the likes of Jackson, Sal Bando, and Joe Rudi, the club captured its fourth consecutive division title by five games over the surprising Texas Rangers. The A's pitchers proved dominant over the Orioles in the League Championship Series, at one point tossing 30 consecutive scoreless innings. Oakland won the series, three games to one.

The 1974 World Series was the first to feature only California teams: the A's and manager Walter Alston's Dodgers. After defeating Los Angeles in five games for his first series title as a skipper, Dark agreed to return to Oakland in 1975. And, despite losing Hunter as a free agent, he guided the A's to yet another divisional title. With a record of 98-64, the A's paced the division with a comfortable seven-game lead over the Kansas City Royals, but the 1975 Red Sox swept Oakland in three games in the playoffs.

On October 17, 1975, Charlie Finley announced that Dark's contract would not be renewed. Dark returned to the Cubs as a coach for manager Herman Franks in 1977 before replacing John McNamara as the San Diego Padres' manager on May 28. Although the Padres played well under Dark, their second-half record could not lift them beyond a final mark of 69-93. Citing a "communication problem," Padres general manager Bob Fontaine fired Dark on March 21, 1978.[19] He was only the second manager in major-league history to be released during spring training.

Although Dark has yet to be enshrined in Cooperstown, and will likely never make the cut, he is a member of the Oklahoma Sports Hall of Fame, the Louisiana Sports Hall of Fame, the Louisiana State University Sports Hall of Fame, and the New York Giants Baseball Hall of Fame. Dark married his childhood sweetheart, Adrienne Managan, in 1946, and the couple had four children: Allison, Gene, Eve, and Margaret. Divorcing in 1969, Dark was married a year later to Jackie Rockwood, and adopted her children, Lori and Rusty. Al returned to baseball as the farm system evaluator for the Chicago Cubs in 1981, and in 1986 served as director of minor leagues and player development of the Chicago White Sox.

At age 86, Dark has 20 grandchildren and three great-grandchildren. He lives in Easley, South Carolina, to which he moved from San Diego in 1983. Today he is involved with the Alvin Dark Foundation, a Christian organization dedicated to financially supporting ministries, and has shown his affinity for the old days by several times traveling to New England for reunions hosted by the Boston Braves Historical Association.

Notes

1. Alvin Dark and John Underwood, *When in Doubt, Fire the Manager* (New York: E.P. Dutton, 1980), p. 32.
2. Tom Meany, *The Incredible Giants*, (New York: A.S. Barnes, 1955), p. 73.
3. Louisiana's Ragin' Cajuns Athletic Network www.athletic network.net
4. *When in Doubt*, p. 36.
5. *Ibid*, p. 42.
6. *The Incredible Giants*, p. 74
7. *When in Doubt*, p. 59.
8. Interview with Alvin Dark, December 18, 2006.
9. *The Incredible Giants*, p. 76.
10. Stein, Fred, and Nick Peters, *Giants Diary: A Century of Giants Baseball in New York and San Francisco*, (Berkeley: North Atlantic Books, 1987), page missing.
11. Jack McDonald, "Alvin Assigns New Lockers in Effort to Kill Cliques," in *The Sporting News*, April 19, 1961, p. 26.
12. Bob Stevens, "Dark Blows Stack—Loses Finger-Tip on Metal Stool," *The Sporting News*, July 5, 1961, p. 9.
13. David Bush, "Turn Back the Clock 1962: When the Giants Lost a Heartbreaker to the Yankees," *Baseball Digest*, October 2002, page missing.
14. Robert Boyle, "Time of Trial for Dark" *Sports Illustrated*, July 6, 1964, p. 28.
15. Alvin Dark and John Underwood, "Rhubarbs, Hassles, Other Hazards," *Sports Illustrated*, May 13, 1974, p. 48.
16. *When in Doubt*, p. 98.
17. *Ibid*, p. 166.
18. Bruce Markusen, *A Baseball Dynasty: Charlie Finley's Swingin' A's*, (Haworth, NJ: Saint Johann Press, 2002), p. 289.
19. *When in Doubt*, p. 230.

Sources

"Dark's First Hit of the Season No. 2,000 for His Career" in *The Sporting News*, Vol. 149, Issue 14. St Louis: April 27, 1960: p. 8.

Boyle, Robert. "Time of Trial for Dark," in *Sports Illustrated*, Vol. 21, Issue 1. July 6, 1964: pp. 26–31.

Bush, David. "Turn Back the Clock 1962: When the Giants Lost a Heartbreaker to the Yankees," *Baseball Digest*. October 2002.

Dark, Alvin, and John Underwood. "Rhubarbs, Hassles, Other Hazards," *Sports Illustrated*, Vol. 40, Issue 19. May 13, 1974: pp. 42–48.

Dark, Alvin, and John Underwood. *When in Doubt, Fire the Manager*. (New York: E.P. Dutton, 1980).

Louisiana's Ragin' Cajuns Athletic Network, www.athleticnetwork.net

Markusen, Bruce. *A Baseball Dynasty: Charlie Finley's Swingin' A's*. (Haworth, NJ: Saint Johann Press, 2002).

McDonald, Jack. "Alvin Assigns New Lockers in Effort to Kill Cliques," *The Sporting News*, Vol. 151, Issue 13. St. Louis: April 19, 1961: p. 26.

Meany, Tom. *The Incredible Giants*. (New York: A. S. Barnes, 1955).

Stein, Fred, and Nick Peters. *Giants Diary: A Century of Giants Baseball in New York and San Francisco*. (Berkeley: North Atlantic Books, 1987).

Stevens, Bob. "Dark Blows Stack—Loses Finger-Tip on Metal Stool," *The Sporting News*, Vol. 151, Issue 24. St. Louis: July 5, 1961: p. 9.

Tourangeau, Dixie. "Spahn, Sain, and the '48 Braves" *The National Pastime*, published by SABR, Vol. 18. 1998: pp. 17–20.

BOB ELLIOTT *by John McMurray*

G	AB	R	H	2B	3B	HR	RBI	BB	SO	BA	OBP	SLG	SB	HBP
151	540	99	153	24	5	23	100	131	57	.283	.423	,474	6	0

A consistent and sometimes spectacular player, Bob Elliott was the biggest everyday offensive threat on the 1948 Boston Braves. He led that pennant-winning team in games played, home runs, and runs batted in. He was very selective at the plate, striking out just 57 times while leading the National League with 131 bases on balls. The performance was not surprising; a year prior, the husky third baseman became the first Boston Brave to be named the National League's top player since Johnny Evers won the Chalmers Award in 1914. Sportswriter Harold Kaese quoted Hall of Fame second baseman/manager Rogers Hornsby as saying, "Bob Elliott *made* the Braves. He's the old-time type who hits and plays his best in the clutch."

It is sometimes reported that the right-handed Elliott was such an integral part of the '48 Braves lineup that New England sportswriters gave him the nickname "Mr. Team." But Kaese, a longtime *Boston Globe* columnist, explained later that "his teammates, without any prompting from the press, began to address him as 'Mr. Team.' If Elliott hit a home run in the clutch, they said, 'Nice going, Team.' And on the bench before games, they'd ask solicitously, 'How's the Team feeling today?'"

A profile of Elliott published by the Pittsburgh Pirates when he was with that team in 1943 had foreshadowed his success with Boston, saying that "his power, speed, and fielding skill and spirit make him look so much like a natural that there is hardly any question that he is destined to rank eventually with the greatest of his time."

Elliott was responsible for one of the greatest hits in franchise history as well—when his three-run home run off Giants hurler Larry Jansen clinched the NL pennant for Boston in 1948. On a 2–1 count in the first inning of the September 26 contest at Braves Field, Jansen threw a slider. "I caught this one hard," Elliott said later. "It was off to right center. I didn't think it would make it.... It went right over the visiting bullpen. We were ahead 3–0." The Braves won the game, 3–2, to end a 34-year championship drought, and Elliott recalled manager Billy Southworth

Bob Elliott entered the '48 season as the past year's Senior Circuit MVP.

telling him: "That's the best base hit you ever got in your life, Bob."

Elliott even looked the part of a hero. He was described by Kaese as "a rugged young man, blond, blue-eyed, and wearing a chin like a chisel," and was well regarded by his peers, fans, and the press. *Boston Daily Record* columnist Dave "The Colonel" Egan, for one, noted in 1952 that that "Bob Elliott has been a big-leaguer off the field and on it for 13 years" and that he has been "a man of decency and integrity."

Robert Irving Elliott was born on November 26, 1916, in San Francisco and grew up in El Centro, California. His parents were Irving Elliott, a plaster plant superintendent, and the former Anne C. Johns; Robert was one of four children. In his early years in California, Elliott was a student at Harding Grammar School, Wilson Junior High School, and Union High School. At Union he played football and baseball, then took up these same sports at El Centro Junior College.

As a teenager, Elliott got a break that set the wheels of his career quickly in motion. According to the 1948 World Series press notes: "One afternoon when Bob was 17 years old, he received an invite to visit the desk sergeant at the El Centro, Cal. police station....The purpose of the invitation was a dark secret until Bob reached the sergeant's desk to discover that he was Jack Stark, a former Coast Leaguer who was interested in the El Centro semipro team and wanted Bob, a good amateur player, to join the team....Needless to say, Bob accepted and soon his playing attracted attention of scouts."

Years later, Elliott recalled: "Jack Stark ran a semipro club at El Centro...and recommended me to [former major leaguer George] Cutshaw. Cutshaw, in turn, told Mr. [William] Benswanger of the Pirates about me. Oscar Vitt, managing Oakland, offered me a contract, but George said, 'You stick with me. I can get you to Pittsburgh.' He was doing some scouting for that club. I figured that with a direct line to the National League, I would have a better chance, so I stuck with Cutshaw, who landed me with the Pirates."

Elliott began his career in professional baseball with Savannah of the Class B South Atlantic League in 1936. In 144 games, he hit 12 homers and knocked in 84 runs while batting .292. Before the 1937 campaign, his rights were acquired by the Pirates as part of a minor-league working agreement. While with Savannah during the '37 season, Elliott showed good speed in legging out 16 triples. He was chosen as a SALLY League All-Star that summer, repeating an honor earned the previous year.

Still just 20 years old, Elliott was sent back for a third season of minor league seasoning in 1938. He played 11 games with Knoxville of the Southern League, then was returned to Savannah to play the bulk of the summer. Now a familiar face to Georgia fans, he batted .325 with 30 doubles, 11 triples, and 12 homers in his third year with the club.

In 1939, Elliott's strong batting performance in the early going propelled him to the major leagues. The Pirates had sent Elliott to Double A Louisville of the American Association to start that season, "with the notation that Bob is a brilliant prospect, just a year out of the majors." In his debut for the Louisville club managed by Donie Bush, Elliott "lashed a triple off the scoreboard" against St. Paul. Bob had another single in that game, and, according to an account on April 27, 1939, "Bush is wondering if like the absent-minded professor, he found right under his nose the power right-handed batter he had been willing to beg, borrow, or steal."

After playing only 14 games with Louisville, Elliott was optioned to Toronto of the Double A International League. In 115 games there in '39, he batted .328 with 27 doubles. Brought up by Pittsburgh at the end of the season, he made his major-league debut on September 2, during an 11–3 win against the Cardinals in St. Louis. All he did in that game was homer into the left-field bleachers and collect three runs batted in. He got his first major-league hit off Clyde Shoun, a single that Cardinals outfielder Enos Slaughter misplayed, allowing Elliott to wind up on third base.

Elliott played in the All-Star game in only his second full season in the major leagues (1941), which was no sure thing since he was hit in the head by a Sam Nahem pitch during a May 24 game. In the Midsummer Classic played on July 8 at Briggs Stadium in Detroit, Elliott made an error in the fourth inning that led to the American League scoring the game's first run in what would be a two-run NL loss. "I cried," Elliott later said. "Real tears, like a kid."

The 6-foot, 185-pound line-drive hitter came to the major leagues as an outfielder, and he played there through 1941 with the Pirates. As he told Jack Hernon of the *Pittsburgh Post-Gazette*, he wound up replacing both Hall of Fame-bound Waner brothers: "The Waners were in their last days when I arrived in 1939, and my first full season, the following year, I was in center

field as the replacement for Lloyd Waner," Elliott recalled. "Then when the club traded Johnny Rizzo to Cincinnati for Vince DiMaggio, I moved over to right field and Paul [Waner] left the club."

Pittsburgh manager Frankie Frisch decided to switch Elliott to third base in 1942 to replace Lee Handley, who had left the team to serve in World War II. When informed of the position change, Elliott reportedly asked, "Am I that bad an outfielder?" As one account noted, "He was not, but the Pirates needed a third baseman." True to his pleasing personality, Elliott said he was willing to "give it a whirl."

As recounted by Arthur Daley of the *New York Times*, Frisch hit some grounders toward Elliott to give the young player some practice at third base: "Elliott gave the first couple of grounders the Pie Traynor treatment, beautiful pick-ups and throws. But the next one struck a pebble and smacked him squarely between the eyes. Down he went—out cold. The frantic Flash poured a bucket of water over him. Bob blinked and sat up.

"Hey, Frank," he said weakly. "Remember what you told me about third base adding five years to my career?"

"Yes, yes," said Frisch.

"I think I lost three of those five extra years already," said Elliott.

Bob experienced a similar moment at third base during a Pirates-Chicago Cubs game on June 21, 1943, at Wrigley Field, when he was decked by a ball hit by Cubs outfielder Harry "Peanuts" Lowrey. According to a contemporary account, "The ball, hitting him on the head after a bad hop, struck with such force that it caromed close to the mound."

Another account of the incident claimed that Elliott was refused for military service in World War II because of head injuries he sustained playing baseball in 1943. In support of the war effort, Elliott joined Elvin "Buster" Adams of the Philadelphia Phillies working for Consolidated-Vultee Aircraft Corp. in San Diego during the 1943 offseason.

While never known principally for his defense, Elliott did develop into what the *Times's* Daley called "a mighty fine third baseman" in spite of his growing pains. A 1951 profile written while Bob was with Boston called Elliott "one of the coolest customers around the hot corner in the National League" and made note of his "sharp fielding." The stats support these claims; although he led the NL with 35 errors at third the year he was moved there (1942), he cut them by one-third the next year and never approached the total again.

Durability was another Elliott trademark. Once he became a regular with the Pirates in 1940, he never played in fewer than 140 games with the team through 1946. He batted in more than 100 runs in every season from 1943 through 1945, and on July 15 of '45 hit for the cycle. His speed was also evident: Elliott hit 10 or more triples in four different seasons with Pittsburgh, and his 13 stolen bases in 1940 led the team. With many of the National League's other top third basemen away during the war, Elliott represented the Pirates at the position in the 1941, 1942, and 1944 All-Star Games, and was named to the All-Star team in 1945, a season in which wartime restrictions forced cancellation of the All-Star Game.

Still, he was never able to bring Pittsburgh as a team to the same level of success that he did later with the Braves. As sportswriter Al Hirshberg said: "Back in Pittsburgh, [Elliott] was known as Jumbo, because he is a gentleman of somewhat ample proportions. But back in Pittsburgh, there was no reason to call him 'Mister Team.' He couldn't pull the Pirates out of the ruck by himself."

In October 1945, there were rumors that Elliott might be traded by the Pirates to the New York Giants. He had come off a strong offensive season in which he batted .290 and knocked in 108 runs despite hitting just eight homers. Although he was approaching 30 years of age, he was clearly the fourth-place team's most desirable player in a potential trade. It is also likely that teams felt his power numbers would improve in a park that was more favorable to hitters than Forbes Field. Moreover, one report alleged, "Elliott is said to have told friends that if Frankie Frisch remained manager of the Corsairs, he would request a change of scene."

That change of scenery took place after Elliott endured a subpar 1946 season, by his standards (.263, 5 homers, 68 RBIs). On September 30, the Pirates traded Elliott to the Braves along with Hank Camelli in return for Billy Herman, Elmer Singleton, Stan Wentzel, and Whitey Wietelmann. Even though Herman would later go on to manage in Pittsburgh, the trade really did not benefit the Pirates on the field, as Herman played in only 15 more major-league games and the other three players appeared in a total of only 127 games for the Pirates. For the Braves, however, it proved one of the best swaps in team history.

According to Al Hirshberg: "[T]he Pirates had two ball players who interested the Braves to no end. One was Ralph Kiner, a rookie outfielder whose 23 home runs led the National League in 1946 and who gave every indication of being well on his way towards fame and fortune.... The other Pittsburgh ball player who intrigued the Braves was Bob Elliott.... Of the two, Southworth's first choice was Elliott, in spite of the slugging potentialities of the youthful Kiner. The Braves manager was thinking about the empty hole that would be left at third base with Herman gone. The Pirates didn't want to give up either of their stars.... [The Braves brain trust] pointed out that the big Californian wasn't happy in Pittsburgh, which was true....

"Finally, they got right down to cases. 'Herman and who...do you want for Elliott?' 'An infielder, an outfielder and a pitcher,' came the reply....'We can use a spare catcher,' commented Southworth. The boys finally agreed on a deal....In return for [Herman] and a half dozen nondescript ball players, the Braves acquired the classiest third baseman in baseball."

In spite of his success with Pittsburgh, Elliott, as Arthur Daley put it, "never did reach his full potentiality until he was traded from the Pirates to the Braves." Daley wrote that Southworth reportedly started envisioning a pennant when Elliott joined the team, and he made a point of motivating his new third sacker:

"'You're a very fine ball player, Bob,' [Southworth] told Elliott. 'You can make all the plays you're supposed to at third base. You have an excellent arm. You run the bases well and are a dangerous long-ball hitter. All you need to achieve true greatness is the added sparkle of more hustle. If you hustle, I'm absolutely convinced that you will win the most valuable player award this season.'

"Elliott hustled. He won the most valuable player award. That was 1947 and the lift he gave the Braves spurred them to the pennant the following season." In fact, that reputation for hustling stayed with Elliott. After the 1953 season, Frank Lane of the Chicago White Sox called Elliott "one of the greatest hustlers I ever saw. Bob played every game as if the championship hinged on it."

Although he finished in the top 10 in the National League's MVP voting in every year from 1942 through 1944, Elliott's performance in 1947 put him over the top. He batted .317, hit 22 home runs, had a career-best 113 RBIs, and seemed to always make the key hit or fielding play when the Braves needed it. In the MVP balloting, Elliott won nine of the 24 first-place votes and 205 total points, outdistancing second-place finisher Ewell Blackwell of the Cincinnati Reds by 30 points. "Mr. Team" became the first NL third baseman ever to win the award as well as the first player from a non-pennant-winning team to earn the NL honor since 1938.

A November 1947 newspaper account remarked that Elliott being voted MVP was "a surprise selection if ever the old circuit had one" and concluded that the "the Boston infielder's all-around record impressed the committee sufficiently to make him the first third-sacker and the first member of the Braves to gain the official most valuable player award of the National League." During his breakthrough season Elliott did not lead the National League in any statistical category, although he was second in batting, doubles (35), and on-base percentage (.423) and sixth with his career-high RBI total.

Another newspaper article, this one from October 13, noted that William H. "Billy" Sullivan, the Braves' director of public relations, had published "a comprehensive account" to "tout the third baseman as the National League's Most Valuable Player. It represents what is probably the most determined campaign on the part of a ball club to swing the writers' ballots in favor of a candidate." The article added: "The unusual part of this letter is that when you finish it, you really are convinced Elliott was the league's most valuable player."

The article said that most clubs would have preferred not to have their player win the MVP award, fearing that it might lead the winner to hold out for more money. Yet, in Elliott's case, he signed a new contract for $30,000 shortly thereafter. He was still far from the six-figure stratosphere inhabited around that time by players like Joe DiMaggio and Ted Williams, but he was among the top-paid players on a club filled with veterans.

After another 100 regular-season RBIs in 1948—capped by his pennant-clinching home run—Elliott had a few more big blows in the World Series versus the Indians. With the Braves trailing three games to one, and a then-record 86,288 fans watching at Cleveland, he hit two homers to pace an 11–5 Boston win in Game Five. In the top of the first inning, his three-run shot off Bob Feller gave Boston a 3–0 lead; two innings later, he hit a solo blast off Feller. The Indians wound up winning the sixth game and the series back in Boston, but "Mr. Team" finished the fall classic with seven hits, five RBIs, and a .333 average.

His Game Five heroics made up for some defensive gaffes by Elliott earlier in the Series. He made three errors at third base during the first two games, and the press was quickly on his heels. It was unknown to the public at the time that Elliott's father was "critically ill," causing Bob to travel to California to be with his dad before the series opened in Boston. Elliott was intent on keeping the matter private at first, but an unnamed teammate revealed the situation to the media. "Maybe [Elliott] thinks it's a personal matter," said the teammate. "Or it may be he's afraid someone will think he's trying to cop an alibi. But it's time people who have been inclined to label him a flop hear it." The teammate said that Elliott and his father had an especially close relationship: "Really, they have been more like a pair of brothers sharing each other's thoughts and ambitions." After Game Two, Elliott played errorless defense and set World Series records for chances accepted at third base (28) during a six-game series as well as the most chances accepted cleanly (25).

Although the Braves fell from their lofty heights in 1949 and never captured another pennant in Boston, Elliott stayed one of the team's top offensive contributors. One highlight for Bob in his remaining years with the club was hitting three home runs in a game on September

Bob Elliott led the majors in base on balls in 1948 with 131; Ted Williams was second with 126.

4, 1949, and his 76 RBIs that season gave him the distinction of having driven in more runs during the 1940s (903) than any player in the majors. He started off the next decade in similar fashion (with 24 homers and 107 RBIs in 1950), but his performance slipped a bit in 1951. Although his offensive numbers were down, he was still chosen as an All-Star that summer, the third time he had played in the game as a member of the Braves and his seventh appearance overall.

After this disappointing campaign came more headaches for Bob in the form of a salary dispute. Ten days before the start of the 1952 season, cartoonist and sometimes sportswriter Gene Mack reported that "Elliott acknowledges that it's a salary dispute that is keeping him and the Braves front office apart. Reports from the spring training camp hinted that the contract offered by the Tribe included the maximum pay cut of 25 percent from Elliott's 1951 stipend."

With the team trying out Willard Marshall at third, Elliott was concerned about his job security, saying: "[Salary] differences have been going on in baseball for half a century. The point is, if they don't want me, they ought to let me know one way or the other." The apparent "indifference" he was receiving from the team was, Bob said, "'bush' in my book."

The timing of his dispute couldn't have been worse for Elliott, coming on the heels of his subpar season and with the team losing money due to a dramatic drop-off in attendance. Thus "Mr. Team" was likely not surprised when, as he approached his 35th birthday, the Braves traded him to the New York Giants on April 8, 1952, in return for relief pitcher Sheldon Jones and $50,000.

During his one season in New York, Elliott was a shadow of his former self. He played sporadically and batted in only 35 runs in 98 games. After the season, he requested and received his release from the team. He told Arthur Daley, "When the season was finished, and [manager] Leo [Durocher] wondered about my .228 average, he naturally figured I was washed up," said Elliott. "Now, I have no beef about the way I was treated at the Polo Grounds. Durocher and [owner Horace] Stoneham were fine. But when I got into only 98 games with only 272 at-bats, and I am not right on that kind of fare. I like to be in there every day. When I play only occasionally, I get rusty."

Elliott came back for one more major-league season. He thought of playing in the Pacific Coast League. "But just lying in bed one night thinking about it, I felt that

I'd like to stay in the majors," he said. "There's nothing like it."

He also thought that St. Louis Browns manager Marty Marion would give him the most playing time, and managed to get himself invited to the club's 1953 spring training camp. After Elliott hit a three-run homer for St. Louis during a 10–6 exhibition loss to the Cubs, team president Bill Veeck was so impressed that he signed Elliott to a one-year contract with the team just before the season began.

The lifetime National Leaguer warmed to the idea of playing in the Junior Circuit for the first time, saying that "new company, different players gave me quite a thrill." As he said at the time, "It has been a lot of fun. It has been profitable too. I have had a happy life in baseball, and never was I thrilled more than I am right now, in the American League."

In his short stay with the Browns, Elliott got his 2,000th career hit. In fact, he later said that the attraction of getting that 2,000th safety was one reason he decided to continue playing in the majors if possible after being released by the Giants:

"I was only 33 hits away from 2,000," he said, "and that was partially it, but mostly it was my belief that I still could play major league ball. And my ability to play capable baseball, I think, depended a lot on the manager. My success, if I have had any this year, is due to the fact that Marty Marion is an outstanding manager.… Billy Southworth was wonderful at Boston because he gave me every chance to be a star. Marty reminds me a lot of Billy."

Bob Elliott had certainly stayed in baseball longer than many expected. Arthur Daley wisely remarked, "Those last five years…belong to Frank Frisch. The Flash gave them to Elliott by making him a third baseman." Elliott said his longevity could also be attributed to good conditioning: "I hunt and I play a lot of golf and am always busy with things around the home, like building a den.…"

Still, his switch to the AL did not rejuvenate Elliott's skills. He played part time at third base with the Browns for 48 games in 1953, and was hitting .250 when on June 13, he was traded along with Virgil Trucks to the Chicago White Sox in return for Darrell Johnson, Lou Kretlow, and $75,000. After battling strained leg muscles during his time with the White Sox, for whom he batted .260 with little pop, he was released by Chicago after the season. Elliott finished his major league career with 2,061 hits, 170 home runs, 1,195 RBIs, and a .289 batting average.

Like many ballplayers in the days before big-salary contracts, he was itching to keep himself in spikes and paychecks when his big league days ended. In 1954 he returned to his native California and suited up for the San Diego Padres of the Pacific Coast League. In 81 games, Elliott batted .256 with 12 home runs and 39 RBIs, and helped the Padres to the PCL pennant by hitting two home runs in a playoff game, one of them the championship clincher.

The popular star next made a quick transition to managing, piloting San Diego in 1955 (a second-place finish), 1956 (seventh place), and into the 1957 season before being replaced by George "Catfish" Metkovich on May 16 with the club in sixth place. He went on to lead the Sacramento Solons of the PCL to a fourth-place finish in 1959, a half-game behind San Diego, before getting the chance to return to the majors and manage the Kansas City Athletics in 1960. Kansas City's owner, Arnold Johnson, died just before the season began, however, and it was a year of upheaval. The A's ended the '60 campaign with a 58–96 record and an eighth-place finish in Elliott's only season as a big-league manager. Two of Elliott's coaches with that team were former Braves, Fred Fitzsimmons and Walker Cooper.

After the Athletics replaced him with Joe Gordon, Elliott went back to the West Coast to coach for the expansion Los Angeles Angels in 1961. This season was Elliott's last in major-league baseball; he went on to work for a beer distributor in Indio, California, while maintaining his home in San Diego. In his spare time, he liked to fish and bowl.

He would not get to enjoy these pastimes for long, however. Elliott suffered a ruptured windpipe in the spring of 1966, and in spite of receiving several blood transfusions and undergoing surgery for hemorrhaging in his stomach and lower esophagus, he died at Mercy Hospital in San Diego on May 4, 1966, at the age of 59. He survived by his wife, the former Iva Reah Skipper (whom Elliott referred to as Skippy); daughters Judith and Cheryl Lynn; and two sisters.

Buried in Greenwood Memorial Park in San Diego, Elliott was posthumously inducted into the San Diego Hall of Champions in January 1967. Thirty years later, on August 30, 1997, he was similarly elected to the Boston Braves Hall of Fame by fans of the long-defunct team who had formed the Boston Braves Historical Association. His daughter Judy accepted the plaque on his behalf, on the same weekend the Braves returned to Boston to play the Red Sox in the first season of interleague play. In this and other years, Judy Elliott made sure her dad was remembered in New England by attending Braves reunions alongside his old teammates—many of whom she had babysat for back in the '40s. She need not have worried, however; nobody who saw her dad perform for that club ever had any trouble recalling "Mr. Team."

Sources

Hirshberg, Al, *The Braves: The Pick and the Shovel* (New York: Waverly House, 1948)

Harold Kaese, *The Boston Braves* (Boston: Northeastern University Press, 2004)

1947 Boston Braves Sketch Book

Rich Marazzi. *Baseball Players of the 1950s*

1960 Sporting News Register

NL Service Bureau, 1948 World Series Press Notes

Schiffer, Don, *My Greatest Baseball Game:* New York: A.S. Barnes and Company, pp. 63–66.

Elliott's biography and World Series statistics on baseball-reference.com, retrosheet.org, and thebaseballpage.com.

Clippings from Elliott's file at the Hall of Fame:

Associated Press, "Bob Elliott, 49, Ex-Braves Star: Most Valuable Player in '47 Dies—Known for Hitting."

Hugh Bradley, "Worry Over Sick Dad Cause of Elliott Lapses." 1948.

"Bob Elliott: Hub's hot corner keeper cools rivals with sharp fielding, solid hitting."

"Bob Elliott, Ex-Star of N.L., Dies at 49 On Coast" *Baltimore Sun*, May 5, 1966.

"Bob Elliott—San Diego, Manager." No citation information given.

"Braves' Officials Praise Elliott: Letter of Many Words from Club Seen as Effort to Influence Most Valuable Player Votes," October 13, 1947.

Robert L. Burnes, "The Bench Warmer," June 7, 1953.

Arthur Daley, "The Comeback Kid," July 6, 1953.

Dave Egan, "Braves Betray Elliott: Lockout Unfair to 'Mister Team,'" March 26, 1952.

"Elliott Hurt By Batted Ball," June 22, 1943.

"Elliott Most Valuable National League Player," November 1947.

"Elliott of Braves Most Valuable in National League Last Season," November 1947.

Gene Mack, Jr., "All-Star in 1951, Elliott 'Forgotten': Baffled by Braves' indifference," April 5, 1952.

Jack Hernon, "Homers Elliott's Trade Mark," *Pittsburgh Post-Gazette*, May 2, 1952.

Tommy Holmes, "Elliott of Pirates Has Right to Kick: Offensively, Bob Outdid Bill Johnson All-Star Selection at Third Base," January 14, 1944.

Harold Kaese, "Elliott Not Too Fond of Playing Outfield, but If Leo Says So…," April 10, 1952.

Harold Kaese, "Bob Elliott, Alias Mr. Team."

Ralph Kiner, "Kiner's Liners," *Pittsburgh Press*, June 19, 1952.

Jim McCulley, "Elliott Losing Jitters, Pays Off for Giants," June 1, 1952.

Obituaries, "Bob Elliott, MVP in 1947, Former Pilot of Athletics," May 9, 1966.

"Pirates Cashing In on Player Shifts," April 23, 1942.

Porter, David L., ed., "Robert Irving Elliott," in *Biographical Dictionary of American Sports*.

"Robert (Bob) Elliott." No citation information provided.

Robert Irving Elliott, Pirate Personalities, Pittsburgh Baseball Club.

J.G, Taylor Spink, "Looping the Loops: Elliott Finds Differences in Two Majors, *The Sporting News*, June 3, 1953, p. 2.

"Split With Phils: Bob Elliott Clouts Grand-Slam Homer," 1945.

Sunday News, May 23, 1948, p. 17. Summary and photos of Elliott's career.

"Veeck Signs Bob Elliott After Home-Run Display," March 25, 1953.

"White Sox Hand Walking Papers to Bob Elliott," 1953.

GLENN ELLIOTT *by Doug Skipper*

G	ERA	W	L	SV	GS	GF	CG	SHO	IP	H	R	ER	BB	SO	HR	HBP	WP	BFP
1	3.00	1	0	0	1	0	0	0	3	5	1	1	1	2	0	0	0	15

G	AB	R	H	2B	3B	HR	RBI	BB	SO	BA	OBP	SLG	SB	HBP
1	2	0	0	0	0	0	0	0	0	.000	.000	.000	0	0

The lesser known and less accomplished of the two unrelated Elliotts who played for the Boston Braves in the late 1940s, Glenn "Lefty" Elliott is best remembered because he wore eyeglasses on the ballfield and surrendered Jackie Robinson's first major-league base hit.

A 5′10″, 170-pound soft tosser from Oregon, "Silent Glenn" Elliott spent parts of three seasons as a relief pitcher for the Braves. From 1947 to 1949 he pitched in 34 National League games, posted a 4–5 record, and compiled a 4.08 earned run average in 90⅓ innings. In Boston's 1948 NL championship season, he gave up five hits and a walk in his only appearance, but allowed just one run in three innings and was credited with a win. At the plate, he was a switch-hitter who couldn't hit from either side; he singled safely just twice in 21 big-league at-bats.

But the crafty lefty enjoyed a lengthy and successful career as a starting pitcher in the minor leagues. Elliott posted a 150–139 record and a 3.47 ERA for five franchises from 1942 to '56. He appeared in 426 contests—mostly with the Braves' Milwaukee farm club or in the Pacific Coast League, served up 2,479 hits in 2,475 innings, walked 692, and struck out 1,229. A graduate of Oregon State College, the scholarly southpaw taught school during the offseason, and worked as a carpenter, sold cars, farmed, and served as a scout for the Phillies before his untimely death from a brain tumor.

Herbert Glenn Elliott was born on the first anniversary of the end of World War I, November 11, 1919, at Sapulpa, Oklahoma, the youngest of Jacob and Julia Goodman Elliott's seven children. Jacob, born in 1868, was a ranch-hand whose family was among the first white settlers in Southern California's Imperial Valley. He journeyed to work with his brother in Oklahoma, and met and married Julia, a Cherokee Indian who was born in Kansas in 1892 (Glenn's Native American heritage was seldom if ever mentioned during his career). The couple produced four daughters and two sons who survived childhood and another son who did not. In 1922, the Elliotts (including young Glenn) moved to California, and eventually settled near Bakersfield. By 1935, Jacob and Julia had split up, and she and her younger children followed an older daughter to Myrtle Creek, a small mill town in a heavily forested region of southwestern Oregon.

A natural lefty forced to write right-handed, Elliott arrived in the Pacific Northwest at the age of 15, and earned letters in baseball, football, and basketball at Myrtle Creek High. He pitched a pair of no-hitters for his high school squad and two more for his American Legion team. Scouted by the Red Sox, Dodgers, Reds, and Yankees, he was regarded as one of the nation's top pro prospects, but instead of signing, elected to attend Oregon State College (now Oregon State University) in Corvallis. Freshmen weren't eligible to play in 1939, but Elliott earned a letter as a sophomore in 1940 when the Beavers posted a 19–5 record and won the Northern Division of the Pacific Coast Conference for longtime coach Ralph Coleman. Elliott lettered in 1941 when Oregon State posted a 15–10 mark, and in 1942, when the Beavers finished 14–8.

After Oregon State's 1942 season ended, Elliott played semipro baseball before he signed a pro contract with Seattle of the Pacific Coast League. The Rainiers farmed him to Vancouver of the Class B Western International League, where the lefty posted a 7–3 record and a 3.35 ERA in 13 games in the summer of '42 despite a sore and twisted arm. He had injured the arm at Oregon State on a day when he pitched in a cold rain. It bothered him the rest of his collegiate career, robbing him of some velocity, and his efforts to compensate further damaged the limb. "While with Vancouver, his arm became so crooked it was difficult for him to pitch and Manager Don Osborne suggested that he take up bowling to try to straighten out his salary wing," the *1947 Boston Braves Sketch Book* later revealed. "After about a year his arm was well straightened out and the soreness gradually vanished."

Seattle recalled Elliott, who compiled a 6–7 record with a 3.84 ERA in 24 games with his "bowling straightened" left arm in 1943. Married briefly, divorced, and the father of a baby daughter, Barbara Ann, Elliott continued to attend classes at Oregon State in the offseason. The next spring, he graduated with a degree in biological sciences, then turned in a 6–6 record with a 3.43 ERA in 25 games for the 1944 Rainiers. "His arm had troubled him so much during the period when it was crooked that he

As the starting pitcher, Glenn Elliott recorded a victory in his only 1948 appearance with the Braves.

spent most of his time as a relief pitcher once it had been straightened out," the *Braves Sketch Book* reported.

By 1945, he was primarily a Seattle starter, his workload continued to increase, and he went 14–12 with a 3.81 ERA. He took a couple of giant steps forward the next year, first to the altar, where he wed childhood sweetheart Audrey Joyce Ady (known by Joyce) of Myrtle Creek on May 15, 1946, and then on the field. Though he compiled just a 12–13 record for the last-place Rainiers in 1945, he pitched 227 innings, 31 more than the season before, had a much stingier ERA (3.26), struck out 49 more hitters (135), and walked just six more (73).

At the end of the season, the Braves purchased Elliott from Seattle on a conditional basis. After an offseason spent teaching in Myrtle Creek, the bespectacled southpaw allowed just five runs in 24 spring training innings, and was named Boston's outstanding rookie of the camp by *The Sporting News*. But as the team played exhibition games on its way north, Elliott began to falter, and failed to find a foothold in the starting rotation. On Opening Day 1947, Elliott was in Billy Southworth's bullpen when Boston's Johnny Sain and two other pitchers suffered a 5–3 loss at Brooklyn. Jackie Robinson, the first African American to play in the major leagues in the 20th century, went 0-for-3 at the plate, but reached on a misplayed sacrifice bunt and scored the winning run in his debut as a Dodger.

Two days later, on Thursday, April 17, Elliott made his first major-league appearance at the age of 27 before 10,252 at Brooklyn's Ebbets Field. With the Braves trailing 7–2, Elliott made his entrance in the bottom of the fourth inning and surrendered three runs. Robinson reached on a bunt single, the first hit of his major-league career, and scored one of those runs (Robinson bunted 42 times in 1947; 19 went for hits). Elliott rebounded to pitch a scoreless fifth inning; then yielded to pinch-hitter Tommy Holmes. In his two-inning stint, Elliott allowed three hits and a pair of walks and recorded one strikeout.

After he gave up Robinson's initial hit, Elliott experienced a variety of reactions. "He would tell us that some people jokingly told him, 'Thanks to you, the color barrier was broken,' " Glenn's daughter Taraleen Elliott Stymer remembered. "For other people it wasn't very funny. They were serious. 'It's your fault.' The story that we heard was that Jackie Robinson's career was a little iffy at that point, and that was kind of a last shot and if he didn't make it [with Brooklyn], he wasn't going to make it [in the major leagues] and that [the bunt single] was kind of what gave him the edge." Elliott didn't dwell on the reaction, and didn't question whether Robinson should be in the big leagues. "I think he was more embarrassed that he got attention for it," Taraleen remembered. "He certainly didn't think it was any big deal. He said that if people could play ball, they should play ball. There was a fair amount of ill will at first; then folks realized [Robinson] was a good ballplayer and that was all they cared about after a while."

Two days after he gave up Robinson's historic hit, Elliott allowed just four safeties in 5²/₃ innings against the Phillies in relief of Red Barrett at Braves Field. And though he surrendered a two-run homer to Andy Seminick, he struck out three and collected his only hit of the season in a 9–2 defeat. On April 27, Elliott suffered a loss, his lone decision of the campaign, when he served up a ninth-inning Jim Tabor home run in the first game of a doubleheader at Philadelphia. In the second game of the twin bill, he pitched the ninth inning to preserve a 4–3 win and record what would today be regarded as a save. He was inconsistent in May, however, and by early June he had allowed 18 hits, eight walks and 10 runs in 19 innings, to post a lackluster 4.74 era for Southworth's squad.

The Braves shipped Elliott to their farm team at Milwaukee, and for the next four months, Elliott was outstanding. Inserted into the rotation by manager Nick Cullop and backed by a keystone combination of second baseman Danny Murtaugh and shortstop Alvin Dark, Elliott compiled a 14–5 record to lead the Brewers to a third-place finish in the American Association regular season standings. Cullop encouraged Elliott to add a screwball to his arsenal, and the results were immediate. He pitched three shutouts, posted a 3.78 ERA, struck out 75, and walked just 45 in 138 innings to earn a spot on the league's All-Star Team. He earned two victories in the American Association playoffs when the Brewers bested the Kansas City Blues four games to two and the Louisville Colonels four games to three. And to cap off the season, Elliott pitched a complete game 9–1 victory in the deciding game of the 1947 Junior World Series as Milwaukee defeated the Syracuse Chiefs of the International League in seven contests. In that championship finale, "the wily southpaw" scattered nine hits and no walks, and allowed only a ninth-inning home run.

After he played winter ball in Puerto Rico, Elliott was back with the Brewers (who listed his birth year as 1922), in 1948. He posted a 14–7 record and a 3.76 ERA, the best in the American Association. He surrendered just 181 hits and 73 walks and struck out 125 in 189 innings; a performance that earned him a callback to pennant-contending Boston the first week in September "for immediate delivery." The move irritated fans of the second-place Brewers, and seemed worse when Milwaukee lost in the first round of the AA playoffs.

Elliott, meanwhile, made just one appearance down the stretch for the "Spahn and Sain and Pray for Rain" Braves. With Boston clinging to a one-game lead over the New York Giants, Glenn was tabbed by Southworth to start the second game of a September 1 double header at Cincinnati. Staked to a 3–0 lead by the Braves in the first inning, Elliott surrendered a single run in the bottom of the first, then shut out the Reds in the second and third. In the top of the fourth inning, he grounded out, collided with Cincy first baseman Ted Kluszewski, and had to leave the game with a 3–1 lead. Elliott had allowed five hits, the run, one walk, and two strikeouts in his three-inning stint, and was awarded a win in accordance with the rules in effect at the time. It turned out to be his last outing of 1948; meanwhile Boston's "other" Elliott, defending NL Most Valuable Player Bob Elliott, led the Braves to the World Series.

Both Elliotts were back with Boston in 1949, and Glenn compiled a 3–4 record with a 3.95 ERA. He appeared in 22 games, hurled 68¹/₃ innings, and gave up 70 hits. The soft-tossing southpaw walked just 27, but struck out only 15. He made his final big-league appearance on Tuesday, September 29, against Brooklyn, in relief of Spahn in a 9–2 loss at Braves Field.

Elliott attended spring training with the Braves in 1950, but was optioned to Milwaukee before the season started. He was less effective for the Brewers than before, posting an 11–12 mark with a 4.50 ERA. He did manage to draw one of two walks given up when Louisville's Bob Alexander pitched a 5–0 no-hitter against the Brewers on July 29, but that wasn't enough to save his job. In August, the Braves sent Elliott to Sacramento of the Pacific Coast League along with cash and a player to be named later in exchange for pitching prospect Max Surkont.

The nearsighted portsider spent the rest of his playing career in the PCL. He appeared in 11 games for Sacramento the remainder of that season and compiled a 3–4 record and a 3.21 ERA. He posted a 15–14 record and a 3.05 earned run average in 33 games for the Solons in 1951, but the seventh-place squad struggled to make ends meet. Sacramento was engaged in a working agreement with the Chicago White Sox, but the parent team terminated it at the end of the season. "In canceling their working agreement with Sacramento recently," *The Sporting News* reported, "the Chicago White Sox paved the way for the Solons to peddle their two bespectacled pitching aces, Lefty Glenn Elliott and Rookie Walt Clough, both of whom will be draft eligible. The Chisox had first refusal on the two players, the first for $35,000 and the second for $30,000. Solon officials hope to use Elliott and Clough as bait for a new working agreement." Manager Joe Gordon speculated that Elliott would be a steal at $25,000, but there were no takers, even at the bargain price.

That made Elliott eligible for the annual draft of minor-league players, and on December 1, the lefty was the sixth player selected, claimed for $10,000 by the Washington Senators. "I have to respect what Joe Gordon, the Sacramento manager, told me about Elliott," Senators skipper Bucky Harris told *The Sporting News*. "He assured me that Elliott could win in the majors, that he is all business out there and has amazing control for a lefthander. 'If Elliott isn't a big winner for you, Bucky, I give up.' Those were Joe's words." Despite the promise, Elliott's final audition for a big-league roster spot went poorly. He suffered from a sore shoulder from the start of spring training, and on March 12, he was smacked on the head by a Mickey Vernon line drive. The Senators absorbed a $2,500 loss when they sold Elliott back to Sacramento for $7,500 before the 1952 season started.

Washington may have given up too soon. Elliott, who joined former Boston Braves teammate Bob Sturgeon in Sacramento, bounced back from the sore shoulder to pitch 254 innings in 40 appearances—both career highs—and struck out 117 batters. He went just 12–18 for the struggling Solons despite a 3.19 ERA, and at the end of the season Sacramento traded Elliott and pitcher Orval Grove to Portland for outfielder Joe Brovia and pitcher Marino Pieretti. At Portland, he was reunited with another former Braves teammate, Jim Russell. Elliott played winter ball for Hermosillo in the Mexican League, signed late in the spring of 1953 with Portland, then posted a 12–14 record with a career best 3.02 ERA over 227 innings in 38 games.

Limited to 28 appearances in 1954 and forced to wear a tightly stitched jacket when he did pitch because of a sore sacroiliac (the joint between the hips and spine), Elliott still managed a 12–14 record and a 3.28 ERA. He appeared in 32 games in 1955, mostly in relief, and posted a 7–6 record and a 3.28 ERA. He was released by the Beavers over the winter, and at the end of the school year found work as a carpenter in Portland, before Sacramento brought him back in late June of 1956. At the age of 36, he appeared in 20 games the rest of the way for the Solons and compiled a 5–3 record.

Elliott was involved in an automobile accident over the winter, and reported to Sacramento's spring training in '57 with an injured arm that prompted him to return home to Myrtle Creek before the season. The Solons tried to persuade him to join them in June, but the arm hadn't healed and Elliott was by then also nursing a bruised leg. He decided to call it a career.

His pitching days behind him, Elliott sold cars, played golf, and watched his favorite spectator sport—basketball. He became the Pacific Northwest scout for the Philadelphia Phillies in 1960, a position he held for the rest of his life. He went to spring training each year, then hit the road in search of prospects. Among the players he signed for Philadelphia was pitcher Rick Wise, who won 188 games in 18 major-league seasons.

In 1964, Glenn and Joyce moved their six children to Stafford, 15 miles south of Portland, where the family farmed and raised livestock. Elliott hunted, fished, collected stray animals—including a skunk—dabbled with breeding Appaloosa horses, and kept his left arm limber. "He used to throw to my mom," his daughter Taraleen remembered. "My mom was a really tiny person. But she would be out there with a catcher's glove, catching him."

"Silent Glenn" also welcomed friends from baseball to the family farm. "Generally he was really quiet," Taraleen recalled. "He was not a real outgoing person, unless you got to know him. As quiet as he was, he and mom both liked to entertain. Lots of baseball people came out to the farm." Among those who visited were former Braves teammate and lifelong friend Johnny Sain, and his wife, Dorothy, and Portland Beavers announcer Bob Blackburn and *Oregon Journal* writer Bill Mylslur and their families. Taraleen also recalled that the kids looked forward to their annual shipment of chewing gum and baseball cards from the Topps Company.

The family's tranquility was shattered by cancer. Just four months after he was diagnosed with a brain tumor, Herbert Glenn Elliott died at Providence Hospital in Portland on July 27, 1969, at the age of 49 (though some media outlets reported his age as 46). "It was a complete shock for the whole family. We had to sell the farm," Taraleen remembered. "My mother, who had been a homemaker, worked two jobs and moved the family to Corvallis, and rented a house near campus. She knew that we were all either in college or going to go to college." Well after she made sure that each of her six children had the opportunity to attend Oregon State University, Audrey Joyce Ady Elliott died at 71 of complications from Alzheimer's disease on August 28, 1993. She was buried at Odd Fellows Cemetery in Myrtle Creek, where Glenn had been laid to rest 24 years earlier.

The couple are survived by sons Jock (born in 1948) of Albany, Kip (1950) of Corvallis, and Bart (1954) of Redmond, daughters Colleen (1951) Thomas of West Linn, Shalleen (1953) Fruits of Tarpon Springs, Florida, and Taraleen (1957) of Philomath, and Glenn's daughter from his first marriage (Joyce's stepdaughter), Barbara Ann Cross of California, and a number of grandchildren and great-grandchildren.

Nearly a half-century after his untimely death, the bespectacled lefty is remembered in his adopted state. The Glenn Elliott Memorial Trophy has for many years been awarded to the Most Valuable Player in Oregon's Metro State All-Star Baseball Game, and in 1991 Elliott was named to the Oregon State University Hall of Fame. The school's website states: "Glenn was one of the most feared pitchers in collegiate baseball in his era." Though his major-league career and his life were short, Glenn Elliott contributed a win to the Boston Braves 1948 pennant pursuit, and made his mark as a minor leaguer, a scout, and a devoted family man.

Sources

Eig, Jonathan, *Opening Day: The Story of Jackie Robinson's First Season* (New York: Simon and Schuster, 2007)

Gillette, Gary, and Pete Palmer, *The 2005 ESPN Baseball Encyclopedia* (New York: Sterling, 2005)

Hamann, Rex, and Bob Koehler, *The American Association Milwaukee Brewers* (Chicago: Arcadia Publishing, 2004)

Lee, Bill, *The Baseball Necrology: The Post-Baseball Lives and Deaths of Over 7,600 Major League Players and Others* (Jefferson, North Carolina: McFarland & Company, Inc., 2003)

Neft, David S., Richard Cohen, and Michael Neft. *The Sports Encyclopedia: Baseball 2004.* 24th Edition (New York: St. Martin's Griffin, 2004)

Peary, Danny, *We Played the Game: Memories of Baseball's Greatest Era* (New York: Black Dog and Leventhal Publishers, Inc., 1994)

Sugar, Bert Randoph, *Baseball's 50 Greatest Games* (New York: Weiser & Weiser, Inc., 1986)

2007 Oregon State University Baseball Media Guide, Oregon State University Sports Information Department, Corvallis, Oregon.

1947 Boston Braves Sketch Book

1947 Milwaukee Brewers Sketch Book

1948 Milwaukee Brewers Sketch Book

The Sporting News

Portland Oregonian.

Pat Doyle, Professional Baseball Players Database

Interview with Taraleen Elliott Stymer by Doug Skipper, August 2007.

Web Sites:

www.baseball-almanac.com

www.baseball-reference.com

www.retrosheet.org

www.minorleaguebaseball.com

www.mlb.com

www.osubeavers.com

JEFF HEATH *by C. Paul Rogers III*

G	AB	R	H	2B	3B	HR	RBI	BB	SO	BA	OBP	SLG	SB	HBP
115	364	64	116	26	5	20	76	51	46	.319	.404	.582	2	1

Jeff Heath was 32 years old and in his 13th big-league season in 1948 when he surprised his critics and helped lead the Boston Braves to the National League pennant. Playing in just 115 games under manager Billy Southworth's platoon system, he hit 20 home runs, drove in 76 runs, and batted a resounding .319. He hit a home run in every ballpark in the National League, in the process becoming the first player to accomplish the feat in both leagues; he had also homered in every American League park with the St. Louis Browns in 1946 and '47. In addition, he played a near-flawless left field for the Braves, leading the league's outfielders in fielding percentage at .991 and making just two errors.

After more than 1,300 games in the majors, Heath was headed to his first World Series (against his original club, the Cleveland Indians) when misfortune struck. Four games before the end of the campaign, playing in Brooklyn's Ebbets Field, he suffered a gruesome injury when he broke his ankle sliding into home plate. After being tagged out by catcher Roy Campanella, he left the field in agony on a stretcher.[1] Heath's season and, for all intents and purposes his career, were over.

The Braves had acquired Heath from the Browns on December 4, 1947, in a straight cash deal. They were no

With their December, 1947 acquisition of lefty slugger Jeff Heath, the Braves hoped to capitalize on the outfielder's power to reach the chummy confines of Braves Field's right field Jury Box.

doubt looking for some extra pop in their batting order to complement third baseman Bob Elliott, who had won the National League MVP award that year with 22 home runs, 113 runs batted in, and a .317 batting average. Heath was coming off a productive 27-homer, 85-RBI season himself with the Browns, although he had hit just .251. He was also coming with a reputation as a difficult personality. The '47 Braves had finished in third place with an 86–68 won-loss record, eight games behind the pennant-winning Brooklyn Dodgers. Although Cal Hubbard, the future Hall of Fame umpire, always said that Heath was the best fastball hitter in the American League[2], it is unlikely that even the most optimistic Braves supporter could have envisioned that his acquisition would prove to be a catalyst to a championship in 1948.

John Geoffrey "Jeff" Heath was born on April Fool's Day of 1915 in Fort William, Ontario, making him at least nominally a Canadian. His family, however, moved to Victoria, British Columbia, when he was a year old, and shortly thereafter to Seattle, Washington. It was there—where his father operated a hardware store—that Jeff grew up and lived his entire life. He attended Garfield High School in Seattle, where he made the varsity baseball team at 14 as a freshman. He went on to star in baseball and football before graduating in 1934. University of Washington football coach Jimmy Phelan pronounced Heath the best high school running back in the country that year. His prowess as a halfback led to numerous college scholarship opportunities, including offers from the Universities of Oregon, California, Washington, and Alabama, and Fordham University, but he opted to give up the gridiron for a baseball career. According to one source, Heath had his heart set on baseball, and injuries to both ankles and a knee from playing high school football cautioned him about the effects that playing this more physical sport could have on his chosen vocation. He did, however, study business administration at the University of Washington for a couple of semesters before his baseball career took off.

In 1935 Heath signed on with Yakima of the semipro Northwest League, where he hit an attention-getting .390 in 75 games. That performance earned the 20-year-old a spot on Les Mann's All-American amateur baseball team, which toured Japan after the season. He hit a cool .483 on the trip, cementing his decision to forgo college football. When Heath returned to the U.S. at the end of the tour however, U.S. customs would not allow him reentry once they discovered that he was a British subject traveling on a British passport. For two days he was confined to the team's ship, docked in San Francisco. Lefty O'Doul, who had helped arrange the trip, finally interceded and got Heath admitted back into the country. Shortly thereafter Heath became a naturalized U.S. citizen, ostensibly to avoid future such problems.[3]

Willie Kamm, a former big-league third baseman then scouting for the Cleveland Indians, had had his eye on Heath and signed him to a professional contract shortly after his return from Japan. Jeff reported to his first spring training in 1936 with the New Orleans Pelicans of the Southern Association, but soon developed an infected hand, which temporarily put him out of commission. The Indians eventually assigned him to the Zanesville, Ohio, Greys, their farm club in the Class C Mid-Atlantic League. Heath was a resounding success as the Greys swept to the pennant by 10 games. He compiled a .383 batting average, with 208 hits, 47 doubles, 14 triples, and a whopping 187 runs batted in, in 124 games. Only the 35 home runs hit by one Walter Alston of the Huntington Red Birds kept Jeff from a Triple Crown, but his 28 round-trippers placed him second in that category. His eye-popping numbers earned Heath a late season call-up with the Indians all the way from Class C. He proceeded to break into the majors by hitting .341 in 12 games and 41 at-bats. Seven of his 14 hits went for extra bases, including three triples.

A right-handed thrower and a left-handed batter, the muscular 6-foot, 200-pounder was understandably starting to be referred to as a "natural."[4] Even so, the Indians decided that a year with the Milwaukee Brewers, their top Double A farm club, would serve Jeff well, particularly since Cleveland was well stocked in the outfield at the time. So after starting the year with the Indians and fighting for playing time, he spent the bulk of the 1937 season with the Brewers—where he hit a lusty .367 in 100 games to finish behind only Enos Slaughter of the Columbus Red Birds in the American Association batting race. While down a bit from the previous year, Heath's power numbers were still formidable: 34 doubles, nine triples, and 14 homers.

All of that set the stage for one of the top debut years in big-league history. In 126 games with the Indians in 1938, Heath slugged 21 home runs, drove in 112 runs, and batted .343, finishing second in the batting title race by just .006 to Jimmie Foxx.[5] He led the league in triples with 18 and was runner-up in slugging (at .602) to only Hall of Famers Foxx and Hank Greenberg. It looked as though a Cooperstown career was in the offing, but it was not to be. Instead, Heath became something of an enigma, putting together very solid big-league numbers, but making one wonder what could have been.

Heath's personality could be quirky, and the reports on his effort during his career were mixed. He was a frequent holdout, beginning after his first full season, when he was unhappy with the Indians' contract offer. Although invited by Cleveland manager Oscar Vitt to work out with the team in spring training while he negotiated, Heath refused, catching the workouts at the club's New Orleans facilities from the stands.

This stance annoyed his teammates, and one night in the Roosevelt Hotel, the veteran slugger Hal Trosky reportedly confronted the issue, asking, "Heath, why don't you stop fooling, sign your contract, and get down to work like the rest of us?" Heath was not intimidated and replied, "Trosky, if you could hit like I can hit, you'd hold out all summer."[6]

Although he finally signed, Jeff remained unhappy through the 1939 season. His batting average fell 51 points to .292 while his home run and RBI totals also plummeted, to 14 and 69. Although he tied a major-league record on July 25 with two pinch hits in one inning, Heath had two particularly forgettable days in a row that summer which showed he had yet to learn to control his temper. First, on August 27, he struck out against the Red Sox' Denny Galehouse and threw his bat in frustration. It bounced about 10 feet in the air and landed in a front-row box seat, where it glanced off *Cleveland Press* editor Louis Seltzer. The home plate umpire, Bill McGowan, promptly tossed Heath from the game despite Jeff's protestations that he meant no harm.

When the furious Heath returned to his dugout, his friend and teammate Johnny Broaca tried to calm him down. Heath told Broaca to mind his own business or he'd knock his block off, whereupon Broaca, who had been on the boxing team at Yale, removed his glasses and took up the challenge. Teammate Harry Eisenstat later recalled that the Indians had a tough time separating the two because they were really going at it.[7] They almost fought again in the clubhouse, but manager Vitt stepped in and threatened to impose a heavy fine against both combatants.

The very next day, Heath fouled out on a 3-0 pitch with the tying run on third base late in the game. A fan in the front row yelled, "Why don't you throw your bat in the stands again?" Jeff responded by walking over and throwing a punch into the chest of the heckler. Fortunately for Heath, neither the umpires nor his manager saw the punch, so he escaped punishment. Afterward he acknowledged that "it was just another blunder in a season full of mistakes," and even admitted that he hurt his hand when he punched the fan.[8]

That same lost season Heath took exception to an article by sportswriter Ed McAuley of the *Cleveland News* suggesting that the outfielder did not always give 100 percent effort and that he was not a very good "team man." The reaction was predictable; Jeff confronted McAuley and advised him that if he ever showed his face in the clubhouse or dugout, Heath would physically remove him. McAuley dutifully reported the threat in the next day's paper and, with cameras rolling, visited the Indians dugout just before the same day's game. Heath greeted McAuley with a big grin and hearty handshake, and all was forgiven. It was later divulged that Alva Bradley, then president of the Indians, had ordered general manager Cy Slapnicka to tell Heath that if he touched a hair on McAuley's head, he would never play another inning of organized baseball.[9]

The headstrong slugger was not always so restrained, however. Bob Feller, who roomed with Heath on the road for several years, recalled an incident that occurred one evening when they were lounging in their room at the New Yorker Hotel in Manhattan and heard a knock on the door. Jeff opened the door to find a shapely young woman, and a man standing behind her back in the shadows, armed with a camera. Recognizing a scam when he saw one, Heath ordered the lady aside and grabbed the cameraman by the shirt and decked him with one punch. He then shut the door and called the house detective.[10]

The 1940 season was even more eventful for Heath than 1939 had been. He did not hit, and quickly fell out of favor with the acerbic Vitt, who thought the underachieving outfielder was wasting his talent.[11] Vitt had in fact become unpopular with most of the team because of his constant criticism, and in August Heath reportedly led what amounted to a player revolt against Vitt, forcing the manager's ouster.[12]

According to Braves teammate Clint Conatser, Heath always maintained that he had been unfairly made responsible for the turmoil. As Conatser told the tale, Jeff's outfield mate Roy Weatherly (who was nicknamed "Stormy") approached him with a list of gripes players had voiced about Vitt. Weatherly asked Heath, as the respected star of the team, to present the list to the front office on behalf of the club. But when management held a team meeting to get the full story, Jeff's teammates kept quiet and left him holding the bag. The press naturally targeted Heath as the ringleader.[13] Perhaps not surprisingly, given all the turmoil that summer, Heath slumped to .219 in 1940 and appeared in just 100 games, many as a pinch-hitter. In two years his batting average had plummeted 124 points and his RBI total had plunged from 112 to 50.

As the reputed leader of the so-called Cleveland Cry Babies, Heath took a lot of abuse on the road. It was tough to predict his reactions to such taunts or to figure out if and when they were even bothering him. Once, a fan in Griffith Stadium in Washington threw a teddy bear at Jeff on the field. Heath laughed, picked it up, and hugged it. He didn't even punch the guy.

The unpredictability extended to Jeff's career, and the up-and-down years continued in 1941. Under new manager Roger Peckinpaugh, Jeff roared back with another tremendous season and was named the starting right fielder for the American League in the All-Star Game. For the year he batted a resounding .340 with 24 round-trippers and 123 runs batted in, just two RBIs behind league-leader Joe DiMaggio. Heath ranked fourth in the American League in batting, third in slugging (.586), second in total bases (343), second in hits (199), and even third in stolen bases with 18. He also led the league in triples with 20 and became the first American Leaguer to hit at least 20 doubles (he had 32), triples, and home runs in the same season. In the years since, only George Brett (in 1979) and Curtis Granderson (2007) have equaled the feat among AL performers.

Heath never again approached those numbers and thus superstardom eluded him. In the very next season, 1942, for example, he slipped to a .278 batting average with only 10 home runs and 76 runs batted in. In 1943 he hit .274 with 18 homers, good enough to be named to the American League All-Star team in that war-depleted year but still a far cry from '41. He was hobbled by a bad knee in 1944, which limited him to 60 games, and after the season he had surgery to repair cartilage damage. Heath worked at a shipyard in Seattle and in early 1944 he was classified 2-B in the wartime draft as an employee in an essential industry.

As his statistics slipped, Jeff grew increasingly frustrated with Municipal Stadium, where the Indians played most of their home games.[14] In the cavernous ballpark, it was 470 feet to dead center field and up to 435 in the power alleys—great for doubles and triples but not for home run hitters. He also continued to squabble annually with the Indians over his contract. During the war the club trained for three years at Purdue University in

Lafayette, Indiana, and not once during this period did Heath sign his contract in time to even visit there.[15]

Heath also had a reputation for not always giving maximum effort.[16] One of his Cleveland managers, Lou Boudreau, recalled that although Jeff would often work hard, he could also get frustrated and then sort of give up. According to Boudreau, Heath had difficulty making adjustments at the plate and did not have the drive to excel. In one game Heath, playing left field, made no move to catch a fly ball that dropped in front of him. Boudreau sent him to the clubhouse after the inning but, desperate for a key hit, recalled Jeff to take his spot in the batting order. Heath responded by slamming the game-winning hit. Afterward, a slightly mollified Boudreau approached his slugger and said, "Great stuff, Jeff. But why didn't you try for that ball in front of you?"

To which Heath replied, "Don't ask me, Lou. I was hoping you'd tell me."[17]

Heath could also challenge Boudreau's patience and authority in other ways. In 1942, when Boudreau was named "boy manager" of the Indians at the tender age of 24, Lou was two years younger than Heath and younger than most of the players on the team. On an early-season train trip, Boudreau and a number of the Indians were in the dining car when Heath began pelting Jim Bagby, who was not known for his good humor, in the back of the head with hard rolls. Whenever Bagby turned around, Heath feigned innocence. Inevitably Bagby caught Heath in the act and reacted by pouring a glass of water on him. Fisticuffs were about to ensue when Boudreau came to intercede from the other end of the dining car, threatening fines if the two didn't cool it.[18]

Heath's longtime teammate and roommate on the road, Bob Feller, said that while Jeff was not a carouser, he didn't take baseball or life very seriously. Pitcher Harry Eisenstat, another teammate, thought that Heath had trouble accepting failure and tended to dwell on the negative. "If he'd go 0-for-4, he'd complain that the pitcher wasn't really that good," recalled Eisenstat. "He'd keep talking about it. When he had a bad day, he wasn't the nicest guy to have around."[19]

On the other hand, Heath was generally popular with his teammates and sportswriters, especially when he was hitting well. He was indeed fun-loving and accommodating to fans. He would willingly sign autographs for children after games and sometimes even take a bunch for a ride in his convertible.[20]

The Braves' chances of besting the Indians in the World Series were dealt a serious blow when Heath suffered a severe injury sliding into home in a meaningless late season game.

Once during the war, the Indians were playing the White Sox in an exhibition game for the sailors at Camp Grant, outside of Chicago. Manager Boudreau put himself in to pitch to save his regular hurlers, and Heath was playing left field. The field had no fence and only a white flag at the end of the foul line in left. One of the White Sox players hit a gargantuan shot near the line in left but well past the end of the line. Heath raced over and back but had no chance at the ball, so he just picked up the white flag and waved it, to the delight of the sailors in attendance.[21]

In 1945, Heath held out until early June, and while he did hit .305 in 102 games that year after ending his holdout, the Indians had grown tired of his act. After the season, they traded him to the Washington Senators for outfielder George Case, who although known for his stolen base prowess was battling knee problems.[22] Unfortunately, Washington's Griffith Stadium was huge as well, and after Heath hit just four home runs in 166 official at-bats early in 1946, the Senators shipped him in June to the St. Louis Browns for two journeymen, outfielder Joe Grace and relief pitcher Al LaMacchia. Jeff played for the Browns for a season and a half, and improved his power numbers but not his batting average in the more hitter-friendly Sportsman's Park. Before too long, he wore out his welcome in St. Louis as well.

As was his wont, Heath fell into several deep slumps with the Browns, to the consternation of his teammates. One day St. Louis second baseman John Berardino popped up with an important run on third base. When he came back to the dugout, Heath simply said, "Nice hitting, John." With his prolonged slumps Heath was the last person to be criticizing a teammate's hitting, so Berardino took umbrage and hauled off and socked Jeff in the chin.[23]

As a further sign of his quirkiness, Heath was very particular about his bats and would not allow teammates to borrow them. "There are only so many hits in a bat," he would say. In 1947 the Browns signed Willard Brown, a Negro League star. Brown arrived without any bats because he was told that the Browns would supply them. Brown found that the team's bats were all too lightweight for his taste, but eventually discovered one of Heath's discarded bats that had the knob broken off. Heath used the heaviest bats on the team, so Brown taped the knob back on the bat. The umpire wouldn't let him bat with a taped-on knob, so Brown just cut the taped-on knob off and used the bat anyway. He slugged a home run with it, off Hall of Famer Hal Newhouser no less. It was the first homer by a black player in the American League and what would turn out to be the only home run of Brown's short-lived major league career.

When Brown came back to the dugout after circling the bases, Heath reclaimed his bat and shattered it against the dugout wall.[24]

The last straw for Browns management occurred on the final day of the 1947 season. The club, mired in last place and desperate for fans, had hired Dizzy Dean to come out of retirement and the radio booth to pitch the last game of the season against the White Sox. After four scoreless innings the Diz retired for good, but the Sox scored five runs against his successors and were ahead 5–0 going into the bottom of the ninth. The Brownies sprang to life, however, and had two runs in and the bases loaded with two outs when it came Heath's turn in the order. The problem was that no one could find him. Manager Muddy Ruel finally dispatched a batboy to the clubhouse and sure enough, there was Jeff singing merrily as he soaped himself in the shower.[25]

Although the Browns were eager to get rid of Heath, he was greeted with enthusiasm in Boston. He had, after all, slugged 27 homers for a tail-end club in '47, third in the American League, and the 320-foot right-field porch in Braves Field seemed made to order for the lefty slugger. No one could have predicted, however, that he would bat a sparkling .319—68 points higher than in the previous campaign—and achieve a .582 slugging percentage (his best mark in seven years). More importantly, given the team's pennant hopes, many of his hits in 1948 were timely. Perhaps none was bigger than that of September 3, when Heath hit a two-run home run against the Phillies to propel the Braves to a 3–1 win and back into first place—where they would remain for the rest of the year.

According to his teammate Clint Conatser, Heath was particularly eager to play in the World Series if his old club won the American League pennant race (the Indians were battling the Red Sox and Yankees to the wire). Conatser related that Heath had always believed he had been wrongfully blamed for the Indians' player revolt of 1940, and harbored a grudge against the organization for accusing him of sabotaging his manager. He repeatedly told his teammates, "If we play the Indians, I will kill them." As Conatser remembers, just before Heath's fateful game against the Dodgers, he had gone to manager Billy Southworth and asked to not play since the Braves had already clinched the pennant. Heath apparently wanted to save himself for the Indians, if they made it to the Series.[26]

Southworth denied Heath's request, as he did any similar pleas from other players, because he wanted to guard against a letdown by his regulars heading into the Series.[27] So Heath played and, according to Conatser, hesitated on the fateful play as he approached home plate, unsure whether he should slide in a meaningless game.[28] When he did slide, he did so awkwardly as Brooklyn's Roy Campanella went to tag him. The result was a compound fracture and a stay for Jeff in Brooklyn's Swedish Hospital.

The fallen warrior was fitted for a cast and crutches and allowed to visit with his teammates at the ballpark during the World Series. But while he was always photographed with a wide grin during this period, he was no doubt silently seething. The Indians, in the end, had toppled first the Yankees and then the Red Sox (in a one-game playoff) to make it to the Series. But Jeff would not get his chance at revenge, and it cost the Braves dearly. His teammates hit just .230 with four home runs against Cleveland's vaunted pitching staff, and the Indians captured the Series in six games.

Heath attempted to resume his career in 1949 after recovering from his catastrophic injury. He made his first appearance on July 16, going 1-for-5 in a 6–1 victory over the Cubs. But the Braves were struggling along in fourth place in their title defense, and Jeff was nagged by his injury. For the rest of the season he managed to hit .306 for the Braves in 36 games and 111 at-bats, but his mobility was reduced and his days as a full-time player were at an end. He did go on one of his hitting tears in August, hitting eight home runs in 18 games—including two in successive innings—but had just one homer in all his other contests combined.[29] The Braves released him immediately after the season, thus ending his big-league days. He headed back west to play for his hometown Seattle Rainiers of the Pacific Coast League in 1950 (where he was reunited with former Braves teammates Billy Salkeld and Al Lyons as well as old nemesis Denny Galehouse) before hanging up his spikes for good and switching to the broadcast booth as a color commentator for the Rainiers.

For all the controversy Heath generated in the American League, he certainly ended his baseball career on a high note with the Braves. Some late-arriving maturity undoubtedly helped, but the Braves thought him a model professional and had trouble believing the stories they had heard about him. (He had even signed his Braves contracts promptly and without quarrel.) Billy Southworth said, "They told me when I got him from the American League that Heath was a troublemaker. If he is, I'd sure like to have eight other troublemakers like him."

He was also active in the community, and was one of a number of Braves players who visited the Boston hospital room of a child ill with cancer as part of Ralph Edwards' *Truth or Consequences* national radio broadcast in May 1948 that launched the Jimmy Fund charity of the Dana-Farber Cancer Institute.[30] The Braves thought so highly of Jeff that when they released him as a player they offered him a job managing one of their farm teams. He declined, however, thinking he might be able to play for the Rainiers for a couple of years in his hometown.[31]

For his time in the majors, which spanned 14 years, Heath had batted .293 and slugged 194 home runs. He also connected for 279 doubles and used his surprising speed to twice lead the American League in triples, totaling 102 three-baggers for his career. And although none of these numbers rank high on baseball's all-time lists, his .509 lifetime slugging percentage and .879 OPS (on-base average plus slugging average) are still in the Top 100—and a strong indicator of his prowess when healthy and focused.

Looking back, Heath showed some introspection in analyzing his time in the game. Asked by Franklin Lewis of the *Cleveland Press* if he would have done anything different in his career if he had it to do over, Heath said, "I wouldn't gag around as much. I shouldn't have popped off. It's all right for little guys to talk loud, but not a big ox like me." *Baseball Digest* published an article under Heath's byline a couple of years after his retirement titled "I Did It the Wrong Way!"[32] It was the lead article of the issue, the cover of which blared "Jeff Heath Confesses: I was a clubhouse lawyer—and I was wrong!" The article itself, however, does not live up to the hype. Heath does admit to youthful "impulsiveness" and being "headstrong" as his "biggest blunder," but the article is in reality an attempted explanation of his behavior rather than an acknowledgment of it.[33]

Heath did not exactly mellow, however, after his playing days, and managed to get into more scrapes. In 1956, while broadcasting a Rainiers game, he swore into an open microphone from frustration over some technical glitches. He later apologized on the air but, when confronted by a station manager in the broadcast booth, responded by throwing him down a flight of stairs.[34] A year later, in 1957, he was accused of knocking down a Seattle construction worker in a brawl in a café.[35] In August of the same year Heath became ill while participating in a children's parade at Seattle's Seafair Festival, and was taken to the hospital with what turned out to be a serious heart attack. He was only 43 years old.

After he recovered, Heath continued to broadcast Seattle ballgames through most of the 1960s. The club's principal sponsor was a hot dog manufacturer, and Jeff became well known for downing hot dogs with gusto throughout the broadcasts.[36] He also continued to be the life of any party. Once after a sports banquet, he was enjoying a nightcap with several of the attendees when the subject turned to sliding. Heath lamented, "They just don't slide like they used to. How many of these players nowadays give you the good hook slide anymore? You want to see a good hook slide? Watch this." Whereupon Heath doffed his trousers, revealing flowered boxer shorts, ran a few steps, and executed a beautiful hook slide on the polished floor.[37]

On an earlier occasion, Heath attended a Hot Stove gathering at which Rainiers' general manager Dewey Soriano introduced Lefty O'Doul as the club's new field manager, succeeding Luke Sewell. Soriano was extolling the virtues of O'Doul, including his vast baseball experience and leadership qualities, when Heath piped up from the back in a loud voice, "Hey, Dewey, isn't that just what you said about Luke Sewell last year?"[38]

Heath became involved in real estate development, and in 1972 actively campaigned against the proposed domed stadium for Seattle, actually wearing a sandwich board and collecting signatures on a Seattle street corner.[39] He was not against a new big-league stadium for Seattle, but thought a domed stadium was unnecessary and that the budget for the proposed Kingdome was totally inadequate to build a first-class facility.

In the end, he wouldn't live to see the Kingdome completed. On December 9, 1975, Heath was stricken with a fatal heart attack and died in Seattle. He was just 60 years old and left behind his wife, Theabelle, two daughters, a son, and six grandchildren.

Heath was a fine ballplayer who could and should have been a great one. He was, until his stint with the Braves, a real enigma. Howard Preston, a sportswriter with the *Cleveland News*, perhaps best captured the man in his obituary of Heath: "He was a mixture of gentleness and brute strength, angel and devil, but withal an exciting fellow for what he might have been as well as for what he was."

Notes

1. Jim Shearon, *Canada's Baseball Legends* (Kanat, Ontario: Malin Head Press, 1994), p.55. *The Sporting News,* October 6, 1948, p. 8. Braves' teammate Clint Conatser recalled that when the Braves ran out to tend to Heath, Campanella was visibly upset and repeatedly said, "I didn't block him. I let him slide through." Brent Kelley, *The Pastime in Turbulence—Interviews with Baseball Players of the 1940s* (Jefferson, North Carolina: McFarland & Co., Inc. 2001), p. 296. Photographs of the horrific injury show Campanella making a sweep tag as Heath's left ankle, away from Campy, is gruesomely twisted. Heath later noted that while he was laid up in Brooklyn's Swedish Hospital, Dodgers pitcher Rex Barney brought him a radio and Dodgers owner Walter O'Malley was a daily visitor, helping to boost his morale. Jeff Heath as told to Arthur Richman, "I Did It the Wrong Way!", *Baseball Digest,* January 1953, p. 5.
2. *The Sporting News,* December 17, 1947, p. 7.
3. Humber, William, *Diamonds of the North—A Concise History of Baseball in Canada* (Don Mills, Ontario: Oxford Univ. Press, 1995), pp. 160, 161.
4. *The Sporting News,* November 17, 1938, p. 5.
5. Heath finished the year on a tear, hitting .350 for the month of August and .387 for September. Shearon, *Canada's Baseball Legends*, 59.
6. *Ibid.*
7. Bob Dolgan, Tribe's Heath a Star Who Flared, Then Faded, *Cleveland Plain Dealer*, May 1, 2001, p. 1D.
8. *Ibid.*
9. *Cleveland Plain Dealer*, December 11, 1975, p.1-D.

10. Bob Feller with Bill Gilbert, *Now Pitching—A Baseball Memoir* (New York: Birch Lane Press 1990), pp. 73-74.
11. Vitt was later quoted as saying that Heath "had as much ability as Joe DiMaggio. [H]e had a fine arm and could hit the ball as far as anybody. He ruined a promising career because of temperament and disposition." Undated story, Baseball Hall of Fame Library, Jeff Heath file, Cooperstown, New York.
12. *The Sporting News*, July 10, 1941, p. 1. For additional accounts of the 1940 Cleveland Indians player revolt *see* John Sickels, *Bob Feller—Ace of the Greatest Generation* (Washington, D.C.: Brassey's, Inc., 2004) , pp. 91-101. Lou Boudreau with Russell Schneider, *Lou Boudreau—Covering All the Bases* (Champaign, Illinois: Sagamore Publishing, 1993), pp. 25-39. Bob Feller with Bill Gilbert, *Now Pitching—Bob Feller* (New York: Birch Lane Press, 1990), pp. 94-103. Lou Boudreau with Ed Fitzgerald, *Player-Manager* (Boston: Little, Brown & Co., 1949), pp. 39-48. Franklin Lewis, *The Cleveland Indians* (New York. G.P. Putnam's Sons, 1949, *republished* Kent, Ohio: Kent State Univ. Press, 2006), pp. 200-13. Bob Feller, *Strikeout Story*, (New York: A.S. Barnes & Co., 1947), pp. 158-205.
13. Boston Braves Historical Association Newsletter, Spring 2008.
14. *The Sporting News*, October 21, 1943, p. 18.
15. *The Sporting News*, December 20, 1945, p. 9.
16. Gordon Cobbledick, longtime sportswriter for the *Cleveland Plain Dealer*, generally defended Heath, calling him "the most misunderstood player in baseball." Even Cobbledick, however, acknowledged that Heath didn't always "hustle to the utmost" and sometimes "fail[ed] to seize the fullest advantage of opponents' misplays." Gordon Cobbledick, Heath Hustles—In His Own Way, *Baseball Digest*, October 1943, p. 60.
17. *Ibid.*
18. Lewis, *The Cleveland Indians*, p. 224.
19. Dolgan, *Cleveland Plain Dealer*, p. 1D.
20. Dolgan, *Cleveland Plain Dealer*, p. 1D.
21. *The Sporting News*, December 14, 1944, p. 10.
22. The previous May the Yankees expressed serious interest in obtaining Heath, but no deal was ever made. May 11, 1945 clipping from the Jeff Heath clippings file, National Baseball Hall of Fame Library.
23. *The Sporting News*, December 17, 1947, p. 7.
24. Bill James, *The New Bill James Historical Baseball Abstract*, p. 683. In another reported incident, Heath objected to teammates using his bats while with the Braves in 1949. Eddie Stanky began kidding Heath about his bat phobia and Heath retaliated by "half-kiddingly" lifting Stanky off his feet on the runway to the clubhouse. *The Sporting News*, September 7, 1949, p. 4.
25. *Ibid.*
26. Boston Braves Historical Association Newsletter, Spring Training 2008.
27. *Ibid.* In 1943, Southworth's St. Louis Cardinals had clinched the pennant with 13 days left in the season. Southworth rested his regulars and the Cardinals won only six of their final 11 games and then proceeded to lose the World Series to the Yankees four games to one.
28. *Ibid.*
29. *The Sporting News*, September 7, 1949, p. 22.
30. The publicity from the show launched the famous Jimmy Fund charity. Wisnia, Saul, *Images of America: The Jimmy Fund of Dana-Farber Cancer Institute* (Arcadia), p. 18.
31. *The Sporting News*, October 26, 1949, p. 20.
32. Heath, *Baseball Digest*, 5. The article was told to Arthur Richman of the *New York Mirror*.
33. For example, Heath mentioned that Earl Averill advised him that he was making a mistake by hitting so well during his first full season because everyone would expect that level of performance thereafter. A year later, Heath related that he understood what Averill meant.
34. William Humber, *Diamonds of the North—A Concise History of Baseball in Canada* (Don Mills, Ontario: Oxford Univ. Press, 199), p. 161.
35. *Ibid.*
36. *Seattle Times*, December 11, 1975, p. F2.
37. *Ibid.*
38. *Ibid.*
39. *Seattle Times*, October 4, 1972, p. B4.

Sources

Boudreau, Lou, with Russell Schneider, *Lou Boudreau—Covering All the Bases* (Champaign, Illinois: Sagamore Publishing, 1993).

Boudreau, Lou, with Ed Fitzgerald, *Player-Manager* (Boston: Little, Brown & Co., 1949).

Caruso, Gary, *The Braves Encyclopedia* (Philadelphia: Temple Univ. Press, 1995).

Cobbledick, Gordon, Heath Hustles—In His Own Way, *Baseball Digest*, October 1943, p. 60.

Dolgan, Bob, Tribe's Heath a Star Who Flared, Then Faded, *Cleveland Plain Dealer*, May 1, 2001, p. 1D.

Feller, Bob with Bill Gilbert, *Now Pitching—A Baseball Memoir* (New York: Birch Lane Press, 1990).

Feller, Bob, *Strikeout Story* (New York: A.S. Barnes & Co., 1947).

Finoli, David, *For the Good of the Country: World War II Baseball in the Major and Minor Leagues* (Jefferson, North Carolina: McFarland & Co. 2002).

Heath, Jeff (as told to Arthur Richman), I Did It the Wrong Way!, *Baseball Digest*, January 1953, p. 5.

Humber, William, *Diamonds of the North—A Concise History of Baseball in Canada* (Don Mills, Ontario: Oxford Univ. Press, 1995).

Jeff Heath player file, National Baseball Library, Cooperstown, New York.

Kaese, Harold, *The Boston Braves* (New York: G.P. Putman & Sons, 1948, *republished* Boston: Northeastern Univ. Press, 2004).

Kelley, Brent, *The Pastime in Turbulence—Interviews with Baseball Players of the 1940s* (Jefferson, North Carolina: McFarland & Co. 2001).

Lewis, Franklin, *The Cleveland Indians* (New York: G.P. Putman & Sons, 1949, *republished* Kent, Ohio: Kent State Univ. Press, 2006).

Shearon, Jim, *Canada's Baseball Legends* (Kanat, Ontario: Malin Head Press, 1994).

Sickels, John, *Bob Feller—Ace of the Greatest Generation* (Dulles, Virginia: Brassey's, Inc., 2004).

Shatzkin, Mike, ed., *The Ballplayers* (New York: William Morrow & Co., 1990)

BOBBY HOGUE
by Diane MacLennan, Bill Nowlin, and Saul Wisnia

G	ERA	W	L	SV	GS	GF	CG	SHO	IP	H	R	ER	BB	SO	HR	HBP	WP	BFP
40	3.23	8	2	2	1	15	0	0	86⅓	88	34	31	19	43	4	2	0	359

G	AB	R	H	2B	3B	HR	RBI	BB	SO	BA	OBP	SLG	SB	HBP
40	21	0	2	1	0	0	1	0	5	.095	.095	.143	0	0

Although the vaunted starting duo of John Sain and Warren Spahn is usually credited with leading the Braves to the 1948 National League pennant, stellar relief pitching from several sources also helped Boston to the World Series that fall. One of the men providing this spark was rookie right-hander Bobby Hogue, who baffled NL batters with an array of pitches—and later did the same in the American League while contributing to a Yankees world title three years later.

Robert Clinton Hogue was born on April 5, 1921, in Miami, Florida. His father was a well-known boxing trainer, Oakley Hogue, and Bobby himself won 36 of 39 amateur fights while strongly considering a career in the ring. He was also a standout first baseman and outfielder at Miami's Ponce de Leon High School.

Former Pittsburgh Pirates outfielder (and future Hall of Famer) Max Carey convinced Hogue and his father that Bobby should sign a baseball contract with the unaffiliated Miami club that Carey managed. He did so, and in 1940 posted a record of 8–11 with a 4.15 ERA in the Florida East Coast League. During the off-season, in an "unknown" transaction, Hogue was sent to the Detroit Tigers' affiliate in the Piedmont League, the Winston-Salem Twins. He pitched two seasons for Winston-Salem, going 9–8 in 1941 (along with a 2.38 ERA) and 17–13 (with a 2.21 ERA) in 1942—a notable achievement, as he was pitching for a last-place team. In later years, he looked back on this as his best year, since he was with a "hapless tail-ender." Winston-Salem was also the scene of what Hogue told *Complete Baseball* was his most embarrassing moment on the field. It came in 1941: "It had rained all morning and muddy Carolina red clay is the slickest stuff in the world. The first man up bunted. I fielded the ball and, honestly, skidded not only off the infield but also into the Asheville dugout. When I finally climbed out, the guy was on third with a triple."

As with so many young players of the era, Hogue spent 1943–1945 in military service during World War II. Given a fondness for boats, he joined the Navy. An amusing Associated Press story tells of how Detroit GM Jack Zeller sent Hogue his contract for '43 and was surprised

Bobby Hogue was another member of the Braves "48 rookie corps that made important contributions to the pennant drive.

not to be asked for a raise. Hogue wrote back, "The contract arrived and I was delighted with the terms, but I won't be able to play for the Tigers this year. I'm in the Navy now."

After three years of service, Hogue hadn't lost his touch. Detroit optioned him to the Dallas Rebels of the Texas League and he pitched very well in 1946 (9–7, 2.43 ERA after taking a couple of months to get back into form) and '47 (16–8, 2.31). Control was one of his strengths, and he walked just 59 batters in 222 innings during the latter campaign, when he also beat Beaumont with a 4–0 no-hitter on June 23. Jack Zeller had now become the chief scout for the Boston Braves, and the Braves purchased Hogue's contract on August 30, 1947 for cash, a player to be named, and options on two other players. Bobby's ERA had been below 2.50 for three straight years, and Zeller deemed him ready for the big leagues.

The 5-foot-10, 195-pound Hogue was 27 years old when he broke into the majors with the Braves on April 24, 1948, the fourth of seven pitchers to see action in a 16–9 loss to the New York Giants. Hogue's was one of the best performances of the game at Braves Field, as he yielded just two hits in 3⅓ innings. A *Christian Science Monitor* story that spring told of when Braves manager Billy Southworth first met the "portly right-hander" at the minor league meetings the previous December. He asked Hogue, "How are you planning to spend the winter?" When Hogue answered, "On a boat," Southworth said, "Well, if that's the case, you better do a lot of brass polishing and deck swabbing to cut down on your weight." Opening spring training without having seen Hogue again, Southworth declared that Hogue, Jim Prendergast, and Ray Hardee were all "hog fat" and needed to work into form. The manager changed his tune, though, when he found that Hogue was in pretty good shape—and despite having blisters on both feet, asked to get some extra work by pitching to the second squad.

The conditioning and determination paid off; Hogue went 8–2 with two saves and a fine 3.23 ERA (well under the league average of 3.84) during his rookie year. He showed his stuff early on in two games against the powerful Giants, the aforementioned April 24 tilt and a May 1 matchup at the Polo Grounds. In the latter contest starter Bill Voiselle had entered the seventh with a one-hit, 6–0 shutout, then suddenly allowed four runs on three hits; Hogue came in with two outs and the bases loaded, and induced dangerous Walker Cooper to pop out, Still referred to as "the roly-poly right-hander," Bobby pitched one-hit ball the rest of the way.

This was just a warm-up. While Hogue pitched primarily in relief, appearing in 40 games and finishing 15 (making just one start), he often hurled four or more innings in bailing out faltering mates. On May 28, for instance, after Johnny Sain was shelled against the Dodgers at Braves Field, Hogue came in with two outs in the third and allowed one run the rest of the game. On July 2 at Philadelphia, when Clyde Shoun was ineffective, Bobby entered in the third and pitched two-hit, shutout ball over the final 6$^{1/3}$ innings to get the 7–3 win. A week later, when Warren Spahn struggled against the Phillies at Boston, Hogue came to the rescue again with four solid frames in earning the 9–4 victory.

Hoping for a spot on the "48 roster, Bobby Hogue shows his pitching form at the Braves Bradenton, Florida spring training camp.

Hogue's best pitch may have been his slider. "That's the one I always use in the clutch," he told the *Christian Science Monitor* that summer. Years later, fellow hurler Dick Donovan told Arthur Daley of the *New York Times* that Hogue had as good a slider as he'd ever seen, but that it was "a natural slider and he couldn't tell anyone how he threw it." Though Hogue claimed his knuckler was self-taught, he may have owed a great deal of credit to 1948 teammate Nelson Potter, for Hogue said years later that he "stole" his knuckler from Potter, a master of the pitch. This was obviously a man with many pitches, and the 1948 *National League Green Book* declared that Hogue's screwball was his best; that he'd learned that one from Frank Shellenback, a minor league pitching great turned big-league coach.

Interestingly, Bobby's one start of the season came between his two stellar relief jobs of early July, and was a brief one—as he lasted just two innings of a 7–4 victory over the Dodgers on the 8th that was remembered more as the game in which second baseman Eddie Stanky severely sprained his ankle. Once back in the bullpen, however, Hogue returned to form as Boston sought to keep its hold on first place. He had five scoreless innings (with five strikeouts) at Wrigley Field on July 16, and after beating the Cubs with three shutout innings on August 5 was already 7–2—just one less victory than the 8–7 Spahn. A few weeks later, the *Christian Science Monitor* noted, "It was reported yesterday that the Braves recently tore up his original 1948 contract and signed him to a new one, naturally at an increase." Hogue celebrated by pitching shutout ball over the final 4$^{1/3}$ innings of an epic 3–2, 14-inning win over the second-place Dodgers in front of 32,499 at Ebbets Field on August 23.

Hogue's eighth win, which gave Boston a 2½-game lead over St. Louis (with Brooklyn slipping to third) was Hogue's final decision of the season. Shortly thereafter, the Braves' two top starters began the run of stellar complete-game outings that led to their "Spahn and Sain and Pray for Rain" fame, and Bobby was not needed much down the stretch. He did not, surprisingly, appear in the 1948 World Series against the Indians either, although his teammates acquitted themselves effectively with a 3.37 composite ERA in the six-game Cleveland victory. (The one hurler not to post an ERA of 3.00 or lower in the Series was fellow knuckleballer Nels Potter [8.44 in two appearances].)

In 1949, Hogue worked a bit less—72 innings in 33 games—but pitched well again, with a 3.13 ERA. He won two and lost two for the fourth-place Braves, again hurling primarily in relief. One concerning stat, however, was that he had lost his edge in strikeout-to-walk ratio (from 43–19 in '48 to 23–25 in '49). In 1950, it slipped again—and badly: he walked 31 while striking out only 15, and saw his ERA balloon to 5.03. Hogue won three and lost five in this campaign, and some later articles vaguely mentioned that he suffered an arm injury in '49. Although it's not certain, this may have been the cause of his slip in control—and, over time, in effectiveness. Despite some very optimistic press during spring training of 1951, Hogue got off to a disappointing start again with the Braves that year. He pitched just five innings in three appearances, compiling a 5.40 ERA before being placed on waivers. He was claimed by the hapless St. Louis Browns on May 13, at the same time that the Braves purchased right-hander Sid Schacht from the Browns. Not long after that, on July 31, the Yankees purchased Hogue's contract at the same time as they bought the rights to Cliff Mapes from St. Louis; the two transactions were part of a cluster of deals involving a number of players. Hogue was sent outright to New York's American Association team in Kansas City, where he appeared in seven games and went 4–0 in 22 innings. On August 20, the Yanks called up two players from the Kansas City Blues, Hogue and a youngster named Mickey Mantle.

As he had in '48, Hogue came up big in a pennant race. The now 30-year-old pitcher was praised by New York manager Casey Stengel and coach Jim Turner for his solid relief work, although *Complete Baseball*'s Ben Epstein termed him a "fat man with a knuckler" and a "misfit" who threw to the "odd anatomy and thick mitt of backstop" Yogi Berra. Hogue surprised everyone by throwing a total of 10 innings of relief down the stretch without yielding a single run. His contributions included 7⅓ innings during three key games in the midst of the Yankees' red-hot pennant fight with Cleveland, and 2⅔ innings of shutout middle relief in two World Series appearances against the Giants. Thanks to his help, the Yanks won the Subway Series in six games for their third straight world championship.

The stout Hogue developed his knuckler out of "sheer necessity," he told Epstein. "I knew it was either rassling, raking leaves or some other business if I didn't add something to my alleged fastball and curve," he said with a grin. "So I just stuck to the standard pitches and adopted the knuckler." Playing around with it for a couple of years, using it as perhaps his third or fourth pitch in 1951, he had a 6–0 record between Kansas City and New York. After two wins and five saves with the Yankees that year, it wasn't until the next spring that Hogue suffered his first New York loss, on May 24, 1952, against the Red Sox in Boston.

Hogue was a solid hitter, and one writer once made the humorous discovery that he had topped three leagues in hitting. This is rather deceiving—he led the American League with a 1.000 batting average in going 2-for-2 with the Browns; led the National League at .500 (2-for-4) with the Braves; and headed the American Association at .600 (6-for-10) with the Blues—but he did bat .233 lifetime in 172 at-bats in the majors, a high mark for a pitcher. He was also a good fielder who didn't make an error in major-league ball until his final season. Not bad for a guy the press called "chunky" throughout his career.

In 1952, however, Hogue's up-and-down stretch in the majors took a final downward turn. He appeared in 27 games with the Yankees, and while he did notch four saves, his 3–5 record and 5.32 ERA prompted the club to place him on waivers in early August. He was claimed again by the Browns, on August 4; moving from the AL penthouse to the outhouse, he threw 16⅓ innings and recorded a record of 0–1 with a very stingy 2.76 ERA for seventh-place St. Louis. It wasn't enough to save his job. On September 27, 1952, Hogue appeared in relief at Comiskey Park in Chicago, giving up one hit and no runs to the White Sox in the last two innings he pitched in the major leagues.

Hogue's pitching portfolio included a slider, screwball and knuckler.

Back to the minors in 1953, Hogue pitched 135 innings for the Toronto Maple Leafs of the Triple A International League, finishing with a record of 8–11 and a 3.60 ERA. He got into just one game in 1954 for Toronto, walking two and giving up three hits as he was touched for five runs (three earned) in zero official innings of work. From here he went on the voluntarily retired list, and then was given his release on August 5.

There was one more try the following year, but Hogue's pro career finally petered out with 33 innings of American Association work for Minneapolis in 1955 (4.64 ERA with a 1–0 record) and five innings for the independent Williston team in the Manitoba-Dakota League. He was still just 34, but it was time to hang up his spikes.

After baseball, Hogue lived in the Florida Keys and continued to enjoy fishing for pleasure. He worked for the *Miami News* for three years and then in the circulation department of the *Miami Herald* for many years, retiring in 1986. Robert Clinton Hogue died on December 22, 1987, in Miami at the age of 66 after a long battle with cancer. He just missed the 40th reunion of the 1948 National League champions in Boston the next summer, but even if his name is largely forgotten by casual baseball fans today, those who watched or played with the Braves in '48 knew full well his value to the club.

Sources

Epstein, Ben. "Knuckle Ball Bob," *Complete Baseball*, September 1952
1948 National League Green Book.
Christian Science Monitor, New York Times
Thanks to Davis O. Barker and Bob Brady.

TOMMY HOLMES *by Saul Wisnia*

G	AB	R	H	2B	3B	HR	RBI	BB	SO	BA	OBP	SLG	SB	HBP
139	585	85	190	35	7	6	61	46	20	.325	.375	.439	1	1

A severe sinus condition kept Tommy Holmes out of the service during World War II, but the chances are that if he had been drafted and sent into harm's way, several hundred fans from one particular portion of Braves Field would have been willing to follow him into action.

Holmes was among the most popular performers in Boston baseball history, and during his career with the Braves, from 1942 to 1952, nobody enjoyed the type of unabashed love he received from the denizens of the 1,500-seat, stand-alone bleachers situated behind his right-field playing spot. Dubbed the Jury Box by a sportswriter who once counted just 12 fans seated there in leaner times, the section with its wooden benches was filled during the club's contending years with a crew of regulars who developed a friendly give-and-take with their hero. "How many hits you gonna get today, Tommy?" a patron might yell, and Holmes would shout back a reply or hold up however many fingers he deemed appropriate. There is no record of his accuracy in forecasting, but the Pride of the Jury Box had plenty of clutch blows at the ballpark—none bigger than his eighth-inning single off Bob Feller that gave the Braves a 1–0 victory in the opening game of the 1948 World Series.

Brooklyn beginnings

A .302 lifetime hitter who set a then-National League record with a 37-game hitting streak in 1945 and was one of the toughest men in history to strike out, Thomas Francis Holmes was born on March 29, 1917, in the Borough Park neighborhood of Brooklyn. One of eight children, known as "Kelly" to his pals, he had a round, ruggedly handsome face and a chunky, 5-foot-10 frame that didn't seem to match his high-pitched Flatbush Irish accent. Dreaming in his early years of being a boxer, he was dubbed "the world's champion juvenile bag-puncher" at the age of 5 and won many prizes in this area through grade school. The rejection of such pugilist hopes by his father (who had been a second for several prizefighters himself) prompted Tommy to focus on baseball as a teenager.

In discussing his early diamond development, the

Tommy Holmes led all Braves batters in 1948 with a .325 average, third best in the NL.

left-handed Holmes always credited Brooklyn Technical High coach Anthony Tarrantino as his first great teacher. "He was the John McGraw of the high schools," he said of Tarrantino, under whose tutelage he hit .613 as a senior in 1935. "In the winter months he used to have me eat my lunch up in the gymnasium. He would draw home plate on the floor, and then we would talk about hitting. He'd show me parts of the plate, zoning and so forth. He was telling me how to reach the outside of the plate, how to reach the inside, and what to look for from a pitcher. He also taught me to have the courage to hit to opposite fields."

When Tech played Tilden High for the city championship, Holmes remembered Tarrantino shouting out, "*There's the best ballplayer in Brooklyn!*" when Tommy got a hit. Since Tilden's lineup included a standout named Sid Gordon who also enjoyed a successful big-league career, such praise meant a lot to Holmes. The confidence his coach instilled in him served Tommy well in the competitive semipro ranks of New York City baseball. "We grew up playing ball, or watching it, all the time," Holmes recalled. "Right in Brooklyn we had the Parade Grounds, which had about 21 fields. One big half-mile square filled with diamonds, and we played there every Sunday.

"I was a Dodgers fan growing up, but I never hated the Yankees. Many times three of us would get 55 cents together, we'd go over to Ebbets Field, and one kid would go through the turnstile and the other two would sneak under after him. I'd get to see a ballgame for under 20 cents. Then there was the Happy Felton program. He was a radio broadcaster who would get the Dodgers ballplayers to come out, and the kids would ask them questions. Then the players would put on kind of a clinic."

Brooklyn had two semipro teams that drew the attention of major-league scouts, the Bay Parkways and the Bushwicks. After graduating from high school, Holmes went seeking a job with the Bay Parkways. "Harry Hess, the manager, told me I was just a kid, but then one day a guy didn't show up and he said, 'Can you play left field?' I said sure, even though I had never played left field in my life. I was a first baseman. Well, I got a couple hits, and the next Tuesday night an owner of the Bushwicks—there were two brothers, Joe and Max Rosner, who owned both clubs—he called and asked me if I would play at Dexter Park for him against Josh Gibson, Satchel Paige, and all of those great Negro League players. I told him sure. I batted against Satchel Paige; I didn't know who he was, but I got a couple of hits." (Although Holmes never mentioned it to this writer, many sources claim he also played for the Bushwicks while still in high school, under the assumed name Thomas Kelly.)

Watching the games in which Holmes suited up against Gibson and Paige's Pittsburgh Crawfords team was Yankees scout Paul Krichell. He called Tommy's father, and as Holmes recalled, "There were no negotiations. We got together, Krichell said 'We'd like to sign your son,' and they gave me a few bucks—not much. I don't even remember what my bonus was. My father just said, 'Sure, sounds good.' I stayed out of the financial end of it. The average, I think, was $500 for a kid like me coming out of high school, and maybe $1,000 or a little more for a college kid with three or four more years' experience."

It was the late 1930s, and the Yankee dynasty started by Babe Ruth and Lou Gehrig was continuing with Gehrig, Joe DiMaggio, Bill Dickey, and Co. New York would win four consecutive World Series from 1936 to 1939, and the club oozed with confidence. "The Yankees always won, and they had no signs," Holmes said. "When I went to spring training with them, I asked what the signs were, and guys would say 'Signs? Just swing the goddamn bat!' I'd say, 'Well, what about....' and they would yell, 'Just swing the bat! If we can hold the opposition to four runs, we'll score seven.' That was the Yankees—bang-bang-bang. They had the power, and they could beat the hell out of you.

"I was told by George Weiss, then the Yankees' farm director, that their philosophy was that hopefully you had three years of playing Triple A ball, or at least two years. I could have come up earlier, but with DiMaggio, [Charlie] Keller, and later [Tommy] Henrich in the outfield, it was tough. Weiss said to me, 'Tommy, don't you sit around. You go out and *play*.' Holmes did as he was told, and put up great numbers. During his first professional season at Norfolk, in the summer of '37, the center fielder batted .320 with 25 homers and 111 RBIs. He made the All-Star team that year, then followed it up with an MVP campaign in '38 when he led the Eastern League with a .368 average, 200 hits, 41 doubles, and 110 runs for the Binghamton Triplets.

This prompted a promotion to the Yankees' top farm club, the Newark Bears—a team then considered to be the equal of many major league squads. All Holmes did there was bat .339 with 10 triples in 1939. His power numbers were down (he had just four homers, and topped 13 just once more as a pro), but it was clear that he was a first-rate hitter. Things progressed further in 1940, as Tommy topped the International League with 211 hits and 126 runs scored while batting .317. He was even better in the playoffs, setting a circuit mark for postseason hits and helping lead Newark to the Little World Series title. On September 13 of that year, the Associated Press reported that Dodgers president Larry MacPhail had supposedly offered the Yankees $40,000 for the hometown hero, but this was never substantiated and Holmes stayed put.

Escape from Newark

By the end of spring training in 1941, having just turned 24 and married his sweetheart, Lillian Helen Pettersen, Holmes was already a veteran of four minor-league seasons, who had shown the talent that normally warranted a promotion to the majors. But Keller, DiMaggio, and Henrich were still manning the outfield for the Bronx Bombers—with reigning AL batting champ DiMaggio in Tommy's position of center—and that left little room for a rookie lacking home run prowess. So after a look-see in spring training, Yanks manager Joe McCarthy sent the youngster back to Newark yet again with a promise: If New York couldn't find a space for him on its roster during the regular season, club management would make every attempt to grant his wish and send him to another big-league organization.

McCarthy was true to his word. Holmes hit .302 with a league-best 190 hits in his third season for the Bears in '41, but with the Yankees' outfield contingent seemingly set for years to come, the organization decided to trade off its still-valuable prospect. Two days after the Pearl Harbor attack, on December 9, 1941, Holmes was sold to the Braves for undisclosed cash and players to be named. The Yanks received first baseman Buddy Hassett a week later as part of the deal, and on February 5, 1942, Boston outfielder Gene Moore was sent Bronx-bound to complete it. The trade still ranks as one of the finest in Braves history; while Hassett played just one more season in the majors and Moore three subpar campaigns, Holmes was among the NL's top hitters for much of the next decade. "I always said it took the best ballplayer in the world—Joe DiMaggio—to run me out of New York," Tommy said, and while he was kidding, there was much truth to the statement.

With a tight budget, a no-frills ballpark, and a club mired deep in the second division, the Braves were the polar opposites of the aristocratic Yankees. Boston was coming off a 62–92 season and a third straight year in seventh place under manager Casey Stengel, and Tommy instantly found himself with a starting center-field job for 1942. Later he recalled that when he asked Stengel, "Who in God's name brought me here?" Casey said simply, "I did. Someday I want to build a whole ballclub around you." Holmes called going from the Yankees organization to the Braves like "living at the Waldorf, then going to live in Povertyville down at the Bowery."

Pearl Harbor and America's entry into World War II made for a long winter, but Holmes was still all smiles come spring. When the Braves started their season at Philadelphia on April 14, Tommy donned jersey No. 1 (which he'd wear his entire career) and batted leadoff in his major-league debut—going 2-for-5 against future teammate Si Johnson in a 2–1 Boston victory. And although the Braves wound up seventh yet again under Stengel, there were two future Hall of Famers on the playing roster all year for the rookie to learn from. Slow-footed catcher Ernie Lombardi hit .330 to capture the league batting title, and former Pirates great Paul "Big Poison" Waner played alongside Holmes in right field. Just a .258 hitter at age 39, Waner still had the knowledge of a man with three batting titles and a lifetime average of .330-plus under his belt. When he collected his 3,000th hit that year during his one full season with Boston, he was just the seventh big leaguer to achieve the feat.

For Holmes, Waner was nothing short of a revelation. Big Poison preached pulling the ball to right field, and in this curious rookie he had an apt pupil. "One day in '42, I took an 0-for-9 in a doubleheader," Tommy recalled nearly 60 years later. "I was in the clubhouse moping around, and there was Paul Waner, who liked his sauce, having a beer. He says, 'What's the matter, kid?' I say, 'Paul, I was 0-for-9 today.' He says, 'Don't worry about that. Just come out in the morning.' This was the beginning of my hitting life. I was a line-drive hitter, same as Paul. He says, 'See that foul line over there? I'm going to show you how to hit it. Never hit the ball where three guys can catch it, not with that wind blowing in at Braves Field. Shoot for the foul lines. If a few go out of play, don't worry about it. You don't pay for the balls.'" (Although Holmes credited Stengel with similar batting tips at the time, he always cited Waner as his chief tutor in later interviews.)

The rookie learned his lessons well. Batting leadoff most of the year, Holmes hit .278, second only to Lombardi among Boston's regulars, and struck out just 10 times in 558 at-bats. He went 10-for-19 in one August stretch against the Dodgers and Giants, broke up two no-hit attempts, and compiled a .990 fielding average to tie for second best in the league. Having not gotten his first big-league shot until he was 25 years old, he was making up for lost time. Even when he dipped a bit to .270 in his sophomore season, he led the league with 629 at-bats and collected 33 doubles and 10 triples. He was above .300 much of the season, often batted third, and later claimed that focusing on learning to pull the ball cost him 50 points in his batting average. It proved a worthwhile sacrifice.

Of course Tommy's mind was likely on more than baseball that summer. With the war in Europe and Japan heating up, married players like Holmes were starting to be drafted, and he got a call in March 1944 to leave spring training and report to Brooklyn for his Navy physical.

Although it was widely reported that he had passed and would be reporting for duty that summer, the call never came. Later, Holmes described an induction scene where examining doctors determined him unfit for duty due to lifelong sinus problems that they feared could be life-threatening in the European climate.

One of a dwindling number of strong young ballplayers left on big-league rosters, and fresh off a winter spent working in the Brooklyn shipyards, Holmes posted his first super season in 1944. Third in the NL with 195 hits, 93 runs scored, and 42 doubles, he also finished 10th in hitting at .309 after staying near the top (and above .330) into late summer. His power totals took a big leap as well: after hitting four and five homers in his first two years in the majors, he slugged 13—ninth in the league. The introduction of the wartime "Balata ball" had hampered slugging league-wide, but Holmes hit the heavier spheres better than most.

Making the feat more impressive was the ballpark Tommy called home. Braves Field was a cavernous park built during the inside baseball era of 1915, just before Babe Ruth ushered in the home run age. Its center-field fence was originally built 550 feet from home plate, and with the wind blowing in off the Charles River just beyond its walls, few on the club had ever managed even 20 homers. Now, seeing that Holmes had some pop in his bat, Braves management brought the 345-foot right-field fences in by 20 feet midway through the '44 campaign to give him an easier target.

Sakes alive in '45

Even with this move, what transpired next took the most optimistic of fans by surprise. Holmes got off to a hot start in 1945 that never let up, and Paul Waner's star pupil reached his peak. Although the Braves stumbled to yet another second-division finish, Tommy astonished the baseball world by leading the major leagues with 28 homers, 224 hits, 47 doubles, a .577 slugging percentage, 81 extra-base hits, and 367 total bases. He batted .352—finishing second in the NL to Phil Cavarretta of the Cubs in a race that went down to the final day—and was also runner-up (to Brooklyn's Dixie Walker) with 117 RBIs. His 125 runs scored placed him third in that department, and he even stole 15 bases (fourth most in the NL) for good measure. Moved to right field to make room for Carden Gillenwater in center, Holmes played in all 154 games and had 13 assists, to the delight of the Jury Box fans now seated just behind him. (Tommy's throwing arm was never considered a strong suit, but he did manage 10 or more assists in seven seasons.)

Making this dominant showing all the more impressive was what Holmes did in the middle of it—establishing a new NL record with a 37-game hitting streak. He started the stretch in scorching fashion with 10 total hits in back-to-back doubleheaders on June 6–7, and kept up the torrid pace into July. He tied and broke Rogers Hornsby's old mark of 33 straight games against the Pirates in another doubleheader that featured rainy, hurricane-like conditions at Braves Field and a homer, single, and four doubles by the man of the hour.

The hits kept coming right up until the All-Star break (which he entered with a major-league-best .401 average), but in his first game after the three-day layoff, Holmes was stopped by Hank Wyse of the Cubs on July 12 at Wrigley Field. All told, he batted .433 during the streak, which lasted as a record for 33 years before being broken by Pete Rose. Even today, while Tommy's breakthrough season has been largely (and unfairly) forgotten by all but fervent baseball historians, his hitting streak still stands as the ninth longest in big-league annals.

Perhaps the most amazing stat of all is that Holmes stepped to the plate on more than 700 occasions in 1945 (636 official at-bats plus 70 walks), and left it a strikeout victim just *nine times* (once swinging). This gave him the distinction of being the first man ever to lead the majors in most homers and fewest strikeouts in the same season, an incredible display of contact hitting in keeping with his career averages. Holmes never struck out more than 20 times in a season, and had more homers than strikeouts on a record-tying four occasions (Ernie Lombardi, Lefty O'Doul, and Ted Williams also accomplished this feat). In fact, Holmes' 122 lifetime strikeouts in 4,992 career at-bats are fewer than many current major leaguers notch in just one season of less than 600 at-bats.

Unfortunately for Holmes and his fans, Tommy's breakthrough summer did not end with a National League MVP award. That honor went to Cavarretta of the pennant-winning Cubs, who despite edging Holmes for the batting crown finished far behind him in every other major offensive category. The native Chicagoan hit just six home runs, missed 22 games with assorted injuries, and as a first baseman did not hold down a crucial defensive position. Still, perhaps overly influenced by the finishes of the Cubs and the sixth-place Braves, writers gave Cavarretta 15 first-place votes to second-place Tommy's three. Holmes was named Player of the Year by *The Sporting News* and Boston sportswriters, however, and the team's management and fans chipped in to buy him a new Packard automobile in a Tommy Holmes Day ceremony at Braves Field on September 2. He celebrated, naturally, by slugging a home run.

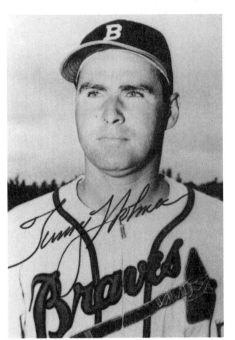

Unlike his fellow Braves fly-chasers, Tommy Holmes was not a part of manager Billy Southworth's outfield platooning.

Braves rise—and fall

With Holmes established as a top star by the end of '45, new Braves president Lou Perini and his ownership group began following through on Stengel's dream of surrounding Tommy with a strong team. Ace manager Billy Southworth (a three-time pennant winner) was brought in from the St. Louis Cardinals, and the war's end along with blockbuster trades brought many new faces onto the 1946 roster, including Warren Spahn, Johnny Sain, and Johnny Hopp. The result was a leap to third place, and Holmes had another standout season with a .310 average, 35 doubles, and a 20-game hit streak. The Jury Box crowd so adored him that when Tommy swapped positions with left fielder Johnny Barrett for one day that year, fans showered Barrett with so many boos and insults that he claimed at game's end, "I'll never go out there again." There was one problem, however. "The owners had doubled my salary to around $30,000 [after '45]," Holmes recalled later, "but then they went and moved the fences back out!" Despite Tommy's 28 home runs and teammate Chuck Workman's 25 during 1945, team statisticians saw that more opponents than Braves sluggers had been taking advantage of the closer right-field target. When the fences went back out, the result was just six homers and 79 RBIs for Holmes in '46. The Pride of the Jury Box would never crack as many as 10 homers again, but Perini and Co. were finding other big bats to do the bashing.

Bob Elliott came on the scene in 1947 and in addition to crushing 22 homers finished just ahead of Holmes in the National League batting race, their .317 and .309 marks placing them in second and seventh place respectively. Tommy's 191 hits topped league MVP Elliott and the rest of the senior circuit, and one of his rare home runs was particularly meaningful—a ninth-inning shot to beat the Giants on August 10, the day his son, Tommy Jr., was born. "I couldn't let the kid think his old man didn't have it in the clutch, could I?" Holmes quipped to sportswriters. (Tommy Jr. later appeared with his dad in a full-color magazine ad for Wheaties.)

Everything came together for the Braves in 1948, and Holmes was a big factor as leadoff man for the NL champions. He placed third in the league with a .325 average (his fifth straight year in the top 10), was second with 190 hits, and made his second All-Star team. The Three Troubadours, a trio of musicians who serenaded players at Braves Field on trombone, trumpet, and clarinet, played the Irish tune "Has Anybody Here Seen Kelly?" when Holmes stepped to the plate. The answer was more folks than ever, as the Braves set an all-time attendance mark of 1,455,439 that summer even as the Red Sox were drawing 1,558,798 of their own while battling for an American League pennant down the road.

And although Holmes batted just .192 in the World Series against Cleveland, he had arguably the biggest hit of the fall classic. With Johnny Sain and Bob Feller locked up in a scoreless pitchers' duel in the eighth inning of Game One at Braves Field, Tommy's roommate, Phil Masi, appeared to be caught snoozing off second base when Feller and Cleveland shortstop Lou Boudreau pulled a pickoff play they had been practicing. It was clear in still photographs taken at a variety of angles that Boudreau had indeed tagged Masi on the shoulder before he could slide back into the bag, but umpire Bill Stewart (a Fitchburg, Mass., native) saw it differently and called Masi safe. Sain lined out, but then Holmes hit a ball past Ken Keltner at third to drive in Masi with the game's only run and send the chilly home crowd of 40,135 into a frenzy. Feller wound up a 1–0 loser despite his two-hitter, and the Braves had a quick edge in the World Series. It was a heady time for the underdogs, but it was short-lived. Boston went on to drop four of the next five games and the series, with Holmes ending the 4–3, Game Six finale at Braves Field with a fly out. As if this wasn't bad enough, Tommy had to head to the hospital the next day for an appendectomy. Then it was back to Brooklyn for his newest offseason job—selling televisions.

Braves management was confident that their team could contend for years to come, but in 1949 the Braves quickly fell back to fourth place. Talk of dissension rocked the club starting in spring training, as players reportedly grumbled about Southworth driving them too hard and seeking too much credit for the previous year's accomplishments. Players later said the disharmony was largely a figment of the press, but there was no denying the dramatic decline in performance by many on the club. Holmes was among them; he batted less than .300 for the first time in six years (dropping all the way to .266), and began getting platooned on a semi-regular basis. He got his average back up to .298 in 1950, when the Braves again contended much of the season, but by then Tommy

Tommy Holmes in a circa 1945 Braves uniform. That season Holmes led the NL in hits, doubles and home runs and established a new NL consecutive game hit streak at 37 games.

was practically splitting time with Willard Marshall. Even though Holmes showed a bit of his 1945 pop with nine homers in just 322 at-bats, his playing career was winding down. The organization had other things in mind for him.

A raw deal

As a player Holmes was popular with his teammates, the coaching staff, fans, and reporters, so it seemed only natural that he might make a success as a manager. He was asked to take over the Braves' farm club at Hartford as player-manager for the 1951 season, and he enthusiastically accepted the challenge. By midway through the year Billy Southworth's health and the big league team's record were both floundering, and with Southworth's stunning resignation on June 19, another request came Holmes' way: How would he like to manage in Boston? He had likely thought it would be years before such an opportunity came, so it was no surprise that Tommy again said yes.

In many ways, his appointment—which also cost Hartford Holmes' .319 bat—was an experiment doomed to fail. Suddenly the youngest skipper in the big leagues at just 34, Tommy took over an underachieving club mixed with veterans like Elliott, Spahn, and Earl Torgeson who had been his teammates the previous year, and raw youngsters like Johnny Logan and Chet Nichols who were getting their first taste of the majors. It was hard for him to establish authority under such circumstances, and his mild-mannered approach and lack of training didn't help. While there were some high points, including a 9–0 victory by Spahn over the Cubs in Holmes' managerial debut and a midsummer stretch in which the club won 14 of 18 games, by year's end his record was a mediocre 48–47 for a team that finished 76–78 overall.

The worst was yet to come. In 1952 the Braves got off to a poor start, and Tommy (cover boy on the first edition of the team scorebook that season) became a convenient scapegoat. Newspaper columnists who had spent a decade praising his playing skills now attacked his tactical moves and coaching prowess at third base, and on May 31, with the club in seventh place at 13–22, he was fired in favor of Charlie Grimm—whose managerial résumé already included 13 big-league seasons and three pennants. General manager John Quinn said Holmes simply needed more experience to be a successful skipper, an odd comment considering that he now had a year more of it than when they had given him the job.

Asked his own feelings, the ever-classy Holmes said of the club that fired him by phone: "They are wonderful people. They probably hated twice as much telling me I was fired as I disliked hearing it. And it's no disgrace to be replaced by Charlie Grimm." In later years he would be more open, telling the *Boston Herald* in 1986: "It broke my heart when they let me go. I was ready to have a home built up there. That was going to be my home. It was a shock. It was like losing your family. I don't think I ever got over that even yet."

In the end, there was a bright spot to the season for Tommy. He signed on two weeks later as a spare outfielder with his hometown Brooklyn Dodgers, and on June 29 he beat the Braves with a pinch single before Boston's second biggest home crowd of the season (13,405). Brooklyn wound up winning the pennant, and Holmes saw his last big-league playing time in a seven-game World Series loss to the Yankees. The Braves meanwhile, finished with a 64–89 record and back in seventh place. Attendance had fallen to 281,000, financial losses were mounting, and the following spring Perini announced he was moving the club to Milwaukee. The Jury Box fell silent.

Although it frustrated his fans that Tommy didn't get a chance to stick as manager long enough to help the Braves flourish after their move—they leaped to 92 wins in 1953, and claimed a World Series title over the Yankees by 1957—in retrospect his exit while the club was still situated in New England seems appropriate. Perhaps more than any other player, Holmes personified the underdog, determined *Boston* Braves. And despite how his career with the team ended, his numbers still shine through. He averaged 185 hits, 36 doubles, and 86 runs scored during his nine seasons as a regular, and ranked among baseball's Top 10 during the 1940s in hits and doubles.

Going home, giving back

His playing career in the majors now finished once and for all, Holmes embarked on a minor-league managerial odyssey during the next several seasons. Lou Perini brought him back to the Braves organization to lead its top farm club in Toledo for 1953, after which he jumped once more to Brooklyn as skipper of its Class A team at Elmira for '54. He summered with Fort Worth of the Texas League in 1955, and with the Portland Beavers of the Pacific Coast League the next year. In '57 he returned home once more to scout New York area high school and college players for the Dodgers, but then later that summer was off to Montreal to manage the Royals of the International League.

Tommy's travels finally stopped in 1959. He was named director of the *New York Journal-American*'s sandlot baseball program, which was later renamed the New York Sandlot Baseball Alliance. (His former mentor Paul Waner had once held the job.) In more than 30 years in this position, Holmes would help teach thousands of youngsters, many from underprivileged backgrounds, the joys of the game. He once claimed that 85 of "my kids" had made the major leagues, and said with pride that "none of my kids, no matter what their ability, sits on the bench."

Back in the spotlight—and Boston

Starting in 1973, Holmes took on an additional role as director of amateur baseball relations for the New York Mets. He became a familiar figure around Shea Stadium during three decades on the job, but likely never would have risen from relative obscurity outside Flushing Meadows had not Pete Rose gotten on a hot streak during the summer of 1978. Once Rose had hit in 30 straight games and was nearing Holmes's record 37-game skein, Tommy's name started appearing in newspaper stories throughout the country for the first time in a quarter-century. "I wish [Rose] luck," Holmes joked to a reporter. "Heck, until two weeks ago nobody knew I was alive."

As fate would have it, the Reds were playing at Shea against the Mets when Rose reached game No. 38 of his streak on July 25. The game was stopped momentarily to honor the achievement, and a teary-eyed Holmes stepped on the field to shake the new record-holder's hand. The gesture impressed Rose, who said of his predecessor, "I only hope I show as much class as Tommy Holmes did when somebody breaks my record. He thanked me for making him a big leaguer again." (Rose eventually made it to 44 games before he was stopped, ironically, by the Atlanta Braves.)

Ten years later, when the '48 Braves were invited back to Boston for a 40th reunion, one of the most popular guests was a still-trim Holmes—sporting his 1986 World Series championship ring earned with the Mets at the expense of the Red Sox. He and his beloved Lillian also made the drive up from their home in Woodbury, Long Island, each year throughout the 1990s to attend the annual events hosted by the Boston Braves Historical Association (BBHA), where he delighted in talking about Waner, Stengel, and other departed colleagues while meeting with fans who had cheered him from the Jury Box half a century before. Holmes was the inaugural inductee into the BBHA's Boston Braves Hall of Fame at the 1993 event; another dinner featured a reunion of Holmes and Bob Feller—who ribbed each other about Game One of the '48 World Series a half-century after the fact. When an original member of the "Three Troubadours" surprised Tommy at one reunion with his clarinet rendition of "Has Anybody Here Seen Kelly?" it brought tears to the old right fielder's eyes.

When ill health prompted Tommy's retirement from the Mets and stopped his pilgrimages to the Hub around 2002, it was if the Braves diehards who remained were losing their hero all over again. Holmes no doubt felt the same way. He always said it was not the batting streak or his hit off Feller that provided him with his greatest Boston memories; those were reserved for his love affair with the 1,500 bleacherites in right field. "Williams, DiMaggio, Musial—they never had what I did," he often recounted proudly. "The other 29,000 fans, if they wanted to give me a boo or two, go ahead. But not if you sat behind me in the Jury Box, I'll tell you that. They were always hollering at me, 'Keep your eye on the ball, Tommy!' 'Try and wait for a good one, Tommy!' Tommy this, and Tommy that.

"I remember when I was on the 28th game of my streak. It was a beautiful day; the sun was all over the place. And this gentleman comes into the Jury Box under the influence of liquor, and starts in on me: 'So you're the great Holmes! You couldn't carry Ted Williams' jock!' Then of course I get up and hit into a double play. Holy geez. So now I go back out to right, and he yells, 'If I wanted to go to the circus, I would have gone to the GAAAH-DEN!' Finally, Marty Marion hits a line drive to me with the bases loaded: 'I have it, I have it, I have it....I can't find it.' It hits the fence behind me, and the guy yells, 'Now I KNOW I'm going to go to the GAAH-DEN, because I have never seen anything like this!'"

Just then, a little fellow in the front row behind me says, 'Tommy, I'm going to take care of this.' He goes and gets Big Dan, the Irish cop. Now you can't arrest a fan for yelling or cursing, but remember, he was needling me about Williams and so on and so forth. I come out the next inning, and the loudmouth is gone. I say 'What happened?' And the little guy says, 'We had Big Dan throw him out of the ballpark!'

"That's the way it was out there. They would do practically anything for me, and I never forgot it."

Still No. 1

The Pride of the Jury Box still had his original Boston Braves uniform, socks, and cap when he died of natural causes on April 14, 2008, at the age of 91. His passing in Boca Raton, Florida, left Al Dark as the last regular from the 1948 National League championship club still alive, as fellow teammates Sain, Spahn, Eddie Stanky, and Bill Voiselle had all died in recent years. Tommy had also been the last living Boston Braves manager for quite some time, owing to the young age at which he held the position.

In tributes that appeared in newspapers upon his death, Holmes' good-guy image shined through. His daughter, Patricia Stone, said her father had been enjoying baseball games on television right up until the end.

She also recounted that "When he played baseball, there would be days he'd leave early and he'd pass children playing and he'd stop to play with them." Son Tommy Jr. said that "he loved every minute of his time in Boston and he received fan mail long after he left." Those family members mourning his loss also included his beloved wife of 67 years, Lillian, two grandchildren, and two great-grandchildren.

Mets Chief Operating Officer Jeff Wilpon called his former employee "one of our sport's truest gentlemen," adding that "his passion for the game and up-and-coming players, along with his 30-year association with our franchise, was unsurpassed." So was his passion for hitting, as evidenced by a story told to the *New York Daily News* by Mets employee Lorraine Hamilton—one of several female front office employees who played on the organization's softball team and received valuable advice from Holmes. "He told me, 'Anyone can hit if they put their mind to it' and he worked with me in the batting cages." What Hamilton probably didn't realize is that she was getting a variation on the same sage advice Paul Waner had once passed down to Tommy at Braves Field so many years before.

Those players still around who played with or for Tommy were just as praising. "He always made rookies like myself and Johnny Antonelli feel like one of the guys," said catcher Del Crandall, a teammate in 1949 and '50. "He was a real pro the way he went about his business, and when I played in Milwaukee, I inherited his uniform No. 1."

Tommy Holmes—No. 1 in your (old) scorebook, and No. 1 in the hearts of Boston Braves fans.

Sources

Author interviews with Tommy Holmes, 1991–2002

Tommy Holmes remarks at Boston Braves reunions, 1991–2002

Assorted Associated Press, *New York Times*, and *Hartford Courant* articles, 1939–1978

"Home of the Braves," *Boston Herald Sunday Magazine*, May 4, 1986

Kaese, Harold, "Boston's Strong Boy," *Sports World*, July 1949

Pave, Marvin, Holmes obituary in *Boston Globe*, April 15, 2008

Rubin, Roger, Holmes obituary in *New York Daily News*, April 15, 2008

Caruso, Gary, *The Braves Encyclopedia*, Philadelphia: Temple University Press, 1993.

Kaese, Harold, *The Boston Braves*, New York: G. P. Putman's Sons, 1948

Honig, Donald, *Baseball Between the Lines*, Lincoln: University of Nebraska Press, 1976

DANNY LITWHILER *by Glen Vasey*

G	AB	R	H	2B	3B	HR	RBI	BB	SO	BA	OBP	SLG	SB	HBP
13	33	0	9	2	0	0	6	4	2	.273	.385	.333	0	2

"Starving for run making power, the Phillies' Labor Day attendance found in their lap a brand new outfielder.

He hit a homer with the bases full. Also a triple, double, and two singles. He batted in six runs in the first game; 2 more in the nightcap....

Dangerous Dan Litwhiler is the name. A slugging schoolmaster from upstate Pennsylvania."

—Unattributed, undated 1940 clipping #9540, "Dangerous Dan, the Pill-Pounding Pedagog" in Litwhiler folder, Giamatti Library, Cooperstown, NY

Dan Litwhiler's major league career began with the Philadelphia Phillies in 1940 and saw him ply his trade as an outfielder with the St. Louis Cardinals, the Boston Braves, and the Cincinnati Reds over the ensuing dozen years. But his playing days, while distinguished, offer only a glimpse of what this man has contributed to the game he so loves.

The evidence, if one cares to look, is out there.

One of his gloves, perhaps the first to ever have its fingers tied together, is on display in the Hall of Records in the Baseball Hall of Fame and Museum in Cooperstown, N.Y. That same museum owns, as another gift from Litwhiler, the prototype of the JUGGS Speed Gun, the first radar gun developed for use as a baseball-teaching tool by Litwhiler and a friend.

The nine years Dan spent coaching Florida State University and the 19 he spent in the same role at Michigan State earned him election to the American Association of College Baseball Coaches Hall of Fame.

He served five years as the international president of the United States Baseball Federation, during which time he worked hard to make the sport an international game.

Later he returned to the Reds as a hitting instructor and consultant, which resulted in his working individually

Danny Litwhiler missed out on playing in his third Fall Classic when he was swapped to the Reds in May.

with every player who appeared in the starting lineup for Cincinnati's 1990 World Series opener.

Perhaps most uniquely, throughout all of his years in the game, he invented more than 100 items, some of which all major leaguers today take for granted, in his efforts to improve the teaching and playing of baseball. And at 91 years old, he was still going strong more than 70 seasons after his first summer in the game.

Born August 31, 1916, in Ringtown, Pennsylvania, Dan was the son of Stephen Luther and Mary (Yeager) Litwhiler. His parents ran a hotel that catered to mining and railroad workers in their tiny town (population 150). In a March 2005 interview he revealed that he was the seventh son of a seventh son, and joked that that might be where he got his penchant for inventions. He also more soberly mentioned that two of his older brothers had died prematurely.

The Litwhilers still had a house full of children as Dan was raised with four older brothers and one older sister, and that doesn't even include the two additional older brothers that his parents adopted when they first believed they wouldn't be able to have children together. "That's the old wives' tale with the Pennsylvania Dutch, which we were," he said. "If you adopt a child you can have your own. They adopted two and soon there was Archie." And then Ida Katherine, and the twins Truman and Sterling, and Woodie, and finally Dan.

Archie, Truman, Sterling, and Woodie all loved baseball and shared that love with Danny. He started out, as all little brothers must, just following his older brothers around and playing batboy, but joined in the games as soon as they would let him.

Ringtown was so small that "we didn't have Little League or anything like that. Our second baseman in high school was a girl; had to have them because there wasn't enough boys. She was good too, Mildred Breisch. Good hitter and a good fielder."

If a Litwhiler said someone could play, you could believe him. Archie, Truman, Woodie, and eventually Danny all went on to star at Bloomsburg State Teachers College, and Woodie even preceded Dan into professional baseball as a pitcher before hurting his arm. Archie, however, was "the family's role model. He was a real gentleman, he was a schoolteacher, everybody liked him. He dressed well, so we had to do the same thing."

Dan would eventually follow both of his brother Archie's professional examples—teaching and playing ball—and achieved a high standard in both fields.

After starring for four years as an outfielder on the college team and graduating from Bloomsburg with his teaching certificate, Dan got his first professional break.

In an age when every town had a number of loosely organized town teams, and when many fairly small towns hosted minor league clubs, the mayor of Charleroi, Pennsylvania—who also happened to be the owner of the Charleroi entry in the Class-D Pennsylvania State Association—came to Bloomsburg to watch some sandlot games in hopes of recruiting talent. Dan had tonsillitis and didn't get a chance to play for the mayor, but Ed Schuyler, a newspaperman in Bloomsburg, recommended the youngest Litwhiler with enough conviction that the mayor agreed to extend an offer. Dan became part of the defending World Champion Detroit Tigers organization.

At Charleroi in 1936, Dan batted .313 in 66 games, demonstrating moderate power and an unlikeliness to either walk or strike out. He earned $75 a month. Good money if you could get it, in a Depression-saddled land, especially for doing something that you surely loved.

The next year, he was sent to Charleston, West Virginia, in the Class-C Middle Atlantic League. When he arrived, manager Iggy Walters wasn't expecting him.

"Where do you play?" Walters asked.

"Outfield."

"You ever play right field?"

"No, I always play left or center."

"Well, you go out to right field."

Five minutes later, Dan came in on a line drive, tried to hold up when he saw he couldn't make the catch, and broke his ankle.

By the time he was able to return to Charleston, his timing was off and he had trouble pulling the ball, but he managed to hit .287 in 48 games, increasing his walks while his power numbers dropped.

In another example of how times have changed, Dan showed up in Charleston for a second season in 1938, only to be told the team had all the players it needed. He was sent to another team that told him it was taking only rookies. Finally a call was put through to Detroit and he was told to report to Alexandria, Louisiana, in the Class-D

Evangeline League. Even there, manager Art Phelan was reluctant to accept Litwhiler until he saw him hit in batting practice. "I just hit ball after ball out of the ballpark," Litwhiler remembered. "I just had an 'on' day."

In his first at-bat before the home fans in Alexandria, Dan hit a home run. It was a harbinger of things to come. In 76 games that season he batted .369 with a .436 on-base percentage and a .556 slugging average, driving in 71 runs and scoring 62. That summer he was chosen to play center field in the Evangeline League All-Star game. He became enough of a fan favorite that a local policeman helped him get a job teaching in an Alexandria high school in the offseason, which eventually interfered with his next step up the ladder.

When the 1939 season assignments for the Tigers organization were being handed out, Dan was already a bit busy as the JV basketball coach, the assistant football coach, and a science and biology teacher at Bolton High School in Alexandria. Detroit assigned him to Toledo, one of the top organizations in its minor league chain. Dan was excited and ready to go, but the school told him that he had to wait until it found a replacement for him in the classroom. So the dutiful educator waited and delayed his reporting time, not wanting to leave either the students or the school in the lurch.

When he finally reported to the Toledo team, he had not had an opportunity to get himself in condition at all, but he was excited about having an opportunity to make a strong impression at this higher level. As Litwhiler later recounted, when he introduced himself to Myles Thomas, Toledo's manager, Myles looked at him and said, "Who are you?"

"I'm Dan Litwhiler."

"Litwhiler? Then who the hell is that out there in right field?"

Litwhiler looked. "It looks like Milt Lenhardt; he was our centerfielder in Alexandria."

Thomas looked at him, "I thought that was you all along."

"No," Dan said, "I'm just getting here. I was teaching school and I had some trouble getting away."

Thomas nodded, "Go on out to right field."

Later Dan confronted Lenhardt, "Say, Milt, how come you took my name?"

Milt shrugged, "Hell, you had a great year last year, I had a lousy one. He called me Litwhiler and I said, 'okay.'"

"He made the team that year too," Litwhiler recalled. "He said he didn't think he would have made it if he'd been Lenhardt."

Soon after, there was another looping line drive that Litwhiler was coming in on, thinking he could make the catch. Suddenly deciding that he *couldn't* make it, he pulled up and tore the cartilage in his knee. Soon after that the Tigers released him without payment.

That could have been the end of Dan's professional career, but before the year was out his brother Woodie had arranged a tryout in front of general manager John Ogden of the Baltimore Orioles of the International League. The Orioles at this time were an independent International League team, and Woodie Litwhiler had met Ogden during his own professional career.

Woodie escorted his brother to Baltimore for the tryout and even pitched batting practice for him. Soon John Ogden exclaimed, "That's enough, you're losing all the balls!" And later, "We'd like to sign you. Go back to your hotel and wait until I call you."

After three days without a call, the brothers, their finances waning rapidly, made their way back to Ringtown. When they got home there was a message for Dan to call a Philadelphia number. Dan dialed the number and was told he'd reached the Philadelphia Phillies. He identified himself and John Ogden got on the phone.

Not one to beat around the bush, Dan asked John why he hadn't called him. Ogden told him, "Because I was working for Baltimore then. If I called you, you'd be under contract to Baltimore now, which wouldn't do me a lot of good if it turns out that you become the player I think you're going to be. You see, I'm the general manager of the Phillies now."

Then he put Philadelphia owner Gerry Nugent on the line. "John says you're going to be a good ballplayer," Nugent said, and then offered Dan a decent contract and full coverage for the knee operation he would need.

"I may have been one of the first ones who played after a knee operation," Litwhiler later recalled. "Maybe I'm wrong, but I don't remember anybody playing after one."

The 1940 *National League Green Book* touts "'Slug' Litwhiler, upstate Pennsylvania Dutchman," though it does not indicate whether he got his nickname from his hitting ability or in reference to his speed on the base paths. Slug never stole more than two bases in a season, and totaled 11 for his career, although as a strong defensive outfielder he was presumably not slow afoot.

The Phillies held their spring training in Miami, Florida, in 1940 and Dan remembers playing "every inning of every game," leading the team in "everything" and getting great press.

"There was no doubt in my mind that I was going to

While with the Cardinals, Litwhiler had played for Southworth's 1943 NL Champs and 1944 World Series victors.

play on Opening Day," he would later say. "Everybody, the fans, the writers, everybody was positive that I was going to play." The clippings seem to back him up; "Phils Expect Big Things of Dan Litwhiler" read one Associated Press headline from that winter. "'He's Our Dark Horse,' Says Johnny Ogden."

The Phillies were scheduled to open in New York against the Giants. Dan got to the train station in Philly in plenty of time but managed to get lost in coffee and conversation with the friends who had come to see him off and so missed the train. A station employee explained that if he took the next train, an express, he would actually beat the Phillies' train to New York. He did so and hid out in the New York hotel lobby until his teammates arrived. Then he tried mingling nonchalantly with his mates.

Jimmy Hagens, the team's traveling secretary, approached and asked where he'd been.

"What do you mean?" Dan asked, "I'm right here."

"You weren't on the train," Hagens observed.

"Yes, I was."

"I still have your ticket."

Dan quickly improvised a story about another car, a friend, the conductor asking for his ticket and Dan telling him that Jimmy Hagens had it, but it didn't fly.

"He knew I was lying," Dan later admitted.

"Doc Prothro (the Phillies manager) never said a word to me, never said one word. So the lineup gets put up and Litwhiler's not in the lineup. I said, 'Uh-oh, something's wrong here.' I didn't say anything to him about it.

"The ballplayers come up and say, 'What happened? What did you do wrong?' I said, 'I have no idea.' They thought I was on the train. They saw me at the station, they saw me at the hotel."

He finally got a chance to play in the season's fourth game back in Philly, pinch-hitting on April 25 with two outs in the ninth and the team down 3–1. He took a major league cut at a hanging curve from Brooklyn's Hugh Casey and hit a major league popup. "Before that ball came down," he'd lament, "I think I was headed for Baltimore."

After some time in Wilkes-Barre (where he hit well) and Baltimore (where he didn't), he made it back to Philadelphia and started off with a 21-game hitting streak.

"By that time Prothro's in love with me," Dan stated, and he finished the 1940 season with a .345 average, five home runs, and 17 RBIs in 36 major league games. He had finally made it. To cap his season, he married Dorothy Lynch, whom he had met on October 10. In 1941, his first full year in the majors, he hit .305/18/66 with 72 runs scored in 151 games. Not only was that a personal best for home runs, but he also managed to hit at least one in every National League park that season. Unfortunately he made 15 errors in the outfield that year as well.

In 1942, Hans Lobert took over as manager of the lowly Phillies, who were coming off a 43–111 season and four straight seasons in last place. He told Dan that he'd noticed that all of his errors the previous year were on groundballs, not on flies or throws. "I'll tell you what you're going to do this year," Lobert told him, "You're going to take second infield practice every day this year. If you don't, it's going to cost you $50."

The results speak for themselves. In 1942, Dan became the first player in major league history to play every inning of every game for an entire season without making an error, which is why his glove is on display to this day in Cooperstown. Indeed, Dan stretched his errorless streak to 187 games before finally making an error. The miscue that broke his streak on May 10, 1943, was the only one he would make that season as he led the league outfielders in fielding percentage for the second consecutive year.

Part of his record could be attributable to his first invention. "I may be wrong," he said in 2005, "but I think that my glove was the first one that had the fingers tied together by rawhide."

It was simply an inspiration he had. "I thought if I tied them together, if I catch a ball, maybe it would stay. Sure enough, during the time of the record, I fielded the ball two times right on the end of the fingers. No way in the world I would have caught [them] if it weren't tied together."

Even so, his errorless streak, like every streak, had a moment of doubt included. In this case, as George Robinson and Charles Salzberg recounted in their fine book *On a Clear Day They Could See Seventh Place: Baseball's Worst Teams*, it happened in the Polo Grounds (though the authors fail to supply a specific date). "The outfield was a quagmire," they report, "when Johnny Mize hit a sinking line drive to left that Litwhiler gloved on a dead run. When he tried to set himself to throw the ball back in, his feet went out from under him and he dropped the ball. Litwhiler assumed the streak was over and it would be 10 years before he knew why the official scorer, who had originally ruled it an error, changed his mind. Mize, who had been hitting .299 coming into the game, desperately wanted to reach the .300 mark, so much so that he ran up to the press box in full uniform to argue with the scorer after the game, convincing him to make the change."

Late in 1942, Dan showed another side of his character that made him a valued commodity in the world of baseball. In the final week of the season, in the ninth inning of a tie game against the Cardinals—who were battling Brooklyn for first place—Dan singled to center, and then stretched it into a double despite the sterling reputation of Terry Moore's throwing arm. The next batter also singled to Moore in center. Litwhiler, not to be dissuaded, rounded third and headed for home. He arrived at his destination just as catcher Walker Cooper caught the throw from Moore and moved to apply the tag.

Litwhiler was knocked unconscious as his head hit Cooper's shin guard; Cooper's shoulder was dislocated in the collision. Litwhiler had won a game for the last-place Phils at the expense of the Cards, who were still fighting for the National League pennant. Billy Southworth, the Cardinals manager, was paying attention.

"If he plays this hard for a last place team," thought Southworth, "how hard will he play for a contender?"

The following year Southworth engineered a trade for Litwhiler.

Despite the fact that his first three years in the big leagues were spent with what may have been the most moribund team of all time (the Phils lost 534 games in five seasons from 1938 through 1942, had only one winning season to boast of since 1917, and had lost 100 or more games half of the previous 22 years), Dan claims that they never lost heart.

"I don't think we felt like we were going to lose," he said. "Like when Hugh Mulcahy pitched, he didn't win a lot of games but I swear he was a great pitcher and you'd just play your heart out for him.... I never felt like we were going to lose this game." (For the record, Mulcahy went 40–76 as Philadelphia's "ace" right-hander from 1937–40, making an All-Star team in '40 while going 13–23.).

During the 1943 season, Southworth was able to put together the trade he wanted, to get Litwhiler for his own squad. On June 1, St. Louis gave up Elvin "Buster" Adams, Coaker Triplett, and Dain Clay to get Litwhiler and Earl Naylor from the Phils. It was a turnaround of the highest order for Dan, who in one day went from the league's worst club to its best.

In 80 games for the 105–49 Cards, Dan hit .279 that year and got to play in his first World Series. Against the Yankees he hit .267 with a double and two RBIs as St. Louis lost the series in five contests.

In 1944, he appeared in 140 games, hitting .264 with 15 home runs and 82 RBIs, the latter representing a personal high for him. The Cardinals went 105–49 again; that year in the World Series, Litwhiler batted only .200, but his four hits included a double and a home run, the latter coming in Mort Cooper's 2–0 shutout of the St. Louis Browns in Game Five. This time Dan and his teammates got their World Series ring as they prevailed in the six-game classic.

Having previously been turned down by Selective Service because of his bad knee, Dan was accepted for "limited service" in the Army in March of 1945. After completing his basic training at Fort Lewis in Washington, he was asked to start a recreation program there. He first organized softball games, which were so popular that he was named recreation director for the 10,000 troops stationed at the base.

In May 1946, Litwhiler was mustered out of the service. He retuned to a Cardinals team that was now being managed by Eddie Dyer and enroute to yet another pennant-winning season. He got into six games, all as a pinch hitter, before the Cardinals sold his contract to the Boston Braves on June 9, reuniting him with his favorite manager, Billy Southworth.

Dan liked Southworth's approach, and it was one he would adopt himself when he started coaching. Southworth taught "exactly how to bunt, exactly how to slide," Dan said. After the trade, Litwhiler hit a solid .291.

He was with Boston on Opening Day in 1947 when the Braves played the Brooklyn Dodgers in a game at Ebbets Field that has been as celebrated as any opener in the history of the sport. Litwhiler went 0-for-3 and scored a run, exactly the same line of box score numbers that were achieved by the game's true star. The other fellow was Brooklyn first baseman Jackie Robinson, and it was his debut in the major leagues. The Braves lost the game by a score of 5-3 as Robinson broke the nearly half-century-old color line in the big leagues.

In a 1997 interview with Ira Kaufman of the *Tampa Tribune*, Litwhiler said, "It wasn't that big a deal back when it happened. I remember Jackie got a great hand from the hometown crowd and you could easily see he had a lot of athletic ability. Nothing ugly happened during the game."

A year later, their paths would cross a little more intimately.

On May 11, 1948, the Braves traded Dan—hitting .273 in the early going after a lackluster .261 mark in '47—to Cincinnati for Marv Rickert. Soon after, Warren Giles, the Reds' general manager, unexpectedly summoned Litwhiler to his office.

"I was thinking I was on the move again," Litwhiler told Kaufman, but when he arrived at Giles' office he found the mayor of Cincinnati and a representative of B'nai B'rith, a Jewish service organization that promotes racial harmony.

"They said there was talk that we could have trouble with Jackie coming to town. They asked me if I would take a picture with Jackie to run in the paper the next day. I asked them, 'Why me?' And they said it was because I was a college graduate and I understood all the implications."

The next day the photo was taken, with Litwhiler and Robinson gazing at a poster that depicts some boys preparing for a game of ball. The poster reads, "What's race or religion got to do with it—HE CAN PITCH!" and was sponsored by the mayor's friendly relations committee.

Nineteen years later, their paths would cross yet again when Dan was coaching at Michigan State and Jackie came to the campus to speak. Litwhiler approached him with a copy of the 1948 photo and Jackie signed it: "Been a lot of water under the bridge since this picture. Good to see you again. Jackie Robinson 1947–1967."

"I'm glad I was there for his debut," Litwhiler told Kaufman, "and I'm proud that I took that picture with Jackie. It makes me feel like I'm part of the history."

The end of the 1948 season must have meant mixed feelings for Dan for a number of reasons. First his former teammates in Boston put together a pennant-winning campaign without him, then went on to lose the World Series. Meanwhile Bob Lemon and Jim Hegan, both former minor league teammates of Dan's, managed to star in Cleveland's World Series victory over the Braves. Lemon started and won two games, while Hegan caught the entire series for the Indians.

Litwhiler stayed with Cincinnati through the 1951 season, although he got into just 12 games that last year, and ended his major league career with a .281 lifetime batting average, 107 home runs, and 451 RBIs over 1057 contests.

In 1952, he played briefly in the Pacific Coast League before taking a job as player-manager of Fargo-Moorhead in the Class-C Northern League. In 1953, he continued wearing two hats, this time for Wilkes-Barre in the Class-A Eastern League. The '54 campaign found him at Jamestown in the Class-D PONY League and Duluth in the Northern League, still playing as well as managing at the age of 38.

That same year, a representative from Florida State University asked Baseball Commissioner Ford Frick to recommend someone to start a baseball program at the university. Frick recommended Litwhiler. It was a marriage made in heaven.

"I didn't like managing pro ball," Dan told Lynn Henning for a 1974 article in the *Michigan State University Alumni Magazine*, "because they don't believe in teaching, they believe in winning....My theory of baseball is 'Teach baseball and then win.'"

His theory was very effective. Over nine seasons FSU's record under Litwhiler was 189–91, as he took his teams to three College World Series. In 1963, he moved to Michigan State, where he would coach for the next 19 years, long enough to become MSU's all-time winningest coach with a record of 488–362 and two Big Ten championships.

It was during his years at Michigan State that Dan Litwhiler suffered a great loss and an important and rejuvenating gain. After an extended illness, Dottie, his wife of many years, passed away. Friends came through in appropriate and timely fashion, however, eventually introducing him to an "attractive redhead" named Pat who, like Dan, had five grown children. Before long they were wed.

Along the way Dan came up with more than 100 inventions to improve the way he taught the game. From the radar gun to Diamond Grit (an absorbent material we've all seen grounds crews spreading on wet infields after a rain delay), from the bunting bat that has only a bottom half (when held horizontally) to encourage proper technique in bunting practice to the unbreakable mirror that allows a pitcher to observe his own motion as he throws. Dan always felt that if he opened the new season with a new invention, his players would begin to feel that they had an advantage over their opponents.

Of course talent also had something to do with it; several of his student-athletes went on to the big leagues, from Woody Woodward and Dick Howser in the 1950s and '60s to Steve Garvey and Kirk Gibson in the '70s and '80s, No matter what their skills, however, all his players gained an advantage from his teach-to-win approach.

In 1958, the U.S. State Department asked Dan to go to Europe as part of an educational exchange. He complied and set up a baseball training program for Holland, Spain, and Italy. Then he sent one of his Florida State players, Ron Fraser, to the Netherlands to coach and develop a team there.

As the international president of the United States Baseball Federation (1977 through 1982), Dan was even instrumental in bringing baseball into the Olympics. He left this role to return to the Cincinnati Reds as a roving hitting instructor and consultant, holding that position through 1988. During this second tenure with the Reds he had another chance to combine the two skills that he was most adept at, teaching and baseball.

In 1999, Dan was in the hospital for six weeks for heart bypass surgery when he received a note from Kirk Gibson.

"Just wanted you to remember that talk you had with me when I was considering 'giving up' baseball," Gibson wrote, referring to an incident when the Michigan State star was weighing a possible career as a pro football receiver. "It's the same in every aspect of life. Keep your chin up and push on!"

Litwhiler has been named to the Pennsylvania Sports Hall of Fame, the Citizens Savings Hall of Fame, and the American Association of College Baseball Coaches Hall of Fame, and has been the recipient of the Lefty Gomez Award for outstanding contributions and distinguished service to college baseball.

If that isn't enough, Bloomsburg State College named their stadium for him: Daniel Webster Litwhiler Stadium. Has a ring to it, doesn't it?

Dan's autobiography, *Living the Baseball Dream*, written with Jim Sargent, was published by Temple University Press in September of 2006. It is a wonderful read.

Sources

My primary source for the material in this essay was a lengthy telephone interview that I conducted with Litwhiler on March 19, 2005. All quotes, unless otherwise attributed, should be assumed to have come from that interview.

My interest in the Phillies of Litwhiler's era was first piqued by the chapter on them in George Robinson and Charles Salzberg's *On a Clear Day They Could See Seventh Place: Baseball's Worst Teams*, Dell, 1991.

Patric Doyle of Old Time Data sent along a detailed profile of Litwhiler's major and minor league playing and managing statistics, for which I am grateful.

The Dan Litwhiler file at the Giamatti Library at the Baseball Hall of Fame in Cooperstown, New York, was rich with hard-to-find newspaper clippings, magazine articles, and correspondence. From that file came such useful articles as:

"Danny Litwhiler: Teacher with class," Lynn Henning, *MSU Alumni Magazine*, May 1974.

"Danny at the Bat," Lillian Arganian, *Spartacade*, volume 1 number 8.

"Baseball's Ultimate Inventor" Lou Pavlovich Jr., *Collegiate Baseball*, October 6, 1995

"Player Recalls Courage," Ira Kaufman, *Tampa Tribune*, April 6, 1997

"Diamond Dust and Diamond Grit," Pierce Lehmbeck, *The Mentor*, September 1957

A ProQuest search for "Litwhiler" from 8/31/1916 to 12/20/2004 turned up 1,861 documents on the latter date. Since then ProQuest has expanded and such a broad search would be mind-numbing. Many of the references, of course, are generated by the name appearing in a box score or in some inconsequential manner in the body of an article, but several of these were vivid and useful references.

A more general web search turned up many interesting things, including Jim Sargent's fine piece "A First Class Big Leaguer Remembers the 1940's," from *Oldtyme Baseball News* (Vol. 8) 1996. Later a fellow SABRite supplied me with Mr. Sargent's e-mail address and Jim helped to put me in touch with Litwhiler. This was a sequence of events I was very grateful for.

Of course, it wouldn't really be a valid baseball essay without the author having referred to the *Macmillan Encyclopedia of Baseball*.

AL LYONS *by Mike Richard*

G	ERA	W	L	SV	GS	GF	CG	SHO	IP	H	R	ER	BB	SO	HR	HBP	WP	BFP
7	7.82	1	0	0	0	1	0	0	12⅔	17	11	11	8	5	1	0	0	64

G	AB	R	H	2B	3B	HR	RBI	BB	SO	BA	OBP	SLG	SB	HBP
16	12	2	2	0	0	0	0	2	4	.167	.286	.167	0	0

Although he was best-known as a pitcher during his five seasons in the major leagues, Al Lyons was called up by the Braves from their Milwaukee farm team in the midst of the 1948 pennant race to fill a possible occasional need in the outfield.

A versatile performer, the right-hander began dabbling in pitching during his second season with the Yankees' farm club at Joplin, Missouri, in 1941 while also playing outfield early in his career.

He appeared in four games as an outfielder for the '48 Braves and was called upon three times as a pinch-hitter and once as a pinch-runner. Lyons also saw action in seven games as a pitcher, with one victory in 12⅔ innings pitched. He did not appear in the World Series.

Albert Harold Lyons Jr. was born on July 18, 1918, in St. Joseph, Missouri, and later relocated with his family to California, where he played baseball at Washington High School in Los Angeles; he was also an All-Southern California fullback on the football team.

He gained the most attention in baseball, where he played for an American Legion team as well as a semipro baseball squad in Los Angeles.

In 1940, he began his professional career in the New York Yankees' farm system with the Joplin Miners of the Class C Western Association in 1940. Among his teammates on the Miners was future Yankees manager Ralph Houk.

As an outfielder, Lyons hit .299, belting 13 home runs and driving in 97 runs. He came to bat 475 times with 142 hits and 94 runs scored.

He returned to Joplin in 1941, and extended his talents to the pitching mound. At the plate, he hit .304 with 10 home runs, 83 RBIs, and 52 extra-base hits, and had an outstanding record in his first season as a pitcher, posting a 5–1 record with an impressive 1.22 ERA, and striking out 48 batters in 43 innings pitched.

That season, Joplin battled Stan Musial's Springfield Cardinals much of the season before catching fire in August. The Miners went on a tear, winning 30 of 41 games for the regular season title.

The multifaceted Al Lyons was called up in mid-season 1948 not only to energize the pitching staff but also to occasionally pinch hit and serve as a potential reserve outfielder.

Lyons moved up to the Binghamton Triplets of the Class A Eastern League in 1942, where he again played the outfield. He had 32 assists and participated in 11 double plays, while hitting .249 with eight home runs and 73 RBIs.

Once he was elevated to the Kansas City Blues of the American Association, one of the Yankees' two Triple-A (then called Double-A) teams in 1943, Lyons continued to showcase his talents as a pitcher and an outfielder under manager Johnny Neun. He went 4–6 on the mound with 80 innings pitched and a 3.49 ERA, while batting .236. He played 78 games in the outfield.

As the wartime 1944 season began, several Yankees pitchers joined the military, including Butch Weinsloff, Marius Russo, and Tommy Byrne. That opened up a pitching slot for Lyons, who appeared in 11 games that season. He didn't record a decision; in 39⅔ innings he allowed 22 runs (20 earned) for the third-place Yankees.

By the time the season reached the dog days of summer in late July, Lyons himself had to report for duty with the U. S. Navy.

In late March of 1945, he participated in a "spring training" three-game series against the New York Giants at the Bainbridge Naval Training Center in Maryland. On the 25th, Lyons held the Giants hitless over 4⅓ innings and also belted a home run to help the Commodores to an 8–4 victory witnessed by some 6,000 sailors. Other Navy men with major league experience in the Bainbridge lineup included Dick Sisler, Stan Musial, and Eddie Miksis.

Lyons spent the entire 1945 season in the military but made the Yankees' Opening Day roster in 1946. On April 24 he was optioned to Kansas City, where he pitched 24 games with a 7–12 record with a 3.67 ERA.

Lyons was called up by the parent club in September and appeared in two games, starting one and carding a 0–1 record. In 8⅓ innings pitched he allowed five runs, all earned.

During the 1947 season Lyons appeared in seven games with the Yankees. He pitched in six games, losing one, while also playing one game in the outfield. On June

1, he won his only decision of the year for the Yankees, beating Cleveland's Bob Lemon, 11–9.

On August 3, 1947, the Pittsburgh Pirates purchased Lyons' contract from the Yankees. At the same time, the Pirates sent second baseman Eddie Basinski to the Yankees' Triple-A farm team in Newark.

The Yankees went on to win the pennant that year, their first since 1943, while the Pirates finished in last place. Nonetheless, after New York went on to beat Brooklyn in the World Series, the Yankees voted Lyons $2,915—half a Series share.

Lyons appeared in 13 games down the stretch for the Pirates with a 1–2 record over 28⅓ innings. He allowed 24 runs (23 earned) on a staff that included Kirby Higbe, Fritz Ostermueller, Ernie Bonham, Preacher Roe, Rip Sewell, Elmer Singleton, Nick Strincevich, and Ed Bahr.

On September 23 at Forbes Field, while appearing in a relief role, Lyons hit his only major-league homer, off St. Louis's Jim Hearn. In that same game, a loss to the Cardinals in which he did not receive a decision, teammate Ralph Kiner hit his 51st homer of the season.

On November 18, 1947, the Pirates traded Lyons with Jim Russell and Bill Salkeld to the Boston Braves for Johnny Hopp and Danny Murtaugh.

When the 1948 season began, Lyons made only one appearance in the early going, pitching 2⅓ innings and allowing three hits on April 24 in a 16–9 loss to the Giants at Braves Field. Three weeks later, on May 13, the Braves assigned Lyons to their Milwaukee farm team in the American Association, where he was 3–1 in 11 games.

He was called back up on July 3 when utility infielder Bob Sturgeon was shipped down to Milwaukee. According to manager Billy Southworth, the move to bring Lyons back would help energize its pitching staff.

"Southworth thinks Lyons will become a 20-game winner," the game notes in the July 3, 1948, issue of the *Worcester Telegram* stated. "It is Southworth's opinion that Lyons was never allowed to concentrate on his pitching with the Yankees and Pirates."

Lyons appeared in only two games with the Braves in July. On the 17th he went 2⅓ innings, allowing two hits and two walks and striking out one in a 4–1 loss charged to Warren Spahn at Chicago. Three days later, he surrendered three hits and a walk in two-thirds of an inning of a 9–6 Bill Voiselle loss to the Cincinnati Reds.

On July 24, outfielder Jim Russell was hospitalized with what was diagnosed as a heart condition and the depleted Braves outfield of Tommy Holmes, Mike McCormick, and Frank McCormick needed some reserve help. Clint Conatser, Marv Rickert, and Jeff Heath all saw some time in the outfield, while Southworth also looked to Lyons to fill one of the outfield spots and called upon him several times in pinch-hitting roles.

On July 31 he came on as a pinch-hitter for Heath in the ninth and drew a walk to keep the inning alive. He

later scored on pinch-hitter Sibby Sisti's bases-clearing triple in the midst of a four-run rally that beat the St. Louis Cardinals, 7–6.

For the next four games, Lyons appeared in non-pitching roles. On August 1, he grounded into a force play against the Cardinals while pinch-hitting for pitcher Nelson Potter, while on August 2 and 3 against Cincinnati he was a late-inning outfield replacement for Tommy Holmes. On August 4, he pinch-hit for Bill Voiselle and flied out. The Braves wound up losing all four of those games, but it would be their last dip for the remainder of the season.

Lyons' last appearance in a major league game occurred during Boston's final regular-season game of 1948. With the Braves playing the Giants at the Polo Grounds, Southworth emptied his bench during an 11–1 rout of New York. Lyons played in center field and right field and came to bat twice without recording a hit.

Overall with the 1948 Braves, he appeared in seven games on the mound with a 1–0 record. He pitched 12⅔ innings, allowing 11 runs, all earned. At bat, he wound up his career as a .293 lifetime hitter in 58 at-bats.

Lyons was not used in the 1948 World Series, but did receive $2,285.40 (out of a $4,570.73 full share) from the pool.

Shortly after the fall classic he was traded by the Braves with a player to be named and outfielder Tommy Neill to Seattle of the Pacific Coast League for pitcher Bob Hall. The Braves later sent first baseman Heinz Becker to Seattle to complete the trade.

Once he arrived in Seattle, Lyons remained in the Pacific Coast League from 1949 until 1952, where he gained the reputation of being a power-hitting, strong-armed outfielder. He belted a total of 76 homers with the Rainiers and had two stars painted on the center-field fence of Seals Stadium in San Francisco to signify two balls that he hit over the 404-foot distant spot.

In 1949, Seattle finished fifth as Lyons led the team with 23 home runs. Then, during the 1950 season, Lyons led the PCL in home runs with 22, including one of the longest blasts ever seen at Sick's Stadium in Seattle, over the center-field fence.

Lyons pitched in 12 games for Seattle in 1951, going 8–0 with a 2.78 ERA. The Rainiers won the Pacific Coast League championship under manager Rogers Hornsby, then captured the Governor's Cup over the Hollywood Stars, three games to two.

At the end of the 1951 season, Lyons was part of a contingent of PCL stars that joined Lefty O'Doul's entourage to Japan to play in a series of exhibition games. The big leaguers in the group included Joe and Dom DiMaggio, Ferris Fain, Eddie Lopat, Bobby Schantz, Mel Parnell, and Billy Martin.

Playing in Shizuoka, Japan, on November 6, Lyons scattered seven hits against a Japanese team over eight innings and also hit a three-run homer to lead the U.S. All Stars to a 6–1 victory.

After playing one more season with the Rainiers, Lyons was traded to the San Francisco Seals along with first baseman George Vico, formerly of Detroit, for catcher Ray Ortieg in December 1952.

After playing the 1953 season and the start of 1954 campaign with San Francisco, Lyons moved to the San Diego Padres. He returned to the mound for the 1954 season, appearing in 21 games with an 8–2 record and a 2.30 ERA.

That season, the Padres and Hollywood Stars played the entire 168-game schedule and ended in a deadlock for first place. A one-game playoff was held at Lane Field in San Diego, with the Padres winning 7–2, spoiling the Stars' bid for their third straight pennant.

In 1955, Lyons began the season with San Diego before moving on to play with Hollywood, where he appeared in 44 games, logging a 10–5 record on the mound with a 5.81 ERA. That was his swan song in the PCL. Through his seven-year career in the league, from 1949 through 1955, he appeared in a total of 1,050 games,with a batting average of .295 and a pitching record of 26–12.

In 1956, Lyons became the player-manager of the Modesto Reds, a Yankees farm team in the Class C California League, but was replaced as manager by Richard Greco on July 26. Lyons wound up the season batting .316 in 63 games and posted a 2–0 record in six pitching appearances.

Before the 1956 season ended, Lyons went on to play in the Man-Dak League, an independent league in Manitoba and North Dakota.

Pitching for the Williston Oilers, he recorded a 2.46 ERA in 44 innings, allowing 37 hits and six walks along with 29 strikeouts in posting a 4–1 record.

Lyons' final season of organized baseball came at the age of 38 in 1957, when he played for the Brandon Greys in the Man-Dak League. He showed he could still wield a potent bat when he homered for Brandon's only run in a 9–1 loss to Williston in the first game of a July 29 doubleheader. In the nightcap, Lyons hit another home run but the Greys lost, 9–8. (That 1957 season was the Man-Dak League's last, as it disbanded at the close of the campaign.)

Lyons later became a scout for the New York Mets. With the Mets he was credited with signing pitcher Dick Selma in 1963 and southpaw pitcher Don Shaw in 1955.

Lyons remained a Mets scout until his early death of a heart attack at age 47 in Inglewood, California, on December 20, 1965. He is buried in Inglewood Park Cemetery.

Sources

http://www.historylink.org/Slide_show/index.cfm?fileId=7123 &frame=14

Milwaukee Brewers Media Guide, 1948.

Story of Al Lyons, The. Capital Publishing Co. John Phillips, Kathleen, GA. 2006.

Western Canada Baseball web site http://www.attheplate.com/ wcbl/1955_20i.htm

Worcester Telegram: Game coverage for 1948 season.

RAY MARTIN *by Jim Gormley*

G	ERA	W	L	SV	GS	GF	CG	SHO	IP	H	R	ER	BB	SO	HR	HBP	WP	BFP
2	0.00	0	0	0	0	2	0	0	2⅓	0	0	0	1	0	0	0	0	14

G	AB	R	H	2B	3B	HR	RBI	BB	SO	BA	OBP	SLG	SB	HBP
0	0	0	0	0	0	0	0	0	0	.000	.000	.000	0	0

With its long winters and cold, rainy springs, New England has never been a hotbed for scouts hunting baseball talent. There have, however, been ballplayers through the years who have overcome these weather woes to shine brightly enough that they can't be ignored. Ray Martin was one such prospect—a pitcher so strong he was toeing the rubber at Braves Field just a few months out of high school.

Raymond Joseph Martin was born in Norwood, Massachusetts, on March 13, 1925. His father was a house painter and later a night watchman at the Charlestown Navy Yard. His mother was a secretary at the Plimpton Press in Norwood. Ray was an only child.

Martin lived across the street from a large field known as White Mike's. It was named for the owner, white-haired Mike Curran. It was there that Ray developed his athletic skills, as his dad would hit fungoes to the neighborhood kids. It was a family affair; his uncle built a backstop and his father made a home plate for the daily games. And the day after a local parish priest, Father MacAleer, made Ray a pitcher for the St. Catherine's School team, his dad came home with a catcher's mitt to help him make the transition from the infield positions he had usually played.

Another major leaguer groomed on the same field was Richie Hebner.

Ray's uncle worked for the Public Works Department and with the Martin house so close to White Mike's, the town stored the playground athletic supplies on the Martin front porch. The family was well supplied with bats, balls, bases, and catcher's equipment. Each of the playgrounds in the community had a ball team, and Ray and the other young players rode their bikes or walked to all parts of Norwood for regular games umpired by the playground instructors. Many of these instructors were themselves former high school athletes.

Opportunities abounded. There was a strong twilight league for boys up to 21 years of age, and there were playground teams for "midgets" (those up to 12 years old) and "intermediates" (ages 13–15). There was also junior high baseball during the school year; the St. Catherine's school Ray attended, which went through grade nine, had a strong spring team as well as a summer CYO squad. Many of the other churches sponsored uniformed teams, as did various social clubs.

Norwood was clearly a good place to grow up if you liked to play ball, and Martin was one of the best in town. In the summer before his senior year of high school, Ray led Norwood to the 1942 state American Legion title under the coaching of John Dixon, who had himself pitched the town to a state championship in 1927 and later made the Boston College Hall of Fame for football and baseball. An assistant coach on the previous year's Legion squad was Marty Callaghan, another Norwood High ballplayer, who had made the majors with the Cubs and Reds in the '20s and '30s.

During Martin's senior year, Norwood also won the state high school title by defeating Dalton High, 3–2, at Fenway Park. Ray, who threw and batted right-handed, was the winning pitcher as he struck out 12 in a nine-inning six-hitter. This completed an undefeated year for the hurler, which included a 23-strikeout game against Boston Trade in a regular-season contest. At one point in that game, he struck out 17 in a row, and the 23 total whiffs broke the state record held by Danny MacFayden of Somerville High. Danny had gone on to pitch for the Braves from 1934 to 1939 (he also pitched for the Red Sox, Yankees, and Reds in a 17-year major-league career) and actually scouted Ray in '43.

In the 1943 high school tourney opener, Ray had defeated Brockton, 1–0, striking out 17 in 13 innings. Then, playing first base to rest his arm, he led Norwood to a 6–4 win over St. Mary's of Lynn by blasting a 425-foot home run to center at Braves Field. He then defeated Arlington, 4–1, striking out another 17 in the Eastern Massachusetts final. (The winning hits against both Brockton and Dalton were made by first baseman Ed Praino, whose

Former local high school pitching phenom Ray Martin ended his big league career with the '48 Braves with two relief appearances.

induction into the Navy was delayed one week so he could play in the tourney.)

After Martin's unbelievable tournament performance, Braves scout Jeff Jones signed the 6-foot-3-inch, 185-pound multisport athlete on June 21, 1943. In signing with the Braves, Ray turned down interest from the other hometown team (the Red Sox) as well as the Yankees, Cubs, and Philadelphia Athletics. His rationale was clear. Joining another franchise would have meant an assignment to the minors and an unfamiliar environment. Columbia University, Boston College, and Holy Cross had also recruited Ray, but the Braves offered both a bonus of $4,000 and a promise that he would go right to the majors. Knowing that he would likely be trading in his glove for a gun and World War II service at the end of the season, he wanted his family—including his grandfather, who never missed a Norwood High School or Legion game—to have the opportunity to see him pitch in Boston.

The majors were a lot different than high school ball, as Braves manager Casey Stengel reminded Martin upon meeting him. "What the hell are you doing here?" he asked Ray. "You should be pitching regularly in the minors." Martin agreed with his manager, as he recalled later: "I didn't know how to use my legs and I only threw with my arm." Despite this indoctrination, he actually did get into two games for Boston in 1943. He relieved in the ninth with the Braves losing to the Cubs, 7–1, on July 2, and retired Lennie Merullo, Claude Passeau, and lifetime .300 hitter Stan Hack on seven pitches. In his one other outing he pitched two innings and gave up three hits, a walk, and three earned runs.

There was then no phone in the bullpen at Braves Field, so Stengel had hand signals for each of his relievers to get loose and to bring them in. Ray remembers there were two pitching rubbers in the unenclosed bullpen, which ran along the right-field line. "Only one had a mound. They were worried the right fielder might run into it so the other rubber was just on a flat spot. It made it tough to adjust when you came in to go back to throwing off the mound."

Amazingly, in addition to his big-league work, the 18-year-old Martin got to pitch to Babe Ruth that summer. The Braves held an exhibition game for the war effort and Ruth, who retired as a Brave in 1935, pinch-hit.

A nervous Ray's first pitch was in the dirt. The second went to the backstop. "Phil Masi, the catcher, called time after The Babe said something to him and walked out to the mound," said Martin "I asked what Ruth said. Masi said Ruth told him to remind me that nobody came to see me and to just throw one where he could get a good swing. I threw one belt high, and Ruth hit a long fly to the warning track for an out. As I passed the clubhouse after the game, I saw Ruth changing and heard him yell out, 'Hey Kid, nice pitch!' as he raised a beer bottle in salute." (Martin also got Ted Williams out twice during his five-inning stint.)

Shortly after that unforgettable moment, Martin's 1943 season ended on August 17 as he entered the Army. When he arrived at Fort Devens, Massachusetts (about 40 miles from Boston), with a trainload of other inductees, he was met by former Braves infielder Ray "Skippy" Roberge, who told him he was being sent to Grenier Field in New Hampshire. When he asked why, Roberge replied, "They need a pitcher." In fact, Martin was told the next day that he could go home and report in five days. His father wound up driving him to Grenier Field, where Ray served as an MP in the Army Air Corps until he was shipped out to Europe in January 1945 with the Ninth Infantry.

His unit marched across Germany, finally meeting the Russians at the German border eight days after the war was over. Martin's most intense battle experience came in March at the Remagen Bridge over the Rhine, where 50,000 Germans were attempting to retreat. "We were under heavy artillery fire and only had about a minute and a half between shelling to get our troops across the bridge," he recalled. "We could only send about a dozen across at a time. Ten days later the bridge collapsed from the effects of the battle. The towers at either end still stand as a memorial." Fellow Braves pitcher Warren Spahn, a platoon sergeant stationed at the bridge, was one of those wounded in this ongoing battle; he just escaped death when the bridge fell moments after he walked off it.

While in the service Martin pitched three times against fellow National Leaguer Ewell Blackwell. One of the games was a 13-inning, 1–0 loss. He also played some hockey while in Germany at the rink Hitler had built for the Winter Olympics, employing skills learned as a defenseman on Norwood High's hockey team. He even got to play some football (his favorite sport) in the service; he had also been the starting fullback for the undefeated 1942 Norwood squad. In addition, Ray was scheduled to pitch in the European Theater of Operations Armed Services World Series that September until he was hospitalized for five weeks in Munich for complications from food poisoning.

Discharged from the service on April 17, 1946, after 33 months, Martin was optioned by the Braves to Evansville of the Three-I League on May 16. There he compiled a 7–9 record, pitching 119 innings, striking out 74, and walking 55 while recording a mediocre 4.69 ERA. The next year he went to spring training with the big-league club, but after not appearing in a game through May was sent to Hartford of the Eastern League to continue his development. He threw 171 innings in a 6–10 season with a 4.63 ERA, and pitched 11 complete games. Despite his lackluster record, he was brought up to the Braves at the end of the minor-league season.

Shortly thereafter, on September 27, 1947, Martin won his first and only big-league game—a 2–1 victory over the Brooklyn Dodgers at Braves Field. The Dodgers had already clinched the National League pennant, but still played Eddie Stanky, Jackie Robinson, Pete Reiser, Spider Jorgenson, Stan Rojek, and Duke Snider that day. Martin, wearing number 24, gave up seven hits, walked four, and struck out two in the complete game. A crowd of 7,720 attended the afternoon contest that lasted a brisk 2:07, and they went home happy as Tommy Holmes banged a two-out single past third in the bottom of the ninth to bring in Connie Ryan with the winning run.

"Billy Southworth, Braves manager, made it easy for me. I didn't know I was going to start until I got to the park," Martin recalled. "There weren't many of my friends there so I wasn't too nervous."

That May, before his demotion to Hartford, Martin had been involved in a bizarre incident at the Polo Grounds. Boston's starting pitcher showed up under the weather from a night of heavy drinking. Ray, at the time, was shagging balls in the outfield. "That's all we ever did. The Braves didn't believe in wasting time on hitting if all you did was pitch. For the regular pitchers, who were expected to go the whole game, it didn't seem to matter since they batted every four or five days. The manager [Southworth] came by and said, "You better get ready. He's in no shape to throw today." Asked who the pitcher was, Martin would only smile.

Shortly thereafter, as Martin was warming up, the scheduled starter appeared and started throwing. "I asked the manager who was pitching. He said, 'He is. He pitches better when he's been drinking anyway.'" The pitcher did pitch—and won.

These goings-on went unreported, but another odd occurrence did make the papers. "The night before that game, our clubhouse at the Polo Grounds was broken into and eight of us had our gloves, spikes, and other equipment stolen," Martin said. "When we were out on the field I saw the clubhouse manager bringing out gloves from the Giants for us to use in the game. We even had to borrow spikes from them. Vern Bickford, another of our pitchers, was one of those to lose his stuff."

On January 8, 1948, the Braves re-signed the now 23-year-old Martin, who again reported to spring training. He threw well in Florida and came north with the big club, but got into only two early games. While he didn't allow a hit over two innings, it was not enough to keep him from being sent to the Braves top farm team, Milwaukee, of the American Association, on April 28. "The manager wanted to bring in players who had been with him in St. Louis. I was the second youngest pitcher at 23. Johnny Antonelli was only 18. The average age of the pitchers was 29."

There may have been another reason why Martin was sent down. In the clubhouse one day Southworth noticed a religious medal hanging from Ray's neck. "He ordered me to take it off. I said no. The medal was given to me by Father Mac (the Norwood priest mentioned earlier who organized youth sports and had died suddenly of the flu). I wore it all through the war. I even told those in the front office about this incident, I was so upset."

Ray went a solid 10–7 in Milwaukee in 144 innings, while back home the Braves won the pennant. He did get to watch the World Series games in Boston, but not in uniform. "My wife and I sat out in the right-field pavilion. I remember saying to her, 'Aren't you glad you knew someone who could get us tickets?'"

After spring training in 1949, Martin was again sent to Milwaukee, on May 8. He went just 6–11 that season, throwing 142 innings with a 4.37 ERA. "I enjoyed Milwaukee…friendly people in the organization and fine coaches. My wife [Claire Canniff, whom he had married in November 1948] was made to feel welcome immediately. Within a day, four of the other wives had taken her under their wings.

"I remember pitching against Minneapolis and getting pounded in one inning. It was as though they knew what I was throwing. When I got back to the dugout a coach said I was tipping my curve. As I took my stretch I was rotating my wrist early. He asked if I knew what I had to do and I said yes. The first time I had a runner on I rotated the wrist and threw a fastball inside. The batter hopped out of the box and started yelling at his dugout, 'That's no curve!'"

It was also in Milwaukee, during Martin's first season there, that he was involved in an unusual play. On July 6, 1948, Kansas City Blues outfielder Leon Culberson (who had earlier played for the Red Sox) stole second when the Brewers catcher, Frank Kerr, missed a pitch and the ball got stuck in umpire Harry King's mask. Kerr tore the mask off, but couldn't remove the ball as Culberson took second and Martin yelled for King to throw the mask (and accompanying ball) to him. The umpires wound up ruling that the ball was still in play and allowed the stolen base.

Martin returned to Milwaukee in 1950. He went 11–13 with a 4.00 ERA in 180 innings. After the '50 season, the Braves told Ray he would be with them in spring training the next year. However, on October 4, 1950, the Braves traded him, along with Mickey Haefner, to Seattle of the Pacific Coast League for Jim Wilson. The righty Wilson had been 21–11 for the Rainiers the previous year, when he led the league in victories.

In Seattle, Ray joined 12 former major-leaguers, including Marv Grissom, Bill Salkeld, Emil Verban, Wes Hamner, and Steve Nagy. Hall of Famer Rogers Hornsby was the manager, and regularly took batting practice. "You could see why he was a great hitter," said Martin. "He had tremendous bat control and put on some real exhibitions in practice. There were some fine players in the league such as Chuck Connors, who played for the Dodgers and also with the Boston Celtics. Jim Rivera was another; he could really run. Gene Baker was a fine shortstop who later played for the Cubs.

"The Pacific Coast League was interesting and very competitive. Every Monday was an off day and you actually played a longer season than the majors. You were usually two weeks on the road. This was still before the majors expanded to the West Coast and there were just 16 major league teams. There were a lot of very good players in the league."

After appearing in nine games during 1951 for Seattle, including a stint on the disabled list in May, Ray was sent to the Atlanta Crackers to specialize as a relief pitcher. He appeared in 30 games, winning three and losing five in 71 innings with a 4.31 ERA. He finished with a flourish, as he pitched no-hit ball in his last nine innings of relief.

Martin's last professional contest was in Atlanta. Dixie Walker, the manager and former Dodger, called him in to hold a 4–2 lead with the bases loaded and no outs. He threw one pitch. It went to the second baseman, who began a triple play to end the game.

With that efficient ending, Ray retired at season's end. "I really hated the minor league bus rides and I did not want to hang around the minors waiting for another shot at the majors," he said. "I basically lost interest. I figured that since I did not have a college education I should take a job with good training. I went to work for General Electric. Skip Roberge was also working there. After a couple of years I went to Picker X-Ray and stayed with them more than 30 years as a sales manager, calling on doctors and hospitals [selling medical supplies] throughout the Northeast."

When he first left organized ball, Martin did some weekend barnstorming throughout New England with a semipro club. "Our team was dressed as a Georgia chain gang. We would pile into two or three cars and play a game on Friday night, two on Saturday and Sunday. We didn't make much money but it was a way to keep playing. Charley Shea, a former Boston College player and Braves farmhand, was our catcher."

Ray, his wife, and their young daughter, Susan, moved to Portland, Maine, for a few years in the late 1950s as Picker expanded into that area. Ray was away most of the week calling on clients; when it was time for his daughter to start school, however, the family moved back to

Norwood. After retiring from Picker he worked part time as a greeter and pallbearer for the Gillooly Funeral Home in his hometown.

For many years, until declining health made it impossible, Ray regularly attended Boston Braves reunions as well as the 2002 SABR convention in Boston (where he was on a Braves panel). He maintained close ties with Boston teammates Tommy Holmes, Sibby Sisti, and Johnny Sain, and even did some baseball card shows with other Braves in the 1980s and '90s. He was inducted into the Norwood High School Athletic Hall of Fame in the late 1980s, and was a frequent guest on the local cable station and at the Norwood Historical Society, speaking on the community's athletic history. He was also involved in youth hockey and baseball coaching during the '60s and early '70s.

He may not have made it big with the Braves, but Martin was still a big winner—and a favorite son—in his hometown. Perhaps his career is best summed up by Dixie Walker's comment to Billy Southworth during the 1947 game that was to be his only major league victory. Southworth asked Walker midway through the game as he passed the Braves dugout what sort of stuff Martin had. Walker replied "He's nobody's cousin!"

Sources

The bulk of the information came from six interviews with Ray Martin from March to June 2007. With me was Charley Parker, the right fielder who threw out the tying run at home plate in 1943 to preserve the win over Dalton in the state championship game. I also used the *Norwood Daily Messenger* from 1942 to 1952 and files of the Norwood Historical Society. SABR links were also useful, particularly with box scores and newspaper accounts of major- and minor-league baseball.

Some facts come from a transcription of Martin's appearance at the 2002 SABR convention in Boston.

PHIL MASI *by John McMurray*

G	AB	R	H	2B	3B	HR	RBI	BB	SO	BA	OBP	SLG	SB	HBP
113	376	43	95	19	0	5	44	35	26	.253	.318	.343	2	1

Although he was a four-time All-Star with the Boston Braves and respected throughout baseball as an excellent defensive catcher and steady hitter, Phil Masi is best remembered for being part of one of the most controversial plays in World Series history.

During the bottom of the eighth inning in Game One of the 1948 Series between the Braves and Cleveland Indians, Cleveland pitcher Bob Feller spun around and threw to shortstop Lou Boudreau to try to pick Masi off of second base. Masi, who was pinch-running for slow-footed starting receiver Bill Salkeld, slid back to the bag and was called safe by umpire Bill Stewart, though most observers believed he was out. The implications became huge moments later when Masi scored the only run of the game on Tommy Holmes' single, thus denying Hall of Famer Feller his best chance to win a World Series contest.

Although the Indians went on to win the series in six games, controversy raged over the play for decades—and Masi made a point of not conceding he was out. Holmes, who was Masi's roommate with the Braves, said, "Whenever I asked Phil [about the play], he always said, 'Tommy, it was close.'" Holmes was on-deck at the time, and he claimed that the play happened too quickly for

"Butcher Boy" Phil Masi became the Tribe's regular backstop in 1943.

him to know for sure. On October 7, 1948, one day after the game, the Associated Press noted that Masi was "not sure" whether he was safe or out. He insisted only that "it was much closer than it looked," adding that: "I would have squawked if I had been called out." In an interview published in *Baseball Digest* in 1978, Masi offered a stronger opinion formed over 30 years by stating: "Feller and Boudreau worked the play very well, but I'm sure I was safe."

Back in '48, bitterness about the pickoff play had remained strong throughout the remaining five games of the series. Feller said that the ump's decision "started a scrap that ran through the series and was picked up lustily by the fans in Cleveland." Writing about the incident for *The Sporting News* in 1990, McCoy also recounted that "Carl Lundquist, a New York sportswriter who was covering the '48 Series for the old United Press, wrote that Stewart 'was as popular in Cleveland as the Mad Butcher of Kingsbury Run,' a mass murderer who was in the news at the time."

Ironically, the decisive run that Masi accounted for in Game One would be the only one he scored in that World Series. Interestingly, and long since forgotten, is that Indians pitcher Bob Lemon and Boudreau picked Boston's Earl Torgeson off of second base in Game Two using the same play. Cleveland won that game 4–1, and after the Indians captured the series it would have been logical for fervor over the incident to die down.

This was not the case. In November '48, the official film of that year's World Series debuted for more than 300 baseball writers and league officials at Toots Shor's restaurant in New York. Writers had hoped that the film, which was made under the direction of former major leaguer Lew Fonseca, would shed light on whether Masi was safe. "The movie showed the play," said one contemporary article, "but in a very negligible way. As Fonseca warned the writers, it showed nothing. The play had been photographed with a wide-angle lense. Fonseca said he had tried to purchase the pickoff incident from the newsreels [that era's equivalent of TV news coverage], but they had no better luck than he had with it."

Further complicating matters, the inconclusive footage led to charges that National League President Ford Frick was "censoring" the film by intentionally removing the frames that might have been embarrassing to Stewart. Frick denied the charges vigorously, according to writer Dan Daniel: "That story involving me in a plot to cut that play out of the film is far more serious than appears on the surface," said Frick. "The yarn attacks not only me, but the integrity of baseball, as well."

Legendary New York sportswriter Joe Williams said that the film was "informally known as "The Mystery of the Missing Play." When the movie debuted, Frick alluded to the burgeoning controversy, making the "facetious" comment, according to Williams, that "this picture comes to you through the censor's office of our league." Yet the film still did not resolve the question of whether Masi was out, much to the dismay of the public. As Williams said in his column:

> "[Y]ou come away from the film wondering just how Fonseca's cameras could have missed this play when they captured in full detail every other key play in the series. Time after time the film is stopped to show by what a narrow margin a runner is thrown out or beats the ball, or breaks up a double play...." [I]t was the most debatable play the series has developed in years. How Fonseca's cameras managed to catch every play but this one will continue to be a mystery as baffling as any the FBI ever grappled with."

Feller, however, had no doubt that Masi was out on the play. In his 1990 autobiography *Bob Feller: Now Pitching*, written with Bill Gilbert, the old ace said:

"We caught Masi napping. Unfortunately, we caught Bill Stewart of the National League, doing the same thing. Lou put the tag on Masi as he slid back into the bag. Neither the Braves nor Stewart knew we had that play in our book, so nobody was looking for it.[1]

"Lou tagged Masi out by two feet," Feller went on. "It wasn't even close. Everybody in the ballpark saw Masi was out—except one—the umpire. We hadn't just picked off Masi. We had picked off Stewart too." Feller added that "the pictures in the paper the next day left no doubt" that Masi was out, although others were of course far less conclusive.

Feller said that Boudreau was thwarted in his attempt to inform the umpires that the team might use the pickoff play, which they had perfected during the season: "Lou told me later that he couldn't alert the National League umpires to the play because [Braves manager Billy] Southworth was in the room during the pre-Series meeting of the managers with the Commissioner. Lou said he should have pulled them aside after the meeting but he didn't and they didn't know to be looking for it in a situation like that.

"In this case, though, our pickoff—or *attempted* pickoff—has endured through 40 years as one of the most controversial plays in World Series history," Feller continued. "And there's this much about it: I get asked about that World Series play everywhere I go, and I have never had even one person tell me that Masi was safe. Ten years later, Bill Stewart told me he blew the call."

As Bob McCoy of *The Sporting News* described in a column on April 16, 1990, Masi had reportedly changed his story about the play shortly before his death a few weeks before. Holmes had received a baseball in the mail to sign from a young fan who had first sent the ball to Masi for his autograph. "The ball came in a box and I just signed it and shipped it back," Holmes told *The Sporting News*. "The kid had enclosed a note that said, 'I have Mr. Masi's autograph, and I'd like yours too.' The kid tipped me off to what Phil had signed. Sure enough, below his signature, there it was: 'I was out.'"

Raymond R. Coffey of the *Chicago Sun-Times* on April 5, 1990 noted that "Phil had refused to talk about the play while Stewart was still alive. But, he admitted now, he was out; the ump blew the call." Masi also acknowledged in his will that he was out, no doubt hoping to put an end to the topic as well as ease his conscience. It may have done the latter, but more than a decade later Feller was still hearing—and talking—about it.

The incident overshadows what was a fine catching career and a fine life for a devoted husband, father, and grandfather. Philip Samuel Masi was born on January 6, 1916 in Chicago, Illinois, and was the lone brother to four sisters. He graduated from Austin High School in Chicago, and he was nicknamed "Butcher Boy" since he was discovered working behind the counter of a Chicago meat market, according to the 1939 National Green book. The incident was later described in great detail by Ed Rumill of the *Christian Science Monitor* in a June 1947 article:

> "He [Masi] had caught high school and sandlot ball around his native Chicago without attracting

a great deal of attention. But one day he was working behind the counter of a butcher shop when in walked the old Chicago White Sox outfielder Johnny Mostil, in search of pork chops. Johnny got his chops all right and the butcher boy got a job. Phil agreed to report to Wausau of the Northern League, the same circuit in which Mostil managed the Eau Claire club. John had seen Masi play high school ball." Rumill quotes Masi as saying, "I was so eager, I wanted to take off my apron right then."

As a 20-year-old in his first professional season, Masi hit .334 with 10 home runs and 61 RBIs in only 96 games for Class D Wausau. In fact, he hit a home run in his first professional contest, and before the end of the 1936 season the hot young hitter was loaned as part of a "gentleman's agreement" to the Eau Claire team, which Mostil managed.

Although he had started as a catcher, Masi was a full-time utility player during his second season with Wausau in 1937. He appeared in 12 games at first base, 20 games at third base, 36 games as a catcher, and 52 games as an outfielder. Wherever he played, he hit, including three home runs and a double in one contest. All told Masi had his finest minor league season at the plate in '37, batting .326 and leading the league with 31 home runs in being named a Northern League All-Star.

Following his 102-RBI performance with Wausau, Masi was purchased by the Milwaukee Brewers, a Cleveland affiliate, and sent to Springfield of the Mid-Atlantic League at the very end of the '37 season. He would get into 12 games there and drive in nine more runs, giving him a fantastic 111 RBIs in just 124 contests that summer.

According to an article published on August 19, 1937: "Observers who have watched the play of Outfielder Phil Masi, purchased by Milwaukee last week from Wausau of the Northern League for 1938 delivery, describe the Italian lad as a Pepper Martin type of performer, with such Wild Horse characteristics as head-first slides, short-cut sleeves, strutting and prancing in a frequently dirty uniform."

Yet, according to Rumill: "[A]bout this time there came a turning point in Masi's career. It seems that Cleveland had originally signed him to a Milwaukee contract, then shipped him to Springfield. This somehow violated the laws of baseball and Commissioner K.M. Landis declared the Chicago boy a free agent."

By 1938, Masi was primarily a catcher. During that season his backup behind the plate was Jim Hegan, who would be the opposing catcher when Masi's Braves and his Indians faced each other in the World Series 10 years later. Hegan would eventually have the longer big league career, but in '38 Masi was the star. While his offensive numbers had fallen a bit for Springfield, Phil's

.308 batting average with 16 home runs and 97 RBIs was enough to convince the Boston Bees (as the Braves were then called) to sign him to a deal. Boston scout Jack O'Connor had his eye on Masi when he became a free agent, and Jack McAllister, another scout for the team, soon offered Masi a contract with the Boston organization. The deal also included a signing bonus.

The Bees already had a surplus of catchers: the '38 Boston roster included veterans Al Lopez, Ray Mueller, and Johnny Riddle. This was tough competition indeed. Lopez was a future Hall of Famer, and Mueller a future All-Star. Masi, however, would not be deterred from the challenge, and Bees Manager Casey Stengel noticed.

According to Rumill: "Masi worked so hard in the sandy soil of Bradenton [in spring training] that Stengel had to push him past three or four other catchers who ranked ahead of him in the Boston backstopping department. It may have been that Phil remembered Thomas Edison's oft-remembered advice: 'Success is five percent inspiration and 95 percent perspiration.' At least, it described Masi's program."

A *New York Times* article from March 10, 1939, recounted a conversation at the Bees' training site in Bradenton, Florida between Fresco Thompson, the manager of the Bees' Hartford farm team, and Stengel. "I'll take a chance on that fellow [Masi]," said Thompson. After watching Masi hit a home run, Stengel retorted to Thomson, "You're very generous. But maybe I'll take a chance on him myself." By the start of the '39 season both Mueller and Riddle had been traded, and rookie Masi was the primary backup to Lopez.

The right-handed hitting Masi debuted for the Braves as a defensive replacement on April 23, 1939 in New York against the Giants. The next month, in his first plate appearance, he hit a run-scoring double off of Bucky Walters. All told, Phil batted .254 with just one home run and 14 RBIs in 46 games during his rookie season, as Lopez played almost every day. Understandably, while Masi did get a game-tying run in the ninth inning of the September 7, 1939 game against Carl Hubbell—hitting the first pitch he saw to center field to score Max West—he did not get much notoriety during his first season. When he slugged a home run off of Brooklyn pitcher Hugh Casey on August 13, 1939, in fact, writer Robert B. Cooke referred to him as "the obscure second-string catcher."

For a while, things did not get much better. From 1940 through 1942 Masi struggled woefully at the plate as a back-up player, posting batting averages of .196, .222, and .218, respectively and never getting more than 180 at-bats in a season. According to Rumill, Stengel used to get "a bit impatient" with Masi "because the kid eventually got so confused at bat, he didn't know whether he was going or coming." Still, the author noted that Stengel's tips helped Masi develop as a hitter while first Ray Berres (in '40 and '41) and then Hall of Famer Ernie

Lombardi (in '42) handled the bulk of the catching duties. And although his offensive highlights were few during this period, Masi in 1941 did break up Whitlow Wyatt's no-hit bid for Brooklyn in 1941 as a pinch-hitter with one-out in the ninth inning.

Masi served as a backup through 1942, but that season ended prematurely for him on August 20 when he suffered a compound fracture of the little finger on his throwing hand and returned home to Chicago to recover. By this time it was already a lost year for Phil anyway; on July 25, his father Andrew Masi had died of a heart attack at age 53. Because Phil then became his mother's sole means of support, he was exempt from military service. This meant he could stay on the Braves roster through World War II, and his patience would finally pay off the next season.

When defending NL batting champ Lombardi was traded to the Giants in early 1943, Masi took over as the team's regular catcher and responded with a .273 batting average in 80 games. He also showed good speed for a catcher, stealing seven bases during that summer. In fact, Masi occasionally was used as a pinch runner throughout his career in Boston, a rarity for a catcher.

Still, it was the 5'10", 180-pound Masi's ability to handle pitchers, rather than his bat, that kept him in Boston's lineup consistently for the next several years. He made just two errors during the '43 season, and tied Lopez (now with Pittsburgh) for the league's top fielding percentage of .991. A 1978 *Baseball Digest* article made reference to his "magnet glove" and how he led the National League in fielding in 1947, 1948, and 1950, while also leading all N.L. catchers in assists in 1945 and putouts in 1946.

This was especially impressive considering that one of Boston's top hurlers during part of this period was knuckleballer Jim Tobin. "I always caught Jim Tobin because I could handle the knuckleball, which was all he ever threw," said Masi in *Baseball Digest*. Masi went on to catch Tobin's 2–0 no-hitter against the Brooklyn Dodgers in April 1944. Rumill praised Masi's defensive work at the time, saying, "Of all the butterfly hurlers in the majors, Jim was probably the toughest to hold. His ball was slower than the others and did more tricks. But Masi gave it a regular battle and held it like a master."

Masi also gained notoriety for his work catching 20-game winners Warren Spahn and Johnny Sain. "Johnny Sain had an outstanding curve ball," Masi noted, "but he was harder to catch than Spahn because he would sometimes shake off the signals. I'd call for a curve, but if the

Masi was known for his solid defense and ability to handle pitchers.

batter shifted his stance, Sain would come in with a quick slider instead. He said he could get the batter out easier that way, and since it worked most of the time, it was okay with me."

Another contemporary but unattributed account found in his Hall of Fame file also praised Masi's defense:

"The outstanding reputation which Masi had established for himself in 1944 and 1945 as among the major leagues' best catchers is being enhanced daily by his fine work behind and at the plate. In the first two months of the 1946 campaign, Phil hit consistently in the vicinity of .300 and turned in a superb job as a receiver. His outstanding work already this season stamps him among the best catchers in the business."

Masi's RBI totals improved in both 1945 and 1946, and he enjoyed his best season at the plate in 1947 as the Braves continued their rise from perennial second-division dwellers to a strong third-place club. In the middle of that '47 season, Rumill made this observation:

"No player in the National League puts more effort into a ball game than does Phil Masi. No man tries harder to win, with a minimum of importance on his own averages. It is foolish to say of a ballplayer that he is a 100 percent team and never thinks of his personal figure. No player living completely ignores his own statistics. But Masi pays as little attention to them as any player you can name."

For others, however, Phil's numbers in 1947 stood out. Masi had career highs with a .304 batting average, which ranked 10th in the National League, 125 hits, and nine home runs. He also struck out just 27 times in 411 at-bats and had 11 sacrifice hits, so even when he wasn't getting a hit, he was usually putting the ball in play (often to the team's benefit). As Coffey said in reference to Masi's 1947 season: "That wouldn't get a guy into the Hall of Fame, which no one understood better than Phil. But it was pretty good." During that summer, Masi also was the catcher when Jackie Robinson had his first at-bat in the major leagues (against Johnny Sain).

While his offensive production tailed off in 1948, Masi still batted in 44 runs and played solid defense for the pennant-wining Braves. He was chosen as a National League All-Star for the fourth consecutive season that summer and got his only career hit in All-Star play. In

Baseball Digest, Masi related how the team celebrated after making it to the World Series: "When we clinched the pennant in 1948, we didn't have a clubhouse celebration because our manager, Billy Southworth, didn't believe in it. No champagne, no anything. So we went out, hit all the Boston nightclubs, and charged our bills to the club's account. Lucky for us, Perini (Braves' owner Lou Perini) accepted them."

Early in the 1949 season, there was a published report of "dissension" in the Braves clubhouse. According to a United Press article datelined April 13, 1949, Manager Southworth claimed that he had originally called a meeting to discuss signals but that stories were soon written about clubhouse turmoil. One allegation was that the players felt that Southworth was taking too much credit for the team's accomplishments, and there were rumors that the club had called a players-only meeting. "I can't understand why all this stuff is coming out," said Southworth.

According to the UP article, Masi contradicted a *Boston Globe* report alleging that there had been such a meeting. Said Masi: "There was absolutely no meeting of that kind held by the players. If there were, [Masi's roommate and team player representative Tommy] Holmes would have known about it and told me."

Amid this mess, at age 33, Masi's offensive production continued to fall in early 1949. Through his first 37 games, the veteran catcher was batting only .210 with zero home runs and six RBIs. With promising 19-year-old Del Crandall available as a potential replacement, the Braves traded Masi to the Pittsburgh Pirates for outfielder Ed Sauer on June 15, 1949. Masi would back up Clyde McCullough and Ed FitzGerald in Pittsburgh for the rest of that season, and to his credit hit much better (.274 in 48 games) after the trade. This showed other teams he could still produce, and on February 9, 1950, he was purchased from the Pirates by the Chicago White Sox in what was described in one account as "being a cash deal involving more than $10,000." The Chicago native was going home.

Playing in the American League for the first time and starting again at catcher, Masi's career was further rejuvenated with the struggling White Sox in 1950. Following a stretch from June 11 to 25 when Chicago won 11 of 14 games, an anonymous major league manager commented: "I'm glad to join the applause for [newly-acquired Chicago players Ray] Scarborough, [Ed] Robinson, and the others, but don't forget the guy who has been the biggest single factor in making the White Sox a tough club—Phil Masi, the catcher. How that guy was ever waived out of the National league (sic), I'll never know.

"He's doing a terrific job of handling pitchers," the praise went on. "His work has been nothing short of inspirational for the whole club. And if you'll check your records, he's been carrying his share of the load at the plate, too....A real hustler and team man, the ex-National leaguer (sic) is acting like he's tickled to death to be performing steadily in his home town."

All told, Masi hit .279 with the White Sox in 1950 and placed fourth on the club in both home runs (with seven) and RBIs (55). He was Chicago's starting catcher again in 1951, but while he still hit well at .271 he was being rested much more. Following that season, when the team acquired the much younger Sherm Lollar in a trade with the St. Louis Browns, Masi became a backup once again.

Phil's career had come full circle by 1952. At age 36 he hit .254, the same average as his rookie season with Boston back in '39, and at year's end he was released by Chicago. Masi finished his major league career with 917 hits, 27 home runs, 417 runs batted in, 45 stolen bases, and a .264 batting average in 1,229 at-bats over 14 seasons.

Masi played one last season in 1953 with the minor league Dallas Eagles before retiring from professional baseball, and he went out a winner. As he explained in *Baseball Digest*: "The White Sox gave me my release at the end of 1952. Not long afterwards the owner of the Dallas Eagles, Dick Burnett, called Paul Richards, the White Sox manager. He said he wanted a catcher who could win the Texas League division championship, the playoffs, and the Little Dixie World Series. Richards recommended me, so Burnett signed me up for the next season. And we won all three."

In a letter published in the *Chicago Sun-Times* on April 15, 1990, Ernie Rossi related this memory of Masi: "As a kid of about 9 years old, I'll never forget watching [Masi play sandlot ball with Rossi's brothers, who also went to Austin High School] and how outstanding Phil was as a catcher. During the summer of 1938, we used to play two or three games of ball at Byford School, at Iowa and Central. Masi came by when the Braves were in town to play the Cubs. He agreed to let me pitch a tennis ball to him. He took one swing—and the ball was still rising as it hit the house across Iowa Street. My friends and I were just thrilled to have a real major leaguer take time to play a little ball with us and be so nice to us. Phil was our hero. I was so glad for Phil to come into my life, even if it was for such a short time...I will never forget him."

Following Masi's death, Raymond Coffey offered this description of the former catcher: "He was a nice guy. Great family man. He'd entertain the grandchildren by going one-on-one against his dog in ice cream cone-eating races. The kind of grandfather we'd all like to be."

Masi, according to Coffey, was "a ballplayer before ballplayers took to being millionaires first and ballplayers second...He was a ballplayer, and more than a ballplayer. A man for all seasons." Art Ahrens was similarly taken with Masi, and described him in *Baseball Digest* during 1978 as "a bespeckled grandfather with thinning gray hair" though "he still retains the trim physique of his playing days."

According to his obituary, Masi worked with a silk-screen printing firm in Chicago called Reliable Printing Company until 1980. Masi and his wife, Lucille (Gentile), had moved to Mount Prospect, Illinois in 1966, where he lived for the rest of his life. He had a daughter, Joanne Dhein, who also lived in Mount Prospect at the time of Phil's death. Masi had seven grandchildren and six great-grandchildren.

"Even as he battled cancer into extra innings [in the summer of 1989]," said Coffey, "Phil had an amplifier hooked up to his bed so he could follow games on TV and radio. And he still dragged himself out to watch his great-grandson's Little League games."

Phil Masi died of cancer on March 29, 1990 at age 74 at his Mount Prospect, Illinois home. His funeral mass was held two days later at St. Cecilia Church. Masi is buried in All Saints Cemetery in Des Plaines, Illinois. He is fondly remembered in Des Plaines as far more than just the guy who should have been called out at second base. After all these years, it's only fair.

Note

1. During a reunion of the Boston Braves Historical Association on October 12, 2003, Paul Stewart, the grandson of Bill Stewart and a former player and referee in the National Hockey League commented: "I led two professional hockey leagues in penalty minutes, then went on to officiate. One thing I learned from making the transition is something none of you players will ever know: Phil Masi may have thought he was out but he wasn't out. You know why? Because the umpire is always right—and so is the referee!"

Sources

Masi's biography and statistics on baseball-reference.com, retrosheet.org, baseball-almanac.com, and baseballlibrary.com.

Clippings from Masi's file at the Hall of Fame:

Ahrens, Art, "Major League Baseball in the 1940s: Phil Masi recalls when the Boston Braves won a pennant almost 30 years ago," *Baseball Digest*, February 1978, pp. 50–56.

"Bees Defeat Giants. 4–3. as Hub Falters," September 8, 1939.

Coffey, Raymond R., "A ballplayer we shouldn't forget," *Chicago Sun-Times*, April 5, 1990.

Cooke, Robert B., "Boston Triumphs 13–6 and 8–2, Piling Up 17 Hits in First Game," August 14, 1939.

Daniel, Dan, "Hannigan Hints Interest in Giants."

Daniel, Dan, "World Series Film Saddens Yankees," December 1, 1948.

"Denies Censoring Movie." Day illegible, but it is from November 1949.

Feller, Bob with Bill Gilbert, *Now Pitching: Bob Feller*. (New York: Birch Lane Press, 1990).

Letter dated April 26, 1990 from Phil Masi's wife, Lucille, after Masi's death.

Letters from Ernie Rossi and Richard S. Williamson in the Chicago Sun-Times, April 15, 1990.

"Masi," obituary in *Chicago Tribune*, March 30, 1990.

"Masi Clouts Homer," April 21, 1944.

"Masi Uncertain About Lou's Tag," October 7, 1948.

McCoy, Bob, "Final Call: 'I Was Out.'" *The Sporting News*, April 16, 1990.

"Movie Pickoff Proves Naught," November 10, 1949.

"No Dissension Ever Says Southworth," April 13, 1949.

"Phil Masi, at 74, was catcher with Boston Braves from 1939–49," *Boston Globe*, March 31, 1990.

"Phil Masi," obituary in *Daily Herald*, March 30, 1990.

"Phil Masi." No publication or date given.

"Philip Samuel (Phil) Masi." No publication or date given.

Program from Funeral Mass at St. Cecilia Church, Mt. Prospect, Illinois, March 31, 1990.

Rumill, Ed, "Phil Masi Arrives," June 1947.

Untitled articles: September 11, 1941; July 2, 1942; February 11, 1947. Also one titled "The Backstop Department" without a publication or title. There is also what appears to be a birth certificate.

"White Sox Buy 2 NL Players," February 2, 1950.

Williams, Joe, "Series Movies Accent Mystery of Missing Play," December 1, 1948.

FRANK McCORMICK *by Sheldon Appleton*

G	AB	R	H	2B	3B	HR	RBI	BB	SO	BA	OBP	SLG	SB	HBP
75	180	14	45	9	2	4	34	10	9	.250	.289	.389	0	0

In three different seasons—1939, 1941, and 1944—Frank McCormick hit home runs more often than he struck out. In his entire 13-year career, encompassing 5,723 at-bats and more than 6,200 plate appearances, the slugging first baseman had just 189 strikeouts—10 fewer whiffs than Ryan Howard achieved in only 529 at-bats during 2007 alone. Only nine players in 20th century major-league history struck out at a lower rate, but McCormick did far more than just make contact. He was also a .299 lifetime hitter, a terrific fielder, and a nine-time All-Star who played on three National League championship teams.

Frank Andrew McCormick—nicknamed "Buck" for Frank Buck, a big-game hunter and movie director—was born in New York City on June 9, 1911, to Andrew (a railroad worker) and Ann McCormick.[1] He played the outfield in sandlot, church league, and high school baseball, and by the age of 17 had decided to become a professional ballplayer. After failing to impress at tryouts with the Philadelphia Athletics, Washington Senators, and New York Giants, McCormick borrowed $50 from his uncle and traveled to Beckley, West Virginia, for a tryout with the Cincinnati Reds in 1934. His sandlot manager suggested that there would be more competition for outfield positions than for first base, so McCormick became a first baseman. This time, he impressed veteran major-leaguer and Cincinnati scout Bobby Wallace and upon signing was sent to Beckley in the Class C Middle Atlantic League. He wasted no time in making an impression; he hit .347 in 120 games during his first professional season, and was brought up to the major-league Reds at the end of the '34 season.[2] He was 23 years old.

McCormick's big-league debut came against knuckleballer Dutch Leonard on September 11, 1934, at Ebbets Field in Brooklyn. He reached first on an error by the second baseman, not a very exciting start. A few days later, however, he got two hits against Hall of Famer Carl Hubbell at the same Polo Grounds where he had failed in a tryout years before.[3] Though he hit .313 in his brief stay with the Reds, he was sent back to the minors in 1935 and it would be three years before he returned for good.

In 1935, McCormick covered some ground, playing for five different teams in five different leagues. He began with Toronto, hitting just .235 in 12 games before being sent to Fort Worth in the Texas League. After just five games playing for the Panthers (hitting just .100), Bill Terry of the Giants worked a deal that sent McCormick to Nashville, though the Reds still controlled his contract. He hit .311 for the Vols, but nonetheless saw duty in Dayton and Decatur before the year was done.

In 1936, McCormick struggled badly during his first few games with the Durham Bulls of the Class B Piedmont League until manager Johnny Gooch suggested a different grip on his bat; he hit for an average over .400 for 12 straight weeks, finishing the season with a league-best .381.

Frank opened the 1937 season with the Reds, but they couldn't find a regular position for him. He played some at second base and one game in the outfield, but when a clear need for a first baseman at their Double A club in Syracuse opened up in mid-May, he was sent there for the rest of the year, hitting .322. He rejoined the Reds on September 19, banging out seven hits his first day back. He finished the season with an average of .325 in 83 at-bats.

After coming up to the big leagues to stay in 1938, McCormick quickly showed that his strong early performances were no fluke. At 6 feet 4 inches and more than 200 pounds, he was much bigger than the average player

Frank McCormick wrapped up a 13-year big league career with the '48 Braves.

of his day, and was a bigger hitter as well. He batted .327 to place third in the National League, led the league in hits with 209—the first of three consecutive years in which he paced the senior circuit in this category—and drove in 106 runs. His production was all the more remarkable considering he had just five home runs.

As he later told baseball historian Donald Honig in an interview: "Six years [after his failed tryout with the Giants] I was a unanimous choice as the National League's All-Star first baseman, and Bill Terry—who'd turned me down at the Polo Grounds—was one of the men who picked me."[4] In fact, this was the first of nine consecutive All-Star selections for McCormick—he was selected in every year in which he played more than 100 games. After the season, on October 8, he married Vera Preedy, who bore him two children, Judith and Nancy.[5]

In 1939, the Reds won the National League pennant, and McCormick had another big year. He batted .332 and led the league in hits (209), RBIs (128), and fielding percentage at first base (.995). Though the Reds were swept in the World Series by the powerhouse New York Yankees, McCormick hit .400 in the Series. That year also, as teammate Billy Werber describes in his autobiography, the eager McCormick was admitted to the Cincinnati infielders' "Jungle Club" and christened "Wildcat." (Second baseman Lonnie Frey was "Leopard," shortstop Billy Meyers was "Jaguar," and Werber styled himself "Tiger.")[6]

In 1940, the Reds won it all and McCormick, who drove in 127 runs and led the league in hits and fielding percentage again, as well as in doubles (44), was voted the league's Most Valuable Player. (Curiously, the American League MVP was also a tall, strapping Bronx native, Hank Greenberg.) Frank hit just .214 in the World Series this time, but strong performances from Werber and pitching aces Paul Derringer and Bucky Walters helped Cincinnati topple the Tigers in seven games. Unfortunately, the joy of the Reds' championship season was dampened by the suicide on August 2 of backup catcher Willard Hershberger, who had been despondent about calling for the wrong pitches in a loss the day before.[7] (He was hitting .309 at the time.)

During the 1941 season, notes Werber, McCormick injured his back attempting a one-and-a-half gainer in a hotel pool, and had to wear a back brace for the remainder of the year.[8] This may well have exempted him from military service. He continued to perform very well, but approached his 1939–40 level of performance again only in 1944, during World War II. The Reds' fortunes also declined. During McCormick's last five years with the club, they never finished closer than 12 games behind the league leader. By 1945, the Reds were reduced to seventh place, 37 games in back of the Chicago Cubs. Through these lean years, McCormick usually batted cleanup for the Reds and wore number 10.[9]

When the war ended, McCormick was sold by the rebuilding Reds to the Philadelphia Phillies for $30,000. That season he led the league in fielding percentage for the fourth time, going a then record-setting 138 straight error-less games at first base (beginning in September of 1945). Though he threw right-handed—a disadvantage for a first baseman—STATS, Inc. chose him as the "retrospective gold glove" first baseman of the decade of the 1940s,[10] and historian Bill James called him "one of the best defensive first basemen ever to play the game."[11]

While McCormick's defense remained stellar, his offensive production slipped in Philadelphia. Early in the 1947 season, hitting just .225, he was released by the Phillies and signed with the Boston Braves. Platooning at first with Earl Torgeson and pinch-hitting, he hit .354 with the Braves. McCormick and Torgeson were as diverse a pairing as can be imagined. Torgeson was a left-handed hitting rookie with a modest batting average but a high on-base percentage, because he drew many walks. McCormick was a right-handed hitting veteran who compiled high batting averages but walked infrequently. Their excellent output—they combined to bat well over .300 with 121 RBIs—was perhaps the best example of manager Billy Southworth's widespread (and usually effective) use of platooning.

McCormick hit .250 for the Braves as a pinch-hitter and part-time sub for Torgeson during their pennant-winning year of 1948, and ended his major league career on a high note with his third appearance in a World Series. His last hit was one of only five against Cleveland's Gene Bearden, who shut out the Braves in Game Three. His last at-bat came three days later at Braves Field when he pinch-hit against Bob Lemon in the seventh inning of the sixth and final game. He grounded out to Ken Keltner at third, and the Braves lost the game and the Series, 4–3. A few weeks later, the Braves released the 37-year-old McCormick.

In 1,534 major league games, McCormick batted .299, with 1,711 hits, 128 home runs, 951 RBIs, and a .995 fielding percentage—the highest of any first baseman in history at that time, and still one of the top 10. Four more hits would have made him a career .300 hitter. During

his eight full seasons with the Reds, he led the team in RBIs seven times, in batting average six times, in slugging average five times, in home runs four times, and in on-base percentage twice. His single-season totals for hits (in 1938 and 1939), doubles (in 1940), and RBIs (in 1939 and 1940) still rank among the top 10 in Reds history.

In each of his nine full major league seasons, McCormick's batting average, slugging average, fielding average, and range factor [putouts plus assists] at first base exceeded the league average.[12] At one point, he played 682 consecutive games—at the time the longest streak since Lou Gehrig's. Bill James reports that because injuries in the minors delayed his ascent to the majors, "he was determined to shake the 'brittle' tag and wouldn't come out of the lineup even when he should have. One time he was beaned in the first inning of a doubleheader, and stumbled around almost in a daze for 18 innings, but refused to come out."[13]

McCormick stayed in the game after his playing days. In 1949 he managed the Quebec Braves in the Canadian-American League, and led them to a 90-win season—34 more than the previous year—and to a playoff sweep and the league championship.[14] Nevertheless, he found himself managing the Lima Phillies (Ohio-Indiana League) in 1950. That was his last stint as a manager, but he continued to be involved with baseball as a coach, scout, and television broadcaster for the Reds and as director of group and season ticket sales for the New York Yankees. [15] He died of cancer in Manhasset, New York, on November 21, 1982.

Frank McCormick backed up Earl Torgeson at first base in 1948.

Notes

1. Albert J. Figone, "McCormick, Frank Andrew 'Buck,'" in David L. Porter (ed.), *Biographical Dictionary of American Sports: Baseball.* (Westport, Conn.: Greenwood Press, 1987), pp. 348–349.
2. Honig, Donald, *Baseball When the Grass Was Real.* (New York: Coward, McCann and Geoghegan, 1975), Berkley Medallion Edition), pp. 221–226.
3. Honig, pp. 226–227.
4. Honig, p. 223.
5. Figone, p. 348.
6. Werber, Bill, and Paul Rogers III, *Memories of a Ballplayer.* (Cleveland: Society for American Baseball Research, 2001), pp. 165–168.
7. Werber, pp. 175–177.
8. Werber, p.217.
9. Richard Wittingham (ed.), *The DiMaggio Albums.* Vol. 1. (New York: Putnam, 1989), p. 251.
10. James, Bill, John Dewan, Neil Munro, and Don Zminda

(eds.), *STATS, Inc. All-Time Baseball Sourcebook.* First Edition. (Skokie, Ill.:, STATS, Inc., 1998), p.2469.

11. James, Bill, *The New Bill James Historical Baseball Abstract.* (New York: The Free Press, 2001), p.452.

12. "Frank McCormick," Baseball Reference.com.

13. *The New Bill James Historical Baseball Abstract*, p.452.

14. Daniel Papillon, "The Quebec Braves: A Baseball Dynasty," in Jane Dorward Finan (ed.), *Dominionball* (Cleveland: Society for American Baseball Research, 2005), p. 114.

15. Figone, p.349.

Sources

Baseball Reference.com.

Albert J. Figone, "McCormick, Frank Andrew 'Buck,' " in David L. Porter (ed.), *Biographical Dictionary of American Sports: Baseball.* (Westport, Conn.: Greenwood Press, 1987).

Honig, Donald, *Baseball When the Grass Was Real.* (New York: Coward, McCann and Geoghegan, 1975).

James, Bill, John Dewan, Neil Munro, and Don Zminda (eds.), *Stats Inc. All-Time Baseball Sourcebook.* (Skokie, Ill., Stats, Inc., 1998).

_____, *Stats Inc. All-Time Major League Handbook.* (Skokie, Ill.: Stats, Inc., 1998).

_____, *The New Bill James Historical Baseball Abstract.* (New York: The Free Press, 2001).

Mulligan, Brian, *The 1940 Cincinnati Reds.* (Jefferson, N.C.: McFarland, 2005).

Daniel Papillon, "The Quebec Braves a Baseball Dynasty," in Jane Finnan Dorward (ed.), *Dominionball.* (Cleveland: Society for American Baseball Research, 2005), pp. 114–117.

Thorn, John, and Pete Palmer (eds.), *Total Baseball.* (New York: HarperCollins, 1989).

Werber, Bill, and Paul Rogers III, *Memories of a Ballplayer.* (Cleveland: Society for American Baseball Research, 2001).

Whittingham, Richard (ed.), *The DiMaggio Albums*, Vol. 1. (New York: Putnam, 1989).

MIKE MCCORMICK *by C. Paul Rogers*

G	AB	R	H	2B	3B	HR	RBI	BB	SO	BA	OBP	SLG	SB	HBP
115	343	45	104	22	7	1	39	32	34	.303	.363	.417	1	0

As a 33-year-old veteran outfielder, "call me Mike" McCormick was a major contributor to the Boston Braves' run to the 1948 pennant. In 343 at-bats in 115 games, the right-handed-hitting McCormick batted .303, to help solidify the Braves outfield. A pinch hitter extraordinaire, Mike stroked six hits in 14 tries off the bench. He started all six games of the World Series, playing center or left field, and hit .261 in the Series (6 for 23) with two runs batted in. All told, McCormick played 2½ seasons with the Braves and was always in the club's outfield rotation.

Myron Winthrop McCormick was born on May 6, 1917, in Angels Camp, California, the spot that triggered the California Gold Rush of 1849 after a mother lode of gold was discovered there. When he was 4 years old his family moved the family to Stockton, 20 miles away. Mike played third base at Stockton High and for the local American Legion team in the summer. He also ran track, winning the Northern California 100-yard dash title as a schoolboy and recording a 9.9 personal best.[1] A Cleveland Indians bird dog and former pitcher named Carl Zamloch (he went 1–6 for the 1913 Detroit Tigers) spotted McCormick while he was in high school. Zamloch was an accomplished magician who could swallow fire, eat glass, and perform a host of magic tricks. As the story goes, he would display his magic to

The Braves purchased Mike McCormick from the Reds in June of 1946.

prospects on the West Coast, thus getting their attention before shifting talk to their baseball futures. It must have been effective, for Zamloch signed McCormick for the Indians at the tender age of 17.[2]

The Indians shipped Mike east to the Monessen Indians of the Class D Pennsylvania State Association for the 1934 season. In 49 games the youngster hit .235 while playing third base. In 1935 he was shifted to the Butler Indians in the same league and began to show major-league potential, batting .344 with 13 triples in 110 games to lead the league in both categories. His 46 errors and .888 fielding percentage, presaged an eventual move to the outfield but his bat earned him a promotion to the New Orleans Pelicans of the Southern Association for 1936. Still only 19 years old, McCormick hit .264 in 62 games in a utility role. He was assigned to the Buffalo Bisons of the International League for 1937 and there, playing first base and the outfield, batted .283 in 139 games and 498 official at-bats.

The following winter Commissioner Kenesaw Mountain Landis entered the picture, ruling that the Indians, under their "gentleman's agreement" with Buffalo, had exceeded their three option years on McCormick under the rules then in force. Landis declared Mike a free agent. He signed with the Washington Senators, who sent him to the Indianapolis Indians of the American Association for the 1938 season.[3] In 99 games in the outfield, McCormick made only one error. He hit only .250 but was affected by a badly sprained ankle suffered while sliding into second base. The injury sidelined McCormick for seven weeks and probably delayed his advancement to the big leagues by a year. He was back with Indianapolis in 1939 and showed his stuff, hitting .318 in 149 games and 547 at-bats.

McCormick's hustle and quick baseball instincts made him a fan favorite in Indianapolis. Once he raced in to catch a Texas Leaguer in shallow center field and then continued on to tag second base for an unassisted double play. Another time, he tagged up at second and advanced to third on a long fly to the outfield. Mike noticed that the opposing outfielder was a little lackadaisical about returning the ball to the infield and so he kept running and scored.

The Cincinnati Reds had won the 1939 National League pennant but of their outfielders only Ival Goodman had really produced with the bat, hitting .323. As a result, the Reds purchased McCormick from Indianapolis, with whom the Reds had a working arrangement. Manager Bill McKechnie's original plan was for McCormick to compete for the left-field job against the incumbent, Wally Berger as well as Lee Gamble, Arthur Luce, and Vince DiMaggio. Spring training injuries to Berger, center fielder Harry Craft, and right fielder Goodman further muddled the outfield picture.

Throughout the spring, however, McCormick performed well both at bat and with his speed in the outfield. The Reds barnstormed north with the Red Sox that spring and in the nine games they played after leaving Florida, Mike hit a lusty .382 with 13 hits, including four doubles, in 34 at-bats. That earned the 23-year-old rookie a spot in the Opening Day lineup against the Cubs in Crosley Field in Cincinnati. In his first big league at-bat, McCormick doubled against Bill Lee into the overflow crowd in left center. He later singled and in the eighth inning with the scored tied 1–1 fielded a hit slammed by Billy Herman as it caromed off a temporary fence near the left-field foul line, wheeled, and fired a strike to Billy Myers at second to nail a surprised Herman.

In his second game, a 2–1 pitching duel between Gene Thompson and Claude Passeau of the Cubs, McCormick drove in the Reds' first run with an eighth-inning double and then scored the winning run on a Billy Myers single.

McCormick's appearance in the 1948 World Series would be the second of three trips to the Fall Classic over the course of his 10-year major league career.

Mike soon slumped at the plate, however, and earned himself a spot on the Cincinnati bench. Harry Craft was also struggling at the plate and McKechnie soon began working McCormick into the lineup in center field. At midseason Mike was hitting only .245 but he quickly picked up the pace and became an outfield regular. He ripped off a 19-game hitting streak and during the last month of the season batted a robust .354 as the Reds pushed to their second straight pennant, winning by 12 games over the runner-up Dodgers. His late surge brought his average for his rookie campaign to an even .300 in 110 games and 417 official at-bats, tops on the club among outfielders.

The 1940 World Series matched the Reds against the Detroit Tigers, who had won the American League pennant by a single game over the Cleveland Indians. McCormick started and played every inning of the seven-game Series in center field, setting Series records, since broken, for putouts and chances accepted. The Reds won the world championship with Mike contributing nine hits, including three doubles, in 29 at-bats for a .310 Series average.

Just 23 years old, McCormick had reached the pinnacle of the baseball world as a rookie, becoming the regular center fielder on a World Series winner. The 1941 Reds had high hopes of a third consecutive pennant, with a team that returned mostly intact. They failed to hit out of the box, however, and McCormick was a chief culprit, starting off only 4-for-40 for an unglamorous .100 batting average and finding himself back on the bench. Just as in his rookie year, however, McCormick began to hit in the second half of the year and regained his regular position, alternating between center field and left field. The Reds never hit as a team, batting only .247 for the year and were never really in the race. They finished third with an 88–66 record, 12 games behind the Dodgers and 9½ games behind the second-place Cardinals.

For his sophomore season, Mike batted a team high .287 in 110 games and 369 at-bats. Although the Reds as a team did not hit, their outfield was especially weak with the stick, with no one else batting over .250. Thus, McCormick was the Reds' top outfielder heading into 1942. He was off to another typically slow start when he broke a bone in his ankle on Memorial Day, sliding into second base on a force play. The injury knocked him out of action for about 10 weeks and limited him for the balance of the season. For the year Mike got into only 40 games, batting .237 in 135 at-bats. Meanwhile the Reds, who hit only .231 as a team, slid to fourth place with a 76–76 won-loss record.

World War II was in full force in 1943 and McCormick received his induction papers just as the season began, even though he was married with a child on the way. He appeared in only four games for the '43 Reds, with just two hits in 15 at-bats, before heading to McClellan Field in California to begin his military service. There Mike played for the McClellan Field Fliers, one of the strongest service teams in the country. The Fliers were able to field a team that included, in addition to McCormick, present or future big-leaguers Gerry Priddy, Ferris Fain, Bob Dillinger, Walt Judnich, Dario Lodigiani, Charles Silvera, and Rugger Ardizoia. Mike, Priddy, Fain, Silvera, and Yankee farmhand Carl De Rose also played on an undefeated basketball team that won the post championship.[4] McCormick served a total of 27 months, much of in the Central Pacific Theater, and completely missed the 1944 and 1945 baseball seasons before his honorable discharge from the Army on October 22, 1945.

McCormick returned to the Reds in 1946, now 29 years old. Once again he got off to a slow start and in early June was hitting under .220. This time the Reds did not wait for his bat to come around but sold him on June 3 to the Boston Braves in a straight cash deal. The change of scenery was to Mike's liking. In his second game with Boston, he homered, doubled, and singled against the Cardinals.[5] With that kind of hitting, McCormick quickly found himself in the Braves' outfield mix. In 164 at-bats for Boston, he batted .262 to raise his average for the year to a subpar .248. The Braves finished in fourth place with an 81–72 won-loss record, 15½ games behind the first-place St. Louis Cardinals.

In 1947 the Braves improved to 86–68 and third place, only eight games behind the pennant-winning Brooklyn Dodgers. Plagued by another slow start, McCormick competed for playing time in left field and center field with Johnny Hopp, Bama Rowell, and Danny Litwhiler. Tommy Holmes, a perennial .300 hitter, pretty much owned right field. As the season wore on, Mike began hitting and by July he was starting four of every five games and batting over .300. Mike tailed off a little but still hit a solid .285 for the year in 92 games and 284 at-bats.

Trying to get more punch in the outfield, the Braves acquired disgruntled outfielder Jeff Heath from the St. Louis Browns after the 1947 season. They also traded outfielder Rowell and first baseman Ray Sanders to the Dodgers for second baseman Eddie Stanky. In a five-player deal with the Pirates, the Braves acquired the veteran outfielder Jim Russell and catcher Bill Salkeld. It was one of those years where every move paid dividends. Heath had a very productive year, batting .319 and providing much-needed power. Stanky was a real sparkplug and was hitting .320 when he broke his ankle on July 8 sliding into Brooklyn's Bruce Edwards at third base. Veteran Sibby Sisti filled in ably for Stanky and rookie Alvin Dark broke in with a bang at shortstop, batting .322 to finish fourth in the batting race and third in the MVP voting while sweeping to the Rookie of the Year Award.

With Heath taking over left field, McCormick played center field, starting mostly against right-handers. He had a strong season, hitting .303 in 115 games and 343 at-bats and was in the lineup every day after Jim Russell was hospitalized with a heart ailment in July. The Braves, behind "Spahn and Sain and Pray for Rain," won the pennant by 6½ games over the Cardinals. Heath broke his ankle in a gruesome play at the plate in Ebbets Field four days before the end of the season. Partly as a result of Heath's injury, McCormick played every inning of the World Series against the Cleveland Indians, starting four games in center field and two games in left.

McCormick hit safely in every game but the first. In that game, a 1–0 Braves victory, he sacrificed Phil Masi to second base in the bottom of the eighth of a scoreless tie. That set up the controversial play in which Masi appeared to be picked off, although the umpire at second called him safe. Tommy Holmes eventually singled to left, scoring Masi with the only run of the game and sending Indians ace Bob Feller to defeat.

Mike went 2-for-4 in Game Two, a 4–1 Boston loss. He then had a pivotal at-bat in Game Six. The Braves were down three games to two and went to the bottom of the eighth inning losing 4–1. They rallied, scoring two runs to chase Bob Lemon, and with two outs had the tying run on third and the go-ahead run on second. McCormick came to the plate against Gene Bearden, who had shut out the Braves, 2–0, in Game Three and had been Cleveland's best pitcher down the stretch. Mike grounded sharply back to Bearden, who snagged the one-hopper and threw to first to end the inning. If Bearden had been a righty instead of a southpaw, McCormick's comebacker may have instead been a two-run single up the middle which likely would have evened the Series and forced a seventh game.

That Series at-bat would be the last one for McCormick in a Braves uniform. On December 15, 1948, Boston traded him to Brooklyn for former Dodgers legend Pete Reiser. McCormick was enthusiastic about moving to the Dodgers and planned on being an everyday outfielder for the Bums.[6] It was not to be. Mike got off to his customary slow start and, bothered by nagging injuries, never got on track at the plate. For the 1949 season he hit only .209 in 55 games and 139 at-bats. The Dodgers won the National League pennant by a single game over the Cardinals before losing the World Series to the Yankees in five games. Mike appeared in only one game as a defensive replacement and did not have an at-bat in the Series.

Nor surprisingly, the Dodgers released McCormick shortly after the end of the Series. He was unemployed until the New York Giants signed him on January 4,

1950. Giants manager Leo Durocher admired McCormick's work and was adding some veterans to a young club. Unfortunately, Mike again struggled at the plate in spring training and the early season and was released on May 19 after only four at-bats. He signed with the Oakland Oaks of the Pacific Coast League and there regained his batting stroke, hitting .314 in 51 at-bats in 18 games. That prompted the Chicago White Sox to pick him up in June. He played the rest of the season for the White Sox, batting .232 in 55 games and 138 at-bats.

On December 11, 1950, the White Sox traded McCormick to the Washington Senators for Bud Stewart, in a swap of veteran outfielders. Senators manager Bucky Harris was happy to have Mike, commenting at the time the trade was made that "there are outfielders playing regularly in this league who are not as good as McCormick."[7] By the end of June 1951, the 34-year-old McCormick was batting .311 and had worked his way into the regular lineup. In one nine-game stretch, he exploded for 14 hits in 28 at-bats. Although he cooled off, for the year he hit .288 in 243 times up, playing in 81 games for the seventh-place Senators. McCormick was also tough off the bench, placing second in the American League with a .467 pinch hitting average (7-for-15).

Even with his productive 1951 season, the Senators opted to go with youngsters like Jackie Jensen and Jim Busby for 1952. On February 1, Washington unconditionally released McCormick, marking the end of his big-league career. Mike split the 1952 season between the Sacramento Solons and the Portland Beavers of the Pacific Coast League, batting .251 in 315 at-bats. In 1953 he was the player-manager of the Wenatchee Chiefs of the Class A Western International League. Mike batted .318 in 280 at-bats but the Chiefs still finished ninth in a 10-team league.

Mike worked as a coach for the San Francisco Seals of the Pacific Coast League in 1954 before becoming a minor-league manager in the New York Giants farm system. In 1955 he managed in two cities in the Class A Eastern League. His club began as the Wilkes-Barre Barons and finished as the Johnston Johnnies after a July 1 move. The 38-year-old McCormick batted .355 in 62 at-bats for the Barons/Johnnies, mostly in pinch-hitting duty. The season marked the end of his playing days.

In 1956, McCormick found himself managing the Lake Charles Giants of the Class C Evangeline League, piloting the club to a fourth-place finish. The next year he split between managing the Springfield Giants of the Class A Eastern League, where he tutored a young outfielder from the Dominican Republic named Felipe Alou, and the Danville Leafs of the Class B Carolina League. The Giants placed him closer to home for 1958 with the Fresno Giants of the Class C California League. There Mike had his greatest managerial success, piloting Fresno to the regular-season pennant with an 85–55

won-loss record. His Giants also won the league playoffs, defeating the Stockton Ports two games to one in the first round and then taking four out of five against the Visalia Redlegs.

McCormick was back with Fresno in 1959 but the club was bereft of talent and finished far in the basement with a dreadful 44–96 record. He was assigned to the Pocatello Giants of the Class C Pioneer League for 1960 and again ended up with a last-place club, although future big leaguer Chico Salmon played for him and led the league in hits.

McCormick retired from baseball after 1960 and went to work for the Ventura Pipeline Construction Company in Ventura, where he had resided since 1946. In 1966 he was elected to the Cincinnati Reds Hall of Fame and was officially inducted on July 28 at Crosley Field. He frequently attended Los Angeles Dodgers games and was in Dodger Stadium on April 14, 1976, to watch the Dodgers' home opener against the San Diego Padres. He suffered a massive heart attack at the game and died en route to the Queen of Angels Hospital. McCormick was only 58 years old. His survivors included his wife, Beverly, two sons, a daughter, and his father.[8]

McCormick's major-league career spanned 10 seasons and six teams. He was an excellent outfielder and a heady baserunner. Although not a power hitter, he hit .275 for his career and played a major role in two pennant winners, the 1940 Cincinnati Reds and the 1948 Boston Braves. Plagued with slow starts at the plate through much of his career, he tended to come on very strong during the last half of the season when the pressure was on. In three World Series, two of which he started every game in the outfield, he batted a strong .288.

Notes

1. Cincinnati Reds Press Release, March 1940, Mike McCormick clippings file, National Baseball Library, Cooperstown, N.Y.
2. *The Sporting News*, April 25, 1940, p. 3.
3. *Ibid.*
4. Unidentified clippings, dated September 23, 1943, and February 24, 1944, Mike McCormick clippings file, National Baseball Library, Cooperstown, N.Y.
5. Unidentified and undated clipping, Mike McCormick clippings file, National Baseball Library, Cooperstown, N.Y.
6. *New York Post*, March 1, 1949, p. 5.
7. *The Sporting News*, July 4, 1951, p. 11.
8. Unidentified clipping dated April 15, 1976, Mike McCormick clippings file, National Baseball Library, Cooperstown, N.Y.

Sources

Allen, Lee, *The Cincinnati Reds* (Kent, Ohio: Kent State Univ. Press, 2006), first published 1948 by G.P. Putnam's Sons.

The Baseball Encyclopedia (New York: The Macmillan Co., 1969).

Caruso, Gary, *The Braves Encyclopedia* (Philadelphia: Temple Univ. Press, 1995).

Honig, Donald, *The Cincinnati Reds—An Illustrated History* (New York: Simon & Schuster, 1992).

Johnson, Lloyd & Miles Wolff, eds., *The Encyclopedia of Minor League Baseball* (Durham, N.C., 1997, 2d ed.).

Kaese, Harold, *The Boston Braves 1871–1953* (Boston: Northeastern Univ. Press, 2004), first published 1948 by G.P. Putnam's Sons.

Mulligan, Brian, *The 1940 Cincinnati Reds* (Jefferson, N.C.: McFarland & Co., 2005).

The 1951 Baseball Register (St. Louis: The Sporting News, 1951).

Werber, Bill & C. Paul Rogers III, *Memories of a Ballplayer: Bill Werber and Baseball in the 1930s* (Cleveland: SABR, 2001).

NELSON POTTER *by Sidney L. Davis*

G	ERA	W	L	SV	GS	GF	CG	SHO	IP	H	R	ER	BB	SO	HR	HBP	WP	BFP
18	2.33	5	2	2	7	9	3	0	85	77	27	22	8	47	4	0	1	332

G	AB	R	H	2B	3B	HR	RBI	BB	SO	BA	OBP	SLG	SB	HBP
18	29	0	11	1	0	0	3	0	3	.379	.379	.414	0	0

Entering the twilight of a 12-year major league career, Nelson Potter joined the Boston Braves in midseason of 1948 and became the top relief man and spot starter for the NL champs with an impressive 5–2 record and a 2.33 ERA. This was his second stint with a pennant-winning team; as a nearly full-time starter, he had been the ace of the 1944 St. Louis Browns staff with a 19–7 record. He was on his way to a 20-win season in that campaign when he became the first player in big-league history to be ejected (and suspended) for throwing a spitball, but always denied "loading up" then or at any time in his career. His screwball and slider were tough enough on batters, and while he is not remembered with the reverence of a Warren Spahn or Johnny Sain, his success with these two legal pitches played a big role in Boston's National League club reaching its first World Series in 34 years in '48.

Born August 23, 1911, in Mount Morris, Illinois, to farmer Irving Potter and his wife, Ida Mae, Nelson was an all-sport high school star—leading both the baseball and basketball teams into state tournaments. In addition to his pitching prowess he captained the football squad and, despite being just 5-feet-11, jumped center for the hoopsters. He even won trophies in track for the shot put and discus. Mount Morris teammate Everett Henderson remembers Potter as a "superb athlete" who was equally proficient in tennis and horseshoes and later in life shooting pool and bowling (after retiring, Potter built and managed a bowling alley).

As an example of Potter's ability to dominate in any sport, Henderson recalls a tournament basketball game when Mount Morris was trailing by five points with less

Nels Potter's abrupt firing by A's manager Connie Mack led to his mid-season free agent signing with the Braves.

than a minute to go: "In those days there was a center-jump after every basket. Nelson said, 'Buck, I am going to tip the ball to you, shoot it to Dopey and then he is going to pass it back to me for the shot.' (Everyone in our small town of 3,000 had a nickname.) We did the same play three times in a row and won the game by a single point."[1]

Potter's son Nelson Jr. similarly recalls his father as a "gifted natural athlete at any sport he tried. He never played a round of golf but he could drive golf balls out of sight. He had not bowled before building the bowling alley but soon carried an average around 200. He was also an expert pool and billiards player who made a modest amount of money playing those sports at a time when money was no doubt hard to come by."[2]

Given his skills, it was not a big surprise when Potter left Mount Morris College in his junior year to sign with the Chicago White Sox after helping the school tie for a 1932 title in the Little Nineteen League (made up of small Midwestern colleges). His son James recounts the story passed down to him: "The local doctor in Mount Morris knew a trainer with the White Sox and through that contact he was given a tryout and inked to a minor league contract."[3]

His first pro experience was likely also Potter's first time struggling on the diamond. Assigned to Waterloo, Iowa, in the Class D Mississippi Valley League, he ended the season with a 5–10 record and a 4.86 ERA. He had no better success the next year, 1933, with Lincoln in the Nebraska State League (4–6, 6.72) but in his second summer with Lincoln he turned around. Potter pitched his only no-hit, no-run game as a pro against Norfolk, and his earned-run average of 1.71 led the circuit. He posted a

17–9 record, struck out 200 in 216 innings, and received honorable mention in league All Star balloting. In a letter recapping his minor-league career Potter described his no-hitter, which was nearly a perfect game: "...[I] struck out 14 men and only pitched to 27 batters. One man walked but the next man hit into a double play."

When the Mississippi Valley League folded, Potter wrote, the White Sox released him rather than pay his back salary. He signed with the St. Louis Cardinals in 1934 and spent three years with farm teams in their organization—one year at Houston (1935), followed by two with the powerful Columbus Redbirds of the American Association (1936–1937). St. Louis did bring him to the big leagues in '36, but he pitched just one scoreless inning before being returned to Columbus for more seasoning. While there, he shared the mound with future major leaguers Mort Cooper and Max Lanier. Potter was regarded as a "right-hand relief hurler de luxe,"[4] appearing in that role in 33 of 44 games pitched in 1937. He went 11–11 with a solid 3.56 ERA, and really shined in the postseason. As Potter later recalled, after once winning three games in three days during the regular season, he pitched in five of seven games against Newark in the Little World Series in 1937. He was a relief pitcher in the first four games and started the seventh and final contest, but was the losing pitcher.

After his playoff heroics, the Philadelphia Athletics took Potter in the Rule V draft and brought him up to the majors the next year. He started 62 games over the next 3½ years before being traded to the Boston Red Sox in midseason of 1941, and while his record with the woeful A's was an unimpressive 20–37, he did have several bright spots. In the spring of '38, for example, he relieved at Detroit with the bases loaded and preserved a one-run lead by retiring the heart of the Tigers' order—Charlie Gehringer, Rudy York, and Hank Greenberg. On August 10 of that year he pitched perfect ball for six innings against the Red Sox, and in a 1940 game he stopped an A's losing streak with a seven-hitter in early May. The same month he hurled the last six innings against the White Sox, yielding only two hits and facing 19 batters to preserve a 3–2 victory.

The A's never rose above seventh place and averaged 99 losses a year from 1938–40. There was little room for pitcher error, and Potter's overall 1940 performance—he went 9–14 with 13 complete games for a 54–100 team—prompted *Washington Post* sportswriter Shirley Povich to note, "The pitcher that's getting a tough break this year is Nelson Potter of the A's. He's pitching great ball and the A's are kicking 'em away for him. He'd win 20 games with a good ball club."[5] Arch Ward of the *Chicago Tribune* wrote, "American League players vote the title of the year's tough luck pitcher to Nelson Potter."[6]

His fortunes were far better off the diamond during this period. On October 10, 1937, "Nels" (one of his several nicknames that also included "Clint" and "Popcorn") married his high school sweetheart, Hazel Park. Nelson Jr, who was born two years later, explains the Clint nickname: "My father was called Clint because, the story goes, during high school he was put upon by a local bully named Clint, and one day he took care of the problem by giving him a thorough enough beating that the bully never bothered him again. After that my father was called Clint."[7]

Such toughness clearly served Potter well, since throughout his baseball career he was plagued by a high school basketball knee injury. As he recalled, "It was a game in Rochelle, Illinois. I had the ball and started to make a quick pivot when one of the heavier opponents ran over my right foot, pinning it to the floor. My knee pivoted, but my foot didn't. It sure ripped hell out of the cartilage." The injury became worse in 1938, and after a dismal 2–12 season with Philadelphia, he decided on surgery. The procedure was not successful (the doctor removed the wrong ligament) and two years later Nels went under the knife for a second time.[8] It required a full year of therapy for the knee to regain its full strength, and Potter developed his own method to strengthen it.

As younger son Jim remembers hearing, "To get his knee back into shape he hunted fox every day that winter (of 1938–39). My mother would drive around with my dad looking to spot fresh fox tracks. He would count how many fox tracks went in and how many went out of the area. More going in than going out meant there was a fox in there, so he chose the freshest-looking track and then my mother would let him out of the car and go home. My dad would track foxes all day long from first light until night and then call my mother from some farmhouse miles from where she left him off. He would have several fox pelts, and then they would do the same thing the next day, all winter long. He and his knee got in excellent shape that winter."[9]

Things weren't perfect, however. Potter told Stan Baumgartner, a sportswriter for the *Philadelphia Inquirer*, that he had to pass up his usual offseason job in a print shop because of the knee trouble. The after-effects of the operation resulted in Potter's being classified 4-F in the draft during World War II. As he assured journalist George Castle: "People asked then, how could you play ball and not serve in the military? I would have served, driven a truck, whatever, but they would not take me."[10]

While recovering from surgery during the 1941 season, Potter was sold to the Boston Red Sox on June 30. Appearing in just 10 games for manager Joe Cronin's club, he compiled a 2–0 record and an encouraging 4.50 ERA (he had been 1–1, 9.26 that year with the A's). Unfortunately, the contending Red Sox didn't see Potter for what he was—a determined pitcher about to blossom into a very successful one. In the spring of 1942, Boston sold Potter's contract outright to Louisville of the American

Association. That proved to be his turnaround year. He won 18 games for the Class "A" Colonels and four of his eight defeats were by either 1–0 or 2–1 scores. He pitched 212 innings, had an ERA of 2.12, and was second in the league with 148 strikeouts while giving up just 59 walks. He even boasted a .303 batting average with several pinch hits during the campaign.

Attributing his mound turnaround to developing a slider to go with his already effective screwball, Potter said he made the move to compensate for his sore arm and knee problems. At the end of the season, the hapless St. Louis Browns selected him in the major league draft for $7,500, an investment that would help result in the long-suffering franchise's first and only pennant. Tommy Fitzgerald of the *Louisville Courier-Journal* noted: "If he had been blessed with a team less puerile at the plate, Nels probably would have bettered that glossy record of 18 and eight.... Potter's specialty pitches are a screwball and a curve. He's not fast, but uses his speed ball so judiciously in the midst of a lot of junk that he succeeds in slipping it by opposing batters quite often."[11]

Potter contributed to the Braves championship effort as a reliever and spot starter.

The 1943 season was Potter's first winning campaign in the big leagues. He pitched in 33 games, both as a starter and reliever, and ended the year with a record of 10–5. He pitched eight complete games and had an ERA of 2.78, good for 10th in the American League. The Browns, however, were not much better than the A's had been a few years before, going 72–80 and finishing sixth in the American League.

The '44 season started on a low note for Potter when he was floored by a bad case of the flu during most of spring training, and failed to pitch even an inning before Opening Day. But he hurled a six-hitter in the third game of the season to beat the White Sox, 5–3, then followed this up with another complete game against Cleveland in a 5–1 victory. Nels had thus contributed two of the eight consecutive wins the Browns registered to kick off the season. In addition to putting the Browns into the uncharacteristic regions of first place, the opening streak also topped the previous record of seven straight wins at the beginning of a season (set by the Yankees in 1933).

Potter also registered the first shutout of the season for the Browns, a 2–0 performance against Detroit in early May. A few weeks later he retired the first 23 Red Sox he faced in a game at Sportsman's Park, and by July 20 he was 9–5 when he took the mound against the Yankees in a game that would end up in the record books. Early in the contest, Browns manager Luke Sewell approached umpire Cal Hubbard to protest that New York pitcher Hank Borowy was moistening his fingers before delivering pitches. That, of course, brought the ump's attention to Browns hurler Potter; Hubbard warned Potter that he was doing the same thing his manager was complaining about, but to no avail.

In an interview the next day, the umpire said, "I warned Potter in previous games and I feel that I have given him every possible break possible. Sewell himself forced the issue last night by kicking about Borowy's pitching methods. The warnings were not prompted by any protest from the Yankee side until after Sewell asked me to warn Borowy."[12] Potter wound up being ejected by Hubbard in the fifth inning and ultimately was suspended for 10 days. The Browns did go on to win the game, however, which helped quiet a crowd of 13,093—some of whom had pelted the field with an assortment of bottles and straw hats after Potter's exit. In a 1982 interview with the *Rocky Mountain News*, Hubbard recalled the inacident in the following manner, "He (Potter) has a wife, and I think he wanted a vacation anyway. They said his wife gave birth to a child nine months later. I gave him the chance to be home." "That's true," said Potter when reminded of the story. "And one thing you can be sure of, I didn't name him Cal Hubbard Potter." (A son, James, was born to Hazel and Nelson on April 19, 1945.)[13]

Many years later, speaking before an audience at a convention of the Society for American Baseball Research, Potter said, "The truth is I have never thrown a spitball in my life. It was a cool, dry night and we were playing the Yankees. I was using the rosin bag, Cal Hubbard said I couldn't go to my mouth with my hands that night. I then blew on my hand. Cal said, 'You can't do that.' I threw the ball in and said there was no rule that says you can't do that. He kicked me out of the game and I got suspended for 10 days."[14]

Potter returned to the Browns' lineup on August 6, winning the second game of a doubleheader against the Indians, 6–4, and helping his own cause with two hits in three trips to the plate. But more trouble—and more headlines—were in the near future. Later that month he fielded a bunt in foul territory and, without warning, he and the Washington Senators' batter, George Case, started swinging fists. Both benches cleared, prompting the police and military police to join the fray and quiet the players; when it was over Case and Potter were tossed and fined $100 by league president Will Harridge. (This time, luckily, there was no suspension.)

Despite all the turmoil, Potter pitched the best baseball of his career after the 10-day spitball "vacation." He went 10–2 in August and September, and the Browns needed all of it during a heated pennant race. St. Louis was tied with the Tigers on September 26, when Potter blanked the Red Sox, 3–0, on two hits. Three days later the Browns ended the defending world champion Yankees' hopes for a repeat with a doubleheader win, Potter shutting out the Bronx Bombers 1–0 in the nightcap. Amazingly, just 6,172 fans attended the Friday twinbill for the Browns, who had been laughingstocks for so long that some folks were no doubt still expecting they'd blow the race. They didn't; two days later, with a team record 37,815 looking on at Sportsman's Park (the Browns' first sellout in 20 years), they clinched the pennant with a 5–2 victory.

The '44 World Series was the first all-St. Louis matchup in the fall classic, and the seventh time that clubs from the same city competed for baseball's highest team honor. It was also the first World Series for the Browns *period* in their 43-year history. Both the Browns and Cardinals played in Sportsman's Park, and Potter worked out a deal with a Cardinals player to share a hotel room during the regular season since they were never in the city at the same time. During the Series, however, one of them had to move, for fear that if the media learned of the situation it might not look good.[15] (Managers Sewell and Billy Southworth had the same roommate arrangement, but theirs *did* make the papers.)

Potter was the starter for the second Series game, and was lifted in the sixth inning for a pinch-hitter with his team trailing, 2–0. He was the victim of two unearned runs, throwing four-hit ball as the Browns made four errors in the game. Potter did not help his own cause as he committed a double error on what should have been a double play on a bunt by Max Lanier. Nels was taken off the hook later when the Browns scored two runs, but they lost in the 11th inning. The Cards won the next two games as well, so it was win or go home when the Browns took the field for the sixth contest. Manager Sewell started Potter, and after three innings he held a 1–0 lead. A three-run Cardinals explosion in the fourth, however, ended both Potter's and the Browns' hopes, and the Redbirds claimed their second championship in three years. It was hard to put blame on Nels, who again was the victim of shoddy defense; two of the three runs against him this time were unearned, and when combined with the two let in through miscues in the first game, left him with a sparkling Series ERA of 0.93 over 9⅔ innings.

As a small consolation, the Browns were voted the number one sports comeback in the United States by the Associated Press and Potter received several votes for American League most valuable player. During the offseason he returned to Mount Morris and worked as a high school basketball referee, claiming it was "great for the legs." And, of course, he spent much of his time on his usual hunting and trapping. (This hobby had once proven extremely lucrative. In his youth he was known to trap as many as 14 muskrats in a single morning, for which he earned the sum of $2.50 per pelt. In his biggest year in baseball, by contrast, he earned $19,000.)[16]

The Browns dropped to third in 1945, but Potter continued his winning ways with a 15–11 record, three shutouts, and a terrific 2.47 ERA (sixth in the league). He helped his own cause during his first game of the season when he delivered a game-winning single in the ninth inning against the Indians, and a month later he scattered eight hits in winning his first shutout of the season, 5–0, over the Red Sox. But in the late spring and early summer, he lost seven consecutive games, before finally winning a 5–1 rain-shortened contest against the Washington Senators. And later in the season he racked up eight wins in a row, topped off with a masterful two-hit shutout against the first-place Tigers on September 24. One of his teammates in that season, the worst of World War II in terms of player shortages, was the one-armed Pete Gray. Although other Browns players ridiculed the .218-hitting Gray and grumbled that his presence on the team was a publicity stunt that cost them a second pennant, Potter had great respect for his teammate and made it a point to visit Pete after they both retired from the game.[17]

As a final reminder that the '45 Browns had lost their magic of the previous year, Potter gave up a ninth-inning grand slam to Hank Greenberg of the Tigers on the last day of the season to help Detroit capture the American League pennant. St. Louis landed in third place with an 81–70 record, but they likely would have been much worse off without Potter; in addition to his stinginess on the mound, he was also one of St. Louis' best hitters with a .304 average (28-for-92).

On April 16, the second day of the 1946 season, Potter faced the Tigers again, pitching against Detroit ace Hal Newhouser in Briggs Stadium. Potter lost, 2–1, as nemesis Hank Greenberg walloped a line drive into the left-field seats for the game-winner. This was a sign of things to come; both Potter's and the Browns' fortunes further declined during the year, with Potter posting an 8–9 record (with a 3.72 ERA) and the team dropping to seventh place. The season was also plagued with the defection of several St. Louis players to the Mexican League, including slugger Vern Stephens. Toward the end of the season Luke Sewell was replaced as manager by Zack Taylor.

Things got still worse in 1947; the Browns ended up in the cellar with a 55–95 record, while attendance dwindled to 320,474, lowest in the league. Potter had a bleak

4–10 record and was used much more as a reliever—starting just 10 games among his 32 appearances. It was also in 1947, however, that Potter, in his role as the Browns' player representative, helped establish baseball's first pension plan. "We made cash contributions to get it started [at the time of the interview in 1986 he noted that he was receiving less than an $800 monthly benefit]."[18]

In May 1948, Browns management declared its intentions to rebuild with a younger team. Potter, then almost 38 years old, was sold back to the Philadelphia Athletics, where he had pitched from 1938 to 1941. The A's badly needed relief help, and Potter started by downing the Yankees twice in three days over the Memorial Day weekend. He relieved starter Lou Brissie in one of the contests with the bases loaded and no outs in the fifth inning, and pitched his way out of the jam without being scored upon. In his first five games with Philadelphia, Potter pitched 14⅓ innings and allowed just three runs while striking out 12. Longtime doormats since their last dynastic run in the early 1930s, the A's were surprising contenders in the American League race thanks in part to the familiar face in their bullpen.

Aging A's owner-manager Connie Mack soon became disenchanted with Potter, however, and fired him before a hushed clubhouse on June 13 after he blew a three-run lead in the space of only five batters. Mack exploded, "Go get your check. You are off the club."[19] Many of the A's players thought the move cost the team whatever chance it had of winning the 1948 AL pennant. As Potter recalled, "Mr. Mack got excited about losing a ball game and flew off the handle. It isn't true, as Mr. Mack inferred, that I wasn't trying my best. I told him I was doing the best I could, but otherwise I kept quiet out of respect for his age. I won two games for him in New York and I saved one in Detroit. He thought I was doing all right then."[20]

Potter quickly left for the Philadelphia airport and a flight home. When asked whether he felt down and out when let go by the A's, Potter responded, "Down and out—no. I knew right then the A's were doing me the biggest favor of my life. Some of the players wanted me to stay around until they could talk to Mr. Mack. But I would not have come back if he had asked me."[21] The firing did in fact turn out to be a blessing in disguise for Potter, as several strong teams lobbied for the versatile right-hander. The AL-contending Indians offered him $15,000, a large sum at the time, but he decided to sign with the National League-leading Boston Braves. It was the right move for both the pitcher and the club.

National League batters had not faced his screwball and slider, which helped Potter build an impressive 5–2 record with an ERA of 2.33 over the final three months as the team clinched its first NL pennant since 1914. He proved to be an effective backup for top starters Johnny Sain, Warren Spahn, and Vern Bickford, starting eight games while relieving in nine others. Pitching his first game as a starter on July 18 against the Pirates, he came away with a 10–2, seven-hit victory in which he helped his own cause with three hits and two RBIs. Nine days later he pitched a 5–1 six-hitter against the same club, and on September 12 he came out of the bullpen to win one of the most exciting games of the year by shutting out the Phillies in the 10th through 13th innings of a 2–1 victory. By year's end he had compiled a fine 8–5 record with three saves and a 2.86 ERA over 28 games and 113⅓ innings with three teams.

Nels later claimed to have taught the screwball to future Hall of Famer Spahn during the '48 season, which no doubt helped Spahnie stay a 20-game winner into his forties. In the World Series, however, Potter's magic wore out. The aging hurler was hit hard by the Indians in two appearances totaling 5⅓ innings, including a Game Five start, as Cleveland took the Series in six contests. He was pleased and honored, however, that the Braves team voted him a full share even though he had been with the team for only part of the season.[22]

The next year, 1949, was Nelson Potter's last in the major leagues; he pitched 96 innings, mostly in relief, and compiled a 6–11 record with seven saves. This dipped his career won-lost record under .500 for his 12 years as a big leaguer, to 92–97 with an ERA of 3.99. He had pitched a total of 1,686 innings and given up a meager 123 home runs, 62 of them coming during his first four-year tour with the A's and prior to his knee operations.

At the end of the '49 season, after finishing fourth, the Braves cast away many of their former heroes including Nels. Potter was picked up on waivers for $10,000 by the Cincinnati Reds, but declined the offer. He told Cincinnati president Warren Giles that he was returning to his native Mount Morris and his job as a pressman, and later explained, "I didn't want to stay in baseball. I traveled for so many years, in a hotel on a road trip, you'd hang up your clothes for three days. So I was happy to hang my clothes in a closet at home."[23]

One downside of Potter's decision to retire is that it prevented a reunion with his Brownie skipper, Luke Sewell, now managing the Reds. In three seasons under Sewell at St. Louis, Potter had pitched 45 complete games in 74 starts, winning 44 times while losing only 23 with an ERA well under 3.00. Instead, back home, Potter coached a Junior American Legion team and played some semipro ball with the De Kalb Blue Sox retiring from the game altogether.

Now free to do what he wanted, where he wanted, Potter stayed close to home and became active in business and politics around Mount Morris. He continued to work as a skilled proof-press operator for several years until he built a bowling alley, Town and Country Lanes, in 1956, after inheriting land adjacent to the site. For a while the family lived in an apartment on the second floor above the establishment, and he later built a handful of homes including one for his family beside the lanes.[24] The road is now named Potter Lane.[25]

For many years this dedicated family man served his community as township supervisor, maintaining 40 miles of rural roads. And for the last few years before his retirement he sold insurance, a job for which Nelson Jr. said he was well-equipped, "as he knew everyone and everyone knew him." Four or five times a year the elder Potter would make the 2½-hour drive to Chicago and see the Cubs, and in 1988 he was named to the St. Louis Browns Fan Club's Hall of Fame. He actually waxed nostalgic with teammates from both his pennant-winning clubs that year, as in August he went to Boston to participate in a celebration marking the 40th anniversary of the '48 Braves' NL championship, sponsored by the New England Sports Museum.

This would be the last time he saw most of his old friends from baseball. Nelson Potter died at his home of a heart attack while watching the Cubs play the Mets on television. The date was September 30, 1990 (the Cubs scored two runs in each of the last two innings and beat the Mets at Shea, 6–5). Potter was 79 years old. His wife, Hazel, had passed away in 1986, and they were survived by three children. Nelson Jr. teaches philosophy at the University of Nebraska, Barbara (now deceased) was a music teacher, and James is an executive with Tootsie Roll. In addition, he had three grandchildren. The memorial service and burial were in his beloved hometown of Mount Morris, and a more permanent tribute came in 2006 when Potter was inducted into the Manchester College Hall of Fame. Son James, representing the family, was in attendance. The inscription on the plaque reads:

Nelson "Clint" Potter Sr. '34 is the first Hall of Fame inductee who attended Mount Morris College before it merged with Manchester College in 1932. Potter was a three-sport athlete-basketball, baseball and tennis, and was key to the Mount Morris offense and the leading scorer during the two years he attended the College.

Notes

1. Interview with Everett "Buckshot" Henderson, March 15, 2007.
2. Interview with Dr. Nelson Potter Jr., April 4, 2007.
3. Interview with James Potter, April 5, 2007.
4. 1938 *Spalding Guide*, p. 143.
5. Povich, Shirley. *Washington Post*, August 6, 1940.
6. Ward, Arch. *Chicago Daily-Tribune*, August 14, 1940.
7. Interview with Dr. Nelson Potter Jr., April 4, 2007.
8. *Ibid.*
9. Interview with James Potter, April 5, 2007.
10. Castle, George. Lerner Newspapers, August 12, 1986.
11. *The Sporting News*, November 12, 1942, p. 9.
12. *St. Louis Post-Dispatch* , July 21, 1944.
13. Berler, Ron. *Rocky Mountain News*, February 22, 1982.
14. Castle, George. Lerner Newspapers, August 12, 1986.
15. Interview with James Potter, April 5, 2007.
16. Interview with Dr. Nelson Potter Jr., April 4, 2007.
17. *Ibid.*
18. Castle, George. Lerner Newspapers, August 12, 1986.
19. Povich, Shirley. *Washington Post*, July 9, 1949.
20. Associated Press, *Philadelphia Inquirer*, June 14, 1948.
21. Birtwell, Roger. *The Sporting News*, August 4, 1948.
22. Interview with Dr. Nelson Potter Jr., April 4, 2007.
23. Castle, George. Lerner Newspapers, August 12, 1968. Unlike many contemporary ballplayers Potter welcomed overnight travel. After a particular rough train ride the night before he was scheduled to start, Potter was queried by a sympathetic reporter as to whether he had been able to get much sleep. Potter responded, "Yes I slept fine. It's a funny thing, but I can sleep better on a train than almost any other place I know." To which Braves trainer Dr. Charles Lack interjected, "Nelson's certainly in the right profession" *The Sporting News*, August 4, 1948.
24. Interview with Dr. Nelson Potter Jr., April 4, 2007.
25. Interview with Everett Henderson, March 15, 2007.

A number of the quotations ascribed to Potter come from a letter he wrote in longhand, in which he recapped his entire minor league career.

JIM PRENDERGAST *by Tom Harkins*

G	ERA	W	L	SV	GS	GF	CG	SHO	IP	H	R	ER	BB	SO	HR	HBP	WP	BFP
10	10.26	1	1	1	2	4	0	0	16⅔	30	20	19	5	3	1	0	0	84

G	AB	R	H	2B	3B	HR	RBI	BB	SO	BA	OBP	SLG	SB	HBP
10	5	0	0	0	0	0	0	0	3	.000	.000	.000	0	0

Those Americans who grew up in the Great Depression, went to fight in World War II, returned home, and went to work bringing the country back to life are now called, thanks to Tom Brokaw, the "Greatest Generation." Such a man was James Bartholomew Prendergast—who also happened to play professional baseball. He worked hard to reach the pinnacle of his profession, used the rights open to him as a citizen to fight the establishment when he felt he was being denied a say in his own future, and even turned to politics as a way of giving back to the country that had given him so much.

Jimmy Prendergast was born on August 23, 1917 in the rough, dockside section of Brooklyn bordering the Gowanus Canal. He was the eighth boy born into a working class Irish-American family; his only sister would soon follow. Their father died while Jim was three or four, and he was raised by his older brothers, two of whom became NYPD officers. His brothers taught young Jimmy to be a fighter. His children remember their father relating tales of his involvement in "pranks" during times of labor difficulties on the Brooklyn docks where some of his brothers were longshoremen and active in their profession's local union.

During his very early years in Brooklyn, Jimmy suffered an accident which may have actually improved his pitching ability. After he burnt his hands on the kitchen stove, doctors spread and stretched them out on boards that separated the fingers while the burns healed. This stretching of his hands may well have helped Prendergast pitch better, as his top pitches were his sinker and curve, both of which are best delivered from a long-fingered grip.

Jim's first serious exposure to baseball was in high school, where he teamed at Brooklyn Tech with his future teammate on the 1948 Braves, Tommy Holmes. Prendergast pitched well at Tech, winning his first game with a shutout. He also showed he could hit for power, and at one point while he was pitching in the Reds organization later on, it was suggested that he consider making the move to the outfield. He preferred to stay on the mound.

Prendergast may have pitched some batting practice at Ebbets Field during his high school days. He did come to know then-Dodgers coach Casey Stengel, who both gave him some tips and steered him towards his first professional contract. After leaving Brooklyn Tech in 1934, Prendergast was signed by GM Bob Quinn of his hometown Dodgers and sent to the Hartford (CT) Senators of the Northeastern League. In the midst of the Depression, with $100 in his pocket, 17-year-old Jimmy left home to seek his fortune in professional baseball.

His sojourn at Hartford proved too difficult for the youngster and, with Quinn's help, he found himself at a more suitable level, playing semipro ball around York, Pennsylvania. While pitching in this region, no longer under Dodger contract, Jim was scouted and signed by Gene McCann of the New York Yankees, who assigned him to the Butler Yankees of the Class D Pennsylvania State Association. He played for Butler in 1936 and also spent some time with the Bassett (Virginia) Furniture-makers of the Bi-State League. Overall he appeared in nine games, pitched 41 innings, and posted a 3–2 record.

The next season saw Prendergast splitting time with Augusta (GA) Tigers of the South Atlantic League and the Palatka (FL) Azaleas of the Florida State League, posting a fine combined 16–10 record with an ERA under

As a rookie with the 1948 Braves, Jim Prendergast was reunited with his former Brooklyn high school teammate, Tommy Holmes.

3.50. In 1938, he toured the country with four teams: he played two games for the Kansas City Blues of the American Association, another 11 in the Pacific Coast League—with both the Seattle Rainiers and the Hollywood Stars, but spent the bulk of his time with the Southern Association Birmingham Barons. His combined totals in 25 appearances were four wins, three losses, and an ERA over 4.50.

In 1939, he joined a team with which he would stay for three seasons; ironically, it was the Arkansas Travelers, again in the Southern Association. Prendergast became a mainstay of the Travelers staff, and his time in Little Rock produced a record of 36 wins versus 43 losses in 120 appearances. He struck out 302 while walking 202, with an ERA around 4.00.

Despite his losing record, the Cincinnati Reds, probably assessing that Jimmy was a good pitcher on a poor team (the Travelers were a second-division club whose combined record during Prendergast's tenure was 198–225), drafted him after the 1941 season. The 1942 *National League Green Book* pointed out that Prendergast had settled down in Little Rock, becoming their biggest winner and "caught the eye of the Cincy scouting staff, peerless pickers of pitchers."

Prendergast was scheduled to attend spring training with the Reds in 1942 but after the Pearl Harbor attack in December of '41 he chose to report to another training venue instead: the U.S. Army Officer Candidate School at Fort Benning, Georgia. The circumstances surrounding his enlistment illustrate the close-knit, protective and supportive family in which he was raised. Jim had received a draft notice earlier, but because he was helping to provide for his widowed mother, the draft board allowed an older brother, Woody, to take his place. When he received a second notice from the Selective Service, another brother, Walter, again offered to be taken in Jim's place. This time, however, Jim decided to enlist and reported to OCS. The Reds placed him on the National Defense List, where he stayed for the duration.

Jim received his commission as a second lieutenant in December 1942 and after a brief furlough in Brooklyn reported back to Georgia. He pitched in the spring of 1943 for the Fort Benning Infantry team managed by Capt. Hank Gowdy, who as a Boston Braves catcher back in 1917 had been the first major league enlistee in World War I. Gowdy later coached Jim with the Reds in spring training, and it was he who reportedly suggested that the hurler consider a move to the outfield. There was more important work to do, however; Lt. Prendergast was assigned to the European theater, where he served in a combat unit that saw action in France, Austria, and Germany. He was promoted to captain, and pitched a little on Army teams when not engaging the enemy.

Returning from military service, Prendergast was re-instated to the Cincinnati roster in February 1946 and reported to the Reds' spring training camp in Tampa. In late March, he was optioned by the team to its top farm club, the Syracuse Chiefs of the International League. He spent two successful seasons at Syracuse; in '46 he was 17–10, and in 1947 he really shined, posting a 20–15 record with a 3.08 ERA while leading the league in wins, complete games (24), and innings pitched (257). Although this superlative campaign didn't prompt a promotion to the Reds, it did warrant interest from the Braves—who purchased Prendergast's contract from Syracuse in November 1947. Braves GM John Quinn was the son of former Dodgers GM Bob Quinn, who had signed young Jim right out of high school. This capped off quite a year for the left-handed hurler; in addition to his mound exploits, he had met and courted the woman who would become his wife and partner for life. Jim and Terese O'Donnell, a registered nurse from Syracuse, were married on November 27, 1947 just a week after he became a member of the Boston Braves.

When the newlywed reported to the Braves spring training camp in 1948, however, he found he was one of many hurlers fighting for final roster spots. With so many pitchers in camp he didn't see a lot of Grapefruit League action, but he pitched well enough in the opportunities he had—most notably an April 2 outing against the Cardinals in which he pitched three perfect innings. After that game manager Billy Southworth commented that he wanted to see more of Jim Prendergast; in addition, it was reported that day that the Braves farmed out two pitchers to San Diego.

In the end, Jim made the club as one of 14 pitchers on the Braves roster. It was expected he would be used primarily in relief, but his is first big league appearance was a start in the second game of a doubleheader against the Giants at Braves Field on Sunday, April 25. It was not a sterling debut. Prendergast surrendered five runs in $2\frac{2}{3}$ innings pitched and picked up the loss as the Braves were shut out by the Dodgers, 6–0.

His next two outings were both in relief of Charles "Red" Barrett. On May 2, using a borrowed glove (his was one of nine gloves stolen when the Braves clubhouse at the Polo Ground was burglarized), Jim pitched two

Prendergast's pitching repertoire featured a sinker and curveball, enhanced by a childhood hand injury that extended his grip on a baseball.

scoreless innings and gave up a single hit in a 5–1 Barrett loss. The next Saturday, against some of his former Syracuse teammates now with the Reds, Prendergast's sinker must have been working well as he retired four batters on "infield taps" and allowed but one hit on a "slow roller."

The following day versus the Cardinals, he relieved Warren Spahn with one out and two on in the seventh. He struck out Terry Moore for the second out, but then gave up three straight hits to Stan Musial, Whitey Kurowski, and Enos Slaughter. When the dust had cleared, four runs had crossed the plate: two charged to Spahn, who got the loss, and two to Prendergast in only one-third of an inning.

This poor showing kept Prendergast out of action for 10 days, but he did manage to survive the final roster cut. His next time on the mound came on the 20th, when the Braves suffered their worst defeat of the year; the Pirates scored 13 runs on 17 hits while not allowing a Boston runner to reach second base. This time Jim relieved Barrett with the bases loaded in the fourth, giving up four hits in another third of an inning. He faced five batters, surrendering two triples and two singles, and his only out was recorded when the pitcher bunted foul with two strikes.

Once again, it was over a week before Jim next toed the mound. This may have been because of his shaky performances or it may have been due to the weather. Although the doggerel, "Spahn and Sain and pray for rain" didn't appear in print until September, during the month of May the Braves were rained out twice—once before and once after back-to-back performances by their two aces.

On May 28 the Braves lost to the Dodgers, 7–5, with Prendergast allowing a single in one inning following Bob Hogue in relief of Spahn. This game was the first of the season in which the Braves donned their "sateen" uniforms. Described by a *Boston Post* writer as "shimmery circus suits" and "musical comedy raiment," these odd outfits with the stripes down each arm were designed to be seen easier by fans during night games. The players disliked them because they were cold in cool weather and hot in warm, and the equipment manager didn't like them because they had to be dry cleaned after each use—yet still shrunk. Jim Prendergast's sateen uniform #38 was sold in the summer of 2006 by Leland's auction house for $6,704.82, an amount which exceeded any annual salary earned by Jim during his professional baseball career.

Red Barrett lost both ends of a June 12 doubleheader at Cincinnati, entering the record books with the dubious achievement. He started and lost the first game, and was on the hook as a reliever in the nightcap. With the score tied in the eighth inning of the second game, Prendergast relieved Barrett in a 9–9 contest and inherited batter Johnny Wyrostek with a 3–0 count. Jim proceeded to throw ball four on the first pitch, a walk charged to Barrett. He then surrendered a single to Hank Sauer, sending Wyrostek to second—and Jim to the showers. Bill Voiselle replaced Prendergast and allowed Wyrostek to score on a sacrifice fly, the run that caused the loss to be charged to Barrett.

The next day, Jim bounced back when called upon to start the second game of another doubleheader at Crosley Field—gaining the win by allowing six hits and three runs in five complete innings. He left the game leading the Reds 5–3, and the bullpen held it for his first (and only) major league victory. The win kept the Braves in a first-place tie with the Giants in the National League race, and showed the respect the team (at least temporarily) had in its rookie hurler.

The Braves' third doubleheader in five days was at home against the Cubs on Bunker Hill Day, June 17. Voiselle was credited with both victories in relief as the Braves rallied twice in late innings. The game was significant outside the pennant race for a reason unknown at the time; famed artist/illustrator Norman Rockwell was there taking photographs for a future *Saturday Evening Post* cover. In producing the lifelike illustrations for his cover art, Rockwell often first took photos on site and used them to paint on canvas in his Stockbridge, Mass. studio. The September 4, 1948 *Post* cover is considered one of Rockwell's classics. Entitled "The Dugout", it shows a sad and despondent Cubs team sitting dejectedly in their Braves Field dugout while visible behind them in their front rows rabid and vociferous Braves fans are delighting in the Cubs' misfortune. Although Prendergast didn't appear in either game or on the magazine cover (no Braves player or coach did), Jim's wife, Terese, was photographed that day along with the wife of coach Freddie Fitzsimmons. In the issue, Rockwell shows the photos he took of the two wives and how he included them among the screaming Braves fans. An issue of this magazine is still a proud possession of the Prendergast family. (Frank McNulty, visiting team batboy for the Braves, can also be seen on the cover standing glumly in front of the dugout in a Cubs uniform.)

The next appearance by Prendergast after his lone win came on June 24 in a mop-up role, as the Braves were trounced 11–2 at home by the Cards. He pitched the last two frames and gave up three hits and two runs. His final outing was on June 29 in another blowout, as he hurled the last inning and a third (giving up three hits) of an 11–3 Cardinals victory at St. Louis. The *Boston Globe* foreshadowed of the end of Jim's stint with the Braves in the same issue in which it reported Jim's swansong. The paper's front page story on June 30 reported that Braves owner Lou Perini had sent his private plane to Rochester, New York to bring to Boston newly signed high-school pitching phenom Johnny Antonelli.

The Braves had offered a large bonus and beat out several other teams to sign the 18-year-old left-hander, who was described by the *Boston Post* as baseball's best young pitching prospect since Bobby Feller. Because Antonelli had to be put on the major league roster due to the "bonus baby" rules of the time, 30-year-old lefty Prendergast became expendable. On June 30 GM Quinn gave Jim his outright release, sending him to the Milwaukee Brewers of the American Association. His final major league stats: 1–1 with a 10.26 ERA over $16\frac{2}{3}$ innings in 10 games.

Prendergast reported to the Brewers promptly and pitched well in 17 games, mostly as a starter. In 87 innings he was 8–2 with seven complete games, an ERA of 3.10, and a strikeout to walk ratio of better than three to one. Despite his good stats, the Braves neither recalled him for the late-season pennant run nor voted him a World Series share. Both Antonelli and Paul Burris, who pitched in just four and two games respectively, did receive shares through the intervention of the commissioner's office.

If the Braves were waiting to see how Prendergast did in a second stint with the Brewers, they could not have been impressed. Pitching with Milwaukee in the first half of the 1949 season, he slumped to 5–8 with an ERA of 4.25. Starting in the second half of the '49 season Jim made a lengthy attempt to reprise his success at Syracuse, but in a season and a half with the Chiefs he posted a 13–23 record with a lofty ERA of close to 5.50 in 51 games.

Although the 1950 season was Prendergast's last in organized baseball, it was not his last as a professional ballplayer; for two winters he also played winter ball in Cuba. As a member of the Marianao Tigres, he played with several past and future major leaguers. Among his teammates were Rollie Hemsley, Sr., Tommy Lasorda, Minnie Minoso, Negro League Hall of Famer Ray Dandridge, and his 1948 Braves comrade, Charles 'Red' Barrett. The team was managed by Cuban legend Dolph Luque.

Jim shared many stories of Cuban baseball with his children, the oldest of whom accompanied him to Cuba to escape the harsh upstate New York winters. American players were treated as celebrities in Cuba, with some featured in cover stories in the Cuban equivalent of *Life* magazine.

Returning from Cuba in 1951, however, Prendergast was not treated like a celebrity by the Syracuse front office. Citing his poor performance in 1950, the Chiefs offered Jim a contract with a significant salary cut—which he refused to sign. On April 25, Syracuse traded him to the Texas League's Beaumont Roughnecks for Ralph Buxton, a journeyman reliever with two cups of coffee in the majors. The drop in level for Prendergast, from AAA to AA, brought with it a reduction of salary from $1100 to $750 a month. Although both the trade and pay cut were permitted under the reserve clause of his prior contract, Jim still refused to sign; when he failed to report to Beaumont, he was suspended from organized baseball.

Ever the fighter, Jim immediately retained Frederic Johnson, the attorney who had successfully represented former Giants outfielder Danny Gardella in his suit involving the reserve clause that then bound players to the teams that owned their contracts. Gardella, who had been suspended by Commissioner Happy Chandler when he jumped to the Mexican League, had his case settled out of court and had been allowed to return to baseball. Prendergast's suit was filed in the Federal District Court in Syracuse in late April 1951, with Jim seeking $150,000 in damages.

Johnson argued that the reserve clause "continually tendered materially to hamper Prendergast in negotiating for salary and employment." The defendants argued that under former rulings organized baseball was exempt from anti-trust legislation, relying upon Justice Holmes' 1922 decision in the Federal League cases that baseball was an "exhibition" and not a "business." Prendergast's case was eventually dismissed in the wake of the 1953 Supreme Court decision in the Toolson case (Toolson, a Yankees minor leaguer, had also challenged the reserve clause). Perhaps not surprisingly, Prendergast would never be employed in organized baseball again.

Although his pro sports career was over, Prendergast held a position in business that he had first obtained thanks to his work in baseball. While pitching for the Syracuse Chiefs he had worked doing sales and promotions for the William Simon Brewery in the Syracuse area, and as his court case was pending Jim worked fulltime for the Buffalo-based brewery. He returned to his Syracuse home on the weekends, a situation which continued for a few years until his growing family seemed to dictate relocation to Buffalo. The Prendergast family grew to eight children, six boys and two girls. Jim stayed involved with breweries and beer distributorships for many years; after leaving William Simon, he subsequently worked for Ballantine, Carling, and Dow.

For Ballantine he served as the company's sports director when they were a major media sponsor of both the Yankees and the New York Football Giants. In this capacity he brought team highlight films to show to various organizations. His son Peter remembers an incident in 1963 or 1964 involving Yankees pitcher Jim Bouton. His father was shepherding the star hurler to an appearance for a Ballantine sales promotion, and had Bouton pick up Pete and his brother at school in his flashy convertible. Imagine the joy in the young boys' hearts as they road around Buffalo with a Yankee hero.

Prendergast was also active in numerous civic, community, and church activities in Buffalo. A lifelong Democrat, he took part in local politics and ran for Tonawanda town supervisor in 1959 and U.S. Congress in 1964 (both times unsuccessfully). He also faithfully coached his sons' youth baseball teams, and was able to combine all these interests in a way that showed both his sense of humor and his competitive spirit. Much to the dismay of his Republican neighbors, he provided his team with uniforms which were proudly and defiantly labeled "Little Democrats." His children said that he frequently took them to see Buffalo's minor league team, but as a former player he found it difficult to simply sit and watch. Retiring from beer sales left Jim feeling restless at home, so he launched a realty agency which his son Joe still runs. In 1994, on his 76th birthday, Jim Prendergast passed away after a long illness, in his home surrounded by his family. It was a fitting end for a true member of the "greatest generation" who also happened to play our national pastime.

Sources

Interview with Peter Prendergast on Monday, August 20, 2007 in Buffalo, NY.

Prendergast clipping file from Giamatti Research Center Baseball Hall of Fame.

MARV RICKERT *by Gene Gumbs*

G	AB	R	H	2B	3B	HR	RBI	BB	SO	BA	OBP	SLG	SB	HBP
3	13	1	3	0	1	0	2	0	1	.231	.286	.385	0	1

Marvin "Twitch" Rickert's career was typical of that of many players in the first half of the 20th century. Before the days of free agency and long-term contracts, Rickert was a useful piece that several clubs plugged in, and then discarded, over his six-year big league career.

The speedy, left-handed-hitting outfielder reached 100 hits only once in the majors, in 1946 with the Chicago Cubs, and never had as many as 400 at-bats in a season. He showed the promise of power in the minor leagues prior to his shot in the big time, but never hit more than seven homers in a season in the big leagues. And even when Rickert played in a World Series—suiting up for the Boston Braves in the 1948 fall classic—his appearance came only as the result of another player's injury. A year later, the Braves were just as quick to sell him off after his best season.

Born in the small (pop. 600) Olympic Peninsula town of Long Branch, Washington on January 8, 1921, Marvin August Rickert came from a family of ballplayers. His father was in the logging business, but a ballplayer on the side. The Long Branch team won the Washington State semipro championship in 1908, with eight Rickerts on the town squad—Marv's father and four uncles among them. The only non-Rickert on the team, Bert Watkinson, was brought into the family through marriage. "He married Uncle Fred's daughter," Rickert told sportswriter Edgar Munzel.

Young Marv was a bit of a legend as an excellent hitter with the Tacoma Tigers of the Western International League in his late teens, and he parlayed that into a journeyman major league career for five different teams.

Signed right out of high school, the 6'2", 195-pound athlete got his feet wet in 19 games as a first baseman for Class B Tacoma in 1938, at the age of 17, but lost most of the year due to a broken foot. He then spent the majority of 1939 optioned out to Boise in the Class C Pioneer League. There he moved full time to the outfield and hit a resounding .354 in 100 games with 14 homers and 75 runs batted in. He spent the entire 1940 season back up a rung with Tacoma and came back to earth somewhat, hitting a still-solid .288 (with 77 RBIs and eight home runs), dividing his time between first base and the outfield.

In 1941, Rickert was on the same pace with Tacoma once more (.284 after 87 games) when he was sold to the Chicago Cubs in August for a sum thought to be in excess of $3,000. Assigned to the Class A Tulsa Oilers, the Cubs' Texas League farm club, to finish the season, and variously described in *The Sporting News* as a "fleet center fielder" and a "sleek right fielder," Rickert hit .230 while getting adjusted to the more competitive league. During the playoffs, however, he tore it up—hitting .750 in six games against the Dallas Rebels.

Rickert really began to blossom in 1942 and batted .310 for Tulsa with nine homers and 73 RBIs, earning himself a call-up to the Cubs in September. He debuted on September 10 and saw duty in eight games, all in the outfield, batting a respectable .269. But like so many other players of that time, just as he got his chance to join

Marv Rickert received a sudden, unexpected promotion to Boston near the end of the season to replace the injured Jeff Heath. Heath's bad luck also resulted in Rickert being granted an exception to participate in the World Series.

a big-league club on a full-time basis, Marv was faced with World War II.

He enlisted in October 1942 and spent three years (1943–45) on active duty with the Coast Guard. It was no easy work, shipping out of Seattle and serving aboard an explosives ship transporting ammunition to American bases in the Aleutian Islands. "I still shudder when I think of it," Rickert told *The Sporting News* in 1946. Later in the war, things got easier when he was transferred from sea duty to coach the Coast Guard baseball team at Seattle, and they posted a spectacular 98–8 record over a two-year span.

Returning to the Cubs after the war ended, Marv joined the club for spring training on Catalina Island and battled two-time home run champ Bill Nicholson for a starting outfield slot. Rickert survived one incident late in the exhibition season when he tried to steal second base with the bases loaded. He got to within 10 feet of the bag when he realized his mistake. Phil Cavarretta tried to score during the confusion, but was cut down at the plate.

All in all, though, Rickert seemed to pick up right where he'd left off and then some, appearing in a career-high 111 games in 1946 and hitting .263 with 18 doubles, three triples, seven homers, and 47 RBIs. Valuable because he could play all three outfield positions as well as first base, he got a chance at regular action after Andy Pafko wrenched his ankle stepping on a baseball before a June 1 game with the Braves. Rickert made the most of the opportunity; he hit a three-run homer that very day, and drove in five runs during a doubleheader against Boston the next day. Perhaps the most memorable moment of his career came later that same month, when he and Eddie Waitkus hit back-to-back inside-the-park home runs on June 23—the only time that has ever been done in the National League. (It was the only time in the majors until Toby Harrah and Bump Wills repeated the feat for the Texas Rangers in 1977.)

Waitkus and Rickert were fast friends. Along with Russ Meyer, they were three fun-loving bachelors who often hung out together. Rickert also had the reputation as one of the team clowns, and manager Charlie Grimm's loose clubhouse gave him plenty of opportunities, it seems. One of his favorite routines was parading around the clubhouse in just his jockstrap, pulling the straps up over his shoulders and prancing around, according to former teammate Len Merullo.

Rickert's playing time diminished in 1947, as he got to bat just 137 times, largely as a pinch-hitter or defensive replacement. After the '47 season he was sold to the Cincinnati Reds; Less than a month into the season, and after just six at-bats (with one single) as a Red, he was traded to the Braves for veteran outfielder Danny Litwhiler and assigned to their Milwaukee Brewers farm club in the American Association. Rickert's time with Milwaukee was notable. While his future teammates in Boston were battling it out for the NL pennant, he batted .302 with 27 homers and 117 RBIs and was named to his league's All Star team.

Once the American Association season ended and the Brewers disbanded, Rickert proceeded home to Tacoma—presumably for the winter. But then Boston starting outfielder Jeff Heath broke his ankle during the last week of the regular season. The Braves purchased Rickert's contract from Milwaukee and ordered him to fly east on the first available plane. He arrived in Brooklyn one hour before the start of the game and was inserted into the line-up in left field. Rickert recorded an RBI when Ralph Branca nicked him on the leg with the bases loaded in the fourth inning, aiding in the Braves' 3–1 victory. He went on to the Polo Grounds with the team and appeared in two of the last three games of the season. Boston petitioned Commissioner Happy Chandler to certify Rickert as World Series eligible because of the late call-up necessitated by Heath's injury. The AL Champion Cleveland Indians gave their consent, and Marv found himself starting in left field in five of the six '48 World Series games.

Rickert had just four hits in the Series in 19 at-bats (a .211 average), but made his presence felt. One of his safeties was one of only two Boston managed off Bob Feller in winning Game One, 1–0. The lone member of the Braves who had ever batted against Rapid Robert before the fall classic, Rickert "always has hit him as though he owned him," Arthur Daley of the *New York Times* wrote after the game. Daley was not exaggerating; a few seasons earlier, when he was with the Cubs, Rickert had faced Feller nine times in spring training and collected six hits.

Two of Marv's other hits in the Series came in Game Four off Indians hurler Steve Gromek, including a solo home run that accounted for the lone Braves tally in a 2–1 loss. Overall, Boston hit just .230 in the Series, which was dominated by pitching and won by Cleveland—which itself hit just .199—in six games.

Daley was also responsible for creating the misimpression that Rickert technically played for "fun" that fall. In his October 11, 1948 *New York Times* column, he claimed, perhaps tongue-in-cheek, that since Rickert was called up after the season ended, he was never placed on the Braves payroll and had arrived too late to have been formally allocated a Series share. Daley categorized Rickert as "the first amateur in World Series history." As mentioned above, Rickert did play in regular season games

for the Braves that would have required compensation. Since the split of the World Series player pool had already been voted on by the players and submitted to Commissioner Chandler's office, the commissioner, by executive order after the Fall Classic, awarded Rickert a one-third Series loser's share of $1,523.58.

Marv was widely praised for his outfield defense in the World Series as well, and after his credible performance, the Braves signed him to the big-league club—a signing deemed a reward—for the 1949 campaign. It came out in February, though, that he'd actually been offered $1,500 less than he'd made in the minors with Milwaukee in '48. The embarrassed Braves agreed to make up the difference, but Rickert said he would not play in the majors for what he was making in the minors. Finally, the team came to terms and Rickert called his new deal "the best contract I ever received."

Everyone was fairly happy by year's end. Rickert appeared in 100 games, primarily in the outfield but also filling in for the injured Earl Torgeson at first base during one time of need. Marv showed good pop in his bat with 18 doubles, three triples, and six homers to go along with 49 RBIs, and his .292 average was his best ever in the major leagues. Among players with 150 or more at-bats, it was also the top mark on the club that summer as the Braves slipped to fourth place.

Rickert may also have been the first major-leaguer to use a batting glove. While with the Braves, he used a golf glove on his right hand while batting. Needless to say, he caught his share of barbs from the opposing dugouts.

After the 1949 season, despite his fine performance, Rickert again found himself on the move when the Braves traded him to the Pittsburgh Pirates in December for $10,000 and a player to be named. The Cubs were sniffing around, but Pittsburgh wanted a fourth outfielder and snapped him up. After just 17 disappointing games with the Pirates in 1950, during which he hit .150 coming off the bench in pinch-hitting roles, Marv was once more unloaded—sent to the White Sox on waivers at the end of May in what would prove to be his final year in the big leagues. Although he played regularly for the Pale Hose, appearing in 84 games, he hit just .237 for a team that went 60–94. This left him with a lifetime .247 average, 19 homers, and 145 RBIs for his major-league career.

Sold outright by the White Sox to the Triple-A Baltimore Orioles in December 1950, Rickert kicked around in the minors for a couple of seasons, even leading the International League in homers with 35 while playing for Baltimore in 1951 and making the All-Star team. He also hit at a hefty .320 clip that season, and the Toronto Maple Leafs tried to pry him loose by offering $20,000 for his contract; Baltimore demurred. He also played very good ball with Almendares in the Cuban Winter League, and was a popular player with Cuban fans.

In late May of 1952, Marv was sold by the last-place

Orioles (now ready to take the reported $20,000) to Toronto in the same league. When he was sold, he was hitting .311 with 25 RBIs in 35 games. Between the two clubs, he batted .262, hit 13 homers, and drove in 68.

By early 1953, Toronto was reported to have given Rickert the opportunity to strike his own deal with a Pacific Coast League club. He was determined to stay on the West Coast, closer to home. He seemed to have worked something out with Oakland in March, but it didn't last long, as the Oaks released him in April. Perhaps he was supposed to have returned to Toronto if he hadn't worked anything out, because when he "failed to report" the Leafs placed him on the suspended list on May 19.

That was it for baseball. The outfielder/first baseman returned to his native Washington, where he remained with his wife, Margaret, and children, Byron and Pamela. He worked for a time as a bartender and later operated a charter boat service.

An unheralded but meaningful honor came Marv's way when he was inducted into the Tacoma-Pierce County Sports Hall of Fame in 1964, along with Cy Neighbors, another local product with a "Moonlight Graham" career. According to the *Baseball Encyclopedia*, Neighbors played in only one game in the outfield for the Pittsburgh Pirates in 1908 and did not record an official at-bat in the majors, the same fate that befell Graham three years earlier. They joined perhaps the most notable former big-leaguer from that area, Jack Fournier, who batted .313 in a 15-year career primarily for the Chicago White Sox, St. Louis Cardinals and Brooklyn Dodgers from 1912 to 1927.

By this point Rickert was employed by the Pierce County Parks and Recreation Department, where he worked from the late 1950s until he retired in 1975. He lived out his remaining days on his farm in Oakville, Washington, and died on June 3, 1978, at the age of 57.

Sources

Theodore, John. *Baseball Natural: The Story of Eddie Waitkus* (Lincoln, Neb.: Bison Books, 2006)

www.baseball-almanac.com, www.retrosheet.org, and *The Sporting News* via www.paperofrecord.com

Chicago Daily Tribune

Los Angeles Times

New York Times

Tacoma News Tribune

Washington Post

Tacoma-Pierce County Sports Hall of Fame, Marc Blau, Director

JIM RUSSELL *by Dave Williams*

G	AB	R	H	2B	3B	HR	RBI	BB	SO	BA	OBP	SLG	SB	HBP
89	322	44	85	18	1	9	54	46	31	.264	.361	.410	4	3

In August 1948, both the Braves and their centerfielder Jim Russell were riding high. The Braves were in first place and Russell, acquired in an offseason trade with the Pirates, was having another strong season leading the team in home runs and RBIs. A switch-hitter with speed as well as power, he was batting .264 with nine home runs and 54 runs batted in through 89 games before a serious heart illness ended his season and effectively ended his career as a productive player.

James William Russell was born on October 1, 1918 in Fayette City, Pennsylvania, the son of James and Lillian Russell. His father was of Irish-Welsh descent and his mother was Swedish. It was not an easy upbringing as money was scarce, his parents were not well educated, and his father was tough on young Jim. The elder Russell supported his family with work in several different coal mines, often

A serious heart ailment disabled Jim Russell in midseason and deprived him of the opportunity to play in the 1948 World Series.

switching jobs because he was a highly sought-after ball player for the teams organized by the mines. Doc Russell, known for Spencer Tracy-type looks and a crusty demeanor, acquired the nickname because he regularly wore a fur cap that was left behind at his home by a medical doctor. The military style fur cap was popular among doctors in the early part of the 20th century, but Doc was more suited to a baseball cap. An outstanding infielder, Jim's father was renowned for his slugging prowess; it was said that he once hit a ball that traveled 400 feet in the air and rolled another 250 feet once it landed.

Young Jim was an energetic boy who inherited his father's athletic genes and was always playing one sport or another. His favorite, of course, was baseball and Jim played whenever he could. As a young boy Jim, a natural right handed batter, learned to switch hit so he could hit his brother Carl's curve ball. Since neither of Jim's parents was well educated this sometimes led to some poor decisions in the care of their children. One cold and wet day, Jim was outside playing ball without being dressed properly for the weather and as a result contracted rheumatic fever, and an infection developed in his heart. For a while there was concern that he would not survive, but in time he recovered and remained in good health until the unfortunate illness, related to his childhood disease, that cost him a chance to play in the 1948 World Series.

Jim lacked the same enthusiasm for his school work that he had for sports, and dropped out of school in the ninth grade to work in the mines like his father. Doc's sister Margaret kept a watchful eye on Jim to keep him out of trouble and encouraged him to pursue his baseball dreams. Aunt Margaret, with whom Jim lived off and on during his childhood and even later while in Brooklyn with the Dodgers, was not shy about giving Jim an occasional tongue lashing to keep him focused. He would always have a fond place in his heart for Aunt Margaret and years later he credited her with helping him become a major leaguer.

As Jim grew and his baseball skills became more polished, he began to attract the interest of area professional teams. He signed his first professional contract with the McKeesport (PA) Little Pirates in 1937 and for the next five seasons played minor league ball in several towns including Butler, Beaver Falls, Youngstown, Springfield (Illinois), and St. Joseph of the Michigan State League. In 1938, while playing for Butler, a Pennsylvania State Association (Class D) entry, he was teammates with Hank Sauer, the eventual 1952 National League MVP. Sauer led the league in batting that year and was named to its All Star team. Russell finished the year with the Beaver Falls squad and was an honorable mention All Star after batting .320. He was also an honorable mention All Star in 1939 with the Mayfield, Kentucky squad of the KITTY League, another Class D circuit, where his team won the regular season championship but lost in the first round of the playoffs. Two of his teammates that year were Vernon "Junior" Stephens, the KITTY League batting champion who later teamed with Ted Williams to make a great slugging duo with the Boston Red Sox, and Charlie Metro who later managed

Jim Russell was the only switch-hitter on the '48 Braves roster.

both the Chicago Cubs and Kansas City Royals. Jim acquitted himself well in this group with a .333 mark.

By 1941 Russell had moved up to Class B and in playing 125 games for Meridian of the Southeastern League, he led the league in stolen bases with 51 and established a new single season record. He finished the '41 campaign with the Memphis Chicks of the Class A Southern Association, but Russell was not wholly pleased with the promotion to a higher league. Although he batted .383 with 10 doubles in 24 games, he expected his salary to be increased commensurate with the jump in competition. He let his displeasure over his pay carry out on to the field and became a target of abuse from the Memphis faithful. When the last out of the season was a fly ball to Russell, he caught it and then heaved the ball with all his might into the bleachers.

During the off-season he was selected by the Pittsburgh Pirates in the minor league draft and assigned to Toronto of the International League (AA) for the '42 campaign. Russell enjoyed a fine season batting .295 with 19 doubles, three triples, three home runs, and 14 stolen bases. The Pirates purchased his contract in September and brought him to the big leagues where he appeared in five games. He made just one hit in 14 at-bats.

Russell had grown into a strong, athletic young man, standing 6'1" and weighing 180 pounds and was blessed with outstanding speed. A switch-hitter, he was instantly one of the fastest players in the majors, even winning a 60-yard dash contest held for major league players in conjunction with the annual relay meet at Purdue University. His winning time of 6.9 seconds was only five-tenths of a second off the winning time posted in the collegiate race. Bob Usher of Cincinnati was second, Allie Reynolds of Cleveland was third, and Mizell Platt of the Chicago Cubs was fourth.

Russell's manager in Pittsburgh was future Hall of Famer Frankie Frisch. Frisch, who gained fame first as a player for John McGraw's New York Giants and then as player-manager of the St. Louis Cardinals whom he piloted to the 1934 world championship, led the Bucs from 1940 to 1946. The Fordham Flash thought very highly of his young outfielder, commenting that Russell had a chance to be as good "as he wants to be." Frisch always appreciated players who possessed good speed and thought Russell to be an excellent defensive outfielder with a fine arm. He also worked with him to teach him how to drag bunt to take advantage of his speed. "Why, that fellow Russell ought to bunt .300 in any league! He actually overtakes and beats the ball when he pulls a bunt down the line!" Frisch exclaimed.

Jim's weakened heart from his childhood illness got him classified as 4F and kept out of World War II. With many major league players now in the service, he took advantage of this opportunity and won the starting center field job with Pittsburgh in 1943. Still just 24 years old, he responded well with a .259 batting average that included four homers and 44 runs batted in while appearing in 146 games. He followed that with the best year of his major league career in 1944 when he batted a career best .312, good for ninth in the senior circuit. He also collected 181 hits, 34 doubles, 14 triples, 8 homers, 66 RBIs, and scored 109 runs. One of his home runs was a grand slam on August 20 against Brooklyn; he became the first Pirate to hit one as a pinch-hitter.

He was developing into a consistent major league player that was noted for his speed and defensive abilities. In 1945 he batted .284, and his totals of 12 home runs and 77 RBIs would have been slightly higher if not for an incident that occurred on Opening Day against the Reds at Crosley Field. Russell came to bat in the fifth inning with two men on base, one of whom was shortstop Frankie Zak. Zak asked for time out from the second base umpire so that he could tie his shoes. However, the ump did not signal time until after Cincinnati pitcher Bucky Walters threw the pitch—which Russell promptly knocked out of the park. The umpire signaled "no play" and a heated argument followed. Eventually, the home run was disallowed and the Pirates went on to lose the game in extra innings by the score of 7–6. A still angry Frisch was said to have subsequently told Zak that he was going to buy him shoes with buttons.

Russell also proved to be somewhat of Braves killer in the 1945 campaign. In a doubleheader on July 6 in which Boston outfielder Tommy Holmes broke Rogers Hornsby's modern day record of hitting safely in 33 consecutive games, Russell had three hits including a homer in the second game. Two days later he had four hits in the first game of another twin bill in a 10–8 triumph and on July 17 he had another four-hit game against the Braves in an 8–5 Pirates victory at Forbes Field. Perhaps Braves management still remembered these feats when they traded for Russell a few years later.

Following the 1945 season he was selected to join a squad of 18 National League players that performed before servicemen in the South Pacific with stopovers in Manila and Tokyo. Headed by Brooklyn coach Charlie Dressen, the elite club featured future Hall of Famer Paul Waner, Ralph Branca, and Buddy Kerr. Also on the team were four players would become teammates on the 1948 Braves; Frank McCormick, Ed Wright, Red Barrett, and Bill Voiselle.

The next two seasons Russell, against a tougher crop of post-war pitchers, produced less impressive and almost identical numbers: eight homers with 50 runs batted across in 1946 and eight home runs with 51 RBIs in 1947. He had another big game against the Braves on August 20, 1947, a day that the Braves passed the million mark in home attendance for the first time in team history, Russell had five hits, among them a double and a triple, and drove in five runs in the 16–10 victory. That year he played center field sandwiched between two future Hall of Famers: Ralph Kiner and Hank Greenberg—and once was quoted as saying neither "could move." Russell liked both men and especially sympathized with Greenberg for all the abuse he took as the game's most prominent Jewish player. He remained friends with Kiner, who later in life would visit Russell's home, but wondered why the seven-time home run champ was elected to the Hall of Fame. Russell felt that Kiner was too one-dimensional as a hitter and a poor outfielder.

The business of baseball became a reality for Russell in the off season of 1947 when on November 18 he was shipped along with catcher Bill Salkeld and pitcher Al Lyons to the Braves for outfielder Johnny Hopp and second basemen Danny Murtaugh. Hopp had batted .288 for Boston in 1947 while Murtaugh was a 30-year-old journeyman who appeared in only three games for the Braves. Murtaugh would gain fame later as manager of the Pittsburgh Pirates for 15 seasons in three different stints including both the 1960 and '71 world champions.

Jim responded by having one of his better seasons and was an important element on a Braves team fighting for their first pennant in 34 years. On June 7 in a game against the Cubs in Wrigley Field, Russell had one of the most memorable games of his career when he tied a National League record with four extra base hits in a single game. He not only homered and doubled from both sides of the plate, but he also drove in six runs as the Braves defeated the Cubs 9–5. Russell also showed a knack for hitting the clutch home run that summer. In a May 15 game against the Dodgers at Ebbets Field he supplied the only run in a Warren Spahn shutout with a home run; this also marked the third consecutive shutout by a Braves' starting pitcher. On July 8—again at Ebbets Field—Russell broke a 2–2 tie with an eighth-inning grand slam that helped end Brooklyn's six-game home winning streak. As he went out to take his position in center field in the bottom of the inning, he was greeted by fans throwing rubber balls and other rubbish. The public announcer in his finest Brooklyn accent shouted, "I thought I made that clear. Please don't throw nothing on the field." Threatened with a forfeit, the crowd complied.

Although Russell's bases loaded blow was overshadowed somewhat in game accounts by the broken ankle suffered by Braves starting second baseman Eddie Stanky in the same contest, it launched a red hot stretch that helped Boston build up an eight-game lead over second place St. Louis by July 18. Then, overnight, Jim's dream season came to an abrupt end. On July 22 Russell was admitted to Christ Hospital in Cincinnati with what was alternately reported by the newspapers as "a slight fever," "an infected tooth," and "a touch of grippe." Upon his release five days later the United Press reported that doctors had "removed an infected tooth and decaying jaw bone which were believed to have caused a fever he had for two weeks prior to entering the hospital." Reports of Russell's weight loss during this period ranged from 10 to 20 pounds or more.

Although he rejoined the team in Boston at July's end, Russell never saw action and on August 13 left for his Pennsylvania home for what the Associated Press deemed "a complete rest upon the recommendation of team physician Dr. Roger T. Doyle." Eventually Jim was diagnosed with subacute bacterial endocarditis, a condition caused by a blood infection from which bacteria made its way into the heart and damaged a heart valve. According to Russell in later interviews, this condition was 100 percent fatal before penicillin; however, with the help of this still relatively new wonder drug, he was able to recover his health—but not his batting stroke. On August 30 it was announced that Russell would miss the remainder of the season and have to stay in Charleroi-Monessen Hospital for at least another three weeks to a month. While the Braves stumbled briefly after both he and Stanky were gone and fell out of first place, they did recover to win the pennant. The Braves received permission from the commissioner's office to add outfielder Ray Sanders to the World Series roster to replace Russell, even though Sanders had just come up from minor league Hartford in mid-September and thus would normally be ineligible. Russell's stay in the hospital was a little longer than expected and he listened to the World Series on the radio in his hospital room. After the Series, manager Billy Southworth visited him and said the team, which hit just .230 versus Cleveland, could have used him on offense and defense.

After proclaiming himself "in perfect health" by mid-December, Russell came back to reclaim his roster spot in spring training of 1949. The feel-good story did not last long, as dissension filled the Braves clubhouse in 1949 and Russell was in the middle of it all. Dave Egan of the *Boston Daily Record,* who was notorious for his battles with Red Sox great Ted Williams, reported that Russell was fined $200 for breaking curfew in spring training, a story that Russell denied. Later in August, Russell and teammate Earl Torgeson got into a fight at a Chicago hotel and both combatants came away injured. Torgeson, who had been out most of the season with a shoulder

separation, suffered a sprained thumb while Russell came away with two black eyes. Manager Billy Southworth did not fine either player as he claimed that no team rule had been violated. It was only a short time after this incident that Southworth took his "voluntary" departure from the team which was plodding along with a 55–54 record. At the end of the season in a meeting to divide the fourth-place money the team would receive, a majority of the players, including Russell, voted to give Southworth only a half-share. Commissioner Happy Chandler stepped in and awarded the embattled manager a full share. The incident spoke volumes about the state of the team and at the end of the season it was apparent that some house-cleaning was necessary. Russell's 120 games played was more than any other Braves outfielder, but he batted only .231, and was traded to Brooklyn on Christmas Eve along with Ed Sauer and cash for Luis Olmo.

Prior to the trade the Braves had asked waivers on Russell, so that when the trade was made his contract was assigned to the Dodgers' top farm club, the Montreal Royals of the International League. Russell balked at the prospect of playing in Montreal; citing the weather as being too cold for him, he threatened to retire. Branch Rickey got him to relent when he promised that he would train with the big club and be given every chance to make the squad, which he did.

On June 5, 1950, the famous Russell temper exhibited itself again as a high hard one by Cubs pitcher Paul Minner in the fourth inning of a game at Wrigley Field sent him sprawling. He thought Minner was throwing at him and after a brief exchange of words, he charged the mound and was ejected. National League President Ford Frick interestingly made the trip to Chicago for the next game though nothing became of the incident and Russell was not fined. In a July contest versus St. Louis he duplicated his feat of 1948 by again homering from both sides of the plate, batting lefty against George Munger and righty versus Harry Brecheen, thus becoming the first major league player to accomplish this feat twice. There were not to be many highlights this season, however, as he hit only .229 while splitting time in left field with Gene Hermanski.

Russell spent the majority of the 1951 season with Montreal; he appeared in just in 16 games for the Dodgers and went 0-for-13 in what proved to be his final year in the big leagues. While in Montreal he roomed with a young left-handed pitcher named Tommy Lasorda with whom he developed a lifelong friendship. In later years both were on the scouting staff of the Dodgers and Lasorda would visit with Russell in his home when in the Pittsburgh area. Lasorda went on to greater fame first as third base coach under Walter Alston and then succeeding him as manager of the Dodgers, a post he held from 1976 to 1995 enroute to the Hall of Fame. It was also during his stint in Montreal that Russell met his future wife

Theresa Mary Coreau of Arnprior, Ontario, whom he married on Halloween of 1951.

Russell finished his playing career in 1952 and 1953 with the Portland Beavers of the Pacific Coast League and then retired back to Pennsylvania. He was hired by the Dodgers as a scout, a job he held until 1960 when he took the same position with Washington; he worked for the Senators from 1961 to 1963. At the same time he was a scout, he also owned Russell Brothers Beer Distributing with his brother Carl which they sold in the mid-1960s. In 1964 he was unanimously selected by the Rostraver Township School Board to fill an unexpired term. He aspired to become the tax collector, but instead became a salesman for Smith-Corona. He still indulged his political interests, however, and won election to the school board in the Belle Vernon Area School District in 1967 and 1971. Keeping up his love of the game, he was also instrumental in bringing American Legion ball back to the area and coached the Fayette City entry in the 1970s.

During this period, Jim would occasionally experience severe chest pains. In June 1977 he had his aortic valve replaced with a pig's valve and it was then discovered that his heart was four times the normal size; by comparison the average athlete's heart is two times the normal size. While in the recovery room, his heart went into atrial fibrillation and the doctor's opened his chest right there in recovery and massaged his heart. After a long convalescence Russell, still employed at Smith-Corona, moved to the Tampa, Florida area. There he became an avid golfer, eventually becoming a 10 handicap, and often played with Hall of Famers Stan Musial and Al Lopez at Feather Sound Country Club in Clearwater.

It was early 1987 when he again experienced a severe health crisis as he underwent mitral valve surgery on March 12. On the day before Thanksgiving he boarded a plane for a long planned hunting trip, but something went wrong and he died on takeoff. He was remembered as a charismatic man with a certain dynamic that people wanted to be around, as well as a devoted husband and father to his three children.

Russell's son Stephen has enjoyed a long career as an educator and since 1976 has been principal of Bellmar Middle School in Belle Vernon, Pennsylvania. He has also had longevity in his second career as a ticket seller for the Pittsburgh Pirates. His career with the Pirates actually dates back to the 1960s when he began as an usher in old Forbes Field. He moved into his position as a ticket seller in 1972 and has been there ever since. One of his passions has been to collect memorabilia of his favorite players, especially Paul Molitor, whom he was fortunate enough to meet. Since 1998 he has been curator of the Mid-Mon Valley All Sports Hall of Fame where one famous inductee was in Stephen's homeroom in 10th grade; football great Joe Montana. Russell is proud of his father and fondly remembers his dad's friendship with Bing Crosby, Stan Musial, Tommy Lasorda, Ralph Kiner, and Chuck Tanner. In the eyes of an admiring son, these relationships help show the measure of the man that was Jim Russell.

Sources
Kaese, Harold. *The Boston Braves, 1871–1953*. Boston: Northeastern University Press, 2004.
Jim Russell player file at the National Baseball Hall of Fame
Interview with Stephen Russell, son of Jim Russell, January 6, 2007
Copy of speech delivered by Stephen Russell at Pennsylvania Sports Hall of Fame induction of Jim Russell, November 4, 2006
Short biography of Jim Russell written by Stephen Russell
2005 ESPN Baseball Encyclopedia
Sports Collectors Digest
Pittsburgh Tribune-Review
Pittsburgh Magazine
SABR Baseball Encyclopedia
Boston Daily Record

CONNIE RYAN *by John McMurray*

G	AB	R	H	2B	3B	HR	RBI	BB	SO	BA	OBP	SLG	SB	HBP
51	122	14	26	3	0	0	10	21	16	.213	.333	.238	0	1

Although he had far from the best year of his career in 1948, Connie Ryan was a valuable utility infielder for the Boston Braves that season—primarily backing up incumbent Eddie Stanky (and later *his* replacement, Sibby Sisti) at second base. Ryan was an intense competitor as well as an occasional sparkplug for the National League pennant-winners, and could be counted on to play solid defense. He was also not averse to a scuffle now and then.

Those qualities stood out to former New York Giants manager Mel Ott, who had scouted Ryan before bringing the young infielder to the major leagues in 1942. "From all the tales that have come on here before Ryan he is a competent and aggressive agent," read one unattributed 1942 newspaper account found in Hall of Fame files. "Ott saw him [Ryan] in New Orleans—his home town too—and admired his fighting spirit as well as his ability. He is a peppery, chip-on-shoulder player like [Dick] Bartell or John McGraw."

Ryan's teammates typically viewed him as pleasant

and gentlemanly. Another 1942 account claimed that Connie was "much more articulate than the average rookie getting his first major league chance, and so humble that he ministers to everybody from the bellhops to the bat-boy."

Yet Ryan's competitiveness occasionally boiled over. In 1940, while playing second base in the minor leagues for Savannah, he had a scuffle with future major league teammate Eddie Stanky, who was then the second baseman for the opposing Macon team. As Ryan recounted years later, "Every time that I went out to my position, I noticed that my glove was in right field instead of near second base [fielders routinely left their gloves on the field between innings in those days]. I figured somebody was kicking it out there, so I watched—and it turned out to be Stanky kicking it.

"I ran over and took a swing at him, and we got into a little scrape before other players tore us apart. The next thing we knew, we were on the way to the Savannah jail. He was fined $100 and I got off for nothing, for some reason. We got back to the park about a half hour later and finished the game."

While Ryan reportedly was "not overly proud of his pugilistic exploits," he was a part of two other incidents during his career that received significant attention from the press. During a 1950 game while with the Reds, he was covering first base on a bunt when Philadelphia's Willie Jones spiked him. When the same thing happened at second base a few weeks later, Ryan went after Jones because Ryan "figured [Jones] was doing it deliberately. I missed with a right and then somebody broke us up." The two became good friends when Ryan joined the Phillies a couple years later, and Ryan eventually smoothed things over with Stanky as well.

In addition, when Ryan was managing in Corpus Christi after his major league career was over, he "set off a real donnybrook" in August 1955 when he "unloaded a right cross to the jaw of Pitcher [sic] Bill Bagwell" of Port Arthur. The incident took place after Bagwell had thrown two pitches close to a Corpus Christi batter following some apparent taunting by Corpus Christi's Rene Vega following a home run.

These episodes notwithstanding, Ryan was remembered as "a good team player" and as "an excellent baseball man." Such compliments were traceable to his rookie season of '42, when an article commented on how he was "an eager and enthusiastic youngster, though a pleasantly restrained and polite one, looking much like [boxing great] Billy Conn and exuding Conn's engaging sureness in himself."

In fact, when he first came to the majors that spring

Connie Ryan had been the Braves regular second baseman prior to the arrival of Eddie Stanky.

with the New York Giants, the 5'11", 175-pound Ryan was reportedly so deferential that he referred to teammates, including Carl Hubbell, as "Mister." At one point, manager Ott took Ryan aside and told him that everyone with the team would prefer that Connie use their respective first names. With that, one newspaper reporter remarked: "Suddenly you remembered who Connie Ryan reminded you of. Another quiet, courteous gentleman from New Orleans, named Mel Ott."

Cornelius Joseph Ryan was born on February 27, 1920 in New Orleans. He was of Irish heritage and had two younger brothers; his father did administrative work for a New Orleans barge line.

Connie's interest in sports was evident from an early age, and the young man played for local American Legion teams in 1935 and 1936. Ryan also saw action on the baseball, football, basketball, and track teams at Jesuit High School in New Orleans, the same school attended by future major league All-Stars Rusty Staub and Will Clark. In addition to becoming the first person ever to receive a full baseball scholarship to Louisiana State University—where his future Braves double-play partner, shortstop Al Dark, would star a few years later. Ryan also played semipro ball in 1938 for Angier, North Carolina, and the next year was with a developmental team in Colonial Heights, Virginia.

Ryan's love of the game led him to leave LSU over the Christmas break of his sophomore year to play pro ball for the Atlanta Crackers in the Southern League. He was reportedly conflicted between a career in baseball or in the legal profession, but elected to chase grounders. While he was optioned to Savannah of the Sally League during that first season, Ryan was sent back to Atlanta in 1941 after batting .316 in 113 games for Savannah. During the '41 season with the Crackers, Ryan batted .300 in 151 games with 83 runs batted in and was chosen as Atlanta's Most Valuable Player.

During that period, player-manager Mel Ott felt that the Giants were neglecting to scout talent from his hometown of New Orleans. The team signed Lucius Caruso, a 19-year-old first baseman also from Jesuit High School, as the first New Orleanian on Ott's watch. "We've been missing a lot of good talent here, but from here out our scouts will spend a lot of time in New Orleans and we'll get more boys like Connie Ryan," Ott later said.

The Giants purchased Ryan's contract from Atlanta on August 7, 1941, and soon began preparing him to be the team's second baseman in place of Burgess Whitehead, who left the team after a subpar 1941 season. According to an unattributed February 28, 1942 article: "The kid from Atlanta reminds some of Billy Conn, others of Larry Doyle, but despite the ballyhoo, he has managed to remain Cornelius Ryan, Jr., with a great deal of dignity for a 21-year-old. The boy moved stylishly at second base yesterday, but it's no time to put the plug in for him. If he's overly praised now, it might have to be said next week that Ryan doesn't look like Ryan did last week. In brief, he's just a rookie."

In spite of the high expectations, Ryan played in only 11 games in 1942, batting .185 with two RBIs. He also committed an alarming four errors. "The boy is very nervous, all tightened up," said a newspaper account of May 20, 1942. "That is plain, and there is no need to go beyond that into the play by play of the rookie's misadventures. Summing up, Ryan has not hit, has not come through on double-plays and has not fielded with assurance."

While noting that Ryan had performed all of these tasks well in the minor leagues, sportswriter Joe King went on to say: "There's a lot of ball-player in him—it will come out again in awhile, but the Giants need it now." The popular perception was that Ryan suffered a nervous breakdown, similar to what Mickey Witek—"the breakdown boy of 1940"—had endured two years prior.

One bright spot in a mostly forgettable abbreviated rookie season was the time Ryan almost turned an unassisted triple play against Pittsburgh. On May 12 at the Polo Grounds, the Pirates' Frank Gustine hit a line drive to Connie in the seventh inning. Rather than touching second base to force Johnny Lanning and then tagging out Pete Coscarart, who were both running on a 3-and-2 pitch, Ryan instead threw to shortstop Billy Jurges, who forced Lanning and tagged Coscarart for the triple play. "Just a few steps," said one report, "and Ryan could have retired the side [himself]."

His part in one of baseball's rarest feats notwithstanding, New York soon optioned Ryan to Jersey City of the International League for more seasoning. And after hitting a disappointing .241 in 112 games there, the highly touted second baseman never made it back to the Giants. On April 27, 1943, Ryan was traded to the Braves along with catcher Hugh Poland in exchange for six-time All-Star catcher Ernie Lombardi. There was some controversy surrounding the deal, with rumors that Boston may have received a secret $30,000 as part of the trade. Yet it was well known that Lombardi was not content with the Braves, and, as one reporter put it, Boston had an incentive to deal "a bachelor who might be called to war any day."

It was a great move for Ryan, as he was the regular second baseman in 1943 for the sixth-place Braves club

A keen student of the game, Connie Ryan would later serve as a major league coach and managed the Atlanta-version of the Braves on an interim basis in 1975.

managed by Casey Stengel and Bob Coleman (who took over during Casey's convalescence from a broken leg). In 132 games during his first full major league season, Ryan batted only .212. He did, however, hit a two-run pinch-hit homer against his former Giants teammates: "With the count two balls and one strike he got hold of an outside pitch and away went the ballgame."

Apparently over his nervousness, Ryan's hitting and fielding the next year improved dramatically, and he was chosen for the first and only time to the National League All-Star team. Ryan played all nine innings of the 1944 All-Star Game at second base, got two hits, and had the lone stolen base of the contest during a 7–1 National League victory at Pittsburgh's Forbes Field.

Exactly two weeks later, and less than two months after the Allied invasion at Normandy, Ryan enlisted in the Navy on July 25, 1944. At the time, his batting average of .295 was second on the team, he was tied for the N.L. lead in stolen bases with 13, and his fielding average was on pace to lead the circuit as well. Duty called, however, and so like many ballplayers during World War II, he traded one uniform for the other while at the top of his game. He wound up playing in just 88 contests that year before heading off for service, yet he made enough of an impression that he still received votes for NL Most Valuable Player that October.

Ryan served overseas during the remainder of the war, and was discharged in January 1946 having missed one-and-a-half seasons. Returning to the Braves, he stepped right back in as the team's starting second baseman for the 1946 and 1947 seasons. The club was much improved; under new manager Billy Southworth, it rose to fourth place in '46 and third in '47. Ryan was a steady contributor on defense and at bat showed surprising pop—finishing among team leaders in doubles both years and placing third in RBIs with 69 in the latter campaign. However, when the team traded for Dodgers second baseman and sparkplug Eddie Stanky shortly before the 1948 season began, Connie became a reserve.

Ryan did play briefly in the 1948 World Series, appearing in two games and striking out in his only at-bat. Still, he was appreciated largely for his defense rather than for his hitting. As baseball historian Arthur Schott noted, "He didn't hit for a big average (.248 in his career), so he had to be an outstanding fielder to stay in the majors as long as he did."

Connie is well remembered for an incident that took place on September 29, 1949 at Braves Field, during his last year with Boston. During a meaningless end-of-season Ladies Day game, as rain fell and the skies darkened at Braves Field, Ryan donned a raincoat while waiting to bat in the on-deck circle. Home plate umpire George Barr saw Ryan's coat and threw him out of the contest for his not-so-subtle suggestion that the game be called.

As Ryan later recounted: "They wouldn't listen to us when we hollered at them from the bench that it was raining too hard to play. They wouldn't even take a hint when we built a little fire out of programs and newspapers in front of the dugout. I thought I'd try to convince them some other way, that's all."

Minus his raincoat, Ryan remained with the Braves until May 10, 1950, when he was traded to the Cincinnati Reds for catcher Walker Cooper—an excellent veteran player whom Boston manager Billy Southworth had previously managed in St. Louis. Ryan started at second base for the Reds through 1951, and proved pretty crafty himself. During a game against the Giants on May 6 of '51, for instance, he infuriated New York manager Leo Durocher when he successfully pulled the "hidden-ball trick" in the 10th inning of a 4–3 contest at the Polo Grounds. New York's Whitey Lockman was tagged out at second base, though he would later argue that his foot was still on the base. "It fooled all the Giants, most of the Reds, the entire press box…perhaps every one of the 27,766 fans, and even an umpire who was a few feet from the scene," said a newspaper report.

The Reds were a dismal sixth-place team, and despite his sharp baseball mind and solid day-to-day contributions—he led the 1951 team with a career-high 16 home runs—Ryan was one of the casualties as the organization sought to rebuild. On December 10 of '51, Cincinnati traded Connie along with Smoky Burgess and Howie Fox to the Philadelphia Phillies for Andy Seminick, Eddie Pellagrini, Dick Sisler, and Niles Jordan. Phillies manager Eddie Sawyer was thrilled to acquire Ryan, saying: "I think Ryan at second with Granny Hamner at short will make a dandy keystone combination."

It did, for a while. Connie hit another 12 homers in 1952, scored a career-high 81 runs, and he and Hamner both turned nearly 100 double plays. A highlight of Ryan's time with Philadelphia was getting six hits in six at-bats during a game at Pittsburgh on April 16, 1953, making him the first Phillies player—and just the 31st in major league history—to accomplish what at the time was a big league record. This was the springboard for another strong year at the plate, as Ryan hit .296 through the first half of the year. But Philadelphia still left him unprotected later that summer, and when released on August 25 he was picked up on waivers by the Chicago White Sox. He played in only 17 games for Chicago (hitting just .222), then was traded back to the Reds with Rocky Krsnich and Saul Rogovin for Willard Marshall on December 10 of '53. His only appearance in his second

stint with Cincinnati, on April 19, 1954, turned out to also be his last game in the big leagues. He finished his 12-year career in the majors with 988 hits in 1,184 games, 56 home runs, 381 RBIs, and a .248 batting average.

Not surprisingly, Ryan's reputation as a tough, heads-up ballplayer helped him to stay in the game. He played the rest of the '54 season in the minor leagues for Louisville of the American Association, then in 1955, played and managed for Corpus Christi of the Big State League. After appearing in 45 games as player-manager for Austin of the Texas League in 1945, his professional playing days were over, but his managerial career was just beginning. Ryan's other minor league skippering stints were with Seattle of the Pacific Coast League in 1958, Oklahoma City of the American Association in 1962, and Twin Falls of the Pioneer League from 1968 through 1970. Ryan was also an interim manager twice in the major leagues: for 27 games with Atlanta in 1975 and for six games with Texas in 1977. Both times the full-time position went to other men, perhaps because Connie's no-nonsense approach worried management. "I am not concerned with anybody's feelings," he was quoted as saying, while the Braves' interim manager. "I would pinch-hit for my mother to win a ball game."

He never achieved fame as a manager at the big-league level, but Ryan did have some other memorable moments while in the non-playing ranks. He was a coach on the 1957 Milwaukee Braves team that won the World Series over the Yankees, and discovered future All-Star Vida Blue while scouting for the Athletics in the 1960s. And perhaps most excitedly, while serving as third-base coach of the Atlanta Braves in 1974, Ryan was the first man to shake Hank Aaron's hand as Aaron rounded third base after setting the new all-time home run record of 715. As a tribute to all his achievements, Ryan was also chosen for both the New Orleans and the Louisiana Sports Halls of Fame.

After his coaching and scouting days were through, Ryan kept busy in church and civic groups during his retirement. He was a member of the executive board of the Ancient Order of Hibernians, the New Orleans Diamond Club, and the Major League Players Association, According to the *New Orleans Times Picayune*, he was also active in the St. Mary Magdalen and St. Clement of Rome Catholic churches.

When Ryan's name comes up today, it's usually by a fan recounting for the umpteenth time the tale of Connie and his raincoat. It's a fun image, but it doesn't do full credit to the man. Ryan could joke with the best of them, but most of the time he was all business whether in the field, at the plate, or making decisions in the dugout. "Connie was a great guy," said Mel Parnell, who pitched for the Red Sox while Ryan was in Boston with the Braves. "He was serious when it came to baseball, and he was a great student of the game."

Connie Ryan died on January 3, 1996 at East Jefferson General Hospital in Metairie, Louisiana following a heart attack. He was 75 years old, and was survived by his wife, Lorraine Chalona Streckfus Ryan, four children, six grandchildren, and a great-grandchild. He is buried in Metairie Cemetery.

Sources

Biographical and statistical information from websites baseball-reference.com, baseball-almanac.com, and baseballlibrary.com.

Clippings from Connie Ryan's player file at the Hall of Fame:

Cincinnati Reds biography, 1951.

"Connie Ryan Discharge Today," January 17, 1946.

"Connie Ryan, Veteran of Baseball Battles, Could Rub Some of His Fight on Braves," December 9, 1956.

"Cooper for Connie Ryan," May 19, 1950.

Daley, Arthur. "Triple Play by Ryan and Jurges Marks 7–3 Success for Ott Team," May 13, 1952.

Daniel, Dan. "Daniel's Dope," April 29, 1943.

"He Reminded You of Someone," Giant Jottings, March 18, 1942.

King, Joe. "Ryan Touted Early as Rookie of '42: But New Giant Retains His Poise," February 26, 1942.

King, Joe. "Nerves Still Wrecking Ryan's Play: Another Rest May Solve His Problem," May 26, 1942.

King, Joe. "Ryan Relieved of Keystone Job on Giants: Witek Takes Over for Jittery Recruit," March 1942.

King, Joe. "Unassisted Triple Play—Almost: Few Steps Would Have Turned the Trick," May 13, 1942.

King, Joe. "Rookie Ryan Key Player of Giant Infield: Ott Banks on Youth To Fill Keystone Spot," February 24, 1982.

King, Joe. "Nerves Still Wrecking Ryan's Play: Another Rest May Solve His Problem," May 20, 1942.

Lewis, Ted. Obituary. "Player, coach, scout Ryan dies at age 75." *New Orleans Times Picayune*, January 4, 1996.

Minor league data, apparently from the 1978 Texas Rangers media guide, provided by the Hall of Fame.

Minshew, Wayne. "Trade Winds Send Players Into Motion," September 20, 1975.

Mitchell, Jerry. "Ott Is Sold on Connie Ryan: Rookie Second Baseman's Fielding Impresses," 1942.

"New Orleans Boys Get Break from Mel Ott," February 4, 1942.

Obituary, "Connie Ryan 75," *Sports Collector's Digest*, February 2, 1996.

Obituary. "Infielder 'Connie' Ryan II, N.O. baseball legend, dies," *New Orleans Times Picayune*, January 4, 1996.

"Ott at Last Gets Slugger He Long Has Been Seeking: Mel's Infield Reserve Strength Reduced to Bartell by Trade," April 28, 1943.

"Redleg in a Rhubarb: One of the reasons Connie Ryan has become Cincy's ace second sacker is because he once went to bat in a raincoat when he was with Boston."

Roeder, Bill. "Giants Not Amused by Connie's Con Game," May 7, 1951.

"Ryan of Braves Goes Into Navy," July 25, 1944.

"Ryan Is 31st To Get 6 Hits"

"Ryan First Phil To Get '6 For 6,'" April 17, 1953.

"Sawyer High on Ryan's Hustle," *Boston Daily Record*, March 17, 1952.

Smith, Ken. "Ryan Homer in 9th Shames Giants, 3–2," *Daily Mirror*, April 29, 1943.

Tagliabue, Emil. "Ryan's Right Cross Starts Corpus Christi Mass Fight: Park Police Stop Melee Between Teams," August 17, 1955.

United Press, "Braves Sign Connie Ryan To Coach at 3d," October 6, 1956.

"Walker Cooper for Braves' Ryan," May 11, 1950.

JOHNNY SAIN *by Jan Finkel*

G	ERA	W	L	SV	GS	GF	CG	SHO	IP	H	R	ER	BB	SO	HR	HBP	WP	BFP
42	2.60	24	15	1	39	3	28	4	314²/₃	297	105	91	83	137	19	5	2	1313

G	AB	R	H	2B	3B	HR	RBI	BB	SO	BA	OBP	SLG	SB	HBP
43	115	11	25	3	1	0	16	1	3	.217	.224	.261	0	0

First we'll use Spahn, then we'll use Sain,
Then an off day, followed by rain.
Back will come Spahn, followed by Sain
And followed, we hope, by two days of rain.
—Gerry Hern, *Boston Post*, September 14, 1948

Nobody would mistake *Post* sportswriter Hern's famous lines for "Casey at the Bat" or even poetry except in the broadest sense, but it sums up most of what many people today know about Johnny Sain. That's unfortunate, because Sain was so much more than someone whose name, fortuitously for Hern, rhymes with "rain"—trainer of fighter pilots, ace pitcher, one of the great pitching coaches, and holder of a little-known but remarkable record attesting to his genius as a contact hitter.

He was born John Franklin Sain in the tiny town of Havana, Arkansas (population 392 in the 2000 Census), on September 25, 1917, to Eva and John Sain. An automobile mechanic and a good left-handed pitcher at the amateur level, the elder Sain would profoundly affect his son's career, encouraging him early on and teaching him to throw a curve while varying his motions and speed.

No one showed much interest in young Johnny as a pitching prospect, and his journey to the majors became a six-year odyssey. According to author Al Hirshberg, Bill Dickey declined the elder Sain's request to talk to his son after watching him pitch in a high-school game because he didn't want to tell the boy he didn't have it. To make matters worse, Bill Terry tried soon after to talk him out of pursuing a baseball career.

After graduating from Havana High School in 1935, the 17-year-old Sain reportedly signed a Class D contract from the Red Sox for $5—and barely survived.

As the story goes, Sain approached Memphis native James "Doc" Prothro, who was managing the Red Sox farm club in Little Rock, part of the Class A1 Southern Association. Prothro sent him to Osceola in the Class D Northeast Arkansas League for the 1936 season, and the 18-year-old gave up a home run to the first batter he ever faced in a pro game, but still managed to win the contest and go 5–3 with a 2.72 ERA. The Red Sox dropped whatever association they had with Osceola in 1937, and the team began an affiliation with the St. Louis Browns. The Indians slipped from second place to fifth (out of six) in 1937, and Sain's 5–8, 4.13 slate reflected the decline. Osceola left the league after the season, and Sain landed with the unaffiliated Newport Cardinals of the same league.

Coming into his own in 1938, Sain finished up 16–4 with a 2.72 ERA for Newport, good for a spot on the league's all-star team. Foreshadowing another of his talents, he also batted .257 with a home run and 14 RBIs. Remaining at Newport, now affiliated with the Detroit Tigers, Johnny had another strong year in 1939, his 18–10 mark accompanied by a 3.27 ERA; in addition, he and teammate Ed Hughes each set the league record for complete games with 27. Sain, who worked hard to become a good hitter and occasionally played in the outfield when not pitching, topped off his fine season with a .315 average, a pair of homers, and 20 RBIs.

Two good years with Newport weren't enough to get Sain to the majors, but he was unwittingly approaching the turning point in his career. It started innocuously on December 9, 1939, when Detroit traded second baseman Benny McCoy to the Philadelphia Athletics for outfielder Wally Moses. Citing corruption and cover-ups in the Tiger organization, Commissioner Kenesaw Mountain Landis nullified the trade and on January 14, 1940, granted free agency to 91 Detroit players and farmhands.[1] Sain was among the fortunate new free agents and one of 23 released players who made it to the majors, although in his case it would take two more years.

Accordingly, 1940 found Sain with the Nashville Vols, a Dodgers affiliate in the Southern Association. His 8–4 mark and 4.45 ERA pale beside the Vols' 101–47 record, good for a .682 winning percentage. The 1941 Vols, no

Johnny Sain made his big league debut with the Braves in 1942 after toiling in the minors for six seasons.

longer a Brooklyn farm club, fell off to 83–70, in second place, and Sain fell much further to 6–12 and a 4.60 ERA. At this point Johnny didn't seem to be going anywhere, but the woeful Boston Braves, possibly on the advice of Pat Monahan or Prothro, and hungry for pitchers, purchased his contract from Nashville and signed him to a major-league contract in March 1942.

Sain made his debut with the Braves on April 24, 1942—in relief—giving up a walk and a wild pitch in 1⅔ innings of a 3–1 loss to the Giants at the Polo Grounds. He picked up his first win on April 29 at Wrigley Field in relief of Al Javery. All told, he went 4–7 with a 3.90 ERA, mostly in relief, for Casey Stengel's last Boston team, a dismal unit that could manage only a 59–89 record and a seventh-place finish.

Even with World War II on, Sain was able to complete the season. Upon receiving his draft notice, he had enlisted for aviation training in the Navy on August 21. However, he didn't have to report until November 15, whereupon he was sent to Amherst College along with fellow big-league inductees Ted Williams, Johnny Pesky, Joe Coleman, and Buddy Gremp. Having completed preliminary ground training by May 1943, Sain was transferred to Chapel Hill, North Carolina, for preflight instruction. After a few months there, he moved on to Corpus Christi Naval Air Training and graduated as an ensign in August 1944. He wound up teaching flying at Corpus Christi through the end of the war, receiving his discharge on November 25, 1945.

The experience proved seminal for the young man, who noted, "I think learning to fly an airplane helped me as much as anything. I was twenty-five years old. Learning to fly helped me to concentrate and restimulated my ability to learn."[2] Shortly before his discharge, on October 1, Sain married Dallas native Doris May McBride. The couple would have four children—John Jr., Sharyl, Rhonda, and Randy.

Service in the war benefited Sain in a variety of ways. For one thing, his arm got some rest. He threw whenever he could, though, and pitched on several teams against stiff competition that often included other major leaguers. He went 12–4 with the North Carolina Pre-Flight team, appropriately named the Cloudbusters, in 1943, but it was a war relief game in Yankee Stadium that July 28 which stood out. The Cloudbusters were facing a team made up of reserves from the Yankees and Indians, whose regulars played a charity, regular-season doubleheader that same day. In the sixth inning, "Yank-Lands" third-base coach Babe Ruth left the box to pinch-hit. Seeing the game as a sort of audition in front of a number of big-league officials, Sain wanted to retire the 48-year-old Ruth, but catcher Al Sabo came out and told him not to throw Ruth any curves and risk embarrassing him. As Sain later said, "Taking away my curveball was like cutting off two of my fingers, but it was Babe Ruth in Yankee Stadium. Then, it became obvious that the home plate umpire wasn't going to call any strikes on him. So I threw five medium fastballs, almost batting practice pitches. Ruth took one, then hit a long foul ball and then walked on the last three pitches." It was the Babe's last at bat in an organized game.

His 24 victories in 1948 marked the third consecutive 20-victory season for Big John.

Another benefit of the war years is that a maturing Sain came to realize and accept that although he was large for his era at 6-feet-2 and 180–200 pounds, he didn't have high-octane velocity. Accordingly, he'd have to rely on mechanics, finesse, and guile, letting batters hit the ball and letting his fielders do their jobs. Moreover, he changed his delivery. Up to and including 1942, he constantly varied his arm action, even occasionally throwing from a crossfire motion. As Sain saw it, there were two problems with this approach: He risked hurting his arm, and it wasn't effective (63 walks in 97 innings with Boston in 1942 were ample proof). After the war, he kept his windmill windup (he was one of the last pitchers to do so) and threw almost exclusively overhand, dropping down to sidearm on occasion if he was ahead of the hitter.

Finally, there was the curveball his father had taught Sain how to throw, on the fly or in the heat of battle. Johnny had a good curve before the war, to be sure, but the knowledge of aerodynamics he'd absorbed as a pilot helped him turn his best pitch into so effective a weapon that he earned the nickname the Man of a Thousand Curves.

Showing no signs of rustiness after a three-year layoff, Sain became a star pitcher and Boston's staff ace in 1946. He turned in a 20–14 slate, a career-best 2.21 ERA, and a league-leading 24 complete games for the Braves, who took a big leap to 81–72 and fourth place under new manager Billy Southworth. Johnny also had the honor on May 11 of pitching the first night game in Boston big-league annals. Facing the Giants in a special "sateen" uniform designed to stand out under the lights, he lost to the Giants, 5–1, in front of 35,945 fans at Braves Field. The pitching highlight of Sain's year, however, came on July 12 at Cincinnati. In the first inning, Grady Hatton hit a pop fly that dropped among three Braves behind third base for a double. No other Red reached base as Johnny beat Ewell Blackwell, 1–0.

Life was improving for the Braves. Tommy Holmes was an effective contact hitter. Bob Elliott, a hustling, hard-hitting team player, was acquired from the Pirates over the winter and won the Most Valuable Player Award in 1947. And there was a decorated war hero, a southpaw who would be the perfect complement to Johnny Sain and a number of other pitchers over a long career—Warren Spahn.

Spahn and Sain became a factor in '47. Spahn had his first great year, going 21–10 with a 2.33 ERA, and Sain was close behind, turning in a 21–12 mark and 3.52 ERA (the relatively high ERA mollified by an outstanding .346 average and only one strikeout in 107 at-bats). At 86–68, the Braves moved up another notch to third place. Sain even became a part of history on Opening Day, April 15, becoming the first major-league pitcher to face Jackie Robinson. Robinson went hitless in three trips to the plate, but the Dodgers still won, 5–3, at Ebbets Field.

Sain's reward for his fine early-season work was pitching in the All-Star Game at Wrigley Field. Replacing the Cardinals' Harry Brecheen in the seventh inning of a 1–1 contest, he contributed to his own undoing. He got George McQuinn to ground out. Bobby Doerr followed with a single, then stole second. Sain had Doerr picked off second but fired the ball into center field, sending Doerr to third. He struck out Buddy Rosar, but Stan Spence, batting for Spec Shea, singled, scoring Doerr with the go-ahead run. The American League held on for the 2–1 win, and Sain absorbed the loss. Nevertheless, it proved a good year, leaving the Braves and their fans reason to be optimistic.

The 1948 season *almost* brought baseball Nirvana to Boston and New England. The Red Sox finished 96–58, two games ahead of the hated Yankees. The bad news was that the Indians under the leadership of Lou Boudreau were also 96–58. The first playoff in American League history—a one-game affair—saw the Sox go down, 8–3, in Fenway Park as Boudreau put on a one-man show with two homers and four hits. However, the Braves, Boston's "other team" and a perennial poor cousin to the aristocratic Red Sox, took the National League flag with a 91–62 mark that would have been good only for fourth place in the American League.

The close pennant race gave rise to Gerry Hern's often quoted (and misquoted) lines about "Spahn and Sain." In a way Hern took advantage of a little poetic license. He got the Sain part right, but at 15–12 with a 3.71 ERA Spahn actually had one of the least effective seasons of his brilliant career, a season more typical of a third or fourth starter than an ace. Vern Bickford (11–5, 3.27) and Bill Voiselle (13–13, 3.63) were a touch more effective.

As for Sain, he was in a class by himself, going 24–15 with a 2.60 ERA. He led the league in wins (24), games started (39), complete games (28), and innings pitched (314⅔). Pitching the Braves into first place on June 15, he beat the Cubs, 6–3. It was a historic moment, as the game at Braves Field was the first to be televised in the Boston area. Appearing in the All-Star Game on July 13, he had three strikeouts (Vern Stephens, Bobby Doerr, and Hoot Evers, all in the fifth) over 1⅔ hitless innings. The year also included an extraordinary streak of personal endurance. From August 30 to September 29, Sain started and completed nine games, winning seven of them. Backed by Sain's efforts, and equally hot hurling from Spahn, the Braves took 20 of their final 26 games to coast to the National League pennant by 6½ games over St. Louis. *The Sporting News* rewarded Sain by naming him National League Pitcher of the Year, and he was runner-up to Stan Musial in voting for the NL Most Valuable Player Award.

Sain was the beneficiary of the controversial Masi pick-off play call in Game 1 of the '48 World Series. He outdueled the Indians Bob Feller in a 1–0 masterpiece.

The year wasn't all roses. During the season the Braves signed 18-year-old southpaw Johnny Antonelli for a sum reported to be at least $50,000. As a "bonus baby," Antonelli couldn't be sent to the minors for two years; but since he almost never pitched, he was taking a place on the roster that most players believed belonged to a proven veteran while pocketing more money than most could make in several seasons. Not surprisingly, the presence of Antonelli and other bonus babies made for tension in major-league clubhouses. All of the Braves were annoyed, none more so than Sain, who took his frustrations straight to owner Lou Perini in the front office. Mounting what he called the "Golden Staircase" that led to Perini's door, Sain told the boss that as a proven pitcher he deserved better treatment than an untried teenager. Perini listened, and before the All-Star Game the Braves gave Johnny a new contract for the remainder of the season—and 1949 as well.

The World Series opened in Boston on October 6, with Sain drawing the nod against the Indians' Bob Feller. It was all a Series contest should be, as both pitchers were at the top of their craft. With the game scoreless in the bottom of the eighth, Bill Salkeld led off with a walk. Phil Masi went in to pinch-run for him, and Mike McCormick sacrificed Masi to second. Feller then intentionally walked Eddie Stanky, with utility infielder Sibby Sisti going in to pinch-run for him. With Sain at bat, Feller turned and fired to shortstop Lou Boudreau in an attempt to pick Masi off second. As the story goes, everyone in Braves Field thought Masi was out—everyone, that is, except second-base umpire Bill Stewart, who had the majority vote and called him safe. Sain lined out, but Tommy Holmes singled past third to score Masi from second and put Boston up 1–0. Sain shut down the Indians in the ninth, and Boston won. Sain had given up four hits on 95 pitches, Feller, two hits on 85 pitches in a game of exemplary efficiency.

After Cleveland won the next two contests, Johnny came back to face Steve Gromek in Game Four at Cleveland and pitched superbly in a 2–1 loss. The Braves staved off elimination in Game Five, but the Indians took Game Six back at Boston, and the Series. Sain was magnificent in defeat—two complete games, a shutout, a heartbreaking loss, nine strikeouts against no walks, nine hits allowed, and a 1.06 ERA.

All told, Sain was arguably the top pitcher in the National League from 1946 to 1948 with a 65–41 record and 2.77 ERA. Indeed, he fit in nicely with his American League counterparts Bob Feller (65–41, 2.75) and Hal Newhouser (64–38, 2.59). Johnny's decline, however, was swift and sudden. He was up and down—mostly down—from 1949 to 1951, going a combined 37–44 with an ugly 4.31 ERA. The kindest thing one can call the 1949 season is a disaster. Spent from his efforts of the year before and a sore shoulder that Sain publicly called the result of his experimenting with a screwball during the spring, he suffered through 10 wins and a career-worst 17 losses with a horrendous 4.81 ERA. He had the dubious honor of leading the league in runs (150) and earned runs (130) allowed. For the only time in his career he walked more than he struck out (75 to 73), and he also surrendered more than a hit per inning (285 in 243 innings pitched), starting a pattern that would continue throughout the remainder of his career. True, he completed 16 of his 36 starts, but he was taking a beating most of the time. In short, there is no way to put the season in a positive light. The defending champs of the National League fell to fourth place with a 75–79 mark.

It wasn't just Sain's ailing shoulder at fault; almost everything went wrong for the Braves in 1949. Billy Southworth, whose demands were grudgingly accepted when his teams were winning, reportedly became intolerable during spring training. Claiming credit the players considered theirs and breaking rules that he set, Southworth put the defending National League champs through two-a-day sessions that totaled six hours and instituted a midnight curfew, complete with room checks on everybody by clubhouse attendant and watchdog Shorty Young. An early-to-bed, early-to-rise type, Sain usually retired by 9:30. Young checked on Sain just once, waking him out of a sound sleep. Furious, Sain said that if it ever happened again, he'd send the offender out the window. A rumor got out that Southworth had checked up on his star pitcher, that Sain had threatened to throw *him* out the window, and that Sain and Southworth weren't speaking. For his part, Sain said he never socialized with his managers.

Although Sain rebounded in 1950 with his fourth 20-win season (20–13), the won-lost record is deceptive. Even in a year replete with heavy hitters, his 3.94 ERA was well off the league pace. While he completed 25 of his 37 starts, he gave up 294 hits in 278⅓ innings. Particularly ominous was Sain's career-high and league-leading 34 home runs surrendered.[3] He was lucky to win more than he lost, largely because he was pitching for a team that went 83–71 in a nice recovery from the debacle of 1949.

All that kept Sain's 1951 season from being a repeat of 1949 was fewer innings pitched, because the figures were pretty proportional (195 hits in 160 innings and a 4.22 ERA). It added up to a 5–13 slate when struggling Boston sold him to the Yankees for $50,000 and a young pitcher who would pay long-term dividends to the Braves and haunt the Yankees a few years hence—Lew Burdette. Sain appeared in seven games for New York, starting four and completing one, while posting a 2–1 mark. The Yanks, won the pennant, and Johnny was brought in to relieve starter Vic Raschi in the seventh inning of Game Six of the World Series with two on and nobody out. He retired the Giants without allowing an inherited runner to score, and worked out of a bases-loaded jam in the eighth. The Giants loaded the bases on three singles in the ninth before Bob Kuzava came in, surrendering two runs but saving the game, 4–3, and the Series for the Yankees. It was hardly an auspicious start for Sain with a new team, especially one that had come to consider World Series titles their birthright (this was their third straight).

Making matters worse, the shoulder injury that had ruined Johnny's 1949 season had never completely gone away. With nothing to lose he underwent a new radiation therapy from a doctor in Dallas, and was so pleased that he recommended it to others. Teammate Eddie Lopat

tried it and was happy. Over the years Whitey Ford had it done five times, and Mel Stottlemyre went Ford one better.

One of many keys to the Yankees' phenomenal success from the late 1940s to the mid-1960s was a genius for resurrecting the careers of players thought to be finished. Johnny Hopp, Johnny Mize, and Enos Slaughter had several productive years added to their careers, and Johnny Sain was a chief beneficiary among the pitching fraternity. How the Yankees did it was brilliant in its simplicity, and one wonders why nobody else figured it out. They made him a spot starter and reliever so that a bit fewer than half of his appearances were starts—16 of 35 in 1952 and 19 of 40 in 1953. He completed half of his starts, 8 in 1952 and 10 in 1953, and relieved superbly the rest of the time. In 1954, his last full year in pinstripes, all 45 of his appearances were in relief, and he saved a league-leading 22 games to become just the second pitcher (after Ellis Kinder of the Red Sox turned the trick the year before) to win 20 games in one season and save 20 in another. Wilbur Wood, Dennis Eckersley, John Smoltz, and Derek Lowe are the only other pitchers to accomplish the feat.

Adapting to his new role, Sain began to pay off in 1952 as both starter and reliever. On May 20, he scattered six hits to beat the White Sox, 3–1. He rescued the Yankees twice at Fenway Park on September 24, coming on in the 10th to preserve a 3–2 win in the opener of a doubleheader, then saving an 8–6 win in the nightcap. Two days later he relieved in the Yankees' 11-inning pennant-clinching 5–2 win in Philadelphia. For the year he was 11–6 with a decent 3.46 ERA and seven saves. He pitched capably but didn't fare well in the World Series against the Dodgers. Taking over in the sixth inning of Game Five for starter Ewell Blackwell with the Yankees leading, 5–4, he gave up the tying run in the seventh and the winning run in the 11th to take the 6–5 loss. The Yankees didn't use him again in their hard-fought seven-game win over their subway rivals.

Now a vital part of the Yankee machine, Sain was outstanding in 1953. Again dividing his duties between starting and relieving, he posted a 14–7 mark with nine saves and a 3.00 ERA while earning a spot on the All-Star team. Once again, the Yankees and Dodgers squared off in the World Series. Relieving starter Allie Reynolds in Game One with one out in the sixth and the Dodgers threatening, Sain stopped the damage, pitched the final 3⅔ innings, and picked up the 9–5 win, even contributing a double and a run scored. He was not as effective in his other appearance, in Game Four, but the Yankees nonetheless captured their fifth straight world championship.

By 1954, Sain was a full-time reliever, going 6–6 with a 3.16 ERA and the aforementioned 22 saves. The Yankees had their best season under Casey Stengel with a

103–51 record, but it was only second-best to the Indians' 111–43 mark, the American League record at the time. Johnny wouldn't get a chance to pitch in his fifth World Series.

Shortly into the 1955 season, after three appearances and a 6.75 ERA, the Yankees determined that Sain was finished. On May 11, displaying neither gratitude nor class, New York pulled off one of the most humiliating trades in the history of the game, sending Sain and future Hall of Famer Enos Slaughter (he was hitting .111 at the time) to the Kansas City Athletics for journeyman pitcher Sonny Dixon and cash. Sain appeared in 25 games for Kansas City, winning two and losing five while posting no saves and an ERA of 5.44. He pitched his final game on July 15 and was released eight days later.

For someone who toiled in the minors for six years, lost three more to the war, and got started at an age when most players are entering their peak, Sain had a fine career: 139 wins against 116 losses,[4] a solid 3.49 ERA; an award as *The Sporting News* Pitcher of the Year; four 20-win seasons; three trips to the All-Star Game; four World Series; the league lead in wins once; the league lead in saves once; and league leads in other categories.

That's just the pitching side of the Sain ledger. An outstanding contact hitter, Johnny had always helped himself with the bat. He sported a .245 career average, led the league with 16 sacrifice hits in 1948 (the first pitcher to lead his league in an offensive category), led his league's pitchers in runs batted in five times, and struck out a mere 20 times in 774 lifetime at-bats. Those 20 strikeouts are extraordinary, the fewest for all hitters with between 500 and 800 at-bats from 1910 (when the National League began keeping strikeout records) and 1913 (when the American League followed suit) to the present.

While his playing days were over, Sain wasn't really through. He returned to Arkansas, to Walnut Ridge, raising his children there. He'd had a prospering Chevrolet dealership in the town since 1952, but at heart he was a baseball man and was happy to get back into the game in 1959 as pitching coach for the Kansas City Athletics. Working with a veteran staff on a team that could do no better than 66–88, he got adequate seasons out of Ned

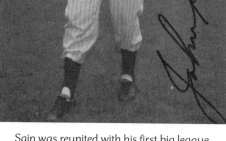

Sain was reunited with his first big league manager, Casey Stengel, when the Braves traded him to the Yankees in late August, 1951.

Garver, Bud Daley, Ray Herbert, and Johnny Kucks. Sain resigned after the season to concentrate on business at home.

Catching on in the same capacity with the Yankees when Ralph Houk replaced the fired Casey Stengel for the 1961 season, Sain showed what he could do with good material. Persuading Houk to go with a four-man rotation, he transformed Whitey Ford from a perennially very good pitcher into a great one. Ford, who credits Sain with rejuvenating his career, posted a 25–4 mark and a 3.21 ERA in 1961, good enough to garner his only Cy Young Award; he followed that up with 17 wins in 1962 and 24 in 1963. Ralph Terry found his groove in 1962, leading the league with 23 wins. Jim Bouton, who calls Sain "the greatest pitching coach who ever lived," had a career year in 1963 with a 21–7 slate and a 2.53 ERA.

Two contradictory versions exist as to why Sain and the Yankees parted company. Sain said in 1993 that he had heard that Houk was going to move into the Yankee front office, with Yogi Berra taking over as manager. Since Sain doubted that Berra would be effective managing recent teammates, he claimed he resigned. His misgivings were well-founded in that Berra was fired after one season despite leading the Yankees into the World Series.

The alternate version is that Houk showed his appreciation for Sain's helping him to three World Series appearances and two world championships in three years by firing him after the 1963 season. The move mystified many people, but Bouton offered a possible explanation: "What general—Houk started thinking of himself as a general—wants a lieutenant on his staff who's smarter than he is?"

After sitting out for a year, Sain joined the Minnesota Twins in 1965. Helping this club to its first pennant, he got Jim "Mudcat" Grant to achieve a 21–7 mark, good enough to lead the league in wins. Under Sain's tutelage, lefty Jim Kaat went 25–13 with a 2.75 ERA in 1966 to lead the American League in wins and help the Twins finish second. Twins manager Sam Mele was so happy with Sain's contribution that he fired him.

Sain moved from Minnesota to Detroit in 1967. Working with manager Mayo Smith's staff that year, he turned Earl Wilson into a 20-game winner for the first and only time in his career. In 1968, Sain crafted his masterpiece—Denny McLain, whose 31 wins were the most since Lefty Grove achieved the same total in 1931, and haven't been challenged since. With just six losses and a 1.96 ERA, McLain took home the Cy Young and Most Valuable Player awards. With lefty Mickey Lolich picking up three wins in the World Series, the Tigers beat the Cardinals and Bob Gibson. Sain kept McLain sufficiently focused and mature in 1969 to go 24–9 and share the Cy Young Award with southpaw Mike Cuellar of the Orioles.

World Series victory aside, Sain and manager Mayo Smith were barely speaking. Sain's tenure with Detroit soured for good in 1969. One day Johnny took some time off to attend to some personal business. In his absence, Smith had the pitchers run, angering Sain, who asked Smith if he wanted to stick with what worked or with what hadn't worked for 25 years. Smith made his preferences clear on June 15, 1969, when he traded Sain favorite Dick Radatz to Montreal for cash. By August 10, Sain was fired.

The rest of Sain's life was taking a bad turn as well. His marriage had fallen apart, as he later explained: "My first wife went back to college and got her degree at age 50 and it changed the tone of our relationship. My life in baseball seemed more and more trivial to her. The divorce was an enormous financial strain on me. I pretty much lost almost everything I had, to the point that I had to declare bankruptcy."

Attempting to dig out from under, Sain spent the 1970 season until late September as farm pitching coach for the California Angels, becoming friends with Angels minor league manager Chuck Tanner. Next, Johnny was off to the White Sox, where he managed to stay for six years, in no small part because Tanner was manager the whole time and had the sense to let Sain go about his business. The approach produced incredible results. Wilbur Wood, who started out as a reliever, became a workhorse starter and won 20 games each year from 1971 to 1974. Wood's ERA in 1971 was a minuscule 1.91, and his work in 1972 earned him *The Sporting News* Pitcher of the Year Award. Reunited with Sain, Jim Kaat won 21 and 20 in 1974 and 1975, respectively. Stan Bahnsen, Rookie of the Year with the Yankees in 1968, reached his peak in 1972 with a 21–16 slate. Making Sain's achievement remarkable is that the White Sox weren't even a .500 club during his tenure, while the Yankees, Twins, and Tigers had all been contenders or pennant winners.

The years on the South Side of Chicago paid an even greater dividend than all those 20-game winners. On July 3, 1972, now divorced, Sain was introduced to Mary Ann Zaremba, the 35-year-old widow of a Chicago policeman, at a club in the suburbs. Johnny was smitten. Mary Ann remembers, "He called me the next day and said, 'You have to marry me.'" That seemed a little impetuous, so they compromised on a date at Comiskey Park on the Fourth. The date must have gone well, for they were married on August 24.

Sain coached Braves pitchers in 1977, but on a miserable team that went 61–101, he had only one first-rate pitcher, future Hall of Famer Phil Niekro. Stints with several clubs in Atlanta's farm system followed, and he went back to the Braves for one final fling from 1985 to 1986 where he was reunited with Chuck Tanner on a pair of second-division teams.

Most of Sain's coaching career followed a pattern: Almost immediate success, the lifelong loyalty and devotion of his pitchers that he reciprocated, inevitable conflict with management, and the search for another job. Often it seems to have been insecurity and jealousy on the manager's part, knowing that the pitchers listened to and respected Sain more than they did him. Sometimes a manager simply thought he knew more or better than Sain, and didn't want to be challenged.

On the flip side, some of the difficulty was Johnny's fault. To begin with, he encouraged pitchers to demand to be paid what they were worth, to mount the "Golden Staircase," as he had done back in 1948. Naturally, this didn't sit well with management. In the second place, he was extremely protective of his charges and wouldn't tolerate interference from anybody, including the manager. His refusal to speak ill of any of his pitchers led Detroit skipper Mayo Smith to conclude that he could never get a straight answer from Sain on a pitcher's physical condition, state of mind, or anything else. Ironically, Houk, Mele, and Smith all won a *Sporting News* Manager of the Year Award with Sain as their pitching coach, then left town not long after Sain's departure.

Always willing to stick up for his pitchers, he further endeared himself to hurlers by not making them run. Some baseball people found this strange, but Sain had two reasons for the tactic, one practical and the other philosophical or pedagogical. On the practical side he noted, "You don't run the ball up to home plate." On the philosophical or pedagogical side, Sain said, "I've always felt that a lot of pitching coaches made a living out of running pitchers so they wouldn't have to spend that same time teaching them how to pitch." On the other hand, he believed that pitchers had to keep their arms strong, so he had them throw almost every day, even after a long stint on the mound the day or night before. To keep pitchers mentally focused, he had, as an example, Wednesday's pitcher chart pitches for Tuesday's game; that way, the pitcher could observe both his teammates and the opposing pitchers and hitters. It seems of obvious benefit, and most managers and pitching coaches now have their pitchers chart the game, but Sain seems to have been the first to make it a practice.

Finally, Sain brought his own brilliant creation to the table. Noted baseball author Roger Kahn described it in *The Head Game*:

The Yankees hired Sain in 1961 as pitching coach. He showed up with a briefcase full of inspirational books and tapes and a machine he was patenting as the "Baseball Pitching Educational Device," which everyone soon called "the Baseball Spinner." Baseballs were mounted on rotating axes—one axis per ball—and you could snap one in a variety of fast-ball spins and the other in rotations for sliders and curves. The baseballs were anchored. Except for rotating, they didn't move. Using John Sain's Baseball Pitching Educational Device, you could practice spinning your delivery at home or in a taxi or in a hotel room without endangering lamps, mirrors, or companions.

What Sain achieved as a pitching coach (sixteen 20-game winners in all or part of 18 seasons) is impressive, given the diversity of talents he worked with. Some, like Whitey Ford and Denny McLain, had experienced considerable success. On the other hand, Jim Bouton, Jim Kaat, Mudcat Grant, and Stan Bahnsen had yet to show how capable they were. Then there was Wilbur Wood, undergoing the transformation from reliever to starter.

The project that best epitomizes Sain at work has to be Denny McLain. The quintessential flake, McLain had all the tools to be a great pitcher except seriousness of purpose, sense, and maturity. Sain took Denny for what he was and worked his magic indirectly. Learning that McLain was working to obtain a pilot's license, Sain helped him prepare for the required tests, and even went up in the air with him. From that basis the two moved to McLain's pitching so smoothly that he was the best pitcher in the American League in 1968 and 1969, winning 55 games, a Most Valuable Player Award, and two Cy Youngs. At 25, he already had 114 wins under his belt and seemed on path for the Hall of Fame. What McLain's career might have been had he had Sain's guidance for a few more seasons is pure speculation, but the train wreck—erratic and criminal behavior; suspensions from baseball; prison for drug dealing, racketeering, and extortion; poor health in the form of obesity and heart trouble; and who knows what else—that has been McLain's life in the almost 40 years since is indisputable. Denny needed grounding, and Sain gave it to him for a magical couple of years.

Out of baseball, the Sains settled down to a quiet life in the Chicago suburb of Downers Grove. John lectured and consulted with various teams and players, happy to talk with anybody who wanted to listen about the fine art of pitching. Mickey Lolich, a beneficiary of Sain's tutelage, could have been speaking for scores of pitchers when he described his mentor: "Johnny Sain loves pitchers. Maybe he doesn't love baseball so much, but he loves pitchers. Only he understands them."

Over the years there has been talk of enshrining coaches in the Hall of Fame. Writing of Sain in *Newsday*, Roger Kahn noted, "The Hall of Fame admits broadcasters, umpires, entrepreneurs, even newspaper writers. For goodness sake, let's enshrine a great coach." Mike Shalin, Neil Shalin, and Brent Kelley, among others, have indicated support for the cause. Former White Sox GM Roland Hemond, Jim Bouton, Jim Kaat, and others have spoken up for Sain. There have been some letter-writing campaigns. Nevertheless, the movement has never gained sufficient traction.

Cooperstown notwithstanding, the Boston Braves Historical Association saw that Sain was honored for his years in their city. Sain, Warren Spahn, and Sibby Sisti were inducted into the Boston Braves Hall of Fame on October 16, 1994. Four years later, on October 4, 1998, the Association sponsored a fiftieth anniversary celebration of the Braves' championship season. Bob Feller came to town, and the two aces revisited their pitching duel and the pickoff play that "failed."

After suffering a stroke on March 31, 2002, Sain spent his remaining years in ill health. On August 31, 2002, he became the seventh player inducted into the Braves' franchise Hall of Fame at Turner Field. Mary Ann wrote an acceptance speech for him; they couldn't attend the induction, but Hank Aaron read the speech at the ceremony in Atlanta.

Johnny Sain died November 7, 2006, in Resthaven West Nursing Home in Downers Grove. Surviving him were Mary Ann, his four children, 11 grandchildren, and two great-grandchildren. Returning to Havana, he was buried in Walker Cemetery after a ceremony attended by many of his former pitching "pupils" and other friends he had made in the game. Several teams sent gorgeous floral arrangements; in death, all the hard feelings were forgotten.

The last pitcher to face Babe Ruth and the first to face Jackie Robinson, Sain started the first night game in Boston and the first game televised in New England, and unleashed the potential of pitchers like Mudcat Grant, Jim Kaat, Earl Wilson, and Mickey Lolich—not to mention starring in a famous poem, appearing in one of the great baseball songs (Dave Frishberg's "Van Lingle Mungo"), and coaching probably the last 30-game winner. In the words of Maxwell Kates "a veritable Forrest Gump in baseball history," Johnny Sain left a rich legacy.

Notes

1. McCoy and Connie Mack made out nicely in the whole affair. Attracting bids from several clubs, McCoy signed with the Athletics for a $45,000 bonus and a two-year contract at $10,000 a year. Mack kept Moses and obtained the second baseman he wanted in the first place.
2. Thomas E. Allen, *If They Hadn't Gone: How World War II Affected Major League Baseball* (Springfield: Southwest Missouri State University, 2004), p. 136.
3. Sain, Ken Raffensberger of the Reds, and Preacher Roe of the Dodgers all gave up 34 homers in 1950. It was the

third highest number of home runs surrendered up to the time. Murry Dickson of the Cardinals gave up 39 in 1948, and Larry Jansen of the Giants was tagged 36 times in 1949. Jansen also gave up 31 homers in 1950.

4. Allen, p. 139. Allen projects a 45–33 slate with a 3.21 ERA for the three seasons Sain missed due to the war, but such projections seem to be enjoyable speculations.

Acknowledgments

Gabriel Schechter, research associate at the Hall of Fame, provided me with copies of the National and American Leagues' daily sheets detailing each of Sain's games and files of pitchers who came under Sain's tutelage.

Bob Brady sent me copies of the articles by Ed Rumill, thoroughly and thoughtfully reviewed my work, and provided me with invaluable material that I had missed.

Jim Sandoval and Rod Nelson, co-chairmen of SABR's Scouts Committee, guided me through the intricacies of scouts, contracts, and franchises—all as they applied to Sain.

Saul Wisnia edited the final version of this article. He made it better.

I'm grateful to them for their kindness, generosity, and friendship.

Sources

Allen, Thomas E. *If They Hadn't Gone: How World War II Affected Major League Baseball*. Springfield: Southwest Missouri State University, 2004.

Bailey, Jim. "Sain stood out as pitcher, excelled as coach." *The Arkansas Democrat-Gazette*. November 16, 2006.

Eig, Jonathan. *Opening Day: The Story of Jackie Robinson's First Season*. New York: Simon & Schuster, 2007.

Fagen, Herb. "Johnny Sain Did It His Way…As a Pitcher and Coach." *Baseball Digest*. December 1993.

Gilbert, Bill. *They Also Served: Baseball and the Home Front: 1941–1945*. New York: Crown Publishers, 1992.

Hirshberg, Al. *The Braves: The Pick and The Shovel*. Boston: Waverly House, 1948.

_____. "What Really Happened to the Boston Braves?" *Sport*. January 1950.

James, Bill, and Rob Neyer. *The Neyer/James Guide to Pitchers: An Historical Compendium of Pitching, Pitchers, and Pitches*. New York, London, Toronto, and Sydney: Simon & Schuster, 2004.

Johnny Sain files at the National Baseball Hall of Fame and Museum in Cooperstown, New York.

Johnson, Lloyd, and Miles Wolff, eds. *The Encyclopedia of Minor League Baseball*. 3rd ed. Durham, North Carolina: Baseball America, Inc., 2007.

Kaese, Harold. *The Boston Braves, 1871–1953*. Boston: Northeastern University Press, 2004. Reprint of 1948 original and 1954 reprint issued by Putnam.

Kahn, Roger. "A Slide Rule Can't Measure a Ballplayer." *New York Newsday*. July 29, 1994.

_____. *The Head Game: Baseball Seen from the Pitcher's Mound*. San Diego, New York, and London: Harcourt, Inc., 2001.

Kates, Maxwell. "Van Lingle Mungo." Baseball Analysts (www.baseballanalysts.com), November 13, 2006.

Kelley, Brent. *The Case For: Those Overlooked by the Baseball Hall of Fame*. Jefferson, North Carolina: McFarland, 1992.

McCann, Mike. "Mike McCann's Page of Minor League History." www.geocities.com/big_bunko/minor.html.

O'Donnell, Jim. "Mind over Matter: Ex-Major League Baseball Star and Coaching Legend Johnny Sain Never Was One To Do Things by the Book. *Chicago Tribune*. October 10, 1993. Reprint from *Chicago Tribune* archives at chicagotribune.com.

Peary, Danny, ed. *We Played the Game: 65 Players Remember Baseball's Greatest Era, 1947–1964*. New York: Hyperion, 1994.

Professional Baseball Players Database Version 6.0

Rumill, Ed. "Johnny Sain—Hero of the Hub." *Sport Pix*. February 1949.

_____. "Twenty for Sain. *Baseball Magazine*. January 1947.

Shalin, Mike, and Neil Shalin. *Out by a Step: The 100 Best Players NOT in the Baseball Hall of Fame*. London, South Bend, New York, and Oxford: Diamond Communications, 2002.

Siegel, Arthur. "Sain Is Product Of Own Planning To Be Box Star." *Sports Parade*. October 13, 1948.

Thorn, John, and John Holway. *The Pitcher: The Ultimate Compendium of Pitching Lore: Featuring Flakes and Fruitcakes, Wildmen and Control Artists, Strategies, Deliveries, Statistics, and More*. New York, London, Toronto, Sydney, and Tokyo: Prentice Hall Press, 1988.

Tourangeau, Dixie. "Spahn, Sain, and the '48 Braves." *The National Pastime*. 18 (1998), 17–20.

Vincent, David, Lyle Spatz, and David W. Smith. *The Midsummer Classic: The Complete History of Baseball's All-Star Game*. Lincoln and London: University of Nebraska Press, 2001.

Westcott, Rich. *Masters of the Diamond: Interviews with Players Who Began Their Careers More Than 50 Years Ago*. Jefferson, North Carolina: McFarland, 1994.

Wright, Craig R., and Tom House. *The Diamond Appraised*. New York and London: Fireside Books at Simon & Schuster, 1989.

www.sabr.org
www.baseballindex.org
www.baseball-reference.com
www.retrosheet.org
www.baseballlibrary.com
www.baseball-almanac.com
www.paperofrecord.com
www.proquest.com

BILL SALKELD *by Dan Mullen*

G	AB	R	H	2B	3B	HR	RBI	BB	SO	BA	OBP	SLG	SB	HBP
78	198	26	48	8	1	8	28	42	37	.242	.378	.414	1	1

In a time before Super Bowls, when the Final Four was merely an afterthought in the sporting landscape, the World Series was truly *the* sporting event that the majority of Americans looked forward to each year. The '48 series was no exception, as a nation checked in by radio, newspaper, and even on television (a new fad) to see the Cleveland Indians and underdog Boston Braves do battle. More folks than ever were also seeing the games live; after Game Four set a new attendance mark with 81,897 fans squeezing their way into Cleveland Stadium, another record crowd of 86,288 showed up the next day to see if Bob Feller and the Indians could close out their first Series win since 1920. The contest would feature three future Hall of Famers on the mound in Feller and Satchel Paige for the Indians and Warren Spahn for the Braves, and would also provide a journeyman catcher with his finest moment.

With the Indians leading 5–4, Braves receiver Bill Salkeld stepped up to face Feller in the top of the sixth inning. A confident swing of the bat later, Salkeld had tied the game with a solo home run, setting the stage for a big Braves onslaught the next inning that resulted in an 11–5 victory. Though the Indians went on to win the Series in six games, that at-bat proved the pinnacle in a career of ups and downs for the 5-foot-10, 190-pounder who was born in Pocatello, Idaho, and raised in Sacramento.

In 1934, the future was so promising that scouts from the New York Yankees had traveled across the country to evaluate the 17-year-old son of Mr. and Mrs. John Salkeld of V Street in Sacramento. So impressed were the Yankees in young Bill Salkeld as a future major-league catcher that the club was willing to offer a $500 signing bonus and allow him to finish high school just to get him signed. So unimpressed was Mrs. Salkeld with the thought of her boy being uprooted to New York at such a tender age that she refused to let her son sign with the Yankees.

Her stance was made easier when Earl McNeely, a 1924 World Series star and the owner of the hometown Sacramento Senators, stepped up to the plate and offered Bill a contract to stay and catch locally for the Pacific Coast League team. McNeely, a former Sacramento player

Overcoming a serious knee injury suffered in the minors, Bill Salkeld backstopped parts of six big league seasons.

himself, was seeking a new hometown hero to help him salvage a club that the banks had foreclosed upon from the previous owner, Lewis Moreing. Salkeld's unique contract contained an arrangement under which he could attend high-school classes in the morning, then head across town to work out with the professional team in the afternoon.

On March 8, 1934, Bill Salkeld's 17th birthday, the contract was sealed. Bill being a minor, it had to be signed by his father, a Sacramento railroad employee. It was John's railroad jobs, in fact, that had taken the family from Idaho to Oregon, Nevada, and finally California. Bill Salkeld was one of very few major leaguers to be born in Idaho. Local press photographers gathered and snapped photos of the Salkelds and Earl McNeely all smiling as they sat behind Bill's birthday cake. The contract was signed, the pictures taken, and only a few bites of cake eaten before Bill headed off to Moreing Field to begin his catching duties.

Athletics had been a huge part of Salkeld's youth. The brother of a local boxing hero, Tex Salkeld, Bill was known in his high school as a terrific basketball star, a football player, and a swimmer. Though sports took up most of his time, he also enjoyed mystery novels and motion pictures. Later in his career, Bill would spend several offseasons as a set builder in the movie industry.

But Salkeld's loyalties were, first and foremost, to baseball, and his idol as a teen was the great Athletics catcher Mickey Cochrane. His proficiency and versatility in that sport were further demonstrated by his simultaneous participation on both his high-school and local American Legion teams. Though he served his school squad as its star catcher, his Legion team used him as a shortstop. After he signed with the Senators, however, the professional club's management requested that Salkeld concentrate solely on catching.

With dreams of making the big leagues filling his head, Salkeld began his pro career just after graduation by catching 89 games for Sacramento in 1934 and batting .255. His sophomore season saw him increase his workload to 111 games and improve his average to .261. That year he was introduced to Max West, a rookie with Sacramento who later patrolled the outfield for the Boston Bees.

Baseball legend Branch Rickey purchased the Sacramento club in 1935, and the personnel on the team changed drastically. This resulted in Bill wearing the uniform of the San Francisco Seals in 1936, a year that totally changed young Salkeld's career and his life.

On July 10, 1936, San Francisco was hosting Portland at Seals Stadium. Salkeld's first season with San Francisco had, so far, been very tough for several reasons. He was saddled with a .211 batting average after three months, and in June he lost his mother. Nevertheless, the 18-year-old was manager Frank O'Doul's choice for catcher again on this night. During the game, Portland slugger Moose Clabaugh was caught in a rundown between third and home. Salkeld held the ball and began chasing the runner back to third. Clabaugh slipped, Salkeld reached out to tag him, but the catcher felt his shin-guard slip and he stumbled into Clabaugh—tagging him out but impaling his right knee on the spikes of the Portland baserunner in the process.

Spike injuries were not that uncommon in baseball, and Salkeld was given immediate medical attention. Unfortunately, the wounded knee did not respond as physicians thought it should. There was no more baseball for Bill in 1936; suffering from a disorder that left his immune system compromised, he was prescribed a blood transfusion to try to preserve the flexibility and use of his injured leg.

Local papers snapped photos, and positive publicity was generated as all of the Seals players and management lined up at Mary's Help Hospital to donate blood and save Salkeld's career. Obviously nervous about liability and poor public relations, Seals management told the media that everyone from the owner to the batboy would be rolling up their sleeves to support their wounded catcher.

Nothing seemed to work. Three solid months of hospitalization spent strapped in a brace that held his leg at a 90-degree angle did nothing to restore the mobility of Salkeld's limb. Doctors assigned by the team's insurance company could not reduce the stiffness in the right knee, bad news for a man who made his living crouching between an umpire and a batter. At one point there was even consideration of amputation.

The 1937 season came and went with Salkeld on the sidelines, and the next year Bill went to work in the furniture business to support himself and his new wife, Lorraine. There seemed no hope for his ever playing baseball again, and eventually doctors told him the same. The newspapers pronounced his career "finis" and reported that a severance check had been given to the former catcher for $5,000.

Frustrated by the seeming certainty that his playing days were over, Salkeld lashed out, stating that he had received far less than that amount. He spoke of lawsuits against the Seals or the insurance company, while still keeping a small hope alive that he might one day play again.

In 1939, Tucson in the Arizona-Texas League offered Bill a managerial role. The Tucson Cowboys were a farm team of the Seals, who in turn routinely sent players to and from the majors. Salkeld would forever be grateful to Charley Graham of the San Francisco club for putting him back in baseball. Working out with his players, Bill found the desert climate good for his stiff knee. Taking the liberty to occasionally insert himself in the lineup as a first baseman, he eventually found his way back behind the plate as well, developing a whole new way of crouching by keeping his right leg extended outward.

At the end of the 1939 season, three years after his last game with the Seals, the San Francisco team had seen enough of Salkeld (then hitting .303) to take a chance on their former backstop and call him up near the end of the season. All told, Bill hit over .300 and played in 120 games that season, good enough for him to be signed as a free agent by the PCL rival San Diego Padres. There he'd catch for the next five seasons as the United States first watched and then entered World War II.

In 1944, the Padres were a last-place team in the PCL and Salkeld's average was an unimpressive .241. But the war had left the majors in need of talent, and the Pittsburgh Pirates were ready to give the now 27-year-old a chance to catch in the big leagues. The Pirates acquired him in September for a next-season delivery of cash and a player to be named later, but he'd have to wait a while longer to suit up for Pittsburgh.

Finally given the chance that seemed a foregone conclusion to a younger Salkeld, he entered his first major-league season in the spring of 1945 with a final roadblock in the form of 36-year-old future Hall of Fame catcher Al Lopez. It was Lopez, a former standout with the Braves and Dodgers, who stood in the way of Salkeld getting a starting job. Salkeld was available because he'd been declared 4-F by the Army, exempt from military service due to an "ailing right knee."

But when an injury limited Lopez's availability, Salkeld took full advantage of his opportunity. He hit .311 while tying outfielder Johnny Barrett for the team lead in home runs with 15 despite finishing the year with just 267 at-bats. The Pirates finished a solid fourth in the NL at 82–72, and the rookie receiver even tallied several votes for league MVP.

In an August 4, 1945, home game at Forbes Field, Salkeld had the finest offensive performance of his career in a loss to the Cardinals. Driving in all five of the Pirates' runs, he also joined an exclusive club as just the seventh catcher to hit for the cycle. Symbolic of his up-and-down

Left to right: Bill Salkeld, Billy Southworth and Warren Spahn. Salkeld's sixth inning homer in Game 5 of the '48 Series tied the score and set the stage for Warren Spahn's win in relief and the Boston Braves' last ever post-season victory.

time in baseball, Salkeld's big moment came with a couple of dubious statistics attached. He still holds the record for fewest lifetime triples by a player who has hit for the cycle, as the three-bagger he needed that day represented one-half of his career total. In addition, Salkeld managed to catch the entire game without being credited with a single putout or assist.

The 1946 season was a disappointing follow-up to his stellar rookie campaign. Although Salkeld hit a respectable .294, his power numbers were way down and his opportunities were limited with Lopez back from injury and fellow catcher Bill Baker returning from the war and joining Pittsburgh's behind-the-plate platoon. Things got much worse in '47, as a frustrated Salkeld struggled through a further diminishing role with the Pirates and finished with just 61 at-bats and a .213 batting average. After 15 homers and 52 RBI his rookie year, he had now totaled just three and 27 in the next two years combined. Salkeld had to be wondering if a change of venue might do him some good, and that offseason he got it. On November 18, 1947, Bill was traded to the Braves along with Al Lyons and Jim Russell in a swap that introduced the Pirates to Danny Murtaugh, who would eventually manage Pittsburgh to victory in the World Series. But in 1948 it was Salkeld who made it to the October classic, along the way catching for Johnny Sain and earning praise as Spahn's preferred receiver. During the '48 regular season Bill hit .242 in 78 contests backing up All-Star Phil Masi. Bill also caught in five games of the World Series, scoring two runs and getting two hits. One, of course, was the thrill-of-a-lifetime homer he belted off of Bob Feller in Game Five.

Unfortunately, time was running out for Salkeld. He played one more season with the Braves, hitting .255 in 66 games during the club's disappointing fourth-place 1949 campaign. Now splitting the catching duties with Masi and 19-year-old rookie Del Crandall, he finished his five-year National League career with a respectable .273 batting average in 355 games. His next major-league appearance was in the American League; with just a week to play in 1949, anxious to get his rebuilding campaign under way, Braves GM John Quinn sold Salkeld on waivers to the Chicago White Sox on September 26. The next spring, on April 21, 1950, Bill started for Chicago and went 0-for-3 at the plate. The White Sox were well stocked with catchers, however, and were five players over the 25-man limit, so GM Frank Lane sold Salkeld to Seattle of the PCL. Bill played the 1950 season for the Seattle Rainiers and the next year with the Portland Beavers. Batting just .192 in 1951, he retired at the age of 34, though there was a swan song in 1953 when he signed a one-year contract as player-manager of the Stockton Ports in the Class C California League. He slugged 13 homers, but hit only .227.

By this time, Bill and Lorraine had three children—Sally, Sandra, and Billy. The family lived in Sun Valley, California, where the former catcher took a job with U.S. Steel. In his spare time he enjoyed golfing, hunting, and keeping baseball scrapbooks. His only active involvement with the game, however, was as Billy's Little League coach.

William Franklin Salkeld died on April 22, 1967, after visiting doctors too late with inoperable cancer, and the 50-year-old was buried at Forest Lawn-Hollywood Hills Cemetery in Los Angeles. Much later, family members recalled some of the baseball memories that he most cherished. He was very honored to be Warren Spahn's favorite catcher in his two seasons with the Braves. He had fond memories of playing exhibition games for a team that traveled to prisons to play the inmates. Then, of course, there was the World Series home run off Feller.

And even with Bill gone, his modest legacy within the game continued. Four years after his death, Salkeld's son, Billy, and daughter-in-law, Elaine, gave birth to Roger Salkeld, who was a first-round pick by the Seattle Mariners in 1989 and made his debut as a pitcher with the team in 1993.

Sources

Baseball Almanac, Retrosheet, Baseball-Reference.com and the *2006 ESPN Baseball Encyclopedia.*
Salkeld family interviews by Michael Kinsley.

RAYMOND FLOYD SANDERS *by Paul Pereira*

G	AB	R	H	2B	3B	HR	RBI	BB	SO	BA	OBP	SLG	SB	HBP
5	4	0	1	0	0	0	0	2	1	0	.250	.400	.250	0	0

Not unlike the lead character in Winston Groom's 1986 novel *Forrest Gump*, Raymond Floyd Sanders (through happy coincidence or, less likely, adroit planning) was able to build a reservoir of memories in baseball, both delightful and unfortunate, that other ballplayers with much longer careers could only envy. In fact, Sanders' appearance in four World Series in just seven years as an active player is simply the beginning.

Sanders was born on December 4, 1916, one of six children, just outside the mining city of Bonne Terre, Missouri. About 40 miles due south of Sportsman's Park, the St. Louis home of both the National League's Cardinals and the American League's Browns, Bonne Terre was also home at the time to the largest known lead ore deposits in the world. Its residents enjoyed a thriving mill-town baseball culture, with several leagues and teams competing for bragging rights on the many playgrounds in and around the community.

Known by friends, neighbors, and, later, teammates as Ray, Gabe, or Sandy, Sanders was a good-looking, popular young man with an outgoing, "easy-does-it" disposition. At 6-feet-2 and 185 pounds, tall and rangy, a right-hander batting left-handed, Ray developed into an outstanding athlete. Although he played no baseball in high school (legendary coach Bert Fenenga would not keep him on the roster, citing his "lackadaisical" approach to the game), he starred for his local American Legion team. After graduating, however, he spent most of his leisure moments playing softball and developed a reputation as an exceptional player on the St. Louis playgrounds. In 1938, having played softball for three years since school, he was discovered and signed by Cardinals scout Walter Shannon, who was also credited with signing Earl Weaver, Harvey Haddix, Ray Fosse, and Terry Crowley, among others.

The Cardinals assigned Sanders, then 21, to their Paducah Indians farm club in the Class D Kitty League. He was one of some 600 players in the Cardinals' vast minor league system, which was composed at one time of more than 30 ballclubs. Ray quickly adapted to being away from home and to the rigors of Depression-era minor-league baseball, and slowly but steadily advanced

One of many ex-Cardinals on the Braves roster, Ray Sanders suffered a horrific arm injury in 1946 that restricted his future playing time to 15 games over the next two seasons and a sole pinch hitting appearance in the '48 World Series.

through the system by demonstrating a powerful bat and a skilled glove at first base, the position he played throughout his pro career.

Except for his first season, when a broken foot shut him down for a month (a precursor to a history of fractures and injuries later in his major-league career), Sanders was either selected to his league's All-Star team or received honorable mention every year until his promotion to the big leagues in 1942. In 1938 with Paducah, he batted .322 while clubbing 13 home runs and 22 doubles, driving in 68 runs, and stealing 10 bases. His ascension to Class C Kilgore (East Texas League) in 1939 led to a .333 batting average with 14 home runs and 95 runs batted in.

In 1940, Sanders was promoted to the Columbus, Georgia, Redbirds of the Class B South Atlantic League. He had an outstanding year; he was the circuit's MVP, hitting .349 with 14 homers, 16 triples, and a league-record 152 RBIs. He continued to move up in the Cardinals ranks and in 1941 at Double-A Columbus of the American Association was selected as the Rookie of the Year. Solidifying his reputation as a run producer, he scored 119 runs while knocking in 120, led the league in doubles with 40, hit 14 homers, and batted .308.

After the 1941 season, Cardinals general manager Branch Rickey made a bold move that directly affected Ray and his promotion to the parent club. Rickey, driven partly by economics (i.e., a sizable contract for the day) and a belief in moving players before their skills eroded, traded popular first baseman and future Hall of Famer Johnny Mize to the New York Giants, essentially for cash. Mize held the Cardinals' single-season home run record with 43 (set in 1940), and at 27 was just two years older than Ray.

The spirit of the Gashouse Gang was alive and well in St. Louis, where they would "pay little attention to how a player hits or fields, so long as he will run through a brick wall after a ball." Mize had missed a number of games with a sore or broken thumb during the 1941 pennant race with the Dodgers, which didn't sit well with manager Billy Southworth. He injured his shoulder later in the season, and his home run production declined accordingly, from 43 in 1940 to just 16 in '41. Trading Mize opened a slot for Sanders, and with his reputation as a slick-fielding, run-producing first baseman, Ray began the 1942 season with the Cardinals.

Sanders' transition to major-league ball was not as smooth as his ascent through the farm system. He was 25 years old when he broke into the majors on April 14, 1942, with a 1-for-4 day, and he split time at first base with another farm graduate, speedster Johnny Hopp. Sanders appeared in 95 games and finished with a .252 average (after never dropping below .308 in the minors), 5 home runs, and 39 runs batted in. Though coming off an excellent 1941 season in which he batted .303, Hopp finished with similar stats in the platoon arrangement. Sanders was superior on defense, though, proving an outstanding glove man around the bag with only six errors in 77 games, while Hopp finished with 14 in 88 contests.

The Cardinals ended the season going a red-hot 43–8, coming from 10½ games back to win the pennant. They then beat the defending champion New York Yankees in five games to take the World Series. This was the first season of wartime baseball; most teams had already lost or were bracing themselves for the loss of key players to the armed forces or the defense industry. The Cardinals, whether by design or need, had successfully absorbed a large influx of rookies in 1942, with Stan Musial assuming Hopp's outfield position, Whitey Kurowski taking over at third base, and rookie pitcher Johnny Beazley winning 21 games. St. Louis fielded the youngest team in the big leagues during 1942 with an average age of 26 and only one regular over 30.

Manager Southworth went with Hopp in the Series, hoping he'd show some of his 1941 form. Sanders pinch-hit in two games. In the ninth inning of Game One, he walked and scored on Marty Marion's two-run triple, although St. Louis lost, 7–4. Sanders popped out to third while pinch-hitting for pitcher Howie Pollet in the seventh inning of Game Four, as the Cards won 9–6.

As World War II ground on and more players left for the war effort, the Cardinals—hoping to salvage their extensive system—even advertised for players with an ad in *The Sporting News*. Sanders, however, wasn't going anywhere. He became a regular for the next few seasons, one of those fortunate young men who could continue to earn a living playing ball thanks to a 4F classification due to a condition that ultimately led to heart disease.

Ray continued to demonstrate deft glove work around first base in 1943, participating in a league-leading 142 double plays and making just seven errors in nearly twice as many chances as in '42. His hitting picked up too, as in 144 games he batted .280 with 11 home runs, 21 doubles, five triples, and 73 RBIs. He further endeared himself to Southworth and fans of "Gashouse" baseball with 15 sacrifice hits, and also walked 77 times. Sanders ended the season with a strong .381 on-base percentage, well above the league OBP of .339.

Not everything was fine, however. On September 6, Sanders suffered the first significant injury of his career when he was struck in the head by a batted ball in a game against Pittsburgh. He was carried from the Sportsman's Park field on a stretcher. He was pronounced fit after being sent to the hospital for X-rays, but missed several games at the urging of the team physician.

For the second year in a row, Sanders went to the World Series on a team that won at least 105 games (actually 106), as the Cards trumped second-place Cincinnati by 18 games. In the Series, though, the Yankees turned the tables and won the rematch in five games. Sanders started each game, batting sixth and playing first base, and hit .294 with three runs scored. He was one of the few heroes for St. Louis, as his two-run homer in Game Two accounted for the winning run in the only victory of the Series for the Cardinals.

Although the season ended on a down note, the year ended well when Sanders married his hometown sweetheart on Christmas Day. Ray and Bernice Magre enjoyed a 39-year marriage, raising a son, James, and a daughter, Sandra.

The 1944 campaign was Sanders' best by far. He played in all 154 games, hitting a robust .295, with 12 homers, 34 doubles, and nine triples, and scoring 87 runs while finishing fourth in the National League with 102 RBIs (all career highs). His on-base percentage was .371, thanks to 71 walks. Ray again demonstrated the Cardinals' trademark of outstanding defensive expertise, leading all National League first basemen with a .994 fielding percentage while participating in a league-leading 142 double plays and two triple plays—14 days apart—in July. His all-around performance earned Sanders a 15th-place finish in voting for the National League MVP; teammate Marty Marion, the club's sparkplug shortstop, won the award. Sanders was named first baseman on *The Sporting News* Major League Baseball All-Star team.

Winning their third straight pennant, the Cardinals helped St. Louis enjoy its first and only "Streetcar Series" as they faced off against their Sportsman's Park landlords, the Browns. "The funny thing about that World Series," said Stan Musial, "the fans were rooting for the Browns, and it kind of surprised me because we drew more fans than the Browns during the season. The fans were rooting for the underdog, and I was surprised about that, but after you analyze the situation in St. Louis, the Browns in the old days had good clubs. They had great players like George Sisler and Kenny Williams, and the fans who were there were older fans, older men, old-time Brownie fans. But it was a tough Series."

The World Series turned into a pitching showcase, with the powerful Cardinals hitting a subpar .240 while the Browns countered with an anemic .183 average. The Series resulted in a postseason record for strikeouts, with the Browns fanning 49 times in six games while the Cardinals went down on strikes 43 times—Johnny Hopp leading the way with eight whiffs.

Despite all the misses, it was an exciting matchup.

The Browns, led by right-hander Denny Galehouse, won a taut pitching duel in Game One, 2–1. Sanders, batting second, went 1-for-3 and did not figure in the scoring. Game Two proved to be another thriller, with Missouri Senator and vice-presidential candidate Harry S. Truman in attendance. Sanders returned to his traditional sixth spot in the order and sparked the Cardinals to a 3–2 victory in 11 innings by scoring two runs—including the game-winner in the bottom of the 11th.

The buildup to his game-winning tally was thrilling in itself. In the top of the 11th, Browns first baseman George McQuinn led off with a "near-home-run" double off a protective screen in right field, but the Cards then cut him down at third base as he attempted to advance on a bunt. Sanders started the Cardinals' half of the 11th with a sharp single. After a sacrifice moved him to second, the Browns intentionally walked National League MVP Marion to set up a double play. Southworth retaliated by sending up top pinch-hitter Ken O'Dea to bat for Emil Verban, and O'Dea delivered a single to right that scored Sanders and tied the Series at one game apiece.

The Browns took the Series lead again by winning Game Three, 6–2, but the Cardinals won Game Four, 5–1, as Sanders participated in two key double plays that seemed to take a lot of energy out of the upstart American Leaguers. Sanders led off the sixth inning for the Cardinals with a single and scored the club's fifth run of the game on a Marty Marion double.

Game Five represented a matchup of the Game One pitchers, Denny Galehouse and the Cards' Mort Cooper. It remained scoreless until the sixth inning, when Galehouse threw one of "only two pitches he regretted" that day—a slider that Sanders blasted over the right-field pavilion to put the Cardinals ahead 1–0. A second Cardinal home run, in the eighth, resulted in a final score of 2–0 and a three-games-to-two Cardinal lead.

The next day the Cards wrapped up their second World Series victory in three years, winning Game Six, 3–1. Sanders contributed this time by scoring in the pivotal fourth inning, when the National Leaguers wiped out a 1–0 deficit with all three of their runs off Nels Potter and Bob Muncrief.

Sanders finished his three-year run of Word Series participation for the Cardinals with a .282 batting average in 13 games, swatting 11 hits in 39 at-bats with two homers. Ever the glove man at first base, he tied the record for the position with five assists in the 1943 Series and also tied a World Series record by recording a hit in each game of the 1944 classic.

Sanders' aggregate postseason reward for appearing in the 1942, '43 and '44 World Series was $15,141, a significant and substantial sum of money at the time (and higher than the average big-league salary during the era). It would have been even higher, but the World Series winner's share in '44 came to just $4,626, the smallest

since 1933, largely due to the limited seating capacity of Sportsman's Park.

In 1945 Uncle Sam accomplished what the National League could not. Although the '45 season saw a trickle of former major leaguers returning from the war, with some, like the Tigers' Hank Greenberg, significantly affecting their teams' fortunes, most teams continued to see their 1945 lineups negatively affected by the loss of players. The Cardinals had the third lowest number of players called up for service through 1944 (23, in contrast to Detroit, which had the most at 36), but were then dealt the loss of Stan Musial for the entire 1945 campaign and star pitchers Max Lanier and Mort Cooper, along with brother Walker (the Redbirds' starting catcher) in midseason of that year.

Even with the loss of these players, the Cardinals still managed to win 95 games and finish just three games back of the Chicago Cubs for the National League title. In addition to the war losses, St. Louis struggled with nagging injuries to Sanders and Whitey Kurowski. Sanders missed 11 games with assorted bumps, bruises and scrapes, and ended the year hitting .276, with a decline in power numbers (29 doubles, three triples, eight home runs, and 78 RBIs, 24 fewer than the year before). Of concern to a club that often employed the sacrifice and hit-and-run, his strikeout total increased to 55, ninth highest in the National League. And, perhaps due to being in less than ideal health, his errors more than doubled, to 19.

Change was in play for the Cardinals after their "disappointing" 1945 campaign. In 1943, owner Sam Breadon had fired his high-paid GM, Branch Rickey, architect of the Cardinals' most successful period to date. (Rickey moved to Brooklyn to run the Dodgers organization.) In the 1945 off-season, again feeling constrained both by stadium capacity and his club's on-field success in 1942 through 1944 (e.g., "You don't pack them in when your club is 15 to 20 games ahead"), Breadon engaged in a bargain-basement sale of players—Cooper, Hopp, and Jimmy Brown to name a few. The owner even decided it was time for the team and Billy Southworth to part company. Manager Southworth was offered a significant increase in pay to manage the Boston Braves, and Breadon let him go. Despite the moves, Rickey and Southworth continued to play prominent roles in Sanders' future.

The return of prewar stars, along with rumors of a "lively" ball, marked the start of the 1946 season. The '45 champion Detroit Tigers, for example, with an influx of players returning from the service, started only four members of their World Series-winning club. It was an unprecedented turnover in the time before the era of free agency.

As a result of this full-scale switch, the Cardinals were flush with talent once again. The return of outfielders Musial, Terry Moore, and Enos Slaughter, along with the addition of Harry Walker in center, helped make the Cardinals the prohibitive favorites in the National League. Additionally, a slugging rookie phenom named Dick Sisler, son of Hall of Famer and local hero George Sisler, was a sensation during Cuban Winter League ball to the extent that he earned mention in Ernest Hemingway's new novel *The Old Man and the Sea*. With Cardinals coach Mike Gonzalez managing Sisler in winter ball and providing first-hand reports as to his abilities, Breadon dreamed of a big box office in St. Louis, and when new Cardinals manager Eddie Dyer chose Sisler as the starting first baseman just before Opening Day of '46, Sanders was relegated to the bench.

Sisler ultimately flopped, hitting only three homers and .260 in part-time play. Manager Dyer, however, didn't call Ray's number. Rather, he threw a first baseman's glove into Musial's locker one day and asked him to make the move for the good of the cause.

Unfortunately, asking Stan Musial to relocate to first base may have had less to do with a desire to get more offense out of an overcrowded outfield than another underlying reason. As Marty Marion later explained: "When he was with us, we used to call Ray 'Dead Body.' He was a big, tall, skinny guy. He was the laziest man I ever saw in my life. The first day in spring training he was sitting next to me. He said, 'Marty, I wish the season was over!' Ray was touted. A St. Louis boy. He had good talent, but he was lazy. He was supposed to be better than he turned out to be."

In the meantime, a number of former Cardinals, including Hopp and Mort Cooper, had found their way to Boston, reunited in '46 with Southworth on what came to be called the "Cape Cod Cardinals." With the St. Louis first base position promised to a young and inexpensive winter ball phenom, and with a future Hall of Famer in Musial as fallback, Sanders was not surprised to find himself on the trading block as well. On Opening Day, April 16, he was pleased to find that he would be joining his fellow Cardinal alumni playing for the Braves. He had been sold to Boston for the then-princely sum of $25,000.

Many ballplayers enjoyed suiting up for Southworth in these years—he was what might be referred to as a player's manager in modern terms—and Sanders was no exception. With his team picked to finish in the second division in the National League, Southworth was anxious to add some punch to what he felt was a weak-hitting Braves lineup. Ray provided a veteran left-handed bat with pop who, it was hoped, could take advantage of the short right field fence in Braves Field while providing two staples of any Southworth team: speed on the bases and defensive skill around first base.

The Braves saw the benefit of Sanders' presence almost immediately, when he collected nine hits in 17 at-bats during an early-season sweep of the New York Giants, and got off to a .321 start. During the early going, though, the "soft" nature of the Braves lineup remained apparent, as Boston was no-hit by Ed Head of the Dodgers on April 23, 5–0. Sanders was in the lineup, batting cleanup, and went 0-for-3.

Sanders' fast start at the plate quickly subsided as he re-established a trend that had begun in 1945; he was struggling against postwar pitching. His average had declined to .243 by the time a series with the Cardinals in St. Louis began on August 20, with just six homers and 35 runs batted in despite the inviting right-field porch of Braves Field beckoning in home games. After Boston lost the first game of the two-game series, the clubs squared off on August 21 in a night game at Sportsman's Park.

The Cards were leading 2–1 in the seventh when third baseman Erv Dusak led off in the bottom of the inning. He laid down an exceptional bunt toward Braves third baseman Nanny Fernandez. Only an outstanding throw would get Dusak at first base. Fernandez charged in, picked the ball up with his bare hand, and in the same motion whipped it across the infield toward Sanders at first base. It was one of the fielding highlights of the game, but the throw was to the home-plate side of first base. Sanders had to reach out to his left, extending his left arm parallel to the baseline, into the path of Dusak, barreling down the line.

Dusak crashed into Sanders' outstretched arm, shattering it so badly that second baseman Connie Ryan, who was nearest to the play, actually went white. By the time Ryan, Dusak, and everyone else in the vicinity had reached Sanders, he was writhing in pain on the baseline. He was carried off the field and taken to St. John's Hospital, where it was determined that he had suffered fractures of his elbow and upper left arm. His arm was actually broken in three places, and the Braves announced that he would undergo surgery and miss the remainder of the 1946 season.

This injury proved devastating. Sanders remained in St. Louis to rehab for more than a year, undergoing a series of surgeries to repair the damage to his left arm. The Braves paid him his full salary in 1947, even though he did not report to Fort Lauderdale for spring training. In fact, he was out of professional baseball for about 18 months, an enormous amount of time for anyone but a figurative lifetime for someone who would be 31 years old upon his return to the game.

In the interim, the Braves continued to build their team, with an eye toward challenging for their first National League pennant since 1914. Coincidentally, on the day Sanders was hurt, the Braves had purchased highly touted Earl Torgeson from Seattle of the Pacific Coast League for $50,000 and four players. Torgeson, a big, bespectacled slugger, proved difficult for Sanders to displace, as he brought with him all the tools—left-handed power, speed, defense—valued by Manager Southworth and initially sought after in Sanders. Torgeson was also seven years younger.

Finally, Sanders' doctors pronounced him fit to rejoin the Braves in spring training of 1948. Torgeson was coming off a superlative rookie campaign and the Boston organization felt it was close to championship form. Sanders was seen as a spare part but, more importantly for Braves management, as a bargaining chip as they tried to close some holes in their team.

On March 6, 1948, the person who signed Sanders to his first professional contract re-entered the picture. Dodgers general manager Rickey, assured by doctors that Sanders would return to being 95 percent of the ballplayer he was prior to his injury, acquired him along with holdout second baseman/outfielder 'Bama Rowell and $40,000 in cash in exchange for Brooklyn's "holler guy"—second baseman Eddie Stanky. Stanky, described by Leo Durocher as a player who "can't hit, can't run, can't field…but all the little son-of-a-bitch can do is win," was seen by the Braves as a missing piece to their infield puzzle who could stabilize double-play partner and acclaimed rookie shortstop Alvin Dark. With 1947 league MVP Bob Elliott at third, sophomore sensation Torgeson at first, and a double-play combination of Stanky and Dark, Southworth felt he had a championship-caliber infield in place.

Several scribes questioned the value the deal held for the Dodgers while seeing it as strengthening one of their chief rivals for the pennant. Others wrote that now Rickey and manager Durocher could move 1947 Rookie of the Year Jackie Robinson from first base to his natural position of second, replacing Stanky, while improving the club's overall infield defense by inserting Sanders at first. "Sanders looks like the Sanders of old," Durocher said during spring training. "And if he still is when the season opens he'll be my first baseman." Durocher was also quoted, however, as saying he intended on keeping Robinson at first and inserting hotshot rookie Eddie Miksis at second to replace Stanky.

But Sanders was carrying a reported 12 or so extra pounds, which affected his quickness, and it was clear that his left arm still had not mended fully. Once Durocher and other Dodgers officials saw Ray wince after swinging at a pitch in a spring training game, he was returned to the Braves as damaged goods. Brooklyn received a $60,000 refund for its trouble.

"I started coming along pretty good in the spring," Sanders later recalled. "Rickey told me to take all the time I needed. 'It doesn't matter if it is June before you are ready to go,' he said. So I took it easy. The arm was quite

Sanders had extensive postseason experience prior to 1948, having appeared in the 1942, 1943, and 1944 World Series with the Cardinals.

stiff at first, and it hurt when I topped the ball or missed completely. But that was only natural after the layoff and operation. It wasn't long before I was playing three or four innings in the exhibition games and doing all right. I was getting my share of hits, too."

"Then all of a sudden I was put on the bench," he continued. "They just didn't use me any more, and no reason was given. I couldn't imagine what was wrong. I finally found out. Rickey had decided to send me back to Boston and take the cash. He gave me that 'old father' business, saying that if I were his son he wouldn't want me to play and jeopardize my arm. I don't know what he was talking about. A lot of doctors had examined my arm and said it was OK. They told me to go ahead and play, that everything was coming along fine. It really hurt when Rickey turned me back. Everyone values his opinion. So in the eyes of the baseball world I was washed up."

Manager Southworth was secretly pleased to have one of his favorite veteran ballplayers back, although few felt Sanders had much left to offer in terms of playing ability. On May 1, doctors in St. Louis who had been monitoring his rehabilitation pronounced him fit to play, though his elbow and arm clearly still were not at "95 percent". Nonetheless, he returned to the Braves as they set to play the Pirates in Pittsburgh on May 5.

The Braves, stacked with infielders, and especially first basemen, assigned Sanders to Buffalo of the International League on May 25 before he got into a major-league game. Sanders fought the assignment, and was re-assigned to Triple-A Seattle (Pacific Coast League) the next day, but his elbow and arm did not permit him to crack the stacked Seattle lineup. He was called back East to play for Hartford of the Class A Eastern League, where he could get enough playing time to determine whether he could help the Braves from the bench.

The Braves, battling for first place with the Dodgers and Cardinals, intended to recall Sanders on September 4 for the pennant stretch. He had hit .329 in 49 games for Hartford, demonstrating his trademark gap power with 17 doubles while driving in and scoring 24 runs. He had also already been through four previous pennant races, played in three World Series, and had seemingly healed sufficiently to recapture his batting stroke.

As fate would have it, on September 3, in his last scheduled game with Hartford, Sanders was hit in the head by a pitch. Sanders said he could tell the pitch was a fastball, but "just couldn't get out of the way" of it.

Doctors kept Sanders in the hospital for a week under observation, and it was not entirely clear that he had fully recovered when he reported to the parent club. Upon arrival, Ray promptly drove in the game-winning run in his first at-bat for the Braves on a bases-loaded pinch single in a game against the Phillies. "A clutch spot," said manager Southworth, "was a chance to restore the confidence of a guy who has power and heart." However, despite the auspicious return to the lineup, Sanders played sparingly, making four more unsuccessful pinch-hitting appearances down the stretch as Boston clinched the NL pennant.

Then came one more big shot. After center fielder Jim Russell was hospitalized late in September with rheumatic fever and outfielder Jeff Heath broke his ankle, Sanders was added to the World Series roster. "Ray is a great guy to have in your dugout," Southworth said. "He can hit the long ball for you and can hit left-handers as well as he does right-handers." Southworth was the only manager Sanders had played for in the big leagues, and rumors were flying that Sanders would play a significant role in the Series between the Braves and the Cleveland Indians. But rumors were all they were. His only appearance was as a pinch-hitter, for pitcher Nels Potter, and he ended Game Two by grounding out to the pitcher with Eddie Stanky at second. The Braves lost the Series to the Indians, four games to two; for his brief appearances during the regular season and the Series, Sanders received a one-quarter World Series share of $1,142.68.

Contrary to the reputation for "laziness" that may have preceded him, Sanders was determined to prove he could still play. He agreed to a contract with the Braves on the eve of spring training in 1949, and put forth a spirited battle with Earl Torgeson for the first base position after Southworth proclaimed that "all berths were open." Then, injuries once again took their toll. On March 30, after struggling with what he felt was a minor wrist ailment, Sanders was placed on the 60-day disabled list once the Braves determined that he in fact had broken his right wrist in an exhibition game. Upon his return on June 18, Sanders appeared in only nine games for the Braves the rest of the year, getting to the plate 21 times with four hits. In 1950 he was demoted to the Triple-A Milwaukee Brewers, and after a season in which he batted just .195 in 159 at-bats, he retired.

It was several years before Sanders connected with professional baseball again, attending a reunion of the 1942 World Series champion Cardinals on July 1, 1962, at Sportsman's Park. In 1966, he signed on as a scout for the Cleveland Indians, before ultimately retiring with his wife to the St. Louis area, scene of their youth and his greatest professional success. But the bad luck that plagued Sanders during his later playing career never quite left him. He suffered from a "weak heart," a malady that had kept him from serving his country in World War II and one that also kept him from attending the 40th reunion of the 1942 champion Cardinals in his hometown in 1982.

But Sanders left the game secure in the knowledge that he had earned a solid place in both Cardinals and baseball history. Immortalized in the 2002 David Finoli book *For the Good of the Country* as a true star of baseball's war seasons, he lived out his years in the company of his wife of 39 years, Bernice.

In October 28, 1983, Ray Sanders died as the result of an automobile accident in Washington, Missouri. He was 66 years old and was survived by his wife and two children.

Sources

Finoli, David. *For the Good of the Country: World War II Baseball in the Major and Minor Leagues.* (Jefferson, North Carolina: McFarland & Company, Inc., Publishers, 2002).

Heidenry, John and Brett Topel, *The Boys Who Were Left Behind: The 1944 World Series Between the Hapless St. Louis Browns and the Legendary St. Louis Cardinals.* (Lincoln, Nebraska: University of Nebraska Press, 2006).

Hirshberg, Al, *The Braves: The Pick and The Shovel* (Boston: Waverly House, 1948), pp. 190–91.

Phillips, John. *The Story of Ray Sanders* (Kathleen, Georgia: Capital Publishing, 2007).

SABR Baseball Encyclopedia

Articles with author cited

Broeg, Bob "Of Ray Sanders And Game He Loved." *St. Louis Post-Dispatch*, November 1, 1983.

Broeg, Bob. "The '42 Cardinals." *Sport.* July 1963.

By Pap. "Batting for Mize." *Christian Science Monitor*, June 25, 1942.

By Pap, "Taking Up Slack." *Christian Science Monitor*, June 29, 1945.

Conklin, Les. "Sanders Going Back To Braves?" *Lowell Sun*, April 14, 1948.

Dove, "With Malice Toward None, *The Hartford Courant*, September 11, 1948.

Eck, Frank. "Durocher Doubles-Decks Dodgers." *Nashua Telegraph*, April 10, 1948.

Golenbock, Peter, *The Spirit of St. Louis* (New York: Harper-Collins), p. 367.

McGowen, Roscoe. "Taylor Tests Arm At Dodgers Camp." *The New York Times*, March 10, 1948.

Rumill, Ed. "In the Dugout with Rumill: Hope Springs Eternal." *Christian Science Monitor*, April 16, 1949.

Rumill, Ed. "Sanders Battles Torgy For First Base Berth." *Christian Science Monitor*, April 6, 1949.

Rumill, Ed. "Big League Trades May Be Underway." *Christian Science Monitor*, April 16, 1946.

Rumill, Ed. "Card Developed Players Pacing Braves." *Christian Science Monitor*, May 14, 1946.

Smith, James F. "Southworth Counts on Sanders To Help Braves Down Stretch." *Titusville (Pa.) Herald.* September 17, 1948.

Articles without author bylines

"Ray Sanders." 1942 National League Green Book, page 55.

"Ray Sanders, Johnny Hopp Battle For Mize's Vacated Post." *Hartford Courant*, March 3, 1942.

"Sanders of Cards Married." *The New York Times*, December 27, 1943.

"Cardinal Defensive Skill Now Officially Recognized." *Christian Science Monitor*, December 12, 1944.

"Sisler Back At 1st for Cards." *Reno Evening Gazette*. April 16, 1946.

"Redbirds Lose to Si Johnson; Sanders Suffers Broken Arm." *St. Louis Post-Dispatch*. August 22, 1946.

"Ray Sanders Not Ready to Report for Training." *Walla Walla Union-Bulletin*. February 4, 1947.

"Ray Sanders Still Ailing." *Lowell Sun*, February 4, 1947.

"Ray Sanders to Be Out Of Action Indefinitely." *Charleston Gazette*. February 22, 1947.

"Cocky Rookie Making Good." *Walla Walla Union-Bulletin*. March 27, 1947.

"Brooklyn Trade Stanky for Sanders, Rowell." *Charleston Gazette*. March 7, 1948.

"Stanky Arrival Awaited By Manager Southworth." *Christian Science Monitor*. March 8, 1948.

"Braves—Dodgers Player Trade." *Christian Science Monitor*, March 8, 1948.

"Ray Sanders Sent Back To Braves." *San Antonio Express*. April 21, 1948.

"Sanders to Rejoin Braves Tuesday." *Lowell Sun*, May 1, 1948.

"Sanders, Post Optioned." *Lowell Sun*, May 20, 1948.

"Ray Sanders Is Assigned To Seattle of Coast Loop." *Hartford Courant*, May 26, 1948.

"Sanders, Due to Join Braves, Felled by Pitch." *Lowell Sun*. September 4, 1948.

"Ray Sanders Leaves Local Hospital Today." *Hartford Courant*. September 7, 1948.

"Ray Sanders Best in Clutch Says Bill Southworth; Big Help for Down the Stretch." *The Era*, Bradford, Pennsylvania, September 23, 1948.

"Ray Sanders To Sub For Jim Russell." *Charleston* (Pennsylvania) *Mail*. September 28, 1948.

"Ray Sanders Substitutes For Russell On Boston List of Eligibles In Series." *Hartford Courant*. September 28, 1948.

"Ray Sanders Accepts Braves Contract; Yankees Announce Yogi Berra In Fold." *Hartford Courant*. February 27, 1949.

"Sanders Out for Six Weeks." *The New York Times*. April 12, 1949.

"Ray Sanders Is Placed On Disabled List." *Hartford Courant*. April 16, 1949.

"Obituaries." *The Sporting News*. November 14, 1983, Vol. 196, Issue 20

"Police Reports: Traffic Fatalities, Franklin County." *St. Louis Post-Dispatch*. October 29, 1983.

St. Louis Cardinals Vintage World Series Film 1943, 1944, 1946 (A&E Television Networks)

www.baseball-reference.com

CLYDE SHOUN *by Bill Nowlin*

G	ERA	W	L	SV	GS	GF	CG	SHO	IP	H	R	ER	BB	SO	HR	HBP	WP	BFP
36	4.01	5	1	4	2	16	1	0	74	77	37	33	20	25	7	0	2	310

G	AB	R	H	2B	3B	HR	RBI	BB	SO	BA	OBP	SLG	SB	HBP
36	21	2	4	2	0	0	6	0	4	.190	.190	.286	0	0

Left-hander Clyde Shoun played for the Braves near the end of a long 14-year career in the majors that saw him make all but the last 16 of his 454 appearances in the National League. Typically used in relief, he started just 85 contests and posted a 73–59 lifetime record with a career 3.91 ERA. Shoun threw 34 complete games, three of them shutouts—and one of those was a no-hitter, just missing a perfect game by the smallest of margins (one base on balls). Above all else, he was a gamer, rebounding several times when it appeared his career was washed out.

At first glance, Shoun's birth and death data look as if they must be wrong. He's listed as being born on March 20, 1912, in Mountain City, Tennessee, but is listed as dying on the same day—and in Mountain Home, Tennessee. And yet he is buried at Sunset Cemetery in Mountain City. This is indeed all correct.

Prior to coming to Boston, Clyde Shoun had pitched a near perfect game no-hitter against the Braves in 1944.

Shoun did indeed die on his birthday, at age 56 on March 20, 1968. He actually passed away in Johnson City, but it was at a Veterans Affairs Medical Center named Mountain Home. The hospital maintains its own ZIP code and mailing address, and it is indeed Mountain Home, TN 37684.

Shoun's family originated in the Alsace-Lorraine region of the Volunteer State, but the oldest ancestor today's family has traced actually arrived in Philadelphia, Pennsylvania by ship in the late 1600s. These forbearers settled in Loudoun County, Virginia, but moved to the east Tennessee county now known as Johnson County when Leonard Shoun was given a land grant. Leonard and his wife, Barbara, arrived in 1792, Barbara pregnant at age 17 and Leonard toting an ax, a pick, and a bundle of clothing. He was 19. They had a large homestead at Shoun's Cross Roads where they farmed—and raised 17 children. When he died, Leonard was said to be one of the most well-to-do men in the county, maybe the wealthiest.

It was good farmland and the Shouns worked the land, with the help of "several slaves" that he owned. Leonard also owned a country store and an iron forge at Shoun's. A Shoun family history written by Carl Neal reports that Leonard's store hauled goods in from Baltimore, and that the pig (or raw) iron came from Lynchburg. Despite being illiterate, he devised a system of symbols to keep his mercantile accounts. He apparently once charged a customer for a cheese when the man had purchased a grindstone, and a bitter argument ensued until the parties realized it was simply that Leonard had neglected to draw a hole in the center of the circular symbol he used to denote the commodities.

Clyde Shoun's father, Leonard's grandson, was a farmer and a logger, working both the fields and the forest on the land. Clyde himself, his niece Dane Brooks remembers, was always known as Hardrock: "They worked hard. It was a different time. Uncle Hardrock was the fifth child of nine living children. There were four that died as infants. There would have been 13. Twelve siblings of Hardrock's, had they all lived. Everybody called him Hardrock. That's all anyone around here ever said. No one ever called him Clyde."

Some interest in sports ran in the family. Clyde's brother Miles played professional basketball for the Firestone Rubber Company team before World War II and the emergence of the NBA. Hardrock, of course, played baseball. "The story is that he could throw a ball so hard that they just called him Hardrock," said his niece. "Before he went there [to the major leagues], he played with some of the local teams here. They were ball players; that's what they did."

Shoun was a southpaw, standing 6'1" and with a playing weight of 188 pounds. He first turns up playing semi-pro ball in South Carolina's Textile Baseball Leagues at Chester, S.C., in 1934, and was signed by Bill Pierre of the Birmingham ball club. Working in the Southern Association during his first year in the pros (1935), he performed very well, with a record of 12–8 and a 3.83 earned run average in 169 innings of work—excellent numbers considering that Birmingham finished seventh in the eight-team Southern Association. He led his team in victories, and the pennant-contending Chicago Cubs purchased Shoun's contract for the stretch drive (a contemporary

Shoun was principally used in relief during the 1948 campaign.

column in the Chicago *Tribune* said he was nicknamed "Duster").

In his August 7, 1935 debut he threw the last two innings of a game the Cubs lost 6–0 to the visiting Pittsburgh Pirates; Shoun allowed one hit and struck out two. He got his first start on August 19, facing the Phillies in Philadelphia. He gave up a run in the bottom of the first, but then pitched scoreless ball through the next six innings. Philly's Joe Bowman had a no-hitter through six, but began to falter in the seventh. Ken O'Dea batted for Shoun in the top of the eighth and doubled. Billy Herman drove in two, the Cubs took (and held) the lead, and Shoun got the win. Overall, he worked 13 innings during the remainder of the season, and finished with a 1–0 record and a 2.84 ERA. The Cubs won the pennant, and Shoun was eligible to play in the World Series. He did not see action, however, in the six-game showdown with the Detroit Tigers—which the Cubs lost.

In 1936, Shoun began the year with the NL champs, but was released back to Birmingham in mid-May. He had appeared in four games and thrown just 4⅓ innings for Chicago, giving up three hits, six walks, and six earned runs. In the Southern Association he got back on track, and was able to get in 17 complete games and over 200 innings of work for manager Riggs Stephenson, post a 15–11 record, and establish an earned run average of 3.44. Birmingham made it to the Dixie Series finals but was eliminated by Tulsa, which scored five runs off Shoun in the first two innings of the deciding game.

For the next 11-plus years, though, Hardrock remained in major league ball. The 1937 season saw him post a 7–7 record and a dismal 5.61 ERA (worst on the staff) for second-place Chicago.

Then came 1938, and things weren't looking that good when Cubs manager Charley Grimm left Shoun in to be pounded for 11 runs on 15 hits in five innings during a March 21, 1938, spring training game against the Pirates. It was a sign of what was to come. Just before the season opened, the Cubs made a play for former 30-game winner Dizzy Dean of the Cardinals, sending Shoun to St. Louis, along with Curt Davis, Tuck Stainback and—oh, yes—$185,000, one of the largest cash sums in a baseball transaction at the time.

The Cubs won the pennant; the Cardinals finished sixth. St. Louis, however, got the best of the deal. A sore-armed Dean went 7–1 that year in limited duty, but his career was essentially over after that. Shoun, meanwhile, became a dependable workhorse for the Cards. His record in 1938 was balanced again, at 6–6, but with a considerably improved 4.14 ERA. He started in just 12 of his 40 games, increasingly being used in relief. And in '39, he was used almost exclusively out of the bullpen, appearing in a league-leading 53 games and earning a league-leading nine saves. He was 3–1, 3.76, and the 53 outings set a new major league record for pitchers, and helped the Cardinals to a strong second-place standing in the NL just 4.5 games behind the pennant-winning Reds.

It was apparently at some point in this second year with the Cards that Shoun made an impression on a future sports broadcaster, Art Rust, Jr. A young boy at the time, Rust approached him for an autograph at the Polo Grounds and was called a "black bastard." In 1976, Rust wrote about this and a couple of other incidents, "These humiliations really shook up this 11-year-old."

Hardrock got a lot of work in 1940, leading the league in appearances again with a record 54, but also earning 19 starts and throwing 13 complete games for third-place St. Louis. He won 13 games and lost 11, with a 3.92 ERA, not bad considering the inconsistency of his use as a starter on some days and a reliever on others. August was the most interesting month. On the 13th, he threw a seven-hitter, holding his former Cubs to one run, while he drove in two at the plate. On August 26, he committed a balk without even touching the baseball. The Cardinals were hoping to pull off a hidden ball trick at second base, with the shortstop holding the ball. Shoun took the mound—and was immediately called for a balk for taking his position without the ball in his possession.

For reasons unclear to us today, Shoun was unsigned as late as February 1941. He lost three weeks to a sprained ankle that year, and was never fully effective, though he still made it into 26 games. His record was 3–5, with only 70 innings pitched, compared with 197 1/3 in 1940. His earned run average had shot up, too, to 5.66. His off-year came at a most inopportune time, as the Cardinals seemed finally poised to win a pennant and held first much of the season before finishing just 2.5 games behind the champion Dodgers.

He faced only seven batters for St. Louis in 1942 before being sold to Cincinnati. There, once again, he rebounded in a major way, putting up a sterling 2.23 ERA over 36 games and 72 2/3 innings despite an uninspiring record of 1–3.

The next year—1943—was most unusual. Shoun started only five games, but won 14 while losing just five. This gave him the league lead in winning percentage among pitchers with 15 or more decisions (.737). Hardrock appeared in 45 games and his ERA was a good 3.06. He also helped himself at the plate by batting .310, his second straight year over .300. The only drawback was that his old teammates in St. Louis went to the World Series in this and three of the next four years through

1946, while Shoun and Cincinnati were never really in contention.

With World War II well under way, Shoun was accepted for service into the Navy after passing his physical in March 1944, but he was not called for duty until after the season—which was a good one. He was 13–10, with an ERA of 3.02 in 202 2/3 innings of work, starting 21 games in his most active season ever. In addition, he entered a very exclusive club by throwing a no-hitter against the Boston Braves on May 15 in Cincinnati. He faced just one more than the minimum, a perfect game spoiled only by a third-inning walk to Boston pitcher Jim Tobin (who himself had pitched a no-hitter just 18 days earlier). Shoun struck out only one batter in a 1–0 game won by third baseman Chuck Aleno's home run in the fifth inning; Tobin scattered just five hits himself. Aleno saw no action in the field, not an assist and not a putout, while first baseman McCormick made eight putouts. The win pulled the Reds into second place, but Cincinnati eventually finished third.

On January 9, 1945, Hardrock was sworn into the Navy at Fort Oglethorpe, Georgia. Not surprisingly, Shoun quickly wound up at the Great Lakes Naval Station playing for the training center baseball team under coach Bob Feller. He was sent to the Pacific, to join Bill Dickey's Navy ballteam in Hawaii. This squad of servicemen athletes featured the likes of Yankee star Joe Gordon at short, future A's standout Ferris Fain at first, and Cards 20-game winner Johnny Beazley on the mound. But despite his inclusion on such a team, which routinely routed other military clubs, Shoun would initially have a tough time regaining his old form after the war.

Back with the Reds after his discharge, Hardrock had a difficult year in 1946. His record was just 1–6, with an ERA of 4.10. He had only five starts and threw just 79 innings. He saw almost no action in the early weeks of 1947, and was sold to the Boston Braves in a cash deal on June 7. He was 5–3, 4.40 with third-place Boston, his best game an 8–0 shutout against his old Cincinnati mates on September 10. When Hardrock arrived in Boston, he was reunited with manager Billy Southworth, for whom he had played in 1940 until he was sold to Cincinnati during the 1942 season. Shoun was certainly not the only Braves player in this boat; so many of Southworth's former St. Louis players joined the Braves during this period, they came to be known as the "Cape Cod Cardinals."

In the pennant-winning year of 1948, wearing number 26, Shoun ran up a 5–1 record primarily in relief (he started just three games) with an ERA of 4.01. His first start came on June 18, and he pitched a complete game against the Reds, winning 5–4. He later beat the Red again in late September, and also notched four saves for the NL champs. Though eligible for the 1948 World Series, he was not called upon in the six-game loss to Cleveland.

On May 11, 1949, it was back to Chicago for Shoun, this time to the White Sox in a cash deal. It was the first time he'd pitched in the American League, and his stay there wouldn't last long—just 23⅓ innings over 16 contests. Shoun compiled a lackluster 5.79 ERA for the Pale Hose, but his final big league game on July 19, 1949 proved memorable. He entered as a left-hand specialist to face Ted Williams in the top of the ninth in a 3–3 game. Two men were on base and nobody out, but Hardrock got Ted to hit a high pop fly to short leftfield. The Red Sox got lucky, though, as Steve Souchock tried to one-hand the ball and missed it entirely. The bases were now loaded with Vern Stephens due up, so Shoun was taken out for a righty, Max Surkont. He promptly gave up a game-winning two-run single.

A week later, when the White Sox left Chicago to travel to Boston, Hardrock was left behind. According to a news story, Sox GM Frank Lane said that Shoun would "remain in Chicago pending disposition of his contract." A few days later, it was announced that he had signed with the Indianapolis Indians as a free agent. The AP dispatch assigned him a third nickname: the predictable "Lefty."

Overall Shoun was 1–1 in major league play in 1949, with a 5.55 ERA, and finished out the year in Indianapolis with an identical 1–1 record (though with a more respectable 3.15 earned run average.) And while his big-league

days were gone, he had one more comeback in him. In 1950 and 1951, he pitched for Oakland in the competitive Pacific Coast League, getting a major amount of work the first year (233 innings, 16–10, 4.56 ERA.) Playing for the Oaks under Charlie Dressen, he helped the team to a first-place finish in the PCL. In 1951, though, he just didn't have it. He started the season 2–4 with a 5.49 ERA, and decided to call it a day. By late May, he'd returned home to Mountain City.

Shoun had a first wife, Anna Mary (her surname was Mary), and they had two daughters—Anna Mary and Linda. Shoun worked the family farm, largely raising tobacco, and owned and operated a commercial dog kennel. The Shouns later divorced and Hardrock married a woman named Pearl.

Niece Dane Brooks recalls her father, Leonard, taking her to a few local exhibition ball games and seeing Uncle Hardrock pitch. Clyde Shoun also served as a city councilman in Johnson City, but he died early of liver problems, after eight months of illness, at the age of 56.

Sources

Interview with Dane Brooks by Bill Nowlin, December 11, 2006.
The Art Rust quotation comes from the *New York Times*, May 9, 1976.
Thanks to Matt Hill.

SEBASTIAN "SIBBY" SISTI *by Saul Wisnia*

G	AB	R	H	2B	3B	HR	RBI	BB	SO	BA	OBP	SLG	SB	HBP
83	221	30	54	6	2	0	21	31	34	.244	.340	.290	0	1

The first four men inducted into the Boston Braves Hall of Fame after its formation by fans of the long-defunct National League club were Warren Spahn, John Sain, Tommy Holmes, and Sebastian "Sibby" Sisti. In order, that's one Hall of Famer, two All-Stars, and one .244 hitter who lasted for 14-plus years in the majors by playing wherever and whenever he was asked. Nobody questioned the selection.

Sisti didn't belong in the class of Spahn, Sain, and Holmes as a ballplayer, yet for the many Braves fans who both watched him perform and attended reunions of the team during the last two decades he *was* the Boston Braves. The sad-eyed, gravel-voiced athlete-turned-truck driver symbolized the team's working-class demeanor better than perhaps any other individual, and delighted in returning to town and greeting old diehards who

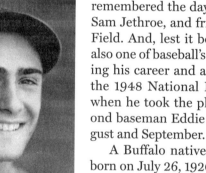

After only a season and a half in the minors, Sibby Sisti joined the Boston "Bees" in 1939 as an 18-year-old rookie.

remembered the days of Earl Torgeson, Sam Jethroe, and fried clams at Braves Field. And, lest it be forgotten, he was also one of baseball's top utilitymen during his career and a key contributor to the 1948 National League champions when he took the place of injured second baseman Eddie Stanky during August and September.

A Buffalo native and an only child born on July 26, 1920, Sisti actually had his initial big-league tryout for Boston's "other team" at the tender age of 15, in 1935. Driven three hours down to Cleveland by area bird dog scout Bill Meyers, he donned a Red Sox uniform and took hitting and fielding practice under the eye of Sox manager Joe Cronin. "I was still a sophomore in high school," Sisti recalled. "It was a big thing for me, because here I was, the first time I had ever been in a big-league ballpark, and I'm working out on the field with these big major leaguers. I had a Boston uniform on, and it was a little big. There was hardly anybody in the stands, because we were working out early before the game. It was a new experience, and being a young kid there with veteran big-league players—guys I had read and dreamed about, more or less—it was a little nerve-racking for me.

"I think I did all right for a young kid," he continued. "I don't remember too much about it, but I do remember taking batting practice. After the last swing, they usually want you to head down to first base, so they can see how you run. I did that. Then they hit me some 15 to 20 groundballs in the infield. That was the extent of it; I was only there one day, and they were just looking. They knew they couldn't sign you at that age, but I guess they were keeping me on their list for future prospects. When the tryout was over with, I had to get dressed and watch the game from the stands with the scout. They wouldn't let you sit on the bench if you weren't a signed ballplayer. Incidentally, that scout, Bill Meyers, was the same guy who signed [Hall of Famer Warren] Spahn for the Braves a few years later."

The Sox didn't sign Sisti, but a few years later an opportunity opened up with Boston's National League franchise. Meyers had told another Buffalo-area scout, Jack Onslow of the Braves (then known as the Bees), about Sisti, and at the beginning of Sibby's senior year at Buffalo's Canisius High School, his father went along with Onslow—a former big-leaguer himself who would later manage in the majors—to meet Bees officials in the Hub. Sibby didn't know about the meeting until he got a call from his dad informing him that he had been signed to a contract with the team's Class A Eastern League club in Hartford, Connecticut. Like any 17-year-old kid, he was more concerned with what the news meant to his immediate situation than the exciting future possibilities.

"I had already played three years of football with the high school, and my father told me the Braves didn't want me to play my senior year," Sisti explained. "So I got in the doghouse a little bit, because I had to tell the coach and the principal that I couldn't play football because I had signed a professional baseball contract. But nobody else knew about it, so I still played basketball and baseball my last year in school. I just didn't play football."

After graduating in the spring of 1938, and before heading out to his first pro season with Hartford, Sisti was called to Boston in June so Bees officials could look over their new signee. "I went up there for three days, and

Sisti stepped into the second base slot upon Eddie Stanky's injury and played an important role in the Tribe's pennant-winning campaign.

the first day I got into town, I had a little batting practice and a little fielding practice," he recalled. "I was still just 17 years old, and naturally, I again had to get off the bench when the game started. I was alone at the time, and didn't know where the heck to go [in Boston], so I just went up and sat in the bleachers of Braves Field. And the ballgame I saw that day [June 19] was when Johnny Vander Meer was trying for his third consecutive no-hitter. I remember Debs Garms getting the first hit off him [in the fourth inning]."

Two days later, Sisti left for Hartford. The speedy right-handed batter hit .293 there, playing a sure-handed third base for manager Eddie Onslow (brother of the scout who signed him, and a former Red Sox coach). That winter, Sibby got a letter from Bees general manager Bob Quinn requesting that he report to spring training in Bradenton with the big-league club in '39. Sisti didn't really think he had a chance yet at the majors; as he recalled, "I had already signed another Hartford contract. They just wanted me to go down to Boston, maybe get in a few games, and get a little experience with a big-league club." Initially, he was right. When the Bees broke camp, Sisti went back to Hartford, this time to play second.

As a Braves farmhand named Hank Aaron would 15 years later, however, Sisti earned a swift promotion because of another man's injury. Boston had traded for Reds shortstop Eddie Miller over the winter, and in June Miller and aging outfielder Al Simmons ran into each other in center going after a Texas Leaguer. Miller broke his ankle, and this on top of other injuries forced the club to call for reinforcements. Sisti was batting .312 at Hartford, and on July 21, 1939, 18-year-old "Sebbi" (as some newspapers then called him) suddenly found himself up with the Bees as the youngest player in the majors. That same afternoon at Braves Field, he made his first trip to the plate in the ninth inning of a tight game against the Cubs. Boston trailed 3–1; a reported crowd of just 2,797 was on hand to witness the moment.

"Everybody remembers their first at-bat in the major leagues," Sisti would recount. "My first time up, [manager Casey] Stengel put me in to pinch-hit for [pitcher] Jim Turner and told me to try to beat out a bunt—because in those days I was a fair bunter. I was facing a guy by the name of Charlie Root, an old-timer. I laid the ball down a little too close to Charlie, and I was thrown out."

In many circumstances a teenager would have been overwhelmed by such a rapid ascension to the top, but the circumstances here were perfect. The Bees were a seventh-place club that wasn't drawing well, so there was little pressure on Sibby to excel right away. Nobody expected him to perform up to Miller's level, least of all manager Stengel. What Casey had was patience and a genuine affinity for Sisti, and he got him into 63 games over the summer. Sibby's first hit came two days after his debut, against the Pirates, and although he batted just .228 with one homer and 11 RBIs in 215 at-bats, the youngster showed his versatility by playing at second, short, and third. Quick and steady defensively, he clearly made an impression; when the 1940 season began, Sisti was Boston's starting third baseman Even his uniform number got an upgrade, from 25 to 1. (When rookie Tommy Holmes came up in '42, he took #1 and Sibby switched to #2.)

Sibby held down the job at third for the next two seasons, hitting a more respectable .251 and .259 although he still showed little power and made an alarming 44 errors in 1941 alone (41 of them at third). But despite a return to their old nickname in '41, the Braves continued to plod along near the cellar. As Sisti later joked, "We finished seventh four years in a row, but we were thankful for the Phillies—because they finished eighth each year." In the midst of the team's travails, Sisti's determination and passion for the game shone through. He and catcher Phil Masi were often spotted by Stengel taking extra batting and fielding practice, and a special relationship developed between the skipper and his young charges on the long train rides from one National League city to the next.

"Casey was always talking with Phil Masi and myself," said Sisti. "Phil was also a young fellow, and we'd talk baseball all the time. You never heard anything but baseball, especially when we got on those trains. Phil and I would be sitting there in the Pullman coach, and Casey would always come around and sit down and start talking with us. He'd talk about game strategy, or he'd tell some stories or what-not. I guess you could say I was more or less one of his pets."

After an eventful offseason that included the Pearl Harbor attack on December 7 and much happier news 20 days later—Sibby's marriage to Norine Barone—more changes were in store. The arrival of rookie Nanny Fernandez to play third base prompted Sisti's shift to second in '42, and even though his average plummeted to .211, he got into 129 games (all but five at the keystone sack). It seemed nothing could keep Sisti down with Stengel around, but World War II did the trick—and Sibby lost the 1943–45 seasons while serving with the Coast Guard. Stengel was fired during this same period, making the task of winning back a spot on the Braves that much harder for Sibby after the war.

"I went to spring training with the team in 1946," said Sisti. "Coming out of the service after three years and going back to a big-league camp, I didn't really know *what* I could do. I played ball my last year in the Coast Guard, but that's like playing with a bunch of semipro or high-school players; it wasn't real good baseball. So, when I got to spring training, I didn't really know what to expect. Billy Southworth was now managing the club, and he told me to work out at third, so I did. I lasted until Opening Day, when he told me he was sending me down to Indianapolis to learn how to play shortstop. I told him I was signed as a shortstop, and I sure knew how to play shortstop. But it didn't do any good; they still sent me down."

If Sibby was miffed by his demotion, he took it out on American Association pitching. Asked about his midcareer foray to the Indianapolis Indians in the summer of '46, Sisti said simply, "I had a pretty good year." He was, in fact, *The Sporting News* Minor League Player of the Year after leading the Triple A circuit in batting (with a .343 mark), hits (203), and triples (14), while scoring 99 runs and knocking in 86. He was back up to the majors in 1947, signing a Braves contract on January 31 for what newspapers reported as "a nice raise in pay," and then earning a role as starting shortstop on a quickly rising team.

He got off to a great start, but unfortunately a freak play soon derailed Sisti's campaign. New third baseman Bob Elliott was out briefly with a thumb injury, and Bama Rowell—normally an outfielder, and much less agile than Elliott—was filling in. Trying to compensate for the loss of range on the left side, Sibby ran over behind Rowell on a grounder in a July 11 game against Cincinnati. Lunging for it, he landed on his left shoulder, suffered three ruptured ligaments, and was sidelined for more than a month. He wound up playing just 56 games, batting .281.

The setback was in keeping with Sisti's career, which had more than its share of bad breaks, literally and figuratively. As Boston sportswriter Al Hirshberg once assessed, "On the few occasions when [Sisti] seemed to have a job wrapped up and won, he got hurt. When Sisti gets hurt, he does the job completely. The most sewn-up athlete in baseball, he carries the scars of 75 stitches on his carcass, giving him the title of 'The Embroidered Man.'" In this case, muscle was grafted from his left leg to strengthen his shoulder, a procedure requiring 24 stitches on his leg and 20 on his shoulder.

When the 1948 season rolled around, a recovered Sibby was once again fighting for a spot in the regular lineup. The club had called up Alvin Dark from minor-league Milwaukee to play short, and Sisti battled hard with the much-heralded rookie before Southworth declared Sibby the starter just a day before the April 20 opener at Philadelphia. This was just the beginning of a roller-coaster year. As Sisti described it: "First I got cut up on a takeout at second base, and that knocked me out of the lineup for a couple of weeks. Dark went in, and he didn't do too well. Then I went in and *I* didn't do too well, so they put Dark back in. This time he clicked, and he stayed there the rest of the year."

Dark wound up batting .322 and being named Rookie of the Year, and Sisti was back on the bench—but not for long. Second baseman Eddie Stanky broke his ankle on July 8, and manager Southworth turned first to Bob Sturgeon and later to Connie Ryan to take "the Brat's" place. Sisti remained patient, and then came July 31. The first-place Braves went into the bottom of the ninth at home trailing 6–3 against the Cardinals, one of three teams on their tail in the standings. Bob Elliott and Al Lyons walked, Clint Conatser and Sturgeon singled, and it was 6–4 with the bases loaded when Sisti came up as a pinch-hitter with one out. Facing Jim Hearn, he rocked a pitch to deepest right-center at Braves Field between outfielders Stan Musial and Enos Slaughter. A United Press account described the scene and its ramifications: "The 31,841 fans stood and cheered at the top of their voices for more than a solid minute as three Tribal base runners flashed around the bases and Sisti, utility infielder, slid madly into third.... By winning, the Braves maintained a 5½-game lead over the now second-place Giants, a 6½-game bulge over the third-place Dodgers, and eight games over the fourth-rung Redbirds."

The clutch hit won Southworth over. Sisti had his starting second base job back again after a six-year hiatus, and he kept it the rest of year with steady play in the field (six errors in 44 games) and at the plate (hitting near .300 down the stretch). Sportswriter Howell Stevens of the *Boston Post* wrote that Sibby "looked like Frankie Frisch in snagging prospective 'Texas Leaguers' in short right." Still, when Stanky returned in late September, Sibby was sent to the bench for the World Series against Cleveland.

While he made just two late-game appearances in the Series, Sisti was on the field for perhaps its two biggest plays. In the opener, he was at first base running for Eddie Stanky in the eighth, and had the best view in Braves Field when Indians pitcher Bob Feller and shortstop Lou Boudreau attempted to pick Phil Masi off second. Masi was called safe, although replays (and Sibby later) suggested otherwise, and Phil was then singled in by Tommy Holmes for the only run of a 1–0 Braves win. The Indians took three of the next four games, however, making Sibby's only Series at-bat, in the ninth inning of the sixth contest, a do-or-die situation. The Braves were down to their last chance of the season, and Sisti, still an adept bunter, was called upon by Southworth to pinch-hit and move the potential tying run from first base to second in a 4–3 game. His bunt attempt resulted in a double play instead, as catcher Jim Hegan caught his pop-up and

Sisti, who assumed the role of "super sub" over the course of his 11-year stay in Boston, became known as "Mr. Boston Braves" through his longstanding efforts in conjunction with the Boston Braves Historical Association to preserve the memory of the departed ballclub.

threw to second to double off Connie Ryan. One out later, the Indians were champions.

Sisti never shirked questions about this dubious incident—nor was he ever forced by Braves fans to wear goat horns as Johnny Pesky or Bill Buckner did after similar miscues for the Red Sox. The public forgave Sibby, perhaps because unlike Pesky or Buckner, he wasn't a star player expected to win, nor was his team. That winter, in fact, he was honored at a Boston baseball writers' dinner with a plaque and a pair of cleats for "filling the shoes" of Stanky during the summer just past, and drew shouts of "No, no!" when he tried to take the blame at the podium for his team's Series defeat. "It was the best thing that ever happened to me in Boston," Sibby later said of the outpouring of gratitude. He was, in fact, so buoyed by the fan support he received after the World Series that he didn't even have any trouble donning uniform #13 in 1951, letting catcher Ebba St. Clair take his old #7.

Although Sisti's playing time waned after this (he appeared in 100 games just twice in his final eight seasons), he developed a sense of humor about his situation. When Boston sportswriter John Gillooly of the *Record-American* wrote that Sibby had been "sitting on the bench so long he had enough splinters in his rear end to start a match factory," Sisti approached Gillooly in the Braves dugout the next day and said, "I have a gift for you in my pocket. This is my manufacturing company." And he gave him a box of matches.

Sisti was equally self-effacing when it came to his .244 lifetime batting average. With the exception of the 1939 season, the sacrifice fly rule was not in force between 1931 and 1954, a span that covered nearly Sisti's entire career. He often joked that he would have had a much higher lifetime average if he had the sac fly on his side. When someone would ask "How high?" he'd shout back, "Hell, at least .245!"

In 1949, with Stanky back at second and Dark entrenched at short, Sisti resumed his role as "Super Sub"—capable of filling in at any infield or outfield spot save for catcher (although, as the team's "unofficial" third receiver, he often caught batting practice). Southworth liked to platoon, and that summer Sibby saw almost equal time in the outfield, second base, and shortstop as well as one game at third base. It was more of the same the next three years; no one position to call his own, but plenty of action at a variety of spots. All told, his career of 1,016 games included 359 at second base, 290 at third, 209 at short, 74 in the outfield, and two games at first. He was never again a full-time starter after 1948, but he did get into 114 contests in '51—and batted a very solid .279. Not surprisingly, given Southworth's faith in him, Sisti was said to have supported the embattled manager during the dissension that reportedly rocked the '49 team.

There would be no chance, however, for Sibby to redeem himself in postseason play. The Braves finished fourth each season from 1949 to 1951, and one by one the stalwarts of the '48 champions disappeared from the box scores. Still in his early 30s, Sisti became the senior member of the club in terms of tenure, and in 1951 and '52 he helped develop his young roommate Johnny Logan into one of the National League's best shortstops. Logan, a loud, tough customer who never backed down from a fight, took an instant liking to the soft-spoken veteran, and the two remained lifelong friends.

"He was a baseball man, and I was his student," recalled Logan. "When I was a rookie, he loved my ability. I asked him, 'Sibby, can you give me some tips?' He said, 'John, remember, if you're a shortstop, just play natural. Don't try and copy anybody. Just play your natural game, and get to know your third baseman and your first baseman.' Sibby Sisti was one of the finest guys that I ever met." At later reunions Logan relished in giving his good-natured roomie "the needle," riding Sibby about his late-night habits of reading Westerns and smoking foul-smelling cigars—which Johnny dumped in the toilet after his friend fell off to sleep.

As Logan progressed, Sisti and the team slumped. Sibby's average fell off to .212 in 1952, and the Braves finished seventh with a woeful 64–89 record. Just 281,278 fans showed up at Braves Field, a far cry from the 1,455,439 who had packed the stands to watch the NL champs just four years before. Still, Sisti was shocked like almost everybody else on the club by what transpired the next March. The team had spent spring training in Bradenton, Florida, as usual, and there was hope that Boston would be a much improved club with promising youngsters like Logan, third baseman Eddie Mathews, and catcher Del Crandall. On March 17, 1953, along with teammate and fellow Buffalo native Warren Spahn, Sisti got permission from manager Charlie Grimm to take a day off and make a quick $100 on an endorsement deal—big money for a guy whose biggest major league paycheck was $12,000.

"Warren and I were up in St. Petersburg making a commercial for Gillette," Sisti recalled. "After I got through with my segment, I went into the other room and was looking at the ticker tape coming out of one of those old globes. I saw that the National League meeting had just concluded, and the Boston Braves were now going to be moved to Milwaukee. I went back into the director where he was shooting Spahn's scene, and I told him that the 'B' on the cap was no good. He says, 'What do you mean by that?' and I said, 'We just moved to Milwaukee.' He just said, 'When we make the announcement and show this commercial on TV, we'll say 'Warren Spahn and Sibby Sisti, *formerly* of the Boston Braves, now of the Milwaukee Braves.' That's how they did it, and the commercials ran that year."

It was only two weeks before Opening Day, and Sisti said the concept of going to Milwaukee was "as green as apple pie to me." In other words, he didn't care for it. He had been in Boston nearly 13 years, and he may as well have stayed there. He had just 23 at-bats during the team's triumphant maiden season in Wisconsin, and appeared in nine games as a defensive replacement (with no at-bats) in '54 before being released and then re-signed as a coach. He was 35 years old.

Sisti was asked to manage in the minors for the Braves the next season, and later spent a decade at the helm of farm clubs in Quebec, Corpus Christi, Austin, and Sacramento. For several of these campaigns he was a player-manager, inserting himself in at various positions and batting as high as .297. Son Michael often came along, taking batting practice with his dad's players and eventually had a short stint in the minors himself. Sibby became an infield-outfield instructor with Phillies minor leaguers for a couple of seasons, coached with the expansion Seattle Pilots in 1969, then shortly thereafter quit the game and returned home to get a "real job" as a truck driver.

"I had a couple of daughters who got married, so I couldn't take it easy," he said with a laugh. "I was no millionaire, and besides, I could make just as much working around Buffalo as I could in baseball as a coach or manager. I had already been in the game nearly 40 years." During travels before and after his playing days, he brought along a baseball that he eventually had signed by an eclectic group including Hall of Fame ballplayers like Hank Aaron and Al Simmons and first-rate celebrities like bandleader Harry James and comedians Abbott & Costello.

A father of five, Sisti settled just outside Buffalo in Amherst, New York, and doted on them and a growing brood of grandchildren and great-grandchildren. He cared for his wife Norine when she became ill in recent years, returned to Boston for a 1988 reunion of the '48 NL champs, and then continued coming back for all but one of the first 14 annual get-togethers of the Boston Braves Historical Association (BBHA)—staying away only after major surgery. Along with his 1994 induction into the Boston Braves Hall of Fame started by the Association, he drew recognition from the Canisius High Hall of Fame, the Buffalo Baseball Hall of Fame, and the Greater Buffalo Sports Hall of Fame. His final BBHA appearance came in 2004 at the age of 84, less than two years before his death on April 24, 2006, in Amherst. As usual, he drew the day's loudest cheers and laughs.

When the 2002 convention of the Society for American Baseball Research in Boston coincided with an Atlanta Braves-Red Sox interleague series at Fenway Park, the Super Sub threw out a ceremonial first pitch at the

June 28 opener to cheers from a crowd that included many SABR and BBHA members as well as other fans whose Braves caps had a "B" on the front. Atlanta's 4–2 win prompted *Boston Globe* writer Bob Hohler to playfully question whether the Sox were under "The Curse of Sibby Sisti." Sibby's fellow first-pitch honoree that night was SABR president Claudia Perry.

Sibby was no Bambino, but he had two unique claims to fame later in life. In 1973, authors Brendan Boyd and Fred Harris ended their popular volume, *The Great American Baseball Card Flipping, Trading and Bubble Gum Book* with a page featuring one of Sisti's cards accompanied by a one-line epitaph beneath it: "Goodnight Sibby Sisti, wherever you are." Most readers probably had no idea.

If they were paying close attention a decade later, however, they found him. In 1983, Sisti was asked to be a technical advisor for director Barry Levinson's popular 1940-era baseball movie *The Natural*. Filmed in and around Buffalo's War Memorial Field, the film told the fictitious story of the New York Knights, a National League team whose struggles on the field and in the stands would be quite familiar to old Braves fans. Sisti helped star Robert Redford (who signed his ball) and other actors with their baseball sequences, and also had a bit part as manager of the Pittsburgh Pirates. An annual highlight of BBHA reunions came when Sibby would reveal the sum of his latest royalty check for his appearance; the checks usually ranged from 65 cents to about four dollars.

In the film's climactic scene, Sisti comes to the mound and calls in a young fireballing reliever to face Redford's Roy Hobbs. A pennant-winning Hobbs home run into the light towers results, and Sisti delighted in telling reunion attendees that after reliving his managerial error again and again on videotape, he had devised a solution. "If they ever make a *Natural II*," he stated emphatically, "I'm going out there again. But this time, on the first pitch, Redford's going right down on his ass!"

Sources

Author interviews with Sibby Sisti, 1991–2004

Johnny Logan quotes from tribute to Sisti at 2006 Boston Braves Historical Association reunion

Boyd, Brendan, and Harris, Fred, *The Great American Baseball Card Flipping, Trading and Bubble Gum Book*, Little Brown & Company, Boston, 1973

Fiorito, Len, and Marazzi, Rich, *Baseball Players of the 1950s: A Biographical Dictionary of All 1560 Major Leaguers*, McFarland & Company, North Carolina, 2003

Hirshberg, Al, *Boston Braves: The Pick and the Shovel*, Waverly House, Boston, 1948.

Hirshberg, Al, "The loneliest player in the majors," *True Baseball Yearbook*, 1953.

Hohler, Bob, "Haunted House," *Boston Globe*, June 29, 2002

Marazzi, Rich, "Goodnight Sibby Sisti, wherever you are!" *Sports Collector's Digest*, July 28, 1995

Pave, Marvin, "Sisti a model teammate," *Boston Globe*, April 29, 2006

"Sebbi Sisti recalled by Boston Bees," *Hartford Courant*, July 21, 1939

Stevens, Howell, "Braves Class of N.L. Once They Got Rolling," *1948 World Series Official Program*

Watson, Earl, "Big leaguer's son lived every kid's dream" *Village Daily Sun*, Nov. 1, 2006

Associated Press/United Press stories, 1939–53

Historicbaseball.com

Baseball-reference.com

WARREN SPAHN *by Jim Kaplan*

G	ERA	W	L	SV	GS	GF	CG	SHO	IP	H	R	ER	BB	SO	HR	HBP	WP	BFP
36	3.71	15	12	1	35	1	16	3	257	237	115	106	77	114	19	1	4	1064

G	AB	R	H	2B	3B	HR	RBI	BB	SO	BA	OBP	SLG	SB	HBP
37	90	10	15	3	0	1	7	6	24	.167	.219	.233	0	0

The fifth-winningest pitcher of all time, Warren Spahn went 363–245 over parts of 21 years from 1942 to 1965. Only by remaining in the game two seasons too long did he fail to finish with an ERA under 3.00 (3.09) and a winning percentage over .600 (.597), and his totals are all the more impressive considering that he didn't record his first big-league victory until he was 25. Spahn should make everyone's list of the 10 best pitchers in baseball history, and was the one "sure thing" Braves fans had to cheer for through the team's final five years in Boston—and far beyond.

Named after both President Warren G. Harding and his own father, Warren Edward Spahn was born in Buffalo, New York, on April 23, 1921, the fifth of six children and the first of two sons to Ed and Mabel Spahn. Supporting his family in the city's blue-collar East End, Ed was a $27-a-week wallpaper salesman who didn't own a car. His family ate meat maybe once a week, and his children stuffed their shoes with newspapers. A good bowler and semipro baseball player but too small at 5 feet 7 and 130 pounds to dream of a big-league career, Ed sublimated his disappointment by teaching the game to left-handed Warren, the most promising athlete in the family. Ed knew there were only so many positions open for a lefty; so just in case Warren couldn't hit well enough to play first base (his favorite position), Ed taught him exhaustively how to throw fastballs and curves from a mound he built in the backyard. "You've got to have control," Ed said over and over. "Without control you're nothing!" Warren nodded and kept dreaming of playing first in the big leagues.

"He insisted that I throw with a fluid motion, and the high leg kick was part of the deception to the hitter," Warren told Oklahoma City's *Daily Oklahoman* in 1998. "Hitters said the ball seemed to come out of my uniform."

The secret of Spahn's future injury-free longevity was the foundation laid by his dad. "He taught me how to follow through with my shoulder and body, how to throw without any strain, how to get the most out of my pitch and out of my weight even when I was a skinny kid," Spahn told sportswriter Bob Broeg. "He taught me how to roll a curveball, how to let it go off my fingers at the last moment. He taught me how to pass my knee by my right elbow.

"I thought it was a lot of drudgery. It was lots more fun just to pick up the ball and throw, but Dad wouldn't let me play catch unless I did it correctly."

Ed and Warren went to Buffalo Bisons minor-league games together, and Warren came to admire Buffalo first baseman Big Bill Kelly, a former major leaguer (A's 1920, Phillies 1928) who hit 149 homers for the Bisons from 1922 to 1930 and earlier had played semipro ball with Ed. Warren's father also instructed him to track the motion of Bisons pitcher Charlie "Lefty" Perkins (A's 1930, Dodgers 1934). "Now, if you want to be a pitcher, watch every move Charlie Perkins makes," Ed told his son. "If you want to be a first baseman, watch Bill Kelly."

Because of his father's connections on the Buffalo club, Warren got to shag balls in practice. When he couldn't remember names, he called all the players "Kelly," and they in turn called him Kelly Spahn. "After those Bison games my dad gave me the option of an ice cream cone or a streetcar ride home," Spahn told the *Tulsa Daily World's* John Ferguson. "Many times we took the ice cream and rehashed the game walking home."

Plainly, the kid wanted to be another Gehrig. When he was 9, Warren donned a uniform for the Lake City Social Club midgets and played with them for three years. He graduated to American Legion ball, always a great training ground for future major leaguers. Eventually Warren was playing first base for three local teams six days

a week. In a dream sequence on the Lake City Athletic Club team, the 110-pound 13-year-old played with his 37-year-old father and handled Ed's hard throws from third. "You'd think he was going to throw it right through me," Spahn told the *Christian Science Monitor's* Ed Rumill. "I weighed only about 110 pounds in those days. But he was teaching me to play hard and it did a lot of good."

When Warren arrived at South Park High School, however, he discovered an All-Scholastic player named Bill Benzerman (who later became a professional wrestler) occupying first base; reluctantly, Spahn took up pitching—this time for good. When his coach asked if he had a favorite uniform number, the ever-contrary lefty said 13. "Thirteen, eh? Not the superstitious kind, I see." "Uh-huh," Spahn said. "Thirteen has always been good luck for me."

The youngster led his high school to two city championships, went undefeated his last two seasons, and threw a no-hitter his senior year, but he was spurned by big-league scouts as too skinny. As fate would have it, a disenchanted Red Sox scout named Billy Meyers disagreed with the popular consensus. Meyers didn't like the deal the Sox were offering one Sebastian Sisti, so he had quit one Boston job and took Sisti with him to the other a few years earlier. (Sibby Sisti would later become a longtime teammate of Spahn's with the Boston and Milwaukee Braves.)

Meyers still worked part time for the Boston Bees (as they were called from 1936 to 1940 before a name change back to Braves) when he wasn't selling tickets for the New York Central Railroad. Impressed by Spahn's control, he signed the young hurler in 1940 (at Ed's insistence, after he graduated from high school), for $80 a month. Because his family couldn't afford expenses, Spahn turned down a partial scholarship from Cornell University and headed straight for the low minors.

Spahn's first pro assignment was the PONY League's Bradford (Pa.) Bees, managed by Jack Onslow. When Spahn asked for number 13, Onslow reportedly replied, "Fella, we don't carry any number 13s. A guy's liable to run into enough tough luck around here without wearing any number thirteen on his back."

Experimenting with a new delivery for an overhand curve after about one-third of the season, Spahn snapped the pitch too sharply and tore several tendons in his left

After over a three season WWII-induced absence from a major league mound, Warren Spahn would resume a pitching career that continued until 1965 and would result in induction into the Hall of Fame in 1973.

shoulder. Warren went home with his arm in a sling, and his father went into a depression. Then, after the youngster returned to Pennsylvania two weeks later, he threw his first hard pitch and tumbled off the mound clutching his shoulder. The trainer said he'd need a year off if he was lucky, and Onslow muttered, "You know, maybe I should have given that fellow number 13 after all." Back home, Ed Spahn reacted by going into a deeper depression and was hospitalized. Young Warren spent the remainder of the summer, the fall, and the winter checking baggage at the Buffalo railroad terminal.

With a 5–4 record, 62 strikeouts in 66 innings, and a 2.83 ERA in his brief stay, however, Spahn had showed promise. He recovered by the next season, only to run into more bad luck. In a 1941 appearance at spring training in San Antonio with the Braves, he suffered a broken and permanently disfigured nose courtesy of a teammate's errant throw. He also got some nicknames he didn't appreciate: Hooks and The Great Profile. Even his father called him Meatnose.

During the mid-'40s and early '50s, Boston's Braves and Red Sox fans were blessed with the presence of two of baseball's premier southpaws — Warren Spahn and Mel Parnell.

"When Dad's nose was broken, John Berardino's nose was also broken the same day," Spahn's son, Greg, recalls. "They sent John to a specialist to have it fixed. They called Dad in and told him, 'Warren, we will send you to a specialist to have your nose fixed, but most people that have that done end up with sinus problems and you're not a very good-looking guy.' The ballclub didn't want to spend the money on Dad's nose. John Berardino being an actor, that was a different story."

Nonetheless, Bees manager Casey Stengel said, "He's only 20 years old and needs work. But mark my word, if nothing happens to the kid, he can be a great one." Stengel also said, "Someday he's going to be one of the best left-handers in the league."

In the summer of '41, playing for Evansville of the Three-I League, Spahn led the circuit in wins (19), winning percentage (.760), shutouts (7), and ERA (1.83). With Spahn throwing 42 consecutive scoreless innings and three one-hitters, Evansville won the pennant. Manager Bob Coleman changed Spahn's delivery to put less pressure on his elbow and Warren's roommate, pitcher Willard Donovan, showed him the pickoff move he would perfect.

According to one legend, the old Hall of Fame catcher Ernie Lombardi warmed Spahn up in spring training of 1942. When he threw one of his best fastballs, Lombardi reportedly caught it barehanded, spat tobacco juice on it, and threw it back harder. Turning his back to rub off the juice, Spahn thought, "I'm not sure I belong here."

Even so, Spahn's smooth overhand delivery and flawless follow-though won raves at 1942 spring headquarters in Sanford, Florida, and he made the Boston club (now the Braves again). But when he failed to brush back Pee Wee Reese in his second big-league outing as Stengel ordered, the manager stalked to the mound and growled, "After your shower, pick up your railroad ticket to Hartford." Spahn reported, wowed the Eastern League with a 17–12 record and a 1.96 ERA, and returned to pitch twice more for the seventh-place Braves.

He had no wins over his 16 abbreviated innings with Boston, but did get credit for an abbreviated complete game on September 26 when Polo Grounds kids who had been admitted for working in a wartime scrap-metal drive swarmed the field and forced the Giants to forfeit a game in which they were beating him 5–2 (no pitcher gets a win in a forfeit). All of this, Spahn knew, was a prelude to war. He enlisted in the Army in October of '42, and in November Buck Private Spahn was shipped to Camp Gruber, 60 miles southeast of Tulsa, Oklahoma, where he learned to be a combat engineer. It is also where he met his future wife when Buffalo friend Roy Reimann introduced him to LoRene Southard, an oil company executive secretary with spectacular business acumen who would later help make Spahn rich.

The lefty had a far rougher World War II experience than most big-leaguers, who spent the conflict out of harm's way with gloves instead of guns, but before entering the fray he too got to play some ball. Pitching in the summer of 1944 for the Gruber Engineers, with Reimann as his catcher, Spahn won his first 10 games—seven on shutouts—and struck out 186 batters in just 80 innings. The winning streak was snapped when he uncharacteristically committed three throwing errors in a 7–1 loss to the semipro Atlas Electrics of Tulsa at Texas League Park on July 30, 1944. He may have had a lot on his mind, because Spahn was shipped to Europe aboard the *Queen Mary* on November 9, 1944. As a staff sergeant in the 276th Engineer Combat Battalion, he arrived in France a few weeks later, and survived for about 10 days on peanut butter sandwiches provided by friendly British soldiers.

Spahn's 9th Armored Division, which preceded much larger groups of Allied troops, was charged with repairing roads and bridges. Spahn fought in the snowy, frozen Battle of the Bulge, getting nicked by bullets on the abdomen and back of the head. Crossing France and Belgium, his division arrived at the Rhine River and the Ludendorff railroad bridge at Remagen on March 7, 1945. While retreating, the Nazis had destroyed every intact bridge but the one at Remagen. The demolitions were in place, but for some reason they had never pushed the plunger. The bridge's defense was crucial to the Allies for delivering men, vehicles and equipment to the German heartland. On March 9, Sergeant Spahn and the 276th were ordered to the bridge to remove the demolitions, repair the bridge, maintain it, and construct a second span for two-way traffic. Working furiously to maintain the girders, Spahn and Co. were bombarded by V-2 rockets while troops, tanks, and trucks crossed above them. A biographer, Al Silverman, later described the scene:

"While the bridge vibrated and twanged like banjo strings, swaying precariously as marching infantrymen tramped across each catwalk, and tanks rumbled across the planked railbed, the units patched holes, bolstered the bridge with heavy supports, repaired damaged flooring and cratered approaches."

Ten days after the first successful crossing, Spahn received an assignment at a meeting over the center of the bridge and walked off to explain to his platoon that they'd be taking over the bridge's security at 4 p.m. At 3:56 a platoon member shouted, "Look at the back! The bridge is falling down!" Possibly overloaded, certainly bombarded, the span slipped into the river, leaving 28 soldiers dead, 93 injured, and Sergeant Spahn with shrapnel in his left foot. Having crossed the Rhine, however, the Americans were able to protect a second bridge and other smaller pontoon bridges they built. Surgeons removed Spahn's shrapnel. On June 1, 1945, he was the only ballplayer given a battlefield promotion, from staff sergeant to second lieutenant. In all, he earned a Bronze Star, a Purple Heart, a battlefield promotion, and a Presidential citation. That made him the most decorated ballplayer in World War II. (Like Spahn, Hoyt Wilhelm earned a Purple Heart, but Spahn alone received the Bronze Star.)

Aged rapidly by his battle experiences into a partially bald and fully-grown veteran, Spahn also built up stamina, concentration, and discipline during this period. "After what I went through overseas, I never thought of anything I was told to do in baseball as hard work," he insisted. "You get over feeling like that when you spend days on end sleeping in frozen tank tracks in enemy-threatened territory. The Army taught me what's important and what isn't."

Typically, Spahn found humor in the grimmest of situations. Because German spies would wear American uniforms, he said, "Anybody we didn't know, we'd ask, 'Who plays second for the Bums?' If he didn't answer 'Eddie Stanky,' he was dead." Spahn had no use for being labeled a hero. "The guys who died over there were heroes," he told his son, Greg. Nor did Spahn cotton to the view of baseball historians who estimated that he lost 30 or 40 wins to service time. "I matured a lot in those [war] years," he said. "If I had not had that maturity, I wouldn't have pitched until I was 45." (A statement like that says much about character. By contrast, the querulous Bob Feller says that if it weren't for *his* wartime service, "I'd have won more games than Warren Spahn.")

Unaware that the war would end just two months later after the dropping of atomic bombs on Hiroshima and Nagasaki in August 1945, Spahn accepted the battlefield promotion, which forced him to remain in the service until the next May and miss the start of the '46 baseball season. Instead, he became the hottest pitcher in Germany that spring; working for the 115th Engineers Group, he allowed one run and struck out 73 batters in four games. And when he returned stateside, the Braves immediately promoted him to the majors, on June 10, 1946. "This is the first time in years I've reported to anybody without saluting," he told new Boston manager Billy Southworth.

Spahn appeared in his first postwar game seven days later—Bunker Hill Day in New England—and gave up one run and four hits in four innings of a doubleheader opener against the Cardinals at Braves Field. "He was all grace," biographer Al Silverman wrote, "kicking his right leg high in the air, his left elbow passing his right knee, just as his dad had taught him, then uncoiling and the ball snapping to the plate out of flapping sleeves and trousers, the ball streaking in and on the batter almost before he could measure it, blazing in like a freight train coming out of the darkness."

In his first start, on July 14, Spahn beat the Pirates, 4–1, and allowed just one runner past second base (Frankie Gustine, who homered). It was his first big-league victory, but Warren was distracted by love. Southworth wanted him to wait until after the season before marrying LoRene Southard—he even offered to be best man and pay for the wedding and honeymoon—but Spahn instead got a day off and married her on August 10. Then, after initial success, he lost four straight. Chuck Dressen, a Dodgers coach, said Spahn was tipping off his pitches. "We can beat Spahn every time he pitches," Dressen crowed. "We know every pitch he throws." Spahn, who would correct the flaw the following spring with help from pitching coach Johnny Cooney, still went 8–5 with a 2.94 ERA over the second half of the '46 season. "Pressure? What pressure?" he said. "If I do badly, what's the worst thing that's going to happen? No one is going to shoot at me!"

Because of his military service, balding pate, and relatively advanced age—he won his first game at 25—Spahn fit in quickly and became an instant elder statesman on the Boston club. "He was born old," a teammate said, and the writers described him as a downright Homeric figure. In a single column, legendary New York sportswriter Red Smith playfully called him "goose-necked, stork-legged," and "a gowky [probably a typo for "gawky"], bat-eared old warrior with the ample nose."

Some pitchers are unapproachable on the days they start. For his part, Spahn played practical jokes. He thought nothing of whacking teammates upside the head, setting their straw hats on fire while they wore them, or leaving mice in their pockets. "When I'm kidding, I'm actually relaxing," he said. "It's my way of coping with pressure."

An act like that can grow old in a hurry if you don't win. But already everyone expected him to be an ace. In a 1942 conversation captured by a Philadelphia sportswriter, Phillies manager Ben Chapman and slugger Del Ennis traded impressions with Giants slugger Johnny Mize:

> Chapman: "Spahn has one of the greatest overhand curves I've ever seen."
> Ennis: "Never mind the curve. What I have to watch for is the change of pace he throws. I swing at it before it is halfway to the plate."
> Mize: "The curve and change of pace are all right, but it's that fastball. It does tricks as it reaches the plate."

Spahn's performance backed up these concerns. In notching a 21-win season that helped the Braves to a third-place finish in 1947, Spahn led the league in ERA (2.33), innings pitched ($289\frac{2}{3}$) and shutouts (7) while getting just 13 runs of support in his 10 losses. Most of the 1948 season was a different story; preoccupied by LoRene's pregnancy, the October 1 birth of their only child, Gregory, and an erratic fastball, he was only 15–12, but Spahn and right-hander Johnny Sain pitched the Braves to a pennant with an incredible stretch run, prompting the "Spahn and Sain and pray for rain" poetry crafted by *Boston Post* sports editor Gerry Hern and repeated around the Hub. The exact words were:

> First we'll use Spahn, then we'll use Sain
> Then an off day, followed by rain
> Back will come Spahn, followed by Sain
> And followed, we hope, by two days of rain.

Beginning on September 6, Spahn and Sain started

The 1948 contributions of Warren Spahn and Johnny Sain to the Braves pennant pursuit were forever memorialized by a Boston scribe's bit of doggerel that created the immortal verse, "Spahn and Sain and pray for rain."

11 of Boston's next 16 games, with Spahn going 4–1 and Sain 5–1. On September 6, Warren threw a 14-inning, 2–1 win over the Dodgers in which he picked off Jackie Robinson twice. It was probably the best-pitched game by any Brave all season, and helped spark a 13–1 stretch by the club that all but wrapped up the NL flag. Facing Cleveland in the World Series, however, Spahn lost his only start, 4–1 in Game Two. "A few inches the other way and a couple of those hits would have been outs," said Sain, who had beaten Bob Feller 1–0 in the opener. "You gave it a good try." "I pitch to win them all, same as you," Spahn replied.

With the Braves trailing three games to one, Spahn won Game Five with $5\frac{2}{3}$ innings of one-hit, seven-strikeout relief before the largest crowd in World Series history until that time—86,288 strong in Cleveland. Back in Boston the next day, Southworth asked the weary Spahn if he had anything left, since the manager had to pinch hit for starter Bill Voiselle in his next at-bat and the Braves were trailing late in Game Six, 3–1 "I'll give it all I've got," Spahn said, but he had trouble warming up. When he relieved in the eighth, the Indians scored an insurance run off him with three straight singles before Spahn stymied the rally with a pickoff that started a double play. The Braves' two-run rally in the bottom of the eighth fell just short; Spahn retired the last four men he faced and struck out the side in the ninth to give him 12 K's in his 12 Series innings, but the Braves lost, 4–3.

Members of the Boston Braves Historical Association sometimes speculate: If Spahn had held the Indians scoreless and the Braves had rallied to win the Series, would they have left town so soon thereafter? No one knows for sure, but the club certainly didn't help matters with an uninspiring title defense. The Braves immediately self-destructed amid dissension, contract disputes, and injury in 1949, finished four games under .500 in fourth place, and began the decline that led to their departure from Boston. Already annoyed by the signing of 18-year-old "bonus baby" pitcher Johnny Antonelli for $50,000 or more in 1948, veteran players balked at Southworth's two-a-day workouts totaling six hours at spring training. Drinking heavily, his nerves in tatters, Southworth had to take a leave of absence two-thirds of the way through the season. Unsatisfied, the players voted him a half-share of their fourth-place Series money. Then, as if things could not get worse, management infuriated players and many

The Boston Braves' righty-lefty, one-two pitching punch of Spahn and Sain would last through 1950.

fans by trading double-play mainstays Alvin Dark and Eddie Stanky for four Giants on December 14, 1949.

But neither these distractions nor even his own salary disputes affected Spahn's concentration: Up to 172 pounds, using his thick wrist and well-developed chest muscles, he went 21–14, 21–17, 22–14 in 1949–51, leading the National League in strikeouts all three years and in wins twice. He could go long—he struck out a then-league-record 18 Cubs in 15 innings on June 14, 1952—and he could talk long. After surrendering a homer to a rookie named Willie Mays, for instance, he said memorably: "He was something like 0-for-21 [actually 0-for-12] the first time I saw him. His first major-league hit was a home run off me—and I'll never forgive myself. We might have gotten rid of Willie forever if I'd only struck him out."

Spahn was not only a jokester. He notably befriended Sam Jethroe, the Braves' first black player, and helped start the Jimmy Fund charity in support of Dana-Farber Cancer Institute. He was also an oracle whose every word on pitching was eagerly awaited. "A pitcher needs two pitches—one they're looking for and one to cross 'em up," Spahn said at one point. On another occasion, he stated, "Hitting is timing. Pitching is upsetting timing." Warren's quotability was a welcome distraction for the 1952 team, which slipped back into the second division when Spahn went 14–19 despite a league-leading 193 strikeouts and a stellar 2.98 ERA (nonsupport again serving as his nemesis). It was his fourth straight strikeout crown.

While negotiating his 1953 contract, Spahn accepted a $25,000 pact but rejected a deal that would have paid him 10 cents for every paid admission over 800,000. That made sense, since the Braves had just drawn a league-low 281,278 in 1952. Spahn looked for another payday when his business venture opened Warren Spahn's Diner just across Commonwealth Avenue from Braves Field. When the team moved to Milwaukee during spring training, however, Spahn took a double loss: the Braves drew 1,826,397 in their first Midwestern season (which would

have meant a $100,000 bonus had he taken the deal), and the restaurant opened without its primary owner.

Financial loss wasn't the only concern Warren took west. For all his success, his popularity with fans, and the respect of the many teammates and opponents he helped, Spahn was an insecure man who never forgot his youth in Depression-era Buffalo. After ripping cartilage in a knee during 1953 spring training, he didn't tell anyone. "I was one of the senior men on the club, and they'd have let me go in a minute if I went on the disabled list," he told *The Sporting News*'s Dave Kindred. Spahn pitched in pain all year, won the Braves' Milwaukee opener and the All-Star Game, and led the league in wins (23) and ERA (2.10). Only then did he have offseason surgery.

The Braves finished second, third, and second their first three years in Milwaukee while rebuilding with players like Hank Aaron, Joe Adcock, Del Crandall, Billy Bruton, and Spahn's new running buddy and prankster pal, pitcher Lew Burdette—who, ironically, had been picked up from the Yankees in a trade for the declining Sain. Spahn remained dominant, but with a chance to capture the 1956 pennant on the season's final day after winning 10 of his last 11 games, he lost a 12-inning heartbreaker to the Cardinals when a double-play ball took a bad hop. He actually cried while leaving the field, and threw his glove at a prying photographer (to whom he later apologized). But the 36-year-old Spahn bounced back in 1957, capturing his only Cy Young Award by going 21–11 with a league-leading 18 complete games and winning six times in 19 stretch-drive days while the Braves took their first pennant in Milwaukee.

Spahn lost the World Series opener to the Yankees, 3–1, but won Game Four, 7–5, in 10 innings. It was perhaps with mixed feelings when he fell sick with the flu that Spahnie watched as Burdette took his scheduled start on two days' rest and beat the Yankees in Game Seven. Although happy to see his buddy win three games and a new car as Series MVP, Warren had no doubt wanted the ball himself.

When both teams repeated as pennant-winners the next year, Spahn (22–11 in the regular season) won Game One of the rematch, 4–3, in 10 innings, contributing two hits and an RBI himself. Then, locked in a pitcher's zone ("All I can see…is a strike zone waving a bat"), he two-hit the Yankees in Game Four, 3–0, to give Milwaukee a commanding three-to-one lead. But called on by manager Fred Haney to pitch on two days' rest, Spahn lost Game Six, 4–3, in 10 innings; the Braves might have won the contest (and the Series) in regulation if Billy Bruton hadn't misplayed a fly ball into a single and third-base coach Billy Herman hadn't sent 37-year-old Andy Pafko to be tagged out at home on a short fly. Many considered Spahn the outstanding pitcher of the Series, but the Yankees won in seven games.

With extraordinary staying power, the 38-year-old

Spahn pitched a league-high 292 innings and went 21–15 for the injury-addled 1959 Braves, who lost the pennant in a two-game playoff to the Dodgers. Then, as the team began slipping, he stayed dominant by throwing his only two no-hitters at the ages of 39 and 40. He fanned 15 Phillies in his first gem, a 4–0 win on September 16, 1960. "All right, just nobody say I've got a no-hitter going," he announced to a shocked Milwaukee bench in violation of the silence code, and he ended with a flourish—starting a spectacular 1–6–3 play for the final out. Seven months later, he faced the minimum 27 batters in a 1–0 no-hit win over the Giants on April 28, 1961, retiring Matty Alou with a spectacular backhanded flip to squelch a bunt attempt in the ninth. (Spahnie allowed two walks in this contest, but double plays wiped out both baserunners, accounting for his 27 men faced.)

This wasn't his only milestone contest of 1961; Spahn won his 300th game with a 2–1 victory over the Cubs before a Milwaukee-record crowd of 48,642 on August 11, making him just the 13th pitcher (and the first since Lefty Grove in 1941) to reach the hallowed mark. Even upon getting there, he was far from done; in perhaps the last extraordinary performance of an extraordinary career, the 42-year-old lefty lost a 16-inning duel with the Giants' 25-year-old Juan Marichal, 1–0, thanks to arch-nemesis Willie Mays' homer, at 12:31 a.m. on July 3, 1963. Despite this setback, Spahn finished the '63 season 23–7, led the league with 22 complete games, and even captured several MVP votes.

Explaining his longevity, the usually loquacious Spahn needed just one word: mechanics. "You've got to be a student of pitching," he stated. "The way I threw, I never tried to put too much strain on my left arm." Whitlow Wyatt, a Braves pitching coach, said, "He makes my job easier. Every pitch he throws he has an idea behind it."

Spahn's longtime catcher Del Crandall told Spahn's son, Greg, a high-school hitting star who had career-ending surgery in college and later became a successful real-estate executive in Tulsa, that his father showed the batter three things: the sole of his right shoe, the back of his glove, and finally the ball. Spahn leaned forward in an almost courtly bow to the hitters, then rocked back, his right leg raised above his head in what *The Sporting News*' Kindred called a five-minutes-to-six position, followed by an overhand delivery that was as smooth and regular as an oil-field pumping jack back home in Oklahoma, where he now owned a ranch. Since every pitch was thrown with the same motion, the batter had no idea what to expect. "Sometimes the motion deceived me, and I was the catcher," Crandall said.

And there was something else. Because of an old separated shoulder from high-school football, the 6-foot-tall Spahn couldn't raise his right hand higher than his shoulder. As he moved toward the plate, his glove rose slowly, and then descended quickly through the hitter's line of vision. "People kept telling me that the motion of the glove really bothered hitters," Spahn told Kindred. "So I kept doing it. Whatever bothered hitters, I was for."

This silky-smooth delivery placed a minimum of pressure on Spahn's arm. He also benefited from revolutionary training habits. In his time, pitchers used spring training to get in shape and babied their arms between starts. Spahn headed to camp in tiptop condition, having spent the winters working on his ranch, and threw between starts. Both practices are common today. The same could be said of Spahn's research habits, since he studied hitters' tendencies and rarely gave them the same pitches from one year to the next. He was no slouch at the plate himself; in addition to his 363 victories, he also had 363 lifetime hits—including 35 home runs.

As time passed, Spahn adapted. When his fastball began to fade, he learned a screwball, and when that wasn't enough, he picked up a slider. When his aching knees betrayed him in 1964, he went 6–13 and had to endure manager Bobby Bragan's insinuation that he was hanging on selfishly because of his $80,000 salary. On November 23, 1964, the Mets purchased Spahn from the Braves to be both pitcher and pitching coach. A week later they signed Yankees catching great Yogi Berra. "I don't know whether we'll be the oldest battery in baseball, but I know we'll be the ugliest," Spahn said.

Warren had truly come full circle, as the Mets manager was none other than his first skipper with the Braves back in '42: Casey Stengel. After finishing sixth or seventh his final six years with Boston, Casey had forged a Hall of Fame career in leading the Yankees to 10 pennants in just 12 seasons. Now he was with a club even more woeful than his Braves; the Mets had lost a record 120 games under Stengel in their maiden 1962 season, and suffered 109 and 111 more setbacks over the next two campaigns.

Although even Spahn could not overcome the hardship of having a club of youngsters and castoffs as his support staff, he was sometimes able to take matters into his own hands. Facing 19-year-old Claude Osteen of the Dodgers during the 1965 season, for instance, Spahn carried a 3–0 lead into the ninth. After the Dodgers scored two runs, Stengel, who had admired Spahn with the Braves and saw no reason to change his mind, asked his elderly pitching coach whom he wanted to bring in from the bullpen. Spahn said he wanted to leave the starter in, and then promptly retired the last three batters.

The miracles quickly ran out, though, and Spahn was released and signed by the Giants in midseason. He left Gotham with another great quip: "I'm the only guy to play for Casey Stengel before and after he was a genius."

Spahn again faltered, but not before he saw Willie Mays get his 500th homer. "I saw your first, Willie, and now your 500th," he said. Congratulations." Released at season's end with a 7–16 record, Spahn later said, "I didn't retire from baseball. Baseball retired me."

Disappointed or not, Spahn stayed in the game. When he pitched three games for the Mexico City Tigers in 1966 and three games for the Tulsa Oilers in 1967, people got the mistaken impression that the 45-year-old was staging a comeback. Actually, he was demonstrating technique to a Mexican team he was coaching, and then trying to improve attendance for an American team he was managing. His Oilers won the Pacific Coast League championship in 1968, and Spahn was voted Manager of the Year. Before being fired in 1971 because he'd refused a promotion to Cardinals pitching coach the previous year and outstayed his welcome, he racked up 372 wins. He scouted and coached minor-league pitchers for the Cardinals in 1971, then spent two unhappy years as pitching coach for the Cleveland Indians. His spirits lifted when the Hall of Fame called. Only the sixth player elected in his first year of eligibility—his appearances for Mexico City and Tulsa kept his name off the ballot two additional years—Spahn was admitted in 1973 along with posthumous induction for his son's favorite player, Roberto Clemente.

Spahn instructed Hiroshima Carp pitchers in the summers of 1973–78, then coached minor-league pitchers in the Angels system for a few years before tiring of travel on "funny little airplanes," as he told writer Rich Westcott, after the 1981 season. Blunt-spoken to the end, he blasted long-haired players and dismissed the idea of a designated hitter, saying, "I think pitchers should be athletes."

On October 16, 1995, Spahn was inducted into the Boston Braves Hall of Fame at the third annual reunion of the Boston Braves Historical Association. In their last day together in Boston, he and Johnny Sain visited what was left of Braves Field and the memories of 1948. Addressing a sizable gathering, Spahn remarked that with that kind of attendance in his day, the Braves might still be playing in Boston.

Thanks to his half-Cherokee wife, LoRene, who got her husband to give up the Buffalo winters and settle in Hartshorne, Oklahoma, Spahn grew rich running a 2,000-acre cattle ranch and leasing some of his land for gas wells. "My mother talked us into buying four beachfront properties in Florida," Greg Spahn says of LoRene, who died in 1978. "They're worth millions now."

In August 2003, the Braves unveiled Shan Gray's nine-foot bronze statue of Spahn kicking high outside Turner Stadium in Atlanta. Ailing from a litany of mostly age-related difficulties—a broken leg, four broken ribs, a punctured lung, internal bleeding, and fluid buildup in his lungs—Spahn, 82, was wheeled in to see the work. "I took great pride in mooning people," he said. "That's the reason I developed that leg kick."

It was one of the last and best memories of Spahn: kicking and joking. He died on November 24, 2003, and was buried in Elmwood Cemetery back home in Hartshorne. Posthumous honors followed. The city of Buffalo renamed the street to Cazenovia Park, his old high school field, Warren Spahn Way. Other statues went up at Bricktown Ballpark in Oklahoma City and the Oklahoma Sports Museum in Guthrie. Finally, the Oklahoma Sports Museum established the Warren Spahn Award in 1999 to honor the majors' leading left-handed pitcher.

Should the award have been named for another lefty: a Grove, Koufax, Carlton, or Plank? Not if winning matters most. Spahn's 363 wins are the most of any lefthander, and he was a consistently reliable pitcher, as his ERA's in the regular season (3.09), All-Star Games (3.21) and World Series (3.05) attest. Spahn also holds or shares modern major-league records for 20-win seasons (13), most years leading the league in games won (8), career innings by a lefthander (5,246), wins in a season at age 40 (21) and 42 (23) and possibly double plays started by a pitcher (82), which is not an official statistic. His 35 homers are the most by a National League pitcher. Spahn won 75 games after the age of 40, and no matter what his age was great in the clutch. During his career he had a .546 April-July winning percentage, followed by a .676 percentage in August-October—a staggering .130 increase.

In SABR's *Baseball Research Journal* No. 32, Eric Marshall White described Spahn as "the most fantastic finisher of them all." And he did indeed look as if he could go on forever. "I don't think Spahn will ever get into the Hall of Fame," Stan Musial said. "He'll never stop pitching."

Sources

Bjarkman, Peter C. *Warren Spahn* (New York: Chelsea House Publications, 1994)

Buege, Bob. *The Milwaukee Braves: A Baseball Eulogy* (Milwaukee: Douglas American Sports Publications, 1988)

Cohen, Richard M., & David F. Neft. *The World Series* (New York: Macmillan, 1986)

Johnson, Richard A. Images of America: Boston Braves (Charleston S.C., Chicago, Portsmouth. N.H., San Francisco: Arcadia Publishing, 2001)

Kaese, Harold. *The Boston Braves 1871–1953* (Boston: Northeastern University Press, 2004)

Porter, David L., editor. *Biographical Dictionary of American Sports: Baseball* (Westport Conn.: Greenwood Press, 1987)

Silverman, Al. *Warren Spahn; Immortal Southpaw* (New York: Bartholomew House, Sport Magazine Library No. 9, 1961)

Thorn, John, Pete Palmer, Michael Gershman, and David Pietrusza, editors. *Total Baseball*, fifth edition. (New York: Viking/Penguin Books USA, 1997)

Retrosheet.org

EDDIE STANKY *by Alex Edelman*

G	AB	R	H	2B	3B	HR	RBI	BB	SO	BA	OBP	SLG	SB	HBP
67	247	49	79	14	2	2	29	61	13	.320	.455	.417	3	0

"Now look at The Brat. He can't hit, can't run, can't field. He's no nice guy, but all the little SOB can do is win."— *Leo Durocher*

Baseball, on the outside, can often be looked at from a clinical point of view. One can analyze and hypothesize and compare and evaluate with some degree of accuracy the worth of a player to his team with statistics. However, every so often, an individual sticks out because of characteristics that inspire his teammates and draw the admiration and respect of fans. Eddie "The Brat" Stanky was one of those: a gritty, scrappy player. Stanky was not gifted with natural talent. He worked long and hard to achieve the success he attained. A little guy who stood at just 5'8", Stanky was small but seemed so much more imposing as he flew into second base with a feet-first, spikes-raised slide to break up a double play.

Eddie Stanky was always aggressive. It was the result of his upbringing. Born on September 3, 1917, to a working class family, Stanky was playing with a baseball from the time he could sit up. In his childhood years in the blue-collar Philadelphia neighborhood of Kensington, Eddie developed the belligerent, enthusiastic, win-at-all-costs attitude that would make him so successful—and reviled—in later life. Stanky wasn't a "tool player," he didn't have an excellent batting average (.243 in his senior year at Philadelphia's Northeast High School), but his drive was exceptional. It distinguished him from everyone else, even at an early age. It seemed that he always had a soccer ball or baseball glove, and impressed everyone with his single-mindedness and aggressiveness in the field. "It was baseball that Eddie came to high school for," said Lester Owen, Stanky's high school coach, "He said he was going to be a pro baseball player. That was that. No one doubted him. He wasn't conceited. He was an ordinary boy with extraordinary ambition."[1]

That ambition helped get Stanky a contract with his hometown Philadelphia Athletics. After high school, Stanky was sent in 1935 to play shortstop for the Greenville (Mississippi) Buckshots of the Class "C" East Dixie League. After a few weeks with the team, Stanky—young, homesick, and discouraged—sent his mother a letter asking for money for train fare home. The response was

Eddie Stanky's conflicts with Dodgers management, together with Jackie Robinson's shift to second base, resulted in the Brat's move to the Braves in March of '48.

stern. Eddie was not welcome back at home—quitters weren't wanted in Anna Stanky's family. Stanky stayed in Greenville, and finished the year with a .301 batting average and 80 runs scored in just 104 games.[2]

Life seemed a bit easier in 1936, when Stanky moved to Portsmouth of the Class "C" Middle Atlantic League. He raised his batting average 35 points and improved in virtually every offensive category. Near the end of the season, he was sent to Williamsport (Class "A" New York-Pennsylvania League) and played the last 11 games and the first 14 games of 1937 before returning to Portsmouth (now in the Piedmont League). Having played shortstop, second, third, and even pitched during his first two years in the minors, he was now made a fulltime second baseman.

Stanky started to come into his own. He had never been a power hitter—and would top 10 home runs just once in his pro career—but he started to find other ways to get on base. In 1938, he hit .283, drew 127 walks and was hit by a pitch 20 times enroute to scoring 110 runs. He lost the discomfort that hindered him in his first year—and also gained an adversary: Yankees prospect Phil Rizzuto. Years later, Pirates manager Billy Meyer said:

It's a good thing [Stanky] and Phil Rizzuto ain't in the same league together: there'd be a battle every time they met. [T]hey started tangling back in the Piedmont League days when Stanky was playing for Portsmouth and Phil was with Norfolk of the Yankees chain. Every time Portsmouth played Norfolk the feature of the game was the fight between Stanky and Rizzuto.[3]

Stanky and Rizzuto would clash often, Rizzuto often coming away worse for wear. "I used to slide head-first," recalled Rizzuto almost 60 years later, "and he broke my nose twice when he slammed a tag on me—and I was already on the base! One time, he slid into second base and I was pivoting in the air on a double play and he grabbed my shirt from behind—and I wound up being turned around and throwing the ball to third instead of first."[4]

At the start of the 1939 season, Stanky was sent to the Macon Peaches of the Sally (South Atlantic) League, where he would star under manager Milt Stock for three seasons. Stock, who was also a part-owner of the Macon club, had played in the major leagues for 14 seasons, and had great affection for his sparkplug ballplayer. Stock saw that Stanky had an excellent eye—but no power. He put Stanky in the leadoff position, and urged him to be patient at the plate. It worked. Stanky was an all-star honorable mention in 1939, and he would make the all-star team in 1940.

Eddie's partnership with Stock went beyond the ballfield. Years later, when Stanky was managing the St. Louis Cardinals, he credited Milton Stock with "planting the seed," that helped him blossom into a successful player and manager. In 1940, it was much less then a forgone conclusion that Stanky would make the majors. In addition to the aforementioned overwhelming odds of the 1930's minor league system and Stanky's lack of talent in any specific facet of the game, it was becoming apparent to all that, despite Stanky's small size, he had a disproportionately large temper. Stanky acknowledged his minor-league career in *Time* as "an unending series of brawls" and quarrels with umpires. Stock taught Eddie to control himself, and told him that being thrown out of games (as happened 15 to 20 times a year) hurt his team's chances of winning. But Milt wasn't the only Stock who had a special relationship with Stanky: his daughter, Myrtle "Dickie" Stock, a striking brunette, would fall in love with her father's little infielder, and they were married on April 11, 1942.

Shortly after the wedding, Stock dealt his new son-in-law to the Milwaukee Brewers of the American Association, where Eddie enjoyed his best—and last—season in the minors. Under the watchful eye of manager Charlie Grimm, Stanky finished the year with the league's best average and garnered its MVP award.

In 1943, the Chicago Cubs made Grimm their manager. It was a big break for Stanky, who was able to join his minor-league skipper in the "big show."

Stanky's inability to back down from a challenge or back down off the plate—would, as expected, lead to a few beanings during his major and minor-league career. The first of the beanings, in the minors, was so severe that it left him with a fractured skull. The resultant loss of hearing from that fastball allowed Stanky to start the year with the Cubs rather then the army. On April 21, 1943, in the first inning of his major league debut, Stanky stepped to the plate against Rip Sewell. He was hit in the head by a pitch.

As the Cubs' starting second sacker that summer he hit an uninspiring .245, although he did place fifth in the NL with 92 runs scored. In 1944, Don "Pep" Johnson arrived to take his place, and Stanky found himself warming the bench while Johnson made the All-Star team. Eddie made a simple demand to Grimm: Play me or trade me.[5] Grimm acquiesced, and Stanky was dealt to Brooklyn for lefty pitcher Bob Chipman on June 6.

In Brooklyn, Stanky replaced the aging Babe Herman at second base, and in 1945, his first full season at the Dodgers, he started to make a name for himself. His hard-nosed style of play ingratiated him with the fans, who loved his spirited approach to the game. Branch Rickey, the general manager who had brought him from Chicago with such ease, encouraged the patience that Stanky expressed at the plate, and he walked 148 times in 1945—a new National League record. Stanky loved small-ball and played it well: he also lead the league in runs scored in '45 with 128, keeping with one of his favorite sayings—"The ants get on base and the bulls knock 'em in."[6]

Brooklyn fans adored him. He was given nickname upon nickname: coach Chuck Dreesen dubbed him "Gromyko," after an argumentative Russian politician who was also a well-known advocate of walking,[7] "Stinky" and "Muggsy" were also popular. However, the most famous nickname, a moniker that would stick with him, was "The Brat." Stanky would claim that the name sprung from a comment by Eddie Murphy of the *New York Sun* in 1945, who referred to him as "The Brat from Kensington, PA." The Brat was Stanky's equalizer. The snarling, clamorous, hot-headed edge to Stanky that came out occasionally in moments of high emotion or tension. The Brat was more of Eddie Stanky's on-field alter-ego, and would emerge at various points throughout his playing career. The off-field Eddie Stanky was less of a dervish, very attentive, and spent much time learning about what it might take to be a major league manager; but "The Brat?" Now there was a hell raiser.

Stanky had taken to Dodgerdom like a duck to water, something the team acknowledged with an Eddie Stanky Day on September 8, 1946. Reporters pointed out that his respect for the Dodger uniform and the team it represented outstripped everything. He exemplified Branch Rickey's nickname for his team: "Ferocious Gentlemen." In Chicago, he was best friends with Lennie Merullo, a Cubs shortstop. In May of 1946, the two were involved in a fistfight so unruly that it nearly "inspired a riot." In September of that same year, Stanky and Goody Rosen, an outfielder who Stanky used to room with, were involved in a similar brawl. The Brooklyn fans loved it.[8]

Despite his tough-guy attitude, Stanky was a colorful and intelligent player, easy to write about, and someone who was respected by old-time writers because of his all-consuming desire to win and never-ending hustle.

In 1947, Stanky was elected to his first All-Star squad. He got 141 hits, scored 97 times, and made just 12 errors at second base in sparking Brooklyn to the pennant.[9]

That '47 season, of course, was also the year Brooklyn general manager Branch Rickey and Jackie Robinson integrated baseball. Peter Golenbock, in his book about the Dodgers, *Bums*, contends that Stanky told Robinson when he reported to the Dodgers that he didn't like him but that they would "play together and get along" because they were teammates. More recent research has challenged this, and Jonathan Eig's *Opening Day: The Story of Jackie Robinson's First Season*, has a picture showing Stanky with his arm around Robinson on the day of his Dodgers' debut. Eig says that "in accounts written shortly after the 1947 season," both Rickey and Robinson "rated Eddie Stanky as Robinson's earliest important backer."[10]

"Dad talked about that first game and Jackie a lot," said Stanky's son Mike. "He was so impressed by Jackie's raw ability and the way he dealt with everything he had to handle, that, despite what's been written over the years, they became really close. I think they both discovered that, despite their obvious differences, they were alike, very much alike."[11]

Brooklyn lost the '47 World Series to the Yankees in seven hard-fought games, during which Stanky hit .240. In the offseason, then making around $15,000 a year, he entered Rickey's office to ask for a $5,000 raise, or 33 percent. Instead, he was offered a 6.5 percent increase and "a million dollars worth of free advice" before a compromise was reached: a 25 percent raise. Then, just days after Stanky had signed a contract, ended his holdout, and reported to the Dodgers' training facility in the Dominican Republic, Rickey traded him, on March 6, 1948, to the Boston Braves, in exchange for utilityman Carvell "Bama" Rowell, Ray Sanders, and $40,000 in cash.[12]

When Stanky learned of his swap to the Braves, he told Dodgers road secretary, Harold Parrott, that the Bums would not win the pennant without him. Stanky and Durocher traded barbs on and off the field for much of the season. Durocher told Boston sportswriters that he'd have "made the same trade all over after what I know now. I need Stanky like I need a third eye." When asked to comment on Durocher's book *The Dodgers and Me*, released that year, Stanky's remarks contained equal venom: "Just like the author. Strictly bush!"[13]

Stanky received the most votes of any second baseman in the NL All-Star voting for 1948, and was hitting well over .300 at the break. But just two days after the midsummer classic, while at Ebbets Field for a July 8 battle against the Dodgers, he collided with Dodgers catcher Bruce Edwards—leaving Edwards with a deep spike wound and Stanky with a broken ankle and a torn ligament.[14] He didn't play again until September 19, when the Braves were close to sewing up their first NL pennant in 34 years, something few had expected at the start of the season. The Braves, with "Super Sub" Sibby Sisti handling most of the second-base duties in Eddie's absence, made Stanky a pennant winner for the second year in a row. The Dodgers finished in third place.

In the World Series, the Braves lost to Cleveland in six games. Despite Stanky's leg being "a little below par,"[15] Boston manager Billy Southworth named him to the starting lineup and played him in each contest. Though it could hardly be regarded as a mistake—Stanky had a .524 on-base percentage, drew seven walks, and knocked

out four hits—it must have been excruciating for Stanky to play during the Series. When doctors operated on him two months later, they removed two bone fragments from his ankle joint. The Brat had played through the pain.

More than 60 years later, it is difficult to say whether Stanky's most significant contributions to Boston's magical run in 1948 were on or off the field. At the start of the season, Southworth assigned Stanky a roommate: rookie shortstop Al Dark. The connection between the veteran and his protégé strengthened throughout the season. Stanky enjoyed the sharp Dark's savoir faire; Dark was equally pleased to have a mentor on the team: "[I'm] particularly happy that Eddie Stanky is with the club," Dark told the *New York Times* during the Series." He's given me more tips on how to play shortstop than Leo Durocher could about gin rummy. And you can say I'm listenin'."[16] Dark was voted the National League Rookie of the Year, the first of many young players Stanky mentored over the next 50 years.[17]

Stanky's experience was now another factor in his worth to a ballclub. If his canniness and ability to unnerve opposing pitchers were important, he had also become a full-fledged clubhouse leader. Rookie Johnny Antonelli, who went right from high school to the major leagues and never had to toil the way that Stanky did, recalls a conversation in a cab the night after the Braves won the pennant.

[Stanky] looked at me and said 'Hey kid, would you have ever lasted nine years in the minor leagues and hung in there until you made the majors?' I said, 'No way; if I couldn't make it in nine years—I'd quit!' I was only 18 years old, so I didn't know what to say.[18]

This respect for Stanky became a problem for Southworth in 1949. As soon as training camp started, the manager began to work his players extra hard. He asserted his authority, and some of the players bridled at this treatment. It was to be the beginning of a long year, filled with controversy, for both Eddie and his teammates.

Over the season, a schism developed. Stanky's play was not up to par with his 1948 season (although he still hit a solid .285 with 90 runs scored), and when All-Star voting finished, he was fourth among second basemen, behind former teammate Jackie Robinson, Red Schoendienst, and Emil Verban. Rumors that Stanky would take over the managing job from Southworth abounded,[19] and Eddie started to develop enemies in the clubhouse. Red Barrett, a player extremely loyal to Southworth, suggested a vote of confidence, but Stanky scoffed at the veteran pitcher's proposal of it. "If Southworth wants a vote of confidence, let him ask for it himself."

On July 23 of 1949, in Pittsburgh, another controversy erupted. Southworth may not have liked Stanky's possible threat to his authority, but he respected The Brat's tremendous baseball knowledge, and allowed him to call plays on the field on his own. On that hot July day against the Pirates, team ace Warren Spahn was pitching. A good hitter, Spahn was able to get on base in the third inning, and stole second when a hit-and-run called by leadoff man Stanky, batting after him, went awry. Later on in the game, Spahn reached first again, and again, Eddie sent him to second on a hit-and-run. This time, Stanky made contact, grounding the ball to third. Spahn made second on a wild throw and went for third, where he was tagged out. Then on the mound in the ninth inning, with a three-run lead, Spahn imploded, giving up a half dozen runs. The Braves lost 12–9.

Reporters immediately searched for the man to blame. Team owner Lou Perini flew to join the team on the road to try to right the sinking ship. The assumption was reached that the reason for the loss was that Spahn had run too much on the basepaths and had been tired during that last inning on the mound. The blame for "exhausting" Spahn was placed squarely on Stanky for calling the hit-and-runs. Leo Monahan of the *Boston American* said Stanky's teammates were grumbling about the Brat's assumed authority. Another writer said Eddie's mates were outraged at his "takeover attitude." Stanky was livid. His response dripped with frustration, and his anger was palpable in every word. As *The Sporting News* reported him saying:

I'm always playing to get another run for my club and prevent the other team from getting runs...so far as taking over, I only do what I can to win the games and leave that "takeover attitude" to second-guessing bushers. I resent the implication that I exceeded my authority in putting on plays. I have always co-operated with any manager I played for 100 per cent. I have always played to win. And that's the way I'll continue until I quit the game.[20]

The hit-and-run incident seems to have encapsulated everything that was wrong with the 1949 Boston Braves' season. Spahn, at the center of this debacle, seemed put off by the idea that his ninth-inning meltdown was due to his running the basepaths too much. "That...is so much hogwash. I don't pitch with my feet. Sure, Eddie gave me the sign. Why shouldn't he? That's his right."[21]

The incident was the low point of the season, and Southworth, reportedly on the verge of a breakdown, left the team on August 16 with the defending NL champion Braves in fourth place at 55–54. They finished 76–78.

After the season, reporters across the nation searched for clues as to what went wrong. *New York Times* columnist Arthur Daley, who had been very kind to Stanky throughout the Brat's career, wrote:

If the rumors are to be believed the team was split into two factions. One was led by Bob Elliott and the other by Eddie Stanky, a brilliant and personable young man who can't miss being a major league manager some day. Don't get the impression, though, that Stanky tunneled under Southworth. It just isn't his nature. But he is a veteran campaigner and an eternal scrapper whose fierce will-to-win didn't click too well in some quarters. At least that's the guess here.[22]

Boston sportswriter Al Hirshberg was of a different opinion:

Stanky wasn't popular with the ball club, but Stankys are never popular with ball clubs. The guy is an intense gamecock, a fighter by nature, who was fighting both the team's battles and his own all season. He never fully recovered for the effects of a broken ankle he suffered in 1948. And he never fully recovered from the realization that he was playing for a losing team instead of a champion.[23]

It didn't matter who was right. The Brat was not long for the Braves, and when Southworth announced that he would be coming back to manage Boston for the 1950 season, Stanky was all but gone from the team.

On December 14, 1949, the axe fell, and Stanky and his roommate/double-play partner, Al Dark, were traded to the New York Giants—managed now by Lou Durocher—for outfielders Sid Gordon and Willard Marshall, infielder Buddy Kerr, and right-handed pitcher Sam Webb. It would prove to be a luckless trade for the Braves.

The rift between Stanky and Durocher was quickly repaired. Durocher was sure that Stanky and Dark would tighten up the Giants infield and that their plucky, effervescent play and good chemistry would make them one of the strongest middle infields in the league.

Durocher let Stanky play the way he wanted to, and Stanky thrived. In 152 games during the 1950 season he hit .300 with a .460 OBP, 115 runs scored, and a league-leading 144 walks. He was named to the NL All-Star squad, was selected as Player of the Year by the New York baseball writers, and finished third in the league MVP voting. More importantly, with free rein and total agreement from his manager, the Stanky style of play flourished. When Durocher traded for Stanky, he spoke of the second baseman's win-by-hook-or-by-crook strategy: "Stanky'll drive the pitcher daffy. He'll drop his bat on the catcher's corns. He'll sit on you at second base, sneak a pull at your shirt, step on you, louse you up some way—anything to beat you."[24]

Perhaps not surprisingly, the Giants improved from a 73–81, fifth-place finish behind the Braves in 1949 to an 86–68 mark and third place during Stanky's first season with the club. His distraction tactics touched such a nerve with opposing players that his very motions evoked action by Commissioner Ford Frick after an August 12, 1950, game in which the Brat, who was on second base, started to wave his arms, mimicking the pitcher's windup, while a Giants hitter stood in the batter's box. Philadelphia catcher Andy Seminick protested so vehemently that a brawl broke out and Stanky was thrown out of the game. Durocher protested the contest and said, "What's wrong with trying to fool the batter, anyway? Everyone tries to do that one way or another." Frick wasn't buying the excuse, and ordered umpires to eject any player who engaged in similar tactics.

Things got even more exciting in 1951, when Stanky hit a career-high 14 home runs and scored 88 runs. The Giants, in what became known as the Miracle at Coogan's Bluff, made a late-season sprint to force a three-game playoff with the Brooklyn Dodgers. In the ninth inning of the third playoff contest, the Brat started the rally that led to Bobby Thomson's famous walkoff home run off Stanky's former roommate Ralph Branca. While Thomson jogged around the bases after his homer, Stanky jumped on the back of his manager, standing in the third-base box. As the two danced jubilantly together down the baseline, all the insults and accusations were forgotten.

Of his fiery third baseman, Durocher said later, "To win a pennant you got to win the tight ballgames. And to win those tight ones, those one-run games, you got to have guys who won't quit till they've won. And you've always got to have one guy to lead those other guys. Eddie Stanky was my guy and their guy. He hated to lose. Eddie Stanky was the big difference in tight ballgames.... We wouldn't have won the pennant without him."[25]

The Giants lost the World Series to the Yankees in six games, Stanky hitting a lackluster .136, but more memorable than his anemic batting average was another run-in with an old adversary—Yankee shortstop Phil Rizzuto. In Game Three, on a hit-and-run that failed, Stanky was thrown out by at least 15 feet, but when Rizzuto, covering second, leaned over to tag him out, the Brat kicked the ball out of his glove. The ball dribbled into center field, and Stanky scrambled to third. The play kept a Giants rally going and ignited a five-run outburst that won the game.[26] It was to be one of the last plays that Stanky would make as a Giant.

Almost 900 miles away in St. Louis, the Cardinals were beginning to lose fans to their National League neighbors, the St. Louis Browns. The Browns were a terrible team, and had won just one pennant in their 50-year history. But in 1951, when flamboyant owner Bill Veeck purchased the last-place club, he started to turn the Browns into less of a baseball team and more of a circus. He hired a 3-foot-7 dwarf to pinch hit (he walked, naturally), set off fireworks, let the fans manage a game using signs that had titles like "bunt" or "take," and hired

While Stanky was regarded as a key component of the '48 championship club, he has also been cited as a ringleader in the subsequent player revolt against manager Billy Southworth.

an old St. Louis hero, Rogers Hornsby, as his manager. Cardinals owner Fred Saigh felt the need to counter, and he decided to fire his manager, Marty Marion, and bring in one of the league's more colorful characters—Eddie Stanky.[27]

In December, the Cardinals sent Max Lanier and Chuck Diering to the Giants for Stanky, who assumed the position of player-manager for what was rumored to be a fine salary of about $37,000. It was an opportunity Stanky had long been waiting for. Just a year removed from one of his best seasons ever, and still in his prime, Stanky began to remove himself from the playing field, appearing in just 53 games in 1952 and 17 in 1953.

Throughout his career, Stanky had observed close up the difficulties of managing. He had seen a succession of his skippers and mentors, despite their accomplishments, take the rap for later difficulties. In St. Louis, he joined a team that had fired nine managers in 25 years.

Determined not to become another cautionary tale, Stanky tried to manage the same way he played: uncompromising and smart. He tolerated no laziness and fined players a dollar for every pound over their reporting weight at spring training. He had fines for players not in the dugout for the first and last pitch of the game, not advancing runners, and other such infractions. He feuded with players who resented his strict style of play, with umpires whose calls he disagreed with, and with the media, who, for the first time it seemed, weren't on his side. Even pitcher Harry Breechen, who was so good to Stanky that first year in the minors, was fined for letting a player bunt on what was supposed to be a pitchout (the fine was eventually rescinded).[28] The Brat was almost dictatorial. "The men will play up to the fullest of their capabilities...I do not plan to let anyone take advantage of me...I am not a martinet—and I am not a sucker."[29]

It seemed to work. Stanky was *The Sporting News'* manager of the year in 1952, when the Cardinals went 88–66 and contended much of the season, and in 1953 the club finished in third place for the second straight year. In 1954, however, the Cards took a dive and finished in sixth place at 72–82. Stanky's old boss and advocate, Fred Saigh, had sold the team under charges of embezzlement; he was about to serve 15 months in prison, and it seemed that Stanky's days were numbered. Eddie was unpopular with his players. Not because he lacked the necessary knowledge of the game, but rather because he demanded too much. "He wanted you to play as if today's game was your first or your last," said one of his players, shortstop Dick Schofield.[30] Like many athletes before and since, Stanky was unable to realize that the way that he had played was not the way that he could manage.

One game from 1954 shows the problems in a nutshell. In this contest, Stanky irritated fans and league officials when he used stalling tactics in order to try to get the game—which his team was losing badly—called on account of rain. In the same contest, he started a bench-clearing brawl when he tackled Philadelphia Phillies manager Terry Moore, a coach Stanky had fired in 1952. The umpires ruled the game a forfeit, and Cardinals fans booed their manager.

That was the beginning of the end for Stanky. He suddenly found himself maligned by the fans, the owner, and many of his players. The end would come just 36 games into 1955, with the Cardinals mired in fifth place. Beer magnate August A. Busch Jr., the Cardinals' new owner, had "decided that Stanky was too much foam and not enough body,"[31] and replaced him with Harry Walker on May 28, 1955.

The Brat had learned much from his mentors, but what he never seemed to learn was that players of the 1950s would never be unquestioningly obedient and that "discipline should be laced with understanding," as columnist Daley of the *Times* put it. In any case, Stanky was done in St. Louis, though he grimly remarked that he would "stay in baseball…even if I have to go to a Class D league."[32]

It wasn't quite Class D, but it was minor league. Stanky took a job managing the Minneapolis Millers of the American Association. The Millers finished in fourth place, and once again Eddie was out of a job. He wanted to return to his beloved New York Giants as a coach, and had the blessing of club president Horace Stoneham, but the Giants pilot, Bill Rigney, said no. Instead, Stanky took a job as a coach for the Cleveland Indians (Leo Durocher had helped him get the job by recommending him to Indians GM Hank Greenberg) under freshman manager Kirby Farrell. Eddie remained there for two years.

In a 1958 article that appeared in the *New York Times*, Gay Talese portrayed Stanky as the last remnant of a bygone era, and Stanky remarked that the players of the 1950s were smarter than they were when he played.[33] To Talese, Stanky was "a supreme individualist in a game that now seems saturated with well-educated and mild-mannered conformists."

Still, Stanky did well in his role as a coach with the Indians. He tried to be a loyal "Organization Man." He taught Indians hitter Bobby Avila the "intentional foul" that had made him such a successful player in his day,

While serving as Chisox manager in 1967, Stanky made his notorious "All Star from the neck down" comment about Carl Yastrzemski, further fueling the latter's Triple Crown Impossible Dream season.

and stayed on when Ferrell was replaced by Bobby Bragan, and then again when Bragan was replaced by Joe Gordon. Future major-league manager Joe Altobelli, who was a part-time first baseman on that Cleveland team, called Stanky the best third-base coach he ever saw.[34] Ultimately, Indians ownership cleaned house, Greenberg was fired, and Stanky left the club at the end of 1958. He returned to the Cardinals as a special assistant to general manager Bing Devine, where his role consisted of "scouting and evaluating major and minor league talent."[35] In 1964, Devine was fired by the Cardinals and moved east to become GM of the Mets. Stanky joined him in New York, but did not stay there for long, as he was quickly hired by the Chicago White Sox to be their manager for the 1966 campaign.

Despite his troubles in the past, the Brat's managerial style hadn't changed. His predecessor in Chicago, Al Lopez, was a gentle, soft-spoken man who had been popular with his players. The difference between Lopez and Stanky was night and day. Lopez treated his players with kid gloves, Stanky rode them and pushed them to be the best they could. Lopez played percentage-driven, orderly baseball that rarely employed aggressive plays like the hit-and-run and delayed steals. Stanky was the exact opposite, managing the same way he had played. By 1960s standards, his methods were almost incomprehensibly aggressive. Where most teams never used more than 60 pinch-runners in a season, Stanky used 144 in 1966 and 127 in 1967.[36]

Unable to adjust to their new run-and-gun style, the White Sox finished the 1966 season in fourth place, 15 games behind the Baltimore Orioles. The players simply weren't used to the expectations and aggressive style—both on the field and in the dugout—of their new manager. Stanky demanded that his players grab every edge they could find, and play fundamentally sound and remarkably crafty baseball. Pretend to tag up on every fly ball, no matter how shallow, so the other team would throw the ball around. The win-by-hook-or-by-crook philosophy was prevalent as well. Eddie taught his players, among other things, how to knock the glove off an opposing player's hand as he tried to tag you out, without making it obvious to the umpires.

By the start of the 1967 season, it seemed as though Stanky and the White Sox had found each other. Stanky had fired many of the coaches he had inherited in 1966, and installed those he thought would help convey his win-at-all-costs philosophy to players. (One of those coaches was his former Indians boss, Kirby Farrell.) Stanky's forceful managing, able pitching staff, and a solid fielding team that made few mistakes helped keep the White Sox competitive deep into one of baseball's most gripping seasons. Embroiled in a battle with Boston, Minnesota, and Detroit for first place, the Brat's pitching-rich team was going strong in late August, tied with the Red Sox for first despite being one of the league's weakest-hitting clubs. Stanky had his players motivated, and playing way over their heads. Centerfielder Ken "The Bandit" Berry, an All-star in that year, literally "ran through fences" for Stanky, at one point throwing his whole body over an outfield wall to snare what would have been a home run for Tony Oliva of the Twins. Gary Peters and Joe Horlen were such an effective one-two punch in the starting rotation that they actually killed the Brat's "incentive plan": buying a suit of clothes for a pitcher every time he pitched a complete game (apparently, after buying seven suits each for Peters, Horlen, and Tommy John in the first half of the season, Stanky cut it out). The team ERA was an incredible 2.45.

But the club just petered out around the end of August, and barely anyone seemed to notice. Because of their lack of fireworks on offense and inconsistent clutch hitting, the White Sox were called dull. Hometown fans, who should have been coming to the ballpark in droves to see the hustle-filled baseball that the South Siders were playing, instead stayed away, something that shocked and dismayed hard workers like Berry. On August 24, after a tough game in Minnesota which the Pale Hose lost 3–2 on a controversial call in the ninth, Vice President Hubert Humphrey waited outside the clubhouse to meet with the White Sox. He ended up waiting there for a long time while Stanky talked to his players. "Humphrey can't hit," said Stanky. "What do I need with him?"

The Brat later apologized to Humphrey, but the incident was indicative of his single-mindedness when it came to his team. Even while the Sox were still in the hunt, it was becoming clear that the little manager was rapidly growing increasingly frustrated. It was no secret that Stanky was reviled by the media. Back in his playing days, he had been colorful, an example of hustle that journalists loved. These days he was a nuisance. Once, after sportswriter Watson Spoelstra asked Stanky a question, the Brat performed a strip tease, ripping off each piece of his uniform and hurling them around the clubhouse while yelling at the unfortunate scribe. Eddie ripped the media, the fans, and—unfortunately—opposing players. In June 1967, Stanky had insulted Boston star Carl Yastrzemski, calling him "an all-star from the neck down." The comment lit a fire under Yastrzemski, whom the White Sox had tried desperately to get in 1965 and '66, and he wound up hitting, in the words of catcher J.C. Martin "everything we threw at him but the rosin bag!"[37]

Still, despite it all, the White Sox went into the last week of the season seemingly World Series-bound. NBC came to Comiskey Park to set up cameras. To win the pennant, the White Sox would have to beat the lowly Athletics in Kansas City and then the cellar-dwelling Senators. But they lost a doubleheader to Kansas City, and then committed two first-inning errors en route to being shut out by the Senators on September 29, eliminating them from contention. (They lost the next two to the Senators as well.) The White Sox finished 89–73 and in fourth place, three games behind the champion Red Sox.

Some players credited Stanky for carrying them into the last week of the season with an anemic team batting average of .225. Third baseman Pete Ward maintained that their aggressive leader "kept us in the hunt."[38] But other players, like J.C. Martin and Ed Herrmann, blamed Stanky for the Sox losing those last five crucial games. He was accused of "overmanaging" and tinkering with the lineup. Notwithstanding the massive letdown that was the end of the 1967 season, Stanky's contract was renewed for four years by White Sox owner Arthur Allyn on September 30, for the "outstanding managerial job he did in the greatest American League race in history."[39]

But the White Sox lost their first 10 games in 1968, and 69 games later, Stanky was asked to resign—replaced, ironically, by old manager Al Lopez. That last part-season was excruciatingly painful. Toward the end of his tenure, Stanky was so frustrated with the White Sox' inability to produce runs that after a third straight loss by one run, he instituted a $5 fine for players who failed in certain clutch situations. It didn't matter; the White Sox finished the season 67–95, and in eighth place.

To sum up, Stanky's short time with the White Sox was marked by controversy and large-scale disappointment. Players had simply changed too much for the little manager to relate to them. It wasn't that Eddie was behind the times; he was a proponent of the designated hitter, and he understood that players weren't the way they used to be. He was simply unable to adjust who he was in a game in which he must have truly believed that the team that won was not the more talented or the stronger hitting club, but the one that had the most "guts and determination." It seemed as though Stanky would forever be an old-timey player stuck in a world he was not advanced enough for.

Back home in Alabama, however, the Brat finally found something that he took great joy in when he secured a coaching job in 1969 at the University of Southern Alabama. After the relative glamour of the major leagues, college ball was different. "I had played in beautiful parks with beautiful locker rooms," he said. "At Southern Alabama, I inherited a rockpile for a ballfield, with no dugouts, a four-foot-high fence around it and no grass in the infield." Stanky transformed that little school and rockpile field into a great college baseball team. For the next 14 years, beginning in 1969, teams led by Stanky at the school went 488–193. He did not have a single losing season. Best of all, Eddie finally changed his win-at-all-costs philosophy. He adopted an "everyone plays" style. "I'm a believer in participation," he said. "The one record I care about came in a game against Vanderbilt in 1971. I played 38 men in one nine-inning game. Everyone got in. Some seasons, I've carried as many as 45 players on a team."[40] Stanky loved coaching students, and later said the biggest thrill was when his players graduated and "their mothers come up and embrace me for helping along their sons. There is something about a mother's tears at graduation. I can't weigh it."

Stanky sent 43 of his players to the major leagues, as his team became a Sun Belt Conference powerhouse. "He brought the University of South Alabama from just about point-zero to a national power in three years," said the school's current head coach Steve Kittrell, who played under Stanky and has led the team for 35 years. "He put South Alabama on the map athletically. He is and always will be South Alabama baseball."[41]

Former players recalled him as an intense manager—intensity was a constant with Eddie Stanky—but, he is also recalled as a skipper who cared about the development and well-being of his athletes. He taught the students the same little things he taught his major leaguers, and emphasized sound fundamentals and hustle. "He taught us so much." said former player Rick Patterson, who served for many years as an instructor in the Mets minor league system.

There was a brief moment in the midst of his years at Southern Alabama where it seemed as though Stanky would resume his major-league managerial career. On June 23, 1977, he became manager of the Texas Rangers, and piloted them to a 10–8 victory. The next day, he quit. He told team president Eddie Robinson, "I can't take the job.... I'm homesick for my family."[42] When Stanky had left the White Sox back in '68, he said that it was a practical rather than an emotional decision. "I don't make emotional decisions," he said then. Nine years later, the decision was purely emotional. "I should have known better, that I have too many other things," he told the *New York Times.* Greeted by reporters back at University of South Alabama, he was asked if he was back for good: "You're damn right I am," he responded.

Stanky weathered a heart attack and open-heart surgery to coach the school for another six years before retiring in 1983. In one of his last games, Stanky showed a flash of his "Brat" persona, being thrown out of the contest for cursing an umpire. "If there is anything I can't stand," he said after the game, repeating one of his favorite sayings, "it's an umpire who doesn't know the rules."[43]

In his interview with Gay Talese in 1958 as an Indians coach, Stanky had said that he believed when he reached old age that there would be a cure for cancer and heart disease. He predicted that he would live to be 79, and that he would not be remembered as "The Brat" in his obituary. As it turns out, he lived to be 83. On June 6, 1999, he died in a hospital in his hometown in Fairhope, Alabama, after a heart attack. His *New York Times* obituary indeed called him "The Brat," which, despite Stanky's prediction, seemed only fitting. He was, all at once, Ed Stanky, the intelligent and gentle mentor who cared about his teammates and players, and the feisty "Brat," who led his team with an all-consuming will to succeed.

Not a hitter of home runs or an accumulator of RBIs, Stanky was someone who absorbed information like a sponge wherever he went; a player who used every ounce of his talent; a man who cared about his teammates and players, irrespective of race. A guy who would kick, semaphore, fight, taunt, dive, slide, stall, scream, sacrifice, hustle, and win for his team. A man with an incredible drive and will to succeed in everything that he did, from Philly to Fairhope and everywhere in between. A real Brat.

Notes

1. "The Brat," *Time*, Monday April 28, 1952.
2. Mama Stanky, was renowned for her toughness. Once, when Eddie was playing catcher in sandlot baseball as a little boy, he was knocked out by a bat when he got too close to the plate. Mrs. Stanky, watching from the stands, was apparently unperturbed by her son's unconsciousness and recommended that the other kids just "throw a bucket of water on him." After he came around, Eddie finished the game. (*Time* article) Stanky also had help from his teammates surviving that first year in organized ball. Pitcher Harry "The Cat" Breechen, in his second season of ball, took Stanky under his wing in Greenville. In the book The St. Louis Cardinals by Rob Rains, Stanky claimed that without the help of Breechen, who would go on to an illustrious career himself, he might never have survived that first year.
3. *The Sporting News*, August 24, 1949, p. 44.
4. Berkow, Ira. "Slick, Slicker, Slickest: Reese, Rizzuto, Dark", *New York Times*, January 22, 1996.
5. *Time*, op. cit.
6. *The New York Times*, June 8, 1999, p. B6
7. Sports of the Times, *The New York Times*, Arthur Daley, Sep. 8 1946.
8. Daley, Sep. 8
9. Stanky was also the team's de-facto leader during that 1947 season, a result of Leo Durocher being suspended for the year by the commissioner's office.
10. "Luther Spoehr: Review of Jonathan Eig's *Opening Day: The Story of Jackie Robinson's First Season* (Simon & Schuster, 2007)" History News Network. Written for HNN, 5/7/2007. http://hnn.us/roundup/entries/38544.html.
11. Fitzpatrick Frank. "The Ground Ball that Changed America," *Philadelphia Inquirer*, April 8, 2007. Stanky was one of Robinson's first defenders, most notably firing back at hecklers on the Philadelphia Phillies bench during the early weeks of Robinson's season. Nack, William. "The Breakthrough," *Sports Illustrated*, May 5, 1997.
12. Sanders, a first baseman, did not play in 1947, a result of a fractured arm in an August 1946 game. The Braves agreed to send along more money to the Dodgers if Sanders was unable to play, and, on April 19, when it seemed that he wasn't, he

was sold back to Boston for a reported $60,000. According to Al Hirshberg, the Braves had been angling for Stanky all summer, and only after a contract was reached with Stanky, had Rickey decided to do business.

13. *Time*, op. cit.

14. Initial reports from the hospital indicated that the injury was a severe sprain. (*New York Times*, July 9, 1948, p.13.)

15. *New York Times*, October 6, 1948, p. 38.

16. *Ibid.*

17. In early November, Al Dark received a surprise present from his mentor at his home in Lake Charles, LA. A diamond-studded ring that his roommate had specially designed and had made for him, inscribed with the words: National League champions." What was the reason for this generous present? Stanky said that "One day last April I remarked to Al that my biggest thrill in baseball was getting to play in the World Series with Brooklyn. Dark said that had been his goal, to play on a world championship team. He said he'd like to wear a world champion ring. I told him that I thought he'd be wearing one before the end of the year. Well, everything worked out—except Cleveland won the World Series.' (*New York Times*, December 1, 1948, p. 40) Stanky made sure that his roommate got a ring anyway. Dark would win that World Series ring in New York.

18. Antonelli interview with Boston Braves Historical Association, October 10, 2004. Stanky spent nine years in the minor leagues.

19. Kaese, Harold. *The Boston Braves, 1871–1953* (Northeastern University Press, 2004), p. 278.

20. Description and quotes come from *The Sporting News*, August 3, 1949, p. 2.

21. Hirshberg, Al, "What Really Happened to the Braves?" *Sport*, January, 1950).

22. *New York Times*, August 18, 1949, p. 25. *Time* magazine said that "As the 1949 season wore on, the Braves split into three or four camps—some for Southworth, some against him, and some just against each other." *Time*, op. cit.

23. Hirshberg, op. cit.

24. "The Incompatibles" *Time*, December 26, 1949.

25. "The Brat", *Time*, op. cit.

26. Despite the adversarial relationship, there was a sense of grudging respect. Rizzuto said of Stanky: "He plays a snarling, dog-eat-dog kind of baseball" *Independent, The* (London), June 15, 1999 by Paul Wadey.

27. It should be noted that this second parting between Durocher and Stanky was much more amicable then the first. Stanky had learned a lot from Durocher, and during his stint with the Cardinals as manager, he was accused of trying to imitate The Lip's managerial style.

28. Rains, Rob. *Cardinals: Where Have You Gone?* (Champaign IL: Sports Publishing, March 2005)

29. "The Brat," *Time*, op. cit.

30. Skipper, John C. *A Biographical Dictionary of Baseball Managers* (Jefferson NC: McFarland, 2003)

31. "Relaxed Redbird," *Time*, June 13, 1955.

32. All quotations in the paragraph are from: Daley, Arthur. "Quick Harvest", *New York Times*, June 6, 1955.

33. The theory that baseball players were more intelligent was one of Arthur Daley's reasons for Stanky's failure in St. Louis. Daley said that Stanky relied on a John McGraw approach that did not work because baseball players had changed too much since the McGraw era.

34. Anderson, Dave. "Hot Seat at the Hot Corner," *New York Times*, December 4, 1980.

35. "Cards Name Stanky as Personnel Chief," *New York Times*, September 26, 1958.

36. Views on Lopez vs. Stanky managerial style: White Sox Interactive Website. Mark Liptak interview with Ken Barry. (http://www.whitesoxinteractive.com/rwas/index.php?category=11&id=2961)

37. White Sox Interactive. Mark Liptiak Interview with J.C. Martin (http://www.whitesoxinteractive.com/rwas/index.php?category=11&id=935)

38. White Sox Interactive. Mark Liptiak Interview with Pete Ward (http://www.whitesoxinteractive.com/rwas/index.php?category=11&id=2413)

39. "Stanky is Given Four-Year Contract," *New York Times*, October 1, 1968.

40. "Infielder Eddie Stanky, 82, Dies; Called 'The Brat' for Canniness," *New York Times*, June 8, 1999. p. B6.

41. University of South Alabama Athletics Website. "Tradition." Released 7/11/2006. (http://www.usajaguars.com/ViewArticle.dbml?&DB_OEM_ID=8300&ATCLID=344409&SPID=3266&SPSID=38527)

42. "Ex-Big Leaguer Eddie Stanky Dies," Associated Press, June 6, 1999.v

43. "Stanky to Retire," *New York Times*, May 8, 1983.

BOBBY STURGEON *by John Morrison*

G	AB	R	H	2B	3B	HR	RBI	BB	SO	BA	OBP	SLG	SB	HBP
34	78	10	17	3	1	0	4	4	5	.218	.256	.282	0	0

For Cubs fans of the 1940s and 1950s, Bobby Sturgeon will always be linked with two other shortstops who broke into the majors during the spring of 1940—10-time All-Star Pee Wee Reese of the Dodgers and seven-time All-Star Marty Marion of the Cardinals.

As the story goes, Cubs manager Gabby Hartnett was pushing the team's front office to acquire a young shortstop, and had his eye on Reese, whose contract the

Dodgers had acquired from the Red Sox for $75,000 and prospects the year before. The front office considered the price for Reese too steep, instead opting for a less expensive option from the Cardinals. The Cards apparently offered the Cubs a choice between prospects Sturgeon and Marion for $50,000. The Cubs took Sturgeon. It was later reported that Hartnett became agitated every time he thought about this decision by the North Siders' management. But while it's true that Sturgeon was no Reese or Marion, he was a solid ballplayer and a key reserve on the 1948 NL champion Braves.

Robert Harwood Sturgeon was born in Clinton, Indiana, on August 6, 1919; he moved to Long Beach as a youngster and lived in Southern California the rest of his life. He attended Long Beach Polytechnic High School, noted for a strong baseball program, and starred on the varsity with future major-leaguers Chuck Stevens and Vern Stephens. Poly High's 1936 team featured Sturgeon as the starting shortstop and took the Southern California title with a 14–4 win over Escondido for the Jackrabbits' first championship. Many consider this team to be the best in the school's history.

In the summer of 1937, Bobby began his career in pro ball with the Cardinals' Class D Albuquerque affiliate in the Arizona-Texas League, having been signed by St. Louis scout Bob Hughes—who was also his American Legion Juniors coach in Long Beach. Turning 18 that summer and receiving $75 a month, Sturgeon excelled as a lanky right-handed-hitting shortstop, batting .298 with 148 hits and 82 RBIs—results that earned him a first team all-star selection. Albuquerque defeated El Paso in a best-of-seven series for the championship and beat the Wink Oilers, champions of the neighboring West Texas-New Mexico League, two games to none, for regional bragging rights. In the second game of the best-of-three series, Sturgeon knocked in the winning run in the bottom of the ninth for a 5–4 clinching win.

Sturgeon's strong rookie performance earned him a promotion in 1938 to a solid Sacramento Solons team of the talent-laden Pacific Coast League, and a role coming off the bench to spell starting shortstop Joe Orengo. Unable to adjust to this new role and his limited playing time, Bobby batted just .122 in 49 at-bats over 22 games with a similar drop in his normally reliable glove work—an .898 fielding percentage.

In early July Sturgeon was returned to Albuquerque after much lobbying by team president Sam Minces, who found his Cardinals in the cellar after the first half of the season. Later that summer, Sturgeon's contract was assigned

Bob Sturgeon wrapped up a six-year big league career performing as a utility infielder with the '48 Braves.

Bob Sturgeon and Phil Masi chatting on the top step of the Braves dugout.

to the American Association Columbus Red Birds by St. Louis general manager Branch Rickey. Sturgeon remained with Albuquerque for the balance of the '38 season, earning a second league all star selection while batting .335 in 52 games.

The next spring Sturgeon reported to Columbus, where he produced a stellar season—batting .297 and leading the league in assists while recording a strong .942 fielding percentage. He caught the eye of several major-league scouts, despite competing for attention with two other American Association shortstops, Phil Rizzuto of Kansas City and Pee Wee Reese of Louisville. That winter the Cubs forked over the $50,000 for his contract at the recommendation of scout Clarence "Pants" Rowland.

Invited to spring training in 1940, Sturgeon quickly impressed manager Hartnett with his slick fielding. By making that season's opening day roster, Bobby, at 20, was among the youngest players in the National League. He appeared in seven games at shortstop, batting .190, before being assigned to Jersey City of the International League in early May. He saw action in 124 games at shortstop for the Double A Little Giants, batting .234. Sturgeon said years later of his Cubs debut and quick demotion, "I was pretty cocky about the whole thing. I made seven errors in my first week and found myself in Jersey."

Sturgeon again broke camp with the Cubs in 1941, spending his first full season in the majors as the Cubs' regular shortstop and batting .245 in 129 games with 45 runs scored and 25 RBIs for new manager Jimmie Wilson's sixth-place club. In an indication of his approach at the plate, Bobby had only nine walks in more than 400 plate appearances. It was a much better year all around for him, though; in October, he married sweetheart Doris Hoke.

The following season, however, was not as fruitful. Sturgeon was relegated to a utility role on the Cubs when rookie Lennie Merullo became Chicago's regular shortstop. He saw action in only 63 games, largely splitting time between second base and shortstop, and batted .247 with eight runs and seven RBIs. That offseason, Sturgeon joined hundreds of other major leaguers in the war effort, enlisting in the Navy and serving for the next three years. About this break in his playing career, Sturgeon recalled, "The time I spent in the Navy counted toward my player's pension, and I had a job when the war was over."

Since his military assignments kept him Stateside, Sturgeon had the opportunity to maintain his baseball skills playing for the Long Beach Major-Minors of the Southern California service league. He also spent time on a 1943 service all-star team with other big-leaguers, including Joe DiMaggio, playing war benefit games around greater Los Angeles.

Upon his return to the majors in 1946, Bobby joined a Cubs team that was coming off its first pennant in seven years and he enjoyed his best season, batting .296 in 100 games for the third-place club. Sharing time again at both short and second, he scored 26 runs and had 21 RBIs. He also hit his only major league home run, a second-inning solo shot into Wrigley Field's left-field bleachers off Howie Pollet of the Cardinals on September 22. Another '46 highlight was the season-ending series in St. Louis, when the Cubs took two of three games to drop the first-place Cardinals into a tie with the Brooklyn Dodgers—bringing about the first-ever playoff to determine the National League pennant. While Bobby enjoyed the outcome, he did not see action, because of a dislocated finger sustained earlier in the week.

The next season, his last with the Cubs, Sturgeon played in 87 games, batting .254 with 16 runs and 21 RBIs. He was again slowed by injury; he broke two ribs on a stolen base attempt by Brooklyn Dodgers rookie Jackie Robinson, who instead of sliding into second threw a take-out block that knocked Bobby halfway into left field. Many felt this was retaliation for a game six weeks earlier when Sturgeon hit Robinson in the chest with a throw on a double-play relay.[1]

A highlight of the '47 season was the 6-to-5 triple play Bobby started on September 1 on a line drive off the bat of Cincinnati's Ray Mueller. Sturgeon caught the liner, stepped on second to double off Eddie Miller, and fired the ball to third, where Peanuts Lowrey nailed Eddie Lukon for the third out. Away from the park, the prominent event for the Sturgeon family was the birth of their only child, son Jim.

That offseason had more changes in store, as Sturgeon was traded to the Boston Braves in late February 1948 for infielder Dick Culler and pitcher Walt Lanfranconi. As a dependable glove man, Bobby was deemed best suited to a backup infielder role—a veteran who could both fill in at second base and back up rookie shortstop Alvin Dark.

While playing shortstop for the Cubs in 1947, Sturgeon suffered two broken ribs as the result of a retaliatory take-out block by the Dodgers' Jackie Robinson on a steal of second base.

He was also felt to be a positive clubhouse influence by manager Billy Southworth based on their time together in the Cardinals farm system. The trade also enabled the Braves to move the outspoken holdout Culler, who was not popular with manager Southworth.

Two highlights of Sturgeon's year with the Braves came first in mid-June, when he knocked in the tying run and scored the winning run in a four-run ninth inning rally over the Reds that propelled Boston into a first-place tie, and then in late July, when he was recalled from a three-week stint with the Braves' Milwaukee affiliate after second baseman Eddie Stanky broke his ankle. Bobby had been optioned to Milwaukee on July 2, when the Braves recalled pitcher Al Lyons from the affiliate, and this time he stayed with the big club the rest of the pennant-winning season. While he was a member of the Braves' World Series roster, he did not appear in the Series; he was, however, awarded a full runner-up share of $4,570 and a championship diamond ring. All told, Bob played 34 games with the NL champs that year, batting .218 with 10 runs scored and four RBIs.

Despite the disappointment of losing the Series, Sturgeon appreciated the work of his close friend Bob Lemon, who won Games Two and Six in Boston for the Indians while sporting a 1.65 ERA. The two had grown up in the same Long Beach neighborhood with Chuck Stevens and Vern Stephens, and the three would come by Lemon's house to help him with his chores, so the future Hall of Fame pitcher could join his friends on the local baseball diamond. Later the two Bobs were groomsmen in each other's weddings.

The exciting summer of '48 was Sturgeon's last season in the majors. The Braves sold his contract to Seattle of the Pacific Coast League that offseason. He was far from through with the game, however. After two seasons in the PCL with Seattle and Los Angeles, batting .272 and .202 respectively, Bobby hooked on with Class B Victoria Athletics of the Western International league in 1951. It was here that he got his first opportunity as a player-manager, taking over the team in midseason for "Kewpie Dick" Barrett.

The next season, Sturgeon was signed as player-manager of the Class C Ventura Braves of the California League. While he batted .329 in 59 games, the team was far less successful, having fallen to seventh place by late July. The club also ran into financial difficulties according to Bob, who resigned on August 2 "to help out" since he was drawing the largest salary.[2] He returned to one of his old haunts, catching on as a second baseman with last-place Sacramento of the PCL and batting .239 in 50 games.

Looking to continue his managerial career, Bob signed on in 1953 as player-manager for a new Class A franchise, the Edmonton Eskimos of the Western International League (who brought organized ball back to Edmonton, Alberta, after a 31-year absence). This was among Bob's most successful years as a manager; he led a team that had no official MLB affiliation other than an informal relationship with the New York Yankees, and a roster that had just two players who had previously played together, to a very competitive third-place finish. Bob also had success at the plate, batting .244 with 45 runs scored and 57 RBIs in 118 games. In '54 he returned for a second season at the helm in Edmonton, logging 97 games as the club's second baseman, batting .269 with 32 RBIs as the Eskimos, a .500 team, finished fifth in the 10-team league.

Seeking to catch on with a major-league organization, Sturgeon signed on as player-manager of the Phillies' Class C affiliate in Salt Lake City of the Pioneer League for 1955. He did not last the season as the defending league champion Bees staggered to a fourth-place first-half record, resulting in Bob's release in early July. Later that month he caught on with the Fargo-Moorhead Twins of the Class C Northern League as an infielder, and his 15 games with the Twins were his last in professional baseball. Even at the mature age of 36, Bob continued to have success at the plate that final summer of a 16-season professional career, batting over .300 in 144 at bats at his two stops.

That offseason Sturgeon worked to secure another managerial opportunity, but with nothing forthcoming that suited him and his family, he took a corporate job in Long Beach with the recreation department of the Douglas plant—an operation that became the major assembly plant for DC-8 jets in the years to follow. He eventually became the sports director for the resulting McDonnell Douglas operation in Long Beach, organizing all the company's sporting events. Bob also logged significant time on the area golf links, and was an enthusiastic supporter of the Angels' teams over the years until his death at the age of 87 in San Dimas, California, on March 10, 2007.

Notes

1. baseballlibrary.com
2. Long Beach Press-Telegram, August 3, 1952.

Sources

Newspaper Articles:
Long Beach Press-Telegram, 1935–1956, 1984
Albuquerque Journal, 1937–1938
Oakland Tribune, 1938
Chicago Daily Tribune, 1939–1948.
Boston Globe, 1948.
Boston Post, 1948.
Walla Walla (Wash.) Union, 1953.
Letter dated May 5, 1989, from Sturgeon to Bob Lemon.
Interview in *Baseball Digest*, June 2000 by Clay Woody.
Obituary from the *Press-Telegram*, March 2007.

EARL TORGESON *by Mark Armour*

G	AB	R	H	2B	3B	HR	RBI	BB	SO	BA	OBP	SLG	SB	HBP
134	438	70	111	23	5	10	67	81	54	.253	.372	.397	19	2

In a 15-year major league career filled with great stories and accomplishments of various stripes, Earl Torgeson was well known for getting in brawls. Even before he reached the major leagues, in the winter before his rookie season, he had faced assault charges for decking two men on a Seattle street who had used vulgar language in front of his wife. The judge threw out the case, telling the assembled, "I would have done the same thing."

Billy Southworth, his first manager in Boston, called him "as fierce a competitor as I've seen in all my years in baseball." Second baseman Roy Hartsfield said, "Torgy is a very humorous fellow—until the ball game starts." In 1948 Torgeson took offense in a preseason "City Series" game at Braves Field when Red Sox infielder Billy Hitchcock got tangled up with him while returning to the first base bag. After it happened again, Torgeson belted Hitchcock in the mouth, causing both benches to empty

and a free-for-all to erupt. The skirmish cost Torgeson his glasses, and after this he would always remove them before a pending confrontation.

Then there was the time in 1950 he was hit in the ribs with a pitch thrown by the Pirates' Cliff Chambers. The very next day Chambers threw one at Torgy's head; believing this action had crossed the line, Earl angrily conversed with the pitcher. The conversation did not go well. After removing his glasses, Torgeson charged the mound and started a multi-player melee. Torgeson played the rest of the season with a broken rib, the result of Chambers' first errant fastball. Fortunately, the second one had missed his head.

A few years later, as as he batted in the bottom of the first on July 1, 1952, at Braves Field, Torgeson's backswing hit Giants' catcher Sal Yvars on the shinguard. After Torgeson lined a single up the middle, Yvars picked up the bat and slammed the handle on the plate, shattering it. Torgeson was stranded on the bases, so he did not return to the Braves dugout until after the Giants were retired in the top of the second. When he discovered the broken bat, Torgeson removed his glasses, then sprinted across the field to the Giants' dugout and slugged Yvars in the face, leaving the catcher's right eye swollen, discolored, and bloody. "Sal and I always have been good friends. But breaking a guy's bat is like slapping him in the face." Torgeson said after this incident, "We may be in seventh place but we don't have to take that insult." Torgy was fined $100 for the fight, Yvars $25. The good friends brawled again on July 18, 1954, after both players had changed teams.

"If I had to do it all over again I wouldn't have been such a character," Torgeson reflected many years later. "I just regret the fact that I'm labeled a bad boy." The second "Earl of Snohomish", following townsman Earl Averill, wasn't really a bad boy—he was well-liked, even by the people he was socking in the mouth. He loved laughing, joking with his teammates, and going out on the town. He played baseball with a passion, and the brawling, the all-out head-first slides, this was part of how he needed to play the game. He paid the price for this passion with seemingly annual game-related injuries.

He was a tall, bespectacled left-handed first baseman who smoked several cigars a day. Observers of the time kept waiting for him to break out with the home run totals, to reach his "potential." In the meantime, he was stealing bases, working the pitcher, fielding his position ably, and otherwise contributing to the cause. Off the field, he was bright and funny, traits which made him successful in several ventures throughout his life. "He just refuses to be dull," is how teammate Gene Mauch once put it. "He won't let himself get in a rut—in his conversation, his actions, or anything else."

Clifford Earl Torgeson was born in the lumber mill town of Snohomish, Washington, on New Years Day of 1924, the second son of Melvin Carl Torgeson and the former Helen Kornelia Gray. Melvin was a carpenter of Norwegian heritage, while Helen was English and Native American. The couple divorced when Earl was very young, but they both remained in Snohomish and stayed involved in Earl's life. Helen was a fun-loving woman who married Harold King, with whom she ran an appliance store in town for many years. Melvin Torgeson remarried as well, to Clara Morris, and built many of the beautiful homes in the Snohomish area. Earl lived off and on with each parent in the small town.

Like many Snohomish boys, Torgeson idolized Earl Averill, the first "Earl of Snohomish", the slugger and

Upon arriving in Boston in 1947 after seasoning in the Pacific Coast League, lefty clouter Earl Torgeson immediately drew comparisons to Red Sox superstar Ted Williams.

centerfielder for the Cleveland Indians during most of Torgeson's youth. Averill would return home every fall and drive around town in his fancy car, causing the boys to stare, vowing that they would follow him to the major leagues one day. Torgeson used to follow his idol around town, staring in the barber's window watching him get his haircut.

Torgeson first played baseball on the aptly-named Averill Field near his home. "I'd leave the house after breakfast and come home just before supper," he later recalled. "All the time, I played ball. I must have been 11 years old when I first played as a semipro." Despite needing glasses as a youngster, he also starred in basketball on a team of much older boys. But his prowess on the diamond, along with the public success of Averill, led townsfolk to petition the school board to prohibit Torgeson from playing football for fear of injury. After playing just two varsity games, he was removed from the gridiron team.

After two years of high school baseball, a year of American Legion, and several years playing semiprofessionally in the area, Torgy signed in 1941 with the Seattle Rainiers on the advice of an old scout named George Hokum. Earl trained with Seattle in '41, but the 17-year-old was soon optioned to Wenatchee of the Class B Western International League. His manager there, Ted Merritt, took one look at the tall, gangly, bespectacled Torgeson and asked, "What in the Lord's name have they sent me now?" His new first sacker hit .332 in 92 games.

In a 1941 late-season recall to the Rainiers, he got to play with the 39-year-old Averill (just retired from the big leagues), and was an impressive 4-for-10 in four games to help the Rainiers win a tough pennant race and capture the Pacific Coast League title. The next year Torgy was farmed out to Spokane (also of the WIL), but a week into the season the Rainiers sold incumbent first baseman Les Scarsella to Oakland and promoted Earl, who had hit .429 in 28 at-bats for Spokane. Now playing in the best league west of St. Louis, he hit .312 with 32 stolen bases in 147 games for Seattle.

Now about those stolen bases. Torgeson was a big man, listed at 6-feet-3 and 180 pounds at the start of his career, and was always expected to hit for more power than he did. Even well into his major league career, Torgeson hit in the power slots of the batting order, as befitting a large first baseman. He never did develop a lot of power, but he had a great batting eye and was very fast on the bases. Had he had a different body but the same skills, he would have been a fine leadoff man.

The 18-year-old Torgy likely would have been sold to

a major league team after the 1942 season had he not been about to be drafted. He served in the Army from January 1943 until March 1946. After a year at Fort Lewis and Fort Lawton in Washington State, Earl saw action in the Aleutians, then in France and Germany. He was injured in the Battle of the Bulge by the blast of a shell that landed in his platoon.

Emil Sick, the Rainiers owner, was a friend of New York Yankees owner Jacob Ruppert, and had promised the Yankees first crack at Torgeson after the war. When the Yankees and Rainiers could not come to an agreement on a deal in 1945, the Braves stepped in and landed Torgeson's option for five players plus the price of exercising the option, believed to be close to $100,000. Torgeson was in France when he learned about the transaction. "He can't miss," said Torchy Torrance, the Rainiers' general manager. "He can hit, run, field, and think, and what else do you have to do? Wait and see what this kid does to big league pitching."

When Earl reported back to the Rainiers in 1946 the season had already begun. Two days before the Braves' option was to expire on August 20, Torgeson dislocated his right (nonthrowing) shoulder. The Rainiers granted an extension, and after the Braves looked him over they made the deal. After 3½ years away from the game, Torgy slumped to .285 in 103 games for Seattle.

When Torgeson reported to spring camp with the Braves in 1947, new teammate Red Barrett called him "the poor man's Ted Williams," as a way of teasing the heralded rookie from the left coast. After a subpar opening series in Brooklyn, Braves' president Lou Perini had to talk manager Billy Southworth out of benching the rookie first baseman. Torgeson responded by driving in 36 runs in his first 30 games, drawing further comparisons to Williams, a fellow left-handed slugger from across town who also wore number 9. "I didn't ask for it," said Torgy. "I didn't know until the City Series that Ted Williams also wore that number."

In one way Torgeson and Williams could not have been more different. While Ted was known for refusing to tip his cap to the fans, after a home run Torgeson would take his hat off and wave it around in the air. His personality personified the differences between the images of the two teams—the Braves being the blue-collar team of the fans, the Red Sox the rich, pampered club of stars. Torgeson became a crowd favorite.

Although he cooled off later in '47 and lost some playing time to Frank McCormick, Torgy ended up hitting .285

Earl Torgeson led Braves and Indians regulars with a robust .389 batting average in the World Series.

with 16 home runs as a rookie—compared with 10 round-trippers total in three minor league seasons—and 82 walks. Billy Southworth wanted to take it slow with his young player, saying, "Torgeson is going to be one of the finest first basemen in baseball, but he's still young and needs confidence. I don't want to rush him. He has a little trouble hitting southpaws, in common with most left-handed batters. If I bring him along slowly, I believe he will be able to eliminate that weakness. But if he gets stopped consistently with southpaws now, he may never be able to hit them well."

The tall man with the spectacles could certainly run the bases. "I'll wager today that he's the fastest man in the National League," said Tigers coach Bill Sweeney, who saw Torgeson play in the Pacific Coast League. Braves first base coach Ernie White added: "I see the best runners in our league tear down the line. And take my word for it, Torgy gets down here the quickest."

Even at a young age, Torgeson quickly became a leader on the club, a guy not afraid to hold court in the clubhouse. Platooning with Frank McCormick in 1948, he slumped to .253 with 10 home runs, but added his typical 81 walks (fourth in the league) and 19 stolen bases (fifth) for the pennant-winning Braves. In the World Series he started five of the six games, missing only lefty Gene Bearden's shutout in Game Three. Torgeson, hitting third in the lineup, hit safely seven times in 18 trips, including three doubles. His .389 average led all regulars from both teams in the Series.

Earlier in '48, Torgeson had contributed to another significant event. On May 22, manager Billy Southworth and several members of the team, including Torgeson, visited a local hospital to surprise a young leukemia-stricken boy from New Sweden, Maine, an event which was later broadcast on Ralph Edwards' *Truth or Consequences* national radio show. Named "Jimmy" to protect his privacy, the 12-year-old was presented with a regulation team uniform and a bat from his fellow Swede Earl Torgeson. Money flowed in for Jimmy's treatment, which spawned the "Jimmy Fund" charity of today's Dana-Farber Cancer Institute which was supported by the Braves until their 1953 departure from Boston and has been championed by lthe Red Sox ever since. For many years, it was assumed that Jimmy had passed away as only 15 percent of the children encountering his type of cancer then survived. But a half-century later, Einar Gustafson, the real Jimmy, emerged from obscurity and became an instant celebrity. He even still possessed his child-sized

Braves uniform and Torgeson's bat, and both were put on display at the Baseball Hall of Fame in 1998.

The 1949 season was far less memorable for Earl. In early May, he made an aggressive attempt to take out Jackie Robinson at second base on a double-play ball, slid clumsily and separated his left shoulder. The injury sidelined him for three months. In August he began working out again, but suffered a broken thumb in a fight after curfew involving teammate Jim Russell and three soldiers—it's not completely clear what happened, and Torgeson would never talk about it. His season was over after just 25 games, in which he hit .260 with four home runs. The following spring he spent several weeks learning to throw again—his former overhand motion replaced with a more accurate sidearm toss. His first-rate play around the bag was now that much better.

Torgeson opened up a sporting goods store in Wellesley, a Boston suburb, with Hank Camelli, a 1947 teammate, and worked there in the off-seasons. He also had become a popular after-dinner speaker and had his own radio show, and later a television show.

In 1950 Torgeson was a full-time player for the first time, playing all 156 Braves' games, coming through with 23 home runs, 87 RBIs, and a .290 batting average. He also walked 119 times, third in the league, and led the senior circuit by scoring 120 runs. Historian Bill James suggests that Torgeson might have been the best player in the National League in 1950. The next season he again played every game (155 this time), finishing at .263 but with 24 home runs and 92 RBIs. He walked 112 times, and stole 20 bases. Despite his fine play, however, the Braves finished fourth both seasons.

Torgeson had been married in 1946 to the former Norma Syverson, a beautiful woman of Norwegian descent from Twin Valley, Minnesota. Norma and three sisters had gone to Seattle during the war to find employment. There she met Earl, and they married when he returned from the service. The Torgesons had two children: Christine and Andrew, who later played two years in the New York Yankees' organization. In the early years of Earl's career the family would accompany him to spring training and then back to Boston for the season.

In 1951 the Torgesons settled in Anna Maria, a sparsely populated coastal island in the Gulf of Mexico, not far from the Braves' spring training site of Bradenton, Florida. Many baseball players and families owned cottages nearby, including Warren Spahn, and many baseball teammates and friends visited often. Torgeson's great friend Fred Hutchinson was also a neighbor there. Torgeson spent many a winter golfing every day with his baseball friends. He also loved to host barbecues, gatherings of friends and teammates eating ribs, or lobsters shipped from Maine and prepared by Earl himself.

Despite his fairly impressive statistics, in 1952 many fans and writers thought Torgeson would lose the position to George Crowe, a rookie (and one of the first black ballplayers on the Braves) who had hit .339 or better his previous three seasons in the minor leagues. Torgeson ended up getting most of the playing time, but had his worst year in the majors—hitting .230 with just five home runs in 122 games. After the season Earl was dealt to the Philadelphia Phillies in a complex four-team swap also involving the Dodgers and Reds. For the Braves, this sequence netted them Joe Adcock, who held down first base for the next 10 years.

In 1953, his first year in Philadelphia, Torgy took most of the playing time from incumbent and close friend Eddie Waitkus and hit .274 with 11 home runs in 111 games. Once again, however, an injury set Earl back. He dislocated his right shoulder in January of '54 when he tripped over his dog one night on his way to bed, and he supposedly kept the incident a secret from everyone other than the trainer and a few teammates. The injury sapped his power, leading to just five home runs and a .271 batting average in 135 gutty games. Near the end of the season he broke his thumb, and he ended up having surgeries to correct both conditions.

The following June, his power still not recovered (just one home run in 47 games), Torgy was sold to the Tigers at the June 15 trading deadline; a few weeks later, the Tigers released Ferris Fain, who had been playing first base. Torgeson played very well in Detroit, hitting .283 in 300 at bats, with nine home runs and nine stolen bases without being caught. He also continued to walk, drawing 93 in his two stops during 1955.

On July 17, 1955, the Tigers and Yankees were tied 5–5 after nine innings at Tiger Stadium. In the bottom of the tenth, Torgeson led off with a walk against Eddie Lopat, took third on a single by Ray Boone, and two outs later (with Bob Turley now pitching) stole home to end the game. "After I reached third," said Torgeson, "I noticed Turley didn't look at me before going into his first pitch." After the ball game, as the story goes, Yankee manager Casey Stengel was approached at the hotel by some autograph hunters who asked for Turley. "He's out at the stadium…winding up," responded the sage skipper.

In January 1956, the convertible Torgeson was driving flipped over on a curve, pinning him beneath the steering wheel. Torgy suffered cuts and bruises but remarkably broke no bones. He was charged with reckless driving while drinking, and with not having a driver's license. All of this netted him a $50 fine. In the season ahead, he hit .264 with 12 home runs in 117 games.

The Tigers moved third baseman Ray Boone across the diamond to first base in '57, making Torgeson a part-time player and pinch hitter. He had just 50 at-bats (.240 with one home run) on June 14 when he was dealt to the White Sox for Dave Philley. Torgeson took most of the playing time from Walt Dropo in Chicago, and ended up having a fine second half—.295 with seven home runs in

251 at-bats. New manager Al Lopez became an immediate booster, praising Torgeson's ability to get on base: "I definitely believe that by waiting out the pitcher, Torgy becomes a better hitter and generally contributes more to our attack."

Over the next two years, however, Torgeson became more of a part-time player for the White Sox. In June of 1958 Chicago made a deal with Detroit for Ray Boone, who got most of the playing time at first base the rest of that season. Torgeson played 73 games there, including 45 starts, but pinch-hit and pinch-ran enough to get into 96 games, hitting .266 with 10 home runs. In 1959 Boone had moved on, but the White Sox first gave the job to rookie Norm Cash, who failed to hit, then turned to Torgeson for a few months, and finally acquired Ted Kluszewski in late August to take over the rest of the way. Torgeson hit just .220 with nine home runs. In the World Series he managed a groundout and walk in his two plate appearances, as the White Sox were defeated by the Dodgers in six games.

Earl was 36 years old entering the 1960 season, and his days as a regular player were over. Nonetheless, he stuck with the White Sox and stayed all year as a pinch-hitter, hitting .263 in 57 at-bats. After going just 1 for 15 through June 15 in 1961, he was sold to the Yankees, for whom he was no better (2 for 18). On September 2, he was released and redeployed as a coach. He was not on the World Series roster as the Yankees defeated the Reds four games to one.

Earl and Norma divorced in 1961 as Earl's baseball career was ending. In 1963 Torgeson married Molly Power from White Bear Lake, Minnesota, and had three more children: Holly, Brad and Tina. Earl is remembered as a supportive father, who attended many of his children's sporting events through the years, sitting quietly in the stands, supporting their wins and losses.

His daughter Christine remembers something else: "He loved to sing. He had a great repertoire of old sentimental ballads which he learned from his mother. He especially loved jazz and the old favorites. All of us kids learned the old songs from hearing him sing them. My mother said that they could go to a club and the next thing you know he had grabbed the mike and was singing a song."

When Torgeson retired from baseball, he briefly worked as a stockbroker with Mitchell Hutchins Brokerage in Chicago. Soon after he owned and operated Camp Forsyte, a sports camp for boys in Westfield, Wisconsin, which sponsored many underprivileged kids from Chicago in addition to the paying campers. In 1965, Earl and Molly moved to Everett, Washington, near where Earl had grown up.

Torgeson took a job as director of parks for Snohomish County. When major league baseball arrived briefly in Seattle in 1969, Torgeson was hired to manage the Newark Co-Pilots in the New York Penn League that summer, and then the Clinton Pilots in the Midwest League in 1970, succeeding Sibby Sisti. (Both ballclubs were Seattle affiliates). He even suited up for the big-league Pilots as a batting coach in the last few weeks of the '69 season. Earl's previous managerial experience had been in Managua, Nicaragua, during a couple of winters in the late 1950s, and this marked the end of his professional career. His Newark team finished 42–34, in third place, while his Clinton club came in at 57–67.

Earl was elected a county commissioner in 1972 and served four years. While in office he fought off several schemes from political enemies. He was also charged and tried for allegedly using county labor and materials to work on his car and summer home, charges which cost him three years and $25,000 to successfully defend. Two later attempts at re-election were unsuccessful. He later worked many years with a timber company, and served as the county's director of emergency management for eight years.

In late September 1990 Torgeson discovered he had leukemia, and he died just six weeks later, on November 8, 1990, at his home in Everett, Washington. He was survived by his second wife, Molly, his five children, and six grandchildren. Edo Vanni, who had played with Torgeson on the 1946 Rainiers, recalled, "He could do everything. He was a happy-go-lucky guy. Nothing worried him. Slumps didn't bother him. He was just a super guy."

When the field at Snohomish High School was named after Earl in October 1990, the citation read, in part: "Your contribution to our youth, through your coaching and personal support, is recognized and respected by everyone in the community. Your fans and the citizens of Snohomish will always remember the values, integrity and courage modeled by you for their children."

Sources

In researching this biography, I relied on the kindness and insight of Christine Torgeson, Earl's daughter. I made heavy use of Torgeson's clipping file at the National Baseball Library in Cooperstown, and the online archive of *The Sporting News* at www.paperofrecord.com. I am also indebted to Bob Brady of the Boston Braves Historical Association.

Other sources of note:

1947 Boston Braves Sketchbook.

Gillooly, John. "Earl of Snohomish II." *Sportfolio*, September, 1947.

Hern, Gerry. "Torgy is a Classy First Baseman." *Boston Post*, April 11, 1952.

Kiersch, Edward. *Where Have You Gone, Vince DiMaggio.* Bantam, 1983.

Miller, Hub. Unidentified clipping, dated August 1947, in his Hall of Fame file.

Obituary. Seattle *Post-Intelligencer*. November 10, 1990.

Paxton, Harry T. "The Jesting First Baseman of Boston." *The Saturday Evening Post*, May 26, 1951.

BILL VOISELLE *by Saul Wisnia*

G	ERA	W	L	SV	GS	GF	CG	SHO	IP	H	R	ER	BB	SO	HR	HBP	WP	BFP
37	3.63	13	13	2	30	5	9	2	215$\frac{2}{3}$	226	93	87	90	89	18	3	1	940

G	AB	R	H	2B	3B	HR	RBI	BB	SO	BA	OBP	SLG	SB	HBP
37	72	2	7	0	0	0	4	4	17	.097	.145	.097	0	0

He was a 21-game winner as a rookie in 1944 and four years later started the deciding game of the World Series, but these feats are not what Bill Voiselle is remembered for today. The right-handed pitcher compiled more than 160 victories in a long career split between the major and minor leagues, but it's the number 96 that remains his claim to fame. This is what Voiselle wore on the back of his Boston Braves uniform, a tribute to the tiny town of Ninety-Six, South Carolina where he was raised and spent most of his life.

Until pitchers Mitch Williams and Turk Wendell both donned "99" late in the 20th century, Voiselle's was the highest number in major league history. Also known as "Big Bill," the 6-foot-4, 200-pound hurler was dubbed "Ol' Ninety-Six" in his Boston days, and the nickname stuck for nearly half a century. Even now, years after his January 31, 2005 death, mentions of Bill's decorated digit routinely pop up in baseball books and trivia games. Making this oddity Voiselle's sole legacy, however, is not being fair to the man. In addition to pitching professionally for two decades, he was immensely popular with teammates and fans and was a beloved member of his community. And while even casual sports fans of this era have heard the refrain of "Spahn and Sain and Pray for Rain" in reference to a (perceived) thin 1948 Boston rotation, those who actually *remember* the '48 season also know the truth: Voiselle—along with fellow starter Vern Bickford—was far more than an afterthought for most of that year.

From the mill to the majors

Born William Symmes Voiselle in Greenwood, S.C., on January 29, 1919, Bill was one of four baseball-playing brothers who as teenagers worked in the local cotton mill when not on the diamond or in class. The story goes that on Sundays, when baseball was forbidden in town, he'd sneak down near the banks of a local river with friends to get in a few innings. Later he starred for a high school team that beat college squads in exhibition games, prompting Red Sox farm club director (and future umpire) Billy Evans to sign the youngster and send him to

A former big league 21-game winner, Bill Voiselle was attempting to regain his former prowess when picked up by the Braves in 1947.

Moultrie of the George-Florida League in 1938.

Four years and six teams later, Voiselle was scouted by Giants Hall of Famer Bill Terry while with Oklahoma City of the Texas State League, and purchased by New York's National League club in August 1942. Although just 7–10 for seventh-place Oklahoma at the time, and primarily a fastball pitcher, the 23-year-old impressed Terry with his exceptional change of pace. His enviable draft status was also a plus. Declared 4F due to a hearing loss, he was ineligible for the military and World War II service.

Voiselle was brought up to the Giants late that season, and made his major league debut against the Cubs on September 1, 1942—throwing a scoreless inning of one-hit, one-walk relief in a 10–5 loss at Wrigley Field. Player-manager Mel Ott gave Bill his first start on the 25th against the Phillies, and the newcomer performed well: allowing three runs (just two earned) in eight five-hit innings of a 3–2 defeat.

After some more minor-league seasoning at Triple A Jersey City in 1943, where he went 10–21 despite a fine 3.18 ERA, Voiselle was brought back up to pitching-thin New York at the tail-end of that year's campaign. As recounted by author Frank Graham in his book, the *New York Giants*, Terry looked at the big right-hander's lofty loss total and asked Jersey City manager Gabby Hartnett, "What's happened to Voiselle? I thought he was the best pitcher in the league. But he lost twenty-one games, and won only ten." Hartnett's reply? "With that ball club, it's a wonder he didn't lose them all. He's ready, Bill."

Gabby was right. Voiselle got a start on September 14, and again accorded himself admirably (five innings, five hits, two runs) in a game called off at 4–4 due to inclement weather. The Giants were mired in eighth place, so he also drew starting assignments at Cincinnati and Pittsburgh during the season's waning days. Voiselle lost the first of these encounters 4–2 despite a complete game two-hitter (Buddy Kerr's two eighth-inning errors cost him two runs), but against the Pirates on the 26th, he finally broke through with his first big-league victory by going the distance in a 4–3, 10-inning win in the second game of a doubleheader at Forbes Field. The Giants had recorded their 91st loss in the opener—the most in franchise history—so it was becoming clear that Voiselle had a future in the starting rotation. His second straight four-hitter, this one a 1–0 loss to the World Series-bound Cardinals on the last day of September, reiterated such thoughts.

Rookie rocket

After a sparkling spring training in '44, the *New York Times* reported that the "strapping right-hander from Ninety-Six, S.C." had been tapped by Ott to start the April 18 season opener at the Polo Grounds. Still officially a rookie, he validated his manager's confidence by going the distance with nine strikeouts in a 2–1 victory over the Braves. Then wearing 17, the hurler known for his aggressive nature on the mound and a friendly, humble demeanor off it was an almost immediate sensation with sportswriters and fans forced to watch the lackluster Giants, who had finished dead last and 49½ games behind St. Louis the previous year. He moved atop the National League pitching charts with three straight victories to begin the season, and sparked the "Ottmen" to an encouraging 7–3 record in April.

Poor defense and a lack of production from sources other than their home-run hitting player/manager plagued the Giants, however, and no pitcher was more snake-bit than Voiselle. He allowed just five earned runs in his next six starts, but 15 New York errors—many of them in the ninth inning of tight contests—resulted in 12 unearned runs and six straight losses. (His teammates scored just seven times during the span). One game from this miserable string stands out: May 23, when he started the first night game in New York since the city's wartime blackout restrictions went into effect three years earlier. Bill lead 2–1 in the ninth inning at Ebbets Field, but lost 3–2 to the Dodgers after two of his teammates ran into each other in pursuit of a fly ball.

Better days lay ahead. Breaking the luckless skein with a three-hitter to top the mighty Cardinals on May 29, new bridegroom Voiselle (he married Virginia Elnora Bowlware on May 26) won five of his next six to reach a 10–7 mark by the end of June. The surprising Giants were hovering around .500 thanks to his efforts, and sportswriters from the normally austere *Times* kept coming up with inventive nicknames for the new ace. In one game account he was "the long, lean, lanky lad," in the next he was "the husky from Ninety-Six." Even in an era when complete games were much more common, his 17 full-distance efforts in his first 21 starts stood out. And while he wasn't usually overpowering—seldom striking out more than five or six men, and usually walking four or five—he kept his underachieving club in almost every game. Even a propensity for allowing home runs did not seem to hurt him; he'd give up a record 31 for the year, but seldom would be beaten by them.

Although Big Bill cooled off a bit by mid-July, he was still picked by St. Louis manager Billy Southworth for the National League All-Star squad to replace injured Cards hurler Max Lanier. "Voiselle's season record is eleven and ten, but might easily have been sixteen and five, for poor support has deprived him of at least six triumphs," Roscoe McGowen of the *Times* declared when news of Voiselle's selection broke. The season's second half proved more of the same, as the Giants struggled through a 13-game August losing streak and the rookie phenom who stopped it continued piling up impressive wins and agonizing losses.

By the end of the year New York had fallen all the way to 67–87, but Voiselle stood out with a 21–16 record, a 3.02 ERA, and an NL-leading 312⅔ innings, 161 strikeouts, and 41 starts. His win total and 25 complete games both ranked third in the senior circuit, and he was fifth in league MVP voting—just ahead of .347-hitting Stan Musial. There were no official Rookie of the Year awards given out until 1947, but the Chicago baseball writers who routinely honored freshmen players during this period picked Big Bill as the top newcomer of '44. *The Sporting News*, then baseball's leading journalistic voice, named him its "Pitcher of the Year." No rookie has ever pitched 300 innings since, a record that is likely to hold up.

Not all is fine

It looked like even bigger things were in store for Voiselle and his team in 1945. The right-hander began the season with a victory at Braves Field, and by the time he beat the Pirates 5–1 before 51,340 fans at the Polo Grounds on May 20, he was 8–0 and the first-place Giants were an incredible 21–5. Then, however, the winning inexplicably stopped for the ace—and New York.

Once again showing the hot-and-cold tendencies that would mark his entire big-league career, Voiselle suffered through his second six-game losing streak in as many years while the club endured an abysmal 5–18 stretch to drop out of first. Ninth-inning meltdowns were once again the culprit in many of Bill's setbacks, but this time the problems were often of his own doing. Sportswriters chided the fallen ace in print for his failure to complete starts, and Ott's attempts to use Voiselle in relief met with disastrous results.

After he finally got another win on June 24, the rest of Bill's season was marked by dramatic inconsistency. In one 12-day stretch of July he threw a shutout against the Reds, was knocked out in the third inning by the Cards, beat the Cubs on a five-hitter, then was rocked over five-plus by the Pirates. By season's end, while the rebuilding Giants had improved to a 78–74 record, Voiselle had declined to a so-so 14–14 mark with a swollen ERA of 4.49 (worst by far of New York's four primary starters). His strikeouts and complete games were both way down from his rookie totals, and he allowed an alarming 249 hits and 97 walks in 232⅔ innings.

The next season was even worse; the Giants regressed

in 1946 back to 61–93—a level of franchise futility topped only by the 98-loss club of '43—and Voiselle was just 9–15. His ERA did improve to 3.74, but he was no longer considered a top-flight starter. How had he fallen so quickly? Many point to a headline-making incident between the pitcher and manager Ott early in Bill's '45 slump. On June 1, Voiselle held a 3–1 lead with one out and one on in the ninth inning at St. Louis. He allowed a Johnny Hopp triple to bring in one run, and after getting his next man, had a one-and-one count on Ray Sanders when play was temporarily halted due to a windstorm.

Bill was still on the mound after the delay, but soon wished he wasn't. Sanders tied the score with a single to short right, after which Whitey Kurowski promptly untied it with a game-winning triple to left-center. Following the game, the usually unflappable Ott announced he was fining Voiselle $500 for not "wasting" a pitch on Hopp—who had notched his three-base hit on an 0-and-2 count. Although Ott had previously warned all his pitchers he'd dock them $100 for not staying away from the strike zone under such circumstances, the added sting of a tough defeat likely prompted him to raise the ante on Big Bill.

Controversy brewed when Dick Young of the *New York Daily News* reported that Voiselle told him he had in fact thrown a "bad ball" to Hopp, who had done a fine bit of hitting to reach out and stroke it to left-center. There was, of course, no video or instant reply to consult, and other sportswriters took Bill's side. (Among other things, he reportedly made just $3,500 at the time.) The public appeal worked, and on June 23 Ott announced he was returning the $500 to Voiselle. It didn't help. Bill started that same afternoon against the Phillies, and allowed four hits and three walks in the first inning before Ott mercifully pulled him out. He did have some strong outings in the months and seasons to come, but Voiselle would never be a consistently dependable pitcher for this manager again.

Reborn in Boston

Off to another lackluster start (1–4) in 1947, he was swapped on June 13 to the Braves along with an undisclosed amount of cash for another struggling young "former ace"—Mort Cooper. Fans and sportswriters speculated that the change in scenery might do Voiselle good. "Ott gives up nothing," the *Times'* Arthur Daley surmised in his influential column. "Southworth may get something." Such hopeful prognosticators proved correct. Voiselle was an encouraging 8–7 over the remainder of the 1947 season, and in 1948 spring training Southworth predicted he could win 20 games.

By now the big right-hander had already become a

When it didn't "rain," Voiselle followed Spahn and Sain in the pitching rotation, delivering 13 victories.

favorite topic for photographers after receiving permission from Commissioner A.B. "Happy" Chandler to wear No. 96, and he was soon making news with his arm as well. He got off to a stellar start reminiscent of his rookie year, notching a pair of shutouts and a 4–0 mark in his first four games to help Boston to the top of the National League. On July 10 he was 10–6, still among the league leaders in victories and on pace to achieve his manager's earlier forecast. Voiselle, and not struggling left-hander Warren Spahn, was the man alongside Johnny Sain at the top of the Braves rotation. [It's unclear whether Voiselle decided on his own to ask for 96, or if Braves PR director Billy Sullivan or someone else thought up the creative idea.]

Then, as the pennant race moved into its final two months, Voiselle suddenly went cold. He lost 7 of 10 decisions to fall to 13–13, and after a 4–3 setback to the Phillies at Braves Field on September 4 was pulled from the rotation. With Sain proving the best pitcher in the league and Spahn regaining his own 20-win form of '47, Southworth had decided to ride these two horses as much as possible down the stretch. Bill never drew another start after the Phillies game, just a few relief appearances at the end of the year. Despite his decent overall ERA of 3.63 compiled over 215⅔ innings, he was an afterthought as the Braves held off Brooklyn and St. Louis to win their first NL championship in 34 years. The poem by *Boston Post* sports editor Gerald Hern that first appeared that month didn't help. It read, in part: "First we'll use Spahn, then we'll use Sain, Then an off day, followed by rain."

Poem or no poem, Southworth knew the team never would have been in position to win without Voiselle's earlier success. The manager still had quiet confidence in Big Bill's arm, and in the third game of the World Series he called on him in a very tight spot. Boston trailed the Indians 2–0 in the fourth inning of Game Three at Cleveland when Southworth yanked rookie starter Vern Bickford with one out and the bases loaded. Voiselle came in, got the dangerous Dale Mitchell on a foul out to third, and then ended the inning by retiring slugger Larry Doby on a groundball back to the box. Cleveland's next seven hitters also went down in order, and while the game's score stayed the same, Big Bill's final line of 3⅔ innings, one hit, and zero walks boded well for future Series work.

When it came, that work was on the grandest stage. The Braves faced elimination entering the sixth contest at Boston, and Southworth—feeling that Game One and Four starter Sain needed one more day of rest, and knowing Spahn was unavailable after pitching long relief the day before—gave Voiselle the ball. The move was questioned in a must-win situation (even a tired Sain, some surmised, would be a more formidable choice), but "Ol' 96" gave a noble effort. He was so jacked up before the game that he was seen at 10 a.m. in full uniform on the grass at Braves Field, checking the wind currents. Seeing that the ballpark's familiar gusts were heading out toward left, he likely feared that Cleveland's right-handed power hitters would take advantage. Still, he matched Indians ace Bob Lemon pitch for pitch in the early going, and the score was 1–1 through five innings at Braves Field.

Then the wind helped do him in. Righty slugger Joe Gordon led off the Indians sixth with a home run to deepest left, and a walk, single, and infield out quickly brought in another run to hush the crowd of 40,103. Now down 3–1, Bill pitched a perfect seventh before giving way to Spahn and finishing his day with a solid line of seven hits, two walks, and three runs allowed. The Indians scored one more off Spahnie in the eighth, and when the Braves fell just short in their late-game comeback, it was Voiselle who took the 4–3 loss. His year had ended on the dourest of notes, but Big Bill could take solace as he collected his healthy $4,570.73 loser's share and headed home to South Carolina. His ERA over 10⅔ Series innings had been a very solid 2.53, and he had made a good case for a return to the rotation in 1949.

Back to the bottom—and the bushes

He did earn back his starting spot the next spring, but Voiselle was again plagued by old problems as he turned 30: inconsistency and bad luck. He beat the Dodgers with a three-hitter on April 25 for his first win, but was shelled by the Giants in his next start and then lost a two-hitter to the Reds. Manager Southworth apparently saw something he didn't like, because Voiselle next went three weeks without pitching before picking up a relief victory against the Dodgers on May 28. Two days later he started and went eight innings for a win against the Phils, raising his record to 3–1, but now Southworth sat him down *for a month* before granting him another start. Again Big Bill showed his stuff with a four-hitter vs. the Giants, but when he was routed by the same club four days later he was shown the bench once more.

By late August Voiselle's record was just 6–3, with four of his victories by shutouts. The Braves were floundering around .500 in what would prove an unsuccessful championship defense, and Spahn, Sain, and Bickford had become the unequivocal "Big Three" of the rotation. Other hurlers like 19-year-old bonus baby Johnny

Bill Voiselle had brief trials with the Giants in 1942 and 1943 before assuming a spot in their starting rotation until his trade to Boston.

Antonelli and forgettable lefty Jumbo Elliott were getting some of Bill's starts, and by now even a gentle giant like Voiselle had reason to be fuming. Southworth's decision to temporarily step down on August 16 due to exhaustion (or a breakdown, depending on the source) was likely celebrated by the folks back in Ninety-Six as another chance at redemption for their hero—who that very year brought some of his big-league friends home and put together a benefit exhibition game for Jackie Spearman, a local woman battling cancer. Interim manager Johnny Cooney did indeed put Voiselle back into a regular rotation slot, but he failed to make the most of it—going 1–5 down the stretch to finish with a 7–8 record and a 4.05 ERA.

When reports broke that Braves players had voted Southworth just a half-share of their fourth-place bonus money, it was assumed that Voiselle was one of those voting in the majority to stiff their former-and-future skipper. In post-mortem discussions of the season, with Southworth due to come back, Big Bill was one of those deemed expendable by the club. Rumors broke of interest from the Cubs, and on December 14 they were verified with Voiselle's swap to Chicago for minor leaguer Gene Mauch and cash. An upbeat Southworth was quoted as saying, "We felt we could give up Voiselle, a possible starter, because I think we'll be set with the addition of Norman Roy, who came up to us from Milwaukee."

Southworth was right, to a point. Roy would win just four games in this, his only big-league season, but Boston still got the best of the deal. By May, *Chicago Tribune* writer Irving Vaughn had dubbed the new Cubs pitcher "hapless Bill Voiseille," and after an 0–4 record and 5.82 ERA compiled over 19 outings, Ol' 96 (he still wore the number) was sent to minor league Springfield (Mass.) on July 13. Less than two years after starting the biggest Braves game in 30 years, he had been unable to hold a job with the NL's seventh-place outfit. Although his final major league record of 74–84 (and 3.83 lifetime ERA) had certainly not reached the level suggested by his rookie exploits, he knew he'd enjoyed higher highs than some hurlers with far better marks.

In most cases this would be the end of the tale, but Bill Voiselle was far from through with baseball. Pitching his home games less than two hours from Braves Field, he went 9–8 with the Triple A Springfield Cubs during the remainder of the 1950 season before being sold into the Brooklyn Dodgers system. He got into 47 games for Montreal in '51, registering a solid 3.48 ERA for the second straight year, and then after one year off came back to spend parts of five more seasons in the high minors. In 1955, hurling for Triple A Richmond, he led the International League with a then-minor league record 72 appearances at age 36 and was briefly reunited with old Braves rotation-mate Vern Bickford. All told Voiselle pitched in 502 bush league contests bookending his 245 games in the majors, with an 88–110 slate more suggestive of longevity than excellence.

Ninety-six reasons to smile

Even when his professional days finally ended after 11 appearances with Tulsa of the Texas League in 1957, Big Bill was hungry for more. He returned to his beloved Ninety-Six with his wife, Virginia, and teamed up again with brothers Jim and Claude on the town's mill club in the semipro Central Carolina Textile League. When he wasn't playing himself, he continued helping organize local charity games. On the mound, he certainly didn't take himself too seriously anymore; on one occasion, after an opponent had collected two straight hits off him, he delivered something different to the plate on the batter's next time up: his glove. As Voiselle laughed with delight, the batter belted a solid line drive.

Because of his fame as "Ol' 96," the town celebrity drew far more interest from autograph seekers than most hurlers sporting a sub-.500 lifetime mark in the majors, and he briefly resurfaced in headlines when pitchers Williams and Wendell took to wearing No. 99 in the 1990s. A few years earlier, Bill traveled to Boston for the 40th reunion of the '48 Braves champions put on by the New England Sports Museum, but most of the time he stayed close to home. "He was a real caring person to all us kids," his nephew George Voiselle recalled. "Teachers would have him talk to students, and he never turned anybody down."

Voiselle also never won a World Series, but was honored by the South Carolina House of Representatives in 2001 for bringing "honor and glory to the State of South Carolina" through his athletic and charitable endeavors. "Everything I got, I owe it to baseball," Voiselle once told *Sports Collectors Digest*. "I'm a little ol' cotton mill boy— never had nothing and never been nowhere." In the end he got quite far on his pitching, but wound up right back where he started and most wanted to be.

"He was just a wonderful guy, and everybody loved him to death," longtime neighbor Bubba Summers stated in one tribute published upon Voiselle's death two days after his 86th birthday in 2005. "If you didn't know him, you really missed out."

For Summers, and the other folks in Ninety-Six, Bill Voiselle was far more than just a number.

Sources

Obituary appearing in Feb. 2, 2005 edition of *Index-Journal* newspaper in Greenwood, S.C. (found on www.thedeadball era.com)

Obituary on www.historicbaseball.com

Assorted *Boston Globe, Chicago Tribune, Christian Science Monitor, Hartford Courant, Los Angeles Times, New York Times, Associated Press,* and *United Press International* articles, 1942–1984.

Obituary at www.retrosheet.org

Stats from www.Baseball-reference.com and *baseballray@aol. com*

Kelley, Brent. "Bill Voiselle Was Key Member of '48 Braves", *Sports Collectors Digest*, July 19, 1991.

Graham, Frank. *The New York Giants—An Informal History of a Great Baseball Club* (Carbondale IL: Southern Illinois University Press, 2002—reprint of 1952 book)

Author tribute to Voiselle, "Farewell to Ol' 96," appearing in Boston Braves Historical Association newsletter, spring 2005

ERNIE WHITE *by Mike Richard*

G	ERA	W	L	SV	GS	GF	CG	SHO	IP	H	R	ER	BB	SO	HR	HBP	WP	BFP
15	1.96	0	2	2	0	8	0	0	23	13	7	5	17	8	0	0	0	98

G	AB	R	H	2B	3B	HR	RBI	BB	SO	BA	OBP	SLG	SB	HBP
16	3	0	0	0	0	0	0	0	2	.000	.000	.000	0	0

More than any other military conflict, World War II took its toll on major-league baseball and its players. And it was while fighting overseas during the Battle of the Bulge that Corporal Ernie White "was pinned down in icy water for a day" and—perhaps as a result—ultimately reported to have lost his fastball.

White was among several members of the St. Louis Cardinals serving in the military then, including Harry Walker, Lou Klein, Al Brazle, and Howie Krist. All told,

10 St. Louis pitchers were called to duty during the war years of 1944–45. Neither Krist nor Johnny Grodzicki sufficiently recovered from wounds suffered in battle and neither won another big league game. Meanwhile, 1942 rookie phenom Johnny Beazley ruined his arm while pitching for an Army team in an exhibition against the Cardinals, seriously affecting his career.

Prewar prospect Hank Nowak paid the ultimate sacrifice. After landing a contract with the Cardinals in 1941, he played for the Camp Lee team in Petersburg, Virginia. He died on the battlefield during the Battle of the Bulge on January 1, 1945.

White was more fortunate, although he also spent the better part of that winter freezing through the same awful battle in the Ardennes. After showing promise in the 1941 season, when he won 17 games for the Cardinals, White came home from the war with what was termed "a dead arm" and never matched the promise of his early career.

Ernest Daniel White was born on September 5, 1916, in Pacolet Mills, S.C., and pitched a total of 12 years of organized baseball. It was while pitching for a textile mill team in Pacolet that the southpaw was discovered in 1937 by Frank Rickey, the younger brother of Branch Rickey and a scout for the Cardinals. He'd already been married; two days after he turned 17, he married Margaret Whitlock.

Soon after signing with St. Louis, the 20-year-old White pitched for both the Martinsville (Virginia) Manufacturers in the Class D Bi-State League and the Asheville (North Carolina) Tourists of the Class B Piedmont League. Asheville played its home games at McCormick Field, which much later was the location for a scene in the movie *Bull Durham* as the ballpark where the Kevin Costner character Crash Davis hit his minor league record-breaking home run with the Tourists, after his release from the Bulls.

White was 0–2 for Asheville (and may have appeared briefly for Martinsville, without recording a decision), and was moved in 1938 to the Portsmouth (Ohio) Red Birds of the Class C Middle Atlantic League. The team was owned by the St. Louis Cardinals, and Ernie's teammates included Walter Alston and Whitey Kurowski.

White made his first big splash with the Red Birds on June 3, 1938, against the Johnstown Johnnies when, according to the 1940 *National League Green Book*, he struck out an incredible 15 batters in a five-inning stint. He finished the season with a 15–6 record and received an honorable mention for the league's All-Star team.

The next season found White with the Houston Buffaloes of the Class A1 Texas League under manager and vice president Eddie Dyer, a former St. Louis pitcher of the 1920s who later managed the Cardinals from 1946 to 1950. White's teammates included Johnny Hopp and Red Barrett, later teammates of his in St. Louis and Boston.

The Buffaloes captured the Texas League championship with a 97–63 record before losing in the first round of the playoffs. The club was loaded with pitchers. In addition to White, the mound corps included future Cardinals Harry Brecheen, Murry Dickson, Howie Krist,

Despite Billy Southworth's best efforts to restore his former Cardinals pitching star to health, Ernie White was only able to take the mound sporadically over the course of the Tribe's 1946-48 campaigns.

and Ted Wilks. Dizzy Dean, a former big league MVP in the waning years of his career, was also with the squad. His great fastball gone, Diz posted a 6–4 record.

On July 18, 1939, White pitched the first no-hitter by a Houston pitcher since 1920, a 2–0 victory over Fort Worth. He was 15–6 and finished second in the Texas League in strikeouts with 149.

From there, a stint with the Double A Columbus Red Birds of the American Association beckoned in 1940. This was the top St. Louis farm club, and Ernie impressed, leading the league in winning percentage with a 13–4 record and in ERA (2.25). Five of his victories were three-hitters.

Early in the season, White was called up to the parent Cardinals, for whom he made an impressive debut on May 9, 1940. Relieving shelled starter Murry Dickson in the second inning, he pitched 7⅓ strong innings of six-hit relief to beat the Phillies, 8–4, at St. Louis—aiding his own cause with a perfect day at the plate (three-for-three with a walk). In eight games with the Cardinals, Ernie was 1–1, starting a contest on May 14 and receiving no decision in a 4–0 loss to the Phillies.

In 1941, White came up to the Cardinals to stay, and his first full year in the majors was by far the best of his big-league career. He appeared in 32 games, starting 25, and compiled a 17–7 record with a 2.40 ERA, third best in the circuit. He finished sixth in the MVP voting. White picked up a victory in his first start, against Boston on May 5, winning 5–1. He pitched back-to-back shutouts against Brooklyn (3–0 on June 15) and New York (6–0 on June 21).

For a while in midseason Southworth used his hot left-hander more between starts, and a 9–2 win over the Braves on July 26 marked Ernie's fourth win in five days—a 20th century major-league record. His other wins in the stretch, all in relief, came against the Giants on July 22, 23, and 24. From July 18 to August 10, in fact, White won eight straight games that he appeared in (including six in a 17-day stretch). Then, after a setback at the hands of Pittsburgh caused in part by his own throwing error, he pitched a 2–0 shutout over the Giants as the Cardinals drew to within a game and a half of the first-place Dodgers heading into the season's final five weeks.

St. Louis wound up finishing second, 2½ games behind pennant-winning Brooklyn, but White had been spectacular. He had career highs in complete games with 12, shutouts with three and strikeouts with 117. In 210 innings he allowed 72 runs, just 56 of them earned.

A sore arm sidelined White for part of the 1942 season as his win total dipped to seven. His arm problems began in spring training while he was trying to develop a curveball. As his arm was coming around in midseason, he was hit by a line drive off the bat of Pittsburgh's Elbie Fletcher, which knocked him out of action for four weeks.

Despite White's setback, the Cardinals won their first pennant since 1934 with a pitching staff led by Mort Cooper (22–7), Johnny Beazley (21–6), Howie Krist (13–3), and Max Lanier (13–8). White appeared in 26 games, starting 19, and posted a 7–5 record. He had seven complete games and one shutout, pitching 128⅓ innings and compiling a fine 2.52 ERA.

After his sporadic accomplishments during the season, the highlight of White's year—and career—came when he was called upon to start the pivotal third game of the 1942 World Series against the American League champion New York Yankees, with the series tied at one win apiece.

Pitching in front of 69,123 fans at Yankee Stadium, White struck out six and did not walk a batter as he hurled a complete-game six-hitter to shut out the Yanks, 2–0. He became the first pitcher since Jesse Haines in 1926 to blank New York in a World Series contest, and St. Louis went on to take the fall classic in five games.

It was hoped that White's brilliant October performance would be the springboard to a return to '41 form, but injuries hampered him again in 1943. In another freakish play, he bumped into the dugout at Ebbets Field on May 18 while backing up a throw from the outfield, suffering a shoulder injury. He was forced to leave the game in the seventh (he still got the 7–1 win), and was ailing the rest of the year. He wound up appearing in just 14 games, starting 10 and pitching five complete games with a 5–5 record and one shutout.

White's continued struggles notwithstanding, the Cardinals captured another pennant and were back in the World Series with the Yankees. This time Ernie's lone series appearance was much less memorable than his big win of the previous year; in the seventh inning of Game Four, he pinch-ran for pinch-hitter Frank Demaree, who had reached on an error. It wasn't until the last game of the Series (won by the Yankees in five contests) that White realized he had broken a bone in his shoulder in that May collision at Ebbets Field.

White missed the entire 1945 season while serving in the Army. As it turned out, future Braves teammate Warren Spahn also saw action at the Battle of the Bulge, earning a Purple Heart and Bronze Star for his heroics. Both made it home without crippling injury, but Spahn's postwar pitching experiences had a much happier ending than White's.

After returning from the war, White was released by the Cardinals during spring training because of his continued arm troubles. The Braves signed him a few hours after his release, however, outbidding several other clubs.

Ernie White served as a Braves coach while attempting to rehabilitate his pitching career.

Apparently teams were still thinking that White might rebound.

Ernie became the fourth player picked up by the Braves from manager Billy Southworth's former team within the year, following Mort Cooper, Johnny Hopp, and Ray Sanders. Soon, former Red Birds Danny Litwhiler and Johnny Beazley also followed suit. Boston sportswriters whimsically referred to the Braves as the "Cape Cod Cardinals" because of Southworth's preference for his former players.

During White's three years with Boston, Southworth attempted to work him back into shape through the unique arrangement of employing him as a coach while also pitching him mostly in exhibition games with the hope that his arm would come around. The on-field results, unfortunately, were not successful. During 1946 White appeared in 12 games, starting just one and notching a 0–1 record in 23⅔ innings. The Braves were developing a pitching staff that would help propel them to the pennant two years later. Johnny Sain returned from the military to win 20 games, and Warren Spahn also collected his first eight of 363 career victories that season after his stint in the war. Boston wound up finishing in fourth place.

White showed occasional improvement, and at the 1947 Hall of Fame game at Cooperstown, he held the Yankees to four hits in five innings. But he pitched in only one regular-season game, against Brooklyn on September 28, when he started and pitched four shutout innings. He allowed just one hit, but Johnny Sain came in and wound up with the 3–2 victory.

When the 1948 season began, the Braves still hoped White could attempt a comeback on the mound. Since it appeared that his arm was on the mend during spring training, he was released as a coach and signed as a player. Freddie Fitzsimmons was brought in to coach, resigning as the general manager of the Brooklyn Dodgers football team.

This time the results were a bit better; Ernie appeared in 15 games, compiling a 1.96 ERA with two saves in 23 innings for the NL pennant-winners. But it was apparently too little too late. His final appearance was as a pinch-runner on October 3, 1948, in a game against the Giants at the Polo Grounds, Boston's final game of the regular season. White didn't pitch in the World Series against Cleveland, and the Braves released him on October 28. He was 32.

Looked at as a whole, White's early success and later struggles make him the consummate "what if" player. His seven-year major league career resulted in a 30–21 record in 108 games, with six saves and five shutouts. He pitched 489⅓ innings, with 57 starts, 24 complete games, and 244 strikeouts. As a reliever he was 5–3 with six saves, and his fine lifetime ERA of 2.78 indicated just how good he could have been had injuries and war not intervened. He was also a strong hitting pitcher, batting .209 in 163 career at-bats, including his stellar 3-for-3 debut.

With his playing days over, White was given a position with the Braves organization managing the Bluefield Blue-Grays in the Appalachian League (Class D) in 1949. He led the club to the regular-season pennant with an 88–34 record as well as the playoff championship. The next season, White moved up to the Evansville Braves of the Three I League (Class B), and brought them in at 56–70. In 1951, he managed the Central League Charleston Senators, in the Cincinnati Reds system.

He settled in and managed the Columbia Reds of the South Atlantic League from 1952 through 1955. Once again, his success was immediate as his Reds won the Sally League regular-season pennant with a record of 100–54 before losing in the first round of the playoffs. The next year they won 92 games to finish second, then won the league playoffs. He skippered the Nashville Vols in 1956, but the team finished last in the Southern Association. He spent one year back in Columbia, now a Kansas City farm team in 1957. Switching to the Milwaukee Braves system, he was equally proficient, copping pennants as manager of the Midland Braves (in 1958) and Austin Senators (in '59). He had less success while with the Yankees organization. Appointed manager of the Augusta Tigers of the Sally League in 1962, he came in sixth, although he did manage future Yankees Pete Mikkelsen, Roger Repoz, and Dooley Womack.

White's one big-league coaching shot outside Boston came when he served as the second pitching coach in New York Mets history in 1963. Coming off their 40–120 maiden season, the Mets moved up to 51 wins and had a vastly improved ERA of 4.12 (it had been 5.04 the previous year). Still, White was back in the minors the next year in a managerial post with the fifth place Williamsport Mets of the Eastern League. Future "Miracle Met" standout Ron Swoboda was among his players there.

That was his last pro managerial stint. Denied a long career in the majors despite his noble comeback efforts, or a cushy coaching spot later on, White was also denied a long, comfortable retirement. On May 22, 1974, while in for surgery to remove bone chips in his knee, Ernie White died in Oliver General Hospital in Augusta, Georgia. The Spartanburg, South Carolina, resident was just 57. He is buried in Pacolet Memorial Gardens in Pacolet, South Carolina.

Sources

Baseball Page, The—Ernie White http://www.thebaseballpage.com/players/stats/whiteer01.

Historic Baseball—Ernie White http://historicbaseball.com/players/w/white_ernie.

http://www.baseballinwartime.co.uk/player_biographies/white_ernie.htm

Howie Pollet by Warren Corbett. The Baseball Biography Project

National League Green Book, 1940

Worcester Telegram: Game coverage for 1948 season

Baseballreference.com—White's minor league managerial record

Assorted Associated Press stories on Proquest.com, 1939–1948

ED WRIGHT *by Bob Brady*

G	ERA	W	L	SV	GS	GF	CG	SHO	IP	H	R	ER	BB	SO	HR	HBP	WP	BFP
3	1.93	0	0	0	0	2	0	0	4⅔	9	3	1	2	2	0	0	0	22

G	AB	R	H	2B	3B	HR	RBI	BB	SO	BA	OBP	SLG	SB	HBP
0	0	0	0	0	0	0	0	0	0	0	0	0	0	0

Midway through the last Saturday afternoon of the 1992 baseball season at Fenway Park, the large electronic scoreboard that sat atop the center-field bleachers flashed a welcoming message to the 73-year-old one-time proprietor of Wright's Exxon Service Station in Dyersburg, Tennessee, who was among that day's attendees. The previous time this man had set foot in the ballpark was as a right-handed pitcher for the 1952 Philadelphia Athletics, but some of the 33,223 fans on hand had likely rooted for him even earlier than that. As the between-innings message noted, Henderson "Ed" Wright was back in town to participate in the first player-fan reunion held by the recently established Boston Braves Historical Association (BBHA).

Ed had earned his spot in this fraternity by virtue of taking his turn on the old Braves Field mound for the Tribe from 1945 to 1948. Unfortunately, he missed this Fenway Park tribute, having just left his third base lower box seat to go underneath the stands and grab a hot dog. Upon returning to his seat, Ed reacted incredulously when told of the honor and only became convinced that it had truly occurred when a BBHA member provided the evidence to him several weeks later in the form of a snapshot of the scoreboard message. That incident was representative of the lack of luck that Ed experienced over the course of his five-year major league career. Although on the Opening Day rosters of the National League champion 1948 Braves and the 1950 Philadelphia Phillies, Ed was unable to reap the glory of either first place finish, ending both seasons in the minors.

Ed Wright was born on May 15, 1919, in Dyersburg (population then well under 10,000) and remained a resident of his hometown throughout his life. He grew up in a large family of 10 children—eight boys and two girls. In high school, Ed started out as a catcher but converted to the mound because of a lack of agility behind the plate. It was a good move; playing local semipro ball, he ran up a string of 16 victories against only two defeats. This attracted the attention of a neighbor, Herbert "Dutch" Welch, who was managing the Jackson Generals in the Class D Kitty League. Welch signed the 17-year-old prospect on March 3, 1938, and Ed made the 50-mile trek to Jackson.

His minor league odyssey began on an optimistic note as Ed won his first two games in organized ball. However, bad luck soon struck. During his next start, a losing effort, he fell ill and was rushed to a local hospital with a ruptured appendix. The ailment resulted in a month's hospital stay and its lingering effects kept him out of the game for the remainder of the season. Making an even briefer professional debut with Jackson that season was 24-year-old righty Ellis Kinder, who had a one-game, three-inning appearance for the Generals. Kinder entered the big leagues with the Browns in 1946, eventually making his way to Boston in time to provide mound help for the Red Sox during the exciting 1948 campaign.[1]

After receiving his unconditional release from Jackson, Ed hooked on with the Jonesboro White Sox of the Northeast Arkansas League in 1939. Poor fortune once

As a rookie with the 1945 Braves, Ed Wright joined the starting rotation in midseason and won 8 games, second best on the sixth place ballclub and, combined with his minor league victories, registered 21 overall tallies in the victory column.

again intervened, however, and he played there only a short time before a severe case of boils caused him to leave the club and return home at July's end. Unbeknownst to Ed at the time, he briefly crossed paths before his departure with a future Boston Braves mound-mate, Johnny Sain. After toiling for several years in "D" ball, Big John was experiencing his second successful season in the league, winning 18 games for the Newport Tigers and being named to the circuit's All-Star team. Within three years Sain would be in Boston, and the two would tally 32 wins for the Tribe in 1946 once Big John returned from military service.

Despite being cut loose twice, Ed still received an offer the following winter to sign with the American Association Milwaukee Brewers. Initially assigned to the Brewers' Class B Madison Blues affiliate in the Three "I" League, he found himself back in the Kitty League after an unsuccessful spring training trial. Restored to health, Ed showed the first signs of his big league potential, winning 17 games while dropping 10 contests for the Paducah Indians during their 1940 campaign. The Indians also possessed another 17-game winner who would go on to the major leagues, lefthander Dave Koslo. Interestingly, one of Ed's victories came at the expense of his younger brother Roger, who opposed his sibling on the hill for the Hopkinsville Hoppers on August 21.[2]

Ed's impressive play resulted in a postseason acquisition by the Southern Association Memphis Chicks. He lasted with the Chicks only for the first month of the 1941 season, however, before being farmed to the Greenville Buckshots of the Cotton States League. A strong performance there (15–10 with 152 strikeouts) led to a further spring audition with Memphis the next year, but still more challenges lay ahead. When the team sought to demote him in June of 1942 to the Southeastern League's Meridian Eagles in Mississippi, Ed balked and demanded to be sent closer to his Dyersburg home where he could continue working as a machinist at a textile mill while playing baseball. After rejecting a compromise offer, a demotion to Hopkinsville in Kentucky, Ed returned home until a deal was struck that transferred him back to Jackson. Despite winning his first four starts there, his happiness was short-lived: the league folded on June 17.

Remaining out of organized baseball through 1943, Ed worked at a war-related job but kept in shape by pitching semipro ball in the Memphis Municipal Baseball Association for the Kroger team, which won the 1943 city championship. In 1944 he sought a spring training invitation from Earl Mann, then general manager of the Atlanta

Crackers. Making the squad, he had a 4–3 record in the Sally League before manager Kiki Cuyler requested his option to the Class B Norfolk Tars in the Piedmont League. During his abbreviated stay in Atlanta, Ed was introduced to teammate and first-year pro Billy Goodman. Goodman would later break into the majors with the 1948 Red Sox and claim an AL batting title with the Crimson Hose in 1950.

In Norfolk, Wright received invaluable pitching tips from ex-big league lefty Garland Braxton. Braxton had broken in with the Braves in 1921 and spent parts of 10 seasons in the majors, and the advice he passed down showed immediate dividends. With an 8–3 won-loss total and a 1.69 ERA for the Tars, Ed attracted the attention of Roanoke Red Sox second baseman/manager Eddie Popowski, who recommended him to the Triple A Indianapolis Indians.[3] The Indians sought Ed's rights for the 1945 season from the Crackers but the original deal was aborted when the player traded to Atlanta voluntarily retired, and a straight sale had to be negotiated. The Indiana-based American Association ball club was owned by the Braves through the B-I-H (Boston-Indianapolis-Hartford) Corp., set up by the major league club's ownership triumvirate—Lou Perini, Guido Rugo, and Joe Maney (*a/k/a* the Three Little Steam Shovels)—to oversee the team's minor league affiliates. Since the Tribe maintained its farm system office in Indianapolis, Ed would have an immediate opportunity to impress club officials.

In addition to being under the watchful eye of the Braves brain trust at Indianapolis, Ed had the good fortune to come under the tutelage of another ex-major league pitcher-turned-teacher. Indians manager Bill Burwell had returned to the bushes after a coaching stint with the 1944 Red Sox, and Ed credited the ex-Brownie pitcher (1920–21) for his own eventual elevation to Boston. "I never knew how to pitch until I got to Indianapolis. Bill Burwell taught me the tricks which enabled me to use the same stuff which I always had, and to do much better with it than had ever been the case previously."[4] Burwell would lead the Indians to consecutive playoff berths before returning to the majors in 1947 as a Pirates coach.

The combination of Wright (13–5) and southpaw Jim Wallace (17–4) provided Indianapolis with a highly effective one-two punch. At one point Ed ran off a string of nine consecutive victories, and on May 17 he pitched a no-hitter on the road against the Casey Stengel-led Kansas City Blues. In this 2–0 triumph, he struck out seven, walked three, and faced only 30 batters.[5] Given wartime player shortages, many of his Indians teammates

Wright bridled at manager Southworth's strict calling of pitches to opposing batters and perceived a bias on the part of his skipper toward former Cardinals hurlers on the Braves mound squad.

surfaced in the Hub for trials with the parent club. Ed's chance came on July 20 when the Braves sent two journeymen, pitcher Ira Hutchinson and infielder Steve Shemo, plus a player to be named later to the Indians for him.

Less than two years after being out of organized ball, Ed Wright was in the big leagues. He joined the sixth-place Boston club just as Bob Coleman was being replaced as manager by coach Del Bissonette. The former Dodger first baseman and apple farmer from Winthrop, Maine, was elevated to the post when his predecessor resigned on July 29 on the heels of an eight-game losing streak. Bissonette took an immediate liking to his new righty and added Wright into the club's shaky starting rotation. Ed moved into the spot vacated by the team's "ace," Jim "Abba Dabba" Tobin (9–14), who was sold to the Tigers in August to bolster the Bengals' push toward the AL pennant. In 15 appearances, the rookie made a terrific impression—winning eight games while losing only three, placing him second to the departed Tobin in total victories on the club. Wright registered an ERA of 2.51 (tops on the club) and completed seven of his starts, including a 3–1, 11-inning victory over the Reds on September 18 seen by just 512 fans in Boston. His biggest first-season thrill came a week earlier on September 10, when he hurled a complete game shutout at Wrigley Field against the league leading Chicago Cubs—the eventual NL champs.

The 1945 season represented Ed's high-water mark as a pro. All told, between the minors and the majors, Wright had gone 21–8 and pitched a no-hitter. Not included in this total was a complete game blanking of the Worcester Nortons semipro team in a night exhibition game played by the Braves in Manchester, New Hampshire, on August 29. And he wasn't through yet; after the season, Ed barnstormed in the South with other major leaguers and then signed on to a post-Thanksgiving USO tour of the Pacific Theater with Ralph Branca, Buddy Kerr, Bill Voiselle, Billy Jurges, Whitey Kurowski, and skipper Chuck Dressen.

The Braves were dramatically transformed by the time the 1946 season began. The Three Little Steam Shovels lured St. Louis Cardinals manager Billy Southworth to Boston to helm the ball club. The team's aggregation of moundsmen was significantly improved with the return of the dynamic pitching duo of Warren Spahn and Johnny Sain from the war. And the team inaugurated night baseball in Boston with the addition of eight light towers at Braves Field. Ed's season started off inauspiciously when he stepped on a ball during a February 20 spring training fielding drill, incurring a severe and nagging ankle injury. His introduction to Fenway Park took place on April 12 for a "City Series" exhibition game against the Red Sox. Ted Williams greeted the big righty with a towering first-inning home run.

Although Southworth came with impeccable credentials (three straight NL pennants and two World Series titles from 1942–44), Wright strained under the direction of the new Braves manager and yearned for former skipper Del Bissonette. After being handed the ball every fourth day the previous season, Ed found his appearances more spread out under Southworth. Wright attributed his treatment to a belief that his new manager played favorites, depriving him of sufficient pitching opportunities to stay sharp enough to replicate his prior season's success. Ed also bridled at Southworth's tendency to rigidly dictate how his staff should pitch to opponents, discouraging any input from his hurlers. Nevertheless, while his ERA went up a full run to 3.52, Ed achieved a respectable 12–9 record to finish third on the club in wins during 1946. He was even more proud of his hitting prowess that season; in 59 at-bats, he accumulated 18 hits for a .305 batting average.

Starting against the Giants at the Polo Grounds that May 24, Ed had been on the cusp of big league immortality when he held New York hitless through seven innings. The first Giant safety came in the eighth when centerfielder Babe Young hit a ball to the mound that caromed off Wright's bare hand to shortstop Dick Culler, who threw too late to first base. Ed still held a 1–0 margin through 8⅔ innings until Johnny Mize stroked the Ottmen's first clean hit, a single, and errors by Tommy Holmes and Connie Ryan allowed the tying run to score. The Braves failed to tally any further runs, forcing Ed to pitch through the 11th. In the bottom of that frame, pinch hitting ex-Brave Ernie Lombardi worked the count to 2–2, and then clubbed Ed's next delivery into the upper left field stands.

There were still bright spots to come that year. Ed recorded two shutouts over the course of the '46 season, the second of which, on September 16, clinched fourth place, securing a first division finish for the Tribe for the first time since 1934. Club president Lou Perini awarded Ed a $100 bonus on the occasion, and Boston finished with an 81–72 record. Nearly one million fans came out to watch the improved club, easily shattering the franchise's previous attendance mark. Wright looked set as a key member of a quickly rising team.

The next spring's annual preseason City Series once again brought an Ed Wright-Ted Williams confrontation. On April 12, 1947, at Braves Field, Ed was on the hill in the ninth when Williams entered the batter's box. Manager Southworth positioned all his fielders to the extreme right of the field akin to the Williams Shift, first devised by the White Sox in 1941 and practiced with regularity

during the '46 season by Cleveland manager Lou Boudreau. Wright, who considered Williams the best hitter he ever faced, got a quick strike past the Splendid Splinter. On the next pitch, however, Williams lined Ed's offering into left field where it rolled to the wall for two bases. As Ed later told the tale, "Williams hit the ball through where the shortstop usually played, but the shortstop was over behind second base!"

When the 1947 season began, Wright followed Sain and Spahn in the starting rotation. On April 19, he scattered eight hits and hurled a complete game victory in the opener of a Patriots Day doubleheader at Braves Field against the Phillies. It would, however, be his only complete-game performance of the year. Unfortunately, severe bouts with tonsillitis disabled Ed a number of times, and adversely affected his performance throughout the season. The illness resulted in a loss of weight and arm strength, and his innings pitched dropped from 175 to 64⅔.

Relegated to exhibition duty, Wright was awarded a win in relief on July 21 in Cooperstown, New York, at the annual Hall of Fame game, a 10-inning contest that ended with a 4–3 Tribe triumph over the Yankees. Despite Ed's ongoing pleas, the Braves declined to consent to surgery until near the end of the season. As a result of his debilitating condition, he started only six times in 23 appearances. In one of those rare starts, on the evening of June 18 at Crosley Field, Wright took the loss when the Reds' Ewell "The Whip" Blackwell no-hit the Tribe. Ed finished with a record of three wins, three losses and a lofty 6.40 ERA, but the Braves took another step up to third place with an 86–68 won-loss record.

Now Wright was hard-pressed just to make the 1948 squad before he could even consider grabbing a spot in the rotation. As part of this quest he participated in one of the more notorious incidents in the history of the Hub's City Series. The third game of the '48 spring exhibition series between the Braves and Red Sox, and the first of the year in Boston, took place on April 16 at the Wigwam before 12,630 spectators. By the time Ed took the mound in the fourth inning, the Braves were behind 11–1 and would eventually be humiliated by a 19–6 whipping.

The Bosox's Billy Hitchcock, pinch-hitting for starter Joe Dobson, grounded to Ed, who fired to shortstop Al Dark. Dark tagged the lead runner, who was trapped between second and third base. Blackie then threw to Earl Torgeson in hopes of catching Hitchcock, who had turned the corner. The throw was low and struck the sliding runner. Torgy fell on top of Hitchcock, preventing his advancement; Hitchcock, meanwhile, grabbed the first baseman's ankles, hindering any attempt to retrieve the errant ball. The pugnacious Torgeson immediately took offense and commenced to pummel his opponent. Both benches cleared and a free-for-all nearly erupted. The origin of this animosity could be traced back to an earlier incident between the pair in Florida. Both of the antagonists were banished and the encounter was said to have created such ill will on the part of the National Leaguers that it served as one of the reasons (besides much bigger bonus checks due to the crowds at Cleveland Stadium) why the Braves later openly rooted for the Indians to capture the American League pennant rather than the Red Sox.

While Ed did secure a spot on the Opening Day roster of the prospective senior circuit champs, his stay was relatively brief. He relieved Spahn in the eighth inning of the latter's 3–1 losing effort during the Braves' home debut on April 23 against the Giants, and pitched scoreless ball for the final two innings. After this Wright made only two other relief appearances, achieving a 1.93 ERA in $4\frac{2}{3}$ innings before being dispensed to the American Association Milwaukee Brewers in May. Now performing for the city that would shortly become the home of the Braves, Ed appeared in 30 games—winning 9 while losing 12 and logging a 5.37 ERA. Unlike today's tradition, where pennant-winning teams tend to honor all contributors with a ring and a representative World Series share, Ed was not included in any such largess in '48. Come October, in fact, all his ties with the Tribe were cut when his contract was sold to the Brewers.

Seeking to enhance his chances for a return to the big leagues, Wright joined the Almendares Scorpions of the Cuban Winter League during the latter part of 1948. Bolstered with American minor league stars such as Chuck "The Rifleman" Connors, Sam Jethroe, and Monte Irvin, Almendares captured the Cuban championship and swept the inaugural Caribbean Series against teams from Puerto Rico, Venezuela, and Panama.

Wright was still just 29 years old entering 1949. Based on a recommendation from his trusted old Braves manager, Del Bissonnette, he got another shot at regular pitching work. Now piloting the Toronto Maple Leafs in the Triple A International League, Bissonette convinced the Maple Leafs to purchase Ed from the Brewers for $10,000. Ed headed across the border for the 1949 season and regained a chunk of his old form. An 11–11 record and a 3.97 ERA, compiled over 39 games, drew sufficient interest from the parent Phillies that Ed's contract was purchased upon conclusion of the season. Again he sought to sharpen his skills by venturing to Cuba to play Winter League ball for Almendares.

Ed performed well during spring training, and Phillies manager Eddie Sawyer added him to Philadelphia's roster. Before heading north, however, bad luck struck Wright once again. In a Florida tune-up game against Washington on March 24, he attempted a sidearm pitch and felt a pop in his elbow after completing the throw. Despite a burning sensation that ran down to his wrist, he continued to pitch. And although he spent the first month of the 1950 campaign with the Phillies, he failed to

appear in a game due to his elbow woes. He did, however, achieve a degree of fame with the eventual NL champs, appearing in the club's official team photo that was used in newspapers and publications throughout the season. Ed stood in the back row between Richie Ashburn and Blix Donnelly in the picture, but he was soon relegated again to Toronto.

Once more, Wright would have to work his way back to the majors. Cold spring weather up in the far north had retarded his recovery in the spring of '50, as in order to throw he had to apply heat to his troubled elbow for 20 minutes. In July, a swap with the Minneapolis Millers, the New York Giants' top minor league affiliate, transported Ed back to the American Association. Beginning the 1951 season with the Millers, Ed marveled at the batting and fielding prowess of the team's new center fielder, a 19-year-old lad by the name of Willie Howard Mays, Jr. In old Nicollet Park, Ed observed the "Say Hey Kid" perform heroics that would eventually lead to the latter's enshrinement in Cooperstown. However, neither Ed nor Willie was destined for a prolonged stay in Minneapolis. Mays departed for New York City after 35 games (and a .477 average) while Wright returned to the International League when he was sold to the Ottawa Athletics. Despite a lackluster 5–6, 3.54 performance there, the pitching-hungry Philadelphia Athletics secured Ed's services from the Giants.

In a last-hurrah effort, Ed made Jimmy Dykes' 1952 Athletics squad and spent the entire season in the bullpen. In 24 games, Wright won two while losing one, but his effectiveness was more accurately gauged by his 6.53 ERA, his 20/9 walks to strikeouts ratio, and his allowing 55 hits in $41\frac{1}{3}$ innings. His final official appearance at Fenway Park occurred on April 19 of that year after a memorable event. In the first game of the Patriots Day doubleheader, Ed came in after seven Red Sox runs had been scored off starter Dick Fowler in the fourth inning, the majority as the result of Don Lenhardt's inside-the-park grand slam.

His second turn in the City of Brotherly Love resulted in another pictorial honor for Wright. Ed was included in the Topps Chewing Gum Co.'s legendary 407-card 1952 baseball set that ushered in the modern era of cardboard collectibles. The set was issued in series over the course of the season and Ed's #368 pasteboard currently commands a hefty premium. This is due, however, to its relative scarcity rather than as a reflection of the achievements of the journeyman right-hander pictured on its front. That year's performance completed his final major league statistics: a 25–16 record over 101 games, 16 complete games in 39 starts, and a 4.00 ERA.

Sensing that the end was near, Ed welcomed his sale to the Memphis Chicks upon the conclusion of the '52 season, given the minor league team's relative closeness to his Dyersburg home. He spent the first part of the

1953 Southern Association campaign with the Chicks and the Chattanooga Lookouts before returning to the Kitty League as the player/manager of the Hopkinsville Hoppers in late July, winning five games and steering them to the playoffs. He stayed in that capacity with the Kentucky franchise until June of the following season, when he sought his release in the face of the league's instability. Fittingly, Ed wrapped up his professional playing career in 1954 with a two-game stint with the Lincoln Chiefs of the Western League. There, for the first time as a pro, he teamed up with younger brother Roger, who was in his second season with the Nebraska-based ball club. Released in July, Ed returned to Dyersburg and entered the service station business.

In retirement, in addition to running his gas station, Wright served as an alderman in Dyersburg and coached Dixie Youth Baseball. Known as "Mr. Baseball of Dyersburg," he guided his 1964 Connie Mack team to the state championship. Also affectionately called "Big Ed," he was much admired for his humility and gentle, caring nature. When asked about his big league exploits by his young players, he would relate that he had once been a part of a starting rotation that included Hall of Famer Warren Spahn and the great Johnny Sain. "The sportswriters called our rotation Spahn, Sain, and pray for rain," he'd then attest. "I guess I was the pray for rain."[6] Reflecting back on his life, Ed always remarked that he would "do it all over again" if given a chance. Acknowledging the changes in baseball's salary structure, he would then add that his only regret was that he "was born 50 years too soon." Imagine the cash he could command today after starting his career 20–12?

Ed died of cancer on November 19, 1995, at 76 years of age and was buried in Dyersburg's Fairview Cemetery. On May 15, 1998, on what would have been his 79th birthday, the beloved local coach was honored posthumously when a 40-acre baseball complex north of town was named Ed Wright Baseball Park.

Notes

1. The pair's paths crossed momentarily in 1948 while respectively performing for Boston's National and American League clubs. On March 31 at Bradenton, Florida, Ed triumphed over Ellis in a 4–1 exhibition tilt.
2. Like his brother, Roger has a link to Boston baseball and the 1948 season. A career minor leaguer, he spent several seasons as a Red Sox chattel, experiencing his finest year (17–6, 2.08) with the Lynn Red Sox of the New England League in 1946. Among his bush league mates who performed at Fenway Park in 1948 were Boo Ferriss (Greensboro, 1942) and Mickey McDermott (Scranton, 1947). Scranton teammates Fred Hatfield and Walt Dropo joined the parent club a bit later.
3. Popowski's association with the Wright family also extended to brother Roger. In 1947, Roger was a member of Popowski's pitching staff at Scranton as Pop ascended the Red Sox minor league managerial ladder.
4. *Boston Braves Sketch Book* (1946)
5. On April 18, 1949, Ed's brother Roger chalked up a 7–0 no-hitter against the St. Petersburg Saints while performing for the Tampa Smokers in the Florida International League, thus adding the Wright brothers to an elite group of siblings who have hurled hitless games in professional baseball.
6. Warner Agee, Dyersburg *State Gazette*, May 17, 1998, p. 11

Sources

Conversations with Ed Wright on a sunny October 3, 1992, at Fenway Park over the course of a Red Sox 7–5 victory over the New York Yankees. It doesn't get much better than that!
Correspondence with Ed Wright during 1993
Correspondence with Mrs. Ed (Florence) Wright in 1998
Brent Kelley, "Ex-Boston Braves' hurler Ed Wright interviewed," *Sports Collectors Digest*, September 4, 1992

BILLY SOUTHWORTH *by Jon Daly*

Billy Southworth was like Casey Stengel's long-lost brother from another mother. Both were born west of the Mississippi, less than three years apart. Both were outfielders in the teens and '20s. Bill James lists each as the other's most similar player. And both became hugely successful managers after long, serpentine routes to the top. They were even traded for each other in 1923. But unlike Stengel, who had no children, lived a long, happy life with a wealthy wife, and has never left the public consciousness, Southworth endured tremendous tragedy in his personal life and had been in danger of being forgotten before his 2008 election to the Hall of Fame.

Billy was born William Harold Southworth on March 9, 1893, near the hamlet of Harvard, Nebraska. According to Billy's daughter Carole Watson, William "Buffalo Bill" Cody may have been the one to nickname him "Billy the Kid" after the gunfighter. Cody was a family friend.

Two droughts and a house fire forced the family to return to Ohio (where his father, Orlando, was originally from) when Billy was about nine years old. Billy went with his younger sister and his mother, Myra Melvina Southworth, by train, while Orlando and sons Ervin, Calvin, Pressley, and Arley made the trek east in two covered wagons. Most references list Billy's given name as William Harrison Southworth; not William Harold. He did not care for either middle name, so he made no attempt to correct this error.

The Southworths settled in Saranac, not far from

Columbus, where Orlando was the village blacksmith, wheelwright, and postmaster. The Southworths weren't wealthy, so they made baseballs out of Billy's socks, improvising as youngsters in poor Latin American countries do today. Young Billy cheered on his older brothers as they played for a town team from nearby Darbyville.

Around 1902, the family moved to the west side of Columbus, Ohio. Another boy growing up in the same neighborhood at this time was Eddie Rickenbacker, who was friendly with the Southworths, Arley in particular. Arley and Eddie would race handmade soapbox racers down the hills of the capital city, an early suggestion of the daredevil skills Rickenbacker would employ as both a World War I flying ace and a race car driver and designer.

Billy left school in his early teens and joined the working world. Like the rest of his family, he took a railroad job. But he also played baseball on Sundays for the Chenoweths, a team in the semipro Capital City League, which at that time included fellow future big leaguers Hank Gowdy and Wally Gerber. The young catcher soon moved up to the Kenton Reds, where a slide into third base hurt his throwing arm. Rather than lose Billy's bat for the rest of the game, the skipper moved him to the outfield. When Billy played for his first professional team—Portsmouth in 1912—they already had two catchers, so he made his position switch permanent.

Southworth played 134 games for the Portsmouth Cobblers in the Ohio State League that year. Batting left and throwing right, he started the 1913 season for Portsmouth, too, but was purchased halfway through the season by Charles Somers, owner of the American League Cleveland Naps. Twenty-year-old Billy made one appearance with the Indians, on August 4 as a late-inning defensive replacement in left field, without either a plate appearance or a fielding chance, before being sent westward to minor league Toledo.

When Billy returned to Cleveland in 1914, he did so with the entire Toledo team. The Naps' ownership brought their farm team's whole roster of players to Cleveland to prevent the Federal League from placing a competing franchise in the city. That spring, the Boston Braves reportedly offered Somers $5,000 for Southworth's services, but were turned down. Billy was married that summer, on June 29. His bride was a preacher's daughter, Lida Brooks, of Portsmouth, where she was a

The Braves ownership triumvirate lured Billy Southworth from St. Louis with an exceptionally rich, multiyear contract.

soloist in the choir of her father's church, and Billy met her there as they sang duets.

Southworth played for Toledo for a year and a half. In early June of 1915, Shoeless Joe Jackson got hurt and Billy the Kid got his second shot at the big leagues. But after 60 games, in which he batted just .220, he was shipped to Portland of the Pacific Coast League, where he finished the season and also played in 1916. It was in Portland that Lida gave birth to a son, William Brooks Southworth. After the '16 season, Portland sold Southworth to Pittsburgh and the Pirates assigned him to Birmingham of the Southern League.

He played for the Birmingham Barons in 1917 (missing almost two months with a broken shoulder) and 1918. The league ended operations in June of 1918—every other minor league folded that season—on account of World War I. Pirates manager Hugo Bezdek called up Southworth. Casey Stengel had just joined the Navy and Billy took over his right-field spot. Billy registered for the draft but was never called.

Bezdek was the only man ever to serve as a major-league manager (Pittsburgh Pirates) and an NFL head coach (Cleveland Rams), but his background wasn't baseball. It was said that his players looked forward to the games because they were easier than his practices. His training methods may have been an inspiration for Southworth's regimented spring camps during his own managerial career, and Billy certainly thrived under them. He batted .341 in 64 games with the Pirates in that war-shortened season, and returned to Pittsburgh again in both 1919 and 1920. He hit in the .280s both years and even led the league in triples, with 14, in 1919.

In January of 1921, the Braves finally snagged Southworth—one of three Pirates traded to Boston, with $15,000, for Rabbit Maranville. Billy wasn't happy to be moving from a winning team to a loser. But he wound up signing a contract a few days later and was named captain of the team. Southworth hit .308 for Boston that year. He was limited to 43 games in '22 due to a dislocated knee, but in 1923 he accumulated a career-high 611 at-bats and hit for a .319 average. After the season, however, he was part of a trade with the Giants. It was a multiplayer deal, with Casey Stengel coming to Boston along with Dave Bancroft and Bill Cunningham in exchange for Southworth and hurler Joe Oeschger. John McGraw had coveted Southworth since 1921, according to *New York Times* sportswriter Arthur Daley. But he waited until Billy had demonstrated that he had recovered from his knee injury.

Southworth and McGraw wound up not getting along, and with Ross Youngs ensconced in Billy's usual position of right field, Billy was shifted to center. He struggled at the plate, batting only .256. The Giants won the pennant in 1924, but Southworth saw duty in the World Series only as a late-inning outfielder in five games and made just one plate appearance (he reached on an error). His one moment of glory came as a pinch runner in the 12th inning of Game One; he scored what proved to be the winning run. His 1925 season was better (.292), but the Giants finished second.

In 1926 Billy started with a bang, and after about a month of the season he was carrying a .442 batting average. But in mid-June, McGraw was looking to strengthen the team, and traded Southworth to St. Louis for a true center fielder, Heinie Mueller. The move backfired for McGraw. Billy was already 33, but 1926 may have been his best year. Not only did he hit, but his hits were timely—including a couple of walk-off home runs a week apart in July.

On September 24, the Cardinals were at the Polo Grounds. Facing Hughie McQuillan, Billy hit an upper-deck home run to right field in the top of the second, giving the Cards a lead they never relinquished. The game-winning hit clinched the franchise's first 20th century pennant. Fifty loudspeakers were set up in downtown St. Louis to carry the radio broadcast, and when the last out was recorded, the business district went wild.

Billy's heroics continued into the '26 World Series, when he came through in the seventh inning of Game Two at Yankee Stadium before a record crowd of 65,000. With the score tied, 2–2, runners at first and third, and two outs, Southworth stepped in to face Urban Shocker and hit his second pitch on a high arc into the right-field bleachers. All told, Billy had 10 hits in the Series (batting .345) and the Cardinals defeated the Yankees in seven games.

It would prove his last great moment as a big-league player. In 1927, Southworth suffered a rib injury and was limited to 92 games. That fall, Cards general manager Branch Rickey offered him a managerial job in the St. Louis farm system. In August of '26, Billy had helped settle a feud between a couple of Redbirds that was dividing the team into two camps, and Cardinals owner Sam Breadon considered him to be a man of managerial timber.

Billy took the position, and as a player-manager with Rochester hit .361 over 124 games in 1928. The Red Wings were picked to finish last in a preseason poll of the International League writers; Rochester baseball historian Brian Bennett writes that the team consisted of young prospects, including future major-leaguer Charlie

Gelbert. But after hovering around the .500 mark early in the season, Rochester caught fire, beating out Buffalo by .001 percentage point for the pennant by going 5–1 in three doubleheaders in three days against Montreal late in the year. Rochester wound up losing the Little World Series to the American Association champion Indianapolis Indians, but Southworth's leadership had turned more heads.

Making it even a more impressive managerial performance was what Billy endured in his personal life during the season. In May of that year, Southworth had had to return home when Lida had two twins die during childbirth. She was never healthy after that. His son, Billy, was 12 years old and approaching adolescence when he was accidentally shot by a playmate as they hunted sparrows that October. A button on young Billy's coat absorbed most of the bullet's impact and he suffered only a minor wound. Later, his father said that he was shaken. "He was only 12, but I looked on him as the closest friend I had," Billy said.

Branch Rickey and Sam Breadon went through managers the way Elizabeth Taylor went through husbands. Hornsby in '26. O'Farrell in '27. McKechnie in '28. Although he won 95 games and the NL pennant, McKechnie didn't make it until Thanksgiving after a World Series sweep by the Yankees. Southworth was named manager of the Cardinals for 1929 as part of a job swap in which McKechnie went to Rochester. Billy was surprised. He had been called to St. Louis to meet with owner Breadon, but he had assumed that the meeting would concern the Rochester club. He would be the youngest manager in the National League at the age of 36, and he found himself in over his head.

As J. Roy Stockton of the *St. Louis Post-Dispatch* recalled, trouble started in Florida during spring training. "Billy Southworth had been one of the gang only two springs before," he wrote, "and he hadn't ever been averse to burning a candle or two at any number of ends." Sam Breadon considered former manager McKechnie too much of a soft touch, and wanted his new pilot to "inject more fight and stricter discipline in the Cardinal team." But Southworth's former teammates didn't respect his authority.

Together with coaches Gabby Street and Greasy Neale, Southworth ran a tough camp in Avon Park, Florida. According to Brian Bell of the *Atlanta Constitution*, no team training in Florida worked longer hours. They even had picnic-style lunches at the ballpark instead of returning to their hotel. Southworth aggravated the players at times, such as one trip from Avon Park to Miami when Billy insisted that everyone take the train. No one was to ride with friends or family in their own cars. The team, catcher Jimmy Wilson in particular, grumbled, and gave their new manager a new nickname: Billy the Heel.

Southworth was the only playing manager in the

National League at the time, but in the limited action he assigned himself he hit an anemic .188. Others did better, and the Cards were in first place as late as June 18 with a .614 winning percentage. A horrendous July, however, saw them fall to fourth place. J. Roy Stockton blamed the pitching staff, saying that it had collapsed, Jesse Haines in particular. Some felt that Southworth had mishandled Haines and the other hurlers. Years later, coach Neale told the *New York Times'* Arthur Daley that he thought Southworth's biggest mistake was allowing the players to decide how to pitch to opposing hitters. *The Sporting News* said the biggest thing that Sportsman's Park fans had against Southworth was his insistence on playing for a big inning. Whatever the cause, the Cards had a 7–15 East Coast swing in July, and when they returned home the mercurial Breadon had Southworth and McKechnie swap jobs again. Billy returned to Rochester, taking Neale with him, while Street stayed in St. Louis, eventually replacing McKechnie.

Back in the minors, Southworth led the Red Wings to another International League title. Flags followed again in 1930 and 1931, and they won the Junior World Series both seasons as well. As Charles Dexter wrote in *Collier's* on October 9, 1943, Billy never believed that his success was due to his own wizardry. He simply had the horses; Rickey had built up quite a farm system. In terms of big-leaguers, Rochester had Paul Derringer, Pepper Martin, and Tex Carleton on the way up, and benefited from George Sisler and Andy High on the way down.

Billy returned to Rochester in 1932, but it would prove a dismal year. The Cardinals added Columbus of the American Association to their network of farm teams. Club president Lee McPhail fired manager Nemo Leibold in July and replaced him with Southworth. The Columbus stadium was only two blocks from where Billy had played sandlot ball a little over 20 years earlier with Chenoweth of the Capital City League. He was to live at home with Lida and Billy, but Mrs. Southworth got sick, Billy started drinking heavily, and the injury-bedraggled Redbirds finished second. The Cards fired Southworth (it was the Depression era and they wanted to go with a playing manager, especially because the American Association set a $6,300-a-month salary cap), and Lida died of a cerebral hemorrhage in the fall of 1932.

Southworth wasn't out of work long. On December 21, the New York Giants announced that they had signed him as a coach for 1933. He'd be on the staff of longtime friend Bill Terry. But Billy didn't make it out of spring training. The *New York Times* said that Southworth suffered a knee injury one Sunday while playing in El Paso. *The Sporting News* ran the same story. In reality, Terry fired Southworth. They no longer got along, and Southworth's drinking may not have helped matters. Writer Tom Meany noticed an unexplained black eye that Terry sported while in Texas. Billy's daughter, Carole, suggested

that Memphis Bill might have called her father by the middle name he detested, Harold.

To his credit, Billy was able to wean himself off the bottle. Daughter Carole didn't believe that her father was an alcoholic; she said he started drinking to fit in with the Giants but had a low tolerance for alcohol. Baseball briefly took a back seat in his life. He got a job with Capital City Products, Inc. as a cottonseed oil salesman, and met a Capital City bookkeeper named Mabel Stemen—a golfer, a horsewoman, and a crack shot. They hunted pheasants together and were married on January 7, 1934. Their daughter, Carole, was born in 1935.

Southworth was friends with pro football pioneer Joe Carr. Carr knew Branch Rickey (he also ran the Columbus ballclub before Lee McPhail) and asked Rickey to give Billy a job in the Cardinals organization again. The teetotaling Mahatma was reluctant at first, but after promising reports of how Southworth comported himself, Rickey hired him to manage at Class B Asheville, North Carolina, for the 1935 season.

He finished first there, and in July 1936 moved up to replace Fred Hoffman as skipper of the Class A Memphis Chicks. As one of the early adopters of the farm system, the Cards not only developed talent for themselves, they had a surplus that helped their Memphis team profit, too. Among the players that Southworth helped develop and sell were Al Benton, Hugh Casey, Carl Doyle, and Coaker Triplett. In August, Billy's name was once again mentioned in connection with a major-league job—this time with the St. Louis Browns. But his old coach Gabby Street got the post instead, and Billy signed on for another season in Memphis.

After the 1938 season, Cardinals manager Frankie Frisch was out after a long feud with Branch Rickey. Ray Blades was promoted from Rochester, and the organization asked Southworth to return to Rochester and take Blades' spot as skipper.

1939 was the fifth full season that Southworth managed Rochester, and it was the fifth time he took them to the Junior World Series. They finished second in the International League, but won the Governor's Cup by eliminating Newark in seven games before losing to Louisville in another seven-gamer. In 1940, Rochester got a good jump out of the gate, but in the National League, the preseason favorite Cards were floundering, a game out of the cellar. As Blades had replaced Frisch, so Southworth replaced Blades. It took 11 years, but Billy the Kid was back.

The Cards were still going through managers the way Henry VIII went through wives. But Breadon hired Southworth without consulting Rickey, and Billy reported directly to the owner. Rickey's role with the Cards was diminished. No longer were players allowed to go to the front office to complain about the manager. No longer did the manager have to follow Rickey's policies.

After Billy assumed the helm, the team caught fire. The Cards were 15–29 when he took over, but went 69–40 the rest of the way. It was too little, too late, however, and they finished in third. It was in 1940 that Billy started platooning. It was a strategy that was in widespread use during his playing days, but it had fallen out of favor over the previous 15 years. In revitalizing it, he would achieve his fame—and eventually his fortune.

According to baseball writer Bill James, Southworth was a reasonable and logical man. He could be self-righteous, but he was warm, quiet, and agreeable. The dictatorial John McGraw influenced how Billy would treat players; he would try the opposite approach. Billy communicated with his athletes and didn't second-guess them. Author Fred Lieb said that Southworth's players would come to him with nonbaseball problems.

Going into the 1941 season, *The Sporting News* had the Cards picked for third behind Brooklyn and Cincinnati. They actually finished in second, and might have finished in first if it weren't for injuries. Perhaps taking this into account, *The Sporting News* named Southworth its major league Manager of the Year. He also kept his job.

By 1942, the U.S. had entered World War II. The Cardinals were unaffected that year, with the exception of drafted pitcher Johnny Grodzicki. This was the team that was known as the St. Louis Swifties. As of June 27, the Cards were in second place behind the reigning champion Dodgers, but they were off the pace by 9½ games. Then, in a humdinger of a pennant race, the Cards went 43–9 in their last 52 contests to top the Dodgers by two games and reach the World Series. After losing the first game of the fall classic, 7–4, to the defending champion Yankees, the Cards went on to sweep the next four and take the title. With that victory and the one in 1926, Billy participated in the Yankees' only two World Series defeats between 1923 and 1953 (a span in which the Bombers won 16 titles).

Going into 1943, the Cards lost the services of Enos Slaughter, Johnny Beazley, and others to the armed forces. But thanks to Branch Rickey's farm system—Rickey himself was now with Brooklyn—they were able to call up capable reserves. The pennant race was a cakewalk, as the Redbirds grabbed the National League laurels with an eighteen-game lead over the circuit. They faced the Yankees once again in the World Series, but this time McCarthy's men got the better of them in five games.

In 1944, the Cardinals were shooting for a third straight pennant under Southworth. The Redbird pitching was outstanding in 1943 and Billy could play more conservatively, one run at a time. He didn't expect the pitching to be as good in '44, and in March told the Associated Press that he was planning to play for the big inning. Harry Brecheen, Max Lanier, and Mort Cooper were still on the starting staff, but Howie Krist and Howie Pollet were now in the service. Southworth's new approach

worked; St. Louis scored almost 100 more runs, and for the third year in a row the Cardinals won at least 105 games and the pennant. They were one of baseball's all-time dynasties, even considering the fact that they were a wartime team.

That year's AL champs were the surprising Browns, and all the World Series games were played in Sportsman's Park. The Browns skipper was Luke Sewell, and due to wartime housing shortages, the Sewells and Southworths shared an apartment. Since one team was always on the road, it was usually a convenient arrangement. Except for the World Series. Fortunately, a neighbor was going to be out of town, so he invited Southworth to use his apartment. The Cards won the Series for the second time in three years.

More dark days, however, lay ahead. On February 15, 1945, Major Billy Southworth Jr. took off from Mitchell Field on Long Island in a B-29 Superfortress. Major W.L. Anken was an observer on the bomber, situated in the top gun turret. Shortly after takeoff, he noticed smoke coming from engine one. He reported this over the intercom to Major Southworth. "Keep an eye on it" was the reply. Those were the last words of William Brooks Southworth. He tried to land at LaGuardia Field. The plane touched the runway, according to Anken, but then clipped the water and somersaulted before bursting into flames and falling into icy Rikers Island Channel of Flushing Bay. Five died in the crash, including Major Southworth. His father and stepmother flew to New York as the Navy searched for his body; it was nearly half a year before it was located. Billy was devastated, but his first questions were said to be about the safety of the five survivors.

At some point in the second half of the '40s, Southworth backslid to the bottle. His son's death may have triggered this. Normie Roy, who later played under him, said that whenever they'd go to New York to play the Giants or the Dodgers, Southworth would visit a park near the crash site and "drink and drink and drink." Young Billy's body was finally found at the confluence of the East River and Long Island Sound on Friday, August 3, and a military funeral was held in Columbus four days later. An excellent minor-league outfielder with movie star looks (who apparently had serious offers from Hollywood), Billy Jr. had been the light of his father's life; now, like his siblings and mother before him, he was gone.

In 1945 star outfielder Stan Musial joined the Navy. Despite this and injuries that befell virtually everyone on the roster except second baseman Emil Verban, the Cards kept close to the eventual pennant-winning Cubs. They finished the season only three games behind, mathematically alive until September 29, the next to last day of the season. The Cards were still a force, if not still champions.

On the opposite end of the National League spectrum were the Boston Braves. For years, the Braves were one of the laughingstocks of the senior circuit. They changed their name to the Bees for a while, but even that didn't help. They hadn't finished in the first division in more than a decade. New owner Lou Perini and his partners sought to change this. According to Richard Letarte in *That One Glorious Season*, Boston general manager John Quinn recommended Southworth to them. Perini and company spoke with Breadon, and were able to secure Southworth's services with a three-year contract paying around $100,000 in all. It was substantially more than the Redbirds could or would pay him. (The Braves also imported enough players from St. Louis, including Danny Litwhiler, Ray Sanders, and Johnny Hopp, that some wags called the team the Cape Cod Cardinals.)

The Braves trained in Fort Lauderdale, Florida, and Southworth brought his combination of flexible and no-nonsense training methods over from the Cardinals. In Brent Kelley's *The Pastime in Turbulence*, pitcher Ed Wright, one of the holdovers, said he thought that Southworth played favorites with his old Cardinals. The results, however, were immediate. The Bostons moved up from sixth place in 1945 to a driving fourth-place finish, just a game out of third. Attendance at Braves Field more than doubled to an all-time high of 969,673.

In February of 1947, managers in the Braves farm system were indoctrinated into the "Southworth System." Billy divided his team into groups and rotated them from task to task. He'd keep his players running and work them from 10:30 in the morning to well into the afternoon. In this way, he differed greatly from his contemporary Joe McCarthy, who would work his Yankees team as a group and be done in a couple of hours.

New York Times columnist Arthur Daley was high on the Braves at the start of the 1947 season. As it happened, the Braves opened the year in Brooklyn as Jackie Robinson made his historic big-league debut. Billy was able to coax an MVP season out of third baseman Bob Elliott, who had been rather indifferent as a member of Frankie Frisch's Pirates. Thanks to Elliott's clutch hitting and the pitching of Johnny Sain and Warren Spahn, the Braves wound up in third place, a good enough finish for Lou Perini to tear up Billy's contract and give him a new five-year deal valued at over a quarter of a million dollars.

The Brooklyn Dodgers were grooming Eddie Stanky for a possible managing or coaching position, but he was looking for more money and Branch Rickey was looking to move Jackie Robinson to second base in 1948. Rickey put Stanky on the trading block, and Southworth and the Braves jumped at the opportunity—picking him up for first baseman Ray Sanders and cash. The team promoted hotshot young shortstop Alvin Dark from Milwaukee of the American Association, and he became Rookie of the Year. Solid rookie pitchers Vern Bickford and Bob Hogue came up and produced immediately. Everything came together nicely.

The Braves hadn't won a pennant since 1914. By September, they (and the Red Sox) had *Time* magazine talking about double pennant fever. The Red Sox fell to the Cleveland Indians in a one-game American League playoff, but the Braves were able to capture the senior circuit flag. It was probably a more impressive job of managing than Southworth had ever done in St. Louis. He had only one future Hall of Famer in Spahn, but was able to win the pennant through judicious use of platooning, or "the Army game" as *The Sporting News* was calling it back then. Southworth just barely missed becoming Manager of the Year, getting 87 votes while Billy Meyer, the rookie skipper of the Pirates, received 89 for bringing the Bucs to a surprising fourth-place finish. The Braves lost the World Series to the heavily favored Indians in six games, most of them close.

Success for the Braves, however, would be short-lived. Cracks in the edifice were forming already in June of 1948. Boston signed a bonus baby pitcher named Johnny Antonelli for $50,000 or higher—more than most, if not all, the Braves were making. Many were veterans of World War II, including Spahn, who had received a battlefield commission during the Battle of the Bulge. Antonelli, in contrast, had just graduated from high school, so there was naturally a little resentment. Stan Musial said that over the All-Star break Johnny Sain threatened a sit-down strike, and the 24-game winner (in 1948) got a raise. And while Southworth would use his youngsters when he managed the Cardinals, he let Antonelli languish on the bench. Then again, according to Bill James, no one really played Bonus Babies except Joe McCarthy and Eddie Sawyer of the Phillies.

The March 28, 1949, edition of *Life* magazine had a feature on how hunky-dory things were at the Braves' training camp in Bradenton, Florida. Meanwhile, columnist Dave Egan of the *Daily Record*, a Boston tabloid, was writing another story, one of a ballclub in revolt. Outfielder Jimmy Russell was fined for staying out past curfew. Sain and Southworth weren't speaking. Spahn wanted to be traded and didn't care if it was to a second-division team. Worst of all, Egan described two near-fistfights involving Southworth, one with a radio announcer and one with a player who was reportedly asked to keep tabs on his teammates. Management and players denied everything, and the storm blew over—for a while.

Against Pittsburgh on July 23, things came to a head. The Braves lost a game to the Pirates as the Bucs came back in the ninth frame against a tiring Warren Spahn. Some blamed the loss on Eddie Stanky; Spahn had reached base three times, and twice Stanky signaled for a hit-and-run play, forcing the pitcher to run and slide several times. One time, Spahn was caught stealing. Southworth said he didn't approve of the strategy, while Stanky said he was allowed to put on his own hit-and-run plays. The loss was part of a bad 5–8 home stand.

August saw the defending champs still hovering around .500. Sain was ineffective, possibly from having thrown more than 300 innings the previous year. His shoulder was sore. The team had also suffered other injuries. The night of August 7, first baseman Earl Torgeson got into a fistfight with teammate Jim Russell in Chicago. Outfielder Russell suffered two black eyes, and Torgeson broke a thumb. This was just as Torgy—one of the team's top hitters—was about to return from a separated shoulder. Southworth then tried to hush up the episode, and he and the front office wound up telling conflicting stories to the press. Discussing the Torgeson-Russell fight one night, the skipper blew up over the phone at Perini. He had also been hostile to the press on that road trip, and this may have been the straw that broke the camel's back.

The Braves brain trust held a meeting on August 15. The next day, Southworth was given a "leave of absence" for the rest of the season. He was whisked away from Boston on Perini's private plane before the press could reach him. The official reason was that the Braves felt he was on the verge of a mental breakdown. Southworth was complaining about headaches, something he never had problems with before. His continued drinking probably didn't help matters. Columnist Bill Cunningham called him "…the first major casualty of the new superpowered, high speed, post-war, extravagantly bonused, high salaried, and heavily box office pressured baseball." Some thought that one reason for Southworth's downfall lay in his starting to believe his own press clippings and taking too much credit for the Braves' success in 1948. In *Paths to Glory*, Mark Armour and Daniel Levitt opine that Southworth may have lost the emotional energy needed to control headstrong veterans of both the war and the ballfield.

There was speculation about whether Southworth would return in 1950. An informal poll of the players conducted on August 17 was unanimously opposed. Harold Kaese of the *Boston Globe* mused that 10 to 12 Braves would have to leave if Billy were to return. One such player was Eddie Stanky, and Kaese mentioned the pepperpot second sacker as a possible manager for 1950. In the meantime, Johnny Cooney was the team's interim manager. One of his first moves was to scrap the platoon system, or, as some in the press called it, the Southworth Shuffle.

About a month after he took a leave of absence, Billy

Billy Southworth watches his players in pre-game practice from his perch in the Braves Field third base home team dugout. The Wigwam's uncovered left field pavilion appears in the background.

received a clean bill of health from a cardiologist in Columbus and said he planned to return in 1950. The Braves ended the season at 75–79 and in fourth place. Dissension may have played a role in their disappointing finish, but injuries—Sain's sore shoulder among them—didn't help. The players awarded Southworth a half-share of their fourth-place money; Bob Elliott and Tommy Holmes voted him a full share, but no one else did. Commissioner Happy Chandler overruled the Braves, using the precedent of Judge Landis awarding Rogers Hornsby a full share despite the Cubs players' wishes in 1932. But the message was clear.

At the winter meetings Southworth said that Johnny Sain and Alvin Dark would remain with the Braves. Sain did, but Dark and his outspoken mentor, Eddie Stanky, were traded to Leo Durocher's Giants for Sid Gordon, Willard Marshall, Buddy Kerr, and pitcher Sam Webb. Seven other Braves became ex-Braves over the winter: Bill Voiselle, Marv Rickert, Bill Salkeld, Jeff Heath, Red Barrett, Nelson Potter, and Ray Sanders.

The 1950 squad was younger and included 20-year-old catcher Del Crandall and Sam Jethroe, the first African-American player for either Boston team. There were also some changes to the spring training routine. Press conferences were no longer lengthy affairs at the hotel cocktail lounge; no more bed checks; golf and swimming were permitted; and sportswriters would travel separately from the team. But despite prodigious slugging by Gordon and Elliott and 59 wins from the trio of Spahn, Sain, and Bickford, the Braves finished fourth behind the Whiz Kids of Philadelphia, the Dodgers, and the Giants.

Early in the 1951 season, the Braves were proving a disappointment. One Sunday in June, Southworth called GM Quinn and president Perini, asking to resign immediately. They had him stick around for a few days before announcing his resignation a half-hour after the first pitch of a Braves-Cubs game at Wrigley Field on June 19. The players didn't know until they found out from fans around the dugout who had portable radios. After bidding a teary goodbye to his team, Billy left on the 10:45 train to Columbus with his older brother, Press.

Historian David Voigt has suggested that one factor that drove Southworth and fellow pilot Joe McCarthy from the game was the tomcatting of the postwar player. In the *Life* article mentioned above, there was a mention of Southworth playing marriage counselor for an unnamed player and his wife. Perhaps the wartime experiences made the players of that era less amenable to the hard-driving managerial approach of Billy the Kid's generation and more accepting of the swinging Leo Durochers of the world. Bill James believes that Frankie Frisch was another victim of postwar sexual mores. The cities were bigger. It was harder to keep tabs on players, and women were more independent and adventuresome than their mothers had been.

Southworth was still just 58, and there were rumors that he might catch on with the St. Louis Browns or Branch Rickey's Pittsburgh Pirates. These came to naught, however, and starting in 1952 he hit the road as a scout for the Braves. He also worked with young players at the minor league camp in Waycross, Georgia. Among his assignments were going to Eau Claire, Wisconsin, to look at an 18-year-old Henry Aaron and scouting the Yankees in preparation for the 1956 World Series (by then the Braves had moved to Milwaukee). In the winter of 1955 he was arrested for drunken driving but found not guilty. His scouting contract ended on December 31, 1956, and he retired to Sunbury. This gave Billy more time to pursue his hobbies, which author Frederick Lieb said included hunting, fishing, bowling, and—at least during the days his son attended the school—Ohio State football.

Although he quit smoking in the late 1940s, Southworth spent his last days battling emphysema. He died on November 15, 1969, at Riverside Hospital in Columbus, and Musial and scout Mo Mozzali represented the Cardinals at his funeral. Billy was laid to rest at Greenlawn Cemetery in Columbus. Mabel survived him for almost 30 years; passing away in 1998.

Until December 3, 2007, Southworth may have been the best manager never to make the Hall of Fame. He received some support in a couple of Baseball Writers Association elections during the 1950s, but was not close to selection. There is no record of how he fared with the Veterans Committee, their votes not becoming a matter of record until 21st century elections. Frankie Frisch dominated that committee during the 1970s. He was a teammate of Southworth's with the Giants and the Cardinals, and Billy managed him for half a season in 1929. There may have been some animosity between the two men, but that is mere speculation. It may be, as Rob Neyer suggests, that Southworth's managerial career was too brief by Hall of Fame standards. Some voters may have discounted his success during the war years. His daughter Carole believes that the untimely death of Bob Hoey in an automobile accident kept her father out of the Hall of Fame. Southworth was a modest man; not one to toot his own horn. But Hoey, a sportswriter for the *Ohio State Journal* in Columbus, planned to write a book on Billy. To this day, there is no book length profile of the man.

This changed in December of 2007 when a panel of the Veterans Committee elected to enshrine Southworth and Dick Williams. Tom Verducci of *Sports Illustrated* mentioned some points in Southworth's favor in an online column:

four pennants
six 90 win seasons
340 games above .500
fourth all-time in winning percentage for managers with over 10 years (.597)

Verducci even invoked the point system that Bill James used to rate managers based on victories and titles. Southworth is rated 19th by this measure and all the top 19 managers are immortalized in the plaque room at the Hall.

The most appropriate epitaph for Southworth is quoted by Harold Kaese (in *The Milwaukee Braves*), coming from the *Boston Globe*: "The Braves were an old club, crabby, bitter, set in their ways. Players who could no longer deliver blamed their ineptness on Southworth. Victory, which sugar-coated the bitterness underneath last season, eluded the crippled Braves and left bare the acrid taste of defeat, futility and animosity. Southworth, one of the great managers, could not cope with the situation. Perhaps he was too aloof, too domineering, too cocky, and while he did not need the friendship of his players, even he could not afford to lose their respect."

Sources

Baseball Dynasties: The Greatest Teams of All Time—Rob Neyer and Eddie Epstein
The Bill James Guide to Baseball Managers—Bill James
The Man in the Dugout—Leonard Koppett
The Milwaukee Braves—Harold Kaese
The Pastime in Turbulence—Brent Kelley
Paths to Glory: How Great Baseball Teams Got That Way—Daniel Levitt and Mark Armour
That One Glorious Season: Baseball Players With One Spectacular Year, 1950–1961—Richard Letarte
Collier's
Life
Atlanta Constitution
Boston Globe
New York Times
St. Louis Post-Dispatch
The Sporting News
Washington Post
Watson, Carole. Personal Interviews, March and April 2007.
www.baseball-reference.comwww.retrosheet.org

The 1948 Boston Red Sox

MATT BATTS *by Bill Nowlin*

G	AB	R	H	2B	3B	HR	RBI	BB	SO	BA	OBP	SLG	SB	HBP
46	118	13	37	12	0	1	24	15	9	.314	.391	.441	0	0

Ten years a backup catcher for five major league teams, Matt Batts was born and raised in San Antonio, Texas. He lived in the north part of the city at the time, but San Antonio has grown so much since he was born on October 16, 1921, that where he lived would be nearer the middle of the city today. His earliest baseball memory is of playing on the gravel streets of the city. "I was always the one that hit the furthest and all of that."

Matt's father Matthew was a fireman. His mother Margaret died when he was about a year old. Keeping it in the family, Matt's father married one of his mother's sisters, Brettie. Matt had no brothers or sisters, though a half-sister Eva came from the union of Matt Sr. and Brettie. She lives in San Antonio today.

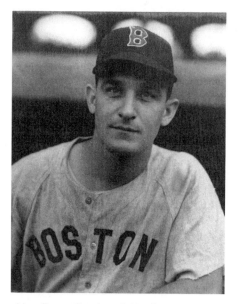

Matt Batts offered a solid backup season in 1948. Courtesy of George Brace Photo.

From the sandlots, Matt progressed through the city's schools. "I played when I was at junior high school, I was quite a hitter. I was pretty good size, you know. Everybody that had a ball club wanted me to play. I would have my bicycle and I'd ride my bicycle across town, or any place to play baseball." The year he started high school, though, the city discontinued its baseball program due to its expense. Unable to play high school ball, he played American Legion ball and in a few other leagues nearby. He was named to the All-State team in Texas for his Legion ball play. "I played with a semipro team that played around San Antonio, out in the sticks. They would pay you a few bucks, five dollars or something, you know. One of the fellows that used to play with Chicago, Art Veltman, lived there in San Antonio. He is the one that got the team together." The teams played around the city, not even traveling to nearby San Marcos, but Batts remembers one road trip when a local sportswriter arranged for a truck loaded with hay in the back and drove the team to Del Rio to play a team on the border.

He started catching in semipro ball, pretty much by accident, really the result of a little clowning around. "We were beating a team pretty bad and we started changing up, you know, different positions, and I told the catcher I wanted to catch, I wanted to see how it was catching. I picked off a runner at first and threw one out at third. I

had always had a great arm. I could throw one from home plate over the left field fence." It's something he never tried at Fenway Park.

He still holds the high school javelin record for the state of Texas. Batts enrolled at Baylor and played on the freshman baseball team—which was good enough to beat the varsity. He left after about a year and a half. "They about run me off," he laughs. "One of the reasons I quit at Baylor was because I had signed a major league contract and didn't tell them about it. I didn't realize at the time that it was against the rules and regulations. I had a deal with the Boston Red Sox that they would pay my way to school and I could still play football and baseball."

Indeed, he had been offered a $2,500 bonus and a new car—quite large at the time—by Red Sox scout Uncle Billy Disch, the University of Texas coach. Veltman, who was a Tigers coach and had wanted to sign Matt, was upset to learn he'd left school and had been beaten out. "He was a great, great, great coach. He was one of the better coaches in the country. He had been after me for some time." Batts signed in 1942 and was sent to Class-C Canton (Ohio) of the Middle Atlantic League. Batts caught and played first base and outfield, batting .294 in 483 at-bats, with 10 home runs and 82 RBIs.

The country was at war, and ballplayers were no more exempt than anyone else. "Mel Parnell was there at Canton with me. He was pitching and we were both friends, because he lived in New Orleans and I lived in San Antonio. It was pretty close, you know. Not too far away. We roomed together there in Canton. We became great friends. When we got back home, some boys that I knew real well that had played ball with me there in San Antonio had entered the service at Randolph Field. One of the colonels over there got them to come and get hold of me and see if I wouldn't sign up instead of just getting drug into anything. With them being there, I said I'd go ahead and join the service."

Matt enlisted in the Army Air Corps at Randolph Field. He became a crew chief, servicing aircraft, mostly trainer planes for the cadets coming through as prospective pilots. His job was to ensure that everything was in shape with the aircraft, ready to go each morning. He served at Randolph Field for the duration of the war, reaching the rank of sergeant. After he was discharged, the Red Sox sent him to nearby Lynn, Massachusetts, to play in the Class-B New England League in 1946. Despite having lost three years to military service, he improved his production at the higher level of play: he hit .337, drove in 86 runs, and hit 12 homers.

In 1947, he was promoted to Scranton in the Single-A Eastern League but appeared in only eight games there. He'd won the job over the first-string catcher, hitting a grand slam in the ninth inning to win one game—but then didn't get to catch another game. "You know how politics are in baseball," he says. "I sat on the bench, and they let some catcher catch that had been there the year before. About two or three weeks passed, so I got hold of the manager [Eddie Popowski] and told him, 'Look, I want to play ball. I don't give a damn where it is.' I wanted to play. He said, well, he couldn't do anything about it. They wanted this boy to catch and I got to let him catch. So he caught."

As it happened, the catcher for the Red Sox International League affiliate in Toronto, Gene Desautels, got hurt. The club asked Boston for a replacement and was sent Matt Batts. When Desautels got better, the manager put him back in, but the team's owner laid it on the line: "You get Batts to catching or you're gone." Matt told the manager, Elmer Yoter, that he had no idea why, that he'd never met the owner. It wasn't the only time Toronto's owner helped out the 24-year-old catcher. "When I was on one of the road trips, my old Chevrolet caught fire and my wife was all scared to death, called me about it. Some people got it put out for her. The owner took my car and had the durn thing all fixed and everything, and paid for it and never charged me a nickel for it." As to the owner, Peter Campbell, Matt says even today, "I never have met him." Matt's wife Arlene notes that they were so poor at the time they could hardly afford a gallon of gasoline.

Late in the season, when Toronto's season was over (Batts hit .262, with seven homers and 40 RBIs), both he and pitcher Cot Deal were summoned to play with the Red Sox. Batts struck out in his first at-bat, pinch-hitting for Harry Dorish on September 10. The following day, he started both games of the doubleheader against the Indians. He was 2-for-4 in the first game with a double and

Batts swinging a bat. Courtesy of George Brace Photo.

a home run, and 3-for-3 in the second game, all singles. He made a bit of a splash, hitting .500 in 16 at-bats for manager Joe Cronin.

Batts was the backup catcher for Birdie Tebbetts in 1948 and did quite well, hitting .314 in his 118 at-bats. From the time he hit the big leagues, Batts never played anywhere other than behind the plate. He felt he saw an improvement on the team under new manager Joe McCarthy, he told Peter Golenbock in the book *Red Sox Nation*: "Coming back in '48, it was more organized than the year before….The difference, in my opinion, was Joe McCarthy. He was super. Oh, yeah. He didn't say much, but you just felt great with the man there. You had the feeling that you had to play your best at all times. Not that he was forcing you. It was just that you had that good feeling."

As Birdie's backup—and roommate for three seasons—had McCarthy consulted either him or Tebbetts before selecting Denny Galehouse as the playoff starter in 1948? He had not, and Batts says that McCarthy never said why he decided on Galehouse. The veteran pitcher had done very well against the Indians in an earlier relief stint, and McCarthy thought the other pitchers were, in Batts' words, "kind of wore out." It didn't work out, but McCarthy was "a great manager. No doubt about it. He was the best that I ever was with."

Batts really enjoyed the 1948 team and enthused about it to Golenbock: "When you woke up in the morning, you wanted to get to the ballpark to play ball, because you enjoyed it, and you loved the people you were with, loved the manager, loved the coaches, and of course, we had great ballplayers." He did admit, though, the team was "upset" about McCarthy naming Galehouse: "The whole 25 ballplayers. I don't think there was one of them that wasn't upset.…We lost some respect for McCarthy, everybody got kind of down on him because of it."[1]

In 1949, Batts got in more games, but didn't hit as well (.242 in 157 at-bats.) "I just had to wait my turn," he says. "The more someone can play, and get up to the plate, and hit every day, every day, every day he can hit better that day, rather than play one day and five or six games later, play another. You're just hitting and missing. You're not going to be a good hitter doing that."

In 1950, Matt got even more work, and improved to

.273, but when manager Steve O'Neill came in to take over from Lou Boudreau (who had succeeded McCarthy), it became less enjoyable. "Steve O'Neill didn't like me for some reason. I thought I was a friend of his, because I knew one of his sons and one of his daughters, you know. Through baseball. When they got him over there, I figured, well, everything's going to be all right." It was not. And early in 1951, he was traded to the St. Louis Browns in a complicated deal that saw the Red Sox acquire Les Moss, while sending the Browns $100,000, Batts, Jim Suchecki, and a player to be named later, who proved to be Jim McDonald. It was, Batts remembers, originally meant to be a three-way deal. St. Louis was supposed to trade him on to Detroit, but that didn't happen until the following February.

He had hoped to get more playing time with St. Louis, but was blocked there by Sherm Lollar. He is blunt about playing for the Browns: "That was the worst place I ever wanted to play." He admits, though, that he did well, hitting .302 with St. Louis in 1951. And he had a number of experiences to look back on later—catching Satchel Paige among them. Bill Veeck was the owner and Batts was there for the Eddie Gaedel game.

After arriving in Detroit, Batts served as backup to Joe Ginsberg in 1952, struggling with a disappointing .237 average and a paltry 13 RBIs. When Ginsberg was sent to the Indians in an eight-player trade in June 1953, Batts took over as first-string catcher, and boosted his average to .278, hitting six homers and driving in 43 runs in 374 at-bats, the most he ever had in major league ball. On the flip side, he suffered the misfortune of being the catcher in the June 17, 1953 game when the Red Sox scored 17 runs in one inning. But back on August 25, 1952 he'd enjoyed being the backstop for Virgil Trucks' second no-hitter of the season.

He missed a lot of time in 1954. He came down ill and was diagnosed as having hemorrhaging ulcers. Never having had stomach trouble of any sort, it was a mystery. "I never had had a stomach ache. I don't know what it was. I know I bled like a stuffed hog, I know that." After two days in the hospital, with the Tigers visiting Boston, Batts determined to check himself out. Told he couldn't leave, he simply absented himself. "I went out the back door, caught me a train and went to Boston, and that's where they found out that I had lost over 70 percent of my blood and they rushed me to a hospital, to the doctor, and I stayed there 30 days in bed. I had to eat baby food for gosh knows how long. About a year."

Batts was traded to the White Sox at the end of May, then traded in early December to Baltimore which in turn sold him to Indianapolis in April 1955, before the season began. "I was going to Baltimore with Paul Richards to be his catcher. One practice in spring training, Richards come up with the idea of pitching the ball underhanded in the rundowns, between first and second, second and third, third and home. Well, old dumb-butted me, when the play got to Pesky and I, Richards asked Pesky, 'How do you like that, Pesk?' And of course, Pesky was smarter than I was. He said, 'Oh yes, that's all right.' He said, 'Batts, how's that with you? Is that all right with you?' I said, 'No, I don't know. They've been throwing the ball overhanded for 150 years. Someone's going to get stung on this game.' Next day, I was gone." The Orioles sold him to Indianapolis on April 12.

Even with Indianapolis, he hit only .231, though when he got a shot with the Reds in early July when Hobie Landrith was placed on the DL and Cincinnati purchased his contract, he posted a .254 average. His career pretty much just petered out. He spent most of 1956 in the Southern Association playing for Nashville (other than three at-bats for Cincinnati), hitting .258. He split time in 1957 between Birmingham and—back where it all began on the gravel streets—San Antonio.

"I just finally retired. I didn't want to bum around in the minor leagues. I was getting up in age. Being sick like I had been, I didn't feel like doing too much. I had been going to spring training all these years, and stopping over in Baton Rouge, Louisiana, and helping the boys in the kids baseball clinic here. I didn't have a job in San Antonio or anything."

He and his wife, Arlene, have two daughters. One of them married the brother of longtime Boston sportswriter Larry Claflin. The family moved to the Louisiana state capital, Baton Rouge. Matt became friends with the sheriff, who initiated a program for juveniles—"instead of the regular deputies arresting juveniles, we would go out and pick them up and talk to them and see if we couldn't get things straightened out." He worked in the district attorney's office, while his wife ran Batts Printing, a business he'd begun with an attorney friend. "We had to buy another press, and then another one. Business got to be so good that I quit the DA's office and went in to help her, and we made it into quite of a great business. We sold it a few years ago and we just retired. We moved out here to the Country Club of Louisiana. Nicklaus built the course out here, and made it a nice subdivision. It's all gated and everything, and I do nothing but play golf."

Note

1. *Red Sox Nation*, pp. 176–77

Sources

Interviews by Bill Nowlin on March 5, 2006 and April 26, 2007.

EARL CALDWELL *by Ray Birch*

G	ERA	W	L	SV	GS	GF	CG	SHO	IP	H	R	ER	BB	SO	HR	HBP	WP	BFP
8	13.00	1	1	0	0	3	0	0	9	11	14	13	11	5	2	1	0	46

G	AB	R	H	2B	3B	HR	RBI	BB	SO	BA	OBP	SLG	SB	HBP
8	3	0	1	0	0	0	0	0	1	.333	.333	.333	V0	0

A right-handed pitcher with a side-arm, almost underhanded delivery, Earl Caldwell, born on April 9, 1907 in Sparks, Texas, spent most of his lengthy professional baseball career in the minor leagues, winning 323 games, beginning with Temple/Mexia of the Texas Association in 1926 and ending with Harlingen of the Big State League in 1954. Caldwell appeared in the major leagues with four teams: the Philadelphia Phillies, the St. Louis Browns, the Chicago White Sox, and the Boston Red Sox, compiling a pitching record of 33 wins and 43 losses and a 4.69 ERA in 200 games. He accomplished a feat few pitchers could claim—becoming a 20-game winner in each of four decades, from the 1920s into the 1950s.

In 1924, while at Holland High School in Holland, Texas, Caldwell responded to the principal's recruitment call for baseball players, thinking that his 6-foot frame would suit him well to try out at first base. The principal, though, who also served as the baseball coach, was desperate for pitching. He took a hoop from an apple barrel and set it on the side of a barn, saying that whoever was the most accurate at throwing balls inside the hoop would be the pitcher on the team. Caldwell threw eight of 10 pitches inside the hoop and, by doing so, set in motion his pitching career.[1]

In 1926, after finishing two years at Thorp Spring College, he took a teaching/principal position in Rogers, Texas. To be eligible for the position, he had to be 21 years of age; he told them that he was born in 1905 which explains why he is sometimes listed as older than he actually was.[2] However, after pitching an exhibition game against Temple/Mexia of the Class D Texas Association, Caldwell left the teaching profession to become a professional baseball player. His performance that day had impressed the Temple manager so much that he signed Earl immediately. Caldwell pitched well for Temple and, within a month, was signed by Waco of the Class-A Texas League. At Waco, from 1926 to 1928, Caldwell compiled a 21—24 record with 24 complete games, earning him a call-up to the major leagues with the National League's last-place Philadelphia Phillies, who purchased him from Waco.

Earl Caldwell with Indianapolis. Courtesy of George Brace Photo.

On September 8, 1928, the slow, easy-going Texan made his major league debut against the Boston Braves, scattering six hits in a 4–0 complete game shutout in the second game of a doubleheader. The Associated Press summary of the game described Caldwell as having a "sweeping curve flung with a side-arm delivery."[3] Reports from the mid-1930s described him as pitching "underhanded." However, his second start, against the Brooklyn Robins, was not as successful, as he gave up 12 hits and nine runs in a 10–0 loss. He followed that up with a 5–3 loss to the St. Louis Cardinals, giving up 11 hits in seven innings while issuing four walks. Despite a promise from manager Burt Shotton that he would be brought back the following year, the Phillies returned Caldwell to Waco in March 1929, where he spent the season earning 21 wins in 291 innings pitched. During the winter of 1928, he began work as plant manager for the Harlingen Citrus Association.

In 1930, "Teach" Caldwell began pitching with Waco once more before going to the Wichita Falls team, also of the Texas League, where he had a 12-game winning streak. In December, his contract was purchased by the Milwaukee Brewers of the American Association. Caldwell spent three seasons in Milwaukee, from 1931 through 1933, during which he lost more games than he won, with an ERA of almost 5.00. In 1934, the Brewers sent him to his third Texas League, San Antonio. Caldwell had two impressive years there, winning 19 games in 1935, with a 2.27 ERA. After six years out of major league ball, he was summoned to the Browns later that season, appearing in six more major league games and winning three, including a 1–0 three-hit win against Schoolboy Rowe and the American League champion Tigers on September 22.

Caldwell spent the 1936 season with a dismal Browns team, winning only seven games while losing 16. After pitching in nine games in 1937 without a decision, Caldwell was sold by the Browns to Toronto of the International League on June 1, posting a 10–12 record for the season there. He spent the next two full seasons and part of a third in Toronto before being sold to Indianapolis of the American Association in May, 1940. Despite a 5–12 win-loss record at Indianapolis, Caldwell had a respectable ERA of 3.56 with six complete games. When asked about his record in the minors after being sent down by the Browns, Caldwell later admitted, "I had an arm that felt like a toothache every time I pitched for the Browns and after I had drifted back to the minors, I was at the point of giving up baseball as a bad job at the end of the 1940 season." However, after playing the next season for a semipro club in Harlingen, Texas, he felt no pain in his arm. "The weather was warm and I suppose that the adhesions in my arm had broken," Caldwell related.

After his stint with the semi-pro Harlingen club, Caldwell signed with Fort Worth, yet another Texas League team. The move proved to be a good one since he had two stellar seasons in which he led the league in innings pitched in both 1941 and 1942. In addition, he posted victory totals of 22 and 21, respectively, with ERAs of 1.57 and 2.33 and placed third in league MVP voting. His former team, Milwaukee, took note of his success and acquired him for the 1943 season. Caldwell continued his winning ways for the Brewers, especially in the 1944 season, when he won 19 games. During the season, Caldwell opined about what he would look for in a young pitcher, saying, "If I were looking for a young pitcher,

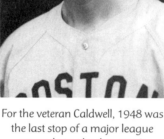

For the veteran Caldwell, 1948 was the last stop of a major league career dating back to 1928. Courtesy of George Brace Photo.

I'd pick a good-sized man, loose, not awkward, who can throw hard. I don't care whether or not he knows how to hold the ball for a curve. You can teach him everything else if he has speed. Remember Bob Feller?"

Caldwell's success in Milwaukee earned him a contract with the Chicago White Sox for the 1945 and 1946 seasons, during which he showed a knack for winning games played under the lights.[4] He didn't lack confidence; at age 38—apparently—he told the Associated Press in February 1945 that he was a better pitcher than ever before and predicted he'd win 15 for the White Sox. He also felt that pitching in the American League would be as easy as pitching in the American Association, declaring that "In the big leagues, each team has more good hitters than in the minors but you always have better fielders and I have always been a big winner when I played on teams with strong infields. Red Sox scout Billy Disch agreed he was good: "Caldwell is a much faster and much better pitcher than when he was with the Browns. Now he would help any big league club."

Caldwell was 6–7 in 1945, but threw over 100 innings, and he blossomed in 1946, when his 13 wins and 2.08 ERA (he was 13–4, used exclusively in relief, and finished a league-leading 37 games) earned him enough votes to finish in 14th place in the AL's Most Valuable Player

balloting. Using his puzzling sidearm delivery, he accomplished this despite suffering a badly swollen thumb that hampered him towards the end of the season. He was, of course, well behind winner Ted Williams, but it was certainly the crowning achievement of his major league career.

During the season, Caldwell, in his practical way of looking at his baseball experience, related, "I feel now like I could pitch nine innings easy, but I probably will last a couple of years longer as a relief pitcher and that suits me. I enjoy the life in major league baseball so until I fade out again, I'll stay at it." When asked to explain how he was doing so well now in the major leagues after so many years in the minors, he stated, "Well, my fast ball—while not fast—has got more stuff on it than it ever had. It's a sinker and makes the hitters top it often and hit on the ground, so there's a better chance for double plays. I don't know why it breaks better than it ever did. I just tinkered with it through the years and finally stumbled on the knack of doing it.

An unimpressive 1947 season began with an uncontested divorce granted his wife Myrtle on grounds of infidelity and was hampered by injuries during the season, but the White Sox kept him on their roster. His poor 1–5 start in the 1948 campaign dampened White Sox interest in him and he was placed on waivers, claimed by the Boston Red Sox for $10,000 on July 26, 1948. Boston sent Mike Palm to Birmingham to make room for the veteran Methusaleh of the mound. Upon arriving in Boston, Caldwell was given number 20 for his uniform, after which he remarked, "Glad they gave me a smaller number. They always kidded me in Chicago that number 46 was not only my number, but also my age." At a later time, when asked about why he has lasted in baseball for so long, he replied, "You remember baseball thrills, old and new; that's why it's such a great game and I guess why I remain young."

After bouncing around the minors for so many years and pitching for so many hapless teams, Caldwell was finally with a team involved in a pennant race. But in a season that would again end in disappointment for Red Sox fans, with a playoff loss to Cleveland, Caldwell appeared in eight games with a 1–1 record and an ERA of 13.00—statistics that signaled the end of his major league career. One shining moment in his dismal year was the attainment of five years in the majors, which qualified him for the players' pension plan.

The 1949 season found Caldwell, by now 42 years old, pitching for the Birmingham Barons of the Southern Association, after being sold by the Red Sox. After a second season there, he moved on to Harlingen of the Class B Gulf Coast League for the 1951 and 1952 seasons, where he won 19 and 20 games respectively; to Lafayette of the Evangeline League as a player-manager in 1953 (still strong, there was one day where he pitched two games in a doubleheader, losing 2–1, then winning, 5–1) and as player-manager for Harlingen/Corpus Christi of the Class-B Big State League in 1954, after which he finally retired from baseball and took a position as manager of the Mission (Texas) Citrus Growers, a co-operative farm association. He served as an agent between the association and wholesale buyers in the North and East. He played his last game on August 2 and threw four-plus innings of relief, yielding only two unearned runs, getting the win—and singling, to spark the come-from-behind rally that saw Corpus Christi win the game.

Author Lloyd Johnson notes one interesting aspect of the 1953 season; Caldwell's son, Earl Jr., served as catcher for his father on the Lafayette team. The two figured in an unusual play where Earl, as the pitcher, was called for a balk on a pitch that Earl, Jr., as the catcher was called for catcher's interference.[5]

Caldwell died on September 15, 1981, leaving behind his wife, Naomi; three sons, James, Larry and Jon; and a daughter, Charlene; Earl Jr. predeceased his father, dying in 1979.

Persistence, determination, and a love for the game seem to be what motivated Earl Caldwell to stay in baseball. In an era when professional baseball players feel slighted when they are sent down for more seasoning, Caldwell survived many trips to the minor leagues without complaint. His attitude toward the game is reflected in this quote by him: "My only wish is that all young players give baseball the best there is in them while playing the game."[6]

Notes

1. "Caldwell Back in Big Time at 39"—Sam Levy, *The Sporting News*, February 15, 1945.
2. "Pitcher Caldwell Quits at 47 in B League; Winner of 391," *Washington Post and Times Herald*, August 3, 1954, p.23. He noted the irony in baseball that most players made themselves out to be younger. "But I was born April 9, 1907, and am 46."
3. "Phillies Upset Braves Twice," Associated Press. September 9, 1928.
4. "Sox Fireman Caldwell Goes Like Blazes at 41," Milt Woodard, *The Sporting News*, August 28, 1946.
5. Johnson, Lloyd, *The Minor League Registry* (Baseball America, 2000)
6. "Earl Caldwell Still Hurling Well at 48," *Washington Post*, June 16, 1953, p.19.

COT DEAL *by Pat Doyle*

G	ERA	W	L	SV	GS	GF	CG	SHO	IP	H	R	ER	BB	SO	HR	HBP	WP	BFP
4	0.00	1	0	0	0	4	0	0	4	3	0	0	3	2	0	0	3	18

G	AB	R	H	2B	3B	HR	RBI	BB	SO	BA	OBP	SLG	SB	HBP
4	0	0	0	0	0	0	0	0	0	0	0	0	0	0

Most people who have become baseball fans since 1990 have never heard of Cot Deal. If they look hard, they will find his major league career summarized in six lines of print in the baseball encyclopedias. If they look harder, they will find something about him as a minor league manager or major league coach in old newspapers or team histories. What has not been written is that Cot Deal spent 50 years in sthe game and, even in his retirement, he continues to be a baseball man.

Over the course of those years, he was a teammate of Ted Williams, Stan Musial, and Red Schoendienst; a minor league manager of Bob Gibson; a pitching coach of Catfish Hunter; and a friend

Deal had a perfect 0.00 ERA in the four innings he pitched in 1948. Courtesy of George Brace Photo.

and advisor to many hundreds, including hall of famers, stars, and ordinary folks.

The same graciousness that has been part of Cot for all those years was extended to a visitor recently as Cot reviewed his years in and outside of baseball in his Oklahoma City home.

The Deal connection to Oklahoma goes back over 100 years, to just after the days of the 1889 Oklahoma Land Rush. The third of four children born to Roy and Ruth Deal, Ellis Fergason Deal arrived on January 23, 1923, in Arapaho, a small town in the western part of the state where Roy Deal taught school. The family eventually settled in Oklahoma City, where Ellis grew up and was called Cot for his cotton-top hair color.

Cot's busiest year was 1954 with the Cardinals. Courtesy of Cot Deal.

All of the children were athletic. The oldest, Roy, Jr., played a season of minor league baseball before retiring due to arm trouble. The youngest, Clarence, was the Oklahoma University third baseman after he came home from being a prisoner of the Germans in World War II. Cot's sister and brothers all live in the Oklahoma City area today.

Cot's baseball skills developed early and, as a 16-year old, he was invited by the Pirates to spend a week in Pittsburgh. The Pirates' manager, Hall of Famer Pie Traynor, is remembered by Cot as "a wonderfully warm man". At the end of the week in Pittsburgh, Traynor gave the last glove he played with to the high schooler. Sadly, after returning home, Cot used the glove in a practice session, put it down to take batting practice, and never saw the glove again.

After signing with the Pirates two years before his high school graduation, Cot spent 1940 with Hutchinson, Kansas, of the Western Association, batting .312 while splitting time between the outfield and third base. The following two years saw him climb the organization ladder to Harrisburg in the Inter-State League before World War II called. As a physical training instructor for the Air Corps, Cot remained stateside until his discharge in 1945.

The next season was spent with the International League's Toronto Maple Leafs, where he became a pitcher and was sold to the Boston Red Sox. Late in 1947 he was called up to the Sox where he lost his only decision, singled in his first at-bat, and drove in his only American League run with a game-winning pinch hit off Bob Lemon.

During spring training in 1948, after earning a spot as a starting pitcher, Cot hurt his arm for the first time. It was an injury that would plague him for the rest of his career. Reviewing his remaining ten seasons, he says, "In my own mind, I don't think I should have ever pitched. I hurt my arm early and never really got over it." Despite the pain, he would eventually pitch in 45 games with the Red Sox and Cardinals, winning three and losing four, and would win another 108 minor league games.

Cot and his sore arm were traded by the Red Sox in 1949 to the Cardinals' Columbus team in exchange for infielder Charlie Harrington. For the next ten years, he established himself in the organization as a pitcher, outfielder, and switch-hitting pinch hitter. Former teammate Vern Benson recalls, "Cot Deal was one of the best competitors I have ever had the pleasure of playing with".

Another teammate, Jack Faszholz, remembers that "Cot could probably do anything that was required on the baseball field."

Cot's one regret from his playing days is that he did not have the chance to be a regular catcher. During spring training of 1951, he asked to be the catcher for Columbus. He earned the job, but a family emergency called him away for a few days and, upon his return, was told by manager Harry Walker that "we need pitching". He then returned to the mound to win 10 games in spite of his sore arm. From then until he stopped playing in 1959, his on-field action would be divided between the outfield and the mound.

Those eleven years in the Cardinal organization saw a number of accomplishments as he moved from player to coach to manager. Among them were:

— Starting and completing a twenty-inning game for Columbus against Louisville on September 3, 1949. In addition to winning the game and giving up just one earned run in twenty innings, Cot also went 4-for-8 at bat.

— Hitting his only major league home run off Cincinnati's Bud Podbielan in 1954.

— Being named player-coach at Rochester under manager Dixie Walker in 1956.

— Being named the first manager of the community-owned Rochester Red Wings in 1957 and reaching the playoffs during his second season.

— Finally getting a chance to be a catcher. He recalls, "My 'most fun' day was the day in Miami in 1957 when, as the manager, with three catchers (Gene Green, Dick Teed, and Bill Schantz) all hurt, I caught Bob Blaylock in a game. We beat Satchel Paige, and I drove in the winning run. I'll never forget it."

— Being honored with Cot Deal Day in Rochester in 1957 and receiving an Olds 88 station wagon.

Among the players Cot managed in Rochester was Billy Joe Bowman, a college all-American who went on to win 56 minor league games and earn All-Star honors in the Southern Association. Bowman says, "I will always remember Cot as one of the few men who would look you straight in the eye whether he be talking to you or you to him and you always felt he cared about you. You will not find many like that in baseball." Jack Faszholz remembers that Cot was "a very self-confident and intelligent man, respectful to all his teammates."

The 1959 season brought excitement and disappointment. The excitement came early on the morning of July 26. The Red Wings were in Havana playing a Saturday night game against their International League rivals, the Havana Sugar Kings. At midnight, a celebration began in honor of the new Cuban government of Fidel Castro. Despite music, fireworks, and gunfire, the game continued and, following an 11th inning argument, Cot was ejected by first base umpire Frank Guzzetta.

Utility infielder Frank Verdi replaced Cot in the third base coaching box, and took over while still wearing his protective batting liner inside his cap. As the twelfth inning began, the tumult increased and gunfire erupted inside the stadium. Suddenly, Havana shortstop Leo Cardenas felt a bullet graze his right shoulder, and coach Verdi was struck by a .45 slug which passed through his cap, deflected off the batting liner through his earlobe and glanced off his shoulder. The umpires immediately suspended the game and the Red Wings left that afternoon for Rochester. Verdi, only slightly injured, stayed with the team and kept his bullet-pierced cap as a souvenir. Had Cot remained in the game, without a batting liner, a very different fate might have resulted. (A fuller account of this event can be found in the author's article, "Gunfire in the Ballpark", found on the *Baseball Almanac* site.)

The disappointment of 1959 came after the next road trip with the Red Wings mired in the second division. In early August, Cot announced his resignation to general manager George Sisler, Jr. and planned to return home for the rest of the summer. Before leaving Rochester, however, he received a call from Cincinnati manager Fred Hutchinson, who asked him to be the Reds' pitching coach. The result was one of baseball's more unusual trades, in which Cot went to the Reds and their previous pitching coach, Clyde King, replaced him as the manager in Rochester.

Joining the Reds would mark the beginning of a 20-year journey across America as manager, coach, and front-office executive for a variety of organizations. The itinerary reads as follows:

1959–1960—Cincinnati as pitching coach.
1961 Indianapolis (American Association) as pennant-winning manager.
1962–1964—Houston as the first pitching coach of the expansion franchise.
1965 New York Yankees as pitching coach.
1966–1967—Kansas City Athletics as pitching coach.
1968—Oklahoma City (Pacific Coast League) as manager.
1969—Oklahoma City (American Association) as manager.
1970–1971—Cleveland as pitching coach
1972—Toledo (International League) as coach.
1973—Toledo as coach and manager.
1973–1974—Detroit as pitching coach.
1975–1977—Out of baseball in private business.
1978—Columbus (International League) as coach.
1979–1982—Oklahoma City (Pacific Coast League) as coach and interim manager.
1983–1985—Houston as outfield coach and defensive coordinator.
1986—Chicago White Sox as assistant farm director.
1987–1989—San Francisco as minor league organization hitting and outfield coach.

For every stop along the way, for every hiring and every firing, there is a story.

The year and a half in Cincinnati would begin a close friendship with Fred Hutchinson that ended end too soon with Hutch's death in 1964 at the age of 45. After the 1960 season, their friendship continued from a distance after Cot was asked by general manager Gabe Paul to manage the Reds' affiliate in Indianapolis. There he led the team to the pennant, but at the price of missing a World Series with the Reds. Ray Rippelmeyer, a 13–8 veteran starter on with Indianapolis, remembers Cot as "one of the best managers I had the opportunity to play for."

When Harry Craft was hired as the first manager of the Houston Colt 45's, he was permitted to choose only one of his coaches. Cot was that choice. Three seasons later, the team changed stadiums, nicknames, uniforms, and managers. Exiting with the manager was his hand-chosen pitching coach.

During his years in Houston, Cot made a profound impression on a promising young pitcher and future manager, Larry Dierker, who recalls: "Like most players in the '60s, I smoked cigarettes. One day, after a workout in Cocoa, Cot saw me smoking and came over with a concerned look on his face. He told me that if I was going to smoke I should at least wait until my heartbeat slowed down and I wasn't breathing hard. I knew it was bad for me and quit a few years later. But my memory of Cot was that he cared more about us as a father than as a coach. I didn't come across many coaches or managers with this admirable quality during my 38 years in the game."

After the 1964 season ended, Cardinals' manager Johnny Keane quit the world championship team to join the Yankees. His first staff selection was to make Cot his pitching coach. The 1965 season marked the beginning of a decade-long Yankee drought and, following a sixth-place finish, Cot was fired.

Shortly after the season ended, Cot was hired by Kansas City A's manager Haywood Sullivan. Before spring training began, Sullivan was hired as Red Sox general manager and his replacement in Kansas City was Alvin Dark. The change proved to be a positive one, as Cot found Dark to be "a very, very smart manager. Of all the managers I ever was with, he was the best 'checker player' as far as making moves". With the A's still a few years away from their dominance in Oakland, Dark and his staff were relieved and another move was imminent.

During 1968 and 1969, Cot managed Houston's Triple-A affiliate in Oklahoma City. Both were losing seasons, and 1969 was particularly difficult as the Vietnam War took thirteen players from the roster. One of the few memorable events was when Cot's oldest son joined the team as a catcher. Randy Deal, a graduate student at the University of Oklahoma at the time, was given permission by the school to take time off to play professional baseball under his Dad. The 89ers finished fifth and Cot was let go at the end of the season.

In 1970, Alvin Dark called and asked Cot to be his pitching coach in Cleveland. When Dark was let go during the 1971 season, Cot stayed on as Johnny Lipon finished out the season.

Lipon moved on in 1972 to manage the Tigers' International League affiliate in Toledo, with Cot as his pitching coach. In 1973, Cot replaced Lipon as manager and then moved up to the Tigers as their pitching coach when they fired Billy Martin and Art Fowler. He stayed there in 1974, when they named Ralph Houk manager. Houk fired Cot at the end of that season, telling the press, "I need someone with a more positive attitude." The 1975 Tigers, with a new pitching coach, finished the season last in their division and with the league's second highest earned run average.

Deal spent six seasons coaching for the Astros. Courtesy of Cot Deal.

From 1975 to 1977, Cot worked in the Oklahoma City area in private business. But baseball beckoned and, in 1978, he joined the Columbus Clippers and their manager, Johnny Lipon, as a coach.

From 1979 to 1982 he returned to Oklahoma City as a coach in the Phillies' organization.

In 1983 he rejoined the Houston Astros as a coach under longtime friend Bob Lillis and, following the 1985 season, he joined Lillis in being terminated despite a 248–238 record for those three seasons.

In 1986, Cot's only front-office experience took place, as White Sox farm director Alvin Dark hired him as an assistant. At the end of the season, General Manager Ken Harrelson and his staff were let go.

The final stop in this long career came with San Francisco as a minor league coach from 1987 to 1989. Following the 1989 season, after fifty years, Cot called it a day and retired.

While baseball has been accused of recirculating managers and coaches from team to team, not every case bears out the "good old boys" syndrome. The people who employed Cot over the years—Fred Hutchinson, Alvin Dark, Johnny Lipon—found his baseball skills and personal integrity to be valuable assets on their teams. The positive comments by players whom he managed and coached testify to his reputation as a teacher and leader. Ray Rippelmeyer recalls that when he "started on a managing and coaching career of my own, I used a lot of what I had learned from Cot Deal."

During his conversations, Cot frequently reflects on the number of former teammates and friends who are no longer alive. Many of the people for whom he had the highest regard—Fred Hutchinson, Allie Reynolds,

Johnny Lipon, "Hoot" Evers, Harry Craft, Mel McGaha, and Mo Mozzali—are gone now. Others remain, and Cot treasures their correspondences. The annual Christmas cards and letters have been replaced to a large extent by e-mail, as Cot's computer skills reveal a man much younger than his nearly 80 years.

Retirement has been good to Cot as he has watched his family grow and succeed. He and Katie celebrated their 60th wedding anniversary on September 23, 2002. All three children, Randy, Elyse, and Donnie, are employed in health-related fields and all live within several hours of home.

Billy Joe Bowman, whom Cot managed in Rochester, has fond memories of the Deals: "I enjoyed every moment I spent with Cot and Katie. They are a wonderful pair and so down to earth." Jack Faszholz adds, "My wife was always impressed with how well-behaved and respectful Cot's and Katie's kids were."

Home for the Deals is a lovely lakeside house in suburban Oklahoma City where they, their dog and their cat entertain frequent visits from the children, grandchildren, and great-grandchildren. Their health has been good despite Cot's battle with prostate cancer beginning in 1989, shortly after he retired. He has long since passed the five-year mark and is officially known as a cancer survivor. He is vocal in recommending that all men over 50 receive an annual checkup. He and Katie recently celebrated their 65th wedding anniversary. In his words, they were "married at 19, parents at 21—and grew up with our kids."

He follows baseball closely. When asked about the differences between baseball in the 1940's and today, he cites several areas:

—The umpires are more powerful and less accommodating than they once were.

—The game has advanced technologically with specialized pitching machines and videotapes.

—The game has become more weighted toward offense with the designated hitter rule, smaller stadiums with less foul territory, and smaller strike zones.

He does not begrudge current players their salaries although he, as a minor league player and major league coach, never approached the incomes they now enjoy. Each winter he went to Puerto Rico to manage in the Puerto Rican League, adding to his income but forgoing his desire to earn a college degree. But the comfort that he and his family enjoy is largely due to his baseball earnings.

In the world of baseball, the term "organization man" is becoming less known in our current era. The names that were synonymous with loyalty—Eddie Popowski, Johnny Pesky, Frankie Crosetti etc.—are harder to come by. Cot Deal was a loyal baseball man; loyal to the organizations he served, loyal to managers who hired him and trusted him, loyal to the fans who supported him.

In his retirement Cot finds pleasure in recalling the "old days," the players and games of many years ago. He is equally comfortable talking about the game today, its problems and its attractions. Although his interests and commitments range widely, Cot Deal is, in the best sense of the term, a baseball man.

This article originally appeared on www.baseballalmanac.com.

Sources

Numerous interviews with Ellis "Cot" Deal, 2002–2007
The Sporting News Baseball Guide, 1941–1960
Total Baseball, Sixth Edition
The Professional Baseball Database, Ver. 6.0

DOMINIC DIMAGGIO *by John H. Contois*

G	AB	R	H	2B	3B	HR	RBI	BB	SO	BA	OBP	SLG	SB	HBP
155	648	127	185	40	4	9	87	101	58	.285	.383	.401	10	2

Who hits the ball and makes it go?
Dominic DiMaggio.
Who runs the bases fast, not slow?
Dominic DiMaggio.
Who's better than his brother Joe?
Dominic DiMaggio.
But when it comes to gettin' dough,
They give it all to brother Joe.
—Parody of Les Brown song: "Joltin' Joe DiMaggio"

It is easy to overlook the remarkable career of Dominic DiMaggio. After all, he lived in the shadow of two famous ballplayers: his brother Joe, arguably the greatest all-around ballplayer of his era, and good friend and teammate Ted Williams, a Red Sox legend. Yet Dom was as solid a major-leaguer as there was in any era, and he was beloved by Red Sox fans. He was a career .298 hitter who played in seven All-Star games. He had a 34-game hitting streak in 1949, still a Red Sox record, and is one of only three players to average more than 100 runs per season throughout his career. For the years he played, he led the major leagues in hits, was second in runs and third in doubles. On the Red Sox all-time list, Dom is seventh in runs scored (1,046), doubles (308), walks, and total bases; eighth in hits (1,680), and 10th in extra-base hits. Many baseball fans will agree with David Halberstam, who in *The Summer of '49* refers to Dom as the most underrated player of his day.

Dominic Paul DiMaggio, the youngest of nine children, was born on February 12, 1917, and grew up in a typical working-class home at 2047 Taylor Street in the North Beach-Telegraph Hill section of San Francisco. Dom and brother Joe used to sell newspapers in downtown San Francisco on the corners of Sauter and Sansone Streets.

The Little Professor Dominic DiMaggio.

The patriarch of the clan, Giuseppe DiMaggio, was a hardworking fisherman from Sicily who spoke little English. Their mother, Rosalee, a former schoolteacher, covered for the boys so that they could play baseball, which their father found frivolous and which violated Giuseppe's code of a strong work ethic. Three of the DiMaggio brothers, Joe, Vince, and Dom, went on to play center field in the major leagues, and it was said of the brothers that Joe was the best hitter, Dom had the best arm, and Vince, who had aspirations to become an opera singer, had the best voice.

In his youth Dom thought of becoming a chemical engineer; he was offered an academic and baseball scholarship to Santa Clara College, but chose instead to follow the path of his older brothers. Vince had set the stage by winning a roster spot on the minor-league San Francisco Seals in the Pacific Coast League at the start of the 1932 season. Vince paved the way for his brother Joe to join the team when a shortstop position later became available.

While Dom was still in high school, Joe was burning up the Pacific Coast League and was sold to the New York Yankees for $25,000. In 1934, as a senior at Galileo High School, Dom was a solid pitcher and shortstop hitting .400. Dom later played shortstop for the North Beach Merchants sandlot team while working at the Simmons mattress factory. He was scouted by the Seals, and later attended a joint baseball camp and tryout for the Seals and Cincinnati Reds. He was immediately called in to the Seals office and offered a contract.

In 1936, Joe made it to the New York Yankees, and in the following year Vince made it to the Boston Braves.

Dom and skipper Joe McCarthy.

Meanwhile, Dom began playing for the Seals in 1937. Dom hit .306 that season, but was still criticized by some who thought he was signed not because of talent, but because of his famous last name. Dom turned down a chance to sit out the last game of the season in order to preserve his .302 average and instead added four points. Dom continued to prove himself with a solid 1938 season, hitting .308; then 1939 proved to be his breakout season. Dom managed to add 20 pounds to his diminutive frame, and with instruction from Lefty O'Doul, the Seals manager, Dom raised his average to .361, finishing second in batting in the Pacific Coast League and winning the MVP award. Dom was first in hits and runs scored and second in stolen bases and triples. A few years earlier, O'Doul had also helped Joe raise his average by almost 60 points. Dominic had high praise for O'Doul in his 1990 book, *Real Grass, Real Heroes*, calling him "... far and away the finest hitting instructor that ever put on a baseball uniform." After the 1939 season, the Red Sox purchased Dom's contract for $75,000.

Lefty O'Doul once again showed his insight into the game by telling reporters in San Francisco that DiMaggio would be a sensation in Boston: "Boston is one town where the fans know and appreciate all-around good ballplayers. Boston is going to idolize Dom" (from *Real Grass, Real Heroes*).

Dominic made his major-league debut on April 16, 1940, and had little trouble adjusting to the big leagues, hitting .301 and scoring 81 runs in 108 games in his rookie season. Going into spring training, Dom was concerned that he might not get to play because Boston was loaded with good outfielders: Ted Williams in left, Doc Cramer in center, Lou Finney in right, and Joe Vosmik, a 10-year veteran, as backup. But Dom, at age 22, had a solid spring and was able to beat out Finney, a .300 hitter the year before, for the starting right fielder's job. Later in the season, Dom was moved to center field, and there he

remained for the rest of his career. The Red Sox showed confidence in DiMaggio by trading Doc Cramer to the Senators during the offseason.

Dom has fond memories of the Red Sox-Yankees rivalry, and especially the media interest in the DiMaggio brothers in center field. He recalls that the newspapers made a big deal out of the first time in 1940 when the Yankees visited Boston for a five-game series. Dom had 11 hits to Joe's nine, or as Dom says, "Twenty hits for the family in one series." One week later in New York, Joe advised his younger brother to move back because the ball carried well in that part of the ballpark. The next day Dom, taking Joe's advice, was able to run down a fly ball hit 460 feet to deep center—off the bat of brother Joe.

In 1941, Dominic went to spring training knowing his role: center fielder and leadoff hitter. After a slow start, which he attributed to tender hands (playing cards in the offseason in his brother Joe's new restaurant in San Francisco instead of fishing with his father) he finished third with 117 runs scored, batted a solid .283, and was named to the All-Star team for the first time. In his first All-Star Game he singled to drive in his brother Joe. The media attention surrounding the DiMaggio brothers, especially with the success of all three center fielders, led to false rumors of a Hollywood movie, and inspired sportswriter Grantland Rice to poetry:

> Out in the olive trail they go —
> Vincent, Dominic, and Joe,
> Lashing, flashing, steaming hot
> In the fabled land of swat.
> Where the big ash sings its song
> For the glory of the throng,
> Or the big mace through the fray
> Sends the apple on its way —
> Watch them as they whirl, careen,
> Over the fields of verdant green.
> Rulers of the batting eye,
> Where their gaudy triples fly,
> In the sunset's shining glow
> Who is it that steals the show?
> Vincent, Dominic, and Joe.

During the '42 season as World War II expanded, many ballplayers were drafted into military service. Around this time Dom was labeled the "Little Professor" because of his 5-foot-9, 168-pound frame, his serious expression, and his glasses—necessary to correct his nearsightedness. Dom earned his second All-Star selection that season while on his way to hitting .286 with 110 runs scored, good for third in the league, 272 total bases, and 36 doubles. Early in the season, Dom tried to enlist in the Navy but was told that his vision was an issue. "I had to fight my way into the Navy," said DiMaggio. "They rejected me because of my eyesight, and for the longest time, I told them I wanted to be in the Navy. I was not about to sit out the war." Despite a 4-F classification, he was able to enlist after completing the season, and left work and home for a three-year stint in the United States Coast Guard. While in the service, DiMaggio played for the Norfolk Naval Training Station team in Virginia and saw overseas duty as well.

Dominic returned to baseball in 1946, along with Ted Williams, Johnny Pesky, Bobby Doerr, and many of the more than 500 professional baseball players who had served during wartime. The Red Sox had an amazing year, finishing 12 games ahead of the Tigers and 17 games ahead of the Yankees, with 104 wins and only 50 losses. Dom was once again an All-Star, hitting .316 and driving in 73 runs. The Red Sox were exuberant about playing in their first World Series since 1918 and very confident.

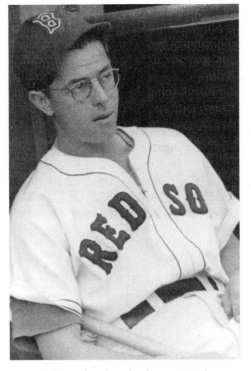

Taking a break in the dugout, 1946.

The Series that year was decided in a legendary Game Seven at Sportsman's Park in St. Louis. In the top of the eighth inning, with a 3–1 Cardinals lead, Dominic came to bat with two outs and men on second and third. With Ted Williams on deck, he knew he would get a pitch to hit and he drove the ball off the wall in right-center. Dom was thinking triple as he hustled around the bases, but he popped a hamstring and hobbled into second base. He was replaced on base and then in center field by Leon Culberson. Ted Williams popped out to end the inning. With the score tied, 3–3, St. Louis took the Series on Enos Slaugher's "mad dash" home from first base after a soft line drive to center off the bat of Harry Walker. Dom believed that if he had been able to remain in the game, the outcome might have been different. He had more experience in center field than Culberson and he was more comfortable with the poor field conditions at Sportsman's Park.

Over the next few seasons DiMaggio was consistently among the league leaders in runs scored, walks, hits, and doubles. In 1947 and 1948, he hit .283 and .285, respectively. In 1948, he was second in runs (127), fourth in walks (101), and fifth in doubles (40). Dom put together the longest hitting streak in Red Sox history in 1949, batting safely in 34 consecutive games. During the streak, from June 26 to August 7, he hit .357 and scored 35 runs. The streak ended against the Yankees on a fly ball to brother Joe. Dom hit .307 that season and finished third in the league in three categories with 186 hits, 126 runs,

and 34 doubles, and he again was named to the All-Star squad.

Dominic met Emily Alberta Frederick in 1943, while playing an exhibition game in Boston to promote War Bonds. Despite a romantic spark between Dom and Emily, he did not see her again until four years later. In 1949 they were married. Emily was not a passionate baseball fan, but she was a passionate community leader. Ted Williams affectionately called her "the Queen" because of her strong personality. Dom and Emily had three children, Dominic, Jr., Emily, and Peter.

1950 was Dom DiMaggio's finest season, with a career high .328 average and 193 hits (both third best in the league), and league-leading marks with 131 runs and 15 stolen bases. In 1951 he continued his hot hitting, putting together a 27-game hitting streak, batting .296 with 189 hits, and scoring a league-leading 113 runs. In 1952 DiMaggio played in just 128 games, but hit a solid .294, and played in his final All-Star Game. After being relegated to the bench the following year and playing in just three early-season games, Dom retired on May 9. The new manager of the Red Sox, Lou Boudreau, had felt that he was past his prime and replaced him in center field with Tommy Umphlett. Dominic had no desire to sit on the bench. He finished with a career .298 average and 1,680 hits.

Johnny Pesky called Dominic DiMaggio "the almost perfect ballplayer, so smart and so talented." Dom was inducted into the Italian American Sports Hall of Fame in 1978, and the Red Sox Hall of Fame in 1995, but he has thus far been overlooked by the Veterans Committee for Cooperstown despite an energetic campaign on his behalf led by former teammate Ted Williams in the 1990s.

Late in his career, Dom expressed concern about the treatment of ballplayers at the hands of some owners. He joined Johnny Murphy, Allie Reynolds, Fred Hutchinson, Bob Feller, Eddie Yost, and others in the early vestiges of a players union, an effort that eventually led to the formation of the Major League Baseball Players Association.

Dominic found success after baseball, as well. In 1953, after he retired from baseball, he founded the American Latex Fiber Corporation along with two partners in Lawrence, Massachusetts. They produced padding for ammunitions packaging, boxcar insulation, and furniture and mattress padding. Dom later bought out his partners and began producing seat padding for the automotive industry. In 1961, he purchased a fire-ravaged company in Pennsylvania and merged the companies to form a new corporation: the Delaware Valley Corporation, and expanded production to include innovative products for the medical, construction, marine and RV industries. The company is still operated by a Dom DiMaggio, although now it is in the hands of eldest son Dominic, Jr.

After Red Sox owner Tom Yawkey died in 1976, DiMaggio headed a group of New England businessmen who put together an offer to purchase the Red Sox. The trust set up to handle the disposition of the ballclub rebuffed a number of offers, in which prospective applicants had invested considerable time and money, leaving a sense that the Haywood Sullivan group had had the inside track all along, resulting a sense of estrangement that lasted for a number of years.

Among other commercial ventures, Dom was involved in the operation of DiMaggio's Restaurant on famed Fisherman's Warf in San Francisco, and in real estate on both coasts. He was co-founder of the Boston Patriots football franchise, and he has actively supported numerous charities. Emily DiMaggio has served as a trustee for Boston's Jimmy Fund for many years. Dom is co-founder (in 1966) and former president of the BoSox Club, now a long-standing fan organization founded to promote interest in the Red Sox and baseball, and to bring closer contact between the Red Sox and the community.

Dom's love for the game of baseball is eloquently expressed in a passage from *Real Grass, Real Heroes:*

> "It was that wonderful sameness, year in and year out. We could always count on baseball to be the same warm and sunny game, on the same fields, in the same cities. We loved baseball not only for

The tablesetters: Dom and Johnny Pesky.

itself but for the secure feeling of continuity it gave you. We felt a loyalty to baseball, because it was loyal to us."

Now over 90, Dominic DiMaggio spends his time between homes in Massachusetts and Florida. He has suffered with Paget's disease since 1962, but he has remained active following the family business and the Red Sox. His sense of humor is evident in his response to a question addressed to him on his 90th birthday:

Ninety tomorrow. Any goals? "Reach 91," he said.

Sources

Halberstam, David. The Teammates: A Portrait of a Friendship. New York: Hyperion, 2003.

DiMaggio, Dominic, with Bill Gilbert. Real Grass, Real Heroes: Baseball's Historic 1941 Season. New York: Zebra Books, 1990.

http://redsoxworld.mlblogs.com/my_weblog/2006/12/dom_di maggio.html. Accessed 1/19/2007.

Zingler, David. "Dominic DiMaggio, Forgotten in Time: August 2002. http://z.lee28.tripod.com/sbnsforgottenintime/id11.html. Accessed 1/19/2007.

http://www.baseballlibrary/ballplayers/D/DiMaggio_Dom.stm. Accessed 1/19/2007.

Browne, Ian. "Dom DiMaggio: Brother of one legend, friend of another." http://boston.redsox.mlb.com/NASApp/mlb/bos/news/bos_news.jsp. Accessed 1/19/2007.

http://www.thediamondangle.com/sitt/dimaggio.html. Assessed 1/19/2007.

Shaughnessy, Dan. "On eve of 90th birthday DiMaggio still on his game." Boston Globe, Feb 11, 2007, www.boston.com/sports/baseball/articles/2007. Assessed June 25, 2007.

www.dvc500.com [Delaware Valley Corp. website]. Accessed June 25, 2007.

JOE DOBSON by Bill Nowlin

G	ERA	W	L	SV	GS	GF	CG	SHO	IP	H	R	ER	BB	SO	HR	HBP	WP	BFP
38	3.56	16	10	2	32	5	16	5	245⅓	237	115	97	92	116	14	1	6	1044

G	AB	R	H	2B	3B	HR	RBI	BB	SO	BA	OBP	SLG	SB	HBP
38	84	9	17	2	0	1	4	6	27	.202	.280	.262	1	0

In the early years of the 21st century, the name of Joe Dobson, a right-handed pitcher who toiled for 10 years with the Red Sox, rarely crops up in discussions of the better Boston players of the past. Nonetheless, his 106–72 record places him ninth on the all-time team list for wins and his .596 winning percentage has him in 13th place among those with 100 or more decisions. Leigh Grossman

succinctly summarized his career: "never a great pitcher, but he was good and consistent for a long time." The only category Dobson ever led his league in was wild pitches, but he was a key component in the pennant-winning year of 1946 and no Red Sox pitcher surpassed him over the following four years when Boston was regularly in contention.

Dobson was a big pitcher for the day, 6'2" tall, with a playing weight of 200 pounds and a shock of wavy hair that earned him the nicknames "Burrhead" and "Curly." Joe hailed from Oklahoma, born in the south-central farm town of Durant on January 20, 1917, a little more than nine years after Oklahoma became the country's 46th state. The youngest of 14 children born to William and Lura Dobson, he moved with his family to Coolidge, Arizona, when Joe was 6 years old. William Dobson was a farmer who turned to carpentry in his later years. Midway between Phoenix and Tucson, it was in Coolidge that Joe was raised and where at age 9 or 10 he lost his left thumb and part of his forefinger in a childhood accident while inexpertly trying to blow up a rock with a dynamite cap a friend had found.

Joe Dobson, 1941.

One of Joe's brothers was a pretty good ballplayer, he recalled. "We'd play catch every day. He'd throw that ball so hard, my hands would hurt."[1] It was during his sophomore year in high school that he began to play baseball. "Before that time I had been content to do all my pitching at prairie dogs and such, just to improve my marksmanship and save money on ammunition." He was helping his dad with carpentry outside of school when he read in the town newspaper that a Dr. Tremble was organizing a team in Tucson and looking for boys who would like to play baseball. He tried out and was added to the team. The first game he pitched, he beat Tombstone. The ballclub came together well and some of the businessmen put some money behind it, naming the team the Tucson Merchants. When Joe won the first game of a doubleheader during the July 1936 Arizona state tournament in Phoenix, he was approached by a Cleveland Indians scout, Grover Land, who asked Joe if he wanted to play pro ball. Joe's feelings at the time reflect those of many: "I would have paid him to sign me up." The Tucson team went on to Wichita for the national semipro tournament and Joe won a couple of games in the semifinals, but they couldn't win it all. Land, though, landed Dobson and signed him to a contract with New Orleans, an Indians farm club in the Southern Association.

His first year in the Cleveland system was spent in Alabama with the Troy (Alabama) Trojans in the Alabama-Florida League under manager Charles Moss. Troy finished second in the six-team Class D league, while Joe posted a record of 19–12 with a 2.27 ERA, leading the league in complete games with 26. He struck out an even 200 batters, walking only 71. His work earned him a quick promotion all the way to the Class A Southern Association, where he pitched in 1938 for Larry Gilbert and the New Orleans Pelicans. At this elevated level, Dobson

was 11–7 (3.29) in 178 innings of work. He made it to the major leagues to stay in 1939, beginning a career that took him right into the 1954 season.

Dobson was hardly a sensation in Cleveland, though. Things started well enough when he was called in to relieve on April 26 after Johnny Broaca had given up four runs to the White Sox in the third inning. Joe gave up three hits and no runs in five innings of work. Manager Ossie Vitt gave him a start four days later in Detroit. He pitched five innings in that game, too, but that didn't go as well: Dobson was tagged for nine runs on 13 hits and lost the 14–1 ballgame. Joe appeared in 35 games, but largely in relief. He had just two more starts, one in June and one in August, and in those, too, the opposition scored into double digits, but the June loss was fully attributable to reliever Johnny Humphries. Dobson threw 78 innings and wound up with a 2–3 record and a 5.88 earned run average.

He pitched an even 100 innings in 1940, and showed some improvement. He ended the season 3–7, appearing in 40 games and recording an ERA of 4.95. The first game he started and won came against the Red Sox on July 21 at Fenway Park. He threw a complete-game, 2–0 shutout, allowing seven hits and walking three, inducing batters to hit into three double plays. Dobson's work that day made an impression on Boston manager Joe Cronin. A few outings earned him recognition in the press, such as a one-hit, 5⅓-inning stint on September 1 termed "brilliant relief pitching" by the Associated Press. Even though Vitt used him often, he felt overlooked. He realized he was, as he put it to Boston sports scribe Johnny Drohan, "just a ball player named Joe.... I couldn't have been any more forgotten had I been a brother to King Tut. I did get in a few ball games but only after all the other pitchers on the bench had been knocked out of there."[2]

A December 12 trade reported at the time as a three-cornered deal brought the pitcher named Joe to Boston. The Red Sox sent Doc Cramer to the Senators for Gee Walker, then traded Jim Bagby, Gene Desautels, and Walker to Cleveland and got Dobson, Odell Hale, and Frankie Pytlak. Dobson was happy to land in Boston. "Joe Cronin probably appreciated me more than the entire Cleveland organization," he told Drohan.

With Bob Feller, Mel Harder, Johnny Allen, and Al Milnar in the rotation, it had been hard to break in as a starter with the Indians, but Dobson had a shot with the 1941 Red Sox as Lefty Grove's career wound down, joining a Boston team with Dick Newsome, Mickey Harris, and Charlie Wagner among the other starters. Dobson showed "hustle and determination and stuff" in spring training in Sarasota.[3] Ed Rumill of the *Christian Science Monitor* predicted early in spring training that "he may turn out to be one of the surprises of the…campaign."[4] For the 1941 season, Newsome won 19, and Wagner and Dobson were second with a dozen wins apiece. Joe didn't last long in his first start, on May 23, but the Yankee Stadium game ended in a 9–9 tie due to darkness. Six days later, he started and won a game against Philadelphia. It had taken him a while to get established, but he became a regular in the rotation and at one point reeled off a string of eight straight victories—something always sure to impress. That winter he could look back at a 12–5 season, with an improved 4.49 ERA, and know that he'd helped the Red Sox to a second-place finish.

Joe credited Frankie Pytlak and Jimmie Foxx with helping turn him around. Joe was 5–5 in mid-August and still struggling with his location when Pytlak told him one day, "Relax, don't try to throw so hard and try to pick your spots around the plate." On another occasion, Foxx said, "Take it easy, Joe. Let up a little. You don't have to strike out every hitter."[5] Nothing special by way of advice, perhaps, but coming from Foxx and coming in a time when coaches rarely gave much real instruction to pitchers, it may have made the difference. Equally important may have been Ted Williams, who had hurt his foot and wanted to take some extra batting practice to help him come back. He asked Joe to throw to him and in the one-on-one pitching repeatedly to a .400 hitter, Joe may have become better able to harness his pitches and develop his control.[6] Author Peter Golenbock added: "They would pretend it was a real game, and Dobson would throw his best. By the time he returned to the Boston lineup as an everyday performer, Williams' batting skills were honed and sharp."[7] Entering 1942, Newsome, Wagner, and Dobson were the three starters on whom the Sox built their hopes. Joe won 11, lost 9, and cut more than a full run off his ERA, bringing it down to 3.30.

With World War II under way, players were starting to leave for military service. Hot rookie shortstop Johnny Pesky was gone, and the entire 1942 outfield (Williams, Dom DiMaggio, Lou Finney) was in the service by 1943 as well. Dobson had a 3-A deferment with a wife (Marguerite Weiss) and young child in the family. He'd spent the winter working construction in his wife's hometown of Nashville. The work kept him in shape and he had another good season on the mound (3.12 ERA), though the team's having lost so many players contributed to a disappointing 7–11 record. The 1943 season started poorly, but after a tonsillectomy in midseason, Dobson came on strong and won six of his seven games after the All-Star break. One, near the end of the season, came on September 24, his last decision of the year. It was a near-perfect game against Cleveland that would have been the first in over 20 years. Leading off the seventh inning, Lou

Boudreau singled into short right field—the only Indian to reach base in the first nine innings. Dobson took the scoreless game through 10 innings, and the Sox won it 1–0 in the bottom of the 10th on back-to-back doubles by Tom McBride and Tony Lupien. Dobson's final start wound up a 3–3 tie against the visiting St. Louis Browns.

Dobson was also a good defensive player. It was only in that final September 29 tie game, the last appearance in his fifth season in major-league ball, that he made his first error, in his only chance of the game. The old American League record had reportedly been Ted Lyons with 88 games. Joe set the new record: 156 games and 153 chances. In 1946, Claude Passeau concluded a stretch of 275 chances without an error, in 145 games. When the "kinky-haired" Dobson had joined the Red Sox, he already had 40 chances in 75 games under his belt but he showed up in spring training with a new glove that Sox pitching coach Frank Shellenback thought was the biggest glove he'd ever seen for a pitcher, looking at first glance like a first baseman's glove. Dobson had had it custom-designed for him, since he lacked his left thuamb and part of his forefinger. The *Monitor*'s Rumill suggested he could distract batters a bit by waving it as he delivered the pitch.[8]

As a batter, Joe wasn't much. He finished 1943 with his second sub-.100 mark, batting just .096. He'd hit one of his two career homers back in 1941 (the other came in 1948) and had only nine career RBIs after his first five years. The first home run came on June 2 during a quite uncharacteristic 3-for-4 day against Bobo Newsom and Bud Thomas; Dobson threw a four-hitter, all singles, for a 9–1 win.

As soon as the season ended, Joe took up defense work at the Bethlehem-Hingham shipyard in Hingham, Massachusetts. Christopher Williams reports that the shipyard "at its peak, when Dobson was employed there, could produce a destroyer escort ship in 25 days, 16 at a time."[9] He was inducted into the Army on December 22 in Boston, and reported to Fort Devens, Massachusetts, on January 12, 1944. He was the 17th ballplayer the Red Sox had lost to the armed services in World War II.

After early basic training, Dobson was transferred to Camp Wheeler, near Macon, Georgia, where he spent the balance of the war. He pitched in 1944 and 1945 for the Camp Wheeler Spokes, and managed the team as well. He later said, "I must have pitched at least 24 games and I lost only three. We had some good games, too. Among members of my club were Cecil Travis, former Senator; Johnny Frye, who tried out at first with St. Louis; Ken Jungels, who was up with Cleveland. We also had some double-A players in our league." Dobson's fellow Spokes also included Bobby Bragan of the Phillies and Johnny Logan, not yet a major leaguer. Though most of Camp Wheeler shipped out to Europe late in 1944, Dobson was one of the more fortunate ones and remained on the base.

In June 1945, Dobson and other players at Camp Wheeler helped conduct a training camp in Macon, Georgia, for young local ballplayers. The team traveled some, playing other bases as far away as California. Cincinnati shortstop Eddie Miller wrote of a game there, "We beat Joe, but he struck out 14 and looked great."[10]

Dobson twice in early 1945 took detours to Fenway Park. While traveling to Washington on detail, Sergeant Dobson parlayed a three-day pass into a visit, where he challenged Red Sox secretary Phil Troy: "Ask me some names of gun parts. I know lots of guns and I know how to pull 'em apart. I can assemble 'em, too, without havin' any parts left, big or little."[11] Dobson was discharged on February 15, 1946, without having seen overseas duty, but just in time to join the Red Sox for spring training. He was one of the last to arrive, but the pitching during the war had kept him in good shape and he was ready to contribute a very good year to a very good Red Sox team.

Fresh out of his Army baseball uniform and into a Red Sox one again, Joe made his first start in an intrasquad game on March 5 and he set down the nine batters he faced, striking out three. For the season, Dobson started 24 games, and relieved in eight more. Just before the June 8 start in Detroit, Joe learned that his father had died in Arizona. His brother told Joe on the phone that their father would have wanted Joe to pitch, so he beat the Tigers that day—taking his record up to 7–1—and then left for the funeral. Back 12 days later, he lost a 2–0 game to the Browns. By season's end, Ferriss, Hughson, and Harris all had more wins but Joe had posted a very strong 13–7 record with a 3.24 ERA, doing his part to bring the team into its first World Series in 28 years, against the St. Louis Cardinals. During the Series itself, he threw one inning of hitless relief in the Game Two loss, righted the Red Sox ship with a complete-game, four-hit, 6–3 win in Game Five, and threw 2⅔ innings of hitless relief in the middle of Game Seven. They were the only World Series games in which he appeared, and he couldn't have acquitted himself much better.

After it was all over, Joe traveled from St. Louis back to Boston, where his wife had a thyroid operation, and then to Arizona, where he and his brother started work building a new home. It was Joe's wife who took credit

Dobson warming up before a 1946 ballgame.

for his win in Game Five. With ongoing shortages from the war years, she said, it was the first steak she'd been able to buy in Boston all year, and she said that it helped her husband. Joe agreed it helped, but said that the real secret weapon was his "atom ball"—which he said was "the pitch I used whenever I got into trouble. It was usually a down-breaking curve that exploded like 'Operation Crossroads.'"[12] He was delayed returning home, when their car broke down in Pittsfield and it was two weeks before it was sufficiently repaired to make the journey. Steaks and auto parts still seemed hard to come by as the nation rebuilt its domestic economy.

The Red Sox looked ready to repeat in 1947, and Dobson was now seen as one of the Big Four. He'd shaken the reputation of a "dazzling spring box operative who faded in early summer."[13] As it transpired, Dobson turned out to be the only starter on the Red Sox that year who didn't seem to come down with a dead arm. Hughson, Ferriss, and Harris all had one problem or another during the course of the season, one that failed to fulfill its promise almost from the get-go. Joe had what might have been his best year—though one could make a good case for 1952. He won a career-high 18 games as part of an 18–8, 2.95 season. By midsummer, newspapers were calling him "Cronin's ace" and one of the few pitchers who had a shot at 20 wins that year. He had another near-no-hitter on September 17 on a blooper of a seventh-inning single to right off the broken bat of Walt Judnich; he settled for a one-hit, 4–0 shutout of the Browns.

Thanks mainly to additional struggles from its pitchers in 1948, the Red Sox were in seventh place at the end of May. A month later, Dobson had nine wins and was named to the All-Star team (he didn't play), but on July 31—with 13 wins under his belt—he was hit in the hand by one of Bob Feller's pitches. He didn't miss a start, nor did he when another Indians pitcher—Satchel Paige—hit him on August 24, but he didn't win a game in four straight starts. When it came to the last scheduled game of the year, and the Sox needed a win over the Yankees to have a shot at the pennant, manager Joe McCarthy gave Joe the start. He kept the game close enough, and Earl Johnson closed it. The Sox won, and found themselves in a tie with Cleveland, necessitating a single-game playoff tiebreaker that the Indians won. There would be no World Series for the Red Sox in 1948. "Curly Joe"—as John Drohan called him—had another offseason job in the Boston area, as agent for a "brewing concern." He'd begun to make his home in Needham, Massachusetts.

All Boston needed was to win one more game to take the pennant in 1949. Joe got off to a lackluster start but he began to come around and won 14 games by year's end. One more would have been nice. The Sox entered Yankee Stadium to play the final two games on the schedule. All Boston had to do was win either game and the pennant was theirs. Mel Parnell started the Saturday game and had a 4–0 lead, but gave up two runs in the fourth and two in the fifth. Dobson pitched four innings in relief, but lost the game on Johnny Lindell's solo home run in the bottom of the eighth. The Sox lost the next game, too. Dobson finished 14–12, his ERA having climbed to 3.85.

Joe finally got a no-hitter late in 1949—very late—it was a postseason exhibition game with the Mickey Harris All-Stars, and he shared the win with Warren Spahn, the two having split the duties to beat the Hartford Chiefs, 7–0.

Dobson won 15 games in 1950, the seventh of the eight seasons he was with the Red Sox that he posted double-digit win totals. He was part of a good staff led by Parnell, Ellis Kinder, and Chuck Stobbs, fronting a powerful team that set any number of records on offense, dampened only when Ted Williams broke his elbow during that summer's All-Star Game. Dobson missed a couple of starts at the end of July, and was sent back to Boston after being hit hard in the side by a Larry Doby line drive. Joe relieved in a dozen games in addition to his 27 starts, but his ERA increased for the fifth year in a row, to 4.18. He finished the year 15–10, second in wins only to Parnell's 18, and the Red Sox finished four games out of first place. Dobson was by no means opposed to working out of the pen. He told Ed Rumill he enjoyed the role and thought he could fashion a new career as a relief specialist. In 1950, he hit a career-best .214 at the plate, with nine RBIs also a career high.

On December 10, 1950, almost exactly 10 years after he'd been traded to the Red Sox, Dobson was dealt to the White Sox (with Dick Littlefield and Al Zarilla) for pitchers Bill Wight and Ray Scarborough. "I wasn't too surprised about the trade," he said. "When you get to be my age, you figure you have only a couple of years left." Many thought the Red Sox had gotten a steal with Scarborough and Wight, but neither panned out as well as anticipated.

The veteran Dobson was GM of the Sox complex in Winter Haven during the 1970s.

Training in Pasadena, California, provided one unexpected bonus; a photograph in the March 21, 1951, *Sporting News* showed Joe strolling arm in arm with Marilyn Monroe with two other White Sox on Marilyn's other arm in the posed publicity shot. He got his first win on May 11, another one-hitter (a pinch-hit double by Bobby Avila in the eighth), against the Indians. He started well, but hit a rough stretch in June and July, getting knocked out of the box six out of seven times, and didn't win a game from July 4 to August 6. He also missed considerable time due to what *Chicago Tribune* writer Ed Burns called "variegated twinges" (a number of minor but still debilitating leg problems) but still appeared in 28 games (21 starts) and put up a 7–6 record with a 3.62 ERA. It was the first time since 1946 that he hadn't won at least 13 games.

The following year, 1952, might have been Dobson's best season of all. He showed up early for spring training in El Centro, California, and worked hard. He lost a 1–0 game to Cleveland's Bob Lemon in his first start, and shut out the Browns with a 4–0 three-hitter in his second. Over his first 34⅔ innings, he gave up a total of one earned run and one unearned run—including another near no-hitter on May 1 that ran for 7⅓ innings before any Athletics batter hit safely. He won that one as a two-hit, 3–0 shutout. The string ended with him getting pounded by the Red Sox on May 6. He won his next four, though, including his third shutout of the young season on May 25. At one point boasting a 7–3 mark, Dobson was 9–5 at midseason. The 35-year-old needed a bit of extra rest between starts as the season wore on, though, and was just 7–7 in his last 14 decisions as the White Sox finished in third place with an 81–73 record. Joe finished 14–10, with a very strong 2.51 ERA, ranking fifth in the American League. Some credited manager Paul Richards with having pushed Joe hard to get in better shape before the season got under way. Dobson was also pitching with a salary that had been cut sharply from 1951, but the cuts were restored in full before the season was over.

After the season was over, Joe took a position as the regional sales manager of a tire distributing company based in Pittsfield, Massachusetts, and did a weekly radio sportscast on Tuesday nights on WBRK.

Dobson began to transition a bit in the spring of 1953 when he helped serve as an instructor in spring training. He was considered the third man in the rotation, behind Billy Pierce and Saul Rogovin. It turned out to be a disappointing season, for both Dobson and Rogovin. Joe finished only three of his 15 starts, even though the White

Sox won every one of his final four starts. Age was beginning to take its toll. He acknowledged that you reach the point where "everything you do out on the field takes effort to the limit of your endurance." His second wife, Maxine, a nurse who never followed sports before she and Joe met in 1945, mused out loud, "I'm wondering if those close fitting baseball caps aren't making our guys partly bald."[14] Joe had lost his first wife Marguerite to a fatal strep infection.] From July 11 to August 5, Joe didn't start at all—put on the shelf. He finished the season 5–5, with a 3.67 ERA.

Finally, after picking up infielder Connie Ryan, Chicago cleared a roster spot by placing Dobson on unconditional waivers on August 25. As a 10-year man, if unclaimed, Joe would be a free agent. He shared his thoughts about finally leaving the game with his best friend among the press, Ed Rumill of Boston's *Christian Science Monitor*. "When a pitcher doesn't have as much stuff as he once had, he's got to have sharp control to win. But if you don't pitch often, you lose that control. That's what happened to me. My arm is as strong as ever." He was gracious in his remarks and didn't blame the White Sox at all for believing that Ryan could do more to help the club. "Baseball has been very good to me," he said.[15] He said he was looking forward to spending time at home. His wife was feeling poorly, and he was tired of traveling.

The Red Sox offered Joe a last hurrah in 1954, announcing Dobson's signing of a free agent contract on January 13. "He's still got some good pitches in his strong right arm," declared GM Joe Cronin. "We expect him to win some games for us and also help teach and guide some of the young pitchers we'll have on our staff." Manager Lou Boudreau added, "I can't believe that Dobson is all through. He's always taken good care of himself." Joe didn't really have enough left. He got into two games, long enough to record eight outs but gave up five hits and two runs and a walk—and one final strikeout, finishing his career just shy of 1,000 with 992 K's. The Red Sox released him on May 8, offering him a coaching contract at the same time. He thought it over for a couple of days and agreed, but then resigned a little over seven weeks later, in early July. He'd worked largely as a "special observer" sitting in the stands and taking notes.

Joe decided to leave baseball—though he was enticed once more to coach for the White Sox in 1955. By October, he was living in Munsonville, New Hampshire (population 231), and spending 12 hours a day, seven days a week operating Joe Dobson's Store, a village general store about 10 miles north of Keene. The store also rented cabins and boats, sold gas, and Joe served as the town's postmaster and head of the volunteer fire department. He termed it a "change of pace." He truly enjoyed the work,

living there with Maxine and an infant daughter, Pam. His 17-year-old son from his first marriage, Joe Junior, was raised elsewhere. It wasn't easy. "Ballplayers don't know what hard work really is," he said. Every day you pitched extra innings, with nobody backing you up in the bullpen.[16] Pam recalls baseballs and bats hanging from the store's ceiling for a little extra decorative flavor.

By 1967, as the Red Sox embarked upon their Impossible Dream season, Joe was the manager and golf pro at the Kearsage Valley Country Club in North Sutton, New Hampshire. The year before, Ted Williams and Dom DiMaggio had earned the club some extra publicity, appearing at a benefit there. Joe had run the course at Laconia before that. He worked at Kearsage for seven years and then in February 1972 moved to Winter Haven, Florida, where he became general manager of the Red Sox complex there and business manager of the Winter Haven Red Sox through 1978.

His wife Maxine passed away in 1976. He later married Dorothy Veness, who survived his passing. After retiring from his work for the Red Sox, Joe and his family moved to his sister's ranch outside Tombstone where he helped with ranch work, fixing fence posts and looking over a herd of 40–50 cattle. In the late 1980s, he moved to Jacksonville and truly retired. It was in Jacksonville that he died of cancer at the age of 77 on June 23, 1994.

Notes

1. Lautier, Jack. *Fenway Voices*, p. 46
2. *Boston Traveler*, June 4, 1941
3. *The Sporting News*, March 20, 1941
4. *Christian Science Monitor*, March 4, 1941
5. *Christian Science Monitor*, March 4, 1942, and *The Sporting News*, January 15, 1942
6. *Hartford Courant*, March 17, 1942
7. Golenbock, Peter. *Red Sox Nation*, p. 135
8. The "kinky-haired" descriptor is from a 1942 *Sporting News* story; the glove is detailed in a March 31, 1941, *Christian Science Monitor* story.
9. E-mail communication from Christopher Williams, January 25, 2008
10. *Christian Science Monitor*, November 17, 1945
11. E-mail communication from Gary Bedingfield, January 25, 2008
12. *The Sporting News*, October 16, 1946
13. Stevens, Howell. *The Sporting News*, February 26, 1947
14. *Chicago Tribune*, July 28, 1953
15. *Christian Science Monitor*, August 28, 1953]
16. Nason, Jerry. *The Sporting News*, October 19, 1955

Sources

Interview with Pam Dobson Garcia on February 6, 2008. Thanks to Gary Bedingfield and Christopher Williams. www.retrosheet.com

BOBBY DOERR *by Bill Nowlin*

G	AB	R	H	2B	3B	HR	RBI	BB	SO	BA	OBP	SLG	SB	HBP
140	527	94	150	23	6	27	111	83	49	.285	.386	.505	3	4

It was Ted Williams who dubbed Bobby Doerr "the silent captain of the Red Sox" and a more down-to-earth Hall of Famer might be hard to find. A career Red Sox player, Doerr's fame enjoyed a renaissance in 2003 with the publication of David Halberstam's book about him and his famous teammates.

Born in the city of Los Angeles on April 7, 1918, Robert Pershing Doerr was one of the four Sox from the West Coast who starred in the 1940s—Williams from San Diego, Doerr from Los Angeles, Dom DiMaggio from San Francisco, and Johnny Pesky from Portland, Oregon. Doerr was born to Harold and Frances Doerr. His father worked for the telephone company, rising to become a foreman in the cable department, a position he held through the Depression. The Doerrs had three children—Hal, the eldest by five years, Bobby, and a younger sister Dorothy, who was three years younger than Bobby. Doerr told interviewer Maury Brown, "If she'd have been a boy, she'd have been a professional. She was a good athlete."

Baseball came early. "We lived near a playground that had four baseball diamonds on it and when I got to be 11, 12 years old, I was always over at the ballpark practicing or playing or doing something pertaining to baseball. And when I wasn't doing that, I was bouncing a rubber ball off the steps of my front porch at home." Manchester Playground attracted a number of kids from the area[,] and a surprising number of them went on to play pro ball. Bobby's American Legion team, the Leonard Wood Post, boasted quite a team. The infield alone boasted George McDonald at first base (11 of his 18 seasons were with the PCL San Diego Padres), Bobby Doerr at second base (14 seasons with the Red Sox), Mickey Owen at shortstop (13 seasons in the major leagues), and Steve Mesner at third (six seasons in the National League.) That was quite a group of 14-year-olds.

Bobby's older brother Hal played professionally as well, a catcher in the Pacific Coast League from 1932–1936. It was Doerr's father who helped bring about Owen's transition from shortstop to catcher in the winter

Bobby Doerr.

of 1933. The team they put together for some wintertime ball didn't have a catcher so Harold Doerr urged Owen to give it a try. Mr. Doerr helped out in other ways, too. During these miserable economic times, the telephone company, rather than lay people off, reduced many people's hours to three days a week—which at least provided some income. "It was just Depression days," Bobby explained. "Sometimes he would buy some baseball shoes for some of the kids, or a glove. Things were tough. Kids couldn't afford to get it themselves, and he had a job…He tried to help when he could from time to time; some of those kids were even having a hard time having meals at home."

Wintertime play was important—unlike Legion ball, the games included people of all ages, including some players who had played minor league ball but wanted to pick up a little extra money playing semipro on the playgrounds. "So when I was 15 and 16, I got to play against pretty good professional ballplayers." That gave Bobby some valuable experience. It also got him noticed.

Doerr told author Cynthia Wilber that his fondest memory as a child was winning the 1932 American Legion state tournament on Catalina Island, winning a regional tournament in Ogden, Utah, then coming within a game in Omaha, Nebraska of playing for the national title in Manchester, NH.

Bobby played high school ball for two years at Fremont High, in 1933 and the first part of 1934, but he'd been working out some with the Hollywood Sheiks and they offered to sign both him and George McDonald.[1] Both were 16 at the time, and in high school. Bill Lane was the owner of the ballclub and Oscar Vitt was the Sheiks' manager. Hal was playing for the Portland Beavers at the time. The Sheiks offered an ironclad two-year contract guaranteeing they would not send Bobby out. Bobby's father let him sign, "but I had to promise that I'd go back to high school in the wintertime and get my high school diploma." He did. Bobby understands that more professional ballplayers came out of Fremont High than any other high school in the country.

Doerr played 67 games for Hollywood in 1934, batting .259, all but six of the 16-year-old's 52 hits being singles. In 1935, Bobby acknowledges he "had a pretty good year"—he hit for a .317 average and added some power, hitting 22 doubles, eight triples, and four home runs. He drove in 74 runs, playing a very full 172-game season.

That winter, the Red Sox purchased an option on the contracts of both Doerr and teammate George Myatt, paying a reported $75,000. Bill Lane moved the Hollywood team to San Diego early in 1936, where they were renamed the San Diego Padres. In July, Eddie Collins came to look over the pair while the Padres were playing in Portland, and took Doerr's contract but declined Myatt. Collins also noticed a young player named Ted Williams and shook hands on the right to purchase Williams at a later time. Doerr improved again in his third year in the Coast League, batting .342 with 37 doubles and 12 triples, though just two home runs. He led the league with 238 hits and scored an even 100 runs.

Doerr was 18 years old when he headed east for his first spring training with the Red Sox, traveling across the country to Sarasota, Florida, with Mel Almada. Doerr made the team in 1937, batting leadoff on Opening Day and going 3-for-5. He had won the starting job and held it until he was beaned by Washington's Ed Linke on April 26; the ball hit him over the left ear and bounded over to the Red Sox dugout. In Wilber's book, Doerr says, "It didn't knock me out, but I was out of the lineup for a few days and Eric McNair got back in. He was playing good ball, so I didn't play too much that first couple of months. The last month of the season I got back in and I played pretty well for the rest of the year." Eric McNair played most of the games at second but by season's end, Bobby had accumulated 147 at-bats in 55 games.

Though he batted just .224, he took over second base fulltime beginning in 1938. The right-hand hitting Doerr (5'11", 175 pounds) batted .289 in 1938, with 80 RBIs, playing in 145 games. He led the league in sacrifice hits with 22. Defensively, he helped turn a league-leading 118 double plays. Only once more did he hit less than .270—he batted .258 in 1947, driving in 95 runs.

Doerr explained to Wilber, "I never did work in the off-season, and I never did play winter ball or anything else. I think it was good for me to get away after a full season.... In those days, I don't think anyone ever got too complacent. Even after I played ten years of ball, I still felt like I had to play well or somebody might take my place. They had plenty of players in the minor leagues who were good enough to come up and take your job, and I think that kept us going all of the time. I hustled and put that extra effort in all of the time."

In 1939, he upped his average to .318 and added some

Ted Williams and the man he called the "Silent Captain" of the Red Sox, Bobby Doerr

power, more than doubling his home run total with 12 roundtrippers. Though his average slipped a bit in 1940 (to .291), he became a more productive hitter, driving in 105 runs, with 37 doubles, 10 triples, and 22 home runs. Again, he led the league in double plays, again turning 118 of them. His 401 putouts also led the AL.

Doerr was named to the first of nine American League All-Star teams in 1941; he played in eight games, starting five of them, and his three-run home run in the bottom of the second inning of the 1943 game, off Mort Cooper, made all the difference in the 5–3 AL win.

Though his RBI total dropped to 93 in 1941, he bumped it back up to 102 the following year, the second of six seasons he drove in more than 100 runs. He led the league in fielding average, too. Come 1943, he played in every Red Sox game all year long (and the All-Star Game), and though his RBI total slipped to 75—a function of greatly weakened team offense—Doerr excelled on defense, leading the American League in putouts, assists, double plays, and fielding average.

Doerr anchored the second base slot for Boston through the 1951 season, missing just one year (and one crucial month) during World War II. The month was September 1944. When the war broke out, Bobby was exempt because he and his wife Monica had a young son, Don. He'd also been rejected due to a perforated eardrum. As the war rolled on, the military needed more and more men and the pressures on seemingly-healthy athletes intensified. After the 1943 season, Doerr took a wintertime defense job in Los Angeles, working at a sheet metal machine shop run by the man who had managed his old

American Legion team. When he left the defense job to play the 1944 season, he received his draft orders and was told to report at the beginning of September. By the time September came around, the Red Sox were in the thick of the pennant race, just four games out of first place—and both Doerr (.325 at the time, his .528 slugging average led the league) and Hughson (18–5, 2.26 ERA) had to leave. The team couldn't sustain those two losses and their hopes sputtered out.

Bobby's .325 average was second in the league, just two points behind the ultimate batting champion, Lou Boudreau, who hit .327. Doerr was named AL Player of the Year by *The Sporting News*.

Because of the war, Doerr missed the entire 1945 season. He had made his home in Oregon and so reported for induction in the United States Army in Portland. He was first assigned to Fort Lewis and a week later reported for infantry duty at Camp Roberts. After completing the months of training, word began to circulate within his outfit that they were being prepared to ship out to Fort Ord, and then overseas for the invasion of Japan. President Truman brought the whole thing to a halt by dropping two atomic bombs on Japan.

After the war, Staff Sergeant Doerr changed back into his Red Sox uniform and returned to the 1946 edition of the Red Sox. He drove in 116 runs, his highest total yet—thanks to the potent Boston batting order. Bobby once again led the league in four defensive categories, the same four as in 1943: putouts, assists, double plays, and fielding percentage.

The Red Sox waltzed to the World Series, but lost to the Cardinals in seven games. Doerr led the regulars in hitting, batting .409 with nine hits in 22 Series at-bats. Babe Ruth, asked who was the MVP of the American League, said, "Doerr, and not Ted Williams, is the No. 1 player on the team."

He averaged over 110 RBIs from 1946 through 1950, with a career-high 120 RBIs in the 1950 campaign. That last full season, he led the league a fourth time in putouts and a fourth time in fielding average. His .993 in 1948 was the Red Sox record for second basemen until Mark Loretta surpassed it with a .994 mark in the 2006 season.

Doerr hit for the cycle twice (May 17, 1944 and May 13, 1947); he is the only Red Sox player to do it more than once. In a June 8, 1950 game, he hit three homers and drove in eight runs. Despite the power demonstrated by his 223 career home runs, his fielding was at least as important. He was always exceptional on defense, more than once running off strings of over 300 chances without an error. He led the league 16 times in one defensive category or another and wound up his career with a lifetime .980 mark—at the time of his retirement, he was the all-time major league leader.

On August 2, 1947, Doerr was given a night at Fenway.

He received an estimated $22,500 worth of gifts including a car.

In early August 1951, in the midst of another excellent year, Bobby suffered a serious back problem. He'd hurt it a bit bending over for a slow-hit ground ball; he felt something give, but continued the game. Quite a while afterwards, he woke up one morning and found he could hardly get out of bed or put on his shoes. He got some treatment but missed nearly three weeks before returning to play. He got in only a few more games. The problem persisted, and he had to bow out after just one at-bat in the first game of the September 7 doubleheader. Fears that it was a ruptured disc proved not the case and surgery was ruled out, but Doerr was told to rest the remainder of the season.

At season's end, Doerr could look back on 1,247 RBIs, a career batting average of .288 and the aforementioned home run and fielding totals, and some 2,042 major league base hits.

Bobby had played most of his career for just two managers: Joe Cronin and Joe McCarthy. He felt Cronin was "firm, but he patted you on the back; he always encouraged you in different ways. That was when I was younger, and was a big help to me." McCarthy was a "much firmer disposition kind of guy" who was admittedly "a little more difficult to play for"—but Bobby recognized that he played some of his best seasons for McCarthy.[2]

He'd played 14 seasons in the majors and had a good career. Though only 33, he didn't want to risk more serious injury and decided to retire to his farm in Oregon. Over time, the back fused itself in some fashion and he found himself able to lift bales of hay and sacks of grain. He began raising cattle, fattening steers for resale, but there was almost no profit in it for the small herd of 100 or so that he could hold on his spread. When Bobby returned to Boston for a night to honor Joe Cronin in 1956, he was asked if he might like to manage in Boston's system. He declined, but did take a position that he describes as "kind of like a roving coach in the minor leagues" beginning in 1957. He is listed as a Red Sox scout for the years 1957–66. He did a lot of traveling, checking out Red Sox prospects in Minneapolis, San Francisco, Seattle, Winston-Salem, Corning, and other locations.

Doing this work for several years, Doerr came to know Dick Williams, particularly after Williams took over as manager of the Toronto farm club. "I got to know him pretty good when he was with Toronto. I have to say that seeing him operate in the minor leagues coaching and managing, and then three years at the Red Sox level, he was the best manager that I saw. Now Joe Cronin was very good. I loved Joe Cronin, to play for. But if I had to pick a manager to take a team that was potentially a winning team, Dick Williams someway was able to put something together[,] and I thought he was one of the best managers I saw."

After he was named Red Sox manager for the 1967 season, Dick Williams asked Bobby to serve as his first base coach. He served for the three seasons that Williams managed, 1967–1969. Doerr agrees that Williams "wasn't the most liked guy. He didn't tolerate easy mistakes. Some way or another, though, the players never got uptight playing for him. He kept a tight ship and to take that club in '67 and put it into a pennant winner, there were so many things he did that he was the best guy I saw." They did not have frequent coaches meetings. "He said what you're supposed to do and he let you do it. You worked with the batter. Nobody ever interfered with what I was supposed to do." Doerr's job was to work with the hitters, as well as coach first. He was familiar with most of the young hitters, having

Doerr as Red Sox coach.

seen them while doing his work as a roving instructor. Eddie Popowski had the same store of experience, and both offered a stable, almost paternal influence to an exceptionally young ballclub. Dick Williams told interviewer Jeff Angus, "He helped me out quite a bit when I was in Toronto. In '67, he was a buffer between people, a soft-spoken guy who could help get the message across."

Second baseman Mike Andrews of the 1967 Sox told the *Boston Herald*'s Steve Buckley, "Bobby Doerr was my mentor. When I was in the minors, I always seemed to improve when he came along. I had so much faith in him that if he told me I'd be a better hitter if I changed my shoelaces, I'd have done it."

After Williams was fired late in 1969, incoming manager Eddie Kasko brought in his new staff for the 1970 campaign.

Several years later, Doerr was named coach for the Toronto Blue Jays, and served them for a number of years as the team's hitting coach. "I really didn't want to go back into baseball," he says, "but they made it so nice for me. Pat Gillick was really good to work with. Peter Bavasi. I was there '77 through '81 and then I worked a couple of years in the minor leagues. More or less spring training, up to Medicine Hat with the rookie team. I didn't do much after '82, '83."

In 1986, Bobby Doerr and Ernie Lombardi were named to the Hall of Fame by the special veterans committee, and were inducted with Willie McCovey in August that year. On May 21, 1988, the Red Sox retired Bobby's uniform number, #1.

Bobby's son Don Doerr later played some college ball at the University of Washington and went into the Basin League in the middle 1960s, pitching for the Sturgis club against future major leaguers like Jim Lonborg and Jim Palmer. Bobby rated his curve ball of major league caliber, but says he "didn't have quite enough fast ball...didn't have quite enough to go far in professional ball."

In his later years, Doerr devoted his life to care for his wife Monica, wheelchair-bound for much of her later years due to multiple sclerosis. Mrs. Doerr suffered two strokes in 1999 and then a final one which brought about her passing in 2003.

Bob Doerr splits his time now between his two properties in Oregon, and has been able to enjoy more time with his son, now retired himself after a successful career as a manager with the accounting firm of Coopers and Lybrand, based in Eugene. Bob visited Boston two or three times a year such as for a reunion of the remaining 1946 Red Sox that kicked off the 2006 baseball season in Opening Day ceremonies. On the 60th anniversary of the first Bobby Doerr Day, the Red Sox held another day for Bobby on August 2, 2007 to honor Bobby at Fenway Park in what he said would be his final visit.

Notes

1. The Hollywood ballclub of the period was popularly known as the Sheiks, though one can find references to them as the Hollywood Stars. Dick Beverage, author of *The Hollywood Stars*, reports of Doerr's timeframe, "The players I've talked to from that era to a man referred to the club as the Sheiks. That was the most popular name. But they were sometimes called the Stars in the papers.
2. Doerr's remarks were made in an interview for the Oregon Stadium Campaign in 2002.

Sourcesv

Interviews with Bobby Doerr, May 8 and 23, 2006
Maury Brown interview with Bobby Doerr, November 13, 2002
Steve Buckley, "The Silent Captain Still," *Boston Herald*, May 22, 2005
Wilber, Cynthia J., *For the Love of the Game* (NY: William Morrow, 1992)
Thanks to Jeff Angus, Mark Armour, Dick Beverage. Maury Brown, Dan Desrochers, Bobby Doerr, J. Thomas Hetrick, and David Paulson.

HARRY DORISH *by Bill Nowlin*

G	ERA	W	L	SV	GS	GF	CG	SHO	IP	H	R	ER	BB	SO	HR	HBP	WP	BFP
9	5.65	0	1	0	0	1	0	0	14⅓	18	13	9	6	5	1	0	2	71

G	AB	R	H	2B	3B	HR	RBI	BB	SO	BA	OBP	SLG	SB	HBP
9	4	0	1	0	0	0	0	0	1	.250	.250	.250	0	0

The small mining community of Swoy-ersville, Pennsylvania, located near Wilkes-Barre, was home to only 5,000 or so inhabitants but gave five ballplayers to the major leagues: Adam Comorosky, Dick Mulligan, Packy Rogers, Steve Shemo, and Harry Dorish. The town also contributed professional athletes in other major-league sports as well. Dorish himself also played football and basketball at Swoyersville High School, and graduated in 1941.

Harry Dorish was not born as Harold, and never had a middle name, but often went by the nickname Fritz. He was born on July 13, 1921, the fourth of five children born to Hritz and Anna Dorish. His oldest brother, John, was a semipro baseball player who reportedly played every position but catcher. With Anna and William preceding him, and sister Mary following, the family was complete. Hritz was a coal miner, whose parents had come from Austria. He died young, of a heart attack in the early 1940s, before seeing his son make the major leagues. William himself was reportedly a good infielder but upon Hritz's death he had to work hard to help support the family.

Hritz's wife, Anna, was Czechoslovakian, her family having also come to America in the late 19th century. She worked in a factory for a while, processing silk, but only for a few years before devoting her life to raising the children. Swoyersville was a community built around the coal mining done at the Harry E. Colliery and many of the workers came from Central Europe, as a look at Census data from 1920 makes clear.

In part for this reason, we cannot be 100 percent sure what Harry's given name truly was. It was not Harold, but was it Hritz or was it Harry? Interviews with his sister Mary Urban, his widow, Eleanor, and his daughter, Barbara Jo German, add the information that his baptismal name was Gregory. The family spoke Slavic languages—perhaps a combination of Russian and Ukrainian. Harry himself completed a questionnaire for the Hall of Fame and cited his parentage as "Russian." Harry's wife, Eleanor Uter, was of Lithuanian ancestry, raised in neighboring Luzerne, and knew Harry from high school days. Due

Harry Dorish, 1956.

to the language barrier, she was unable to talk with Harry's mother.

Harry was 5'11" and 197 pounds. He was often described in the press as "a chunky right-hander" and at times as "pudgy" or as "powerfully built." He was quiet—one account termed him "reticent" and another "retiring rather than aggressive by nature, at least off the playing field." After throwing back-to-back no-hitters in high school, striking out 16 against Plains and 18 against Jenkins Township, he quickly got the attention of Red Sox scout Joe Reardon, who signed Dorish as soon as he graduated. Dorish reported to Class C Canton in the Middle Atlantic League, where he appeared in 21 games (7–6, 3.23 ERA) and saw some action in the playoffs against Akron.

Dorish pitched for the Scranton Miners (Eastern League) in 1942, his second year in pro ball, and "Schoolboy Fritz" posted a very promising 12–8 record, with a 2.07 earned run average. *The Sporting News* remarked on his "perfect control" in a 2–0 July shutout of Williamsport. By January 1943, he'd been added to the Double-A roster of the Louisville Colonels, but also added to the wartime National Defense Service roster—one of 17 Louisville players so registered. Harry had volunteered for the Army and was assigned as a cook at Camp Shelby, Mississippi.

Camp Shelby was an active camp during World War II and served as home for both the famous Japanese American 442nd Regimental Combat Team and a number of Women's Army Corps (WAC) units. It also housed a large convalescent hospital and had a prisoner-of-war camp which contained captured members of Germany's Afrika Corps.

Dorish advanced within the ranks, attached to a Medical Corps unit sent to the South Pacific, but also got in a fair amount of baseball. A 1944 news story datelined—as many were—"Somewhere in the Pacific," reported that Sgt. Dorish held a record of 20–3 while stationed and pitching on an undisclosed island. He'd won one game in good part by striking out 24 batters. He was mustered out of the service in January 1946, just in time to make spring training.

As a wartime article made clear, Harry was remembered by *The Sporting News* as a "hurler with unusual speed."[1] Pitching for the Colonels (of the Louisville variety), Dorish hadn't lost his touch, and was 11–4 (3.14) at year's end. Louisville won the American Association pennant and Harry won a couple of the championship games, even driving in a couple of runs in one to help his own cause. By October, he was officially added to the roster of the Boston Red Sox. The Sox were looking forward to 1947, after falling just short of winning the 1946 World Series, and felt they had a trio of new pitching prospects who could bear fruit: Harry from Louisville and both Mel Parnell and Tommy Fine from Scranton. The *Boston Post*'s Jack Malaney described Dorish in early April as "outstanding among all the rookies Manager Joe Cronin looked over." He noted that Harry had gotten off to a slow start at Louisville, only reaching full stride by midsummer. "When he got going, there wasn't any stopping him. He was especially brilliant in the playoffs and Junior World's Series…Harry has plenty of stuff, but no special fancy stuff, and he specialized on control."[2] His 4–1 record in playoff action secured him an invitation to spring training.

Dorish was so "retiring…by nature" that he had joined the Red Sox train on the way to spring training as it passed through Philadelphia and no one knew he was aboard the train until the following morning. His main pitches were what the *Christian Science Monitor* called a "heavy fast ball which comes in on a right-handed batter, a sharp breaking curve, a deceptive slider and a baffling sinker."[3] Tex Hughson raved about Harry at the end of March, "Dorish throws that fast sinker ball, an effective pitch at Fenway Park, where the hitters try to lift everything against the high wall in left field." Dorish was tagged as a starter coming out of spring training, and the Sox were picked to repeat for the pennant, Dorish and Parnell joined forces to blank the Braves on three hits in a preseason City Series game.

Dorish's big league debut came on April 15, 1947, when he picked up a win on Opening Day. Tex Hughson started and was perfect through the first five innings, mowing down 15 Washington Senators at Fenway Park, but surrendered single runs in the sixth and seventh before coming completely unglued in the eighth and giving up four more runs. The Red Sox had fortunately accumulated a 6–2 lead over Early Wynn and so the game stood tied when Dorish was called on in relief. The bases were full and there were two outs. He got the final out in the eighth, but only after seeing a "tainted hit"—a wind-blown fly—fall in behind Eddie Pellagrini, Johnny Pesky, and Ted Williams behind third base. It went for a double and scored the runs that tied it for Washington. The Red Sox scored a go-ahead run in the bottom of the eighth; Harry pitched a scoreless ninth—two grounders and a strikeout—and got the win. After the game, manager

Joe Cronin said, "Didn't Harry Dorish step in there and do a nice job? He had all the coolness and poise of a veteran."[4]

Just four days later, Dorish won his second game, again in relief of Hughson. He let in one run in the eighth, in part due to his own throwing error, but Philadelphia's 2–0 lead was erased by a ninth-inning Ted Williams home run and the Red Sox won the game in the 10th on Dom DiMaggio's two-out bases-loaded single. Harry had held the A's hitless in both the ninth and 10th innings. After a third win in relief, Cronin gave him his first start on May 16 and he shut out the Browns for six innings before giving up a three-run homer. He held on to win the 12–7 game against the Browns. But he lost his share of games, too. Dorish appeared in 41 games for the Red Sox in 1947, starting nine of them and finishing 12 (two complete games) and posting a record of 7–8. His 4.70 ERA was one of the highest on the staff, but he ate up 136 innings and impressed enough to be invited back under new manager Joe McCarthy in 1948.

It was but for a brief stay, however, as Harry spent most of the season with the Birmingham Barons. Designated for the bullpen from the get-go, he was 0–1 for Boston in nine appearances, used only infrequently. In mid-July he was sent down to Birmingham when Mike Palm was elevated to the big-league club. Dorish was 9–4 for the Barons in 99 innings of work with a 3.45 ERA in the Southern Association. The team won the Shaughnessy playoff, upsetting pennant winner Nashville in part due to the slugging of Walt Dropo and the 9–0 shutout Dorish threw in the fifth and deciding game. In the Dixie Series that pitted the Southern Association winner against the Texas League winner, Dorish lost the opener but Birmingham beat the Fort Worth Cats 5–3 in the fourth game of the five-game series.

In 1948, Harry and Eleanor Uter married. They'd known each other since high school days, but Harry wanted to wait until he'd become established in the game. He came to spring training a little heavy in 1949 and was seen to be in some disfavor as a result. He got a little early-season work, but when Boston had to cut down to the 25-man limit he was optioned to Louisville on May 18. He toiled for the Colonels for a couple of months, recalled on July 24 but not used by McCarthy late in the season. McCarthy was later criticized for utilizing neither Dorish (2.35 ERA) nor Frank Quinn (2.86) but relying on the then less effective veterans Tex Hughson (5.33 ERA) and Earl Johnson (7.48). Harry's year-end stats showed him with just eight innings pitched and no decisions. With Louisville, he'd been an unimpressive 3–3, 5.10. Only a few weeks into the 1950 season, he was sold to the St. Louis Browns for an undisclosed amount of cash. The Browns were 58–96 that year, and Harry's 4–9 was in the same range with a poor 6.44 ERA. One of the low points was starting against the Red Sox on June 7, chased after 2⅓ innings while Boston racked up a 10-0 lead through the first three frames on its way to a 20-4 victory—overshadowed by the next day's 29-4 slaughter of St. Louis. The high point might have been a move just five days earlier that has Dorish still in the record books: he was the last American League pitcher ever to steal home plate. It came on the front end of a double steal that he worked with Ray Coleman. He hit one of his seven career extra-base hits—all doubles—and drove in a run as well in his complete game, 9-3 win over Washington.

The Browns wanted Harry to develop a curveball, and sold him to Toronto at the end of the season, but the White Sox selected him in the November 1950 Rule V draft. Toronto hadn't officially announced the sale, since they were waiting for some pictures to be sent from St. Louis, and Chicago GM Frank Lane later admitted that he had overheard Browns owner Bill DeWitt tell Commissioner Happy Chandler that the Browns were releasing Dorish. After a few rounds of drafts, there was no one left on Chicago's wish list so when it was their time to select, Lane recalled what he'd heard and said, "Dorish of Toronto." That left it to the Browns to explain how a player apparently still on their roster had been drafted by another major league club [See, among other sources, *The Sporting News* of October 1, 1952]. White Sox manager Paul Richards was even more pleased during spring training when Harry did well: "He has been retiring the hitters with such ease it looks almost ridiculous," Richards said. "It's still early, but he certainly has earned himself a good long look."[5]

Harry made the club and was subject to an interesting Richards tactic on May 15 that was told and retold over the years. With Dorish pitching with a one-run lead, and Ted Williams due to lead off the bottom of the ninth, Richards wanted lefty Billy Pierce to pitch to Ted, but he wanted Harry to face the rest of the order. So he beckoned in Pierce, but positioned Harry at third base in place of Minnie Minoso. Ted soon popped up and Dorish took over on the mound again, while Floyd Baker came in to play third. The Red Sox did score one run, but Nellie Fox's two-run homer for the White Sox broke the tie in the top of the 11th and Harry held on to collect the win.

Richards started Harry four times, but preferred to use him in relief. "Dorish is the kind of pitcher you can't gauge quickly, but the hitters catch up with his stuff when

Another 1956 shot of "Fritz" Dorish.

they have several innings to look him over," Richards said.[6]

During the season, Harry and Eleanor tragically lost their seven-month-old daughter, Rozanne, to dysentery at home. Harry had come down with a sore arm a couple of days before and took off a couple of weeks before returning to action. By year's end, Dorish was 5-6 with a 3.54 earned run average. The couple later had two other children, Gregory, who played well in high school ball but suffered bad knees and today works painting houses, and Barbara Jo, a speech language pathologist at the Delaware School for the Deaf.

Dorish was often used in long relief. In 1952, he pitched 91 innings in 39 appearances, with just one start. He led the league with 11 saves and had an 8-4 record with a very good 2.47 ERA. He readily credited part of his turnaround to Paul Richards, who taught him the "slip ball" during spring training, a variation of the palm ball. "I never learned as much pitching in my entire career as I have in the two years I have been with the White Sox," Harry said after the season. "Nobody ever showed me much of anything about the finer points of pitching before.... Coaches on the other clubs might give you a few tips now and then, but they wouldn't work with you over any extended stretch. Richards is different. He sticks with you. When you're pitching, he'll tell you what you're doing wrong even if you happen to be getting them out."[7] The man General Manager Frank Lane called "our star relief man last season" had been headed back to the minors before he picked up the palm ball. Harry called the pitch "The Thing" and pledged to keep it a secret. His favorite pitch remained the sinker, though. It was the sinker that troubled Ted Williams so much that, during Harry's first years with the Red Sox, The Kid had refused to bat against Dorish in batting practice.[8]

Heading into 1953, Paul Richards said he felt that Dorish, Aloma, and Kennedy gave the White Sox the "most reliable bullpen in the league." But in both 1951 and 1952 Harry "had to carry virtually the entire bullpen load for the early months in both seasons. It unquestionably affected his later effectiveness."[9] Edgar Munzel of the *Chicago Sun-Times* called him "one of the best in the business." In 1953, Dorish got in his most work ever, though, and was 10-6 (3.40 ERA) with 145⅔ innings of work (including six starts), and in 1954, he threw over 100 innings again, this time with a 6-4 mark and a 2.72

ERA. In 1955, though, the White Sox traded him to the Orioles for catcher Les Moss (and apparently included $25,000 in cash as well). Chicago was looking for more in the way of offense, and Harry's mentor Paul Richards was the GM and field manager in Baltimore. Dorish was 2–0 with a 1.59 ERA at the time of the trade to the last-place O's. With Baltimore, he shared bullpen duties with George Zuverink and was 3–3 with a 3.15 ERA.

Harry finished his pitching career with the same team he'd begun with: the Red Sox. After 19⅔ innings in 1956 with Baltimore without a decision, and a couple of months after receiving 12 stitches in his heel after being spiked by Clint Courtney, he was placed on waivers and claimed by the Red Sox on June 25 for the $10,000 waiver price. The Sox needed help in the bullpen and summoned Dorish. Harry didn't see a great deal of action, and was 0–2 with a 3.57 ERA. Minneapolis GM Rosy Ryan tried to get Dorish from the Red Sox in August, but Harry had to consent and declined to accept the transfer. On October 9, 1956, he was given his unconditional release.

Not ready to give up yet, Dorish signed on with the San Francisco Seals for 1957. Fortuitously, he may have saved a woman's life during the March 22 earthquake that hit the Bay Area. A *Sporting News* bit says he was near the team hotel when he saw a woman standing in front of a large plate glass window and "acting instinctively, grabbed her out of harm's way just as the window fell with a crash to the sidewalk."[10] Just two days later, the Red Sox played an exhibition game against the Seals in San Francisco and eked out a 5–4 win in 10 innings. Harry had started and kept it close. Harry started the regular season nicely with a 3–0 Opening Day shutout in the Seals' final season and got off to a 3–0 start in wins and losses, but wound up as 9–12 with a 3.32 ERA in the Pacific Coast League. He played for Minneapolis in 1958 (3–3, 2.23) and started 1959 with the Millers, too, but was acquired by Houston—only to be cut loose "to make room for new arrivals." He appeared in only four games combined, for a total of eight innings with the two clubs. His final decision was a win. It was the end of the road as a professional player. He'd appeared in 323 major league games, with a 45–43 record and a career 3.83 earned run average.

Harry promptly took a scouting position with the Red Sox. When newly-named manager Johnny Pesky appointed Dorish as his pitching coach for the 1963

Harry with his son Gregory.

edition of the Red Sox, Harry had been a regional Sox scout for three years (1960–62), and had helped out Pesky as Seattle's pitching coach during spring training when Johnny managed the Rainiers (1961–62).

Harry is not credited with any signings as a scout, and it appears that his work was more as a talent evaluator and roving instructor. One of the pitchers Harry helped in the spring of 1961 was Dick Radatz. According to Radatz, Pesky had Harry work with him in an effort to convert Radatz to relief work: "Because of the fact that I was a one-pitch pitcher, and that being the fastball, they taught me how to warm up rather quickly as opposed to maybe taking 15 minutes to come into games on a minute's notice."[11] Pesky says it was Dorish's idea that led to the birth of The Monster, who had a great—if brief—run as an overpowering relief specialist. "It was a wonderful suggestion," Pesky told writer Hy Hurwitz. Radatz told Hurwitz, "Harry is the guy who introduced me to the bullpen."[12]

When Sam Mele took over as Twins manager after the 1961 season, he reportedly considered Harry as pitching coach but Harry continued to work for the Red Sox. And when Pesky was named Sox manager after the 1962 season, Harry had his ticket back to the big leagues. Pesky replaced Sal Maglie with Harry as his pitching coach.

The first notable change that Dorish introduced in Red Sox preparation work was to require the pitchers to run a lot, to keep them stronger and in better shape. Pesky and Dorish agreed on another innovation—which has since been adopted widely: the following day's starting pitcher would be the one to chart the current day's game and discuss the results with the catchers and coaches.[13] The emphasis on running may have hurt Harry's longevity with the ballclub. Pesky says that some of the pitchers complained to GM Mike Higgins, who fired Dorish the very day the last game of the 1963 season was rained out. Higgins didn't do it himself, though. He forced Johnny Pesky to fire his friend. Higgins' drumbeat to fire Dorish had started about a week before the end, and tore up Johnny, who tried to plead with the GM. Being forced to fire a colleague whose work he admired was, he said, "the only thing I resent in my whole baseball life."[14] Bob Turley was installed in Harry's stead.

Harry quickly found work scouting for Houston,

which he did for three years through 1966. In February 1967, he was named manager of the Jamestown (New York-Penn League) Class A farm club of the Atlanta Braves. In November, Braves VP Paul Richards named Dorish as pitching coach for the Braves beginning with the 1968 campaign, replacing Whit Wyatt. Among the Braves hurlers who credited Harry for important help were Ron Reed, Cecil Upshaw, and Phil Niekro, who praised both Harry and manager Luman Harris: "They changed my motion," Niekro said. With his altered delivery, Niekro said, he was able to stop aiming his knuckleball and just let it go. "I throw the knuckler harder and with better control."[15]

After four years with the Braves, Harry was offered the proverbial role of "another job in the organization" when Lew Burdette was named to take over pitching coach duties in 1972. In this case, the new position was a rather similar one as pitching instructor in the minor league system. Dorish did that for two seasons, then moved to the Cleveland Indians system in the same capacity. He worked for the Indians from 1974 through 1976. No reasons were given for the dismissal of Dorish and two minor league managers at the end of the 1976 season. Lee Stange took his place—but resigned just a month later to become major league pitching coach for the A's. Harry hooked on with the Pirates in January 1977, replacing Larry Sherry—who'd been elevated to the big league club—as their minor league pitching coach starting in 1977.

In November 1981, Harry joined yet another organiza-tion, signed by the Cincinnati Reds as their minor league pitching instructor. He held the position through 1988.

After fully retiring from the game, Harry enjoyed a much quieter life, partly as an avid golfer frequently on the links. He did occasional volunteer work with the Make-A-Wish Foundation, but in later years suffered from a progressive neuro-muscular disease. He never reached the point of becoming wheelchair-bound and died of complications on the last day of the millennium, December 31, 2000.

Notes

1. *The Sporting News*, November 18, 1943
2. *The Sporting News*, April 9, 1947
3. *Christian Science Monitor*, March 11, 1947
4. *Christian Science Monitor*, April 16, 1947
5. *The Sporting News*, March 28, 1951
6. *The Sporting News*, July 4, 1951
7. *The Sporting News*, October 1, 1952
8. See, for instance, Bob Holbrook's column in the July 11, 1956, *The Sporting News*.
9. Edgar Munzel of the *Chicago Sun-Times*, writing in *The Sporting News*, March 4, 1953
10. *The Sporting News*, April 3, 1957
11. Bill Nowlin, *Mr. Red Sox*, p. 190 (Rounder Books, 2004)
12. *The Sporting News*, January 19 and February 16, 1963
13. *Mr. Red Sox*, p. 205
14. *Ibid.*, p. 221
15. *The Sporting News*, May 10, 1969

Sources

Interviews with Eleanor Dorish, Barbara Jo German, Mary Urban, and Leonard Urban, all on October 7, 2007.

BOO FERRISS *by Bill Nowlin*

G	ERA	W	L	SV	GS	GF	CG	SHO	IP	H	R	ER	BB	SO	HR	HBP	WP	BFP
31	5.23	7	3	3	9	13	1	0	115⅓	127	71	67	61	30	7	7	0	518

G	AB	R	H	2B	3B	HR	RBI	BB	SO	BA	OBP	SLG	SB	HBP
31	37	4	9	1	0	0	6	6	6	.243	.349	.270	0	0

You won't find David Ferriss in the Cleveland, Mississippi, telephone directory—but if you were to look up Boo Ferriss, you'd find him. "A lot of people down here hardly know my real name," he says. The nickname came when he was a baby and tried to say the word "brother" and it came out "boo." He was born David Meadow Ferriss, though, on December 5, 1921, at Shaw, Mississippi. He batted lefthanded, but threw righthanded; he probably could have thrown ambidextrously, but never had the chance. He broke into baseball with one of the best starts any pitcher ever had and played on the great Red Sox teams of the late 1940s before suffering arm problems that cut his career short.

Boo grew up in with a love of baseball he inherited from his father, William Douglas Ferriss, who had played semipro ball and then managed several semipro teams and also worked as an umpire. He was a farmer, raising cotton, and worked as a cotton buyer as well. Boo's mother also worked as postmaster in the town of Shaw for some 30 years. Shaw is about 10 miles south of Ferriss's home today.

There were three children in the family—a brother seven years older and a sister five years younger. Will D., the brother, favored football and played in both high school and college. Growing up, Boo played on an open lot right by the side of the house where children in the area played. "In the summertime, of course, there wasn't any organized Little League or anything in those days. We just chose up and we'd play all day and knock off for lunch, and come back in this open field."

There was no junior high school in town; Shaw High School started in the seventh grade, so Boo was playing high school baseball in the seventh grade—against some kids who were quite a few years older. "I was always out there throwing the ball around with them and everything. I really wasn't on the team, but one day the coach got short-handed and he called me out of the stands to play second base. In the eighth grade, I became the regular second baseman.

"One game there, as I started playing some, a runner came into me at second base and I guess dumped me and I fell on my right wrist and broke it. I was always throwing the ball around, outside the house and against the steps and everything with my right hand, so that summer I had my right hand in a cast and I started throwing lefthanded, just to keep active. I loved to get out in the yard and throw a ball—a tennis ball—outside the house and the steps, so I developed some talent throwing lefthanded also." Batting was different, though. "I never batted right in my life. I don't know how I started that. It just came natural to me."

At coach Jim Flack's suggestion, he began pitching a couple of years later and worked from the mound the last 2½ years of high school, playing second base when not pitching. Shaw played round robin style in a county baseball league of around 10 schools. Football and basketball were more popular school sports in Mississippi at the time, but Ferriss fortunately came from an area that preferred baseball. Shaw won the county championship his last couple of years, in his junior year winning the Delta championship in an area that covered about a dozen counties. There were no state playoffs at the time.

By his senior year, he'd begun to attract attention of both college scouts and some major league scouts, in particular from the Indians, the Giants, and the Yankees. "The pro scouts told me they would sign me—it was open stock back then. There wasn't any such thing as the draft. I could have gone pro, but my dad said, 'You're going to college. You're not ready for pro ball.' I knew I wasn't. Mississippi State offered me a full scholarship for baseball. It was the first one they had ever had [offered one] for baseball. The coach there—Dudy Noble—was highly regarded in college baseball circles and had had several major leaguers to go out of there, namely Buddy Myer with Washington, Hugh Critz, Giants and Cincinnati, Willie Mitchell, I think with Cleveland, and a good number of other folks. That was Depression years, so my daddy was thankful for that full scholarship. I had offers from Ole Miss, Alabama, Tulane, and Mississippi College,

David "Boo" Ferriss.

but I went to Mississippi State on that full scholarship and was very thankful for it."

Freshmen weren't allowed to play varsity ball, but he played on the freshman team, then varsity ball in 1941 and 1942. For the most part, he played first base when he wasn't pitching—and he had to carry two gloves because of an idiosyncrasy that confused some of the other teams: he played first base lefthanded, then pitched righthanded. "I guess I was saving my right arm," he says. Ferriss did pitch a little lefthanded in semipro days, but never in professional baseball.

It was after finishing his sophomore year that the Red Sox offered him a nice deal, sending him to Brattleboro, Vermont, to play Northern League baseball, what was called a "college league." It was an eight-team league and he recalls playing against Sam Mele (Burlington) and Chuck Connors (Bennington). That was the summer of 1941. He hadn't signed a professional contract, but the Red Sox were scouting him, knew he had some potential, and their support gave them a bit of a foot in the door. Scout Neil Mahoney made the arrangement.

Brattleboro's manager was Bill Barrett, a former major league outfielder and by then a Red Sox scout. "We had players from Holy Cross and Georgetown and Seton Hall. Harvard, all around. Oklahoma. It was a great experience and I got to see my first major league game. I saw Lefty Grove win his 300th game. Bill Barrett took us in the clubhouse, got to meet Ted Williams, Bobby Doerr, Dom DiMaggio—later my teammates—Jimmie Foxx, Lefty Grove, and all those great names. That was my first major league game. Then after the season was over in early September, the Red Sox wanted me to come down and pitch batting practice for them and stay with them. I stayed with them a week and pitched batting practice in Fenway, and Joe Cronin took me to Yankee Stadium. Ted took me down, walked me down to Times Square and all. That was such a great experience for a small-town boy from Mississippi. September of '41."

So Ferriss was with the Red Sox for a week as he saw Ted Williams in some of the last days of his .406 season, though he'd had to return to college before Ted's dramatic final weekend in Philadelphia. Boo completed his junior year and then signed with the Red Sox in early June of 1942 for a bonus of $3,000—a good amount at the time. "And my dad had them put in the contract that whenever I spent 30 days with the big club, I'd get a bonus of $6,000. So a few years later, I was fortunate to pick up that bonus after being there 30 days." The Sox sent him to their Class B Piedmont League team in Greensboro, North Carolina. As a pitcher for manager Heinie Manush, he was 7-7 with a 2.22 ERA, striking out 98 while walking 53. Manush had him play outfield in several games, too.

Greensboro won the pennant and Ferriss won the MVP award in the playoffs. A couple of months after returning to college, he was drafted. He joined the Army Air Corps as a physical training instructor. Basic training was in Miami and then he was sent to Randolph Field, Texas, where he stayed for the duration, a little more than two years. There were a lot of Army air bases around San Antonio and there was an eight-team league so he got to play a lot of baseball in the area. One of his teammates was later Boston batterymate Matt Batts. The San Antonio Aviation Cadet team from Kelly Field was the big rival; that team featured Enos Slaughter, Howie Pollet, and Del Wilber. "Randolph was kind of considered the 'West Point of the Air.' The main thing there, I got to play for a former major leaguer, Bibb Falk. He was one of the finest baseball men I ever crossed paths with in my entire career." Falk was head coach at the University of Texas, 42 years old, but volunteered to join the service and took Ferriss under his wing. So in 1943 and 1944, Ferriss played for the Randolph team.

Ferriss in 1945, when he had a 21-10 record.

He left the service earlier than expected because his asthma kicked up. It's something he'd suffered most of his life. A couple of times in high school, he'd had to lay off from a game or two. In January of 1945, Corporal Ferriss developed a severe case at Randolph Field and it put him in the hospital for some six weeks before he was finally discharged in late February. Back in Shaw, under the care of his hometown doctor, he got better and the Red Sox asked him if he would be able to try spring training with Louisville. He gave it a shot and it worked out well. Cincinnati manager Bill McKechnie saw him pitch a couple of exhibition games and called up Joe Cronin, saying, "There's a kid down here in Louisville and if you don't like him, I'll purchase him for Cincinnati." A lot of baseball's best players were still in the service, so Cronin took notice. Ferriss was scheduled to pitch the second game of Louisville's season, against Toledo. "About 2:30 I was in my room and there was a knock on the door and it was Nemo Leibold, the manager for Louisville. He came in and said, 'Hey, kid, get your bags packed.' I thought he

was sending me down. He told me, 'You catch a 5:30 train to Washington. You're joining the Red Sox.' That was a great moment, for sure. I was on that 5:30 train."

Cronin had just broken his leg, and Del Baker was running the Red Sox. "I had to pinch myself every day to realize where I was, because a month ago I had been in a hospital bed in Randolph Field, Texas, and here I was in the major leagues." The third game of the team's visit to Philadelphia was a Sunday. Ferriss went to church and came to the park a little late, and found the warmup ball in his locker. Thinking there'd been a mistake, he took the ball over to Baker and was told, "Kid, you're in today." Facing Bobo Newsom. Bob Garbark was catching, and Ferriss couldn't find the plate. He walked the first two men on eight pitches. After two more balls—now 10 in a row—Baker came out but Garbark spoke up: "Del, this kid is throwing good. That ball is moving, it's live, and he's just missing. Stay with him." The next pitch was a ball, too, as Ferriss remembers it, but Bobby Estalella reached for it—and popped it up. Next up was Frankie Hayes, and Ferriss walked him on four pitches. It had now been 15 pitches and he knew that not one of them had been a strike. The bases were loaded for Dick Siebert. Finally, he got one over, got the count up to 3–2 and then Hayes hit a ball right back toward the mound—hard. "It bounced out in front of me but bounced over my head. I couldn't catch it and it was headed right over the bag to center field. I thought it was a base hit and I figured I would be back on that train to Mississippi or somewhere. Anyhow, Skeeter Newsome...good-fielding shortstop, been around...he was shading Siebert a little over toward second. He went over and got the ball, the grounder, and stepped on second and threw to first for a great double play to end the inning."

What happened in the second inning? "The next inning, I came out and I walked the first two men again. Oh, that crowd was really hollering. Baker come out again after I walked Hayes in that first inning and, once again, Bob Garbark said, 'Stay with him, Del. Stay with him. He's just missing a little bit.' I'm thankful for Garbark for staying with me. I got the next guys out. Long story short,

I went on to pitch a 2–0 shutout over Bobo." Despite the rockiest of starts, Ferriss had thrown a five-hit shutout in his major league debut. And he collected three hits at the plate to boot, his first three times up. "The second time, after the hit, Bobo was hollering at me! 'Who are you? I never heard of you. Where'd you come from?' The third time he came over almost all the way to first base and cussed me out. Oh man, scared me to death. Cussed me out and told me next time up, if I came up again, I was going to hit the dirt. But Dick Siebert told me, 'Oh, kid, that's old Bobo. Don't pay any attention to him. You're doing all right.' That was my introduction to major league baseball."

His second outing was just as impressive. Before a packed house at Fenway Park, he shut out the Yankees, 5–0, on seven hits. He'd pitched two complete games in the major leagues and still not surrendered a run. After four scoreless innings of his next game, making it 22⅓ consecutive scoreless innings at the start of a career, he finally gave up a run, about halfway into a game in Detroit. He won it, though, 8–2, and he kept on winning—eight straight, beating every team in the league the first time around. Four of them were shutouts.

He finished 1945 with a 21–10 record and a 2.96 earned run average, pitching for a seventh-place ball club. The difference between the '45 team and the 1946 one was like night and day, and Ferriss improved to 25–6 (his .806 winning percentage led the league), with a 3.25 ERA. Both years, he threw 26 complete games. The Sox made the World Series and Ferriss got the start in Game Three. Another shutout, 4–0, a six-hitter. He couldn't turn the trick in Game Seven, though. The Cardinals scored once in the second and twice in the fifth, and Joe Dobson came on in relief. The Red Sox tied it up, but lost it on Slaughter's mad dash in the eighth.

In mid-season 1947, Ferriss suffered a serious shoulder injury. While he battled through a couple more seasons, he was never again the same pitcher. It happened July 14 during a night game in Cleveland. Neither team had scored and George Metkovich was up with the bases loaded in the bottom of the seventh. Ferriss went all out, breaking off a curveball and something snapped in his shoulder. Bobby Doerr hit a solo home run in the top of the ninth to win the game, but Ferriss was damaged. He kept pitching. "Pitched pretty well," he allows. "But I didn't have as good a fastball, by any means. I had to do a little more finesse work. I finished up, I believe, 12–11."

Ferriss never had a losing record, but it was all downhill from there. He only made nine starts in 1948. "They did everything they possibly could to help me with my shoulder, but it just took away my power in '48, I was kind of a spot starter and reliever. Had some good moments. I got the save on the last day of the season when we won and the Indians lost to win the pennant. Fenway was going wild; the scoreboard showed the Indians losing

Ferriss, Joe Cronin, and Mickey Harris.

to Detroit. I came in the seventh inning against the Yankees with the bases loaded and one out. I pitched the rest of that game. That was about as much pressure as you could have."

In 1949, he appeared in only four games, all in relief. His arm was "completely dead. I just couldn't throw. They worked on it and worked on it, did everything they knew, the medics did and everything." He'd pretty much gotten past the asthma except for one attack in August 1945. He stayed with the ballclub throughout the 1949 season, and through spring training in 1950. He threw the ninth inning of the 1950 opener; the Yankees were already ahead, 13–10. Ferriss gave up two runs on two hits—and didn't pitch again in major league ball. Joe Dobson had tried to get him to pitch left-handed, but he never did. He was sent to Birmingham. The team thought the warmer weather could help. It was the first time Ferriss had been back to the minors since Greensboro. Playing for manager Pinky Higgins, he still couldn't throw hard and had to rely on finesse. He wasn't a power pitcher any more. Southern Association batting wasn't as strong as major league batting, and Ferriss won 10 and lost seven, with a 3.66 ERA.

The next year, Higgins was promoted to Double A Louisville and Ferriss went to Louisville and pitched there in 1951 and 1952, winning seven games both years but seeing his ERA climb to 5.25 and 4.71. His last year, 1953, he coached and worked with the pitchers, throwing just two innings (and giving up four earned runs.) In 1954 Ferriss again worked as a coach, which paid off when Higgins became manager of the Red Sox in 1955. Ferriss became his big league pitching coach, from 1955 through 1959, working with pitchers such as Frank Sullivan, Ike Delock, Willard Nixon, Tom Brewer, Mike Fornieles, Bill Monbouquette, and (the first year or two) Mel Parnell and Ellis Kinder. "I was fortunate to get those years in, to give me a total of almost 11 years in the major leagues. I left on my own accord. Our children were back and forth with school. Go to spring training, then back to Shaw—still making my home in Shaw—and we had children getting on up, eight or nine years old."

The Ferriss family had a son and a daughter. It was their daughter Margaret who was the athlete, competing in high school basketball and tennis. She is now administrator of the Mississippi Sports Hall of Fame and Museum, located in Jackson. David Junior is a medical doctor with CYGNA, working as an administrator in health management.

Boo himself took a position as athletic director and baseball coach with Delta State University in Cleveland, Mississippi and coached 26 years, until he retired in 1988. There was about an 18-month stretch in the middle when he was athletic director at his alma mater, Mississippi State, but the long tenure before and after were with Delta State. "We won three Division Two World Series and played for the national championship in '78. We went in '77, '78, and '82. In '78, we played Florida Southern for the national championship. They beat us in the final game. We finished two years in third place" Jim Miles, Stewart Cliburn, Barry Lyons, and Scooter Tucker were among DSU alumni who made it to the majors.

He very much enjoyed his time coaching college ball. "Had a winning record. Had the top record in Division Two for a good number of years there. Good experience working with young men and being a part of their lives. That's a very enjoyable and rewarding experience and I wouldn't take anything for it."

Inducted into the Red Sox Hall of Fame in 2002, Boo has made a number of trips to Boston in recent years and keeps in touch with several of the players from his era.

A decent batter, he averaged .250 in 372 at-bats and even did some pinch-hitting. His only home run came his first year, on June 29. It was the top of the ninth, off Johnny Humphries, a two-run homer into the right-field stands at Comiskey Park, giving the Red Sox a 4–2 win and giving him his 11th victory of the year. He's one pitcher who can look back at his major league career and know that he was almost never taken out for a pinch-hitter.

Boo Ferriss's brother Will was a salesman who served in the war, going into the service station and trucking business in Shaw after the war. He died in 1972. His sister Martha Ann Ferriss Parker was an excellent tennis player, in the Tennessee Tennis Hall of Fame. Their father died in 1943 and never had the chance to see Boo play professional ball. "He kept up with me, encouraging and everything, when I was in Greensboro and all, but he didn't see me play. That was a sad point in my life, because he would have loved that. He and I just dreamed always of being a major league player and I was fortunate to attain that and he would have loved that."

Source

Interview with Boo Ferriss, March 6, 2006

DENNY GALEHOUSE *by Glenn Stout*

G	ERA	W	L	SV	GS	GF	CG	SHO	IP	H	R	ER	BB	SO	HR	HBP	WP	BFP
27	4.00	8	8	3	15	7	6	1	137⅓	152	68	61	46	38	10	2	0	595

G	AB	R	H	2B	3B	HR	RBI	BB	SO	BA	OBP	SLG	SB	HBP
27	42	6	7	0	0	0	1	8	13	.167	.300	.167	0	0

Denny Galehouse was born on December 7, 1911, 30 years to the day before Japan bombed Pearl Harbor. For Red Sox fans, however, Galehouse is a reminder of another day of infamy—October 4, 1948, the date of the infamous playoff game between the Red Sox and Cleveland Indians to decide the American League pennant. For despite a 15-year major league career with the Cleveland Indians, St. Louis Browns, and the Red Sox during which the right-handed pitcher won 109 games and lost 118, he is best remembered in Boston for being the starting and losing pitcher in the playoff game against Cleveland. Ironically, until that game, Galehouse had a well-deserved reputation as a pitcher who thrived in the pressure of the postseason.

A native of Marshalltown, in northeastern Ohio, Galehouse grew up in nearby Doylestown, just southwest of Akron. After graduating from Doylestown High School in 1928, Galehouse pitched for several local semipro teams before being signed by scout Bill Bradley of the Cleveland Indians. Galehouse began his professional career in 1930 and spent two seasons with Johnstown in the Mid-Atlantic League, improving dramatically in 1931. He pitched for the Fort Wayne Chiefs of the Central League in 1932 and his 136 strikeouts led the league. His 14–6 record earned him a promotion to the New Orleans Pelicans of the Southern Association in 1933.

Galehouse went 17–10 for New Orleans that season and emerged as a top-flight pitching prospect. In the postseason playoff he defeated the Memphis Chicks twice, the second time by a shutout, as the Pelicans captured the Southern League title. Then, in the Dixie Series against Texas League champion San Antonio, Galehouse pitched three times in six days, starting and winning two games, to finish the season with a total of 21 victories.

During spring in 1934, Galehouse impressed Indians manager Walter Johnson and earned a spot on the

Cleveland roster. He made his major league debut on April 30 against the White Sox in Chicago, pitching one inning of relief in a 20–10 Cleveland loss, giving up two hits, a walk, and two earned runs while facing seven hitters. After that single appearance he was returned to New Orleans.

Despite a 12–10 regular season record in 1934, Galehouse had a slightly better earned run average and again emerged as a postseason star for the Pelicans, shutting out Galveston, 2–0, in the finale of the Dixie Series as New Orleans captured its second consecutive Series title. Before the start of the 1935 season, Galehouse was loaned to Minneapolis of the American Association in a deal that landed the Indians outfielder Ab Wright. Galehouse was 15–8 for Minneapolis, and later got into five games for the Indians, including the first start of his major league career, on September 29, earning a 7–4 win in the first game of a doubleheader against the Browns for new Indians manager Steve O'Neill.

In the spring of 1936, Galehouse was out of options and reached the major leagues for good. Although he didn't throw hard, he was an early practitioner of the slider and a pitcher whose success depended upon control. For the bulk of his career he served as a back-of-the-rotation starter and swingman, capable of both starting and relieving. Galehouse went 8–7 in 1936 with a 4.85 ERA in 36 appearances while starting 15 games, and in 1937 was 9–14 while starting 29 games and throwing 200⅔ innings, second in both categories to teammate Mel Harder.

On December 15, 1938, Galehouse was traded to the Red Sox along with Tommy Irwin in exchange for outfielder Ben Chapman, the first of Galehouse's two stints as a member of the Red Sox. Galehouse went 7–8 in 1939 and 9–10 in 1940 before being sold to the St. Louis Browns.

In St. Louis, Galehouse put together the best seasons of his career. In 1942, pitching against rosters depleted by the war, he picked up a career-high 12 victories and 24 decisions. In 1943, Galehouse had a career-low 2.77 ERA, going 11–11 for manager Luke Sewell.

After the 1943 season, Galehouse went to work six days a week at the Goodyear Aircraft plant in Akron, Ohio, earning a deferment from the draft because he was over the age of 26, married with a child, and his job was classified as essential to the war effort. He kept in shape by serving as pitching coach for the Cuyahoga High School baseball team and made an occasional appearance pitching for a local semipro team. As he told author William Mead in *Baseball Goes to War*, in addition to his work on the assembly line, Galehouse worked with the Selective Service "trying to get draft deferments for employees. It was my job to determine who was essential and who was not."

In High School baseball mid-May of 1944, the Browns, in need of pitching, persuaded Galehouse to become a so-called "Sunday pitcher." For the next three months, Galehouse left Akron after his Saturday shift, traveled all night by train to wherever the Browns were playing, pitched the first game of the Sunday doubleheader, then immediately returned to Akron and put in another full six-day work week at the factory before repeating the process the following weekend. In July, when it became clear that the Browns had a chance to win the pennant, Galehouse learned that if he quit his job at the Goodyear plant he was unlikely to be drafted until the fall. He joined the Browns full time for the balance of the season and helped St. Louis capture the pennant and earn the right to play the Cardinals in an all-St. Louis World Series.

Denny Galehouse, in a 1948 photograph.

Galehouse was manager Sewell's choice to pitch Game One and he didn't disappoint, scattering seven hits to beat Mort Cooper, 2–1, in a complete game, losing his shutout with two outs in the ninth inning on a sacrifice fly. In Game Five, Galehouse pitched nearly as well, striking out 10 and again going the distance but losing 2–0 after giving up solo home runs to Ray Sanders and Danny Litwhiler. Cooper struck out 12 in the game, and the combined 22 strikeouts, which Cardinals shortstop Marty Marion blamed on the number of fans in Sportsman's Park's center-field seats who wore white shirts that day, stood as a World Series record for 19 years before being broken by Sandy Koufax and several Yankees pitchers in Game One of the 1963 World Series. Unfortunately for Galehouse and his teammates, the Browns fell to the Cardinals in six games.

Galehouse was drafted into the Navy in April of 1945 and spent most of 1945 pitching for the Great Lakes Naval team in Chicago, which was coached by his old Cleveland teammate Bob Feller. Galehouse rejoined the Browns in 1946 and after a slow start was purchased by the Red Sox on June 20, 1947. Over the next three months, he was terrific for manager Joe Cronin, going 11–7 with a 3.32 ERA.

In 1948, under new manager Joe McCarthy, Galehouse resumed his accustomed role at the back of the rotation for the Red Sox, making 26 appearances and 14 starts with an 8–7 record. But when the Red Sox and Indians ended the regular season tied for first place, Galehouse was destined to pitch one more game. One day after the end of the regular season, on October 4, 1948, the Red Sox and Indians met in a one-game playoff in Fenway Park to decide the American League pennant.

One day earlier, after the Red Sox beat the Yankees, 10–5, behind Joe Dobson and several relievers, Boston manager Joe McCarthy told the Boston *Herald*, "Frankly I don't know who I'll pitch [in the playoff]....We had men working in the bullpen all afternoon. I'll have to find out who did what, who was ready." Most observers expected McCarthy to pitch either Mel Parnell, who had three days' rest, was 15–8 for the season and had already beaten the Indians three times in 1948. Ellis Kinder, 10–7, was also well-rested and had won four of his last five starts. In many subsequent interviews, Parnell has said that when he arrived at Fenway that day he expected to pitch, only to be told by McCarthy that the manager had changed his mind and decided to pitch Galehouse, something Parnell always believed was a "total surprise" to Galehouse.

But in a 1989 interview, Galehouse's first ever about the playoff game, he told the author that he "had a pretty good idea the night before" that he was going to pitch. According to Galehouse, McCarthy sent "another player" around to talk to several Sox pitchers about starting the playoff game. "I'm not at liberty to say anything and I never will about who was asked to pitch," he said. "But the others that were asked all had some little reason maybe why they thought they weren't able to do it. They shall remain nameless. I was the only that said, 'If he wants me to pitch, I'll pitch.'"

Birdie Tebbetts admitted to the author that he was that player sent around by McCarthy, but refused to give any details about what was said to him that evening. "I've never told that story and I don't intend to," he said. "I'm gonna be avoiding it until I write it myself. I've got it on tape." But neither Galehouse nor Tebbetts ever revealed before either died what truly happened that night.

When Galehouse arrived at Fenway Park, he found the ball placed in his glove, McCarthy's traditional method of letting a pitcher know he was starting that day. Despite the fact that Galehouse was, at best, Boston's fifth starter that season, there was some logic to McCarthy's decision. Galehouse had been successful in the postseason and earlier in the year, on July 30, he had pitched 8⅔ innings of two-hit relief against the Indians in Cleveland.

Joe McCarthy later told author Donald Honig that his other pitchers were "all used up" following a grueling regular season and that Galehouse "had pitched a great game against the Indians the last time we were in Cleveland." In fact, however, Galehouse had made two subsequent appearances against the Indians and been hit hard. Moreover, over the final two weeks of the season he had pitched only twice and been belted each time.

Neither was Galehouse well-rested. As the Red Sox outlasted the Yankees on October 3 to earn the right to meet Cleveland in the playoff, Galehouse recalled that McCarthy had sent him to the bullpen in the fourth inning and told him to stay loose. "So I threw six innings [in the bullpen] the day before....That's something that hasn't been brought out at all."

Whatever led McCarthy to make his decision, Sox fans know what happened next. In the first inning Galehouse retired the first two Cleveland hitters and then Lou Boudreau hit a wind-blown home run into the net over the left field wall to give the Indians a 1–0 lead. Then Boudreau led off the fourth inning with a single, Joe Gordon followed with a hit, and Ken Keltner hit a home run to give the Indians a 4–1 lead and chase Galehouse. Cleveland pitcher Gene Bearden and his knuckleball held Boston at bay and the Indians went on to win, 8–3, to capture the pennant.

Galehouse, despite becoming, in the minds of some fans, the "goat" of the game, had no regrets. Despite warming up the day before, he felt he had good stuff that day, saying, "I did the best I could."

Just a few weeks into the 1949 season the Red Sox, as if trying to erase the memory of the loss, released Galehouse. He pitched the remainder of the 1949 season with Seattle in the Pacific Coast League, going 10–12 with a 4.09 ERA, then went 6–7 (4.38 ERA) for Seattle in 1950 before retiring.

Galehouse returned to his home in Doylestown, where he was often referred to in the local press as "the Pride of Doylestown" and to his wife, Elizabeth, two sons, Denny Jr. and Jerry, and his daughter, Jan. He was hired by the Red Sox as a scout covering the Midwest, a position he held for the Red Sox, Tigers, Mets, Cardinals, Dodgers, and Padres for the next 48 years, often driving 40,000 miles or more each in year in search of prospects. "It's not enough for a fellow to be able to run hit, run, throw, and field to be a ballplayer," Galehouse once said of his approach. "He's got to have the heart that goes along with being a great competitor."

One of his most notable signings for Boston was St. Louis high school pitcher Frank Baumann. The most sought-after player in the nation in 1952, Baumann was persuaded by Galehouse to sign with Boston for a bonus of $85,000. Unfortunately, Baumann never fulfilled his promise.

Although Galehouse was disappointed to have lost the playoff game, before Boston lost the 1978 playoff game to the New York Yankees, the 1948 playoff game against Cleveland was rarely brought up by baseball historians or anyone else except in passing—no one interviewed him on the topic until 1989. Most published profiles of Galehouse gave greater weight to his performance in the 1944 World Series. But after the 1978 playoff game and, particularly, after the publication of Dan Shaughnessy's *Curse of the Bambino* in 1990, that changed. Thereafter Galehouse readily admitted to reporters that "When people find out who I am, that's [the playoff game] all they want to talk about."

Yet he was hardly haunted by his performance. Galehouse took great pride in his play during the 1944 World Series, his 11 grandchildren and six great-grandchildren,

and in the fact that he earned a paycheck from the game of baseball for nearly 70 years.

Galehouse passed away from heart disease on October 14, 1998. The San Diego Padres, for whom he worked for the final 18 years of his career, still honor their top scout each year with the Denny Galehouse Award.

BILLY GOODMAN *by Ron Anderson*

G	AB	R	H	2B	3B	HR	RBI	BB	SO	BA	OBP	SLG	SB	HBP
127	445	65	138	27	2	1	66	74	44	.310	.414	.387	5	5

The late 1940s Boston Red Sox consisted of larger-than-life, highly paid, talented baseball men who could accomplish just about anything "except win pennants," reported Al Hirshberg in a 1951 article in the *Saturday Evening Post* on Billy Goodman. Goodman, who had made his major-league debut with the parent club in the spring of 1947, was "notable chiefly for what he is not. He is not a glamorous slugger, not a colorful, flamboyant personality, not a magnet for autograph hounds," wrote Hirshberg. In fact, "he is built like an undernourished ribbon clerk.... Billy Goodman neither looks nor acts like a baseball star. He just goes out every day and plays the game."[1]

Billy Goodman.

And play the game he did, for 16 years in the major leagues with the Boston Red Sox, Baltimore Orioles, Chicago White Sox, and Houston Colt 45s. He finished his major-league playing career with a lifetime .300 batting average.

Beginning as early as high school, Goodman is remembered for being an extraordinarily versatile player—a characterization that distinguished him throughout his baseball career. His versatility originated from his very early years; being the youngest and smallest in the neighborhood, Billy played where he was told to play. Billy often said that "playing regularly" was his goal, which usually meant playing wherever and whenever he was asked.

Billy played every position on his high school team at one time or another. During his senior year he was part of a so-called "reversible battery" with a teammate, pitching one day and catching the next. Earl Kelly, sports editor of the *Concord Tribune*, in Goodman's North Carolina hometown, told Hirshberg that he recalled Goodman once pitching a game left-handed and doing very well. Goodman was naturally right-handed. He was a left-handed batter.

Hall of Famer Eddie Collins, the Red Sox vice president and general manager in 1947, compared Goodman

to a former teammate and baseball standout, Jimmy Dykes, who was considered one of the most versatile players of his time. Collins, a tough critic and perfectionist, described Dykes as "the best until the kid [Goodman] came along."

William Dale "Billy" Goodman was born March 22, 1926, in Concord, Cabarrus County, North Carolina, the second of three sons of Fred and Martha Goodman. As a major leaguer, he was listed as 5'11" and 165 pounds, but during the season often fell below 150 pounds. Billy's father, Fred, was a prosperous dairy farmer, owning more than 300 acres of pastureland, which Billy worked much of the time during his younger years on the farm. The Goodman roots ran deep there, with an uncle owning comparable farmland nearby, and the grandfather, C.J. Goodman, owning the original family farmstead farther up the street. A few hundred yards south of the Goodman homestead was the home of the Littles, who owned a coal and oil business in Concord. Margaret Little,[2] a childhood sweetheart, and Billy, grew up together and were married in October 1947.

Goodman, who was simply known as "Bill" until he entered major-league baseball, was a three-sport star for Winecoff High School.[3] He played four years of high school basketball, football, and baseball. He was the high scorer and captain of the high school basketball team his junior and senior years, and he was a triple-threat halfback star on the football team. But baseball was his real love and his goal was to play professionally.

Although Goodman was voted the best all-around athlete at Winecoff High, he was not remembered as a particularly outstanding baseball man. He did not hit for power, even then. Sports editor Kelly, a three-sport star athlete himself, once described Goodman as "steady and dangerous, but he was never spectacular."[4] He did the little things, consistently and essentially, when his team needed a key hit and runs to stay in the game. It was just assumed that he would come through for them, and he usually did.

When the North Carolina State League (Class D) suspended its operations due to the war, the semipro independent four-team Carolina Victory League was formed. After high school in the summer of 1943, Billy joined the Concord Weavers, and helped win the championship that year. Billy played some outfield and was their star second baseman. The manager of the club, former minor league star, Herman "Ginger" Watts, invited young Goodman—who was 17—to play with them. Hirshberg described the league as being "well covered by the professional scouts."

Claude Dietrich, a seasoned scout for the Atlanta Crackers of the Double A Southern Association, spent the summer of '43 signing up many of Watts' charges for the Crackers. Feeling his job was done, Dietrich was admonished by Watts for missing the best player on the team, Goodman. It wasn't the first time he was overlooked, and it wouldn't be the last. Billy's outward appearance was not the look of major league promise. Larry Woodall, the former scout and later publicity chief for the Red Sox, observed, "Goodman can make a monkey out of a scout. He doesn't look as if he can do anything right when you first see him. You have to watch him for a while before you realize that he can't do anything wrong."5

Dietrich pursued Goodman right away, signing him to a Crackers contract in December 1943 for $1,200, the same year Billy's mother died.6 He joined the Atlanta team in April 1944, under manager and future Hall of Famer Kiki Cuyler. Goodman was listed on the roster as an outfielder though he had been mostly a second baseman for the Concord team. Billy made a good start in professional ball, making the All-Star team that year and batting .336 in 137 games. He was the runs scored leader with 122.

Goodman entered the Navy at the end of the '44 season and was sent to the South Pacific theater, notably the Ulithi Group of the Western Carolines and Guam, where he was placed in the athletic department. He was discharged from the service in June of 1946, and promptly went to Atlanta to see if he still had a job with the Crackers. Billy re-signed and "went to work" the very next day. Cuyler was still managing and gave Goodman the first-base job.

After a week's trial at first base—where he got a base hit his first time at bat, then failed to hit his next 22 times—Goodman was shifted to the outfield and went on a tear, finishing the season batting .387 in 86 games. The Crackers won the Southern Association pennant, then went on to cop the playoff championships against New Orleans and Memphis, winning both seven-game series four games to three. Atlanta played Dallas of the Texas League in the Dixie Series—resumed after a three year lapse—and lost four straight. Goodman went 28-for-67 in 18 playoff games (.418).

This was convincing enough for the Red Sox to purchase Goodman's contract from the Crackers on February 7, 1946, for $75,000. It was thought to be the highest dollar amount ever paid for a Southern Association player. Goodman said he learned of the deal through an *Atlanta Journal* photographer who wanted to take pictures of him for the paper.

Billy was told to report to Red Sox manager Joe Cronin at Sarasota, Florida, in March, 1947 for spring training. Cronin told him he would remain an outfielder. The Red Sox had a championship team returning for the '47 season, so little regard was given Goodman that spring. He was used mostly in pinch-hit roles.

Billy's first look at major-league pitching was in a Red Sox intrasquad game that spring against their stalwart moundsman, Boo Ferriss, a 25–6 performer in the championship year of '46. His first time at bat, as *Globe* reporter Roger Birtwell described it in an April 2, 1947, *Sporting News* article, Goodman reached for an outside pitch by Ferriss and with "the ease of a grocer's clerk reaching for a package of biscuits, ripped a line double to left."

Interviewed at his Cleveland, Mississippi, home in July, 2007, Ferriss exclaimed about Goodman: "Oh, he could hit. You know [he was] a wiry guy, wasn't very big, not a long-ball hitter. He hit very few home runs, but he could swing a bat. And he was versatile. He was playing when I was coaching. I was very close to Billy....He was like [Johnny] Pesky. He could spray that ball. He could hit....You looked up and he was on base."

When the 1947 major-league season opened Goodman was on the bench. He played in 12 games with two hits—both singles—in 11 at-bats. In June, Billy was optioned to the Sox' Triple A Louisville farm club, joining them in June. There simply was no room for him on the big club. Goodman started in the outfield for the Colonels, but took over at shortstop on July 15 when Strick Shofner pulled up lame. Billy never relinquished the position, batting .340 for the year and finishing among the top five American Association hitters.

Harry "Nemo" Leibold—a "clean" member of the 1919 Black Sox—was Louisville's manager in 1947, and the club finished in second place behind Kansas City with an 85–68 record. In the American Association playoffs, Louisville beat Minneapolis four games to three, but lost the championship to Milwaukee in seven games.

It was at Louisville that Goodman began his multifaceted duties fielding several different positions. As he put it to J.G. Taylor Spink of *The Sporting News*, "Mr. Spink, I used up my paychecks buying myself new gloves for the various positions to which I was shifted."7

His successful season at Louisville prompted the Red Sox to give Billy another try and he was back with them again in Sarasota for '48 spring training. It was a new opportunity with a new manager. Longtime New York Yankees manager Joe McCarthy came out of retirement to join the Red Sox for 1948. McCarthy recognized Goodman's talents, but, as with other Red Sox managers, the dilemma was where to play him. The Red Sox were strong at all positions with high hopes for another pennant. When the 1948 season opened Billy was once again perched on the bench.

He saw little action at the start, except for occasional fill-in work for Bobby Doerr and Johnny Pesky at second and third. When the Red Sox spiraled into a nose-dive on their first Western trip—winning only one of their first seven games—and had plummeted well down in the standings, McCarthy became desperate and sought change. McCarthy told Goodman to borrow a first baseman's mitt and take over the position for their regular, Jake Jones, who was not hitting. Billy started at first base against St. Louis on May 25, and remained there for the rest of the season, batting a solid .310 with a .414 OBP, and a .993 fielding percentage (eight errors). He was declared the club's Rookie of the Year by the Boston chapter of the Baseball Writers Association of America.

The Red Sox beat the New York Yankees on the last day of the season, tying the Cleveland Indians for first place. The American League's first-ever playoff contest was played the next day, October 4, at Fenway Park. Boston lost to the Indians, 8–3. Goodman went 0-for-3 with a walk, striking out twice against a hot Gene Bearden.

In spite of Goodman's exceptional rookie year, McCarthy had his eye on a big strapping kid from Moosup, Connecticut—Walt Dropo, an untested first baseman who could hit baseballs out of sight. McCarthy made Dropo the starting first baseman in 1949, and Goodman was riding the bench again. The 1949 season saw the Sox suffer a slow start, and Dropo was not working out well. Neither was Stan Spence, the right fielder. McCarthy made some moves: In early May Dropo was shipped to Sacramento, the Sox purchased steady batsman and highly regarded outfielder Al Zarilla from the Browns, moving him to right field, and Goodman was put back on first base. The Sox began to improve.

The 1949 season was a bittersweet year for the Boston team; they climbed into first place on September 30, only to lose their final two games of the regular season—and the pennant—to the Yankees. It was another year of heartache for Boston.

Billy had a good year, batting .298, but missed several games in August because of a fungus condition he had contracted with the Navy in the South Pacific, affecting his hands and legs and causing general weakness. It led to blisters on his hands, making hitting difficult because of an inability to hold the bat with any strength.[8] Goodman received strong fan support in the AL All-Star voting, placing second to starting first baseman Eddie Robinson of the Washington Senators. He substituted for Robinson at first base in the eighth inning of the July 12 midsummer classic, but he did not have an at-bat.

Based on his solid performance, Billy had first base locked up going into the 1950 season. For the first time, he felt he was a "regular." But fate once again struck; in the April 30 game with the Philadelphia A's, Billy sustained a chip fracture to his ankle in a collision with Ferris Fain. He was batting .333 at the time. Walt Dropo was called up from Louisville and performed phenomenally, crushing home runs at a steady pace and hitting for average. Dropo won American League Rookie of the Year honors. Goodman, meanwhile, lost the first-base job.

Goodman's strength—and resiliency—was his ability to play almost anywhere defensively, infield or outfield, which enabled him to be in the lineup more often than was expected of him. When Boston players went down with injuries, Goodman was there to spell them, and he performed well most of the time. He returned to action from his own injury on May 24, substituting for second baseman Bobby Doerr, who was hurt. He played so well there that he remained in the lineup for a while after Doerr had recovered; but McCarthy reinserted Doerr upon their return from a road trip so that he could take advantage of Fenway's left-field wall.

Then third baseman Johnny Pesky went down, and Goodman filled in for him so admirably that there was speculation that Pesky had lost his job. By June Billy had already played all four infield positions, going counter-clockwise around the diamond as each regular dropped out because of injury.[9] But Pesky returned and Goodman went back to his "sub" role as a one-man bench.

On July 11, Red Sox slugger Ted Williams fractured his elbow in the All-Star game. New Red Sox manager Steve O'Neill, having replaced McCarthy, first tried Clyde Vollmer in left. After a few games, Vollmer slumped, and O'Neill replaced him with Goodman on July 16. Billy had a sensational run and appeared to be made for the left-field duties. In one stretch of eight games, he struck for 32 hits, a .531 pace, and was playing left field "as if to the manner born," wrote Shirley Povich of the *Washington Post*, on July 28, 1950. On August 15, Dropo was beaned by the A's Hank Wyse, knocking him out of the lineup. Goodman took over at first with Vollmer going to left. Dropo returned in four days, and Goodman—who was batting .354—returned to left field.

Goodman was the league's leading hitter and naturally people began to wonder what to do with him when Williams returned. The rest of the team was hitting well and the Sox were on a roll, winning 44 of 61 games during Ted's absence from the regular lineup, their .721 clip placing them two games behind the league-leading Yankees. There was reportedly some resentment among the players, knowing that temperamental slugger Williams would displace their best-hitting handyman.

But Johnny Pesky came to Goodman's rescue. He went to manager O'Neill a few weeks before Williams' return and offered to sit down in order to keep Goodman in the lineup. It was a selfless gesture, and one that paid off for Goodman. Not only was Billy playing exceptional ball, but he would not obtain the requisite number of at-bats to win a batting title if he did not play regularly for the balance of the season. Goodman went to third base on September 15, replacing Pesky. He went on to win the AL batting title with a .354 average. He is recognized as the only major-league player ever to win a batting title without having a regular position. The Sox finished third, four games behind the first-place Yankees.

For his heroics on the diamond, Goodman was recognized as a candidate for the 1950 top male Athlete of the Year by the Associated Press. He finished 11th in the voting—Jim Konstanty of the Philadelphia Phillies won the award—among many sports notables of the day, amateur and professional. Goodman also finished second in the league MVP voting to New York shortstop Phil Rizzuto.

Astonishingly, over the winter there was talk that there might not be everyday room in the lineup for the 1950 AL batting champion. Manager O'Neill characterized Goodman as a bit of a pleasant dilemma. The Boston press labeled it the "Goodman problem." O'Neill rationalized that Goodman should play every day; yet, when asked what he would do with his other stars, and whom he would sit down, O'Neill countered that Goodman would be his "number one utility man while still playing regularly every day."[10] Only days later, the Red Sox traded right fielder Al Zarilla, a .325 hitter in 1950, to the White Sox. O'Neill confided that this was done to provide steady work for Goodman in the lineup. True to his word, O'Neill started the season with Goodman as a regular in the outfield, batting second.

The Red Sox got off to a bad start, losing their first three games. O'Neill showed no patience and quickly began to juggle his lineup, including sitting down Walt Dropo, who was not hitting. He moved Goodman to first base. Billy again rotated through the season between three infield positions—first, second, and third—and some outfield. He received ample playing time in '51, but did not reach the level of achievement that he did in 1950, finishing the season batting .297. The Red Sox finished in third place, 11 games behind the first-place Yankees.

The year 1952 was as a period of change for the Red Sox, with a new manager, core players either leaving or aging, and vacancies needing replacements. Bobby Doerr

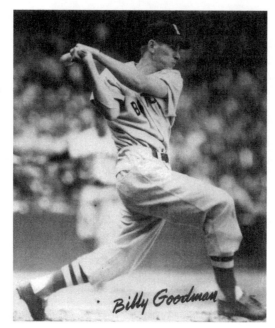

Goodman's .354 average made him 1950 AL batting champion.

called it quits at the age of 33 toward the end of the 1951 season, and Steve O'Neill was replaced by Lou Boudreau in the offseason. Ted Williams was recalled to military duty because of the Korean War and reported on May 2. And both Pesky and Dropo were traded away in midseason. There were holes to fill.

The foremost dilemma for Boudreau—"the game's greatest manipulator," wrote Shirley Povich of the *Washington Post*—was whom to call on to replace future Hall of Famer Bobby Doerr.[11] Boudreau juggled his lineup with regularity throughout the year, favoring youth over experience, speed and defense over power, and constant platooning. Goodman played three infield positions—mostly at second base—and some outfield.

Billy had more plate appearances (513) than any other Red Sox player, and was second only to future Hall of Famer George Kell—acquired in the midseason Pesky trade—with a .306 batting average to Kell's two-team average of .311. The Red Sox had little to cheer about, however, finishing in sixth place, 19 games out of first.

The next season, 1953, was not looking to be a much better year for the Red Sox, but it was a happy one for Billy Goodman because Boudreau made him his full-time second baseman. This was the first time in the major leagues that Billy could call a position his own, and he was doubly pleased because he was taking over from his idol, Bobby Doerr.

Interviewed at his Oregon home, Bobby Doerr described Goodman warmly: "He [was] just a very, very fine person and a darn good ballplayer. He was like the perfect guy to be on a ballclub because he could play so many different positions. If he was [playing] utility he was great when he went in [to a game]....He played a good first base. He didn't have the power that first basemen generally have, but he was always on base and ran the bases good. [He was a] good fielder....As a utility player he was perfect in that way, too. He could go in any time and do a good job."[12]

On May 9, 1953, Billy got into his first dispute with an umpire over a close call, and became so enraged that he had to be restrained by teammate Jimmy Piersall, who wrapped his arms around the flailing second sacker and bodily carried him from the field. Goodman sustained cartilage damage to his ribs from the "hugging" incident, and was sidelined for nearly a month. Boudreau later remarked that Goodman's absence was a factor in the Red Sox not being a contender in 1953. Casey Stengel agreed, commenting that Goodman's absence "changed the whole complexion of the first division."[13]

The Yankees won the pennant again. Boston finished in fourth place, 16 games out of first. In spite of his injury and long absence, Goodman had a good year, batting .313, tied for third with Minnie Minoso in the AL batting race. He was named to the AL All-Star team as the starting second baseman. He went 0-for-2 with a walk, and was caught stealing.

Goodman played on mediocre Red Sox teams from 1954 to 1956, finishing fourth each year. He continued his steady play, batting .303, .294, and .293, respectively, while often being used in utility roles.

Goodman and teammate at spring training in Sarasota.

In 1957 there was a career year change for Billy. He was being used sparingly by manager Mike Higgins. Baltimore's Paul Richards had had his eye on Goodman since 1955; on June 14 Billy was traded to the Orioles for pitcher Mike Fornieles.

Richards regarded Goodman as the Orioles' ultimate utility player, using him at all infield positions—mostly third base—as well as in right and left field, a total of six fielding slots. Billy stroked a home run—one of 19 he hit for his entire major league career—in his debut with Baltimore. He hit well for the O's, batting .308. The Orioles finished in fifth place, 21 games behind the first-place Yankees. On December 3, the Orioles traded Goodman, Tito Francona, and Ray Moore to the White Sox for Larry Doby, Jim Marshall, Jack Harshman, and Russ Heman.

Billy played solid baseball in 1958 for manager Al Lopez, mostly at third base, and batting .299. Chicago finished 10 games behind New York, in second place.

The "Go-Go" White Sox were the American League champions in 1959—their first Series since the infamous 1919 "Black Sox" scandal—and were known mostly for their speed, defense, and solid pitching. "Powderpuff hitters," they were called. Goodman, who batted .250 during the regular season, platooned at third base with Bubba Phillips.

The White Sox (6-to-5 favorites going into the Series) lost, four games to two, to the Los Angeles Dodgers. Goodman played in five of the six games, starting in three of them, and in pinch-hit roles. He went 3-for-13—all singles—batting .231 for the Series.

Chicago used Billy sparingly in 1960 and 1961 as a utility player and pinch-hitter. The White Sox did not equal their success of 1959, finishing third in 1960 and fourth in 1961, 23 games behind the Yankees. Goodman played in just 30 games in 1960 and 41 in '61, hitting .234 and .255, respectively.

Almost 36 years old, Goodman went to spring training with the White Sox in 1962, but he was given his unconditional release on April 3. On May 15, he signed with the expansion Houston Colt .45s of the National League. He played in utility roles once more, appearing in 82 games and batting .255. He was released after the season.

In the spring of 1963, Goodman signed on as player-manager of the Durham Bulls of the Class A Carolina League at the invitation of his old Orioles manager, Paul Richards, now Houston's GM. He left that assignment toward the end of the 1964 minor-league season, going to Houston's rookie camp in Cocoa, Florida, as manager-instructor, where he remained through '65.

In the winter of 1966 Billy caught on with his old team, the Red Sox, who hired him as a "special scout." In 1967 he joined the Kansas City Athletics as an instructor.

In the winter of 1968 the Atlanta Braves hired Goodman as a minor-league instructor, and on April 3 he was elevated to the parent club as the first-base coach, where he remained through the 1970 season. On September 28, the Braves announced they were not rehiring Goodman for 1971.

In 1973, Goodman joined the Kansas City Royals at their Baseball Academy in Sarasota, Florida (Goodman's home town), as an infield and hitting instructor. The Royals closed their academy in the spring of 1974, but retained Goodman on the payroll along with a few other instructors. Billy stayed on as manager of one of their rookie league clubs of the Gulf Coast League, the Academy Royals.

In May 1976 the Atlanta Braves hired Billy, again, this time as an instructor in their minor-league system. In June he joined the Braves' Triple A Richmond club as batting instructor.

Goodman's widow, Margaret, says that between 1977 and 1982 Billy was retired from baseball, playing golf, fishing, hunting, and gardening, and doing some occasional work with her in her antiques business—her store, the Babe Ruth Auxiliary, and in their other commercial properties. He appeared for an old-timers game, the Cracker Jack Old-Timers Baseball Classic, in July 1982 at RFK Stadium in Washington. Billy and Margaret also owned a 30-acre orange grove which they sold before he died.

Billy became ill with multiple myeloma in 1983, and died on October 1, 1984, in Sarasota. He was 58. He is survived by Margaret, of Sarasota; daughter Kathy Goodman Simpkins of Concord, North Carolina; and son Robert Goodman—named after Goodman's good friend, Bobby Doerr—of Bradenton, Florida. Margaret has three grandchildren—all girls—ages 24, 17, and 16 in 2007. Asked if she ever remarried, Margaret's response was a decided "Oh no. We grew up together and there's one love in a lifetime, and I had him."[14]

Billy Goodman played in 1,623 games in his major-league career, collecting 1,691 base hits and a .300 lifetime batting average. He played in two All-Star games and one World Series. He ranks 10th all-time for OBP in a season by a rookie, with a .414 percentage in 1948. In 1969, Goodman was honored by his native state, North Carolina, by being inducted into their Sports Hall of Fame. He is also a member of the Boston Red Sox Hall of Fame, inducted in 2004.

Notes

1. Hirshberg, Al. "That Modest Young Guy in the Outfield." *Saturday Evening Post*, March 17, 1951, p. 34.
2. *Ibid*, p. 142; Spink, J.G. Taylor. "Goodman Proves Right Man at First Base." *The Sporting News*, September 22, 1948, p. 4. Goodman's wife, Margaret, was known as "Evelyn"—she was born Margaret Evelyn Little—throughout her youth and during Billy's early years in baseball. Billy said in his 1948 interview with J.G. Taylor Spink, "My wife was Evelyn Little." According to Margaret—in interviews in May, September. and October 2007—her first name took hold when they moved to Sarasota, Florida, and started their businesses there. She used the given name, Margaret, on all formal documents, and it stuck.
3. Hirshberg, Al. op cit, p. 142. Billy Goodman was called "just plain Bill," in Concord, where he played high school and semipro ball, as well as with the Atlanta Crackers. According to Goodman's widow, Margaret, the name Billy took hold while he was with the Red Sox, but she does not remember how it got started.
4. Hirshberg, Al. op cit, p. 143.
5. *Ibid*.
6. Troy, Jack. "Goodman, Expert Cook, Gives Hot Plate Service to Crackers." *The Sporting News*, June 22, 1944, p. 6. Atlanta scout Claude Dietrich, tells the tale of the first time he encountered Goodman "wearing an apron" cooking a rabbit in the Goodman home. Dietrich was startled by Billy's slight appearance, accentuated by his donning of an apron. Father Fred Goodman later explained that Billy took over the kitchen duties as "chief cook" after his mother's death that year.
7. Spink, J.G. Taylor. op cit, p. 4.
8. Birtwell, Roger. "Whattaman Goodman—and What a Man!" *The Sporting News*, September 13, 1950. p. 3. Goodman was plagued with a chronic fungus—a so-called "saltsea fungus called "jungle-rot"—the Birtwell article says. It made him generally weak, and "affected his hands so much he couldn't get a firm grip on his bat." Margaret Goodman recalled the circumstances, saying that Billy "had to wear special things on his feet and he had something on his hands when he batted.…It was always with him."
9. Birtwell, Roger. op cit, pp. 3, 6. Nowlin, Bill. *Mr Red Sox: The Johnny Pesky Story*. Rounder Books, 2004. pp. 136–138. Goodman briefly filled in for Vern Stephens at shortstop, "on one occasion," before he subbed for Pesky, thus effectively playing at every infield position, moving counter-clockwise around the infield.
10. O'Leary, Steve. "Goodman Problem Tackled by O'Neill—He'll Be a 'Daily Sub.'" *The Sporting News*, November 29, 1950. p.15.
11. Povich, Shirley. "This Morning, with Shirley Povich." *Washington Post*, April 17, 1952 p.18.
12. Bobby Doerr interview, June 5, 2007.
13. Hurwitz, Hy. "Boudreau Bubbles Over Bosox Babes—and His New Pact." *The Sporting News*, October 7, 1953. p. 7
14. Margaret Goodman interviews, May, September, and October, 2007; Bobby Doerr interview, June 5, 2007. Goodman's widow, Margaret, was not entirely certain about the years 1977 and 1982. She did feel that Billy was most likely fully retired at the time and engaged in recreational pursuits along with his occasional assistance in her antiques business. Doerr—who maintained some contact with Goodman—expressed a similar opinion.

Sources

Nowlin, Bill. *Mr Red Sox: The Johnny Pesky Story*, Rounder Books, 2004.

Bresciani, Dick. Boston Red Sox Vice President Publications and Archives.

Thorn, John, and Pete Palmer, eds., with Michael Gershman. *Total Baseball* (4th edition), *The Official Encyclopedia of Major League Baseball*, Viking Press/Penguin Group, 1995.

Neft, David S., and Richard M. Cohen, *The World Series*, St. Martin's Press, 1990.

Stout, Glenn, and Richard A. Johnson, *Red Sox Century, The Definitive History of Baseball's Most Storied Franchise*, Houghton Mifflin Company, 2004.

Contributing writers: Nemec, David; Hanks, Stephen; Johnson, Dick; Raskin, David; Gilbert, Thomas W.; Cohen, Andy; Glickman, Joe; Green, Danny; Shea, Stuart. *The Baseball Chronicle*, Publications International Ltd., 2004.

Hirshberg, Al. *Saturday Evening Post*, March 17, 1951, pp. 34, 141–144.

Spatz, Lyle, editor. *The SABR Baseball List & Record Book*, (New York: Scribner, 2007 p. 349.)

Johnson, Lloyd, and Miles Wolff, eds. *The Encyclopedia of Minor League Baseball*, Baseball America, Inc., 1993.

MICKEY HARRIS *by Ryan Brodeur*

G	ERA	W	L	SV	GS	GF	CG	SHO	IP	H	R	ER	BB	SO	HR	HBP	WP	BFP
20	5.30	7	10	0	17	1	6	1	113 2/3	120	73	67	59	42	10	1	2	505

G	AB	R	H	2B	3B	HR	RBI	BB	SO	BA	OBP	SLG	SB	HBP
20	32	6	2	0	0	0	1	10	6	.063	.286	.063	0	0

"Me a pop-off? Aw, that's bunk."—Mickey Harris, *Boston Post*, May 20, 1941

Mickey Harris in 1941.

Mickey Harris is well known for an impressive amount of self-confidence and for posting a 17–9 record as one of the key components of the starting staff that carried the 1946 Boston Red Sox to their World Series showdown with the St. Louis Cardinals. After his impressive All-Star '46 season, Mickey struggled to work through arm troubles that kept him from having any further success as a starting pitcher. He did, however, pitch well as a reliever for Bucky Harris's Washington Senators in 1950 before he retired from baseball in 1953 at the age of 36.

Maurice Charles "Mickey" Harris was born on January 30, 1917, in the Belmont Park section of Queens Village, New York. He batted and threw left-handed, weighing in at 6 feet tall and 195 pounds during his playing years. His father, Maurice Sr., was himself a semipro infielder in the New York area. Mickey had a sister, Gertrude, and one brother, Robert.

It was in the infield that Mickey, as his father preferred to call him, got his start. At Public School 109, Jamaica Industrial High School, Harris found himself planted at first base, but when circumstances in a doubleheader required a new pitcher, Harris took the mound and never went back.

His semipro career began in the Queens-Nassau League, where he used the extra $5 to $10 a game the pitchers earned to supplement his day job of "spraying paraffin on milk containers for a dairy company."[1] In 1937, either through his own motivation or on the recommendation of his peers, the 19-year-old left-hander decided to pursue the next level, ending up at one of Bill Terry's tryout camps for the New York Giants. In an attempt to launch some modicum of a professional career, Harris received permission to toss batting practice for the Giants, hoping to have his talent noticed. Unfortunately for Harris, the gambit did not pan out.

After Harris had spent two months working out with the Giants, his mother contacted the club's front office in an effort to prevent her son from risking the possibility of losing his paying day job.[2] The contact finally got Terry's attention. Mickey was quoted in a May 20, 1941, *Boston Post* article: "He [Terry] told me that he hadn't known I was jeopardizing my job in order to try out, and advised me to go back to work.... Naturally, I was hurt that nobody paid any attention to me for two months."

Having had his immediate hopes of joining up with the major leaguers dashed against more realistic prospects, Harris continued to pitch in the Queens-Nassau League. His ability caught the eye of Red Sox scout and former big league umpire Jack Egan, who was helping to construct the new Boston farm system under the watchful eye of Farm Director Billy Evans.[3] Egan scouted Harris from the sidelines, and saw the lefty serve up a game-winning grand slam. Harris later recounted the event for Boston sportswriter John Drohan:

"I'm pitching out on the Island for the Queens Alliance club. We're playin' the Belair Civics. The score is tied in the ninth when they load the bases on me. Then I throw my home run ball and everybody walks out on me.

"An old guy with gray hair comes up to me. When he asks me what I threw the batter, I think he's a nosey fan. I told him a hook. He then asked me what my best pitch was. I told him my fastball. 'Then why didn't you throw it?' he says.

"I got the red-ears anyways, so I says, 'Well, if you can do any better, here's my glove.' But the old guy says, 'Now, don't lose your head. I'm Jack Egan and I scout for the Red Sox.' I says, 'Oh, yeah? I'm Lefty Grove.' But he shows me credentials enough to convince me he's the McCoy."[4]

Harris ended up signing a contract for $100 per month and a bonus of $100. "I held out for an extra $50 bonus and got it," he recalled.[5] The contract was with the Red Sox affiliate in Clarksdale, Mississippi, in the Cotton States League. Egan initially attempted to skip the entry-level Clarksdale and place Harris in Little Rock of the Southern Association in 1938, but Harris was rejected.[6] It was in the Little Rock spring training camp in 1938, however, that Harris heard his first words of encouragement from a member of a major league front office.[7]

In a training camp outing, nerves caused Harris to walk seven straight men. Out from under this cloud Billy Evans pulled a silver lining for the club's young addition: "You were throwing the ball faster to the seventh man than you were to the first and that was what counted with me. You're going to be all right."8

Back pitching with Clarksdale for the 1938 season, Harris posted a 17–18 record. The following year, 1939, Harris found himself at the next level for the Scranton Miners in the Eastern League. There he greatly improved his control and improved his record to 17–4, shared the league lead in winning percentage with a mark of .810, and led in strikeouts with 148 in 184 innings pitched. As his control improved, so did his chances of making the big club in Boston.

Harris's 1939 season is most remembered for helping solidify the cocky image he would carry with him for most of his playing days. In the 1939 Eastern League playoffs, Harris demonstrated the full force of his confidence. Wrote Hub Miller of *Baseball Magazine*:

"In the process of pacing Scranton to a pennant, the pride of Queens Village beat the Springfield club half a dozen times. But when the two rivals came together in the playoffs, Springfield won a close decision. Spencer Abbott, the Springfield manager and no shrinking violet, devoted the afternoon to giving Harris a verbal going over. Spencer used every word in a ballplayer's book.

"Of course there wasn't anything the young Harris could do about it. He had to stand out there and take it. But as he walked past the Springfield bench at the end of the game, he stopped and pointed a finger at Abbott, said: 'You had your innings today, Abbott. But remember this. Next year you'll still be down here, riding the same old busses and I'll be in the big leagues. And every time I go through Springfield on the train I'll stick my head out the window and wave to you.'"9

Indeed, Harris's prophecy came to pass the following season. Early in 1940, Red Sox manager Joe Cronin decided to carry Harris, on the strength of his 17–4 season at Scranton, and on the show Harris put on at camp. "The Bosox pilot [Cronin] decided to have a look at the young southpaw and as the training period progressed, it was evident that Mickey had a live fastball, a sharp curve, and good control."10 Still, Mickey's overconfidence again got higher billing than his pitching talents, as he was overheard remarking in training camp, "The pitchers on this ballclub don't look so hot. Winning twenty in the American League ought to be a cinch." His image was further aided by an ill-concealed phone call home, in which he informed his parents that he would be replacing established Red Sox left-hander Fritz Ostermueller. Cronin cracked down on the fresh young southpaw for the remainder of camp, though Harris would come to have the last laugh, as he made the 1940 team.

Harris won his Red Sox debut in Fenway Park on April 23, 1940, against the Washington Senators and hurler Dutch Leonard, 7–2. He followed up with a win at Philadelphia over George Caster, 7–3. From there, he slumped, losing his next two starts to the Browns' Denny Galehouse and Cleveland's future Hall of Famer Bob Feller, and earned a no-decision against the Yankees' Spud Chandler. The sudden drop-off stemmed from the most rookie of mistakes: Harris was tipping his pitches.11 Cronin shipped Harris back to the Scranton Miners in July; in his first major league stint, he'd posted a 4–2 record. As if to demonstrate to the skipper that his decision was ill-informed, Harris went on to post an Eastern League-leading ERA of 2.25.

Harris's first full season came the following year, in 1941. Harris himself acknowledged early in the spring that he had been unprepared for a full season the previous year:

"My trouble last season?" remarked Harris, "That's easy to answer.... In one word. Inexperience! I wasn't ready....

"I knew from the outset, even after winning those early games, that I needed more seasoning. Joe (Cronin) wanted me to throw overhead, because he felt it was my best pitch, and I felt the same way myself. Then from lack of experience, I found myself serving up too many fat pitches, like the day in St. Louis when they hit three homers off me.

"Yes, I knew my own faults and defects, and I'm sure that Cronin did the right thing sending me to Scranton. There I worked regularly, improved my overhead delivery and won 10 out of 15 games....

"I'm frank to admit that I still have a lot to learn, but I know that I'm much better equipped right now than a year ago this month, and I sure hope I stay with the Sox this time."12

Harris did remain in Boston for the entire 1941 campaign. He had matured enough to finish the year with a mark of eight wins and 14 losses, and even managed to be selected for the 1941 All-Star team, where he witnessed Ted Williams' historic game-winning home run to right field at Briggs Stadium in Detroit. Still, the excitement of his debut season was overshadowed by the onset of World War II.

In May 1941, Harris was classified 1A by his draft board in Queens, available for unrestricted military service. There were enough volunteer student reclassifications, so Mickey was assured that he would not likely be summoned until that fall. His brother, Robert, offered to serve in Mickey's stead in attempt to help along the fledgling major-league career, but "[t]he Army wouldn't buy the deal and so Mickey lost some of his best baseball years."13

On October 14, 1941, a month after his originally anticipated draft date, Harris was called into active service as Private Maurice Harris, 83rd CAAA (Coast Artillery Anti-

Harris warming up in Sarasota during spring training.

Aircraft) at Fort Eustis, Virginia. Harris was stationed in the Panama Canal Zone, far from the concerts of Europe and the Pacific, and seemed to take his service requirements in stride. Said Harris to an unidentified journalist that November, "I'm still young and I'll be back."

Harris maintained his form by pitching for the Balboa Brewers in the Panama Canal Department Army League. His professional experience held him head and shoulders above most of the competition, as Harris led his Brewers to the Canal Zone League championship in 1942. To cap it off, Mickey attained the highest pitching honor in baseball, tossing a perfect game. On April 12, 1942, he retired all 27 batters of the Canal Zone All-Stars on only 67 pitches, striking out five, in a 9–0 victory for Balboa. Said Harris, "The greatest thrill I ever got in baseball came to me in the Army, when I pitched that perfect game in Balboa. I got more kick out of that than I did out of winning my first professional game, or even winning my first full game with the Red Sox."[14]

Unfortunately, Harris injured his pitching arm in 1943, and was unable to help the Brewers repeat as Canal Zone League champions. Still, he managed to help the Brewers regain their top spot in 1944, and set a Canal League single-game strikeout record by whiffing 20 hitters on March 27, 1945.

Additionally, the 26-year-old Harris married Dorothy Elizabeth Baumann in St. Mary's Catholic Church in the Canal Zone on August 6, 1944. They had three boys: Richard, William, and Kevin.

Mickey confidently returned from the Army after his heroics in the Canal Zone League. Crowed Harris, "I'll win 25 this year. Yeah, I know that I wasn't facing DiMaggio, Keller, Heath, Boudreau, and a lot of other big league clouters down there but if a pitcher has control with a good amount of stuff, he can win in fast company. When I went into the Army, lack of control bothered me. I have that now and I'm just telling you that I'll win 25. Check with me next September 30."[15]

Upon returning from his time in the military, Mickey found himself an integral part of the rotation that helped carry the Red Sox to their first World Series appearance since 1918. Although he didn't end up reaching his 25-win prediction, Harris did manage to win his first seven starts of the '46 campaign en route to a 17–9 season record. He was unable, however, to come through when it counted most, losing both of his World Series starts to the St. Louis Cardinals.

Harris pitched Games Two and Six, losing to St. Louis lefty Harry Brecheen in both games. Although the final score in Game Two was 3–0, Harris himself was responsible for only one of the runs. Mickey bore more responsibility in Game Six, handing over three of the four Cardinal runs in the third inning. The real culprit in both losses was a Boston lineup unable to push across any runs.

In addition to being his best season, 1946 would turn out to be the only season in which Harris would win 10 games or more. The two closing World Series losses marked the beginning of the end for Harris's career. In 1947 his playing time was limited to 52 innings as the result of arm troubles that Harris claimed originated during a spring training start against the Cincinnati Reds.[16] In 1948, Harris threw 113 2/3 innings but managed only a 7–10 record. A healthier Harris started the 1949 campaign, but after posting only two wins in 37 2/3 innings for Joe McCarthy's Red Sox, he and outfielder Sam Mele were shipped to the Washington Senators for right-hander Walt Masterson.

In Washington the early returns on Harris were equally disappointing. He wrapped up 1949 as a starter for the Senators but managed only two more wins against 12 losses for the capital club, continuing the downward trend. In 1950, however, Mickey's career picked up some unexpected life.

The Washington manager was none other than Bucky Harris, the man responsible for converting Yankee hurler Joe Page into a reliever. During spring training, Bucky reportedly walked up to Mickey and said, "Look, you've always been a starting pitcher. From now on, you're a relief pitcher." Bucky's explanation was simple: "The guy's got the temperament. . . . He's cocky and confident. He's the kind of guy who loves a fight and loves to show how he can get out of trouble. He's got stuff and he's been around the league for a long time. And he's never going to do me much good as a starter. That's for sure."[17]

By August, Bucky knew his decision to convert Mickey had been a success: "That man has saved at least 15 ball games for me," he told a Boston sportswriter. "He's pitched in maybe 35 or 40. Sometimes, if my pitchers are going well, I don't use him for a week, and sometimes I need him every day for a week. It doesn't make any difference what I ask him to do. He does it, and that's what counts. You know what? With Page having a bum year, this guy's the best relief pitcher in the American league. Outside of that Konstanty pitcher over in the other league, he's the best relief pitcher in baseball."[18]

As it turned out, Harris did indeed save 15 games in 1950, to lead the league. He also led the league in appearances, toeing the rubber in 53 games and finishing 43 of them. The key to his success as a reliever was to eliminate his weakness as a starter, namely, his inability to pitch more than a few good innings because of his arm troubles.[19] Add a "newly developed slider pitch,"[20] and Harris found some late life in his new home.

He had a mediocre season on a mediocre team in 1951; Washington's most successful pitcher was Connie Marrero, with 11 wins. His career in Washington lasted one inning longer, and eight days after the 1952 season began, the Cleveland Indians purchased Harris's contract from the Senators for $10,000. At 35 years old, Harris was on his way to his third major league club. His stay in Cleveland would be even shorter than in Washington. After tossing 46 innings of relief for the Tribe, Harris found himself placed on waivers at the close of the season. When no claims were submitted, Mickey received his unconditional release on March 27, 1953. With that, his career in professional baseball came to a close, as Mickey announced his retirement that spring.

"I figured I might have one or possibly two years left in the majors," said Mickey, "and I concluded that I'd be better off to get out while I'm still young and healthy."[21]

After his baseball career ended, Mickey held jobs as a car salesman in North Cambridge, Massachusetts, as the Western New York salesman for AMF bowling equipment, and as a maintenance worker for Holy Sepulchre Cemetery and Alexander Hamilton Insurance Company. Both maintenance positions were held in his home of Farmington, Michigan, where he had lived for 15 years.[22]

Mickey Harris died of a heart attack suffered while bowling on April 15, 1971. He was 54 years old.

Notes

1. Shirley Povich, "Call for 'Mr. Trouble!'" *Baseball Digest* (September 1950): 90.
2. Jack Malaney, "Harris, Red Sox Hurler, Labels 'Pop-off' Tag as Bunk, but Mickey's No Mouse in Standing Up for His Rights," *Boston Post*, May 20, 1941.
3. Peter Golenbock, *Red Sox Nation* (Chicago: Triumph Books, 2005) 101.
4. John Drohan, "Mickey Whistles While He Wins—So Does His Fastball." Mickey Harris Player File, A. Bartlett Giamatti Research Center, National Baseball Hall of Fame and Museum.
5. Summary of Mickey Harris's signing and career, May 1971. Mickey Harris Player File.
6. Povich, "Call for 'Mr. Trouble!'" 91.
7. Jack Malaney, "Red Hot Rookie of Red Sox: Harris Makes Grade on Hill in Hurry," *Boston Post*, April 11, 1940.
8. Malaney, "Red Hot Rookie."
9. Hub Miller, "The Whistler From Queens," June 1947. Mickey Harris Player File. A. Bartlett Giamatti Research Center, National Baseball Hall of Fame and Museum.
10. Malaney, "Harris Labels Tag as Bunk."
11. Malaney, "Harris Labels Tag as Bunk."
12. Fred Knight, "Hash, Harris Ready to Make Comebacks," March 3 1941. Mickey Harris Player File, A. Bartlett Giamatti Research Center, National Baseball Hall of Fame and Museum.
13. "Brother Bob Offered To Serve in Army." Mickey Harris Player File, A. Bartlett Giamatti Research Center, National Baseball Hall of Fame and Museum.
14. Tom Meany, "Mickey Harris Had Biggest Thrill in Canal Zone," *PM Syndicate*, July 8, 1942.
15. Quote from Mickey Harris predicting success in 1946, March 1946. Mickey Harris Player File. A. Bartlett Giamatti Research Center, National Baseball Hall of Fame and Museum.
16. Hy Hurwitz, "Mickey Harris Ordered Not to Touch Baseball for Next Two Weeks," 26 June 1947. Mickey Harris Player File, A. Bartlett Giamatti Research Center, National Baseball Hall of Fame and Museum.
17. Al Hirshberg, " 'Fireman' Harris Haunts Red Sox" August 19, 1950. Mickey Harris Player File. A. Bartlett Giamatti Research Center, National Baseball Hall of Fame and Museum.
18. Hirshberg, "Harris Haunts Red Sox," August 19, 1950. Mickey Harris Player File.
19. Hirshberg, "Harris Haunts Red Sox," August 19, 1950. Mickey Harris Player File.
20. Povich, "Call for 'Mr. Trouble!'"
21. "Mickey Harris Quits Game," 1953. Mickey Harris Player File.
22. "Maurice 'Mickey' Harris," *Farmington Observer*, April 21, 1971, 14B.

Additional sources

Daniel, Dan. "Daniel's Dope." *World Telegram*, October 7, 1946.
Eberenz, Leo J. "3 in Row for Harris in Canal Zone Finals." May 25, 1944. Mickey Harris Player File. A. Bartlett Giamatti Research Center, National Baseball Hall of Fame and Museum.
Feldman, Chic. "Of Mickey Harris Late Pitching Idol." *The Scranton Tribune*, April 24, 1971.
Grossman, Leigh, ed. *The Red Sox Fan Handbook, Everything You Need to Know to be a Red Sox Fan or Marry One, Updated for 2005*. Boston: Rounder Books, 2005.
"Harris, Red Sox, Is Rated Class 1A of Army Draft." May 28, 1941. Mickey Harris Player File. A. Bartlett Giamatti Research Center, National Baseball Hall of Fame and Museum.
"Harris, Ex-Red Sox, Married in Canal Zone." *United Press*, August 7, 1944.
"Harris, Mele For Masterson." *United Press*, June 13, 1949.
"Harris, Mickey C," *Detroit Free Press*, April 17, 1971.

BILLY HITCHCOCK *by William Akin*

G	AB	R	H	2B	3B	HR	RBI	BB	SO	BA	OBP	SLG	SB	HBP
49	124	15	37	3	2	1	20	7	9	.298	.341	.379	0	1

Billy Hitchcock spent over forty years in professional baseball as a player, manager, scout, coach, and minor league executive. For nine seasons, between 1942 and 1953, he was a utility infielder with five major league clubs. He had stints as manager of Detroit, Baltimore and Atlanta in the 1960s. During the decade of the 1970s he served as the highly respected president of the Southern League.

Born William Clyde Hitchcock on July 31, 1918, in Inverness, Alabama, he was the son of James Franklin Hitchcock, clerk of the circuit court of Bullock County, Alabama, and Sallie Louise Davis. The family of five boys and two girls included an older brother, James, Jr., an All-American football player who played briefly in the majors.

Billy starred in two sports at Alabama Polytechnic Institute (now Auburn University). The 6'1", 185-pound All-Southern Conference tailback led Auburn to its first bowl game, the Bacardi Bowl in Havana, where he scored Auburn's only TD, a 40-yard run, in a 7–7 tie against Villanova. As captain and shortstop on the baseball team he led the Tigers to their first conference baseball title.

In his teen years Hitchcock played summer ball at Union Springs, Alabama, in the Dixie Amateur League (1933), Abbeville, Alabama (1934 and 1935), Greenville, North Carolina, in the semi-pro Coastal Plain League (1936), and a textile mill team in Langdale, Alabama (1937). After Hitchcock's graduation in 1938, Johnny Nee signed him for the New York Yankees. However, a knee injury sustained playing football kept him from playing until the following year.

The Yankees started Hitchcock at the highest level, with Kansas City of the American Association. With Phil Rizzuto as the Blues' shortstop in 1939 and 1940, Hitchcock moved to third base. He showed good speed, fielded cleanly, and hustled, but his .263 and .268 batting averages in 1939 and 1940 did not impress. With Vince DiMaggio (46 homers and 136 RBIs in 1939) and Rizzuto, minor league player of the year in 1940, Kansas City needed little from Hitchcock.

In 1941 Hitchcock emerged as a big league prospect. A knee operation after the 1939 season improved his range, and his marriage to former Auburn co-ed Rebecca Rice of Opelika, Alabama, prior to the 1941 season gave him security. With Rizzuto's promotion to New York, Hitchcock

Billy Hitchcock seen in 1949.
Courtesy of George Brace Photo.

moved to shortstop. He batted a solid .296 with 59 RBIs and 24 stolen bases. Joe Williams reported in The Sporting News "at least six big league clubs are after him" (*TSN*, 9/11/1941).

Detroit acquired Hitchcock from the Yankees and made the rookie their shortstop for 1941. He made his debut April 7, 1941, and that first game remained his greatest baseball thrill. Even though he hit only .211 in 1941, at 23 he seemed destined to have a long career ahead of him.

Hitchcock, who was a lieutenant in the Army reserves, got the call to report for active duty in early August 1941. He served in the Army Air Force and advanced to the rank of major by the end of World War II, earning the Bronze Star for service in the Pacific and three battle stars.

When Hitchcock returned to baseball in 1946, the Tigers had given their shortstop job to Eddie Lake. Hitchcock played only three games before Detroit sold him to Washington, where the great pre-war shortstop Cecil Travis had to switch to third base because of his war injuries. Hitchcock hit a disappointing .212 as the Nats shortstop.

For the next three years Hitchcock settled into a utility role. Washington sold him to St. Louis, where in 1947 he hit his first home run but batted only .222. The Browns traded him to Boston with Ellis Kinder for pitcher Clem Dreisewerd and infielders Sam Dente and Bill Sommers. He contributed a tidy .298 average in the BoSox' pennant drive in 1948, but fell back to .204 in 1949.

In the early 1950s, Hitchcock logged three solid seasons with the Philadelphia Athletics. After Boston traded him for catcher Buddy Rosar, he became Connie Mack's regular second baseman in 1950. He batted a quite respectable .273, with personal highs in doubles and triples. In 1951 he compiled a .306 average, the only year he hit over .300 in either the major or minor leagues. On September 9 he had his best day, hitting two triples and a double while driving in five runs. The following year, as the regular third baseman, his average dropped to .246, but he posted his major league high of 56 RBIs.

Detroit reacquired Hitchcock in 1953 in a trade for Don Kolloway, but he played only 22 games for the Tigers, batting .211, the same as he hit for them in his rookie season twelve years earlier.

The Tigers organization liked Hitchcock and believed the affable Alabaman had a future in the game. They appointed him as manager of their Triple A farm club in Buffalo (International League) for one season, 1954, and then brought him to Detroit as a coach. He stayed in that position for the next seven years under six different managers. In 1960 the Tigers and Cleveland pulled off one of the strangest deals in baseball history, trading managers. Jimmy Dykes left Detroit for Cleveland, and Joe Gordon came to the Tigers. Detroit had a game to play before Gordon could reach the club, and Hitchcock managed for one game, a Tigers victory.

After seven years as a coach, Hitchcock got the opportunity in 1962 to manage in the majors. Lee McPhail, president and general manager of the Baltimore Orioles, thought his young team would perform better for an easy-going manager than for authoritarian Paul Richards. Brooks Robinson remembered, "Billy was the nicest guy you ever wanted to meet, but we didn't play very well under him" (Peary, 579). In fact, the 1962 Birds were awful. Their wins declined from 95 to 77. In retrospect, it is surprising Hitchcock stayed at the helm for 1963. In his second season, the Orioles got off to a good start and were in first place at the end of May, but they swooned in June, losing 22 of 30 games. The Orioles did recover enough to finish with 86 victories against 76 loses, but fans were disappointed, and Baltimore quickly replaced Hitchcock with drill-sergeant Hank Bauer. After the team added Frank Robinson and Jim Palmer, Bauer would lead the O's to the pennant in 1966.

Hitchcock's managerial stint at Baltimore ended with a 163–161 record. His 1963 team was built around fielding and speed. They led the American League in steals and fielding average, but pitching let them down.

Another chance to manage came in 1966 and 1967. After Hitchcock's firing, McPhail kept him on as field coordinator and scout for the Orioles. Then John McHale hired him as scout for the Milwaukee Braves in 1965. When the team moved to Atlanta in 1966, Billy became a coach under fellow Alabaman Bobby Bragan. After winning 84–88 games the three previous seasons, the Braves slumped in Atlanta. Following a 52–59 start under Bragan, McHale handed the reigns to Hitchcock. His mild-mannered approach seemed to pay off, as the Braves suddenly became the hottest team in the league, finishing with a 33–18 record under Hitchcock. Hank Aaron's 44 home runs and 127 RBIs helped.

The high expectations engendered by the strong finish in 1966 could not be met in 1967. The club fell to seventh with a 77–82 record. The season resembled the 1963 season in Baltimore in that the Braves played well the first half of the season, only 3.5 games back on July 22. Then they nose-dived, finishing 24.5 games behind the league leader. Hitchcock's managing style differed sharply from his approach at Baltimore. The Braves, old and slow, relied on an offense that played for one base at a time. They led the NL in home runs, but were ninth in stolen bases, played leaky defense, and had poor relief pitching.

Hitchcock announced his retirement after the 1967 season. In winters he had helped in his father-in-law's hardware store in Opelika. Now he would run the store, but his retirement from baseball proved short-lived. When John McHale moved from the Braves to the expansion Expos in 1969, he persuaded Hitchcock to serve as special assignment scout and then director of minor league instruction for Montreal.

Early in the 1970 season, Sam Smith, who had headed the Southern League since its rebirth in 1964, died of a heart attack. Montgomery general manager Woody Parks urged Hitchcock to consider the position of league president, and the owners quickly elected him. Hitchcock's only stipulation was that the league headquarters move to Opelika. He acted to reorganize the league. He abolished the Dixie Association, a quasi-merger arrangement with the Texas league, brought in additional teams, set up a divisional format with a post-season playoff, and in 1976 the league introduced a split season. The addition of Nashville in 1978 pushed league attendance over 1,000,000 for the first time, up from 333,500 when Hitchcock took office, and it rose to 1,761,192 when he stepped down in 1980. Under his leadership the "Southern League enjoyed growing popularity, extraordinary attendance, and financial stability."[1]

Hitchcock continued to live in Opelika. His first wife died in 1973, and in 1976 he married Bette Ann Miller of Opelika, a widow with five children. He played slow-pitch softball until he was 60, but his major retirement avocation has been golf, a sport he has enjoyed throughout his adult life. He combined his love of golf with his commitment to bettering his alma mater by establishing Auburn's Billy Hitchcock Golf Tournament, which has become a premier collegiate golf event. Auburn has returned his loyalty by naming its renovated baseball field Hitchcock Field. In 2003 Baseball America named this 4,090-seat facility the best college stadium in the country.

Notes

1. O'Neal, Bill. *The Southern League: Baseball in Dixie, 1885–1994* (Austin: Eakin Press, 1994), pp. 161–162

Sources

Devaney, John, "A Study of Player Discontent," *Sport*, February 1967, p. 18.

Greene, Sam, "Billy Hitchcock: Hardwareman to Tool Up the Orioles," *Baseball Digest*, February 1962, pp. 63–65.

Hitchcock File in the A Bartlett Giamatti Research Library at the Hall of Fame contains dozens of clippings from *The Sporting News* between 1939 and 1980.

James, Bill. *The Bill James Guide to Baseball Managers* (New York: Scribner, 1997)

O'Neal, Bill. *The Southern League: Baseball in Dixie, 1885–1994* (Austin: Eakin Press, 1994)

TEX HUGHSON *by Andrew Blume*

G	ERA	W	L	SV	GS	GF	CG	SHO	IP	H	R	ER	BB	SO	HR	HBP	WP	BFP
15	5.12	3	1	0	0	11	0	0	19⅓	21	14	11	7	6	0	0	0	84

G	AB	R	H	2B	3B	HR	RBI	BB	SO	BA	OBP	SLG	SB	HBP
15	2	0	0	0	0	0	0	0	0	.000	.000	.000	0	0

Tex Hughson was a big right-handed power pitcher out of the University of Texas who principally wore the number 21 during his tenure with the Red Sox (he would also be assigned the numbers 29, 15, and 27) and, like his numerical counterpart and fellow Longhorn Roger Clemens four decades later, was the dominant Red Sox hurler of his era; and when healthy, was one of the top starting pitchers in the big leagues. Were it not for military service and arm problems that drastically shortened his career, Hughson would in all likelihood have been on course for Cooperstown immortality and the Red Sox might not have suffered for 86 years between world championships. However, it is unlikely that Hughson would ever complain about the circumstances that shortened his time in baseball as he went on to be a dominant positive force in his Texas community of San Marcos.

Hughson pitched his entire big-league career for the Red Sox during the decade of the 1940s, compiling a record of 96–54, good for 11th place on the Red Sox career wins list. With a .640 winning percentage, he ranks fourth on the Red Sox all-time winning percentage list among pitchers with at least 100 decisions, ahead of Clemens (.634) and behind only Pedro Martinez (.760), Joe Wood (.676), and Babe Ruth (.659). When he was healthy and at the top of his game, he was the man the Red Sox wanted on the mound against the opposition's ace. Red Sox teammates Bobby Doerr and Johnny Pesky are reported by writer Oren Renick to have named Hughson as the man they wanted on the mound in a crucial game.

Cecil Carlton Hughson was born to Cecil "Pop" and Ada (Rowland) Hughson on February 9, 1916, in Buda, Texas and grew up in Kyle in Central Texas, 20 miles south of Austin. There he was exposed to the rugged life of a cattle rancher and farmer by his father, who operated the family-owned Hughson Meat Company.

After graduation from Kyle High School (in a class of only 11 to 13, according to his daughter Jane Hughson), he pitched at the University of Texas at Austin for legendary coach William J. "Uncle Billy" Disch, whose teams

Tex Hughson in 1942, the year he posted a 22-6 record.

went 465–115–9 during Disch's career from 1911 to 1939. Tex lettered in baseball in 1937 and compiled an 8–2 record, earning First Team All-Southwest Conference honors. In June 1937, Hughson was signed by the Red Sox. After several years of acquiring expensive major-league talent the Red Sox had changed course—farm director Billy Evans was acquiring home-grown talent that eventually contributed to the team's 1946 pennant winner, including Ted Williams, Bobby Doerr, Dom DiMaggio, Dave "Boo" Ferriss, Hughson, Mickey Harris, Earl Johnson, and Johnny Pesky.

Hughson went to Moultrie of the Class D Georgia-Florida League and got his feet wet in 1937 with a record of 8–6 (2.33 ERA) and a good ratio of strikeouts (76) to walks (38). In 1938, he starred for the Canton Terriers of the Class C Middle Atlantic League, compiling a league-leading .759 winning percentage (22–7, 3.93 ERA) while striking out 129 and walking only 64 in 205 innings. His 22 wins also led the league. He finished the 1938 season with the Red Sox-owned Rocky Mount team in the Class B Piedmont League. In 1939, Tex moved up to Class A ball, teaming with Mickey Harris at Scranton in the Eastern League, but finished 1939 and played in 1940 for the Louisville Colonels of the then Double A American Association, the minors' highest classification.

In 1940, Hughson finished 7–11 with a 2.91 ERA for Louisville but got the parent club's attention in the post-season, finishing 5–0 in the playoffs, first helping the Colonels eliminate Columbus and then beating Newark, the Yankees' International League farm team, twice in the Little World Series. Prior to his playoff run, Tex so impressed Cincinnati Reds scout Jewel Ens in tossing a three-hit shutout against Indianapolis that the Reds reportedly offered the Colonels $50,000 for him. "Broadway Charlie" Wagner is credited by sportswriter John Drohan with having sold Red Sox manager Joe Cronin on promoting Tex to the big club in 1941.

On April 16, 1941, the 25-year-old Hughson made his major league debut in relief for the Red Sox in a 12-inning contest against the Washington Senators at Fenway

Park, a game won 8–7 by the Red Sox. Then he spent some time with Louisville, going 7–1, but was back with the big-league club on July 6 to make his first start. It came against the Senators at Fenway in the second game of a twin bill, facing off against Washington's Bill Zuber.

Tex surrendered two doubles and a single to open the game. Pitching coach Frank Shellenback was running the team, as Joe Cronin had left the game to be with his wife, who was giving birth to a son, and Hughson is said to have pleaded with Shellenback to leave him in the game. Tex settled down after the shaky start en route to a 4–3 complete-game win, his first win as a big-leaguer. He compiled a 5–3, 4.13 record in 12 appearances and 61 innings in his first season. His eight starts included four complete games.

Another 1942 image of Hughson.

The biggest obstacle he would face in his career was not the opposition's bats but the health of his pitching wing. In mid-August 1941, Hughson pulled his deltoid muscle, putting him on the shelf for the rest of the season.

Hughson emerged as the ace of the Red Sox in his breakout 1942 season (the "pitching sensation of the league this season," according to Jack Malaney of the *Boston Post*), in which the Red Sox won 93 games, their most since 1915. Tex completed 22 of his 30 starts, his first start not having come until May 16 (after he again experienced arm troubles in the spring), an amazing number considering his final win total. His career-best 22 wins, against only six losses, led the American League and tied the Cardinals' Mort Cooper for the major league lead. Hughson also led the league in complete games, innings (a career-high 281), and strikeouts (113). His ERA was an exceptional 2.59. Tex was 5–1 against the World Series-bound Yankees. According to Oren Renick, Tex relished the opportunity to face the Yankees throughout his career. "I would rather beat the Yankees once than any other team twice," he told Renick. "They were the best, and they were cocky, particularly in New York with those Yankee pinstripes on. It was as if you ought not to beat them. You ought to just go out there and rather politely lose."

Tex was named to his first of three All-Star teams in 1942, although he did not enter the game to pitch since starter Spud Chandler of the Yankees and the Tigers' Al Benton were the only two pitchers used by AL skipper Joe McCarthy in its 3–1 win at the Polo Grounds in New York. Hughson was named to *The Sporting News* All Rookie team along with pitchers Johnny Beazley of the Cardinals and Hank Borowy of the Yankees. He was also selected to *The Sporting News* Major League All-Star Team.

The 1942 Red Sox finished second, nine games back of the Yankees. Their progress was dramatically affected from 1943 through 1945 by World War II and the military draft, probably more so than any other major-league team. According to Glenn Stout, only Bobby Doerr, Jim Tabor, and Hughson remained in 1943 and '44 from the 1942 starting team (Tony Lupien was with the Sox in 1943 but was traded in 1944). By 1945, even Doerr, Tabor, and Hughson were in the service. No Red Sox regular player hit over .300 in 1943. Hughson led the pitching staff in wins with a 12–15, 2.64 record in 266 innings. His 20 complete games led the league. Hughson was felled by a Jimmy Bloodworth line drive in a game against the Tigers that broke his pitching thumb. His inability to grip the ball properly upon his return explains why he won only one of his last 10 decisions in the year. It is thus no surprise that the Red Sox fell to 68–84, 29 games back of the Yankees. Hughson was selected to his second All-Star team. He earned the save in the game, won 5–3 by the American League at Philadelphia's Shibe Park, allowing a pair of runs and five hits in three innings.

Hughson dominated again in 1944, compiling an 18–5, 2.26 (career-best ERA) record, his .783 winning percentage and 9.43 WHIP (walks and hits per inning pitched) leading the league and keeping the Red Sox in contention for the AL flag. Selected to his third and final All-Star team, Hughson was the pitcher of record in the AL's 7–1 loss at Forbes Field in Pittsburgh. After retiring the side in order in the fourth in relief of starter Borowy, Tex allowed four runs, three of them earned, on five hits in the fifth.

On August 9, 1944, Hughson pitched his final game before leaving the team for military induction, defeating the White Sox with a 9–1 four-hitter at Fenway, the ninth game he had won that year by allowing only one run. After the game, the Red Sox stood in second place, 6½ games behind the St. Louis Browns. With the loss of Hughson, coupled with the further loss within a couple of weeks of both AL Most Valuable Player Doerr and catcher Hal Wagner to the military, the Red Sox folded, losing 29 of their final 50 games, including 10 in a row in September, as the Browns won their first and only American League flag.

At the time of his induction into the military, the 6-foot-3, 198-pound Hughson was in the prime of his career. He coupled power pitching with superb control and a masterful knowledge of what to throw to which hitter. The *Neyer/James Guide to Pitchers* lists Hughson as having thrown a sinking fastball, hard curve, slider, screwball, an occasional knuckleball, and a changeup. He admitted to having thrown an occasional spitter as well to throw the hitter off balance. He was said to have absorbed everything he could relating to pitching. "Youth and experience never go together," Tex told sportswriter Al Hirshberg. "If they did, we would all be great before we were 21. I want the advantage of youth, plus the knowledge of experience.... Once I knew a wise old Dutchman who told me something I will never forget. We are too soon old and too late smart."

Writing in *The Sporting News*, Shirley Povich quoted an anonymous umpire talking about the AL pitchers at the time of Hughson's August 28 induction into the military: "Tex...was the best. With his stuff he should have won every game he pitched. He got licked usually when he got mad. It upset him when a .220 hitter hit one of his good pitches. If he had kept his temper, they'd never have beaten him. Hughson threw everything. And whatever he threw, he had control. His catcher needed more signals than any catcher. If Hughie was behind in the count on a hitter, he didn't have to ease up to get the ball over like other pitchers. He poured the next two in there. He was the only fellow in the league who could throw the ball and let the batter do the worrying." On Hughson's return from the war in 1946, former Tigers general manager Jack Zeller called him the greatest right-hander in the game at that time, saying, "Compared with...Hughson, the others are only throwers. He has an arm, too, but he puts more headwork into his pitching. He is one of the most cunning pitchers in years." In giving the nod to Hughson, Zeller bypassed Bob Feller, Spud Chandler, Dave Ferriss, and Jack Kramer. In 1948, Joe DiMaggio named Hughson and Virgil Trucks as the pitchers who gave him the most trouble.

Originally intended for induction into the Navy, Hughson wound up in the Army. Much of his war effort was directed toward improving the military morale through baseball at postings ranging from Texas to Hawaii to the Marianas Islands in the Pacific. Tex, by his own admission, "fought World War II with a bat and a glove." In a letter to manager Joe Cronin from Saipan, Tex addressed preparations for the play of a three-team Army Air Force league called the Marianas League, which would feature major league players in the service: "We have been busy building our own tents to live in and our own park to play in. The ball park certainly is no beauty, but will answer the purpose. Of course, there is no grass and the seats for 'customers' are made exclusively of bomb crates, of which we have plenty here." Hughson hurled the first three innings of the Marianas League All-Star game, held in September 1945 and won 3–2 by the American

Hughson with Charlie Wagner, 1942.

League. His 73rd Wing Bombers, managed by former Red Sox outfielder Buster Mills, won the Marianas League championship.

On January 17, 1946, the Red Sox received great news in the form of Ted Williams being put on the inactive list by the Marine Corps, Dom DiMaggio being released from the Navy, and Hughson being mustered out of the Army Air Forces. With their return, along with DiMaggio, Doerr, Pesky, Jim Tabor, and Wagner, the Red Sox busted out of the gate and never looked back, winning 41 of their first 50 games, including 15 in a row from April 25 through May 10, and opening up a 10-game cushion over the Yankees.

Tex won the April 16 season opener in Washington, 6–3. He and 1945 rookie sensation Dave Ferriss teamed up to become the Red Sox' first pair of 20-game winners since 1935. Ferriss won 25 games to lead the Sox. Hughson was 20–11 with a 2.75 ERA in a career-high 35 starts, his ERA half a run per game better than that of Ferriss. Hughson's 172 strikeouts established a career high. He led the league in fewest walks per game with 1.65. He tossed six shutouts, including four won by 1–0 scores. The fourth of those 1–0 nailbiters occurred on September 13 at Cleveland, breaking a six-game Red Sox losing streak and clinching the AL flag, a game won by Ted Williams' only career inside-the-park home run, one of only two hits given up by opposing pitcher Red Embree. Tex allowed only three hits of his own in a game reported to have been completed in an hour and 28 minutes. The Red Sox won the American League pennant by 12 games over the Tigers with the Yankees a distant third, 17 games behind.

Hughson faced off against Howie Pollet and the St. Louis Cardinals in Game One of the 1946 World Series at Sportsman's Park in St. Louis on October 6. Tex retired the first six Cardinals in order. The Red Sox scored the first run in the second inning on a Pinky Higgins single that scored Rudy York, who had been hit by a pitch. The Cardinals tied the game in the sixth when Red Schoendienst singled and Stan Musial doubled him home. The Cardinals took a brief lead in the eighth. Whitey Kurowski singled and was driven home on a Joe Garagiola double to center. Hughson was removed after the eighth inning for a pinch-hitter. His line was seven hits and two earned runs over eight innings with five strikeouts and two walks. The Red Sox tied the game in the ninth on singles by Higgins, Rip Russell, and Tom McBride. York homered in the 10th off hard-luck 3–2 loser Pollet. Earl Johnson closed out the contest with two hitless innings and got the win.

Hughson didn't fare well in his second start of the Series, Game Four at Fenway Park. After a one-two-three first, Enos Slaughter opened the second with a homer, one of his four hits in the game. (Kurowski and Garagiola each collected four hits as well). Tex was knocked around for six runs, three of them earned, on five hits with one strikeout in two-plus innings of a 12–3, 20-hit Cardinals win.

Hughson's third and final appearance of the 1946 Series came in Game Six in St. Louis. Intended to be saved along with Ferriss for a possible Game Seven, Tex came on in relief of starter Mickey Harris in the third with the Sox trailing 3–0. He scattered two hits over 4⅓ innings, striking out two and walking one in the Red Sox' 4–1 loss, which evened the Series at three victories apiece. Hughson's history of arm problems made him unavailable for the deciding seventh game.

After their Game Seven loss to the Cardinals in 1946, the Red Sox saw no reason why they couldn't return to the World Series in 1947. But injuries to the previous year's big three of Hughson, Ferriss, and Harris thwarted the Red Sox' repeat pennant aspirations. Joe Dobson won 18, but Hughson, Ferriss, and Harris won only 29 games combined after totaling 62 in 1946. Each of the three developed a sore arm in the spring. Ferriss went down in late August with a badly cut toe, which was slow to heal. Harris had a bad shoulder that limited him to six starts. The season had started promisingly for Hughson. He retired the first 15 Senators he faced in the season-opening 7–6 victory. On April 24, he tossed a two-hit, 1–0 shutout over the Yankees. Then the physical troubles began again. In May, he became hindered in his pitching efforts by numbness in the tip of the middle finger of his pitching hand. It was also speculated that he had a chipped bone in his elbow. On September 3, in the first game of a doubleheader, Hughson was removed from the game in the fifth with numbness and circulatory trouble in his arm. "The circulation went out completely; I was in terrible pain," he said. He was sent to a specialist, who determined that surgery was necessary.

This surgery was performed at a time when orthopedic surgery was relatively primitive and long before the days of arthroscopic surgery. Writer David Falkner says the first time Hughson heard the term "rotator cuff," years later, he thought it was a type of French shirt. Apparently an overdeveloped muscle had cut off circulation in his pitching arm, an injury similar to that later experienced by both J.R. Richard and Whitey Ford. Hughson's season was over. He was 12–11 with a 3.33 ERA in 29 games and 189⅓ innings, with 13 complete games and 119 strikeouts. The 1947 Red Sox finished in third, 14 games behind the Yankees. Hughson had offseason surgical procedures on his shoulder and his elbow, and the nerve in his right shoulder responsible for the numbness was severed.

Still recovering, Hughson made slow progress in the spring of 1948. New manager Joe McCarthy was reluctant to put his trust in the rehabbing Sox ace. After pitching in two innings of relief against the Browns on May 8, Hughson was optioned to the Austin Pioneers of the Class B Big State League, 30 miles from his San Marcos home. He hoped that the Texas heat would aid his recovery. Hughson went 4–0 for Austin. He discovered that by warming up slowly and for a long time, he could throw "pretty hard without ill effects." He found curves and sliders to be harder to toss without strain. On July 12, Hughson was recalled by the Red Sox. He pitched the ninth inning of a 3–1 loss to the Tigers on July 17, retiring the side in order. He was used exclusively in relief, 19⅓ innings pitched in 15 games, winning three and losing one with a 5.12 ERA. A Red Sox fan could only dream of what a healthy Hughson could have contributed to the 96-win Red Sox squads of 1948 and 1949, each of which lost the pennant by just one game.

Of Hughson's 29 appearances in 1949, only two were starts, one each in in April and May. He was 4–2 with a 5.33 ERA in 77⅔ innings, finishing 17 games. Mel Parnell won 25 games and Ellis Kinder 23. McCarthy wore out both pitchers down the stretch. He used Hughson sparingly in relief for a period, then overused him causing his elbow to swell up. Hughson's final major league appearance came in the final game of the season, in Yankee Stadium with the Red Sox and Yankees tied for first, in the bottom of the eighth with the Yankees up 2–0 and Hughson not having pitched in a game in four weeks. Hughson reportedly said: "They're really scraping the bottom of the barrel." He got Joe DiMaggio to hit into a double play, then gave up singles to Johnny Lindell and Billy Johnson. Hank Bauer ran for Lindell and went to third when Ted Williams bobbled Johnson's hit. Cliff Mapes was intentionally walked, bringing up rookie second baseman Jerry Coleman. Hughson threw hard, high, and inside on Coleman's hands. Coleman managed to dump the ball into no-man's land near the foul line between right fielder Al Zarilla and second baseman Doerr, Zarilla missing the catch, according to the *Boston Herald's* Arthur Sampson by "the width of a gnat's eyebrow," clearing the bases and giving the Yankees breathing room in their 5–3 win, which painfully wrested the pennant away from the Red Sox. Ted Williams recalled the play in David Halberstam's *Summer of '49*: "Tex makes a good pitch. A damn good pitch....I can still see it with my eyes closed....It's funny how you can remember something so painful so clearly."

Hughson resented McCarthy's reluctance to give him the opportunity to reclaim his position as the staff ace. "The only man in baseball I completely disliked was Joe McCarthy," Hughson told sportswriter George Sullivan. "I asked to be traded and said I wouldn't be back in 1950. So they sold me to the Giants....I refused to report. I didn't want to live in New York, and I didn't want to start pitching in a new league at my age (then 34). So the Red Sox sent Jack Kramer to the Giants instead and I retired. The same day McCarthy quit in June 1950, Bobby Doerr called me in Texas while I was buying cattle and said they wanted me to go back. 'No, I'm retired for good,' I told him. Yes, I had arm problems my last three seasons. But I'm positive I could have pitched some more. I wouldn't when McCarthy was there, though, and when he was gone it was too late."

Along with his 96–54 career record, Hughson had a 2.94 ERA, 10th on the Red Sox all-time list among pitchers with at least 1,000 innings. He struck out 693 and walked only 372 in 1,375 2/3 innings. His 99 complete games place him 10th on the Red Sox all-time list, and his 19 shutouts place him in a tie for seventh place on the list. The 13 consecutive wins at home in 1944 tie him with Ferriss for the Red Sox record in that department.

Hughson was inducted into the Longhorn Hall of Honor in 1970 and the Texas Sports Hall of Fame in 1987. On November 14, 2002, he was inducted into the Red Sox Hall of Fame, his son Stanley accepting on behalf of the Hughson family. Hughson and the 1946 team were honored at a reunion dinner in 1986 at which he was awarded a World Series ring and a Red Sox jacket which his daughter Jane said he was very proud of and wore all over town.

After retiring from baseball, Hughson became a successful real estate developer in San Marcos. His development of family ranch land was called Hughson Heights and included a tribute to Fenway Park in its Fenway Loop. The front license plate of his car reportedly announced "Boston is baseball." Hughson became a frequent contributor at Red Sox spring training camps and maintained relationships with Pesky, Doerr, and Williams. In 1952, he founded Little League Baseball in San Marcos and in 1954, while serving as the vice president of the San Marcos School Board, successfully moved to integrate the local high school after the United States Supreme Court decision in Brown v. Board of Education found racially separate but equal public schools to be unconstitutional.

Hughson was one of the first to introduce the French Charolais breed of cattle through the family-owned Hughson Meat Company, founded by his father in 1946 and in which the family remained involved in ownership into the 1970s. The company, which provides beef products to the grocery, restaurant and hotel industries and to the public through a retail outlet in San Marcos, is still in business.

Hughson died of kidney failure at Central Texas Medical Center at the age of 77 on August 6, 1993, and was buried in San Marcos Cemetery. With his first wife, Roena Moore, he had two daughters, Dixie Moffitz, born in 1941, and Jane Hughson, born in 1954, and a son, Stanley, born in 1944. Several years after Roena's premature death in 1968, Hughson was married again, to Gladys Watson, who was with him at his death. He was also survived by a brother, Bruce; a sister Mary Helen Conway; and six grandchildren.

Sources

The Associated Press.
Baseball-reference.com.
Boston Red Sox Media Guide 2007.
Falkner, David, "That Farewell to Arms Feeling", *The Sporting News*, May 20, 1996.
Gentile, Derek, *The Complete Boston Red Sox* (New York: Black Dog & Leventhal Publishers, Inc., 2003)
Gillette, Gary and Pete Palmer, *The Ultimate Red Sox Companion* (Hingham, Mass.: Maple Street Press, 2007)
Golenbock, Peter, *Red Sox Nation* (Chicago: Triumph Books, 2005)
Halberstam, David, *Summer of '49* (New York: William Morrow and Company, Inc., 1989)
Hirshberg, Al, *The Red Sox, The Bean and The Cod* (Boston: Waverly House, 1947)
www.Hughson-Meat.com.
Interview with Jane Hughson, December 2007.
James, Bill, and Rob Neyer, *The Neyer/James Guide to Pitchers* (New York: Simon & Schuster, Inc. (Fireside), 2004
Lieb, Frederick G., *The Boston Red Sox* (New York: Van Rees Press (Putnam), 1947
Linn, Ed, *The Great Rivalry*, (New York: Ticknor & Fields, 1991)
Looney, Jack, *Now Batting, Number...* (New York: Black Dog & Leventhal, 2006)
New York Times.
Nowlin, Bill, *Day by Day With the Boston Red Sox* (Cambridge, Mass.: Rounder Books, 2006)
Paper of Record.com.
Proquest Historical Newspapers.
Renick, Oren, "Cowboy on the Mound: The Tex Hughson Story," *San Marcos Daily Record*, Septembevr 5, 2004
Retrosheet.org.
Snyder, John, *Red Sox Journal* (Cincinnati: Emmis Books, 2006)
Stout, Glenn, and Richard A. Johnson, *Red Sox Century* (New York: Houghton Mifflin Company, 2005)
Tan, Cecilia, and Bill Nowlin, *The 50 Greatest Red Sox Games* (Hoboken, N,J,: John Wiley & Sons, 2006)
TexasSports.com.
The Sporting News.
Sullivan, George, *The Picture History of the Boston Red Sox* (Indianapolis/New York: The Bobbs-Merrill Company, 1980)
Thorn, John et al., *Total Baseball, Sixth Edition* (New York: Total Sports, Inc., 1999)
Walton, Ed, *This Date in Boston Red Sox History* (Briarcliff Manor, N.Y.: Scarborough House, 1978)
The Washington Post.

EARL JOHNSON *by Bill Nowlin*

G	ERA	W	L	SV	GS	GF	CG	SHO	IP	H	R	ER	BB	SO	HR	HBP	WP	BFP
35	4.53	10	4	5	3	21	1	0	91⅓	98	49	46	42	45	7	0	2	402

G	AB	R	H	2B	3B	HR	RBI	BB	SO	BA	OBP	SLG	SB	HBP
35	31	2	3	0	0	0	3	1	9	.097	.125	.097	0	0

Among all the ballplayers who served in World War II, Earl Johnson was the real military hero. Unlike some, he had his better years after the long layoff for the war, peaking in 1947, but began to lose his edge just as the Red Sox entered two seasons (1948 and 1949) when one more win would have made all the difference.

The "smiling Swedish southpaw" (a phrase found by Jack Kavanagh) was born in Redmond, Washington on April 2, 1919. But he wasn't Swedish. In fact, his grandfather Hjalmar Johansen was one of the most famous polar explorers from Norway who sought the North Pole with Fridtjof Nansen on the boat *Fram*. Nansen and Johansen became icebound and had to take dogsleds to survive; they returned a year later and folks thought they were dead. Their return created a major sensation; they became national heroes. Later, Johansen joined in an expedition with Raoul Amundsen to seek the South Pole. An Oslo museum has preserved the *Fram* for today's visitors. The family name Johansen was Anglicized to Johnson after arriving in America. Earl was the third of three sons born to George Johansen (who emigrated to the United States from Narvik) and Love Lillian Glass, originally from Canada. The three boys—George, Chet, and Earl—some 16 years later had a sister, Norma Jean. Love Lillian was a homemaker, but worked for a while for Seattle's Bemis Bag Co. George Sr. played some semipro ball at first base before taking up his life's work.

"Papa George" Johnson worked as an installer for the Pacific Northwest Telephone Company for 35 years, explains his daughter-in-law Elsie J. Busch, herself of Swedish origin. Elsie's husband George Jr. was the eldest of the three boys, born in 1914. George Jr. played baseball from grade school on, and for all four years at Seattle's Ballard High School but graduated in 1933 during the depths of the Depression and earning an income was of immediate necessity. He did play some semipro ball in California, also at first base, but was able to secure a position as lineman with the telephone company. After he and Elsie Granstrom had their first child, George Jr. was able to transfer to inside wiring work working as a PBX installer and no longer needed to climb poles. The

Earl Johnson in 1941.

couple raised a daughter, Diane, and a son, David. Elsie worked 28 years for an insurance company.

The middle boy Chester was born 16 months before Earl, and had a long career in baseball, ultimately making the major leagues only very briefly near the end of 1946 with the St. Louis Browns. Chet was a left-handed pitcher, like his younger brother, and also played at Ballard High. After graduation in 1935, he worked in the shipyards and attended the University of Washington before finally being scouted and signed by Red Killefer. He began with El Paso in 1939 and played for Tacoma and Bakersfield, as well as three Pacific Coast League teams: San Francisco, San Diego, and Seattle before World War II was over. His brief stay with the Browns only saw him pitch 18 innings in five games, with a 5.00 ERA. He spent 1947–49 with Toledo and Indianapolis in the American Association and then played 1950 through 1956 back in the Coast League with San Francisco and Oakland, and the last five seasons with Sacramento. He won 204 games and lost 215.

Chet was also known for his comical pitching antics in games that were lopsided affairs. "I loved to see the fans have a good time. My purpose, though, was to make the hitters laugh with me or get so mad that they'd lose their concentration and swing at anything I threw." After baseball, he worked for Seattle Fuel, and later became a salesman for Cudahy Bar-S Meats until his retirement. He also refereed college basketball and football games, and worked with Earl as a pitching instructor at a summer baseball camp in Oliver, British Columbia. Chet and his wife Nancy Lee Rowe had two boys, Bill and Dick—both of whom played ball quite a bit but never to the point of becoming professional—and two daughters, Martha and Theresa.

Earl Douglas Johnson also attended Ballard High. Though in grade school he'd only played softball, he played exceptionally well in high school and was fortunate in being able to receive a baseball scholarship to attend St. Mary's College in Oakland, California, the college that produced so many major league ballplayers over the years. Pitching at such a showcase school, and at one point winning a reported 24 games in a row, it was no surprise that he caught the attention of scouts from several teams. Earl also played a little semipro ball in Bremerton, Washington in 1939. Red Sox scouts Billy Disch and Ernie Johnson (no relation) are credited with his signing around Christmas time 1939.

He was an imposing 6'3", 200-pounder. Earl was assigned to Boston's Class-B Piedmont League affiliate in Rocky Mount NC and pitched very well, with a 12–6 record and a 2.67 ERA. He got off to a great start, but Bob Considine wrote that Johnson "was beaten six straight times, trying to win his thirteenth victory for Rocky Mount, and when Heinie Manush, his manager, came up to him one night and said 'looks like you'll never win another in this league, kid,' Johnson thought he was through. But Manush added, 'So the Sox just phoned me to send you to Boston—so you can win there.'"[1]

Though still just 21 years old, Earl got a quick promotion to the major league ballclub, simply because (in the words of the *Washington Post*'s Shirley Povich) manager Joe Cronin "doesn't know where his next winning pitcher is coming from and can blame his club's failure to be in the league lead on the worst pitching in the circuit." By season's end, no starter had won more than 12 games and the staff ERA was a high 4.89. Yawkey spent some considerable sums trying to buy good pitching, but Povich wrote, "The best young pitcher to come up with the Red Sox in several years is no fancy-priced minor leaguer, but Rookie Earl Johnson, the left-hander Boston signed fresh out of St. Mary's College in California."

The young lefty's major league debut came at Fenway Park in the midst of an eight-game losing streak on July 20, 1940 in relief of Lefty Grove. The Red Sox scored once in the bottom of the first but the veteran Grove was unable to retire a Cleveland batter in the top of the second; he left the game having surrendered four runs. Earl Johnson came on in relief and threw five scoreless innings before the Indians got to him for three runs to break a 4–4 tie. The final score was 9–6 Cleveland. Johnson had walked three and allowed five hits in the six full innings he pitched. He appeared in relief again, and earned his first start in the July 28 doubleheader, beating the St. Louis Browns, 3–1. He walked one and gave up four hits in five innings, relieved by Emerson Dickman.

In his third start, against the Yankees in Boston, Johnson was hit hard off the shin by a batted ball during the first inning and had to leave after completing the inning. The bruise healed quickly enough that he was brought back in the first game of the next day's doubleheader, throwing three innings in relief and getting the win. Three days later, on August 10, he threw his first shutout, scattering eight hits in 8⅓ innings before Jack Wilson came on to retire the last two Senators. Povich praised Johnson, as "a loose-jointed blond kid who vaulted into the majors this season." Only two Senators had reached third base—though Johnson did have to work his way out of a seventh-inning situation which saw the bases loaded and nobody out. His "out pitch" was a "wide-sweeping curve" that he threw to good effect. He got the Senators again, with a five-hit 4–2 win eight days later, sandwiched around a loss to New York. Johnson won a 6–1 four-hitter in Cleveland in mid-September. By season's end, Johnson had a 6–2 record with a 4.09 ERA. Looking ahead to 1941 spring training, Jack Malaney wrote in *The Sporting News* that Johnson "finished the American League season in brilliant style."

With Mickey Harris and Johnson on the Red Sox, Cronin felt free to let Fritz Ostermueller go. At the end of March, the Sox traveled to Havana for a series of four games, the first against a team of Cuban all-stars and the other three against the Cincinnati Reds. Johnson pitched the first game against the Reds, allowing just four hits in six innings. When May rolled around, he began to hit his stride once more and was pitching well when he came down with a sore arm. He only started once in June, and only lasted three-plus innings. By early July, *The Sporting News* observed, "Johnson very definitely is on the shelf, and there is no telling when he can get off." Doctors diagnosed an unusual cause: "He has bad teeth, which were found to be bad, extracted, and they even dug into his jawbone. When the Sox left home last week, he was left behind in the care of the club physician."

In late August, the same periodical noted that he'd last pitched well on Decoration Day (now Memorial Day); the soreness in his arm had gone away, but he'd been unable to regain his control since rejoining the rotation on the 10th. Johnson's totals at the end of his first full year in the majors were just 4–5, with a 4.52 ERA. Little did he know that he would miss four full seasons to service in the United States Army. He drew a high number in the draft lottery, and even before Pearl Harbor prompted the massive expansion of the American armed services, he knew the Army was in his future. He was inducted at Seattle on January 5, 1942, and sent a terse telegram to Sox GM Eddie Collins: "Inducted into Army today. Best regards." Private Johnson was posted to Camp Roberts, California and had made corporal by the summertime—and was pitching well for the Camp Roberts baseball team. For 1942, he was on the National Defense List with the Red Sox, a status he maintained for four full years—more than most ballplayers. And unlike most ballplayers, after going through training, Earl Johnson saw combat duty.

While still in training, he married Jean Taintor in 1943.

Johnson served in the Army, as did Paul Campbell, Tommy Carey, Joe Dobson, Bobby Doerr, Danny Doyle, Dave Ferriss, Al Flair, Any Gilbert, Mickey Harris, Tex Hughson, Roy Partee, Jim Tabor and Hal Wagner. Partee took part in the invasion of The Philippines.

Sgt. Earl Johnson served with the 120th infantry (30th

Division) and landed in Europe 21 days after D-Day. "We were a replacement unit," he told the *Providence Journal*'s Bill Parrillo. "We had to go through Omaha Beach to get there.... The wreckage was still there, the burned-out tanks and half-sunken ships and assault boats that were just so much twisted steel." Several times, he came across groups of dead bodies—from both sides—still unburied. He was a rifle platoon sergeant, involved in liberating many towns in France and Belgium. Unfortunately, he witnessed the results of the Malmedy Massacre in Belgium, where 150 American prisoners had been killed by Nazis. Johnson fought in five major conflicts and took part (as did later Sox manager Ralph Houk) in the famous Battle of the Bulge. For heroism in combat, Johnson was awarded the Bronze Star, a Bronze Star with clusters, and the Silver Star, and received battlefield commissions promoting him to lieutenant.

Johnson's citation for the Bronze Star reads: "On September 30, 1944, in Germany, during heavy concentration of hostile fire, a friendly truck was struck by an enemy shell and had to be abandoned. The fact that the vehicle contained vital radio equipment made it imperative that it be recovered before falling into enemy hands. Sergeant Earl Johnson and several other members of his unit were assigned to this hazardous mission. They courageously braved a severe hostile fire and were completely successful in dragging the vehicle over an area in plain view of the enemy." The Bronze Star with clusters was awarded after he helped urge a tank crew to drive through a minefield on its way to wiping out a German position which had pinned down his men.

"Lefty" Johnson's Silver Star required another soldier to pitch in relief of the Red Sox southpaw. The two were fighting hedgerow by hedgerow in France when they noticed a German tank laying in ambush—with its hatch open. Johnson threw two hand grenades at the tank—but missed with both. The other soldier—who'd supposedly never thrown a baseball in his life—tossed one and scored a direct hit. "Gee," Johnson remarked later, "If I only had that kid's control, what a pitcher I would be." The blast killed all five German tankers. Johnson's platoon started the Battle of the Bulge with 36 men, but ended with only 11.

With the war over in 1945, Lt. Johnson was demobilized and joined many other Red Sox veterans coming back for another year of baseball. In Earl's case, he'd missed four full years—more than anyone else on the Bosox. Unlike many others, he'd not been playing service baseball; he said he hadn't touched a ball the whole time. Cronin pinned his pitching hopes largely on the returning Tex Hughson, sophomore Dave Ferriss, and Mickey Harris. Jim Bagby looked promising. Of both Bill Butland and Earl Johnson, Jack Hand wrote in the *Washington Post* late in spring training, both had been "slow rounding into shape because of their war experiences." Earl told Bill Parrillo that his fastball was gone: "I had to

learn how to become a pitcher instead of just a thrower. I developed a slow curve and a changeup and a slider. That first year, they put me in the bullpen; they didn't like the fact that I couldn't throw hard anymore."

Johnson got into it early, and after Ferriss got battered around in the second start of the season, Johnson came on and three 5⅓ innings of relief, allowing just three hits, and got the win. The "blond southpaw hurler" (Associated Press) won the May 21 game by throwing five full innings of hitless relief and doubling in the winning runs in the eighth inning. Though he started 12 games during the year, he was primarily used in relief and all five of his wins came as a reliever. Earl finished the season 5–4, with a 3.71 ERA in 80 innings of work.

Preparing for the World Series, as they waited for the National League's scheduled three-game playoff to resolve the pennant, Johnson started a "warm-up" game to keep the Red Sox in playing shape, as the Sox played against a team of American League All-Stars. Bill Zuber and Jim Bagby each pitched three innings, too, and the Red Sox won, 4–1. His relief pitching had been "strong" early in the season, but had "tapered off alarmingly in the last two months," wrote Arthur Daley of *The New York Times*. But Johnson picked up an important tip during the tune-up games, Daley reported, when Hank Greenberg "sidled up" to him on the bench. "Earl," Greenberg confided, "There's something I have to tell you now that you're about to go into the World Series. For the past two months you've been telegraphing every pitch you've thrown and the boys in our league have been teeing off on you." Greenberg explained what Johnson had been doing wrong.

During the 1946 World Series, Earl pitched a hitless ninth and tenth innings in Game One and got the win. In Game Six, he allowed the final run of the game pitching to the Cardinals in the eighth inning, but the Red Sox only scored once and lost, 4–1. After Slaughter had scored to put the Cardinals ahead to stay in Game Seven's eighth inning, Johnson—who probably should have been pitching instead of Klinger—was brought on and got the final out. When he was due up with two outs in the top of the ninth, Cronin had Tom McBride bat for him and McBride grounded into a force play to end the game, and the Series. Johnson was a lifetime .187 hitter with 13 RBIs in 171 career at-bats.

Earl's brother Chet was about a year and a half older, and also a left-handed pitcher. He made the majors with the St. Louis Browns and appeared in five games during September 1946. He got three starts but no decisions. Though the two were on opposite benches during two games, they never faced each other. Earl started the September 19 game, but Chet's second start came two days later against the White Sox. Chet's major league career ended after his start in the final game of the year. Earl went on and had his best year in 1947. His first start of '47 came on July 12, against Greenberg's former team, shutting out Detroit, 2–0, on six hits, while going 3-for-3 at the plate.

His next start came on July 19, and in the bottom of the first inning, Johnson surrendered three consecutive singles. The bases were loaded with nobody out. Johnson got out of it, and never allowed another hit for the rest of the game, the only Browns baserunner coming on his one walk. The final was 1–0, Red Sox. Johnson was involved in three more 1–0 games in 1947, and he started every one of them. He lost a two-hitter to the Senators on August 6, 1–0, on an unearned run. Allowing just three singles ("two of them scratchy affairs"), Johnson turned the tables on Washington with a 1–0 win. Then the Yankees got a superior effort out of Bobo Newsom, who held the Sox scoreless and Johnny Lindell hit a walk-off single in the bottom of the ninth for a 1–0 Yankees win on August 16.

Johnson won his 10th game on September 6, a 4–3 win over the Athletics. A week later, on the day that Red Sox veteran and paraplegic war hero Sy Rosenthal was honored with a "Day" at Fenway Park, there was stiff competition between two pitchers who had both seen combat and Johnson beat Bob Feller with a four-hitter, 3–2. Earl finished 1947 with a 12–11 record and a 2.97 ERA, having thrown 142⅓ innings in 45 games, 17 of which were starts.

In 1948, Johnson was used almost exclusively in relief, though he had one start in April and two in May. Appearing in 35 games overall, he posted a 10–4 record, but with a distinctly higher ERA at 4.53. He'd begun to lose effectiveness. In 1949, he appeared in 19 games with a 3–6 record and a 7.48 ERA. In 1950, he got into just 11 games, was 0–0 and had an earned run average of 7.24. On July 5, Earl was given his outright release to Louisville—though the A.P. reported that he would remain on the Red Sox roster for 12 more days so that he would become a 10-year man and thus eligible for his pension. Boston called up pitchers Willard Nixon and Dick Littlefield.

The Tigers took a chance on Johnson, signing him on November 15, 1950. He pitched just 5⅔ innings for them in 1951, in six games, with no decisions and with a 6.35 ERA. His last major league game was on June 3, 1951. With two outs in the top of the ninth inning, Johnson was asked to get the third out, but walked one batter and was touched up for two hits, then removed. The Tigers released him on June 15.

Johnson signed with the Seattle Rainiers to play in the Pacific Coast League. He finished out the '51 season with as 8–3 record (3.43 ERA) in 17 games, seven of them complete games. His last year as a player came in 1952, finishing his career with Seattle working as a reliever; he was 0–2 with a 4.70 ERA.

Earl is listed as a Red Sox scout in the team's 1953 spring training guide starting that year, and served as a fulltime West Coast scout for Boston until he retired following the 1985 season. At one point, while working with the Red Sox in March 1965, he also served as a pitching coach for the Mexico City Red Devils.

Earl and Jean had two children, Sally and Earl Jr. Neither showed particular interest in baseball. Sally worked in a restaurant in Iowa and Earl Jr. remains self-employed as a general contractor.

When he wasn't following baseball in the Seattle area, Earl looked after the laundromat he owned in Ballard. Earl's sister-in-law Elsie Busch recalls all the trouble it gave him at first. "He used to have all these machines and they were spending all their time on repairing them, until he finally took them all out and put in Maytags. It was just like an advertisement. Put in Maytag and you won't have to call the repairman." There were 10 or more machines in the laundromat and he owned it until his death. Earl suffered a minor stroke in the early 1990s and died in Seattle on December 3, 1994. His wife Jean survived him until her death in July 2006.

Thanks to Elsie J. Busch and Dick Bresciani for assistance in putting together this biography.

Notes

1. *Washington Post*, March 23, 1941

JAKE JONES *by Dick Thompson*

G	AB	R	H	2B	3B	HR	RBI	BB	SO	BA	OBP	SLG	SB	HBP
36	105	3	21	4	0	1	8	11	26	.200	.276	.267	1	0

Jake Jones made one of the loudest debuts in the history of the Boston Red Sox. After Joe Cronin swapped slumping first baseman Rudy York—who had knocked in 119 runs for the AL champs in 1946—to the visiting Chicago White Sox for Murrell Jones on June 14, 1947, York's first response reportedly was, "I've been traded for who?" Streaming into Fenway Park for a doubleheader the next afternoon, bewildered Red Sox patrons were referring to their new player as "Muriel." After the games the same fans were calling Cronin a genius, for Jones drove in seven runs and homered in both games of the Red Sox sweep. With the nightcap knotted at 4–4 in the ninth, Jones arrived to the plate with the bases full and two down. Ted Williams and Bobby Doerr had drawn intentional passes in the inning so Jake was on the spot. His former mates in the visiting dugout were letting him have it, hollering that he couldn't deliver in the clutch, but they couldn't have been more wrong. Producing under fire was Jones' forte and he sent the first pitch into the left-field screen for a walk-off grand slam.

Jake almost did not receive full credit for his game-winning blast. "Bobby Doerr, who was on first base when Jones hit the ball over the fence," reported the *Boston Globe*, "ran down to second base, touched the bag—and then headed to the clubhouse.

"Just as Doerr reached the vicinity of the pitcher's box, he saw Coach Del Baker waving at him and suddenly realized that—although the winning run was scored—a rookie's home run was at stake.

"He then turned back and resumed his trip around the bases.

"If Doerr had not turned back, it would have changed the score of the game to 5–4—instead of 8–4."

Jones was surrounded by reporters after the game. Tex Hughson told them he had played a hunch, stating, "He'll hit a home run on the first pitch" to his teammates as Jake walked toward the plate. Johnny Pesky looked at Jones and said, "He's strong. I'm glad he is on our side." When someone said that Jones had a pretty good day, Eddie Pellagrini exclaimed, "Pretty good day! That's a pretty good week."

Impressive as Jake's day had been though, it was far from his best effort. That had come several years earlier when he flew a Hellcat off the USS *Yorktown* in the Pacific. Jones's final tally in aerial combat was seven planes shot down, and the highly decorated ace had rung up one of the most impressive war records among all ballplayers in the military.

James Murrell Jones was born in rural Epps, Louisiana, on November 23, 1920. His parents were Luther A. Jones Sr. and Della Virginia Moore Jones. His childhood was spent in Epps and nearby Monroe, Louisiana. Family and friends called him "JM" or Murrell, the nickname "Jake" being hung on him either in the minor leagues[1] or the military,[2] depending on the source. His Boston teammates simply called him "Jonesy." Following his graduation from high school in 1938 he began his baseball career in Louisiana with the semipro Clarks Lumbermen. In 1939, he hit .321 with 14 home runs and 103 RBIs for Monroe in the (Class C) Cotton States League, and in1940 he put up .301/16/75 numbers for Shreveport in the (Class A1) Texas League.

Jones was on the fast track to the majors. In addition to his powerful bat, he displayed an innate ability to scoop up low throws around first base. "Jones reached his defensive peak in the Texas League all-star game at Beaumont," wrote the *Shreveport Journal* on August 14, 1941, "when he practically saved the hides of the southern

Murrell "Jake" Jones. Courtesy of George Brace Photo.

division team with sensational fielding feats on bad throws. He was so nearly the whole show that he was acclaimed the most valuable player in the game and will receive a trophy designating him as such."

A number of big league teams were bird-dogging Jones: the Pirates, Yankees, Giants, and White Sox were reported as the interested parties, and his 20 round-trippers by early August—he led the Texas League with 24 for the season—had not escaped the notice of at least one Hall of Famer, for "Detroit's immortal Harry Heilmann has labeled Jones as one of the greatest natural hitting prospects he has ever seen."[3] With rumors about that "he might draw $75,000 from the pocketbook of a big league magnate,"[4] Jones was sold to the Chicago White Sox for $25,000 on August 23, 1941.[5]

His major league debut came a month later, on September 20, and he went hitless in his first six games, totaling 21 at-bats over parts of two seasons, until breaking through with two safeties against Washington's Early Wynn on April 30, 1942.

Sent back down to the minors for additional seasoning, Jones enlisted in the Navy during the summer of 1942. Despite never having gone to college, he was selected for flight training—the assumption being that, like Ted Williams, his quick reflexes made him superbly qualified for the task, and on August 1, 1943, Jones was commissioned an ensign. Jake told his son that he played basketball at the University of North Carolina while in the service and information received from the military's National Personnel Records Center in St. Louis lists his place of entry into the service as Chapel Hill, North Carolina.

The USS *Yorktown* (CV-10)—nicknamed "the Fighting Lady"—was the second aircraft carrier of that name to serve in World War II, the original (CV-5) being lost at the Battle of Midway. Jones joined the ship in time for her second deployment to the Pacific.

For two weeks in November 1944, the *Yorktown* launched air strikes on targets in the Philippines in support of the invasion of Leyte. It was during this action that Jones was awarded his first Air Medal. His citation, signed by Vice Admiral J. S. McCain, the grandfather of Arizona Senator John S. McCain III, read as follows:

"For distinguishing himself by meritorious acts while participating in an aerial flight as pilot of a carrier based fighter airplane assigned to strike against enemy installations and shipping in the vicinity of the Philippine Islands on 14 November 1944. He performed his assignment as wingman for the Air Group Commander in an outstanding manner and destroyed an enemy fighter during our

Fixing type styles (missing "extract" styles) and reflowing text
from page 245 to end of Jones section.

attack. His skill and courage were at all times inspiring and in keeping with the highest traditions of the United States Naval Service."

Promoted to lieutenant junior grade, Jones quickly picked up a second Air Medal.

"For meritorious achievement in aerial flight as pilot of a fighter plane in Fighting Squadron THREE, attached to the USS *Yorktown*, in action against enemy Japanese forces in the vicinity of the Philippine Islands, December 14, 1944. Participating in a strike against the enemy, Lieutenant Junior Grade, Jones pressed home a daring attack against three enemy fighters, destroying one, inflicting severe damage on another and forcing the third to flee. His skill, courage and devotion to duty were in keeping with the highest traditions of the United States Naval Service."

The November 2001 issue of *Naval History* magazine printed an article written by Rear Admiral MacPherson B. Williams, U.S. Navy (Retired), who had been the Yorktown's Air Group Commander.[6] The article was entitled "I Was Alone in Enemy Territory" and it was about his harrowing experience in evading capture after being shot down.

"It was 16 December 1944. The U.S. Navy Task Force was 150 miles east of the Philippines. As the air group commander in the USS *Yorktown*, 'The Fighting Lady,' I was leading the morning strike. We launched and rendezvoused over the pocket destroyer on the starboard bow and headed west toward our objective, climbing for altitude and testing our guns on the way. We were at 15,000 feet when we topped the cloud cover of the eastern shore of Luzon and saw the wide expanse of the Manila Plain below.

"Over Nichols Field, our target, we peeled off, delivered our bombs, and ducked low to Manila Bay to get under their flak. We then turned south beyond Sangley Point and the ruins of Cavite Navy Yard to join up over Laguna del Bey...

"With 40 minutes to spare, I released the three section leaders to browse on their own and join me, over Laguna del Bey, in 30 minutes.

"My wing man, Jake Jones, and I went up the Pasig River to Marikina Air field, where reconnaissance photos had shown there were hidden Japanese aircraft. The low level attack we delivered resulted in a small antiaircraft hit in my engine. Realizing trouble, we headed toward the hills on the eastern side of Manila Plain. The fire in my engine got bigger and finally into the cockpit with me. Having no choice, I bailed out...."

Williams suffered painful burns to his arm when he bailed out, but landed safely. He spent several weeks behind enemy lines before he was able to reach friendly forces.

As for Jones, 10 combat missions flown between January 3 and January 15, 1945, in the vicinity of Formosa, China, French Indo-China and Nansei Shoto earned him his third and fourth Air Medals. A week later, he won his first Distinguished Flying Cross. Highlights of that citation are as follows:

> "For heroism and extraordinary achievement in aerial flight as pilot of a fighter plane in Fighting Squadron THREE, attached to the U.S.S. Yorktown, during action against enemy Japanese forces in Formosa on January 21, 1945. Participating in a long instrument flight, Lieutenant Junior Grade Jones carried out a low altitude attack in the face of intense antiaircraft fire, scoring rocket hits to set a large hostile oiler on fire and contribute to the success of the mission...."

On February 16 and 17, the *Yorktown* launched strikes on mainland Japan near Tokyo where Jake downed five enemy planes to win the Silver Star and another Distinguished Flying Cross. Years later he told his son that he flew back to the *Yorktown* from one of those missions with a hole in wing that was big enough for a man to climb through. The citation highlights, the Silver Star first and then the second Distinguished Flying Cross, are as follows:

> "For conspicuous gallantry and intrepidity in action against the enemy during the first carrier based strikes against the Japanese homeland on February 16, 1945. While flying a carrier based fighter plane he countered aggressive, determined and skillful attacks by numerically superior enemy fighters. He succeeded in shooting down three of these enemy fighter planes. After air opposition had been neutralized he, with his wingman, made low-level rocket and strafing attacks against air field installations, securing destructive hits on each of six hangers....
>
> "For heroism while participating in aerial flight against the enemy during the first carrier based strikes against the Japanese Homeland on February 17, 1945. While flying a carrier based fighter plane as section leader in his Air Group Commander's division, he countered the attacks of aggressive, determined and numerically superior enemy fighters. In this action he shot down two of these attacking planes. His skill and courage were at all times in keeping with the highest traditions of the United States Naval Service."

Jones returned home a hero. He received a week of shore leave in New York City, where he appeared on the Kate Smith radio show. Legendary sportswriter Grantland Rice, quoting an anonymous shipmate, wrote of Jones:

> "A great guy and one of the best flyers I ever saw. Jake was on the FIGHTING LADY, one of the

fightingest carriers in the war. And Jake was one of the fightingest pilots in the outfit—his record was seven Jap planes shot down in combat and, in addition to this, he was responsible for the sinking of at least four Jap ships. His war campaign included the Philippines, Formosa, China, Iwo Jima, Okinawa and missions over Tokyo. It was over Tokyo that three Jap flyers ganged up on him and he got all three.

Commander George Earnshaw and ace pilot Jake Jones during World War II.

"Jake got to play some baseball between flights, but not too much. I recall once when he came back from a flight and we had quite a party that night. It was on the island of Maui. Next day Jake played ball and got two home runs and a triple, to break up the game. He certainly could put the wood against that ball."[7]

Commander George Earnshaw, a former pitching ace for Connie Mack's great Philadelphia Athletics World Series squads of 1929–1931, was a shipmate on the Yorktown and several photos of the pair, probably used by the Navy for publicity purposes—think "two major leaguers at war"—are known to exist. It is likely that Earnshaw was Rice's anonymous source.

Jake's older brother, Major Luther A. Jones Jr., piloted a B-29 named the *City of Monroe* in over 20 combat missions in the Pacific Theater of Operations. Luther was awarded two Distinguished Flying Crosses and three Air Medals. The *City of Monroe's* bombardier was Hollywood actor Tim Holt.[8]

Returning to baseball after the war, Jones was the only legitimate power threat on the White Sox team that finished last in the American League in 1946 with just 37 round-trippers. Veteran Hal Trosky opened the season as the starting first baseman but manager Jimmie Dykes soon moved Jones into the lineup and on May 3 his first major league home run proved to be the game winner versus the Philadelphia Athletics. His second home run, a two-run shot at Comiskey on May 15 which countered a Ted Williams round-tripper, was the big blow in a 3–2 victory over the Red Sox. His walk-off double on May 22 produced a 5–4 victory over Philadelphia.

Though Jones had returned unscathed from the Second World War, he did not have the same luck on the baseball diamond and on May 26, 1946, he suffered a season-ending fracture of his left wrist and elbow when Detroit shortstop Eddie Lake ran into his outstretched arm. Shortly after the season *The Sporting News* reported that Jones was having trouble straightening out his surgically repaired arm and was a carrying around a bucket of sand for several hours a day for physical therapy.[9]

Manager Ted Lyons started his 1947 spring training sessions at Pasadena, California, unsure of who his first baseman would be. In addition to Jones, he looked at veterans Trosky and Joe Kuhel before opening the season with Don Kolloway. Jake saw little playing time in April but in May he had four doubles and three home runs for the still punchless Chicago squad. Then his bat went silent. Streaky as they come, Jake was capable of carrying the team when he was hot, but extremely impotent with the bat when he was cold. At the time of the trade to the Red Sox, his batting average was .240.

In his first 11 games with the Red Sox, all played in Boston, Jones hit .302 with four doubles, three home runs, and a triple. His swing was tailor-made for Fenway Park, where in 1947 he hit .276 with 12 doubles, three triples, 14 home runs, and 57 RBIs in just 254 at-bats. In 321 at-bats away from Fenway that year, he hit .206 with nine doubles, one triple, five home runs, and 39 RBIs. He scored 39 runs in Boston and 26 elsewhere.[10] Three players hit 10 or more home runs in Fenway Park in 1947. Ted Williams had 16, Jones 14, and Bobby Doerr 12. Jake hit one in Boston while with the White Sox, but after the Jones-York trade on June 14, the leading Fenway home run hitters were Jones with 13, Williams with 11, and Doerr with 10.[11] "Too bad he can't carry the left field fence with him on the road," said the *Boston Globe* of Jones on September 10, 1947.

The line on Jake was that he didn't show much emotion on the field and he chased low outside curves. His response to the first was simple: "When you have to fly through a lot of flak, you don't scare easily on a baseball field." Pitcher Dizzy Trout described Jones's predilection for the slow curve: "He misses a couple of curves by a mile and you feel certain you've got him, and then he makes a monkey out of you by blasting the ball out of the park."[12]

Soon the opposing teams started stacking the deck. "Jones is strictly a pull hitter and teams like the Chisox, Yankees, Indians, and Tigers shift their infields on him, bunching their men on the left side of second base, just the opposite of the way they play Ted Williams."[13]

Jake was capable of delivering the big hit. While with Chicago in 1947 he had at least two game-winning at-bats; a fly ball that produced the deciding run in a 3–2 victory over Washington on May 18 and a 10th-inning single that accounted for a 9–8 victory over the Yankees on June 9. Jake's base hit following Ted Williams' triple delivered a 7–6 victory over Washington on July 5. His ninth-inning

Jones exploded on offense in his first 11 games with the Sox. Courtesy of George Brace Photo.

triple against Washington's Early Wynn on August 12 resulted in a 2–1 Boston win. The next day Jake hit back-to-back homers with both Bobby Doerr and Sam Mele in a 10–3 victory over Washington. On September 1 he drove home all four Boston runs in a 4–1 win over the Yankees. His three-run homer on September 9 was the vital hit in a 5–3 victory over Detroit. Jake's 19th and final round-tripper of the season, on September 17, accounted for the first two runs of Joe Dobson's one-hit, 4–0 masterpiece over St. Louis.

On July 27 the Red Sox swept a doubleheader from the Browns at Fenway. In the sixth inning of the first game, Jake topped a foul ball that dribbled down the third base line. Though there was no chance that the ball would be fair—and as third baseman Bob Dillinger was about to pick it up—pitcher Fred Sanford threw his glove at the ball. Umpire Cal Hubbard, despite a vehement protest from the Browns, awarded Jones a triple on the 60-foot foul, basing his decision on the fact that the word "foul" was missing from the rule regarding the situation. Baseball's Rules Committee later amended the wording.

Jones was involved in another odd play, coming in the same August 12 game against Washington which was previously mentioned. With Washington batting in the fifth, and with Rick Ferrell on third and Early Wynn on second, Joe Grace hit a sharp grounder to Jake, who stepped on first to record the second out of the inning. Ferrell had held third on the play, but Wynn, not paying attention, took off for the same occupied bag. Seeing both runners standing on the same base, Jones sprinted across the diamond and tagged both runners. The umpire signaled that the final out of the inning had been recorded and Jones was credited with an unassisted double play, one out recorded at first base and the other at third.

Joe McCarthy replaced Joe Cronin as Red Sox skipper after the 1947 season. The former Yankees skipper did not share the same opinion of Jones's ability as Cronin

and in December, two months before spring training, announced that outfielder Stan Spence would be his first baseman in 1948.[14] Oscar Fraley, a writer for the United Press who covered the Red Sox spring camp in Sarasota, wrote:

"So Jones sits it out in spring training even though he hit 19 homers last season compared to 16 for Spence and knocked in 96 runs compared to 73 for the former Senator.

"A left-field hitter, Jones is a dangerous batter in the Red Sox home park, and while he may not impress McCarthy, he received a tidy tribute from Cronin last winter when McCarthy was on his shopping spree.

"For about that time, Joe DiMaggio bumped into Cronin and, kiddingly, asked the Red Sox general manager when Cronin was going to purchase him from the Yankees.

"Cronin said the Red Sox might trade Jones for joltin' Joe, which struck Demag—and a lot of others—something like swapping a Rembrandt for a comic book.

"But Cronin pointed out that DiMaggio only hit one more home run last season than Jones and only knocked in one more run, which is a fair measure of measuring a player's value. Still Jones gets the deep freeze, without benefit of explanation, as Marse Joe oils the buttons labeled with stars."

Shirley Povich of the *Washington Post* also interviewed McCarthy on his two big infield decisions, the other being the more remembered Pesky-Stephens issue:

"I was talking to one of McCarthy's former Yankees the other day at St. Petersburg, and he had some comment on McCarthy's big decision to shift Johnny Pesky from shortstop to third base, instead of Vernon Stephens. 'We thought the Red Sox were going to be tough to beat,' said the big Yankee, 'but if McCarthy plays 'em that way, we'll lick 'em.'

"So at Sarasota yesterday I asked McCarthy about that and he wasn't perturbed at all. 'I didn't move Pesky because he couldn't play shortstop,' he said. 'Why don't my friends let me do the worrying? Pesky and Stephens are interchangeable, anyway. If my move is wrong; I'll be the first one to know it.'

"Anyway, McCarthy is vastly more excited about another development in the Red Sox camp. He's babbling, almost, about the showing of Stan Spence as his first baseman. The former Washington outfielder who hasn't played more than 50 games at first base in his big league career, is now the sensation of Sarasota and has the first base job all to himself.

"McCarthy handed Spence a first baseman's mitt the first day he reported, and now he's ready to open the season with him. In fact, Murrell Jones, the Boston first

YESTERDAY'S HERO — By Gene Mack

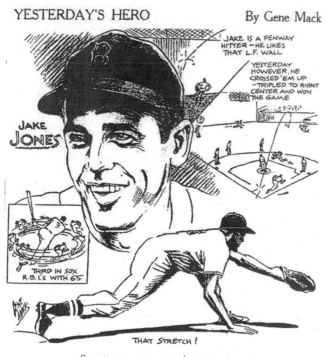

Sports page cartoon depicting Jones'
August 12, 1947 game-winning triple.

baseman of last season, has seen so little action in the exhibition games that he's about to ask somebody to introduce him to McCarthy so his presence in camp can be noted."[15]

Spence got off to a slow start so on April 29 McCarthy inserted Jake into the lineup, and though Jones hit a two-run homer in his first start, neither he nor Spence could make a bold enough statement with the stick. On May 8 the *Lowell Sun* wrote:

"Baseball fans are all talking about the strange case of Jake Jones. This big, curly-haired first sacker has become a real problem. Lately the fellow has looked helpless at the plate. It seems that he couldn't hit his mother-in-law with a base fiddle at two paces. Yet, he can stretch like a rubberneck at a burlesque show when it comes to playing first base.

"Time and time again Jake's two-way stretch puts a girdle to shame as he makes almost impossible double plays. He saves his infielders errors at least twice a game, yet he is as lost as two-year-old in a subway when he gets to the plate.

"Jones has become a real problem. Stan Spence opened the season at first base but he isn't half as fancy around the cushion as Jake. They are both hitting at a tremendous .222 clip...."

With Boston's record being 12–17 on May 25, McCarthy gave utility infielder Billy Goodman the first baseman's mitt. Spence moved to the outfield, where he sometimes hit cleanup between Williams and Stephens,

and Jake rode the pine, remaining with the club all year but seeing virtually no action in the second half of the season. He did receive a full player's share of second-place money, $1,191.71, and in January of 1949 was released to Louisville of the American Association.

Jones played that one last season, hitting .243 with 18 homers and 69 RBIs for Louisville and then San Antonio in the Texas League. He returned to his hometown, where he owned a 400-acre cotton farm and operated a flying service, doing mostly crop-dusting work. He was recalled to active duty during the Korean War, and helped train pilots. Married twice and having raised five children and two stepchildren, Jones passed away in a local hospital in nearly Delhi, Louisiana, on December 15, 2000, at the age of 80. His widow, Mary, and son Chris were interviewed for this story. They said that Murrell was a quiet man who didn't like publicity. He wouldn't initiate conversation regarding baseball or the war, but didn't shy away from either topic if asked. He continued to fly without incident until, to the great relief of his wife, he gave it up in 1980. Not unexpectedly, Jake and Ted Williams, sharing mutual interests in flying, baseball, and fishing, were great friends. Ted once forgot to return some borrowed fishing tackle and that gave Jake a story that he would use for the rest of his life—not that he didn't have plenty of his own—as he jokingly told his friends that the great Ted Williams still owed him fishing equipment.

Notes

1. *The Sporting News*. May 7, 1947.
2. *Ibid*. June 25, 1947.
3. Unidentified clipping in Jones's Hall of Fame file.
4. *Chicago Daily Tribune*. November 28, 1941.
5. *The Sporting News*. August 23, 1941.
6. The article had originally appeared in the *U.S. Naval Institute Naval History Magazine*. Williams died in 1990.
7. *Syracuse Herald-American*. September 8, 1946.
8. From the history of the 39th Bomb Group. WWW.39th.org.
9. *The Sporting News*. October 30, 1946.
10. As tabulated from Jones' day-by-day logs from the Hall of Fame. Assistance provided by Bill Deane.
11. SABR's Tattersall/McConnell Home Run Log. As provided by David Vincent.
12. *Lowell Sun*. September 13, 1947.
13. *Ibid*.
14. *The Sporting News*. December 17, 1947.
15. *Washington Post*. March 30, 1948.

Additional sources

Interviews with Mary Jones and Chris Jones
Aviation and Military Museum of North Louisiana. Website www.ammla.net.

ELLIS KINDER *by Mark Armour*

G	ERA	W	L	SV	GS	GF	CG	SHO	IP	H	R	ER	BB	SO	HR	HBP	WP	BFP
28	3.74	10	7	0	22	3	10	1	178	183	84	74	63	53	10	2	2	762

G	AB	R	H	2B	3B	HR	RBI	BB	SO	BA	OBP	SLG	SB	HBP
28	62	8	6	0	0	0	4	8	18	.097	.200	.097	0	0

Ellis Kinder's best year was 23-6 in 1949.

In January 1956, a few months after Ellis Kinder had been sold by the Boston Red Sox to the St. Louis Cardinals after eight years in the Hub, his friends threw him an Appreciation Night at Boston's Sheraton Plaza Hotel. In attendance were the governor, the mayor, several former teammates, and 600 assorted guests. Birdie Tebbetts, who had caught Kinder in the late 1940s and was then managing the Cincinnati Reds, served as toastmaster. Birdie had caught Hal Newhouser and Dizzy Trout in Detroit, Mel Parnell in Boston, and Bob Lemon, Early Wynn, and a late-career Bob Feller in Cleveland, but he told the gathered throng that he never caught a better pitcher than Kinder. Furthermore, in a nod to Kinder's reputation off the field, his old catcher added, "There'll be places explored in National League cities this coming season that were never heard of by ballplayers."

This was Ellis Kinder: well-loved by teammates and fans, more than a bit reckless off the field, and a great pitcher, one of the best pitchers in Red Sox history, both as a starter and a reliever for eight years. All that, and he didn't get to the majors until he was 31, or develop into a star until he was 33. "Old Folks" was late to the party, but he sure knew what to do once he got there.

Ellis Raymond Kinder was born on July 26, 1914, in Atkins, Arkansas, about 50 miles northwest of Little Rock. The second son of Ulysses and Iva Kinder—at the time of the 1930 census there were three other sons—his father was a farmer of corn and cotton, struggling to feed and clothe his large family. Ellis was picking cotton in the fields by the time he was 10 years old. Kinder later recalled working 5½ days a week in the fields, then going fishing on Sunday with his mother.

Kinder attended public school through eighth grade. He played baseball occasionally, and was good enough to play on the high school team while still in grade school. He continued to play sandlot ball on the weekends after he had left school behind. On March 28, 1934, still working the fields, the 19-year-old Kinder married Hazel McCabe. Soon after, he began work driving a tractor for a road contractor. By 1937, Kinder's parents had both died,

and Kinder was responsible for his wife and daughter and three siblings.

That summer he was first recruited by Hartel Gilliam, the owner of the Jackson, Tennessee, club in the Class D Kitty League. Kinder turned down the offer of a job because he could not afford to work for $75 a month for four months. With a steady job, extra income from an occasional ballgame, and six dependents, he stayed where he was. In 1938, he turned Jackson down again. In August of that season he went to Jackson during his two-week vacation and pitched three innings for the club, allowing four hits and two runs in a single game.

The next season Ellis's boss told him he'd hold his job for him if he wanted to join a team for the summer. Reporting to Jackson for full-season duty in 1939, Kinder put up a 17–12 season, with a 3.59 ERA over 223 innings. Despite his success, his advanced age was enough to keep him in the low minors in 1940, when he recorded a 21–9 record, leading the league with a 2.38 ERA, a league-record 307 strikeouts, and 276 innings pitched.

The New York Yankees were sufficiently impressed to purchase his option for $5,000 and assign him to Birmingham of the Southern Association in 1941. After he split six decisions through June, the Yankees released him and he returned to Jackson, where his family now lived. Back home, Kinder recorded an 11–6 record with an impressive 2.88 ERA.

Kinder pitched for Jackson (Mississippi) of the Class B Southeastern League in 1942, finishing 6–2 with a 2.88 ERA (again), then for Memphis in the Southern Association (2–3, 5.52). After the 1942 season he retired from professional baseball, and took a better-paying job back home in Jackson as a pipe-fitter with the Illinois Central Railroad. Kinder had lived in poverty his whole life. He grew up poor, and he was still poor, earning a small wage while supporting a large extended family. As much as he loved baseball, he needed the money.

In 1944 he was offered a contract to return to Memphis by manager Doc Prothro. Prothro was surprised when Kinder turned him down again. "I need pitchers," claimed Prothro. "The Illinois Central Railroad needs pipe-fitters," responded Ellis. Two days later, Prothro substantially upped his offer, and Kinder put his uniform back on. It is not known how the Illinois Central Railroad dealt with the loss of their pipe-fitter.

Kinder was the star of the 1944 club, finishing 19–6 with a 2.80 ERA. Memphis lost in the seventh game of the playoff finals to Nashville, with Kinder taking the loss in the final game. The more famous player on the 1944 Memphis Chicks was outfielder Pete Gray, who led the league with a .344 batting average despite not having a right arm. At the end of the season, the contracts of Gray and Kinder were purchased by the St. Louis Browns, though Gray's acquisition understandably garnered most of the headlines and press. Though Gray played the 1945 season with the Browns, Kinder did not, instead serving a year in the Navy, being discharged in March 1946.

Kinder finally got to the big leagues with the Browns in 1946, just shy of his 31st birthday. Fully matured, the right-hander stood 6-feet-1 and weighed 195 pounds, with penetrating blue eyes and sharp facial features that made him look much younger than he was. Mainly a mop-up pitcher as a rookie, Ellis got into 33 games and finished 3–3 with a 3.32 ERA. The following season he joined the starting rotation and began the year with five straight wins, but tailed off to 8–15 and a 4.49 ERA for the lowly Browns. His most famous moment in his rookie season might have been during a game in 1947 when a dead fish, likely dropped by a gull passing overhead, landed on the mound behind him as he prepared to pitch to Bobby Doerr in Fenway Park.

On November 18, 1947, Kinder was traded to the Boston Red Sox, along with infielder Billy Hitchcock, for three players—pitcher Clem Dreisewerd and infielders Sam Dente and Bill Sommers—and $65,000. This deal, along with an even larger one for Vern Stephens and Jack Kramer the day before, made the Red Sox instant favorites for the pennant after their disappointing 1947 season. Newly hired manager Joe McCarthy was ecstatic about the news, telling the press, "Kramer and Kinder are sure to help the pitching situation. [General manager] Joe Cronin has certainly helped a situation that didn't look too promising." In January, McCarthy added, "From the reports I've heard on Kinder, he may be as important and perhaps help us more than the others. I understand he has great stuff."

Kinder arrived in Sarasota several days late, with a reputation for enjoying drinking and chasing women, and reportedly did not tend to his training regimen with as much enthusiasm as Joe McCarthy would have liked. After his manager bawled him out in the hotel dining room one morning after a late night on the town, Kinder got with the program a bit more, though his off-field activities did not slow down. McCarthy grew to tolerate Kinder's lifestyle once he saw that Ellis showed up every

day ready to pitch. As teammate Maurice McDermott later recalled, "[McCarthy] never asked Kinder what he'd done the night before. He always knew where Kinder was—in bed with a bottle and a blonde."

Kinder hurt his arm in New Orleans just before the start of the regular season, and missed a few weeks with his right arm in a cast. He started pitching well in mid-summer for the resurgent Red Sox, winning 10 of his 17 decisions over 28 games and 178 innings. After the Red Sox lost the season-ending playoff game to the Indians, Kinder lamented, "If it hadn't been for my arm trouble, we'd have won this easy. Well, I'll show them next year. I'll win 20 games or more for this club and we'll win the pennant."

In the spring of 1949, Red Sox catcher Birdie Tebbetts predicted a 20-win season for Kinder, a prognostication that was not taken seriously despite Tebbetts' closeness to the situation. After all, Kinder was nearing his 34th birthday and had just 21 major league wins under his belt. Kinder had a great spring, and began the season in the starting rotation. Like the rest of the team, Ellis started the season somewhat slowly before kicking it into gear in the early summer. After a loss to the Browns on June 9 dropped his record to 4–4, Kinder embarked on a stretch of pitching that made him the best pitcher in the game. He won six straight games before suffering a loss in relief on July 24. Kinder then won his next 13 starts during the Red Sox' valiant fight for the pennant. By September McCarthy was even using Kinder in relief between his starts, a season total of 18 appearances out of the bullpen.

The Red Sox finally caught the Yankees on the next-to-last weekend of the season, and the two clubs fittingly were tied going into the final contest at Yankee Stadium on October 1. Kinder, 4–0 against the Bombers and working on a streak of 19 consecutive victories as a starter, got the assignment for the Red Sox against Vic Raschi. Kinder allowed a run in the first inning, then shut the Yankees down, but trailed 1–0 entering the eighth frame. When it was Kinder's turn to bat, with the club in desperate need of some offense, McCarthy pinch-hit the little-used Tom Wright for his great pitcher. Wright walked, but was retired when Dom DiMaggio hit into a rare double play to end the brief threat. Kinder's replacements, Mel Parnell (who had pitched the day before) and Tex Hughson, allowed four runs in the bottom of the eighth, and the Red Sox' subsequent three runs off Raschi and Joe Page in the ninth were not enough. Kinder's removal in this game was perhaps the signature moment of the season for the Red Sox, and remained a controversial one for decades in Boston. Joe McCarthy, whose moves always seemed to work out when he managed the Yankees, unfortunately found that in Boston his most important decisions, right or wrong, did not pan out. On the train ride back to Boston after this final game, Kinder, apparently quite drunk, sharply criticized his manager, further eroding McCarthy's reputation in Boston.

After the season Kinder was named the American League pitcher of the year by *The Sporting News*. There was no Cy Young Award in 1949, but since his award was voted on by the nation's sportswriters, there is a good chance Kinder would have won the Cy Young Award had there been one. His greatest competition came from his teammate Mel Parnell, who was equally heroic during that season. The 1948 and 1949 clubs are unfortunately remembered for failing to win on the final day of each season, but both teams had to come from behind to force those final games, especially in 1949. This team was 35–36 on July 4, and 61–22 thereafter. Their two ace pitchers were a big reason for the turnaround, Parnell finishing 15–2 after this date, and Kinder 16–2. A couple of extra runs on October 1 in New York and it is not hard to imagine Ellis Kinder as the league's MVP and the history of the Red Sox forever altered. But those runs were not forthcoming.

During his early years in the majors, Kinder had operated a taxi business back home, often after spending a few weeks barnstorming with fellow major leaguers. After the 1949 season, Kinder first barnstormed with a team run by Dick Sisler, then returned to Jackson, according to the *Sporting News*, "exercising and working on motor repairing." He barnstormed again in later years.

After two straight harrowing pennant race losses, Kinder joined a 1950 club again expected to contend. Kinder was beset with a series of injuries that season, breaking a rib shagging flies in the spring, and suffering a bad back in midsummer. Always a quick healer, Ellis started out in the rotation, but was converted to the bullpen in midseason, ending up 14–12 in 48 games, with a 4.26 ERA. Manager Steve O'Neill, who took over for McCarthy in July, liked using Kinder as a bullpen weapon during the pennant race.

One of Ellis's career highlights took place on August 6, 1950, when he beat the White Sox 9–2. Kinder hit a grand slam off Billy Pierce and drove in six runs in all, a record for AL pitchers at the time. Ellis loved facing the White Sox, as this game came in the middle of a club-record 18 straight victories for Kinder over Chicago, a streak that lasted from 1948 to 1953.

His personal life made the news that offseason. His wife, Hazel, was granted a divorce in court in Jackson on January 11, on a charge of desertion, a charge Ellis did not contest. Mrs. Kinder was granted full custody of their three children: Charles, Jimmy, and Betty. On January 16, Kinder married Ruth Corkery in Boston, after a courtship that was likely longer than the five days he was single. His second marriage, by all accounts, did not slow him down much.

The 36-year-old Kinder was now a full-time relief pitcher, and his career was in some ways just getting started. In 1951 Kinder led the league with 63 games pitched, a team record, finishing 11–2 with a 2.55 ERA. In the middle of a big three-game series in New York in early July, O'Neill could not resist starting Kinder, and Ellis responded with a complete game 10–4 victory, notching 10 strikeouts. On July 25, Kinder entered a tie game in the eighth inning in Chicago, and pitched 10 shutout innings before his club finally pushed across a run in the 17th inning for the win.

"Old Folks" getting loose on the sidelines.

Kinder was an early pioneer in the evolution of the ace relief pitcher. Although there were many examples of pitchers who starred in this role for a few years, it was likely the use of Joe Page by the Yankees in 1949 that cemented the belief that having a star in the bullpen had become a necessity for success. The conversion of Kinder, one of the best starters in the game, to a relief pitcher in 1950 was a bellwether moment in the story. By late 1951, O'Neill could say that Kinder was too valuable to start and be taken seriously. Bobby Doerr, nearing the end of his long career with the club, said, "In all the years that I have been with this team, we have never had a relief pitcher like Ellis. The way he can come in and stop a rally or hold a lead is something at which I marvel. He is just as good as Page was for the Yankees two years ago."

For his efforts, Kinder received two first-place MVP votes in 1951. In January he was honored as the team's

MVP at the annual writers' dinner in Boston. That off-season, he stayed in Massachusetts, working at a sporting goods store in New Bedford.

In 1952 Kinder worked for another new manager, Lou Boudreau, who had to learn how to use his newfangled pitching weapon. Boudreau chose to use Kinder in both starting and relief roles and, coincidence or not, his star pitcher was soon bothered by a few injuries. A sore back sidelined him briefly in early May, then he hurt himself while breaking up a fight between teammate Jimmy Piersall and New York's Billy Martin on May 24. He hurt his back again in June and was finally shut down for two months. Between and around the injuries, Kinder finished the 1952 campaign with just a 5–6 record but with a 2.58 ERA in 23 games, including 10 starts.

After the 1952 season, at a party in Siesta Key, Florida, Kinder suffered a wound to his stomach when he either was cut with a knife or fell on a drinking glass. He was taken to the hospital, but refused treatment and walked out. How much the erratic and suddenly fragile 38-year-old had left as a pitcher was certainly in doubt.

Ellis Kinder had a lot left, it turned out. He pitched just one inning in spring training in 1953 due to a prolonged bout of flu, and was used gingerly at the start of the season. He ended up pitching in 69 games, breaking the league record set by Ed Walsh in 1906, winning 10 of 16 decisions, and posting a microscopic 1.85 ERA. He also hit .379 (11 for 29). When manager Boudreau approached the mound to bring in Kinder, he put his hand on his head signifying a crown—for the king of relief pitchers. Bill McKechnie, the longtime major league manager, and at the time the Red Sox pitching coach, commented, "He's got a heart, a head, and a low sharp breaking slider that's as tough a pitch to hit as anybody throws." For the second time in three years, Kinder was named the team's Most Valuable Player by the local press corps.

In 1954 Kinder hurled 48 games, split his 16 decisions, and posted a 3.62 ERA over 107 innings. He was sidelined with various ailments, including a throat infection early in the year and later pneumonia. On July 15, in a ceremony at home plate, Kinder was made an honorary member of the City of Boston Junior Firefighters.

The following season Kinder turned 41, yet he improved his ERA to 2.84, finishing 5–5 in 43 games. He had become quite famous for his success at such an advanced age, acquiring the nickname "Old Folks." He attributed his success to pitching every day: batting practice, long toss, or in game action. He caused a bit of a stir when he responded to a question about legalizing the spitball by saying, "Bring it back. I've got a dandy one already."

On June 13, 1955, Kinder was involved in a near-fatal car accident long after curfew. He said he swerved to avoid a dog, and then crashed his vehicle into a telephone pole. When asked what a dog was doing out wandering around at 2:30 in the morning, Kinder only laughed.

Typically, he received just a few cuts and bruises and was pitching within a few days. On September 3, Kinder came into a bases-loaded situation in the eighth inning, tossed 4 2/3 scoreless innings, then drove in the winning run in the bottom of the 12th.

In December Kinder was sold to the St. Louis Cardinals for the waiver price. The Red Sox felt they could make the deal because of the emergence of a few young relievers, including Ike Delock, Leo Kiely, and Tom Hurd. Still, the popular Kinder was caught off-guard. "There is nothing wrong with my arm, and there's no reason I can't help the Cardinals next year," Kinder said. "I've enjoyed playing in Boston, where the fans have been wonderful to me. And I must say that Joe McCarthy and Mike Higgins were the best managers I ever played for."

Ellis Kinder Night was on January 24, when he was lavished with gifts and praise. Jimmie Piersall spoke of the support Kinder had given when he struggled with mental health issues in 1952 ("like a big brother to me"), Governor Christian Herter called him a wonderful example to all ballplayers, and Tebbetts said, "Never in all my baseball career have I ever heard Kinder say anything bad about any player, manager, or umpire." Kinder received telegrams from Ted Williams, Rocky Marciano, and a poignant one from Mrs. Georgiana Agganis, the mother of Harry Agganis, Ellis's teammate who had died tragically just months before. Kinder concluded the night by saying, "Baseball's been very good to me. I've had a lot of thrills, and tonight is one of the biggest."

Kinder starred early for the 1956 Cardinals, causing manager Fred Hutchinson to say, "As far as I'm concerned he's earned his salary already." Vinegar Bend Mizell, after winning two games saved by Kinder, said, "If anything happens to him, ah'm gonna pack my bags and go home." He slumped briefly in June, and despite his 2–0 record and 3.51 ERA was sold to the White Sox on July 11. In Chicago, he pitched well again, finishing 3–1 with a 2.73 ERA in 29 games.

Kinder held out briefly in the spring of 1957, which may have helped speed the end of his career. After just seven innings in spring training due to a leg injury, and one scoreless appearance in April, he drew his release when the White Sox had to reduce their roster to 25 in mid-May. He signed with the San Diego Padres of the Pacific Coast League in June, but pitched just twice. After a few fruitless weeks hoping to find a job, Kinder soon realized his career was over.

The marriage of Kinder and Ruth did not last long, and after his career ended, Ellis moved back to Jackson and soon had moved in with Hazel, his first wife. Kinder worked hard his whole life, and quickly returned to a life of labor. He hired himself out to perform carpentry, roofing and other home-improvement jobs. He struggled to control his life-long battle with alcohol, and his struggle was often in vain.

He was in poor health for a few years before undergoing open-heart surgery, a rare procedure in those days, in the fall of 1968 in a Memphis hospital. While recovering, he watched that year's World Series between the Tigers and Cardinals, but he suffered a reversal and died on October 16, 1968. The 54-year-old Kinder was laid to rest at Highland Memorial Gardens, in Jackson, Tennessee.

In an article written shortly after his death, Harold Kaese recalled the heart and competitiveness of Ellis Kinder. "Tip the lid to Tex Hughson, Dave Ferris, Mel Parnell, and Jim Lonborg, but if the Red Sox had to win one game, my pitcher would have been Kinder," wrote Kaese. Kinder, like teammate Vern Stephens, who died just 18 days after Ellis, did not live to see his great Red Sox teams from the late 1940s become the stuff of nostalgia. While many of his ex-teammates could make a living in the 1980s and beyond selling autographs and writing books, Kinder and Stephens, two of the greatest players on those teams, have faded from memory. No more.

Sources

In researching this story, the author relied heavily on *The Sporting News* historical archive accessed at www.paperofrecord.com, and Kinder's clipping file at the National Baseball Hall of Fame Library in Cooperstown. I spoke with Maurice Stansell of Jackson, Tennessee, who knew Kinder during and after his career. His minor league stats came courtesy of SABR's Ed Washuta. Important other sources included:

Obituary. *The Sporting News*, November 2, 1968.

Steve O'Leary. "Wonder-Kid Kinder 'Just Starting' at 35." *The Sporting News*, September 28, 1949.

Harold Kaese. "Vern and Ellis Among Sox Best." *Boston Globe*, November 6, 1968.

Roger Birtwell. "Kinder, Ex-Pipe-Fitter, Fits in Well as Bosox' Sub Starter for Kramer". *The Sporting News*, April 27, 1948.

Milton Richman. "'Guts of Iron' Kinder". *Baseball Digest*, November 1949.

Hy Hurwitz. "Fans, Friends, Players Give Kinder Big Night." *Boston Globe*, January 25, 1956.

Roger Birtwell. "Story of Kinder, Pitcher Unusual." *Boston Globe*, January 24, 1956

Gerry Moore. "Kinder to Start, Relieve, Too, He Learns at Dinner." *Boston Herald*. January 25, 1956.

JOHN HENRY "JACK" KRAMER *by C. Paul Rogers III*

G	ERA	W	L	SV	GS	GF	CG	SHO	IP	H	R	ER	BB	SO	HR	HBP	WP	BFP
29	4.35	18	5	0	29	0	14	2	205	233	104	99	64	72	12	0	3	891

G	AB	R	H	2B	3B	HR	RBI	BB	SO	BA	OBP	SLG	SB	HBP
29	73	7	11	1	0	1	8	10	21	.151	.253	.205	0	0

After winning the American League pennant by 12 games in 1946, the Boston Red Sox had slipped to third in 1947, finishing 14 games behind the champion New York Yankees and two games back of the second place Detroit Tigers. In an attempt to improve their hitting and pitching the Red Sox pulled the trigger on a blockbuster trade with the St. Louis Browns on November 17, 1947, acquiring 30-year-old right-handed starting pitcher Jack Kramer and slugging shortstop Vern "Junior" Stephens in exchange for seven players (catchers Roy Partee and Don Palmer; pitchers Al Widmar, Jim Wilson, and Joe Ostrowski; infielder Eddie Pellagrini; and outfielder Pete Layden) and a reported $310,000 cash.[1]

Both Kramer and Stephens would respond with terrific years and would be key ingredients to the Red Sox chase for the pennant in 1948 which they lost in a one game playoff to the Cleveland Indians. Kramer would become the team's leading winner, compiling a record of 18 wins against only five losses, including a clutch 5–1 victory over the powerful Yankees on the last weekend of the season. It would be Kramer's career year and last real hurrah. Plagued by a sore arm, Kramer could win only

Jack Kramer. Courtesy of George Brace Photo.

six games while losing eight in 1949 when the Red Sox would again fall just short of the pennant.[2]

At the time the Red Sox acquired Kramer, he was a 12-year veteran of professional baseball and had pitched for the Browns since 1939. He had been born on January 5, 1918 in New Orleans where he grew up. By 1934, Jack was the catcher for the Skelly Shamrocks, his American Legion team, until he tried pitching one day in the second game of a doubleheader. He threw only fastballs and had no real wind up, but a three-hit shutout was the result. Thereafter Kramer was mostly a pitcher. During his last year at Warren Easton High School in New Orleans he caught the first game of the season but pitched thereafter, losing only one game. His mound prowess caught the attention of Lenny Mock, a New Orleans native who happened to manage the Lafayette White Sox of the Class D Evangeline League, an affiliate of the St. Louis Browns.

Mock arranged a tryout and signed Kramer for the 1936 season. Jack was raw and wild and Mock came close to releasing him. Ray Cahill, a Browns scout, saw something in Kramer, however, and urged patience. He worked with Kramer and changed his delivery to overhand from his previous herky-jerky three-quarters delivery. Kramer finished the year with seven wins and 11 losses and an unattractive 5.60 earned run average but was signed nonetheless for 1937. There the virtue of patience showed itself as Jack improved to 12–9 and dropped his earned run average 2½ runs to 3.03 to help Lafayette into a tie for the pennant with the Rayne Rice Birds. He struck out 147 batters in 175 innings and was rewarded with a late season call-up to the Des Moines Demons in the Class A Western League.

Kramer advanced to the San Antonio Missions of the Texas League for 1938 and, only 20 years old, won 20 games while losing only 11. In 242 innings he allowed only 201 hits and put together a sparkling 2.42 earned run average. His great performance in the fast Texas League earned him promotion to the woeful St. Louis Browns for the 1939 season. The '39 Browns, under manager Fred Haney, who would almost 20 years later lead the Milwaukee Braves to two pennants and a world championship, could win only 43 games while losing 111 and finishing deep in the American League cellar, a whopping 64½ games out of first place. Kramer's nine wins tied Vern Kennedy for the club lead. He also suffered 16 defeats and his earned run average was an unsightly 5.83 which nonetheless was slightly below the team's 6.01 ERA. His strikeout to walk ratio was a backwards 1-to-2, with only 68 strikeouts and 127 walks in 211⅔ innings. He still showed promise, throwing two shutouts and pitching 10 complete games.

Kramer struggled even more in 1940, going 3–7 with a 6.26 ERA before the Browns shipped him to Toledo of the American Association. He wasn't any better with the Mud Hens, finishing with a 1–6 won-loss record and an unhealthy 6.86 era. The pitching deprived Browns gave him another shot in 1941 and he compiled a 4–3 record in 29 games, all but three in relief. Still plagued by wildness, Jack walked 40 and struck out only 20 in 59⅓ innings while his ERA remained above five. Kramer roomed with utility infielder Ellis Clary at the Melbourne Hotel in St. Louis during the 1941 season and Clary recalled that Jack called his mother in New Orleans every night.

With World War II on in full force, Kramer spent 1942 working as a shipfitter at the Delta Shipyard in New Orleans where he was able to pitch an occasional Sunday semipro game. Then he enlisted in the Navy in January 1943 and volunteered for the rigorous Seabee training at Camp Peary near Williamsburg, Virginia. His sinuses, which had first been a problem in Toledo in 1940, kicked up with all the plunging in and out of water in Virginia's marshlands that was required of him, landing him in the post hospital. After a month's stay there the Navy gave him an honorable discharge on May 14 and he headed home to New Orleans to further recuperate.

Kramer rejoined the Browns on June 22, 1943 and appeared in three games as he worked his way back into pitching shape. The Browns played an exhibition game on August 5 with Toledo, still their top minor league affiliate, and left Kramer with the Mud Hens. It was a wise decision, for there, in his second stint in Toledo, Jack turned his career around and never looked back. After losing his first start to the Kansas City Blues 3–1, he reeled off eight straight wins, including two-hit and three-hit shutouts. He even topped those performances on September 11 when he threw a no-hitter against the Louisville Colonels. It was the first no-hitter ever at Parkway Field which had opened in 1923. He finished the year with the Mud Hens with an 8–2 record and an impressive 2.46 earned run average. Improved control helped immeasurably, he struck out 59 and walked 26 in 84 innings of work.

The 1943 Browns had finished in sixth place with an uninspiring 72–80 won-loss record. In 1944, however, the baseball gods looked down with favor on the historically hapless franchise. With the war at its peak, the Brownies roster was favored with a number of 4-Fs who were frontline players, including Vern Stephens, George McQuinn, and Al Zarilla.[3] In addition, they had three key players who had been discharged from the service—Kramer, Gus Mancuso and Sig Jakucki, who was working as a paper hanger in Houston when the Browns signed him.[4]

The Browns entered the season with uncertain pitching to say the least. Manager Luke Sewell selected Kramer to pitch the April 17 opener against the Tigers in Detroit even though his lifetime record was 16–26 and his earned run average was close to six. But Jack was superb, beating Dizzy Trout 2–1 and shutting the Tigers out until allowing Pinky Higgins' home run with two out in the ninth. That win was the first of nine straight Brownie victories to start the season, blowing by the Yankees' record of seven straight wins to open a season, set in 1933. Kramer also won the fifth and ninth of those victories, defeating the White Sox 5–2 while hitting a two-run homer over the 402-foot sign in left-center and then conquering Cleveland, 3 to 1.

The Browns stayed in first place until May 11 when the Yankees took over, but eight days later St. Louis reclaimed the lead. They were in and out of the lead, embroiled in a tight pennant race with up to four teams. Kramer won five in a row to start the season before slumping. At the All-Star break the Browns were 45 and 34 and in first place by 2½ games. They won 10 in a row in early August to open a 6½ game lead over the Yankees but by Labor Day had surrendered the lead to those same New Yorkers. Although the Browns briefly slipped to third place in early September, they refused to wilt and showed the resiliency necessary to hang in there.

On September 16, Kramer threw a one-hitter at the White Sox to propel the Browns back into the lead. It was short-lived, however, as the next day the Tigers won a doubleheader over New York to regain the lead and virtually eliminate the Yankees from contention. Heading into the final weekend of the season, the Browns found themselves one game behind the Tigers, with four games against the tough Yankees at Sportsman's Park while Detroit hosted the cellar-dwelling Senators. Kramer pitched the crucial first game of the Friday doubleheader and prevailed 4–1, contributing a key double to the Browns' offense. The Browns, behind continued outstanding pitching, went on the sweep the vaunted Yankees while

Kramer throwing before the game.
Courtesy of George Brace Photo.

the Tigers could only split their four games with Washington. Their performance vaulted them by a single game to the first and only pennant in franchise history.

Waiting for the Browns in the World Series were the powerful, by wartime standards at least, Cardinals, who had won 105 games and swept to the National League pennant by 14½ games. The teams split the first two games and Kramer started the pivotal third game against rookie Ted Wilks for the Cardinals. Wilks had broken in with a bang, winning 17 while losing only four, but the Browns drove him from the mound with four runs and five hits after two were out in the third. Kramer pitched a strong game, striking out 10 and allowing only two unearned runs to win 6–2 and propel the Browns into a two-games-to-one lead.

Unhappily for the Brownies, the Cardinals then won three straight to win the Series four games to two. Kramer pitched two scoreless innings in a losing cause in Game Six to bring his series total to 11 innings and a perfect 0.00 earned run average. For the regular season he had won 17, lost 13, with a sparkling 2.49 earned run average in 31 starts and 257 innings.

Kramer held out until late March the following spring, looking for a $5,000 raise. He got something less than a $3,000 increase but still started the season strong, winning his seventh game in mid-June. Thereafter a groin injury hampered him but he tried to pitch through it. Jack finished 10–15 for the season, but with a solid 3.36 ERA. The drop-off in his performance, however, certainly had an impact on the Browns, who finished in third place with a solid 81–70 record, six games behind the Tigers. It may also have had something to do with the fact that he was tipping his pitches and at least the rival Tigers picked it up. According to Les Mueller and Red Borom, Kramer turned his glove one way when throwing his fastball and another when throwing his curve, making it easy for the batter to know what pitch was coming.[5] As a result, Kramer rarely got past the fifth inning against Detroit, and since the Tigers won the pennant by only a game and a half over Washington, may have been a significant, if unwitting, contributor to their pennant run.

Kramer was not above enjoying himself in the dugout and did a mean Bugs Bunny imitation. One-armed outfielder Pete Gray was on the Browns in 1945 and, according to teammate Ellis Clary, Kramer would sit in the dugout and in his best Bugs Bunny voice say, "Eh, don't look now, Doc, but there's a one-armed man out there in center field." Everyone on the bench would crack up and later, when it was quiet, Kramer would repeat the line in case anyone had missed it.[6]

The spring of 1946 the Browns attempted to cut Kramer $2,000, evoking an angry reaction from Jack who indicated that the club was fully aware of his injury the previous year. He ended his holdout on February 27 and joined the club for spring training in Anaheim, California. The Browns struggled from the start and won only 66 games, finishing in seventh place, 38 games out of first. Kramer was one of the few bright spots, leading the team with 13 wins against 11 losses with three shutouts and a 3.19 ERA. In May and June the Yankees repeatedly tried to acquire Kramer but manager Muddy Ruel would not let him go. He was selected to the American League All-Star team for the first time and only time of his career. All-Star manager Steve O'Neill tabbed Kramer to pitch the last three innings of the 12–0 American League laugher in Fenway Park and he responded with three hitless innings, striking out Phil Cavarretta, Marty Marion, and Del Ennis in the process.

Kramer had Hollywood good looks and by now had an earned reputation as a clothes horse. It was said that he couldn't pass a mirror without stopping to admire himself. He apparently also had quite a pair of rabbit ears. One afternoon the Indians, led by one of their coaches Del Baker, were quickly on his case, giving him a considerable going over from their dugout. In the second inning, Kramer plunked player-manager Lou Boudreau in the ribs with a fastball. As Boudreau trotted to first, Jack strolled over toward the first base line and said, "If you don't keep those guys on the bench quiet, I'll stick one in your ear the next time you come to bat. You're the boss so let's see you shut them up."[7]

Kramer was well known for his competitive drive and generally did not like to be removed from games he started. Once when Browns manager Luke Sewell took him out of a game against the Red Sox in Fenway Park, Kramer became so mad that he fired the ball far up into the stands. One wag remarked that it was his best throw of the day.

The 1947 Browns continued the team's slide, this time falling all the way to the American League basement. The club, under Muddy Ruel, could win only 59 games. They were led by Kramer's 11 victories, the only Brownie hurler with double digit wins. But Jack lost 16 times and his earned run average was an unsightly 4.97. For the first time since 1941 he walked more men than he struck out and gave up more hits than innings pitched.

One of his teammates on the Browns was the equally temperamental Jeff Heath, a burly outfielder who would play a key role for the 1948 Boston Braves pennant winners. Heath and Kramer were not shy about agitating each other about poor performances during that long, losing season. Before a game in Detroit, Kramer complained to Heath about poor offensive support and Heath reminded Kramer about how many times he had been knocked out of the box recently. Finally Heath said, "Okay, we'll get you a three run lead today. Let's see if you can hold it."

Heath proceeded to go hitless but John Berardino drove in three runs with a bat comedian Joe E. Brown had just given him. Kramer did his part, pitching a four-hit shutout to beat Detroit 3–0.[8]

After winning the 1946 pennant, the Boston Red Sox had slipped to third place in 1947, finishing 14 games behind the Yankees. Shortly after the season, the team named the veteran skipper Joe McCarthy manager, with Joe Cronin moving upstairs to full-time general manager. The new brass did not waste much time shaking up the roster. Before Thanksgiving, the BoSox outbid the Indians and made two deals in two days with the financially strapped Browns, first securing Kramer and slugging shortstop Vern Stephens for seven players and a reported $310,000.[9] With starters Tex Hughson, Dave (Boo) Ferris, and Mickey Harris all nursing sore arms and contemplating surgery, the Red Sox counted on Kramer to step into the starting rotation in 1948.

It didn't begin well for Kramer, who reported to spring training recovering from the flu which inflamed his back. He also suffered with what was described as a "bad leg." In any event, he was not able to make his first start for the Red Sox until May 1, defeating the Yankees 8–6. After losing his second start to Detroit 8–3, Kramer threw a six-hit shutout against the White Sox on May 11, winning 8–0. But two rough outings followed and with the Red Sox thrashing around in seventh place, Joe Cronin reportedly put Kramer on waivers. It is uncertain whether no one claimed him or whether the Red Sox revoked the waivers, but Kramer remained with the Red Sox. It is often said that some of the best deals are the ones teams do not make and keeping Kramer was a prime example of that maxim. He proceeded to reel off 11 straight victories through early August to propel Boston into pennant contention. Although passed over for the All-Star team, at the end of his streak Jack's won-loss record stood at 13–3.

At some point during his streak, Kramer went on a clothes shopping spree. According to teammate Birdie Tebbetts, Kramer announced in the clubhouse that he had just purchased two suits, half a dozen trousers, and four sport coats. The clothes were being altered and he couldn't wait to show them off. He said, "Best looking set of clothes you'll ever see, but you bunch of hillbillies wouldn't know the difference, so what the hell."

On the day Kramer picked up his new clothes from the tailor, Tebbetts told Ted Williams, "Kramer is coming in soon and he'll be wearing his new clothes. No matter what I say to him, I want you to agree with me." Ted said, "OK, I'll do it."

Shortly Kramer did come waltzing in decked out in a flashy sport coat and greenish trousers with a knife crease. He stood in the middle of the clubhouse with all eyes on him and turned in a circle with his chest out and said, "All right you assholes, what do you think?"

Tebbetts went up to Jack, felt the material, and said, "Gee, they are beautiful, Jack. Must have cost you a fortune. What do you think, Ted?"

Williams said, "Yeah, they're beautiful, Birdie. Must have set him back a pile of dough."

Then Tebbetts stood back and frowned and said, "Wait a minute, Jack. The left sleeve is longer than the right."

Williams said, "Yeah, you're right Birdie. They are uneven."

Then Tebbetts reached up and adjusted Kramer's collar and said, "Jack, your collar is riding up."

Williams came up and looked at it and said, "That's right, Birdie, but have you looked at the trousers? The cuff is riding too high."

Kramer walked to the mirror, staring at his cuffs and turning this way and that while his teammates were muffling laughter. Finally, he stomped off cussing out his tailor while his teammates guffawed behind him.[10]

On August 4, with his winning streak still intact, Kramer was forced to leave a start against the Browns in the third inning with a sore shoulder but under the rules then in place was credited with the victory, his 11th in a row. After a no-decision against the Yankees six days later, Kramer lost to the Senators 5–4 on August 14 to end the streak. On August 20 he beat the Senators 10–4 to bring the Red Sox within three games of the league lead. His arm, however, was clearly bothering him. He lost to the White Sox in a short outing on August 27 and at one point threw only two innings in a ten day stretch before beating the Tigers 10–1 on September 1 to record his 15th win of the season. The win kept the surging Red Sox in front of the pack by a single game in one of the tightest pennant races in history.

On Labor Day, four days later, Kramer threw another strong game, defeating the Senators in Washington 2–1 on a four-hitter to complete a sweep of a doubleheader. The win ran Jack's record to 16–4 and kept the Red Sox a game ahead of the Yankees and a game and a half in front of the Indians. Joe McCarthy then tabbed Kramer to start at home against the Yankees on three days rest but the Bronx Bombers chased him in the sixth on their way to a 6–2 lead. The Red Sox came back to tie the game 6–6 in the eighth inning before Joe DiMaggio's grand slam home run in the 10th inning won it for New York and cut Boston's lead to 2½ games.

Kramer's next start was shaky as well. On September 14 he lasted only into the third inning and left trailing 4–1 in what was eventually a 17–10 loss to the White Sox. The blowout defeat cut the Red Sox's lead over the Yankees to a single game. Three days later in Detroit Kramer tried again in the second game of a doubleheader and was again knocked from the box early, this time after 3⅔ innings while behind 6–3 in a game Boston was to lose 8–6. It was his third unsuccessful try for his 17th win and enabled the Cleveland Indians to climb within one-half game of the lead with the Yankees only a game back.

By the time of his next start on September 25 the Indians, Yankees and Red Sox were in a dead heat, all three with 91–56 records. On a Saturday afternoon before 66,500 in Yankee Stadium, Kramer hooked up in a crucial game against Allie Reynolds, also seeking his 17th win of the season. The Red Sox scored two runs in the first without a hit, thanks to two Yankee errors, and buoyed by great defense, Kramer pitched a complete game 7–2 victory. The Indians kept pace behind Gene Bearden with a win over Detroit.

Kramer's next and final start came on Saturday, October 2, in the Red Sox's 153rd game of the season. It was also against the Yankees, this time in Fenway Park, with both clubs one game behind the Indians with two to play. Cleveland was playing its last two games against Detroit in Municipal Stadium, knowing that the pennant race could not be decided until all three teams had completed the 154-game season. But the loser of Saturday's Red Sox—Yankee contest would be virtually out of the race.[11]

Facing Kramer was Tommy Byrne, a southpaw who had defeated the Red Sox 6–2 the previous Sunday. In the first Kramer retired lead-off hitter Phil Rizzuto but allowed a single to right by Tommy Henrich. Bobby Brown, who had tripled and doubled against the Red Sox the previous weekend, got hold of one but Dom DiMaggio was able to track it down in deep centerfield. Kramer then bore down and struck out Joe DiMaggio to end the inning. It was only DiMag's 30th kayo of the season.

The Red Sox struck quickly in the bottom half of the inning as Byrne walked Johnny Pesky with one out and Ted Williams deposited a fastball into the bullpen in right for a 2–0 lead. In the third, Pesky walked again and Williams doubled him to third. Stan Spence singled sharply to right to score both and stretch the lead to 4–0. Boston tallied another run in the fourth on a sacrifice fly by Vern Stephens to bring the score to 5–0. Meanwhile Kramer had retired 12 Yankees in a row until Tommy Henrich's single in the sixth. New York finally scratched out a run in the seventh on a double by DiMaggio, a ground out by Berra, and a sacrifice fly by Johnny Lindell.

The 5–1 win was Jack's 18th of the year against only five losses and knocked the Yankees out of the pennant race. The Indians, behind Gene Bearden, defeated Detroit 8–0 to maintain their slim one game lead. The next day, Sunday, the Red Sox again beat the Yankees, this time 10–6 in a seesaw ballgame, while Detroit knocked Bob Feller from the box to win 7–1 and drop Cleveland into a tie for the pennant with the Red Sox.

The playoff game was the next day, Monday, and if Kramer were to pitch it would be with only one day of rest. According to a report in *The Sporting News*, McCarthy looked to his veteran right hander to start the playoff game but Kramer did not respond positively.[12] His season was over, as the Red Sox went with the veteran Denny Galehouse and Cleveland, behind the remarkable Bearden, won the playoff and the pennant, 8–3.

Kramer had been instrumental in lifting the Red Sox into the pennant race and had won two huge games at the end of the season to give his team a chance to win it all. His winning percentage of .783 led the American League. For the year he threw 205 innings in 29 starts and 14 complete games. His 233 hits allowed and 4.35 earned run average attest to the fact that he received excellent offensive support when he pitched. But the fact remains that without his winning streak early in the summer and clutch wins the last week of the season, the Red Sox would have not tied for the pennant.

Kramer parlayed his memorable 1948 season into a $30,000 contract for 1949, one of the top salaries on the team. In spring training he apparently won a contest for the best dressed player on the team, a title he savored. He was called Handsome Jack or Alice by his teammates, the latter because he wore only silk underwear which he insisted on washing himself. One story that made the rounds was that Kramer had bought one suit because the salesman told him it was the only one of its kind in the world. When he later saw someone else wearing the same suit, he gave his away. He was so enamored of his wardrobe that he sometimes would change clothes two or three times a day, leading teammates to call him "a fruit basket."

Teammate Matt Batts remembered Jack as an inveterate complainer who was very picky about everything. For example, he would always send his food back in a restaurant if it didn't suit him. His locker was next to Kramer's in the Boston clubhouse. One afternoon Batts came in and found his sports jacket on the floor. He asked Ellis Kinder, whose locker was on the other side of Batts', how it got there. Kinder told Batts that Kramer had tossed it down because he didn't like it that the sleeve of Batts jacket protruded into Kramer's adjoining locker.

When Kramer came in to the clubhouse, Batts confronted him and Jack admitted to throwing Batts' jacket on the floor because the sleeve was hanging over into his locker. Batts bided his time and a few weeks later Kramer wore his white cashmere sports coat to the ballpark. After he hung it in his locker and went onto the field, Batts grabbed it, threw it across the clubhouse floor and left it there. When Kramer came in the two almost came to fisticuffs.[13]

Red Sox coach Mike Ryba was known for his selection of an American League All-Ugly Team each year. His selections were the cause of much anticipation and discussion among the league. More than once Ryba picked Kramer to his all-ugly team, just to bring him down a notch or two.

Unfortunately Jack struggled mightily in '49 with a sore arm and at the All-Star break had only one victory against four defeats. The Red Sox hung tough with the Yankees even without Kramer, thanks to great years from Ellis Kinder and Mel Parnell on the mound and astounding offensive production from Ted Williams, Vern Stephens (both of whom would drive in an eye-popping 159 runs), and Bobby Doerr. After a mediocre start, the club went 36–10 from July 5 through the end of August to come within 3½ games of New York. Kramer had a brief resurgence in August, going 3–0 for the month.

Handsome Jack was known to show off from time to time. During the season Kramer asked rookie catcher Matt Batts to warm him up in front of the dugout before a night game on an evening when he was not scheduled to pitch. Batts was not very happy about it since warming Kramer up would cause him to miss batting practice. The crowd was filing in and Red Sox owner Tom Yawkey and other executives were nearby. Batts thought Kramer was exaggerating his motion and preening for the audience a little more than necessary. As Jack delivered a pitch,

Batts dropped his catcher's mitt and caught the ball barehanded. Batts returned the ball to Kramer but Jack made no effort to catch it. Instead he just turned around and walked away. It was the last time Kramer asked Batts to warm him up.[14]

The Red Sox again lost a taut pennant race, this time on the last day of the season, 5–3 to the Yankees on a two-run home run by Tommy Henrich and a three-run double by Jerry Coleman. Kramer struggled to a 6–8 record and a dismal 5.16 earned run average. He threw only 111⅔ innings and could start only 18 games.

Joe McCarthy was clearly tired of Kramer's act and in February 1950 the Red Sox sold Jack outright to the New York Giants for a reported $25,000. Under the rules then in place, all the American League clubs would have had to pass on Kramer for him to be sold to the National League. Kramer had, at a minimum, his feelings hurt by being dumped by the Red Sox and lashed out at Joe McCarthy, calling him "the most ornery man I know" and accusing him of "railroading him out of the league only because he had a personal grudge" against him.[15] He promised that he would make McCarthy regret the sale.

By most accounts, his Boston teammates were glad to see Jack go, some referring to him as "a grand opera." Birdie Tebbetts, the Red Sox regular catcher, was particularly harsh, alleging that Kramer "never delivered when we needed him. His attitude was all wrong from the time he first joined up. All he cared about the game of baseball was the money he could get out of it to buy fancy clothes and cars and strut as Handsome Jack. He didn't really care for the game and he certainly didn't care for anybody on this squad."[16] Another "star" teammate said, "The best thing Joe Cronin ever did for this club was to get rid of that drone bee. Joe [McCarthy] knew what a bad influence the guy was on team morale. We have peace and harmony now that he's gone."

Veteran Boston sportswriter Harold Kaese labeled Kramer as temperamental, high strung, sensitive, and self-centered.[17] When Kramer learned of the quotes attributed to Tebbetts, he found it hard to believe that Birdie had said those things about him. But, Kramer went on, if Tebbetts had said those things, they were lies. A man had to defend himself, he said, and he "gave my best for Boston. I always have and always will. Man, I couldn't sleep nights if I didn't and I can always sleep nights."

Kramer couldn't understand why someone "in the same business" would talk about another like that because "it gets no one any satisfaction." He then couldn't resist responding to Tebbetts' supposed quip about his wardrobe: "I don't know why Tebbetts brought up the subject of clothes and automobiles. He has more clothes than I have and he can afford better automobiles."

Then Handsome Jack attempted some humor, "I'll say this about clothes. Birdie may have more clothes than I have, but mine fit me a lot better than his fit him."[18]

On the other side of the deal, Giants' manager Leo Durocher was sold on Kramer's reputation as a good competitor.[19] But it is unlikely that McCarthy regretted the sale. Kramer went 3–6 for the Giants in 1950 in 35 games and only 86⅔ innings. His ERA was a respectable 3.53 but he walked more than he struck out and gave up more than a hit an inning. He was used mostly in relief and as a spot starter, with nine starts and one complete game.

In August Kramer cost the Giants a win on the base-paths, of all things. In a game against the Phillies in Shibe Park, Kramer found himself on first base late in a tie game. Jack Lohrke singled to right-center and Kramer only made it to second base on a play that should have sent him to third. Whitey Lockman followed with another hit and Kramer was thrown out at the plate, preserving the tie. The Giants went on to lose in extra innings. After the game, Leo Durocher was headed to Kramer's locker to give him the what for when he found that several Giants were already there, accusing Jack of not hustling and costing them the ballgame in loud, angry voices. For his part, Kramer offered no excuses.[20]

Not surprisingly given his history, Kramer held out in the spring of 1951 balking at a proposed pay cut. The Giants and Durocher found it amusing that someone who had won three games was holding out and made it clear that they really didn't care much if he signed or not. Kramer did sign on March 7, accepting a $15,000 salary, a reduction of $3,000 from the previous year. He reported to spring training but it was not long before he got himself into the doghouse. First, Durocher ignored him for a week or so after he announced that he was ready to pitch, following his late reporting due to his holdout. After finally pitching two innings against the Cardinals, he reported sick for another exhibition game, claiming stomach problems. The Giants were short-handed in the bullpen at the time and the team doctor could find nothing wrong with Jack.

The following day, on the train to Mobile, Alabama, Durocher talked with Kramer, telling him to stop acting like a prima-donna and to get ready to contribute to the team. Durocher told the press that Kramer's problems were all in his mental approach to the game. He referred to a great batting practice Kramer had recently thrown and said, "The guy can pitch if he wants to pitch. Larry [Jansen] and I thought it was one of the greatest pitching shows we've ever seen."[21]

Durocher must have struck a chord with Handsome Jack. On April 3, the day after his heart-to-heart talk with Durocher, Kramer threw five scoreless innings in an exhibition game against the Boston Braves, allowing only one hit. Then a few days later Kramer threw a complete game in Dallas against the Cleveland Indians, winning 10–3. He shut the Tribe out for six innings, running his spring training stretch of scoreless innings to 13.

Once the season began, however, Kramer was ineffective. In four appearances, including one start, he pitched 4⅔ innings, giving up 11 hits and eight earned runs. On May 17, the Giants gave the 33-year-old his unconditional release.

That same day, Kramer walked into Yankee Stadium and asked Casey Stengel for a tryout. Casey apparently did not recognize Jack at first and thought that he was an unknown who had been sent down to the field by George Weiss, the Yankee general manager. It soon was straightened out and Kramer pitched batting practice for the Yankees. Stengel asked his players to tell him if Kramer had any stuff left and the "tryout" went on for 11 days, with Jack pitching batting practice each day. Finally on May 28 the Yankees signed Kramer and put him on the roster, sending rookie pitcher Tom Morgan down to the Kansas City Blues to make room.

One Yankee teammate Kramer knew was Bobby Brown, the Yankee third baseman. Dr. Brown had attended medical school at Tulane and become friendly with Kramer, the New Orleans native, in the offseasons. When he joined the Yankees, Brown knew that if he wanted a new suit, all he had to do was ask Kramer or Allie Reynolds and they would come along and buy three suits to his one.[22]

Unhappily, Kramer could not regain his mound form. He appeared in 19 games for the Yankees, starting three, while compiling a 1–3 won-loss record and a 4.65 earned run average. The Yankees, headed for their third straight American League pennant, ultimately decided that Jack wasn't going to help them. The world champions released him on August 30, ending his big league career.

Handsome Jack returned to his native New Orleans after ending his baseball career, where he eventually worked selling milk, which he believed was "the greatest food in the world," to grocery chains. He was elected in 1967 to the prestigious Diamond Club of New Orleans. Jack Kramer passed away in New Orleans on May 18, 1995 of a brain hemorrhage at the age of 77.

In 12 big league seasons, Kramer won 95 games and lost 103 and thus ended up a sub-.500 pitcher. His career earned run average was an unimpressive 4.24, he walked more men than he struck out, and gave up more than a hit an inning. But he helped the St. Louis Browns to their only American League pennant and was a driving force in the Red Sox near run to the 1948 pennant.

Probably the best dresser in the game, Jack could be a persnickety and difficult teammate. He seemed to wear out his welcome, particularly when he was not pitching well. He struggled with arm trouble for much of the end of his career and his attitude was often suspect. He likely did not make the most of his considerable ability but he certainly left lasting impressions in Red Sox and Browns baseball history. When he was on, he was a very good pitcher and often delivered clutch wins for his ballclubs.

Notes

1. One day later the Red Sox raided the struggling Browns again, acquiring right-handed starter Ellis Kinder and infielder Billy Hitchcock for pitcher Clem Dreisewerd, infielders Sam Dente and Bill Sommers and another $65,000 in cash.

2. In 1949 Vern Stephens would top his 1948 numbers (29 home runs, 137 runs batted in) with one of the best years ever recorded by a shortstop (39 home runs and 159 runs batted in).

3. Eighteen of the 1944 Browns' 33-man spring roster were classified 4-F, the most in major league baseball. Thirteen 4-Fs ended up playing for the Browns the entire season. Bill Borst, *Still Last in the American League—The St. Louis Browns Revisited* (West Bloomfield, MI: Altwerger & Mandel Publishing, 1992), 67.

4. The '44 Browns listed 15 players serving in the armed forces but only two, Walt Judnich and Steve Sundra, were considered regulars. In contrast, for example, the Yankees had lost every starter from their 1942 world championship team to the military. William B. Mead, *Even the Browns—The Zany, True Story of Baseball in the Early Forties* (Chicago: Contemporary Books, Inc., 1978), 118–19.

5. Smith, Burge, *Nine Old Men and One Young Left Arm—A Journey Back Into the History of the 1945 Tigers*, pp. 142–43 (unpublished manuscript on file with the author).

6. Golenbock, Peter, *The Spirit of St. Louis—A History of the St. Louis Cardinals and Browns*, pp. 298, 314.

7. *The Sporting News*, Feb. 12, 1947, p. 28.

8. *The Sporting News*, Sept. 17, 1947, p. 16.

9. The following day, November 17, 1947, the Red Sox acquired pitcher Ellis Kinder and infielder Billy Hitchcock for three players and another $65,000.

10. Tebbetts, Birdie with Morrison, James, *Birdie—Confessions of a Baseball Nomad* (Chicago: Triumph Books 2002).

11. The loser of the Red Sox-Yankees game on Saturday would have to hope that Cleveland dropped both games with Detroit. Then it would have to win on Sunday to force a three-way tie.

12. *The Sporting News*, March 22, 1950, p. 20.

13. Golenbock, Peter, *Fenway—An Unexpurgated History of the Boston Red Sox*, pp. 174–75.

14. *Ibid.*, p. 175.

15. *New York World Telegram and Sun*, Feb. 27, 1950, p. 22.

16. *The Sporting News*, March 22, 1950, p. 20.

17. *The Sporting News*, March 8, 1950, p. 3.

18. *The Sporting News*, April 5, 1950, p. 36.

19. *The Sporting News*, March 8, 1950, p. 9.

20. *The Sporting News*, August 30, 1950, p. 12.

21. Unidentified newspaper clipping dated April 3, 1951 from the Jack Kramer file of the National Baseball Library, Cooperstown, New York.

22. Telephone interview with Dr. Bobby Brown, September 11, 2007.

Sources

Borst, Bill, *Still Last in the American League—The St. Louis Browns Revisited* (West Bloomfield, MI: Altwerger & Mandel Publishing 1992);

Golenbock, Peter, *Fenway—An Unexpurgated History of the Boston Red Sox* (New York: G.P. Putnam's Sons 1992);

Golenbock, Peter, *The Spirit of St. Louis—A History of the St. Louis Cardinals and Browns* (New York: Avon Books, Inc. 2000);

Halberstam, David, *The Summer of '49* (New York: William Morrow & Co., Inc. 1989);

Heidenry, John & Topel, Brett, *The Boys Who Were Left Behind* (Lincoln: Univ. of Nebraska Press 2006);

Kaiser, David, *Epic Season—The 1948 American League Pennant Race* (Amherst: Univ. of Massachusetts Press 1998);

Kramer, Jack file, National Baseball Hall of Fame Library, Cooperstown, NY

Levy, Alan H., *Joe McCarthy—Architect of the Yankee Dynasty* (Jefferson, NC: McFarland & Co., Inc. 2005);

McDermott, Mickey with Eissenberg, Howard, *A Funny Thing Happened on the Way to Cooperstown* (Chicago: Triumph Books 2003);

Mead, William B., *Even the Browns—The Zany, True Story of Baseball in the Early Forties* (Chicago: Contemporary Books, Inc. 1978);

Smith, Burge, *Nine Old Men and One Young Left Arm—A Journey Back Into the History of the 1945 Tigers* (unpublished manuscript dated 2007 and on file with the author);

The Sporting News, various issues 1939–51;

Tebbetts, Birdie with Morrison, James, *Birdie—Confessions of a Baseball Nomad* (Chicago: Triumph Books 2002).

BABE MARTIN *by Bill Nowlin*

G	AB	R	H	2B	3B	HR	RBI	BB	SO	BA	OBP	SLG	SB	HBP
4	4	0	2	0	0	0	0	0	1	.500	.500	.500	0	0

Babe Martin was born Boris Michael Martinovich, the son of a professional wrestler, Iron Mike Martin (Bryan Martinovich). Both of Boris' parents were born in parts of the former Yugoslavia, his father in Montenegro and his mother in Serbia. They each emigrated to the United States and settled in Seattle in the Pacific Northwest. At least one geographically-challenged sportswriter once dubbed him the "Hungarian hot-shot."

When wresting, the senior Martinovich adapted his surname to the circumstances. He wrestled in Montana in Chicago, and in any number of other places. If he was wrestling in an Italian area, he took the name Martini. In a Scottish or Irish area, he became McMartin or O'Martin. "Dad could speak a number of European languages, being born over there," Babe said, adding "When he married mother, that was the end of his wrestling."

Boris had two brothers and two sisters, Lola and Olga. Brother Robert was the only other one interested in sports, but it wasn't something he pursued past college. He became part-owner of a Budweiser distributorship in Florida, while brother Bryan—who'd boxed and wrestled a bit professionally before going into the service—became a jeweler in St. Louis. Boris married the former Mildred Slapcevich of St. Louis in 1943. He never legally changed his last name, but still generally goes by the name Martin. His sons, though, prefer to stick with Martinovich.

His mother prompted a family move to Zeigler, Illinois, in the southern part of the state, due to a conflict with an in-law. Born on March 28, 1920, Boris was just one year old at the time of the move. "The only type of industry at that time in southern Illinois was coal mining so my dad went to work in the coal mining business. A shaft caved in on him. He survived that, but died about three years later. He just died. Back in 1926, they didn't know how or what a person died from." Boris was three at the time of the accident, and the family moved on to St. Louis.

Boris's mother was very supportive of his ambitions when Boris showed athletic inclinations early on. "I played on sandlots, glass, and gravel fields, under bridges, wherever I could go ahead and play on. Playgrounds, wherever, you know. In the summertime, I'd be gone early in the morning and come home at dusk". Martin was a good ballplayer, good enough that "they took me out of grammar school, seventh grade, to play on the ninth-grade high school team."

As the youngest in his family, he was called Baby. "They called me Baby for years. And then as I got a little bit older, it got to be a little bit embarrassing so they called me Babe." He was Babe all through high school and beyond.

Though he was both a catcher and outfielder in pro ball—and only a catcher during his brief time with Boston in the majors, he began as an infielder. "As I grew, I got larger. If it had been today, I never would have consented to be a catcher. I could play first base. I was a pretty good infielder; although I was big, I could have moved to third base. But you know, back then, you did what you were told. If they wanted you in the outfield, you moved to the outfield. Today they don't take that...."

Martin played for McKinley High School in St. Louis in 1936–38, and his high school coach was Lou Maguolo, who scouted in the area for the St. Louis Browns. Maguolo later retired from coaching and became a full-time scout, working in that capacity for the New York Yankees. Babe was all-district in basketball and also played three years on the school's football team.

Boris Martinovich, a/k/a Babe Martin, with the St. Louis Browns. Courtesy of Babe Martin.

Martin graduated from high school in 1940 at age 20 and most sources show him as signing with the Browns then. "Actually," Martin confides, "I signed in high school unbeknownst to anybody. I signed in 1938. They gave me a job working in the Browns office at $100 a month and I worked out with the Browns and Cardinals. Back in the '30s, I guess '37, '38, '39, we didn't have any money. So $100 a month, bringing that home for my mother...my brother Bryan was really the only one that was working at the time. I was working in the office...office work. Answering the telephone at the switchboard. I wasn't very good at that, but mostly I was on the field. I was working out."

He kept active until he graduated from McKinley, when his signing was announced and he was sent to play ball in Palestine in the East Texas League. The franchise "blew up" and relocated in Tyler, where for the first time he began to play games behind the plate.

It was at Tyler that he was beaned by a pitcher named Bob Crow. "I was in the hospital for about seven days. He told me it was an accident. When I got out, they thought it was better for me if I didn't have to face pitchers in the East Texas League. I guess they figured maybe I would be afraid to get up there. We didn't have helmets or anything." Martin had secured a hit off Crow his first time up. Next time, he took a fastball right above the left eye. Martin had been hitting .274 at the time. He was sent to another Class C team, St. Joseph in the Michigan State League, to finish out the year. When he got there, he learned that Crow had bragged that he "showed that rookie so-and-so not to get a base hit off me. To be honest with you, I looked for Bob Crow for a number of years after that, trying to go ahead and find that...because he said he intentionally hit me. You know, if you intentionally hit a guy in the head, you've got to answer for that with your hands, you know. And I was pretty good with my hands." He never found Crow, and that might have been fortunate for the pitcher. Martin hit .235 the rest of the year. As late as August 1944, writer Don Wolfe said that Babe still suffered head pains.

In 1941, Martin had a terrific year, catching and playing in the Northeast Arkansas ball club in Paragould, Arkansas, hitting .353 to lead the league, with 54 RBIs in 75 games. In 1942, he played in the Three-I League for Springfield, Illinois, at four positions: catcher, outfield, and the two infield corner positions. He batted a very strong .325 with 12 homers and 63 RBIs in 345 at-bats. In September, he enlisted in the U.S. Navy and was stationed at Lambert Naval Air Station right there in St. Louis.

"When I got there, when I was signing up, a chief petty officer saw my résumé and he said that we're trying to start a baseball team. He said, 'Would you like to play baseball here at Lambert Field?' I said, 'Sure, I'd love to.' And then he asked me if I knew any other ballplayers that were going in the service, and I said, 'I sure do.' 'Well,' he said, 'If they're about ready to go, tell them to come on out.' So I was able to get some of the ballplayers who were with the Browns and the Giants and whatever and they came out to Lambert Field. Some of them went to the South Pacific later to play with the major league ballplayers out there. I stayed with Lambert Field, and got hurt playing. I got a ruptured quadricep in my left thigh. We beat Great Lakes in 1943, I think 1–0. Mickey Cochrane was their manager. I think Johnny Mize was playing first base at the time, but we had a pretty good baseball team out at Lambert Field."

Because of the quad injury, and duodenal ulcers, he spent four months at Great Lakes Naval Hospital before being discharged in April of 1944. His right thigh was said to be three inches shorter in circumference than his left. The Browns fitted him with a brace that he "used all of '44 and almost all the rest of my career. While I was playing. It was a brace that I had a belt to keep on. I put it on my left thigh from my knee up to my groin." Martin was also reported to keep a quart of milk in the dugout during ballgames so he could help keep the ulcers under control. Taking care of himself helped do the trick. Martin hit .350 in the American Association, playing for the Toledo Mud Hens, with 14 homers and 72 RBIs. He had five hits in the All-Star game and at year's end was voted both the MVP of the league and rookie of the year, though he will still say that he believed Johnny Wyrostek more deserving of the MVP award. At the end of the year, he was called up to St. Louis. He was now playing in the same Sportsman's Park where he'd worked out as a kid. He debuted with a two-for-three game against the visiting Red Sox, and then hit a pinch single his only other time up. He batted .750—three hits in four at-bats with a run batted in.

And he had a better than front-row seat for the 1944 World Series. All in all, "it was really a great feeling. It was my dream. And I was able to sit on the bench, in uniform, during the World Series, although I was not allowed to open my mouth en route under any circumstances. Those were the orders, if I was to sit on the bench. I saw the whole Series between the Cardinals and the Browns. It was great to watch it." A couple of years later, he went to

Martin with his catcher's mitt.
Courtesy of Babe Martin.

every game of the 1946 World Series, as well. Did he root for the hometown team? "I was an American Leaguer, if you remember. I really concealed myself pretty good on that Series."

In 1945, he had his first true taste of major league ball, but it was tough to get into a rhythm because of the start-and-stop nature of the work assigned him. The ball club had a big gate attraction in Pete Gray. Martin was completely candid in his remarks: "The Browns brought up a guy by the name of Pete Gray. He was a one-armed ballplayer, and there wasn't one ballplayer—and I know this is all being taped—but I can tell you that there wasn't one fellow on the ball club that was happy about Pete being there and playing. Pete played almost every game in center field for the Browns and he took Mike Kreevich's place. He would take my place. He would take Milt Byrnes' place. He would take…he was a ticket draw. Pete, God bless him, he couldn't throw anybody out. It was automatic first-to-third for a runner, but it was like Nelson Potter said (who was a great pitcher for us that year), that cost us…that really cost us the pennant. People would think that's sour, but that was the feeling at that time. I don't think any of us were envious. We thought…at least I thought I should be playing. Going in one game and out another game wasn't the way to go to get yourself started." Babe got into 54 games, all as an outfielder, and accumulated 185 at-bats, but only an even .200. At the end of July, the Browns added Lou Finney and Martin was sent down to Toledo, where he played for the Mud Hens and hit .300 in nine games.

In 1946, Martin played for the Pacific Coast League's Oakland Oaks, under manager Casey Stengel. "I tried very hard to go ahead and do a good job for Casey and I wasn't able to achieve that [.244 in 82 at-bats], so the Browns brought me back and sent me to Toledo, and I finished out the season in Toledo in '46." With Toledo, he appeared in 50 games and batted .265. At the tail end of the season, he came back to the Browns, getting into three more games. He had two hits in nine times up.

He had a very good year catching for Toledo in 1947, batting .319, with 15 homers and 64 RBIs, and in November he was taken in the Rule V draft by the Red Sox. Babe spent all of 1948 and 1949 with the Red Sox, but it cost him a great deal of playing time. In 1948, he got just four at-bats all season long and in 1949, he got just two. "I was the third catcher under Birdie Tebbetts, who was the first catcher, and a young guy by the name of Matt Batts—an excellent catcher. He was the second catcher, and I was the third catcher. I worked very hard to stay there. I really worked very hard. At the end of the '49 season, [Red Sox GM] Joe Cronin sent me to Louisville. I had a telephone call from Mr. McCarthy—who was our manager, Joe McCarthy—who told me he had nothing to do with me being sent to Louisville. That was Mr. Cronin's idea. He was the boss."

Martin split 1950 between Louisville and Toledo. "Louisville sold me to Toledo. The Red Sox...Mr. Cronin didn't want me for some reason, so they sent me to Toledo." He was back in the Browns system again. It wasn't a good year, and he hit only .211, with just 13 RBIs in 152 at-bats.

The next two years were spent in the Texas League, playing for San Antonio. There he played some first base the first year, and caught, batting .261 in 1951 and boosting that to .329 the following year. Although he'd played a large part of his career behind the plate, Martin says he'd never truly been taught the craft—not as unusual in the era as one might think today. And for the first time, he began to play first base. "I think I more or less learned how to really catch in 1952. It took a little while. I had no real instructions on how to catch. I just more or less had to learn by myself, with the exception that the Browns had a great former big league first baseman by the name of Jack Fournier. He was a good one."

1953 was again spent doing very little, but at least it was doing very little while on a major league roster, this time again with the Browns. He was the third catcher on the staff once more, and as in 1949 was hitless the only two times all season long that he got a chance to bat. In July, he was told to report to the Toronto Maple Leafs but elected to retire instead. Come 1954, "they told me they couldn't afford to pay me the $5,000 that I was making in '53 and sent me back to Toledo. That's when I quit for the season." He never reported to Toledo and was placed on the disqualified list. The St. Louis Browns still held his contract, though. The franchise moved to Baltimore in the offseason, and as the Browns became the Baltimore Orioles, Martin says, "I was able to secure my release. Mr. Artie Ehlers, who was the first general manager, was kind enough upon my request to give me my release so I could go ahead and get a little bonus and a salary playing with some minor league ball club." The club was Dallas, and it was Martin's last year in organized ball.

Babe was back in the Texas League in 1954, and played for Dallas for half a year, batting .262, but then just quit. He had an interest in brother Bryan's jewelry business and that appealed to him. The owner of the Dallas club wanted him to manage, but "I just told Mr. Burnett, the owner of the ball club, 'Man, at this age, for me to go ahead and take care of high school kids and drive a bus'—this is what we did back in those days, the manager drove a bus—'No, I don't want to be a part of that.' That was the end of it."

The jewelry business didn't work out well, and he lost the money he'd invested, in large part because his brother had too many friends and was too generous, selling jewelry at very little over cost—not securing enough of a profit for the business to survive. Babe got a job working for Highway Trailer Corporation out of Edgerton, Wisconsin. He went into the truck/trailer business as a salesperson based in St. Louis. "I did very well in that. To be honest with you, I don't think I sold a trailer for the first year or two, but after that people knew that we were going to stay in business and that I was going to be their trailer salesperson, I think everything turned out real good. That was the best job I ever had, outside of being a real estate broker, which I later became.

"When I left baseball I wanted to make sure that my children had their college education." One spring training, umpire Dusty Boggess urged Martin to become one of the men in blue, saying he saw it a sure thing that Martin reach the majors by 1954. "But my wife was a very sick woman, and I had to get home to my children. I was able to send my three children to school, which was the most important thing to me. I'm very proud, they're all three each very well off with their own businesses and I'm very proud of them."

What about the 2004 World Series? "My goodness, don't even ask me. The people who own the St. Louis ball club...Bill DeWitt, the general managing partner, was our batboy back in the '40s. His son belongs to our 1–2–3 Club. Bill the third. I had a lot of empathy for the Cardinals, but I played with the Red Sox. Dom DiMaggio, Johnny Pesky, Bobby Doerr, Sam Mele, Boo Ferriss...I'm in contact with those guys all the time. Dom DiMaggio treated me like a first-team player. Pesky. Doerr. Ted Williams. Everybody had tremendous respect for one another.

"I'll tell you something, I was very, very happy for the Red Sox. They needed that, and I'm very happy for them. I would never want to root against the Cardinals. Stan Musial and I are very good friends. Red Schoendienst and I are good friends. I don't root against the Cardinals on anything, but I'm very happy for the Red Sox. They're my team, but I love the Cardinals because I'm very close to the owners.

"One thing I regret is that I didn't stay in baseball to become a major league umpire. I would love to have done that. I'd love to have stayed long enough to have qualified for a pension. I had an opportunity to do that. But I love these guys. We've always been friends."

Sources

Interview with Babe Martin done March 3, 2006 by Bill Nowlin.

Leib, Frederick. "Socking Babe Martin Sacks Up Association's Most Valuable Title," *The Sporting News*, October 26, 1944.

Wolfe, Don. "Babe Martin, Fugitive From Hospital, Builds UP Healthy Bat Mark In Toledo," *Toledo Times*, August 1944

WINDY MCCALL *by Bill Nowlin*

G	ERA	W	L	SV	GS	GF	CG	SHO	IP	H	R	ER	BB	SO	HR	HBP	WP	BFP
1	20.25	0	1	0	1	0	0	0	1⅓	6	3	3	1	0	1	0	0	11

G	AB	R	H	2B	3B	HR	RBI	BB	SO	BA	OBP	SLG	SB	HBP
1	0	0	0	0	0	0	0	0	0	0	0	0	0	0

John William "Windy" McCall grew up about three blocks from Holly Park in San Francisco. He'd bring a bat and a glove and hop in a neighborhood game. "If you didn't get chosen, then you hung around until someone went home for lunch." McCall played a year in American Legion ball and a year in high school. Born July 18, 1925, he grew up in the Mission District. He was 16 when Pearl Harbor was attacked.

Mac's father was a housebuilder and a remodeler, but his mother had her hands full with three children at home—two boys and one girl. John was the only one who played ball. "My brother didn't want to get his hands dirty. He wound up as a pretty good high school teacher, in chemistry and physics." His father, John Patrick (Jack) McCall, used to bring him around to weekend games in San Francisco. "I played for the San Francisco Seals Juniors when I was 17. We had about eight teams in San Francisco. I won the batting title in Legion ball when I was 17 with the Zane Irwin Post." The Seals Juniors were a semipro team that played in Seals Stadium on Saturdays. "I got to play there, but not to pitch. I played the outfield. Because I was a hitter. That's the way I started. Got an early graduate from high school, and I was six months, one season at USF when I joined the Marine Corps."

Johnny McCall graduated from Balboa High School in January 1943 and had a scholarship to play center field for the University of San Francisco, but never pitched there. Nor did he pitch in high school, but he did catch the eye of Brooklyn Dodgers scout Charlie Wallgren. The left fielder for USF was future Red Sox teammate Neill Sheridan. Bill Renna, who played for Boston in 1958 and 1959, was the team's right fielder. Later in 1943, after playing a little semipro ball in San Mateo, McCall signed with the Brooklyn Dodgers, as an outfielder, and was assigned to Olean but never reported. He said he never reported "because I am now a private in U.S. Marine Corps Reserve." Just two weeks after signing—still just 17 years old—he had joined the Marine Corps. And he received a "nasty letter from Rickey"—Branch Rickey—who wrote that McCall should have requested permission. The

John "Windy" McCall.
Courtesy of Windy McCall.

armed services wanted ballplayers, as entertainment for the troops, and Rickey could have set it up for him through the Dodgers.

The new recruit joined the Fourth Division, assigned to the Pacific theater, and served in locations from Iwo Jima to Okinawa. Naturally, Private McCall played a little baseball in the service, a couple of games on Maui but mostly after he'd been given MP duty on Okinawa. "We got to play some. No one could throw hard enough, I guess. I had a good arm. I started pitching there." McCall was a lefthander.

"We were floating reserve off of Iwo [Jima], but the third or fourth day, we had too many guys on Iwo—really, too many targets—so they changed our ship into a hospital ship and they didn't break up our replacement battalion. They shipped us all back to Maui and Honolulu. They had to rebuild the 4th Division because of all the casualties. The company I joined only had seven men left. They broke us into battalions—replacement—and then we went by LST from Hawaii from Saipan/Tinian. Maneuvers again, and then we were going to go into Tokyo Bay when they dropped the atom bomb. So I wound up in Okinawa as an MP.

"We were cleaning up Okinawa because they still had Japanese living in caves and coming out at night and stealing food and things like that. The day I left Okinawa, the 16th of May, we had 12 that we got living in a cave. One was an officer and all the rest were in uniform. They had their rifles all ready. They gave up because they didn't have any airplanes around. When the interpreter told them the war was over, they couldn't believe it."

McCall was reinstated in organized baseball on July 11, 1946, but didn't play professionally that year. He did play some semipro ball in California, pitching some, and even played against [Jackie] Robinson's All-Stars, a black barnstorming team, as they toured the West Coast. When he left the Marine Corps he was 21 years old. His parents had had to sign for him when he was 17, but now he was a free agent and could sign with whichever club he pleased. He chose to sign for the same scout, Charlie Wallgren, but Wallgren now was working for the Red Sox. "I got a bonus this time. I didn't get a bonus from Brooklyn. I went to spring training in '47." It was a $6,000 bonus, half on signing and half at the end of the season. It was a good bonus for the era.

Assigned to Roanoke, a team in the Class B Piedmont League, McCall played under manager Pinky Higgins. "I pitched batting practice a couple of times and played in the outfield a couple of times. I asked him, 'Hey, we've got a doubleheader next weekend. Lynchburg. I'd like to pitch the second game of the doubleheader.' He said, 'Fine. Pitch batting practice tomorrow and you can pitch on Sunday.' So I did. And I won. And I won 17 games. We won the championship." McCall was 17–9 with a 3.78 ERA, and won three more games in the playoffs. In 219 innings, he struck out 198 opponents and was named to the Piedmont League All-Star team.

His record at Roanoke earned him another visit to spring training, and this time he picked up his nickname—from Ted Williams. He'd explained the nickname to the United Press, "I guess they think I like to talk. Names don't hurt much, though. Base hits hurt more." Remembering Williams almost 60 years later, he said, "In 1948, we were in spring training and about the last week of the season, Ted gets two or three dozen baseball bats. He looks them over. This is after a game, and I happened to be there with Ellis Kinder. Ted would pick up the bats with the closeness of the grain, the little curlicues. I was kidding him about hitting, and he said, 'These are my good bats.' He picked out about eight or nine and he puts his number on them, #9. Johnny Orlando, the clubhouse guy, put a big 'P' on them. He said, 'Have your choice. You can have any of those, but not mine.' I picked out a couple. In the conversation, I told Ted, 'You know, I'm pitching batting practice tomorrow. I'm scheduled. Are you going to hit against me?' He said, 'Yeah.' I said, 'Well, bring up your good bats.' So I pitched batting practice to him. About a week later, we got to going north. I think we got to Knoxville, and somebody asked me, "Have you seen the Boston *Globe*?" I guess Ted had told this sportswriter that he knew about me, said, 'The windy one told me when I was pitching batting practice to bring up some of my good bats.'"

"I told him, 'I can hit, too.' And he said, 'Well, you're not going to hit on this club.' I said, 'No, I know. I signed as a pitcher.'" Windy did hit .667 for the Red Sox in 1949, but finished his years in the majors with a .146 average.

McCall worked a better deal than Mickey McDermott on his contract. "Joe Cronin [the general manager] called me to the office. He waited till two days before the opening of the season and he calls me upstairs and he says, 'Here's your contract. You earned it.' I said, 'Good' and I looked at it and I said, 'No, I'm not going to sign this.' I said, "Well, you've got $5,000'—which was the minimum—'and then if I'm optioned, they've got $4,000.' I said, 'I want five across the board, whether I'm optioned

or not. You said I made the team.' So he said, 'Well, I don't know. I'll think about it.' When I hit the bottom of the stairs—his office was on the second floor—the secretary yelled at me, 'Come on back. I think Joe wants to talk to you again.' He put the five/five. So I went down and I told McDermott. He said, 'I'm probably not going to make the team anyway.' They offered him a contract, but it was a five/four. He signed it. The next day, he went to Scranton on option. I hung around for 20 or 30 days and then I went to Louisville."

McCall pitched well in spring training. His last work was to throw the final four innings of a City Series game against Warren Spahn and the Boston Braves. Spahn won the game, 3–2, but all three runs had been the responsibility of fellow rookie southpaw McDermott. Windy's major league debut came on April 25, 1948—a starting assignment in Yankee Stadium. He didn't last long, giving up a first-inning three-run homer to Joe DiMaggio. After McCall allowed six hits total, and a walk, Sox manager Joe McCarthy called on the bullpen and brought in Harry Dorish. "They were really Texas Leaguers, a couple of them. DiMaggio.... I shook off a curveball and Birdie Tebbetts called time. He says, 'I want your curveball on 3 and 2. This guy's a hitter.' So I threw the curveball. I should have thrown a fastball. I did well against him in spring training." The Red Sox lost the game, 5–4, with all four Red Sox runs coming in the top of the ninth. McCall was assigned the loss. And he was assigned to Louisville the very next day. He was recalled in September but saw no game action. All told, McCall spent about a month with the major league club.

Windy got some work in with the Colonels, though, pitching 183 innings with 149 strikeouts. He gave up 182 hits and ran up a 4.67 ERA, with a 9–12 record.

In 1949, McCall started the season with Boston, pitching in the City Series again, a couple of times against the Yankees, and let in just one run in five innings during a game with the Tigers that ended in a 14–14 tie after 13 innings. In mid-May, when the rosters had to be cut down, McCall departed to the minors, optioned to Seattle on May 19. Contractually, he was returned from Seattle on July 11, then assigned to Louisville four days later. With the Red Sox, he'd pitched 9⅓ innings, and lowered his ERA from 20.25 to 11.57. He was 0–5 with Seattle in the Pacific Coast League and 5–2 with Louisville.

McCall wished he'd had a chance to play more for the Red Sox, and regrets both the lack of a pitching coach and Joe McCarthy's shortcomings in dealing with pitchers. "I never really got to play for the Red Sox because of Joe McCarthy. I'm down there [during 1949 spring training] and I'm playing catch with Ellis Kinder—off the field, during batting practice—and he's showing me his changeup. He had a hell of a changeup, Ellis did. And McCarthy saw us and he walks down...all the way down in the corner in right field, off the field, and he yells at

Kinder, 'Get your ass in right field and shag the flies.' It's batting practice. And, 'Mac, I want to talk to you.' We walked all the way down to home plate. Before we got about halfway, Joe says to me, 'You know, with your fastball and curveball, you don't need a changeup.' Well, when he said that, it kind of sunk in that he didn't know anything about pitching. And he didn't. We never had a pitching coach in those years.

"Fireman Murphy. They made him farm director. [Right at the end of the 1949 season] he says, 'I understand you told one of the guys you'd rather get traded because we don't have a pitching coach.' I said, 'That's right. You don't.' I says, 'Trade me.' So they did. They traded me to Pittsburgh." It was a conditional deal; the Pirates could send him back at any time until the first 30 days of the regular season had expired.

In spring training for Pittsburgh, about two days before the season started, he got hit hard in the hand by a line drive that pretty much ended his major league aspirations for 1950. He got into two games, 6⅔ innings in all, but he was black and blue all the way up the arm and the Pirates decided to send him down to Indianapolis. It was his third and final option, so the big league club didn't call him back. He played all of 1951 for Indianapolis (10–9, 4.53) and started 1952 there as well, but was moved to Birmingham in the Southern Association fairly early in the year when the Red Sox bought his contract back on May 29. With Birmingham, McCall was 10–8, with a 4.89 ERA.

Before the season in 1953, he was purchased by the San Francisco Seals and got the chance to pitch in the ballpark he'd played in as a youth. For the Seals, despite seeing his season end with a broken finger in mid-August, McCall won 12 and lost 7 with his best earned run average ever: 3.04. In October the New York Giants made quite an offer for him, trading Frank Hiller, Adrian Zabala, Chuck Diering, and $60,000 cash to sign up Windy. Sportswriter Joe King mused that after a commitment like that, McCall "would have to stink to be cut loose." King later dubbed McCall "the boy with the talented tonsils."

In 1954, he started to get a chance to perform, pitching 61 innings in 33 games with four starts. He also earned his first major league win on August 22, pitching two innings in relief as the Giants came from behind in the bottom of the ninth to beat the Pirates, 5–4. His record

Windy unwinding with the Pirates.
Courtesy of Windy McCall.

was just 2–5, but he had a very good 3.25 ERA. Working under Leo Durocher again in 1955, McCall got six starts and threw four complete games. He was 6–5, with a 3.69 ERA, and more or less pitched about the same in 1956, a 3.61 ERA with a 3–4 record. He started with the Giants again in 1957, but after just three full innings of work was sent to the Seals again, and then to Miami in the International League. All of 1958 was with Miami, as was the start of '59, though McCall spent most of the '59 season with Seattle again, back in the Coast League. "I think I lost about three or four feet off my fastball. The Coast League was a pretty good league."

After baseball, McCall worked for 25 years in sales for Bekins Van and Storage in San Francisco, almost exclusively commercial work, though he did help move Willie Mays at one point. Whenever Bekins had a call from a ballplayer, they gave the job over to McCall. In 1980, the McCalls moved to his wife's home state of Arizona. There, Windy got into real estate, working as an agent for U.S. Home. The McCalls have a daughter and two sons. Sandy McCall might have had pro baseball potential, but he had a scholarship to Stanford and he really enjoyed golf. The golf coach at Stanford told him he'd ruin his golf swing if he played baseball, too, so he quit baseball. McCall's other son was more of a swimmer.

Asked about his lifetime batting average of .146, Windy says, "It should have been a lot more. With the Giants, I didn't really have a chance to hit. We had Dusty Rhodes, Bobby Hofman, Bill Taylor—all pinch-hitters. They all hit .300. And then we picked up Hoot Evers from Detroit on waivers, too, and he was quite a hitter." But his thoughts returned right away to pitching: "It's too bad we didn't have a pitching coach with the Red Sox. We all could have used some guidance. We had a guy like Boo Ferriss. He had a sore arm, and [McCarthy] started him all the time. He should have started McDermott or McCall, but, you know...."

"I always wondered if I'd stayed in baseball.... I know I could hit."

Sources

Interview with Windy McCall by Bill Nowlin on February 26, 2006

MICKEY MCDERMOTT *by John Vorperian*

G	ERA	W	L	SV	GS	GF	CG	SHO	IP	H	R	ER	BB	SO	HR	HBP	WP	BFP
7	6.17	0	0	0	0	5	0	0	23⅓	16	18	16	35	17	2	1	3	114

G	AB	R	H	2B	3B	HR	RBI	BB	SO	BA	OBP	SLG	SB	HBP
7	8	2	3	1	0	0	0	0	0	.375	.375	.500	0	0

Maurice Joseph McDermott, Jr. was a hard-throwing southpaw teenage "can't miss" prospect who devolved into a journeyman reliever. Slated as the next Lefty Grove, Mickey McDermott played 12 seasons in the big leagues with the Red Sox, Senators, Yankees, Athletics, Tigers, and Cardinals. He spent the first half of his MLB career in Boston where he never had a losing season.

Hall of Fame Pitcher Warren Spahn once remarked, "The two greatest athletes I ever saw play baseball were Ted Williams and Mickey McDermott."

A lifetime .252 batter who had 127 pinch-hit at-bats and nine career home runs, the colorful free-spirited strikeout artist with a 98-mph fastball detoured from the promise of Cooperstown due to wildness on and off the field. *New York Times* sports writer Arthur Daley labeled the left-handed hurler a "triple-threat...a man who can pitch, hit, or sing." No doubt the fun-loving McDermott's passion for nightclub performances and Catskills gigs took their toll on his baseball career.

Mickey McDermott was born on August 29, 1929, in Poughkeepsie, N.Y. He had five siblings. His father, Maurice McDermott, Sr., was a police officer and former minor league first baseman with the Hartford Senators (Eastern League). Senior lost his roster slot to a Columbia University man—Lou Gehrig. McDermott the younger shared his father's love for the game and even played his position at first base. All until St. Mary's Grammar School coach John Shannon noticed that the 12-year-old could, in McDermott's words, "...toss the ball across the diamond with curves as impressive as Rita Hayworth's, so he switched me to the mound."

At 13, Mickey went to his first baseball tryout camp, held by the Brooklyn Dodgers in Newburgh, New York. Dodgers scout Mule Haas wanted to sign him but upon learning his tender age begged off and bought him lunch instead.

Ferrara Trucking Company had less concern with child labor laws. Mickey pitched for the company team, facing other semipro teams and, at times, major leaguers like Hank Majeski and Bobby Thomson, playing under

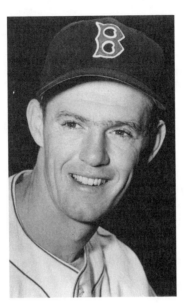

Mickey McDermott.

aliases. Ferrara paid $50 to $75 per contest. McDermott remembered, "After the game my father would generously peel a single off the wad for me and take the rest to the nearest bar."

Pitching for St. Patrick's High School, McDermott set Catholic Conference marks, averaging 20 strikeouts per game. Against St. John's Academy, he struck out 27 batters—a particularly remarkable achievement given that regulation games were seven innings long and not a full nine. His catcher dropped a considerable number of third strikes and was unable to throw to first base in time so the out did not count and Mickey would have to face another batter. Such feats drew Red Sox scout Bill McCarran's attention.

In 1944, McDermott Sr. doctored Mickey's birth certificate, making the 15-year-old appear a year older, and—promptly—Red Sox property. This initial act begot a tangled web of multiple birthdates among baseball-related records as McDermott stuck to the story—or as close as he could. Boston manager Joe Cronin did learn of the father's scam but the two men arrived at a final resolution. Mickey's arm earned $5,000 and two truckloads of Ballantine Ale for Senior. The Sox got a sure phenom, or so they thought.

McDermott was immediately sent to the Red Sox' Eastern League farm club, the Scranton Miners. Piloted by Elmer Yoter, Scranton's 1945 team finished fifth and just shy of .500 ball (.493). McDermott went 2–5 with 3.31 ERA in 69 innings, giving up 71 hits and getting 42 Ks.

On July 14, 1946, McDermott threw his first professional no-hitter, against the St. Louis Cardinals' Eastern League outfit, the Albany Senators. Mickey sealed the road victory by striking out player-manager Rip Collins. McDermott completed the year 16–6, with a 3.29 ERA, 175 innings pitched, 136 hits, and 144 strikeouts. Scranton dominated the Eastern League and finished 96–43. The Red Sox farm club defeated the Wilkes-Barre Barons in the playoff semifinals and swept the Hartford Chiefs to win the Governors' Cup.

In 1947 he was promoted to Boston's Triple A affiliate

in Louisville (American Association) but control problems led him back to Scranton. With the Keystone State club now skippered by Eddie Popowski, McDermott found the strike zone. In 132 innings pitched, Mickey notched a 12–4 record with four shutouts, a 2.86 ERA, and a league-leading 136 strikeouts. In a postseason contest at home against the Utica Blue Sox, McDermott gained his second Eastern League no-hitter. In the top half of the ninth, future Philadelphia Phillies legend Richie Ashburn walked. Advanced to second on a fielder's choice, Ashburn got to third on a fly ball and scored the game's only run on a passed ball. McDermott was tacked with the no-hit loss.

Mickey moved onto the 1948 Red Sox roster and maneuvered into the media matrix of the day. At spring training in Sarasota, Florida, he was photographed for *Life* magazine. The picture's caption read, "The baseball rookie, his face reflecting the eternal glow of optimism...a far more reliable harbinger of spring in the U.S. than the first robin..." McDermott always felt the image was unflattering, highlighting his ears and a silly grin on his face. "Man, what a dumb-looking shot," he commented ruefully. "I couldn't get a date for a month."

Publish? He would have paid the cameraman to burn it.

Imagine his further shock when Norman Rockwell's "The Rookie" became a *Saturday Evening Post* cover. Rockwell painted Ted Williams, Dom DiMaggio, Jackie Jensen, and Billy Goodman apprehensively gazing at a gawky newcomer in the clubhouse. Teammates, fans, and folklore pegged the rook as Mickey. Then on April 24, 1948, McDermott made his major league debut. He appeared in seven games that year. Two months into the season he had pitched 23⅓ innings, striking out 17 but walking 35. Sox manager Joe McCarthy sent him back to Scranton.

Disappointed with the move, McDermott adjusted and gained more control, averaging 13 strikeouts a game. On September 16, 1948, in the Eastern League playoffs, he threw his third no-hitter, an 8–0 victory over Utica.

Southpaw McDermott posing mid-pitch.

With September the parent club's expanded roster included McDermott as well as Willard Nixon.

For the 1949 season McDermott inked a pact at $5,000 and was assigned to the Triple A Louisville Colonels. On May 24, in the second game of a doubleheader, he fanned 20 St. Paul Saints, setting an American Association record that would never be broken; the circuit folded in 1962.

In the following four games, McDermott kept throwing K's and established another milestone: the most strikeouts over a five-game set, 93. The lucky numbers (after the 20 on May 24) were 19, 18, 17, and 19. Eleven games out of first place, Boston called up the Louisville farmhand.

Sox skipper McCarthy slated Mickey as his starter in a June 17, 1949, nightcap of a twin bill against the Chicago White Sox. Before 31,466 of the Fenway faithful, McDermott went eight innings and gave up three hits with nine walks and five runs. But thanks to Junior Stephens, Ted Williams, and Matt Batts hitting home runs with runners aboard, the Red Sox amassed enough runs to give Mickey a 10–8 triumph.

Sportswriter Jack Malaney wrote of Mick's next start, "Come what may during the remainder of the season Maurice 'Slats' McDermott was proclaimed a major league pitcher deluxe last night at Fenway Park by 28,080 fans who watched him start and finish his second major league pitching chore...The 20-year old southpaw marvel recalled only last week from Louisville, limited St. Louis Browns to three hits and shut them out...Facing only 28 batters, young McDermott was (as) near letter perfect as Marse Joe McCarthy and his severest critics could ask."

Mick competed 1949 with a 5–4 record, including two shutouts, and with the world on a string. As he remembered, "I was suddenly the cinnamon toast of Boston—the new Lefty Grove, the new Herb Pennock...the new messiah who would lead the Red Sox not just to the pennant but to the World Series as well." He already had fan clubs. Women clamored for his autograph—and affection. He simply was a man-about-town, a bon vivant, a nightclubber and lounge singer who happened to be a rising Red Sox star. From 1950 to 1952, the free-spirited McDermott partied, drank, enjoyed his multiple female companions, and kept his singing gigs a-going whether at Steuben's in Boston or at Grossinger's in the Catskills. During this period on the mound he notched a 25–20 win-loss record. His annual baseball salary was around $7,500 and his music act commanded $500 weekly. I assume this was in the off-season?

1953 was a zenith year on the diamond. On April 28 at Briggs Stadium, McDermott garnered his second win of the year by holding the Detroit Tigers to three hits in a 2–0 shutout. Back in Boston on May 16, McDermott tossed a two-hitter, shutting down the Indians, 1–0. On August 12, in the City of Brotherly Love, the lefty got his 12th victory in a 10-inning contest, edging the Athletics 3–2. He also performed at the plate with two hits in four at-bats, swatting a single in the 10th and scoring from second on a hit by Hoot Evers.

Mickey went 18–10 in 1953. But late in the season some off-the-field incidents made him a marked man. He slugged a sportswriter and soon after that used foul language in front of a woman outside of Fenway. The woman was Tom Yawkey's wife, Jean.

On December 9, 1953, his world stopped. He was exiled from the first tier of the major leagues to baseball Siberia. Boston traded McDermott and Tom Umphlett to the American League's doormat, the Washington Senators, to obtain Jackie Jensen. Commenting on the swap, Arthur Daley wrote in the New York Times, "McDermott is a left-handed baritone who could sing a lot better than he could pitch—until last year.... Perhaps now he is now over the hump and along the road to stardom. But Bucky Harris, rather than Boudreau, will benefit from it. From the Boston standpoint it's important to remember that the Sox had been a mite lopsided as far as left-handed pitchers were concerned, especially since Fenway Park has not been deemed particularly healthy for southpaws. They have Mel Parnell and Bill Henry. In the immediate future Leo Kiely, a fine youngster ... is about to be sprung. Frank Baumann, $85,000 bonus player, is due to advance from Louisville to the varsity. McDermott would have been a fifth left hander and was the most expendable."

Mickey didn't see the trade that way. His last contract read $12,500. The Nats offered $19,500. McDermott held out. If he didn't sign, the trade would not be completed. Two weeks before spring training's start, the 1953 American League batting champion, Washington's Mickey Vernon, sat down with McDermott, and Mick signed. But playing for the 1954 Nation's Capital nine was an ugly experience. Rather than giving the local team a lift, the once 18-game winner racked up a 7–15 record. Even the USA's Chief Executive noticed the debacle. President Dwight D. Eisenhower was quoted in the sports section as inquiring, "What's wrong with McDermott?" Mick always maintained, "What's wrong, Mr. President? Washington! That's what's wrong."

McDermott felt he pitched in too many one-run contests or opposing club slugfests during his time with the Senators. Even his musical career suffered. In his autobiography (written with Howard Eisenberg), A Funny Thing Happened on the Way to Cooperstown, Mick penned, "I came back in town in the winter of '54. I called on Joe Schneider (of Steuben's). 'Season's over,' I said. 'Want to book me for a few weeks?' Joe's answer came straight from the pocketbook. 'Moishe, 18 and 10 in Boston? Oh, what a beautiful voice! Seven and fifteen in Washington? You don't sing so good no more.'"

In December 1955, the trade winds began to swirl around the Capitol, the Big Apple, and the globe. Washington Post scribe Shirley Povich reported on December 6 that the Yankees were seeking the whereabouts of world traveler Casey Stengel in order to consult him about a proposed 10-player exchange engineered between Yanks GM George Weiss and Nats president Calvin Griffith. A cable was dispatched to Stengel somewhere in the Middle East. En route from Athens to Palestine on an around-the-world tour, Casey was asked to contact Weiss at the major league winter meetings via transatlantic phone.

On Christmas in Paris, Stengel announced to the media, "What's been going on back there for the last months? I've been out of touch since I left Manila." Informed that the Yankees were reportedly seeking McDermott for young lefty Bob Wiesler and some rookies, Stengel shook his head and indicated he would debate those terms with GM Weiss when he returned to New York. Casey said, "Now if I know Chuck Dressen, he'll want about five young players for one feller like McDermott. That don't make sense to me. Everyone wants to get more than their players are worth when they deal with the Yankees. They figure we've got all that surplus material—and they're right. But there ain't no use in us giving it away."

On February 8, 1956, the multiplayer switch happened. McDermott and shortstop Bobby Kline became Bronx Bombers in exchange for Lou Berberet, Bob Wiesler, Herb Plews, and Dick Tettelbach and a player to be named later. The later player was Whitey Herzog. In a clubhouse before reporters, Mickey let out a "whoopee" and said, "...Naturally it will be nice playing for a championship team." The free spirit happened to be in Sarasota, Florida, visiting the Boston Red Sox camp, when he made that declaration.

New York Daily News columnist Jimmy Powers asked, "Did the Yanks grab themselves another pennant when they stole Mickey McDermott?" Mickey told Arthur Daley, "A pitcher dreams of being with a team like this ... They can make the runs for you and they can come up with the double plays to get you out of a hole." In March 1956, the New York Times columnist declared that

McDermott, Gus Niarhos, and Tom Wright, 1952.

McDermott was pennant insurance. Daley argued that Stengel's original knock on the southpaw was a strategic device, solely to improve the Yanks' trade position.

Mick's roommate, Hank Bauer, initially gave him an icy reception, slamming the door in his face. The Yankees outfielder had always hit well against the southpaw and was not pleased to learn Mick would be wearing the pinstripes.

Before the welcoming gesture, Bauer exclaimed, "McDermott, you bastard. There goes 50 points off my average." Nonetheless, the Big Apple agreed with McDermott on and off the playing field. A good hitter himself, Mick faced Baltimore's knuckleballer Harold "Skinny" Brown and drove a gopher ball 420 feet into Yankee Stadium's center field. In the second game of the 1956 World Series, McDermott pitched three innings and got a hit off Brooklyn's Don Bessent. He also enjoyed the Manhattan night scene. And he appeared on Arthur Murray's TV show in a jitterbug competition matched against Mickey Mantle.

Yet McDermott ended the year 2–6. Stengel's initial concerns had resurfaced on April 7 in Mobile, Alabama, in an exhibition game against the Phillies McDermott could not start due to food poisoning brought on by a reported "light snack" of oyster stew, a grilled cheese sandwich, pickles, and beer. During the season Stengel had to assess a $200 fine against McDermott for his involvement in an off-the-field altercation in Boston.

On February 19, 1957, the Bombers dealt Mickey, Rip Coleman, Milt Graff, Billy Hunter, Tom Morgan, Irv Noren, and a player to be named to the Kansas City Athletics for Art Ditmar, Bobby Shantz, Jack McMahan, Wayne Behardi, and players to be named later. The Yanks sent Jack Urban and the A's posted Curt Roberts and Clete Boyer to complete the transaction. At the time some baseball observers noted the cozy and less than arm's-length relationship between the two franchises. Athletics general manager Parke Carroll had been business manager for the Newark Bears, New York's top farm club. A's owner Arnold Johnson had ties with George Weiss and

Yankee ownership. Upon the trade's announcement, aware of the organizational dynamics, Cleveland general manager Hank Greenberg sharply remarked, "It must be great to have your own farm system in the same league."

McDermott became the first A's pitcher to hit a pinch-hit home run. He batted for Wally Burnette in the seventh inning against the Indians on August 10, 1957, and connected off Tribe twirler Mike Garcia. Earlier, on June 20, 1957, against the Washington Senators, Mick belted a seventh-inning home run into Griffith Stadium's left-field bleachers. Bob Addie of the *Washington Post* reported, "It was no puny poke, carrying four or five rows into the bleachers—a good test even for a right-handed hitter. Mickey, of course, is a southpaw by trade." These plate performances may have lessened McDermott's hill appearances. *Washington Post* sports columnist Shirley Povich wrote on August 11, 1957, that "the Athletics are in earnest about converting Pitcher Mickey McDermott into a first baseman and have arranged for him to play winter ball in Mexico at the end of the season." Mick ended 1957 having pitched in 29 games with a 1–4 record and a 5.48 ERA. Whatever plans the Athletics had about returning McDermott to his grammar school baseball team position changed.

On November 20, 1957, Kansas City swapped McDermott, Billy Martin, Tom Morgan, Lou Skizas, Tim Thompson, and Gus Zernial to the Tigers for Bill Tuttle, Jim Small, Duke Maas, John Tsitouris, Frank House, Kent Hadley, and a player to be named later. The Tigers sent Jim McManus to seal the trade. When the trade was made, A's skipper Harry Craft said he was convinced the deal would help the team, but McDermott tossed only two innings in the major leagues for 1958 and was 5–6 with Triple-A Miami. He drew a suspension on August 21, 1958, for missing a game. Miami manager Kerby Farrell, who had recommended the suspension, said, "Naturally we hate to lose a player at this stage of the game but this club is built around an organization and when we have a ballgame I expect my players to be there." During the 1958 season, Casey Stengel was asked about his former 1956 charge. When informed by a pack of reporters that McDermott had said the Yankees didn't give him any chance to pitch, Casey replied, "I noticed that whenever McDermott was given a chance to pitch, the manager got fired." The Ol' Perfessor's crack may have been a foreshadowing of McDermott's diminishing time as a pro pitcher.

With 1959's arrival, McDermott, by then the property of the Charleston, West Virginia, club of the American Association, was sold to the Dallas Eagles of the Texas League. He refused to sign with Dallas and the dispute hit the newspapers. He got a phone call from Miami Marlins GM Joe Ryan. Owner Bill Veeck had the International League club, now affiliated with the Baltimore Orioles, sign Mickey, Virgil Trucks, and the ageless Satchel Paige for the '59 campaign. Piloted by Pepper Martin, Miami finished in seventh with a 71–83 record. McDermott notched a 3–7 record in 70 innings, with 43 strikeouts, 32 walks, and a whopping 5.66 ERA.

Mick hoped to turn things around, and from 1958 to 1960 he played winter ball in Mexico, Cuba, and Venezuela. In later years, he called the experience "souse of the border," and thus he didn't advance his playing skills and continued his reckless partying ways off the field. With typical McDermott luck, he was on the field in Cuba with teammate and future Cincinnati Red Leo Cardenas when pro-Castro forces commenced shooting up the ballpark, and he played in Caracas when an assassination attempt was made on Venezuelan President Romulo Betancourt.

Still trying to return to the major leagues, McDermott signed for 1960 with a Double-A club, the Little Rock Travelers of the Southern League. He went 13–11, pitching 172 innings with 98 strikeouts, 87 walks, a 4.40 ERA.

In 1961 he was briefly picked up by the St. Louis Cardinals. In St. Petersburg on March 28, Mick blanked the Milwaukee Braves on four hits with a 1–0 win. On April 9, he was added to the roster. But on July 9, in the Bay area, the Cardinals indefinitely suspended him for violating curfew. He had violated curfew 10 days earlier. On July 21, the Cards sold him to Kansas City.

On August 10, 1961, McDermott appeared in his last major league game, at Baltimore's Memorial Stadium before 6,027 fans, where a four-inning relief stint resulted in two wild pitches, six walks, and three earned runs in an 8–0 loss to the Orioles. On August 15, the A's pink-slipped him. No other MLB club sought his services. Every major league team that selected Mickey had done so in the hopes he would blossom into their ace given his talent. Now the project was over.

With his major league career silenced, McDermott played some minor league ball, drank more, took odd jobs, and lost out on three failed marriages. His fourth wife, Betty, succumbed to breast cancer in 1996.

In 1967, the California Angels hired him as an assistant coach and batting practice pitcher but he was gone by the 1968 season. Mick tried his hand at running a bar but drank up any profits. Good friend Billy Martin got McDermott an Oakland A's scouting position, and McDermott submitted the initial report on Mark McGwire to the Athletics front office. Upon Martin's firing as A's manager in 1982, Mick was sent packing as well.

The dismissal led to a business partnership with Tino Barzie in the field of player representation. Their agency advocated for ballplayers like Tony Armas, Marty Barrett, Mario Guerrero, Candy Maldonado, and Alejandro Pena. However, McDermott's heavy alcohol use caused the firm to dissolve.

In 1991 Whitey Ford got a 5 a.m. telephone call. His startled wife could not believe what was happening. Ford handed her the phone to her and said, "Listen for yourself, you can tell it's McDermott. He's so drunk he thinks he won $7,000,000 in the Arizona lottery." Actually, McDermott was telling the truth. His poor health, legal problems due to numerous DWIs, and the lottery victory all combined to help keep McDermott sober for the remainder of his life.

His memoir was published in April 2003 but sadly on August 7 he died in Phoenix, AZ of congestive heart failure and colon cancer.

About his life, Mick wrote, "My reincarnation as a pitcher is doubtful....So at age 74, maybe it's time to sit down, tune in to whatever brain cells I've got left, and figure out where I got lost on the road to the Baseball Hall of Fame. Hey maybe what I've got to say will help a couple of kids find their way into it."

Sources

McDermott, Mickey, with Howard Eisenberg. *A Funny Thing Happened on the Way to Cooperstown* (Chicago: Triumph Books, 2003).
McDermott questionnaire from Hall Of Fame #4736
American League Questionnaire undated
Web sites www.retrosheet.org, www.baseball-reference.com, www.baseballlibrary.com
New York Times
Washington Post

SAM MELE *by Bill Nowlin*

G	AB	R	H	2B	3B	HR	RBI	BB	SO	BA	OBP	SLG	SB	HBP
66	180	25	42	12	1	2	25	13	21	.233	.292	.344	1	2

Sam Mele won the World Series for the Twins in 1965, but just a year and a half later was fired by the team—and the Twins wound up the season tied with the Tigers, just one game out of first place in the American League.

The record books show Sam Mele as born January 21, 1923, at Astoria, Long Island, New York. He was really born a year earlier, in 1922. "I'll tell you why," he confides.

"I had two uncles in the major leagues [Tony and Al Cuccinello.] They told me cheat a year on your age because you'll last a year longer in the big leagues. So I did." The tradition is a venerable one. The Cuccinellos are his only major league relatives; Sam was well aware of Dutch Mele, but there was no relation. Sam's mother, Anna, was a Cuccinello and the two were her brothers; Anna herself was born in Avellino, Italy, as was Sam's father, Antonio. They met in America.

Antonio worked for Consolidated Edison but had an accident early on, and the utility company made him a maintenance man so he didn't have to do anything too strenuous. Anna Mele was enterprising and borrowed "something like $2,200 or $3,200—she bought an apartment house. What did she know about real estate, coming from Italy, you know? It was a thriving place; it was a six-family house and that was where I was born and lived almost all my life." She kept busy managing the house, and the couple's seven children.

The house was in the city, but there was a dirt road in front as young Sabath Anthony Mele grew up. "Completely dirt. We used to play stickball with a rubber ball and a broom handle. We played all the time until they paved the road. We used to have to hide the goddamn stick because the cops would come and break it. The neighbors, I guess, would complain. You could break some windows. Then we'd have to get another broom handle. If you could hit on a dirt road, you could hit in the damn major leagues, the way the ball bounced. Up and down, all directions."

Sam played high school baseball his sophomore year, but Bryant High School stopped offering it after his first season. The story he heard at the time was that the principal's son had been hit and killed by a baseball, but he doesn't know if that ever truly occurred. There was, however, a boy on the team that year who played for a team out on Long Island called Louona Park, in the Queens Alliance League. Sam and his brother played for them one Sunday, a doubleheader. His brother Al got about seven hits and Sam got six. "Oh Christ, I thought I was something. The following weekend I went out again, didn't get a base hit. Come home, threw my uniform on the floor, and my mother chewed my ass out. About being a quitter. Now of course, she tells her brothers, Tony and Al. Major leaguers. And one by one, they chewed my ass out about you don't ever quit. And my uncle Tony, I'll never forget, he said he had gone, I forget, I think, 8-for-30 in the big leagues, but there's always another day, you're going to play again and again and again. As you went in our apartment, there's a transom. So I come home one day and there's a goddamn noose hanging down, and they said, well, if you're going to quit, why don't you just hang yourself?" Tough love?

There was a lot of baseball talk around the house. Sam remembers Al Lopez in particular, who came by for years. "I used to listen to them talk baseball. Christ, it was amazing. When I went away to play ball, I knew more than the damn managers that I played for because

Sam Mele.

of those guys. My uncle was very friendly with Babe Ruth. I'll never forget, I met him at Bayside Country Club, and he was so big—or maybe I was so small—I was looking up to him like he was God. I didn't realize how great a player he was. I was too damn young."

Growing up in New York at the time, one would think Sam would have been a Dodgers fan or a Giants fan, or a Yankees fan with all the great Italian players they had. No, Sam was a Tigers fan. "When I played in '46, when I went to play for Cronin—I went to spring training with Cronin—he said, 'Did you ever see Lazzeri play?' I said no. 'He was one of the smartest and greatest ballplayers you'd ever meet in your life. Being Italian, you're Italian. Yankee Stadium wasn't that far from where you lived, and you never went to see him play?' Oh Christ, he told me off. I never did see Lazzeri. But he couldn't tell me enough about him."

Sam's oldest brother, Dominic, played first base for Erie, but was the only other one in the family to play baseball. "We had four boys and three of us would sleep in one bed, my older brother in the other because he had a job. My mother would want him to get his rest. So we three guys had to sleep in the one bed. He ended up as a mailman in the office."

Because both of his uncles played second base, Sam saw himself as a second baseman, too. That's not what his uncles saw. "When they saw me play they said, 'Get the hell in the outfield.'" In fact, basketball was more his sport than baseball and he attended New York University on a basketball scholarship. He'd played professionally when still a high school student "and they caught me. They banned me for a year in high school. But then I went on a basketball scholarship." NYU's baseball coach, Bill McCarthy, was friendly with Red Sox scout Neil Mahoney. McCarthy drove Sam up to Fenway Park more than once and he had the opportunity to work out with the Red Sox before regular batting practice. He was batting against the likes of Herb Pennock and Bump Hadley.

"I remember one day taking batting practice, and they said, 'Take five swings.' I had about three swings, and then I took a pitch. This voice behind the cage asks, 'Why'd you take that?' And I said, 'Well, I thought it was outside.' And the voice says, 'You're right, but it was high enough for a strike.' So when I got out, finished hitting, I walked around and this guy called me over and it was Ted Williams. He explained to me about batting, and from that day on, whenever I'd see him...he took a great liking to me for some reason. In spring training in '46, I'd take my batting practice and run to left field and talk to him about hitting.

"Then I asked him about fielding—one question—and he said, 'No. You go to center field. Ask that guy.' Which was Dom DiMaggio."

This was during his first year at NYU. The Red Sox were accommodating, putting him up at a "nice hotel" in Boston. After two or three visits, there was some real interest. The Washington Senators made him an offer, but for very little money. The Cubs offered him $1,000. Al Cuccinello acted more or less as his agent, and Neil Mahoney had told them, "Don't sign with anybody until I talk to you." Mahoney brought Sam and Uncle Al to the Hotel Commodore in New York and introduced him to Red Sox owner Tom Yawkey. Sam was about to go into military service, and Yawkey told him, "We'll give you $5,000. We'll give you $2,500 now and we'll give you the rest when you come out." That was too good a deal to pass up.

Mele entered the Navy's V-12 program, signing up as a Marine. He was sent to train at Yale, and played baseball there under Red Rolfe. The club had a 14–1 record, but as far as going to classes...that wasn't his strong suit. "Finally the teachers said to me, 'Look, you're either going to play ball or you're going to go to class.' I was there about four months and they shipped me out to California, and I played on the Marine Corps team out there. We had no-name guys on the team, and we used to play against DiMaggio, Walter Judnich, and against the Navy with Barney McCosky, Rizzuto, all those big name guys." He served from July 1943 to very early 1946.

He was first formally signed by the Red Sox in 1946, watched their first homestand from the press box and was sent out to Louisville. "I think my first game in Minneapolis, I went 4-for-6, but being a young player in that league—Triple A—I guess I had a lot to learn about the pitchers. [He hit .226 in 53 at-bats.] Then they sent me to Scranton, and I got the Most Valuable Player award in that league. I had a hell of a year down there. There must have been about seven of us that went to the big leagues that year." Mele hit .342 with Scranton, leading the league, ranking first with 154 hits, 226 total bases, and 18 triples.

In 1947, Mele made the Boston ballclub and played 123 games as right fielder, and one game at first base, with only two errors all year long. Playing for Joe Cronin in his last year as skipper, Sam hit for a very strong .302 average with 12 homers and 73 RBIs. His debut

Mele drove in 25 runs in the 1948 campaign.

came on Opening Day; batting seventh, he was 2-for-2 at the plate. It was a very good first year. One of Sam's favorite memories came during his first game in Yankee Stadium. His parents had never seen him play ball, and he got them box seats. "And I hit a damn home run off of Floyd Bevens [April 22, 1947]. As I'm rounding second, I can see the box seats. And they're smiling. Never got up, never clapped or anything. Just smiling. As I'm rounding third, I take a look again over there. I'll never forget the look on their faces. Two Italian immigrants. Yankee Stadium. Never saw a game. Oh, brother!"

In December, the Sox traded for lefthanded batter Stan Spence and it was thought that he and Mele might platoon. Joe McCarthy took over as manager in 1948, and his relationship with Mele got off to a difficult beginning in spring training. "I'm taking batting practice and I had a style like Joe DiMaggio—not that I hit like him, but a wide stance, short stride...and this voice behind the cage—I'd never met McCarthy—says, 'How're you going to hit like that?' I'm saying to myself, well, shit, I just hit .302. I get out and he calls me over and says, 'You have to have your feet closer together, and take a long stride.' Well, you know, Joe McCarthy, with all those winning teams, he must know what he's saying. So I tried that and goddammit, I could never get back to my old style. I went to New York after that to play and Tommy Henrich—I'll never forget it—says, 'What the hell are you doing with your batting style?' And I told him what had happened. He says, 'Goddammit, you were a good-looking hitter. I don't know why the hell they would change you.'"

"McCarthy didn't play me, hardly. I don't know why and I'm thinking it could have been Opening Day in Fenway Park. I lost a ball in the sun and the Athletics beat us. I don't know if he ever held that against me, although he told a writer—a New York writer, and it's in a book—he said Henrich would have stuck that ball in his ass. Now I called that writer and then wrote him, and he never answered me. It was a line drive in right field. I had my glasses down, shielded my eyes, and the next thing I know, the ball went right by my head—pshoooo—and I said, that's the real story. Never mind about Henrich sticking it...he couldn't have caught it either. If a ball is in the sun, you don't have a chance. Well, anyway, I'm not playing hardly at all in '48."

Mele found himself in the doghouse for another reason, too. In early

July, on the train to Philadelphia, he and Ted Williams were playing around mock-sparring with each other. A few hours later it was discovered that Ted's cartilage had become separated from a rib; Williams missed two full weeks. Then, on September 17 in St. Louis, Mele tore up his foot trying to steal third in the fourth inning and was out for the rest of the year.

The story of Mele's injury requires a little delicacy. Joe McCarthy was known to have imbibed to excess. "He's riding the horse," folks would say. White Horse scotch. It got so bad that they locked him in his room and coach Del Baker managed the game. Mele doubled in three runs in the first inning, then got on base in the fourth. Birdie Tebbetts got a hit, too. By now McCarthy had appeared in the dugout and Baker was in the coach's box. Joe Dobson was up and Baker conveyed the sign for a double steal. Mele was hurt, badly, sliding into third base. Mickey Harris called for a stretcher, and when McCarthy came across the field, he looked down at Mele and said, "Since when do they have to take ballplayers off on a stretcher?" Mele, angered, fired back, "F—- you, you son of a bitch, I'll walk." McCarthy then blustered at Baker, "Why would you go for a double steal with a pitcher hitting?" and so forth. As Mele tells it, "Del Baker was good enough to say, 'Hey, you gave me the sign, whether you know it or not.'" The players insisted Mele take the stretcher, but he was out for the season. "I couldn't even put a shoe on."

Mele had far fewer plate appearances in 1948 and, performed poorly, batting just .233. Stan Spence didn't do much better, batting .235. All the Red Sox needed was one more win that year and they would have won the pennant.

In 1949, two months into the season, Mele had been in just 18 games for Boston, batting just .196. On June 13 he was traded to Washington, with Mickey Harris, for pitcher Walt Masterson. In 78 games for the Senators, Mele batted .242. He got in a fairly full year for Washington in 1950, accumulating 435 at-bats, and hit for a .274 average, driving in 86 runs. 1951 was equally good, with the very same .274 batting average, a league-leading 36 doubles, and 94 runs batted in. Early in 1952, despite batting .429 at the time (in 28 at-bats), the Senators traded Sam to the White Sox (on May 3) for Jim Busby and Mel Hoderlein. For the White Sox, he hit .248 the rest of the year, driving in 59 runs. Six of those RBIs came in one inning of one game, when he hit a three-run homer and a three-run triple in the fourth inning of the June 10 game against Philadelphia.

Chicago had Sam Mele for a full year in 1953 and, for the third time in four years, Mele batted .274. He drove in another 82 runs. Shortly before spring training of 1954, the White Sox traded him to the Orioles (with Neil Berry) for Johnny Groth and Johnny Lipon. He was batting .239 in limited action, and finally was offered on waivers in late July. The Red Sox claimed him, and Mele rejoined his original team. Lou Boudreau was managing the Red Sox and found a role for Mele, who responded by hitting .318 over 132 at-bats in 42 games.

He had a hard time getting going in 1955, though, and was hitting only .129 in his first 31 at-bats. The Red Sox sold him to Cincinnati on June 23. For the Reds, he hit just .210. Released by them in mid-January 1956, he was signed a couple of months later by the Cleveland Indians. He appeared in 57 games (114 at-bats) and batted .254. He also drove in 20 runs, the last runs he would drive in as a major league ballplayer. He was released by the Indians on Opening Day of 1957.

Sam spent a couple of years playing minor league ball—.265 for Indianapolis in the American Association, in 370 at-bats, and more limited action in 1958 (.322 in 59 at-bats for Indianapolis, then .216 in 134 at-bats for the International League team in Buffalo).

After 1958, Mele turned to coaching, working for Washington in 1959 and 1960, and moved with the Senators to Minnesota beginning in 1961. On June 6, the Twins asked him to temporarily replace manager Cookie Lavagetto, who was fired 2½ weeks later. Mele became manager and served the Twins for six years. In his first full year managing the Twins, Mele had tremendous success, bringing the 1962 Twins to a second-place finish in the 10-team American League, just five games behind the New York Yankees. The Twins won 91 games in 1963—the same total as in 1962—but the Yankees won eight more games, so the third-place Twins finished 13 games out of first. After a significant dip to sixth place in 1964, the Twins took the American League pennant in 1965, winning 102 games and coming in a full seven games ahead of the second-place White Sox.

The "usually mild-mannered Mele" (Associated Press) was involved in one unfortunate incident during the '65 campaign. During the July 18 doubleheader with Los Angeles, he got into it with umpire Bill Valentine and his left hand connected—or nearly so—with Valentine's jaw. There was clearly some pushing and shoving. Mele said he didn't remember hitting the umpire, but news reports quoted him as saying, "He had his finger stuck in my face. I know that." He later said, with a wink, "I tripped, I stumbled into him. I guess I stumbled into him first." Mele was fined $500 and suspended for five days.

The 1965 World Series pitted the pitching and speed of the Los Angeles Dodgers against the pitching and power of the Minnesota Twins. On paper, the Twins had the edge offensively and took the first two games at home, 8–2 and 5–1, defeating the Dodgers' duo of Don Drysdale and Sandy Koufax. Los Angeles took three games in a row in their home park, as Bob Allison, Harmon Killebrew, Tony Oliva, and AL MVP Zoilo Versalles arguably underproduced; the Dodgers pitched around Killebrew; he drove in only two runs. Ron Fairly drove in six runs in the Series for the Dodgers, but Mele was able to take the

Twins all the way to Game Seven, in Minnesota. The final blow was Lou Johnson's solo home run off Jim Kaat, while Sandy Koufax threw a complete game, three-hit shutout.

The 1966 Twins won 89 games, good enough for second place, nine games behind Baltimore, but when the team seemed to struggle in the first part of 1967, Mele was fired and Cal Ermer was named manager. The Twins were an even 25–25 on June 9 when Mele was shown the door. They finished up in second place, just one game behind the Red Sox.

Boston owner Tom Yawkey had remained friendly with Mele over the years, and had often told him, "If anything happens to you in Minnesota, you call me, immediately." After returning to his home in Boston, he called on Yawkey, who hired him on the spot. Mele worked in the Red Sox system for 25 years.

"I was an instructor in the minor leagues, ran the minor league camp, hitting instructor, baserunning, bunting, and then when the spring training was over, they sent me all over the damn country double-checking players that the scouts had recommended. I did that for a long time. Then in the fall, they had like an instructional league, and I used to run that." Working as a cross-checker, he first met Jim Rice. Sox scout Mace Brown took him to Anderson, South Carolina, to look at Rice.

"Now there's a Detroit scout in the stands," Sam remembers, "and Rice didn't show up for three innings. So the scout said, 'Christ, he don't want to play'—so he left. Mace Brown and I talked to Rice after the game. He had worked at a variety store. His replacement didn't show up, so he stayed on to help the owner. We called the owner; he said, 'That's exactly true.' Houston was after Rice, too,

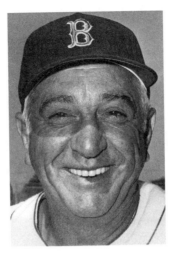

Sam worked in the Boston system for 25 years as a scout and instructor.

but when they took a pitcher, the Red Sox pounced and signed up Jim Rice. He was a driven pupil in the instructional league. "You know how, as an instructor, you've got to get the kid and say, 'Let's go, we've got extra work to do'? He used to grab me, every day. Every day. I didn't get him; he got me. And we became great, great friends.

"He went to Winter Haven in that league. I'd go down to watch him. He had power to all fields. All fields. Now watching these few games, he's trying to pull everything. Pull everything. Pull everything. So I talked to him after the game. The general manager was a pitcher, who thought he was a hitter. He'd try to tell the kid, you've got to pull the ball for Fenway Park, the Wall. I told him after the game, I said, 'You don't have to worry. You're not a dead pull hitter. You can hit balls to right center, right field, center field, left center, left field. Your power is all over.'" That's what he did his whole career.

Sam Mele's time with the Red Sox ended on a sour note, when GM Dan Duquette said he'd been telling Cleveland how to pitch to Boston's hitters. Far-fetched as that might seem, it apparently led to the Red Sox parting ways with a longtime scout. As of 2007, physical ailments have begun to afflict him. He's had his hip socket go out twice, suffered a ruptured disc in his back, and has macular degeneration in his right eye. The only contact he's had with new ownership is to have received a Red Sox watch after the team won the 2004 World Series. "What the hell. I gave it to one of my kids."

Source

Interview with Sam Mele done April 15, 2006.

WALLY MOSES *by Doug Skipper*

G	AB	R	H	2B	3B	HR	RBI	BB	SO	BA	OBP	SLG	SB	HBP
78	189	26	49	12	1	2	29	21	19	.259	.340	.365	5	2

A speedy line-drive-lashing lefty with a strong arm, veteran Wally Moses joined the Red Sox midway through the 1946 season, shored up right field during Boston's run to the American League pennant, and batted .417 in four World Series games. A well-liked and respected Georgian who spent 41 seasons in the majors, 17 as a player, 16 as a coach, three as a scout, and five more as a hitting instructor, Moses contributed solid outfield play on a part-time basis to Boston's 1947 and 1948 AL pennant pursuits.

By the time he joined the Red Sox, the 5-foot-10, 160-pound Moses was in the twilight of a productive playing career. In 2,012 games, all in the American League, he collected 2,138 hits and batted .291. A top-of-the-order slap hitter, Moses laced 435 doubles, 110 triples, and 89 home runs. He drew 821 walks, stole 174 bases, and scored 1,124 runs, and was a two-time All-Star. A stellar and fearless fly chaser who sometimes struggled with grounders and often dropped to one knee to field them,

Moses possessed exceptional range and a strong arm. He collected exactly 4,000 career putouts and dealt 147 career assists.

Between 1935 and 1951, he turned in some of baseball's least predictable seasons. Moses spent his first seven big-league campaigns with Connie Mack's Philadelphia Athletics, and batted better than .300 in each of those seven seasons—but never did so again during the rest of his 17-year career. In 1937, Moses blasted 25 home runs—but he never hit more than nine in any other year, and smacked just 64 in his other 16 seasons. Mack dealt Moses to the White Sox before the 1942 campaign, and a year later the fleet-footed outfielder stole 56 bases—35 more than his next best season and nearly a third of his career production. Moses also tied for the league lead with 12 triples in 1943, and two years later he belted an AL-best 35 doubles and led the league's outfielders in putouts.

Wally Moses hit .417 for the Red Sox in the 1946 World Series. Courtesy of George Brace Photo.

The easy-going lefty spent 2½ years with Boston before he went back to Mack to close out his playing days and launch his coaching career in Philadelphia. Between 1952 and 1970, Moses served five different teams. As a player, he had hit with an open stance and a grip so loose it looked as though he might drop the bat. As one of baseball's first—and most respected—full-time hitting coaches, he taught batters to take a short stroke, direct the ball with the bat, and run to first base fast; and was adept at correcting flaws in a hitter's swing. "I'm a closed-stance guy," Red Sox hitting guru Johnny Pesky said, "but Wally Moses had much success teaching his open-stance style." Involved in baseball into his 60s, Moses served as a hitting instructor for several seasons after his coaching career was over, still able to lace lengthy line drives in batting practice, dissect and correct a swing, or spellbind a crowd with tales of hitters and hitting, past and present.

"In our days, we weren't averse to taking a good rip now and then," Moses once told the *New York Daily News*. "With two strikes against us, most of us would concentrate on guarding the plate and meeting the ball. That's where the difference comes in now. Today the guys keep swinging from their heels, regardless of the count."

Wallace "Wally" Moses, Jr., was born October 8, 1909, in Uvalda, Georgia, the first child of Wallace Moses, Sr. and Martha Louise "Mattie Lou" (Smith) Moses, both natives of Georgia. Although baseball references list his birth year as 1910, the United States Census of that year, taken on April 10, indicated that Wallace, Sr. and Mattie Lou were living with their six-month-old son, Wallace, Jr., and her parents in nearby Tattnall County. Wallace,

Sr. was employed as a retail sales clerk. Three brothers and a sister followed, the family moved to Vidalia, Georgia, today famous as home of the Vidalia onion, and Wallace Sr. and Mattie Lou separated. After Wally graduated from high school in Vidalia, he left home and journeyed 12 miles west to play baseball at Brewton-Parker College in Mount Vernon, Georgia, from 1926 to 1928, and then toiled for local teams. It was reported that in 1930 he stole eight bases in a game and hit a pair of bases-loaded triples in the same inning. According to legend, he was "discovered" by Georgia native Ty Cobb, who had been asked to umpire a sandlot game. Moses embarked on his professional career with the Augusta (Georgia) Wolves of the short-lived Palmetto League in 1931. A 1936 *Sporting News* story suggested that New York Giants manager John McGraw saw his name and dispatched a scout to meet Moses in search of a "Hebrew player" who could be a box office star in New York. The speedy youngster of Scots-Irish and English descent pointed out that he wasn't Jewish, the scout replied "Ah, hell!" and didn't sign him. Moses reportedly had stolen 22 bases and Augusta led the Class D Palmetto League when it folded in July. The young lefty moved on to the Elmira (New York) Pioneers in the Class B New York-Pennsylvania League.

Moses returned to the South for the 1932 season. He toiled for the Monroe (Louisiana) Drillers of the Class D Cotton States League before that circuit disbanded in July, then the Tyler Sports of the Texas League, who played the second half of the season in Texas after a mid-year fire destroyed their ballpark in Shreveport, Louisiana. The Sports moved back to Shreveport and jumped to the Dixie League, but Moses stayed in the Texas League, and led the Galveston Buccaneers to a second-place finish in 1933 and the league championship the following year. Near the end of the season, on August 9, 1934, Connie Mack's Philadelphia Athletics purchased Moses, and directed him to report the next spring.

Moses joined a franchise in rapid decline. Mack had guided the Athletics to three consecutive AL titles and two world championships between 1929 and 1931 and a second-place finish in 1932. But as the Great Depression deepened and box office revenues plummeted, Mack, past age 70, sold off the stars, and by spring training of 1935, first baseman Jimmie Foxx and outfielder Roger "Doc" Cramer were about the only holdovers from those great teams. The A's were about to embark on a stretch where they would finish last in the AL nine times in 12 years, and never out of the second division in that stretch.

Moses was a bright spot. The Georgian made his major-league debut on Wednesday, April 17, 1935, in a 4–2 Opening Day loss to the Senators at Griffith Stadium in Washington. Splitting time with another Southern lefthander, Alabaman Lou Finney, in right field, with Cramer in center and with Indian Bob Johnson in left, Moses hit .325 with five home runs and 21 doubles, and 60 runs scored. His season ended on August 17 when he crashed into a wall at Chicago's Comiskey Park and fractured his left wrist, but he was still named the AL's top rookie by baseball writers.

The showing was impressive enough that the always cash-strapped Mack—who had already pocketed $150,000 in a deal that sent Foxx (and offered Moses) to Boston—shipped Cramer to the Red Sox before the 1936 season in a deal that netted $75,000; Mack installed Moses in center field. The depleted A's lost 100 games and finished last, but Moses responded by batting a career-best .345, rifled 202 hits, including 35 doubles, 11 triples, and seven homers, stole 12 bases, scored 98 runs, drove in 66, and amassed a career-best 396 putouts.

He was called "Wallace" by the venerable Mack and dubbed "the Georgia Express" by *The Sporting News*. "If a spectacular dive over the turf is necessary to snare a fly ball seemingly out of his reach, Wally dives," the baseball bible reported. "Moses is a little fellow who hustles every minute." Teammate Bill Werber called him the league's premier leadoff hitter and the fastest man getting from the batter's box to first base. Moses hustled to the altar that winter. On December 2, 1936, he married Billie Mae Haines, a native of Houston, Texas, whom he had met when he played in the Texas League.

With little more than Moses and Johnson, Philadelphia managed to climb out of the cellar to seventh place in 1937. Moses enjoyed the finest season of his career, when he batted .320 and slammed 25 home runs—the only time he hit more than nine. "I reported late to Mexico by 10 days," Moses told baseball biographer Norman Macht. "Connie Mack sent two pitchers to throw for me for extra hitting, Bud Thomas and Al Williams. I was a straightaway or up-the-alleys hitter, always swung from the end of the bat. The pitchers were throwing pretty good, so I had to shorten up on my grip about three inches, and they pitched inside to me and I found when they pitched me high and tight, I could pull the ball, so that year, I hit 25 home runs. I'd always been a low-ball hitter, so the AL pitchers kept pitching me high and tight, and now I could pull it." Along the way, he collected 208 hits, and became the final A's player of the 20th Century to reach the 200 mark. He also achieved career highs with 154 games played, 48 doubles, 86 runs batted in, 357 total bases, and a .550 slugging percentage.

That summer of 1937, Moses became one of the first baseball players to grace a Wheaties cereal box and was named to the American League team for baseball's fifth All-Star Game. Moses and his ex-teammate Cramer sat on the bench while Dizzy Dean took an Earl Averill line drive off his toe and Lou Gehrig homered to lead the AL to an 8–3 victory at Griffith Stadium in Washington.

Though he hit a respectable .307 and scored 86 runs, the 1938 season was a disappointment. Moses held out for a second straight spring, this time for a month, and settled for a two-year $12,500-per-season deal instead of a big raise from the taciturn Mack. He joined the team in Atlanta on its way north in early April, but suffered a devastating injury sliding into home in his second game. "The next spring a catcher fell on me in Portsmouth, Virginia, and broke my shoulder and I could never swing the same again," Moses told Macht. "It ruined my career." He managed just eight home runs, slugged only .424, and drove in but 49 runs. The Athletics lost 99 games and finished dead last in the American League; then lost 97 more in 1939. Moses represented the Athletics at a game that marked the opening of Baseball's Hall of Fame in 1939 and again batted .307, but battled a spring training ankle injury, played in only 115 games, homered just three times, slugged only .423, and drove in but 33 runs.

Looking to cut costs again, Mack moved Moses to Detroit in a trade for Benny McCoy, a reserve infielder, on December 9, 1939. But a month later, on January 14, 1940, Baseball Commissioner Kenesaw Mountain Landis declared 97 players in the Tigers system, including McCoy and pitcher Johnny Sain, free agents because of signing improprieties and a subsequent organizational cover-up. The edict nullified the trade, Moses returned to Philadelphia, and Mack ended up with McCoy anyway when he won a bidding war for the second sacker's services. Moses and McCoy played together for the Athletics, who managed to lose 100 games and finish eighth, while the Tigers went on to win the 1940 AL title. Moses injured his ankle in an exhibition game at Lafayette College in Pennsylvania, but still batted .309 in 142 games in 1940, hit nine homers, and scored 91 runs, one on a 10th-inning game-winning steal of home in the second game of an August 20 doubleheader with the White Sox. In 1941, Moses injured his shoulder in an automobile accident while traveling from "boiling out" in Hot Springs, Arkansas, to spring training in Anaheim, California. Moses and Athletics outfielder Al Simmons were traveling in Simmons' new car. On February 24, outside of Lubbock, Texas, Moses tried to pass a slow moving school bus, but the bus turned and Moses drove into the ditch to avoid it. The car rolled once and landed right side up. Simmons, a future Hall of Famer, was unhurt, but Moses missed the first month of the season. He rebounded to hit .301 (the last time he would exceed .300) in 116 games. Philadelphia lost 90 more times.

Mack was unhappy with the outcome, and impatient with Moses. Never tolerant of holdouts, the Tall Tactician had grown more annoyed each time his fleet outfielder stayed home in hopes of a better contract. Mack seemed to shop Moses to other AL teams yearly, and trade rumors had swirled since the Georgian's rookie season. A story circulated that during one of the holdouts, a reporter commented to Mack that Moses' only weakness was fielding groundballs in the outfield. Moses often dropped to one knee, which allowed runners to take an extra base. Mack reportedly replied, "Yes, but that's a strong weakness." The Grand Old Man of Baseball wasn't interested in negotiating another contract with Moses. Two days after the Japanese attack on Pearl Harbor and exactly two years after he traded him the first time (the voided deal with Detroit), Mack once again dealt Moses. He sent the seven-year veteran to Chicago for outfielder Mike Kreevich and pitcher Jack Hallett on December 9, 1941. Fiery White Sox manager Jimmy Dykes, who had played third base for Mack, moved the 31-year-old Moses from center to right field and gave him the green light on the base paths. In his first season with the White Sox, Moses hit .270, with 28 doubles and 16 stolen bases. He also smacked seven home runs to lead the White Sox, who bopped a total of 25—11 fewer than Ted Williams slugged for the Red Sox that season.

A year later, Moses stunned the baseball world when he stole 56 bases—40 more than he had ever stolen before in a full season, and 53 more than two years earlier under Mack. "Connie Mack wouldn't let me run," Moses remembered. "I stole a few bases my first year, but Connie Mack said, 'Wally, I don't want you to run. You got Cramer, Foxx, and Johnson behind you. They might hit one and you can walk around.' But when I went to Chicago with Dykes, he told me to run. 'We have to steal runs,' and I had speed. Joe Kuhel was my roommate and he'd steal on guys I'd get thrown out on. I asked him, 'What do you know that I don't know?' He started pointing out things pitchers did." On May 5, in the second game of a doubleheader at Cleveland, Moses swiped home in the top of the 11th inning in a 5–2 White Sox win, his second career steal of home in extra innings, to tie Tony Lazzeri's major league record. He would have had a third that season, but teammate Don Kolloway managed to get hit by the pitch. As a team, the White Sox stole a league-leading 173 bases and were dubbed the "Wild West Boys." Moses earned his own moniker—"Peep Sight"—because

Moses with the other Sox.
Courtesy of George Brace Photo.

of his patience and keen batting eye, and though he finished second in the AL to Washington's George Case, who stole 61 bases, Moses tied the New York Yankees' Johnny Lindell for the league lead with 12 triples. By most other measures, the 1943 season was a disappointment. Moses hit a paltry .245, slugged just .337, and grounded into nine double plays, his worst total since that statistic had been tabulated, starting in 1939.

Like his 25 home runs in 1937, the 56 stolen bases in 1943 turned out to be an aberration. Moses did steal 21 bases—the second-highest total of his career—in 1944, bounced back to hit .280, and clubbed three of Chicago's team total of 23 home runs. He also suffered a pulled groin muscle that would bother him for several seasons. While Moses toiled on the home front, his brother Harry, a pilot in the Eighth Air Force, spent the summer in a German POW camp, interned for 20 months after his plane was shot down on a bombing mission. The war came to an end in 1945, but not before more than 500 major league baseball players had served in the military. It looked as though Moses might join them that summer. Until then, all professional baseball players had been automatically classified with a draft status of "PA." or "Professional Athlete," subject to the draft regardless of physical condition. Through the efforts of Illinois Representative C. Melvin Price and new Commissioner Happy Chandler, a former senator, that practice was changed and baseball players were evaluated on an individual basis. Moses, who had a bad shoulder, Senators pitcher Dutch Leonard, and Yankees pitcher Allie Reynolds were among those who were called up before the 1945 season, but received deferrals from service.

Moses batted .295 in 1945, sixth in the war-depleted AL, led the league with 35 doubles, and was second with 15 triples and 168 hits. The fleet-footed outfielder also managed 11 steals, the last time he posted double figures, and led the American League in putouts with 329. Because of wartime travel restrictions, major league owners canceled the 1945 All-Star Game, scheduled for Fenway Park. After the season, the Associated Press asked NL and AL managers to nominate standouts from the two leagues. With 13 of the 16 pilots voting, Moses was named to the AP's AL team.

Moses was also popular with other players. Ted Williams related an incident that occurred early in the 1946 campaign: "Now, Wally Moses was a nice quiet little guy, never raised his voice at anybody. He was traded to our club afterward and everybody liked Wally." Williams added that during a game between the White Sox and Red Sox, umpire Nicholas "Red" Jones cleared the Chicago bench, and Moses pleaded, "Red, I've been in the big leagues 11 years. This is my 11th year in the big leagues. [It was actually his 12th.] I've never been thrown out of a game in my life. Honest to Pete, I never said a word to you on the bench. I was way over in the corner. I never said a word." Williams remembered, "And old Red Jones, I'll never forget.... He said 'Wally I want to tell you. It's like this. It's just like a raid on a whorehouse. The good go with the bad.'"

Moses was back with the White Sox in 1946 when many of the players who had served in the military returned. But after Dykes was fired just 30 games into the season, new manager Ted Lyons moved Taffy Wright to right field and Moses became surplus. The White Sox waived him, and on July 23, league-leading Boston claimed him. "Words couldn't express my happiness," Moses said. "I'm glad to get my nose out of the mud." With Williams in left and Dom DiMaggio in center, the Red Sox needed a regular right fielder, having employed George Metkovich, Tom McBride, Leon Culberson, and Johnny Lazor. Though he hit just .206 with a pair of home runs, Moses led off, which allowed DiMaggio to bat third, was solid defensively, and played in 43 of Boston's remaining 63 games, as the Red Sox finished 12 games ahead of second-place Detroit. "Veteran though he is," manager Joe Cronin said, "Wally can still fly as a runner, as he proved. He is still a skillful sun fielder."

With lefty Howie Pollet on the mound for the Cardinals in the World Series opener, Moses sat until Cronin inserted him as a defensive replacement with one out in the 10th inning at Sportsman's Park in St. Louis. The fleet outfielder gloved a fly ball off the bat of Enos Slaughter to preserve a 3–2 Boston win. With lefty Harry Brecheen on the mound for the Cardinals, Moses did not appear in Game Two, a St. Louis win. Back in Boston, against righty Murry Dickson, Moses drew a walk in four plate appearances and flagged down a pair of fly balls in the Red Sox' Game Three win. Leading off against righty Red Munger in Game Four, Moses became the 23rd player to collect four hits in a World Series game, but the Cards pounded out 20 of their own and beat the Red Sox, 12–3. Moses flied to center in the first, singled to right in the third, singled to center in the fifth, singled to right in the seventh, and singled in the infield in the ninth. He was stranded each time and, despite the four safeties, was back on the bench against lefties for Game Five at Fenway, a 6–3 Boston win, and for Game Six, a 4–1 Cardinals win at Sportsman's Park.

Moses singled to center, his fifth straight hit, to lead off the decisive Game Seven in St. Louis, and scored the game's first run on DiMaggio's sacrifice fly. But he was retired his next three times up, and struck out with a pair of runners in scoring position in the top of the eighth. And after Slaughter scored the run that gave St. Louis the lead for good in the bottom of the inning, Moses was on deck when McBride grounded into a force play to end the Series.

Although the Red Sox lost the Series, Moses felt at home during his time in Boston and was popular with his teammates. "I remember Dom DiMaggio and Ted Williams coming to our house," daughter Judith Moses Latham, born in 1938, remembered. "Ted Williams was considered a very antisocial person, but he and my father had a very good relationship. There was a picture taken one afternoon where he and I were sitting at our piano bench playing 'Chopsticks' together."

Back with Boston in 1947, Moses hit .275, lost playing time to rookie Sam Mele, and the Red Sox slipped to third place. The next year, Mele and Moses shared time with off-season acquisition Stan Spence, a three-time American League All-Star, and all three struggled to hit for new manager Joe McCarthy. Moses batted just .259, with two homers in 78 games. Spence hit 12 home runs, but batted just .235 and Mele managed just a meager .233 average. Along the way, McCarthy grew frustrated with his team's injuries and chastised Moses when he found him on the training table with a stiff neck.

On November 15, 1948, the Red Sox issued the veteran outfielder his release. Two weeks later, Moses rejoined his old mentor, Connie Mack, in Philadelphia. After more than a decade at the bottom of the AL standings, the Athletics had posted winning records in 1947 and 1948 for the Tall Tactician. Moses appeared in 110 games and batted .276 as Mack's regular right fielder in 1949, alongside left fielder Elmer Valo and center fielder Sam Chapman. The Athletics finished 81–73, good for fifth in the AL. On July 26, Moses collected his 2,000th career hit, off Joe Ostrowski of the St. Louis Browns. The only other active hitter who had reached the milestone was former White Sox teammate Luke Appling; Joe DiMaggio joined the group the following year.

Moses was 40 in 1950, and other than the 43-year-old Appling, no AL player was older than him. He hit .264 in 88 games, but the Athletics floundered, and the 87-year old Mack released the reins after five decades as Philadelphia manager. "Earle Mack (Connie's son) contacted me and offered me the job of managing the A's when Connie Mack was going to retire," Moses told Macht. "I knew I couldn't do the job. I recommended Dykes." Dykes took over in 1951, and though Appling had retired, Moses was again the league's second-oldest player, behind St. Louis Browns pitcher Satchel Paige, who was thought to be 44. Moses, listed at 40, hit just .191, played his final game on September 30, 1951, and was released on January 21, 1952. "In 1948," Moses said later, "when Boston released me, Connie Mack asked me to come back and told me I would have a job with the A's as long as he was there." True to his word, Mack made Moses a coach. "He didn't want to be a manager," Moses' daughter remembered. "He didn't have the temperament for it. He regarded being a manager as political. He knew where his strongest area was, and he went for it."

In his final years as a player, Moses did indeed discover his strength. He tutored the A's hitters, including first baseman Ferris Fain, the 1951 AL batting champion and *The Sporting News* Player of the Year. With Moses in uniform as a coach in 1952, Fain, a pesky slap hitter, captured another batting title. After a disappointing 1953 season, Eddie Joost replaced Dykes as manager in 1954. It was a disaster. Moses was caught in the middle of hostility between Joost and outfielder Gus Zernial, the Athletics slid to 51–103, Joost was dismissed, and the franchise was sold and moved to Kansas City for the 1955 season.

Moses remained in Philadelphia, hopping to the National League to assist new Phillies manager Mayo Smith, another Mack protégé. While there, he told *Time* magazine why star pitcher Robin Roberts avoided intentional walks. "'Take a .333 hitter,' says the Phillies' Coach Wally Moses. "Well, he's only going to get a hit once out of three times. Take Willie Mays: he comes up about 500 times a season, and he hits 50 homers. Hell, that's only one in ten. It'd be silly to walk him. Well, Roberts figures those are pretty good odds.' " Despite the words of wisdom about pitching, he spent more time with the batters, including Richie Ashburn, another slap hitter who won NL batting titles in 1955 and 1958, and 1957 NL Rookie of the Year Ed Bouchee. "I didn't speak much to Mayo Smith," Bouchee said. "But I talked a great deal to his hitting coach, Wally Moses. Smith was a so-so manager who was much too iffy if I had a problem. Smith would be helpful, but I talked more to Wally Moses than him."

On July 22, 1958, Smith was fired and replaced by Eddie Sawyer. Mayo moved to Cincinnati the next year, brought along Moses, and guided the Reds for 80 games before he was fired again in midseason, replaced by Fred Hutchinson at the All-Star Break. Moses stayed on under Hutchinson through the rest of the 1959 campaign and the 1960 season before Smith came calling once more.

This time Mayo was an assistant to new Yankees manager Ralph Houk, and Moses joined a coaching staff that also included Johnny Sain, Frankie Crosetti, and Jim Hegan. Among Moses' pupils that season were Roger Maris, who hit 61 home runs, and Mickey Mantle, who slugged 54. The Yankees won the American League pennant handily and rolled over Hutchinson's Reds in the World Series. In 1962, the Bronx Bombers again won the World Series, a 4-games-to-3 nail-biter over the San Francisco Giants. Moses served as a Yankees scout from 1963 to 1966, was a frequent visitor to Toots Shor's

restaurant on West 51st Street, then returned to the dugout in 1966 when Houk was summoned from the front office 20 games into the season to fix the floundering franchise.

When the season ended, Smith took over the Tigers and Moses joined him. Detroit finished second to Boston in 1967 in a four-team race that wasn't resolved until the season's final day. The next year, the Tigers won the AL title and rallied from a 3–1 deficit to stun the Cardinals in the World Series. "Wally Moses was Mayo's top assistant and knew the game well," star pitcher Denny McLain later related. "Moses coached us on how to signal to each other when Mayo was asleep at the wheel." Smith, with Moses at his side, managed two more seasons before he was ousted in favor of fiery Billy Martin. Moses elected to retire, but the Phillies persuaded him to come back as a batting instructor. He hung up his spikes for good after the 1975 campaign, and he and Billie continued to reside in Philadelphia.

In retirement, Moses pursued lifelong hobbies. "He enjoyed hunting with bird dogs," daughter Judith remembered. "He made furniture. He had a need to know how things worked and understand how they were put together." In addition, "He was a very good ice skater. He read a lot and he played cards. He was a card shark. He had an almost photographic memory." Judith also recalled, "He had an absolutely glorious voice. He had a deep speaking voice and singing voice. I remember when I was three years old, we had an old style Victrola (record player). He played (Russian classical composer) Sergei Rachmaninoff and he sang beautifully."

Growing up, Judith enjoyed a close relationship with her father. "He was phenomenal with young people," she remembered. "He was someone who would listen to you talk. He was a fantastic listener." When home for the summer from boarding school, she attended a number of games, though girls weren't allowed in the dugout. "He was a tremendously positive person," she remembered. "He took part in my school activities and other activities, when he could."

"My father was an incredibly reliable person," Judith said. "He always gave 200 percent. Today he would be called a workaholic. And he was very generous. He had been poor after his parents separated and he was always happy to help someone else. He was also very hard-headed—that's a family trait. He had a terrible temper at times. One shouldn't cross him. But he was very fair with me. He did have some of the shortcomings of many people who come from the South, but that changed as he got older. He was not thrilled with Jackie Robinson, but that changed."

As time went on, Moses worked with a number of young hitters, black and white. "He wanted to help someone get better," Judith recalled. "He would help someone until they got it right. He would work with a batter to capture what he could do well. He had a tremendous ability to instill confidence in other people, especially young people." Although Moses didn't have a big ego, he was highly competitive. "He was never a self- important person," Judith said. "He didn't want the limelight. He just wanted to win. A good illustration of that was when I was a teenager. I said, 'Daddy, it was just a game.' He said to me, 'With that attitude you will never be very good.'"

Never a quitter on the ballfield, Moses, a two-pack-a-day smoker from his teens, gave up tobacco when he encountered health problems in 1978, though the damage was done. Afflicted by chronic lung problems through most of the 1980s, Moses developed cancer, had a lung removed, suffered from emphysema in the other, and relied on bottled oxygen in the final years of his life. His health deteriorated badly, he and Billie moved to Vidalia, and Wally entered a health care center. On October 10, 1990, two days after he celebrated his 80th birthday (it was actually his 81st), he died at the Meadows Regional Medical Center in Vidalia after he suffered a stroke. He was survived by his wife of 53 years, Billie Mae (Haines) Moses, a native of Houston, Texas. After Wally's death, Billie moved to Savannah, Georgia. She passed away in 2002, and is buried alongside him, near his parents and several family members, at Vidalia's Pine Crest Cemetery. Wally and Billie's daughter, Judith Moses Latham, of Arlington, Virginia, is an international radio broadcaster in the Public Affairs Unit of the Voice of America's English Language Division. Judith, who was born in 1938 while Moses was a member of the Athletics, is the host of *International Press Club*, a weekly program that captures reaction by media analysts to U.S. foreign policy, and was a regular contributor to the former documentary program *Dateline*. Judith's son, Ernest "Tiger" Hargraves Latham III, was Wally and Billie Mae's only grandchild, and was the recipient of Wally's World Series ring.

Before he died, Moses was selected to the Philadelphia Baseball Wall of Fame in 1988. From 1978 to 1993, one former Athletics player was selected each year, and a plaque hung in their honor at Veterans Stadium. After the Vet closed, the 25 plaques were relocated in March 2004 to the Philadelphia Athletics Historical Society in Hatboro, Pennsylvania. In 1989, Moses was inducted into the Georgia Sports Hall of Fame.

Sources

Armour, Mark L. and Daniel R. Levitt, *Paths to Glory: How Great Baseball Teams Got That Way*. Dulles, VA: Potomac Books, 2003.

Gillette, Gary, and Pete Palmer, *The 2005 ESPN Baseball Encyclopedia*. New York: Sterling, 2005.

Golenbock, Peter, *Red Sox Nation: An Unexpurgated History of the Red Sox*. Chicago: Triumph Books, 2005.

Halberstam, David, *The Teammates: A Portrait of a Friendship*. New York: Hyperion, 2003.

Halberstam, David, *Summer of '49*. New York: William Morrow & Company, 1991.

James, Bill, *The New Bill James Historical Abstract*. New York: The Free Press, 2001.

Keri, Jonah, ed. *Baseball Between the Numbers: Why Everything You Know About the Game Is Wrong*. New York: Basic Books, 2006

Kuklick, Bruce, *To Everything a Season: Shibe Park and Urban Philadelphia*, 1909–1976. Princeton, N.J.: Princeton University Press, 1991.

Kuenster, John, *The Best of Baseball Digest: The Greatest Players, the Greatest Games, the Greatest Writers From the Game's Most Exciting Years*. Chicago: Ivan R. Dee, 2006.

Lee, Bill, *The Baseball Necrology: The Post-Baseball Lives and Deaths of Over 7,600 Major League Players and Others*. Jefferson, North Carolina: McFarland & Company, Inc.,2003.

Lieb, Fred, *Connie Mack*. New York: Van Rees Press, 1945.

Lindberg, Richard C., *Total White Sox: The Definitive Encyclopedia of the World Champion Franchise*. Chicago: Triumph Books, 2006.

McLain, Denny and Eli Zaret, *I Told You I Wasn't Perfect*. Chicago: Triumph Books, 2007.

Maiorana, Sal, *A Lifetime of Yankee Octobers*. Chelsea, MI: Thomson Gale, 2002.

Mead, William B., *Even the Browns: The Zany, True Story of Baseball in the Early Forties*. Chicago: Contemporary Books, Inc., 1978.

Morris, Peter, *A Game of Inches: The Stories Behind the Innovations That Shaped Baseball. Chicago: Ivan R. Dee, 2006*.

Neft, David S., Richard Cohen and Michael Neft. *The Sports Encyclopedia: Baseball 2004*. 24th Edition. New York: St. Martin's Griffin, 2004.

Nowlin, Bill, *Mr. Red Sox: The Johnny Pesky Story*. Cambridge, MA: Rounder Books, 2004.

Nowlin, Bill, and Dan Desrochers, *The 1967 Impossible Dream Red Sox: Pandemonium on the Field*. Cambridge, MA: Rounder Books, 2007.

Peary, Danny, *We Played the Game: Memories of Baseball's Greatest Era*. New York: Black Dog and Leventhal Publishers, Inc., 1994

Peterson, Richard, *The St. Louis Baseball Reader*. Columbia, MO: University of Missouri Press, 2006.

Porter, David L. *Biographical Dictionary of American Sports: Baseball*, Revised and Expanded Edition, G-P. Westport, CT: Greenwood Press, 2000.

Sheed, Wilfred, *My Life as a Fan: A Memoir*. New York: Simon and Schuster, 1993.

Stout, Glenn, and Richard A. Johnson, *Red Sox Century*. Boston: Houghton Mifflin, 2000.

Sultans of Swat: The Four Great Sluggers of the New York Yankees. New York: New York Times Company, 2006.

"Wally Moses: He Was a Premier Leadoff Hitter," Norman Macht, *Baseball Digest*, February, 1991, pages 79–83.

Williams, Ted, and John Underwood. *My Turn at Bat*. New York: Pocket Books, Inc., 1970.

Time magazine, May 28, 1956.

Interview with Judith Moses Latham by Doug Skipper, August, 2007.

Special thanks: Judith Moses Latham and Norman Macht

JOHNNY OSTROWSKI *by David Laurila*

G	AB	R	H	2B	3B	HR	RBI	BB	SO	BA	OBP	SLG	SB	HBP
1	1	0	0	0	0	0	0	0	1	.000	.000	.000	0	0

Johnny Ostrowski shares the same Polish ancestry as Carl Yastrzemski, but his Red Sox career was in many ways the polar opposite of that of the Hall of Fame legend. While Yaz accumulated a team-record 11,988 regular season at-bats over 3,308 games, Ostrowski is one of 12 position players to appear in only one game, with a single at-bat, in a Red Sox uniform. He did so in 1948, striking out as a pinch hitter in the second game of an April 19 doubleheader.

Born on October 17, 1917, in Chicago, John Thaddeus Ostrowski grew up in the Windy City and attended Tilden Tech, the same high school that later produced Red Sox infielder Chico Walker (1980–84). The youngest of three children, he was born to immigrant parents and grew up with his family's native language, Polish, spoken at home. Ostrowski attracted the attention of professional scouts while playing in Catholic Youth Organization leagues and was signed as an amateur free agent by the Brooklyn Dodgers.

Johnny Ostrowski played seven years in the major leagues. Courtesy of George Brace Photo.

Ostrowski, who batted and threw right-handed, started his professional career in 1939 with the Superior, Wisconsin, Blues of the Class D Northern League. He got off to an auspicious start, homering in his first at-bat as a Dodgers farmhand. He went on to hit a respectable .268 for the season, although he also led the league in strikeouts.

In 1940, Ostrowski moved on to the Class D Alabama State League. Playing for the Troy Trojans, he had his best professional season statistically, hitting .341 and leading the circuit in RBIs and total bases. He was named to the All Star squad. Despite his banner season, which saw him promoted to Class B Macon for the final 11 games, his days in the Brooklyn system were numbered. Under the rules in place at the time, Ostrowski became Cubs property after the season when Macon's minor league working agreement with the Dodgers expired and he was picked up by Chicago.

Ostrowski spent the 1941 campaign with the Cubs' South Atlantic League (Class B) affiliate, the Macon Peaches. Now 23 years old and in his third professional season, he again put up solid numbers. Among the highlights were a league-leading 20 triples and a game in which he drove in six runs in one inning. One of Ostrowski's Macon teammates was Eddie Stanky (a future big-league star), the Peaches' regular shortstop.

Ostrowski split the following season between the Peaches, where he hit .242 in 68 games, and Jackson of the Class B Southeastern League where he hit .294 in 46 games. Ellis Kinder, his future big-league teammate, appeared in nine games for Jackson that season.

In 1943, Ostrowski was picked up by the Pacific Coast League's Los Angeles Angels, considered by many to be among the greatest minor league teams in history. Starting most weekday games at 12:15 p.m. to accommodate war plant swing shift workers, the Angels rolled to a record of 110–45. Ostrowski was a big part of the team's success. Playing right field, he hit .282 with a league-best 21 home runs, five of which came in consecutive games. One day after his long-ball streak came to an end, he recorded a five-hit game. Earlier in the season, on April 30, he hit for the cycle in an 11-inning game, recording a single, two doubles, a triple, and a home run. Ostrowski made his big-league debut in late September, appearing in 10 games for the Cubs and hitting .207 in 29 at-bats. One of his six hits was a triple. During the offseason, Ostrowski worked as a carpenter.

In 1944, Ostrowski returned to the Pacific Coast League, where he spent most of the season. He had another solid campaign for the Angels, batting .282 with 10 home runs and 67 RBIs. He again received a call-up to the big leagues, but appeared in only eight games with the Cubs, banging out a pair of hits in 13 at-bats.

The 1945 season followed along the same lines for Ostrowski, as he again made a brief appearance on the Cubs' roster while spending the bulk of the season in the minor leagues. He did, however, have a change of scenery as he spent the summer with the Kansas City Blues of the American Association. Away from the PCL for the first time in three years, Ostrowski hit a solid .297 with 13 home runs and 99 RBIs. He saw action in seven games for Charlie Grimm's pennant-winning Cubs, garnering three hits in 10 at-bats.

Ostrowski finally earned meaningful playing time at the major-league level in 1946, appearing in 64 games. With longtime Cubs third baseman Stan Hack finally starting to slow down at the age of 36, Ostrowski played 50 of his games at the hot corner, hitting .213 in 160 at-bats. Among his 34 hits were the first three round-trippers of his big-league career.

The 1947 season offered promise, as Hack's days as a regular third sacker were over, but Ostrowski was unable to earn the starting job in spring training. Instead, the Cubs moved outfielder Peanuts Lowrey to third base, and Ostrowski found himself back in the Pacific Coast League yet again. Continuing to show that he could hit in the minor leagues, he batted .292 while hitting 24 home runs and driving in 119 runs. He shared the Angels' Most Valuable Player award with pitcher Jess Dobernic.

After the season, Ostrowski—now 30 years old and a veteran of nine professional campaigns—became Red Sox property when he was selected in the Rule 5 draft on November 10, 1947. He made his lone Boston appearance on April 19 in the second game of a Patriots Day doubleheader against the Philadelphia Athletics. Wearing the number 27 on the back of his uniform, Ostrowski pinch-hit for Ellis Kinder in the eighth inning and struck out against left-hander Lou Brissie. (Brissie, it should be noted, was a war hero, having survived an attack in World War II that left him with German shrapnel in his leg. Ostrowski, meanwhile, did not serve in the military as he had been designated 4-F due to a perforated eardrum.) Connie Mack's A's were victorious in both games of the season-opening twin bill, winning by scores of 5–4 and 3–2.

While Ostrowski was walking to the plate for his only at-bat as a member of the Red Sox, Korea's Yun-Bok Suh was on his way setting a new world record in the 51st running of the Boston Marathon with a time of 2:25:39.

Ostrowski remained with Joe McCarthy's Red Sox for nearly a month, but never made it back onto the field. As is still the case today, players taken in the Rule 5 draft have to stay on the big league roster for the entire season or be offered back to their old team. With no playing time to be had, he was returned to the Cubs' organization on May 15.

Ostrowski was assigned to the all-too-familiar Los Angeles Angels, who played their games in the PCL's version of Wrigley Field (the Angels and Cubs were both owned by Philip K. Wrigley). He spent the next two seasons there, hitting .295 in 1948 and .318 in 1949. His 32 homers and 90 RBIs in 1949 attracted the attention of the crosstown White Sox, who acquired him from Los Angeles on August 4 for infielder Bobby Rhawn and cash. Back in the big leagues, Ostrowski made it into 49 games with

In his one at-bat for the Red Sox, Ostrowski struck out. Courtesy of George Brace Photo.

the South Siders, hitting .266 while filling in for the injured Gus Zernial in left field. In 158 at-bats, he logged career highs with nine doubles, four triples, and 31 RBIs. One of his teammates was former Red Sox outfielder George "Catfish" Metkovich.

In late April of 1950, White Sox general manager Frank Lane traded Ostrowski and cash to the Yankees in exchange for outfielder Dick Wakefield. Wakefield refused to join the Chisox unless they restored a $5,500 pay cut forced upon him by New York after he was dealt from Detroit the previous winter. Ostrowski had been immediately assigned to the Yankees' Kansas City farm club. Lane called off the transaction on April 30, with the support of Commissioner Happy Chandler. Tired of the temperamental outfielder's act, the Yankees sold Wakefield's contract to Oakland in the PCL in late May. Ostrowski remained in his native Chicago.

Ostrowski split his time between two cities in 1950, playing in 21 games for the White Sox and 55 with the Washington Senators. He was shipped to the Nation's Capital on May 31 as part of a six-player transaction that included three All-Stars: Eddie Robinson, Ray Scarborough, and Cass Michaels. On September 22 he was waived back to the White Sox, where he finished out his final big-league season, appearing in a single game for his hometown team. Ostrowski hit only .232 for the season, although he did establish career highs in hits (44) home runs (6), games (77), and at-bats (190).

His big-league days now behind him, Ostrowski spent the 1951 season north of the border, playing 127 games for the minor league Toronto Maple Leafs. Plying his trade in the city where Babe Ruth hit his first professional home run, Ostrowski hit only .215 with 13 home runs and 56 RBIs.

Ostrowski returned to the friendly confines of the PCL for one last time in 1952, playing for the Sacramento Solons (61 games) and the Oakland Oaks (77 games). He was managed by Hall of Famers at each stop: Joe Gordon in Sacramento and Mel Ott in Oakland. Ostrowski responded by batting .258 and hitting 22 home runs with 69 RBIs. Ostrowski finished his playing career in the Southern Association, suiting up in 22 games for the Memphis Chicks, a White Sox affiliate led by Hall of Famer Luke Appling. He batted .281.

A minor leaguer for the majority of his 14-year career, Ostrowski played in 816 Pacific Coast League games, homering 124 times, driving in 474 runs, and posting a .287 lifetime batting average.

Overall, Ostrowski played parts of seven seasons in

the big leagues, debuting on September 24, 1943, and playing his final game on October 1, 1950. He saw action in 216 games, batting .234 with 14 home runs. He spent most of his time in the outfield (108 games) but also saw time at third base (66 games) and had a one-game stint at second base with the Cubs in 1946. The Chicago native was one of 163 players to have played for both of his hometown teams, the Cubs (1943–1946) and the White Sox (1949–1950).

Ostrowski was one of 41 players who have been selected by the Red Sox in the major league portion of the Rule 5 draft, and one of two taken in 1947. The other was catcher Babe Martin, who spent all of the 1948 season on the roster despite appearing in only four games.

After baseball, Ostrowski was a sales representative and drove a truck for Material Service Corp., an Illinois refuse company, retiring in 1980. A member of the Chicago Alumni Association and the Knights of Columbus, he was very active coaching in youth baseball programs in Chicago. Ostrowski died on November 13, 1992, at the age of 75 and is buried in Resurrection Cemetery in Justice, Illinois.

Sources

http://www.baseball-reference.com/o/ostrojo01.shtml
http://www.baseball-almanac.com
http://web.minorleaguebaseball.com/milb/history/top100.jsp?
   idx=13
http://oaklandoaks.tripod.com/
The Sporting News
The *Chicago Tribune*

MIKE PALM *by Bill Nowlin*

G	ERA	W	L	SV	GS	GF	CG	SHO	IP	H	R	ER	BB	SO	HR	HBP	WP	BFP
3	6.00	0	0	0	0	0	0	0	3	6	2	2	5	1	0	0	0	20

G	AB	R	H	2B	3B	HR	RBI	BB	SO	BA	OBP	SLG	SB	HBP
3	3	0	0	0	0	0	0	0	1	.000	.000	.000	0	0

Mike Palm is one of the relatively few Red Sox players to have been born in the city of Boston. Richard Paul Palm's date of birth was February 13, 1925. After moving to a suburb, he picked up his nickname in high school, where Belmont High's baseball coach was Myron "Mike" Palm, a former Penn State athlete who started calling his prospect "Mike."

It was in infancy that "our" Mike's family left the Jamaica Plain section of Boston for Watertown, and it was in junior high school in Watertown that he first became a ballplayer—under the tutelage of junior high school coach Bob Daughters. The same Bob Daughters who had made the major leagues with the Boston Red Sox, ever so briefly, for one game in 1937. "He encouraged me and made a pitcher out of me," Mike recalled in mid-2007. "I had a pretty good arm. That was the start of it. He was new in the school system. He'd just gotten through with the Red Sox. He was a heck of a guy. We all loved him as kids."

Mike's father had been a pitcher, too. Paul Palm had pitched semipro ball in the Brockton League, an industrial league in eastern Massachusetts. Paul was a printing instructor at Wentworth Institute. His wife was a schoolteacher, who taught elementary school until the three children—two girls and a boy—were born. Mike says his father was pretty good ("I used to carry his clippings around"), but he didn't learn that much from him.

Mike Palm as a Colonel.

"In those days, dads didn't have a lot of time to spend with his kids because they were working so hard. I was always interested in sports, though. Not that I played a lot growing up, because we went down to Nantucket for the summer and there wasn't much baseball down there." But his dad did give him a start, and then he met up with Coach Daughters.

The boy who grew to become a 6'3½" right-hander was a real fan, who took in a number of games as a kid. His grandfather took young Mike to both Braves Field and Fenway Park, and Mike saw Babe Ruth hit one of his last home runs, in Ruth's brief time with the Braves in 1935.

Palm was signed by the Red Sox while still in high school. The family moved to Belmont after Palm finished ninth grade. Often striking out as many as 18 batters a game, he earned an invitation to one of the school prospects tryouts that Hall of Famer Hugh Duffy used to host at Fenway Park. "I worked out with them and showed them what I had and they signed me while I was in high school," Palm recalls. The scouts credited with his signing are a very impressive trio: Hugh Duffy, Neil Mahoney, and Herb Pennock. It was 1943. There was no bonus money involved. Assigned to Allentown in the Inter-State League after graduation and awaiting induction into the Army, he saw only a couple of weeks of duty—a total of one inning in two appearances. He walked four batters and let in two runs. He went off to war with a professional ERA of 18.00.

During World War II, Palm spent 2½ years in the Army Air Corps serving first at an airport in Casablanca and then in India for six months after the Japanese surrender, forgoing baseball for both 1944 and 1945. He worked doing manual labor, but wound up inspecting the baggage of soldiers transiting through Casablanca on their way home from different fronts. His job was to relieve them of field glasses, pistols, ammunition, and other prohibited items. "It was sort of a dirty job," he regrets, but Pfc. Palm was glad to be part of the process that brought soldiers home. And it worked out well in one regard: "I got out in time for spring training."

Mike spent the next two years in the Piedmont League pitching for Class-B Roanoke, the first year for Eddie Popowski and the second for Mike Higgins. In 1946, he was 13–8 with a 2.56 ERA in 179 innings of work. The next year, he threw 197 innings and posted a 14–8 record but his ERA climbed to 3.65.

Beginning with Birmingham in 1948, he posted an identical record (14–8) at Double A, but had improved considerably. He was leading the Southern League in ERA (2.20), both as a starter and a reliever, when he got a midseason call to report to the big-league club in Boston. Birmingham, he remembers, was in a "hitter's league" with a lively ball, so his ERA meant even more.

His first appearance came on July 11, 1948, in Philadelphia. The Red Sox had won the day's first game, 9–8, in 10 innings when Dom DiMaggio doubled home Billy Goodman and they held the lead. In the second game, DiMaggio homered as he had in the first game and Johnny Pesky hit a three-run homer, but the Athletics racked up a six-run inning off Mickey Harris and that did in the Red Sox. Wearing uniform number 20, Palm relieved Harris with two outs in the bottom of the sixth, and surrendered three hits before closing out the inning. In the seventh, Mel Parnell took over relief duties. The game ended after 7½ innings because of Philadelphia's Sunday curfew law. Mike's memories remain vivid: "I was a little wild, you know—nervous as hell…in a big league uniform." He roomed with Boo Ferriss on the road and stayed with his family in Belmont while the Red Sox were at home.

Palm's second game was a week later, in Boston, on the 18th—again it was a doubleheader, this time against the visiting St. Louis Browns. Boo started for Boston but gave up seven hits in his 2⅔ innings of work. The Red Sox

Palm was a Greater Boston boy who made the hometown team.

were behind 4–0. Mike Palm completed the third inning and pitched the fourth, allowing just one hit—though he walked three batters. At the plate, the Red Sox came alive and scored six times in the bottom of the fourth. With a 6–4 lead, McCarthy brought in Earl Johnson to pitch. He scattered three hits in five innings of work, letting in just one more run. The six additional runs the Red Sox scored in the sixth proved pure gravy. Johnson was awarded the win, even though Palm had left with the lead.

The last time Palm pitched in the major leagues was in yet another twin bill, a day/night doubleheader against the White Sox at Fenway Park on July 20. Boston won the afternoon game, 3–1. In the night game, Ferriss again fared poorly, hammered for six hits in 1⅔ innings. The White Sox scored five runs in the second, and Palm was once more brought in to close the inning. He allowed two hits and walked two in 1⅓ innings, giving up one run in the top of the third, but once the Red Sox had scored five runs in the bottom of the third and made it a close game, he gave way to Earl Johnson. Palm was again hitless at the plate. Chicago scored three more runs, but the Red Sox scored once in the eighth and three runs in the bottom of the ninth to take the game, 10–9.

He didn't pitch again for Boston, other than throw a little batting practice to Ted Williams. "Maybe they didn't like what they saw, or whatever. They were right in the middle of a pennant fight." As it happens, Mike was shipped back to Birmingham to take part in another battle for the pennant. "They sent me back to Birmingham. We finished the year and won the Dixie Series down there. I won four games in the (league) playoffs. Then we beat Fort Worth for the title. We were big heroes in Birmingham that year. They paraded us through town and showered us with gifts and everything. It was pretty nice."

Though Mike didn't know it at the time, his major league career was over. He'd thrown a total of three innings in three games, walking five and striking out only one. Giving up six hits and two earned runs, he had an ERA of an even 6.00. At the plate, Palm had three at-bats, striking out once and never getting a major-league hit. "I remember Dom DiMaggio telling me, 'You should take a pitch or two.' I was up there swinging at the first pitch, and probably shouldn't have been. I wasn't any shakes as a hitter. I remember in Birmingham I got three hits one night. I think they sent that pitcher down the next day!" As it happens, he never fielded a ball in the majors, either, so he does not have either a batting average or a fielding average.

In early 1949, Red Sox manager Joe McCarthy cited Palm as a prospect but he saw little playing time in spring training and spent two subpar years with Triple-A Louisville in the American Association. Palm posted records of 9–8 (4.47) in 1949 and 3–7 (6.57) in 1950. In 1949, in Louisville, he married his wife, Marie, from Belmont— Anita Marie Denish. Midway during the 1950 season, he was demoted to Double A (1–3, 7.10 ERA.) After the 1950 season, Palm was traded to the White Sox for Bill Evans, effectively sold to Sacramento in the Pacific Coast League. He pitched in three games, a total of five innings, giving up five earned runs. "I quit out there. I went out of there with my wife and we had a little baby, and she was pregnant with the second one. I spent five years at it. I figured I wasn't going to be in the Hall of Fame. It was time to go to work."

Fortunately, he had other options awaiting him. "I thought it was time to get out. I had a job to come to. I ended up selling printing ink. My father was associated with the same company that hired me, and I spent 25 years with that company. I was around the Boston office. I used to cover the state of Maine for the company and the South Shore and North Shore. We ended up with eight kids, just about one a year over ten years." With eight children, did any of them try baseball? "They took up golf, really. They were pretty good in baseball but the golf bug bit them. They were caddies over here in Hadley and so they went the golf route."

Mike's wife passed away suddenly in 1991. He is retired and living with one of his daughters on the South Shore. Both daughters are homemakers. One son is a pipefitter, another is a housepainter, and three work in various aspects of the printing trade. Another son, who had worked in sales, died in the early 21st century. Mike watches games on television, and remains a Red Sox fan, but doesn't head into games. He's on the Red Sox alumni mailing list, but doesn't take any active role in alumni events.

Source

Interviews with Mike Palm done October 14, 2000, July 15, 2007, and August 16. 2007, by Bill Nowlin.

MEL PARNELL *by Bill Nowlin*

G	ERA	W	L	SV	GS	GF	CG	SHO	IP	H	R	ER	BB	SO	HR	HBP	WP	BFP
35	3.14	15	8	0	27	5	16	1	212	205	87	74	90	77	7	4	3	916

G	AB	R	H	2B	3B	HR	RBI	BB	SO	BA	OBP	SLG	SB	HBP
35	80	6	13	1	0	0	8	1	11	.162	.173	.175	0	0

Lefthander Mel Parnell devoted a full decade to the Boston Red Sox, from 1947 through 1956, winning 123 games while losing just 75. He ranks first among left-handed Red Sox pitchers in total wins for the ball club, the number of games he started (232), and the number of innings pitched (1,752⅔). The New Orleans native performed exceptionally well in Fenway Park, a ballpark thought to be unkind to southpaws, compiling a 71–30 mark there. In his final season, 1956, he threw a midseason no-hitter against the White Sox, also at Fenway.

Melvin Lloyd Parnell was born on June 13, 1922, in New Orleans. His mother, Anna Mae Trauth Parnell, was a housewife. His father, Patrick Louis Parnell, was the chief maintenance man for the *Panama Limited*, the Illinois Central Railroad's million-dollar train which ran from New Orleans to Chicago. The *Panama Limited* was an all-Pullman-car train, a companion to the *City of New Orleans*, which was its daytime equivalent—it featured chair cars and had no sleeping accommodations. Patrick Parnell was based in New Orleans and his job was to have the train ready to move every morning; he did that for 30 or more years. Mel had one sister, Dorothy Parnell.

"My dad and I were like brothers when I was growing up," Mel recalls. "He took me to a lot of ball games. We used to go see the local ball club, a Double A team here in New Orleans, the New Orleans Pelicans. He and I would go see a lot of their ball games. During spring training, the Cleveland Indians used to train here in New Orleans and the New York Giants used to come in. On weekends, we'd always catch their exhibition series. At that time, Bob Feller was the young 17-year-old rookie right out of high school pitching for Cleveland and the star pitcher for the New York Giants was Carl Hubbell. They were the complete opposite of each other. Usually those two used to face each other on Sunday and it was a great exhibition to see those two perform [at Heinemann Park]."

Growing up, Mel had the opportunity to play in a number of city parks. "We had a lot of baseball parks around New Orleans. Any direction you'd go into, you could go into a baseball park. It was a very popular sport here. As a youngster, I was playing with people much older than I was. Everyone kept telling my daddy, 'That kid's going to be a ballplayer.' Of course, that was my big ambition—to be a ballplayer. After signing a contract, my ambition was to get to the top and make the major leagues.

Fortunately, no one ever tried to "correct" his natural left-handedness, though when he first began it was as a first baseman. It wasn't until his senior year in high school, when the team was short a pitcher, that coach Al Kreider asked him if he'd want to try pitching. Saying, "I'll play anything. I just want to play," he became a moundsman. "They kept telling me my ball was pretty much alive and that encouraged me more and more into pitching."

It was in high school that coach Kreider gave him his nickname. "I was strictly a lowball pitcher. I threw a lot down in the dirt so he gave me that name 'Dusty' and it stuck with me."

American Legion ball was strong at the time and Parnell played in Legion tournaments as well as for the Samuel J. Peters High School team. It was quite a strong team, and Parnell was such a talent that he was asked to sign his first major league contract before he'd even graduated. Red Sox scouts Eddie Montague and Herb Pennock weren't the only ones following him. He was perhaps wise not to take the first offer. "I was strongly scouted by the St. Louis Cardinals. Branch Rickey used to come out to my house and talk to my father. I told my father, 'Don't commit to them,' because I had been told by many other fellows who had signed with the St. Louis Cardinal organization that it was a tough organization. They had so many ballplayers that you were pretty much a number and not a name. That didn't interest me. I was skeptical of that. My high school team, seven of us signed professional. Six signed with the Cardinals. I was the only one who didn't.

"Red Lavigne, who was an outfielder and the hot prospect; his real name was Edward. Ray Yochim, a pitcher. They were the two top prospects of the fellows who signed with the Cardinals. Ed Montague and Herb Pennock, the Red Sox scouts, were coming in to see Red. The general manager of the New Orleans ball club—a fellow by the name of Vincent Rizzo—he suggested to the scouts, 'I want you to see the little skinny left-handed pitcher that's pitching today.' He brought them out to the ball park, and that day I pitched and I struck out 17 and that's when the Red Sox became interested in me. Naturally, after my career, I was happy that I signed with the Red Sox. I had no regrets. However, the first time I walked on the mound in Fenway Park and looked at that left field fence being so close, I thought maybe I made a mistake. As it turned

Marvelous Mel Parnell was 40–15 in 1948 and 1949 combined.

out, everything turned out well for me and I was very happy to be a member of the Red Sox." The 17 strikeout game was only the fifth game he'd ever pitched.

Parnell had missed a couple of years of school due to illness and injuries, but it was just a short while before he turned 19 that he signed. He first played professional ball in 1941 for Centerville, Maryland, a Class D Eastern Shore League team with which the Red Sox had a working agreement. He was initially sent to Owensboro, Kentucky, another Class D club with a Red Sox affiliation. "When I got there, I was a little skinny kid, 130 pounds. The manager was Hugh Wise, a former Tigers catcher. He said, 'What are you supposed to do?' I said, 'Well, I'm a pitcher. A left-hand pitcher.' He said, 'Well, I don't need left-hand pitchers. I have four.' He contacted the Red Sox and they suggested that I go to Centerville. I never played at all in Owensboro. He was overloaded with left-hand pitchers. He needed right-handers. In Centerville, we had Eddie Walls and then Eddie Popowski. I knew Eddie since that time. We kind of strung along together."

In Centerville, Parnell threw 48 innings, winning four and losing four, posting an ERA of 4.13. He got his feet wet. After finishing up school and graduating in February 1942, he put in a full year with Canton, working under manager Pat Patterson. He had an excellent season, with a 16–9 record after 204 innings of work. His ERA was a spectacular 1.59; he ranked a close third in the Middle Atlantic League.

World War II was, of course, looming at the time and the draft board had been in touch. Not wanting to be taken as a foot soldier, Parnell enlisted in the Army Air Corps. Because he was good at baseball, he earned a pretty soft berth. "The Air Force commander at Maxwell Field, Alabama, wanted to have a good baseball team there and I was one he kept shuffling around to keep me from going overseas. He wanted some entertainment on the base for the benefit of the other fellows, and of course baseball was part of that. I was moved around to various different sections of the Air Force to protect me for baseball." Mel helped train pilots for combat, putting them through their paces with calisthenics and other physical education work. He also did some maintenance work and other duties. He kept getting assigned different tasks, moving from department to department, in order to keep him nearby and available to play ball. "When I first enlisted,

I went to Blytheville, Arkansas. That was a military base that was pretty much new there. Then from there I went to Keesler Field in Biloxi, Mississippi. I went to B-36 school there. Of course, the B-36 [a giant bomber] never did get into use during the war. From Keesler, the commanding officer at Maxwell Field requested my transfer over to Maxwell Field, Alabama. I stayed there for the duration. I enlisted to be a pilot at one time, but the government had too many pilots and they washed us out. There was something like 32,000 pilots they washed out and I happened to be one of them. It was winding down toward the end of the war and there wasn't that big a need for pilots." Parnell ended up as a staff sergeant.

After the war, like with many ball clubs, the Red Sox had so many players coming out of the service that they didn't know where to send them all. Parnell suggests that for many, their assignment was somewhat arbitrary. "They pretty much just split us up by names and half went to Scranton, Pennsylvania, in the Eastern League and the other half went to Louisville. I was one that went to Scranton and we had an outstanding team. I led the league in earned run average and we had a fellow by the name of Tommy Fine that led the league in wins and we won the pennant by 19 games. Truthfully, we had a better team than they had at Louisville. The Red Sox had so many good ballplayers that they couldn't protect them all. Teams were taking some of the better talent away from them because they didn't protect the guys." Parnell's league-leading ERA was 1.30, and he finished the season with a 13–4 season for Scranton. He struck out 111 and walked only 49. He earned himself a promotion to the big league club.

In 1947, Mel trained with the Red Sox and found himself one of six pitchers vying to fill two slots on the staff. There were four veterans, Harry Dorish, and himself. He and Dorish got the two slots. With Boston, Parnell appeared in 15 games (50⅔ innings) and struggled, with a 6.35 ERA, two wins, and three losses. One of those losses came in his April 20 debut. Boston had won the first four games of the year, but Parnell was tagged for three runs in the bottom of the first by the Washington Senators and lost a 3–1 ball game—even though he pitched scoreless ball on just three hits over the next six innings. The Red Sox managed only three hits. He couldn't complete the fifth his next time out, but left with the Sox on top and it was Harry Dorish who couldn't hold the lead. Parnell got his first major league win on April 30 in Detroit, throwing a complete game four-hit, 7–1 win over the Tigers. He got a little more work, but was optioned to Louisville on July 9 to make room for Sam Dente. Parnell suffered a broken finger not long after arriving and figured in only four games, not that effectively.

Come 1948, though, he really took off. Suddenly, he was a major league pitcher who posted a 3.14 ERA and a 15–8 record, throwing 16 complete games. What happened? "In '47, I was moving into a pretty set pitching staff. They won the pennant the year before and they were pretty well solid. I didn't get very much work. I guess (manager Joe) Cronin probably figured it would be better if I went down to Louisville, where I could pitch more and get some more experience. When I came back in '48, I fit right in with the rest of the pitching staff, and of course some of the guys that were on that '47 staff like Tex Hughson, he developed arm problems. Some of the other fellows, they kind of fell off and didn't have a very good year. That gave me the opportunity to move right in." There were indeed a lot of sore arms on that staff. "That gave me a chance to move in and to get into the rotation. Once I got there, I worked hard at it and developed well enough to continue on as a starting pitcher." Having the chance to get regular work in made all the difference, he thought, as did both an extra year of maturity and his learning to adjust to the caliber of player in big league baseball.

Joe McCarthy was the manager in 1948. "I liked McCarthy's style of managing. He was tough. He was the boss and you knew it. If you committed a wrong, he wouldn't show you up in front of anybody. It was just you and him. That I appreciated." McCarthy was predictable, too. Mel had a regular slot in the rotation and could plan for his starts. It made a difference. He threw 212 innings in 1948. Like many veterans, he harbors a little disdain for today's pitchers. "Today it's kind of ridiculous the way they handle pitching—guys pitching five innings and they don't want to go over 100 pitches. We used to throw 150 and it wasn't any different. I think they're being babied too much now."

Many pitchers of the day realized later that they'd largely had to make it on their own. There were no large coaching staffs, nothing in the way of even moderately sophisticated training programs. Did he get much of in the way of instruction? "Not too much. No, not too much. We had an old catcher that was a coach and he really didn't know anything about pitching. In all fairness to him, he was an old-timer and no doubt during his day, no doubt he was a good catcher. Catching and pitching is a different ball game. Larry Woodall. Larry, he did his best, but he just didn't understand pitching. Only a pitcher can understand what he goes through with the arm problems and stuff like that. Catchers can't tell you that."

Did Parnell ever have the benefit of a pitching coach during the years he played? "Well, we had Boo Ferriss come up under Higgins, at the end. We had some help with pitching coaches. We had Paul Schreiber and John Shulte. Schreiber had a pretty good knowledge of pitching. Johnny Murphy was in the bullpen with us. He helped us a lot. We got Johnny Murphy from the Yankees under Cronin. That was early '47, I think he came to us and he was a big help to a lot of the young pitchers. He was the old fireman for the Yankees. He was very helpful to all the young pitchers. We'd sit in the bullpen and talk with him and you could get a lot of knowledge from him."

There is one 1948 game he still wishes he had had a chance to pitch. He fully expected to start for the Red Sox in the one-game playoff for the pennant, October 4 against the Indians at Fenway Park. He's been asked about it so much, he says, that he could write a book about it. "That game I thought was my game. The whole ball club thought it was my game. My family kept telling me you've got your biggest game coming up tomorrow, better get in bed and get some sleep, so I was in bed the night before at 9 o'clock. I got to the ball park the next morning, and as pitchers do during batting practice, you take your time getting dressed because there's no hurry to get out on the field You're not going to shag flies or anything. So I'm taking my time getting dressed and all of a sudden, McCarthy comes up from behind and puts his hands on my shoulders. He says, 'Kid, I've changed my mind. I'm going with the righthander instead of the lefthander today because of the elements.' The wind was blowing out. With that, he calls Don Fitzpatrick, the clubhouse guy, and he tells Don Fitzpatrick to go out on the field and get Denny Galehouse to come into the clubhouse. Galehouse comes in, McCarthy tells him he's the pitcher, and his facial expression changed completely. It was a shock to him. The reason he did that was because Galehouse had pitched well against Cleveland in our last series in Cleveland, and McCarthy was thinking maybe we'd get the same performance.

"So, with that, I then got dressed and I ran out on the field during the latter part of the batting practice and everybody was asking, 'What are you doing out here?' I said, 'I'm not pitching.' They said, 'You got to be kidding.' I said, 'I'm not kidding. I'm dead serious. Galehouse is the pitcher.'"

The Indians thought it was a deception to catch them off-guard. Even during the first inning, Cleveland manager Lou Boudreau sent a man underneath the stands to see if Parnell was warming up, thinking that McCarthy might be trying to get a left-handed lineup and then come in with Parnell in the second inning. That might have been a great ploy, but it was not to be. "McCarthy had his mind made up, he played a hunch and it didn't work. A lot of people said that nobody wanted to pitch it. Hell, we all wanted to pitch it. That was a big game. If you pitch that game and win it, that meant something for you. It was a golden opportunity for whoever got it, to pitch it and win it. If you lost it, nothing would be said about it other than you got beat. But if you won it, it meant a hell of a lot to you." Galehouse got through the first three innings well enough, but imploded in the fourth, and the Red Sox managed only five hits, losing 8–3.

Parnell pitched even better in 1949, the year that was far and away his best. He won 25 games and lost only seven, with an ERA of 2.77. The 25 wins were one

Parnell and Pesky read about the Sox
taking the lead in the 1949 campaign.

more than the previous Red Sox record by a left-handed pitcher, Babe Ruth's 24 in 1917. It was built on a heavy workload, just shy of 300 innings. "That was the year that everything worked well," he summed up. Though Birdie Tebbetts was Boston's primary catcher, Parnell preferred working with the younger Matt Batts, both in '49 and '50. "Birdie was getting on in age and his arm wasn't as good as in his heyday. With a runner on first base, Birdie became a fastball catcher just in case the runner was running. Matt Batts was different. He was calling whatever pitches were working best for me. I figured I had a lot more working for me, working with Batts than working with Birdie."

Like the year before, 1949 came right down to the very last day of the season. The Red Sox traveled to New York that last weekend needing to win either one of the final two games to take the flag. Parnell pitched the first of the two, the Saturday game. The Red Sox had a 4–0 lead after three innings, but Joe DiMaggio's ground-rule double started a two-run rally in the fourth, and three straight singles brought the Yankees to 4–3 and drove Parnell from the game. Joe Dobson closed the gate, but another run scored in the process, tying the game. The Yankees won it in the eighth on Johnny Lindell's home run, and won the Sunday game, too.

Despite both years being as good as one could expect, the Red Sox fell just short both times. And, oddly, Parnell walked more batters than he struck out both years, and his 134 walks in 1949 set a Red Sox record. He ascribes the high walk totals to Fenway's short left field fence and having to pitch very carefully, and the lack of foul territory. "I wanted to make them hit my pitch, not get his pitch to hit. I pitched a lot inside to righthand hitters at

Mel with Birdie Tebbetts, 1949.

Fenway, which lefthanders wouldn't do." He kept them from extending their arms and maybe cut down on runs, but walked more in the process. "I pitched a little different ball game at Fenway than I did on the road. I wasn't a power pitcher. I tried to make the hitter hit my pitches. And I kept the ball in the lower part of the strike zone. The lack of foul territory at Fenway Park was even more important. Any foul ball has a good chance of going into the seats, so you lose a lot of outs. You would get outs in other ballparks, where the hitter is getting another swing of the bat at you in Fenway."

In 1950, the Red Sox scored a ton of runs—1002 runs to the 804 scored by their opponents. The team won 94 games but wound up in third place, four games out of first. Parnell appeared in a career-high 40 games and had the best ERA of any Sox pitcher, 3.61. He put up an 18–10 record, with 31 starts and nine relief appearances, throwing 249 innings—second only to the 295⅓ innings he threw in 1949.

In 1951, Parnell was a very good 18–11 (3.26), despite a team that fell apart in September, but he really flattened out in 1952 (12–12, 3.62). The year started out well, with a three-hit Opening Day shutout of the Washington Senators, but was severely hampered by bursitis. A couple of weeks off beginning in late June helped. He was 12–8 after the first week of September, but lost three in a row—even to the Senators, whom he had beaten 17 consecutive games before a September 20 loss. He did hit his only major league home run, though, on September 15, a fifth-inning solo homer off Lou Kretlow in Comiskey Park.

His last really good season was 1953, when he posted a record of 21–8 with a 3.06 ERA. One thing Red Sox fans savor in Parnell's 1953 season—he shut out the Yankees four times. Parnell appeared in only half as many games in 1954, though, when he was hit in the left arm by his former roommate Maury McDermott. They were

pitching against each other in Washington and planned to have dinner together after the game, but one of McDermott's pitches sailed in and Parnell threw up his arm to protect himself. It hit him in the wrist and broke the ulna bone. That accident hastened the end of his career. "Lou Boudreau was the manager and Boudreau kept trying to get me back into action much quicker than I should have. I think for that reason, my arm never really developed to the point that it should have. I came back too soon." Parnell's record in 1954 was a very disappointing 3–7, though his ERA wasn't all that bad at 3.70. The Red Sox team was pretty poor, too, winning just 69 games and losing 85, finishing 42 games out of first place.

He pitched only 46 innings in 1955 (2–3, 7.83). He fought his way through those seasons, and then rebounded a bit in 1956, his last year as a major league pitcher, with a 7–6 record and a 3.77 ERA. It was in that final year, on July 14, that he threw his 4–0 no-hitter against the White Sox, the first Red Sox no-hitter since Howard Ehmke's in 1923. "The no-hitter was naturally the thing you dream of, but never expect it to happen. I've heard a lot of guys that pitched no-hitters say that they didn't know they were going for it. I don't believe that. You have to know. If a guy hits a ball off you, you know what he hit. You got fans in the stands that are screaming and yelling. You've got that big scoreboard in the ball park that tells you what's happening inning by inning, how many hits have been hit off of you and everything, so you have to know what's going on.

"From the seventh inning on, every out that was made, the fans are jumping up and yelling. My right fielder, Jackie Jensen, comes to me in the seventh inning, he says, 'Look, fellow, you're going on a no-hitter. Don't let them hit the ball to me in right field. I don't want to be the guy to mess it up for you.' I said, 'Jackie, forget it. All I'm looking for is a win.' The final out was hit back to me. Walter Dropo was with Chicago, an ex-teammate. Dropo hit this ball to the first base side of the mound. I came down off the mound, caught the ball, ran to first base, and made the play unassisted. When I get to first base, Mickey Vernon, our first baseman, says to me, 'What's the matter, fellow? You don't have confidence in me?' I said, 'I've got all the confidence in the world in you but I was afraid if I threw it I might throw it away.'

"Going toward first base, the throw I would have had to make would have been a soft throw. A soft throw is easier to miss than a harder throw. If it doesn't hit right in the pocket of the glove, you could lose it."

Mel Parnell's career ended with an elbow operation to try to fix a torn nerve. He figures today that if the Tommy John surgery had been available to him at that time, he might have had as much as another four or five years in his career, but it was not to be.

After a couple of in-between years, Red Sox farm director Neil Mahoney asked him to manage a team in

Alpine, Texas in 1961. It was a team stocked with bonus kids from California, and what he called "a great setup. The ball park was a beautiful ball park. It was a miniature major league ballpark pretty much. They were big money kids. The following season, I went up to York, Pennsylvania in the Eastern League and managed there. The year after that, I went up to Seattle and managed in Seattle. After I got to Seattle, I realized that I was getting tired of that kind of travel and wanted to get home with my family and stay at home. So I retired. After I was home, Curt Gowdy called me and asked me if I would join him in the broadcasting booth, which I did. I regard Curt as one of the greatest."

Parnell began broadcasting on television in 1965 and worked through a couple of lean years, but was on hand for 1967's Impossible Dream season. "It was a great experience, really. It was great to see the ball club being a winner. It was a thrill winning it all on the last game of the season, and seeing the fans—how they reacted—was fantastic, I thought. Just a fantastic year. We had some good ballplayers on that ball club."

He took an offer to work as a broadcaster in Chicago in 1969, but after the first year didn't like it there. He tried to get out of the second year of the two-year deal but they wouldn't let him go, until he found Billy Pierce for them and the station agreed to take Pierce as a substitute. From that point on, Mel remained in New Orleans. He had a deal with Chrysler that allowed them to use his name on an automobile dealership, Mel Parnell Plymouth. He then moved into a completely different field, with a start-up pest control business which he built from scratch, P&T Pest Control. In time, he turned the business over to his sister; she ultimately sold it.

A lifetime .198 batter, his 4-for-4 day on May 23, 1951, was an aberration. Parnell has just one major league home run, hit in 1952 off Lew Kretlow. "He was a fastball pitcher, threw about 100 miles an hour. Hit it in the biggest part of the ballpark. You always remember those good things! I had two .300 years. One year, I was a little higher than Williams, and I always used to kid him, "Well, Bush, I out-hit you."

Mel's wife had worked as a secretary, but after marriage she stayed home to raise their family. The Parnells have three daughters and a son, Mel Jr., an orthopedic surgeon. All four offspring work in the medical field. "My oldest daughter's a nutritionist. The second oldest daughter's a nurse anesthetist. The youngest one's a critical care nurse, who works in intensive care. They just took to that for some reason. The youngest daughter had a background in accounting. She went into the accounting field and she didn't like it. She came home and said she felt like she'd like to be a nurse, and I said, 'Well, if that's what you want, let's go for it,'—and she did.

Mel Jr. was always interested in baseball, a left-hand pitcher, too. He played in high school, in Legion ball, in college, but from his freshman year in high school had his heart set on becoming a doctor.

Adversity has dogged Parnell in later years. He's suffered a stroke, had some heart trouble, beaten back cancer, and got a bad back—on top of which he lost his house and two others he owned to Hurricane Katrina. Fortunately, he was well-insured and has taken it all philosophically. As he told the Associated Press in 2005, "It could be worse."

Sources

Interviews with Mel Parnell done December 31, 1998, and October 13, 2006.

JOHNNY PESKY *by Bill Nowlin*

G	AB	R	H	2B	3B	HR	RBI	BB	SO	BA	OBP	SLG	SB	HBP
143	565	124	159	26	6	3	55	99	32	.281	.394	.365	3	6

Johnny Pesky's career got off to an unparalleled start, and could have propelled him into the Hall of Fame had World War II not pulled three prime years out. Pesky set a rookie record with 205 hits his freshman year (1942) but then served in the Navy for the next three years. When he came back, he twice more he produced over 200 hits, in the Red Sox pennant-winning year of 1946 and in 1947. Had he managed over 200 hits for each of his three missing years, there is every possibility this lifetime .307 hitter could have made the Hall.

Born John Michael Paveskovich in Portland, Oregon on September 27, 1919, Johnny Pesky (he changed his name legally in 1947) was the son of Croatian immigrants. His father Jakov never did really understand baseball, but he and Johnny's mother Marija were both supportive of their middle of three sons when he took to hanging around the Portland Beavers ballpark located a few blocks from the family home. Johnny was just one of the kids around the park, but groundskeeper Rocky Benevento invited him in and put him to work. Before too long, Johnny was one of the visitors' clubhouse kids—and clearly recalls hanging up the laundry of Pacific Coast League players only a year or two older than himself—players with names like Ted Williams and Bobby Doerr.

Johnny had an older brother Anthony, a younger brother Vincent—who spent a little bit of time in the

Yankees' system—and three sisters: Anica (Ann), Milica (Millie) and Danica (Dee.) Jakov worked in the sawmills until asthma forced him to retire. The older children took jobs; Vincent was the youngest and Johnny next-to-youngest. There was enough money coming in that it freed up the two boys to play some baseball.

From an early age, Johnny was doing everything he could to better himself at baseball. The young middle infielder also played American Legion ball, and on a number of city teams in Portland, as well as on some semipro teams. Before he'd graduated from Lincoln High School in Portland, he spent the summer of 1937 with the Bend Elks in the town of Bend, Oregon and led the league with a .543 average. The team won the state league title. Both the summers of 1938 and 1939 were spent with the Silverton Red Sox. Both the Bend and Silverton teams were summer league teams associated with local timber companies. Surprisingly, Boston Red Sox owner Tom Yawkey owned the Silver Falls Timber Company, so Johnny was actually with the Red Sox (albeit the Silverton Red Sox) even before Boston's scout Earl Johnson signed him. Twice Johnny was part of a Northwest team that went to Wichita and competed nationally. The Silverton team won 34 games and lost two, and sometimes played exhibition games against touring teams like the House of David aggregation and the Negro League Kansas City Monarchs.

Johnny was offered $2500 as a bonus by the St. Louis Cardinals, but signed with Boston for $500, because Johnson had so impressed Johnny's parents. They felt he'd look out for Johnny if he signed with the Red Sox. Johnson had offered an additional $1000 if Johnny stayed in the organization for two years. His pay was $150 per month, and the Sox sent him the full thousand after just his first year.

Johnny's first year in pro ball, after signing with Boston, was 1940 in Rocky Mount, North Carolina, playing for the Rocky Mount Red Sox of the Piedmont League, under manager Heinie Manush, who Johnny credits as a major influence. Johnny hit a club-leading .325. He had 55 runs batted in but, ever the table-setter, scored 114 times. Pesky led the league with 187 hits and 16 triples. That .325 average placed him third in the league.

In 1941, Pesky progressed from Class B ball in Rocky Mount to Louisville where he played for the Colonels, again hitting .325. Louisville was a Double A team in the American Assocation, managed by Bill Burwell. Pesky hit for precisely the same average—.325, and once again led the league in hits, this time with 195. He won the MVP

Mr. Red Sox, Johnny Pesky.

award in the American Association for 1941.

By year's end, he was bound for Boston, offered $4000 for his first year's salary. Johnny joined the Sox for spring training just three months after Pearl Harbor. War loomed large over all of baseball, and during Johnny's rookie year; he spent three evenings a week beginning in May taking classroom for the United States Navy where he was in training to become a Naval aviator, in the same program as teammate Ted Williams. Pesky won the shortstop spot in spring training and was assigned number 6. Despite the need to balance baseball with Naval training, Johnny Pesky finished the season with a .331 batting average, second only to Ted Williams (.356) in the American League. He led the league in sacrifice hits. There was no "rookie of the year" award yet. That same year, The Sporting News named Johnny the shortstop on All Star Major League team. Johnny came in third in MVP voting, behind Joe Gordon and Ted Williams.

Tom Yawkey had his own prize for Pesky. At season's end, there was a $5000 bonus for the rookie shortstop—enough to buy his parents a home in Portland. Johnny Pesky never forgot Tom Yawkey's generosity at a time when Johnny was off to military service, perhaps never to return. Yawkey won fierce loyalty from many of his players; with gestures like this, one can understand why.

WWII took three years out of Johnny's baseball career, but while in the Navy he met his future wife, Ruth Hickey. She was a WAVE who Johnny met while serving as an Operations officer in Atlanta. Ruthie and Johnny remained very happily married for more than 60 years. In 1953, they adopted a five-month old son through Catholic Charities—David Pesky, who was born in December 1952. Like a lot of ballplayers, Johnny had many opportunities to play baseball during the war and even played in the AL vs. NL All-Star Game at Furlong Field, Honolulu in 1945.

In 1946, the war over, Johnny and the Red Sox won the pennant, and took the fight right down to the 9th inning of the seventh game of the World Series against the St. Louis Cardinals. Johnny hit safely a league-leading 208 times that season, with a .335 average (third in the league), scoring 115 times (second behind Ted's 142.) The Series was a disappointing one for Pesky, as it was for two other players, named Musial (who batted .222 in Series play) and Williams (.200). And generations of baseball aficionados have heard that "Pesky held the ball" on a key play in the eighth inning of Game Seven, allowing Enos Slaughter to score the winning run from first

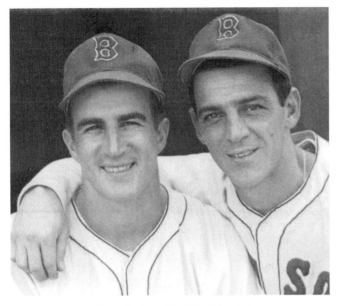

Johnny Pesky with Eddie Pellagrini.

base on Harry Walker's hit to left center. Cardinals 4, Red Sox 3. Films of the play do not show a clear hesitation, and perhaps sportswriter Bob Broeg was right in arguing that credit should go to Slaughter for his "mad dash" around the bases rather than blame being assigned Pesky for what was, at most, momentary surprise that Slaughter was streaking toward the plate rather than secure at third.

The following year, Pesky again collected his 200 hits (207 this time around)—the third year in a row he'd led the league. He and Dom DiMaggio were the table-setters for Ted Williams, and the speedy Pesky was usually discouraged from stretching a single into a double, because a double just meant the other team would walk Ted to fill the unoccupied sack at first. Pesky was a clever infielder as well; three times he pulled the rare hidden ball trick, and would have done so a fourth time had the pitcher not stepped off the rubber at the wrong moment.

The Red Sox came within a game of winning the pennant both in 1948 and 1949, and were only four games behind in 1950. These were some great Red Sox teams. Pesky's place, though, never seemed secure—a strange spot to be in for a top-ranking shortstop. When Johnny joined the team for spring training in '48, he was unsure where he'd be playing, since Boston had acquired Vern Stephens from the St. Louis Browns and it looked like Billy Goodman—another infielder—would make the team. Stephens contributed 137 RBI in '48; clearly manager Joe McCarthy's decision to play him proved wise. (Stephens led the league in RBI in '49 and '50. Goodman stuck, and hit .310. In 1950, he won the AL batting title with a .354 average—with a bit of an assist from Pesky. Johnny approached 1950 manager Steve O'Neill late in the season and offered to take himself out of the lineup so that Goodman could accumulate the necessary at-bats to qualify.)

The problem was an embarrassment of riches. There were just too many good hitters on these Red Sox teams. Johnny Pesky's average fell off sharply in 1948, down to .281. Almost certainly part of the reason was that McCarthy slotted Stephens in at short, and shuffled Pesky over to third. He put a brave "team face" on it, but being asked to learn a new position was unsettling. So, too, was the pay cut Joe Cronin imposed on him after the 1947 season. All he'd done was led the league in hits for each of his first three years, but Cronin cut his $20,000 pay down to $17,500 for 1948. "They asked me how many home runs I hit and how many runs I had knocked in," Johnny explained fifty years later. This was certainly a discouraging situation, and Pesky did pop a career-high three home runs in 1948. He may have been pressing more than a little.

1949 saw a bit of a rebound, his average back up to .306 and, earning an even 100 walks, elevated his on-base percentage to .408. Johnny, always a team booster, allowed, "What a lucky guy I am. Instead of wearing these shoes, I'd probably be shining them for some other guy in the Coast League." There were endless rumors, though, about trades said to feature Pesky. From time to time, he admits, these rumored trades proved distracting for him.

The 1950 season was a tremendous year offensively for Boston. Pesky hit .312, walked 104 times and boosted his OBP to a solid .437. His fielding at third base drew frequent accolades in the Boston press. Scoring 112 runs, he joined teammate Ted Williams as the only other player to have scored 100 or more runs each of his first six seasons of major league ball. This was the year Pesky, in effect, took himself out of the lineup so that Billy Goodman could have a shot at the batting title. Boston Herald sportswriter Bill Cunningham wrote, "The sporting part about his gesture is that he made it for the man who took the job away from him." Years later, in 1985, the *Lynn Sunday Post* editorialized that Johnny Pesky led the majors in "Most Friends."

By 1951, though, the bloom was off the rose, and when the Marines called Williams back in 1952 to fly combat in Korea, the golden days were gone. There were signs that Pesky was slowing a bit. He only stole two bases each in '50 and '51, down somewhat from earlier years. He maybe wasn't getting to as many balls as an infielder as he had earlier. Lou Boudreau had been brought in by Yawkey, and was projected as the shortstop. Even though Pesky's career .316 average at the time ranked him fifth among active players, here he was—once again—having to fight for a spot. Johnny got off to a slow start, but wound up the season at .313. Boudreau hit .267.

Johnny's 1952 season began poorly, and he was hardly ever used by Boudreau, now the manager and seeking a "youth movement" in Boston. Hampered by injuries,

Johnny being taken for a ride by Vern Stephens, 1951.

he was hitting a pitiful .149 when he was traded to the Tigers in a monster deal. Boston sent five players to Detroit, a full 20% of the 25-man roster. In exchange for Pesky, Walt Dropo, Fred Hatfield, Don Lenhardt, and Bill Wight, they got four Tiger players (Hoot Evers, George Kell, Johnny Lipon, and Dizzy Trout). Johnny pulled it together a bit and hit .254 for Detroit. 1952 truly was a sub-par season.

He cracked 300 at-bats in 1953, and hit .292 but he was in decline. After appearing in 20 games for the Tigers in '54, Detroit traded him to Washington, where he finished his playing career with a .246 mark between the two teams.

Johnny Pesky wound up his major league career with a .307 average, and an on-base percentage of .394.

His life in baseball, though, was just entering a new phase. Johnny coached with the Denver Bears in the Yankees organization in 1955, then managed five different minor league teams for the Detroit Tigers from 1956–1960.

Most of his 60-plus years in baseball, however, have been with the Red Sox. After his years with Detroit, the Red Sox called him back following the 1960 season. Johnny managed the Sox' Seattle minor league team in 1961 and 1962, and managed the big league Boston Red Sox in '63 and '64. As manager, he brought some fire to the position, after years of yawns under the likes of Pinky Higgins. Some felt he was a little too fiery; he had a few run-ins with "Dr. Strangeglove" Dick Stuart, who committed 29 errors at first in 1963—but hit 42 homers and

had collected a league-leading 118 runs batted in. He also clashed with Carl Yastrzemski a number of times, and Carl made clear his discontent. As much as anything that may explain Yawkey's refusal to find a position for Pesky within the organization when Higgins finally dismissed him late in 1964. Yaz was like a son to Yawkey, and Higgins was one of Yawkey's drinking buddies. Pesky had originally been brought in as manager despite Higgins' opposition.

When relieved as manager, Pesky hooked on with the Pirates and served as a major league coach for two years, while managing the Pirates' Columbus club for a third.

From 1969–1974, he served as a broadcaster for Boston, working with Ken Coleman and Ned Martin as a color commentator. Though he worked hard at improving himself, he never felt comfortable except during rain delays when he could really stretch out with stories about players from his era.

During the same period, Pesky called on clients for the Sox, initiating a fledgling marketing department for the club, working in tandem with former catcher Bob Montgomery. Johnny Pesky probably appeared at more banquets and events around New England than any other figure in Red Sox history.

He's also one of the only people in baseball to have a part of a ballpark named after him. Fenway's famed "Pesky Pole"—the right field foul pole—was given the nickname by Sox broadcaster Mel Parnell. A former teammate, Parnell was poking a little fun at Johnny's lack of power—he hit just 17 home runs, and only six at Fenway—every one of which went out past the right field foul pole, now the shortest distance for a home run in major league ball.

From 1975–1984, he was first base coach under Sox skippers Darrell Johnson, Don Zimmer and Ralph Houk. From 1985 to the present, Johnny has been a special assignment instructor, evaluating players at lower levels in the Red Sox system, but also working with generations of Red Sox players at spring training and at Fenway. As late as 2003, Johnny Pesky—"Mr. Red Sox" in the eyes of decades of New Englanders—could be found on the field at Fenway before games, hitting fungoes to infielders and generally serving as a goodwill ambassador throughout the region.

It was a good year in 2004. Not only did Johnny enjoy some extra attention when his biography *Mr. Red Sox* was published, but he was able to revel in the Red Sox finally attaining the Holy Grail of Baseball, a world championship. For three years he proudly wore the championship ring the Red Sox presented him on the day that he and Carl Yastrzemski walked across the field to hoist the 2004 World Series banner on the Fenway Park flagpole. After the Red Sox won the Series again in 2007, he sported a second companion ring.

Johnny Pesky is a charter member of the Boston Red Sox Hall of Fame.

Sources

Most of the information for this article was gleaned from many hours of conversation with Johnny Pesky, who gave unsparingly of his time as I worked on the book *Mr. Red Sox: The Johnny Pesky Story* published by Rounder Books in 2004. In addition to the newspapers cited in the text, I consulted *Total Baseball* (7th edition) for statistics, and the microfilmed records of the Boston *Globe* newspaper for the years of Pesky's career. Other information was provided by personal interviews with Ken Coleman, Bob Montgomery, and Vincent Paveskovich.

NEILL SHERIDAN *by Bill Nowlin*

G	AB	R	H	2B	3B	HR	RBI	BB	SO	BA	OBP	SLG	SB	HBP
2	1	0	0	0	0	0	0	0	1	.000	.000	.000	0	0

Neill "Wild Horse" Sheridan was a classic "cup of coffee" major leaguer who saw brief duty in just two major league games, with the Red Sox in 1948.

Neill was born November 20, 1921 in Sacramento, CA. His father, Sol, worked for the California State Employment Service, and the family lived in Berkeley. His mother, Helen, went to her hometown of Sacramento for the birth of her son, but rejoined Sol, and young Neill was raised in the Bay Area. When Neil was ready for high school, Sol Sheridan was transferred back to the state capital and Neill went to Sacramento High School. He excelled in football at halfback and earned a scholarship to the University of San Francisco.

As a youngster, he'd always played baseball. "I've been playing since I was five years old. [Our family] were friends with Myril Hoag, who played with the Yankees. He got a ball for my brother Bill and me, from Babe Ruth and Lou Gehrig, and Hoag of course. I was about eight or ten years old. Hoag was from Sacramento. We were living in Berkeley at the time, but our families were friendly." The Yankees became his favorite team.

Bill was two years younger, and both played on Berkeley playgrounds. Neill recalled, "We didn't have any television or anything else. We had lots of fun and we played a lot of games." Fun was one thing, but by the time it came to high school, Neil began to take part in school athletics. He went out for baseball at Sacramento High, but notes ironically that there was a very strong Legion team feeding players to the school at the time and he couldn't make the team. He went out for track instead. And, as noted, he earned a football scholarship to USF. It wasn't the most structured program. "At that time, USF didn't have any schedule or anything like that. Mostly the younger part of my career was probably semipro. I could play and there were always a lot of teams around San Francisco in those days, so I played a little bit of that."

Wild Horse Sheridan with the Sacramento ballclub, 1954. Courtesy of Neill Sheridan.

He'd just turned 20 at the time of the attack on Pearl Harbor. "I enlisted in the Marine Corps with the rest of our class. There were probably 12 or 13 of us." One of whom was Windy McCall, a left-handed pitcher who also appeared briefly with the Red Sox. McCall was in the class behind Neill.

Sheridan got a medical discharge from the Marines because of asthma. The discharge happened even before boot camp, when Neill suffered an asthma attack. He returned to the recruiting office, but they wouldn't take him because of his asthmatic condition. A visit to the draft board got him nowhere, either, so he went to work for the Kaiser shipyard in Richmond, California, working in the employment office, doing the same sort of work as his father did for the state.

The asthma didn't hold him back from baseball, though. There was a shortage of players during the war years, and the head of one of the unions Sheridan dealt with was a friend of 11-year major league veteran Lefty O'Doul. This led to a tryout with the San Francisco Seals, and the Seals signed him, in time to get one at-bat in 1943. In 1944, he played most of the year at Chattanooga, though, batting .326 in 236 times at bat. He joined the Seals again later in the season, getting in 150 at-bats and hitting .293 over 42 games. Though ineligible for the Pacific Coast League finals, he hit .444 (12 for 27) against Oakland during the semi-final series.

Throughout, he played the outfield, though he'd begun semipro ball as an infielder. "I started out as a shortstop. I picked off a few people in the seats, and so I figured I better play in the outfield."

The right-handed Sheridan was the first player to sign his 1945 contract with the Seals and signed onto marriage to Elizabeth Frank the same week. Ms. Frank was the daughter of Utah's state treasurer. Sheridan played exclusively for the Seals from 1945 through the 1947 season, with averages of .290, .269, and .286, showing some extra power in 1947 (16 homers, matching the total of all his prior years) and 95 RBIs. It was while with the Seals he picked up the nickname "Wild Horse," dubbed that by an older player named Ray Harrell who played for Seattle. "The way I ran, I guess my legs kind of went askew."

Sheridan understands that the New York Giants sent as many as four or five players to the Seals to get an option on his contract. A June 1945 news story indicated that the Giants could exercise an option on him for $30,000, but they never pulled the trigger. Joe King, writing in March 1945, may have indicated part of the reason. "Sheridan is not a screwball, but he is on the temperamental side, according to coast information. He had to ride the bench several times last year as chastisement. He is fast, daring, colorful, and, at 22, is a wonderful prospect. The Giants will know better about him by August."

Sheridan played in the PCL All-Star Game in both 1946 (a home run, a double, and five RBIs) and 1947 (two singles).

The day before the end of the 1947 Sox season, Boston dealt what *The Sporting News* termed "plenty of cabbage" and two players to be named later (Tommy Fine and Strick Shofner were named late in October) to San Francisco to obtain Sheridan in a September 25 transaction.

It wasn't as though the Red Sox needed a left fielder, but Sheridan had somehow caught the eye of the Red Sox and they worked out a way to bring him into the Red Sox organization. A later issue of *The Sporting News* reported rumors that the signing might presage Dom DiMaggio's departure from the Red Sox. Sheridan himself says, "I never did figure out why they signed me, because they had five established big league players to start with. We ended up in a playoff for the pennant."

Sheridan went to spring training with the big league ball club. He opened the season with the big league club, renting an apartment in Boston for himself, his wife, and their daughter and infant son. About a week after they moved in, in early May, he was optioned back to the Coast League, to Seattle. With Williams, DiMaggio, Spence, Mele, and Moses, "they figured out that they didn't need six outfielders." *The Sporting News* asked him how he'd gotten along with manager Joe McCarthy, and Sheridan said that McCarthy had only spoken three words to him all spring: "Nice going, kid" after he'd thrown out Dom DiMaggio taking a big turn at first base during an intrasquad game.

Sheridan had a very good year for Seattle, hitting .312, hitting 17 homers, and driving in 82.

In the final two weeks of the 1948 season, Sheridan was summoned to Boston. Sam Mele had hurt his right ankle sliding into third base. X-rays proved negative, but Mele was expected to be out for a week. The Red Sox at the time held just a one-game lead over the Yankees with 14 games to play. Sheridan's debut came on September 19. It was in the second game of a doubleheader in Detroit.

The Tigers won the first game, 4–3, in 12 innings. The score was 6–6 after six in the second game, and Wild Horse Sheridan was put in to run for Bobby Doerr when Doerr reached base but strained a leg muscle. No one knocked him in, though, and the Tigers scored twice in the bottom of the seventh to win a game called after eight innings on account of darkness.

One week later, he came in to pinch hit for Boo Ferriss in the top of the ninth, facing Tommy Byrne of the Yankees. New York had a 6–2 lead. "The first pitch Byrne threw me, I hit out of the ballpark foul. But in spring training the year before that, we played against the Yankees and I hit against Byrne and I got a couple of hits off him that day, so I guess McCarthy had an idea maybe I might get a hit off him if I was lucky. I was called out on strikes. Birdie Tebbetts was on second, and I asked him afterward, 'Was that a strike, Birdie?' And he said, 'No.' But that's the way it goes."

Sheridan stuck with the team, staying right through the playoff game against the Indians. He'd done well against Gene Bearden in the Coast League, but the Indians built up such a big lead early on that the game felt like a lost cause. The season over, Sheridan was sent back to Seattle in time for the PCL playoffs, but "Oakland wouldn't let me play because I wasn't there in time…they could have let me play if they'd given their permission, and consequently Seattle didn't win the playoffs."

Seattle was home for Sheridan in 1949, a little bit of a decline but still a respectable .259 with 14 homers and 67 RBIs. It was back to San Francisco for 1950, where he hit .288 with 12 homers and 54 RBIs in 319 at-bats. 1951 was a year he split between the Seals (.204) and Minneapolis (.306.) "When Willie Mays went to the Giants, I went to Minneapolis and took his place."

The next year was an off-year, Sheridan hitting just .219 in 1952 in limited action for Toronto in the International League and .221 in the second half for Texas League San Antonio. He played for Oakland leading off 1953, but "Oakland ran out of money after about the first month of the season, and so I ended up in Sacramento and I played there for two years. That was about the end of my career." But not before having at least one more very good night. "One night in Sacramento, one of the fellows was supposed to run against a horse. Well, he pulled a muscle or something so he couldn't do it, so I ran against the horse and beat the horse. It ran between stakes, you know. It was fairly easy for me beating the horse, because the horse had a harder time going around the stanchions. The same night, I had a couple of home runs. I was pretty proud of myself that night. I pulled a hamstring the second year I was in Sacramento and they released me."

He hit .293 in '53, but only .153 in 22 PCL games for Sacramento/San Francisco in 1954. Sheridan moved to play for the Victoria (BC) Tyees in the Western International League. He played outfield until the Victoria franchise folded on August 2. Sheridan didn't miss a beat; he flew to Vancouver, signed as a free agent, and played in the August 3 in a Caps uniform. For Victoria/ Vancouver, Sheridan appeared in 95 games, driving in 76 runs and wound up his pro career batting .308 on the year. "Actually, I did pretty well in Vancouver and we won the championship [but] there wasn't any prognosis that I was going to end up back in the big leagues. I went to work in the retail grocery business, and I retired there in 1982. Black's Market, Orinda, California. We had a pretty good-sized supermarket and the fellow that I worked for put me in charge of the liquor department, and I worked doing that and the general run of things you do in a grocery store."

He thinks back to his brief time in major league ball a bit wistfully: "I think if I'd have gone to a team that really needed somebody—the Philadelphia Phillies or Athletics, or the Washington Senators...." Though a Yankees fan as a youngster, though, he remains a Red Sox fan today.

Sheridan's son, who was a bit of an artist, died in the middle 1990s, but his wife and daughter remain, and he enjoys three granddaughters and five great-grandchildren. He enjoys hearing from the Red Sox alumni office and was very pleased when Boston finally won it all in 2004. "I think it was wonderful, especially for the fans that have been so loyal."

Sources

Interview by Bill Nowlin done February 26, 2006
Unattributed news stories in Sheridan's Hall of Fame player file.
King, Joe. "Sheridan, Coast Flycatcher, Adds Color to Giants" unidentified news clipping in Hall of Fame player file.
The Sporting News

STAN SPENCE *by Mark Armour*

G	AB	R	H	2B	3B	HR	RBI	BB	SO	BA	OBP	SLG	SB	HBP
114	391	71	92	17	4	12	61	82	33	.235	.368	.391	0	0

Stan Spence had the misfortune of being a young outfielder for the Red Sox at a time when the team was developing Ted Williams and Dom DiMaggio. A trade to the Washington Senators gave him his opportunity to shine, and his five years in the nation's capital landed him on four All-Star teams as one of the best players in the American League. A late start cost him a long career, but he had plenty of thrills during his time in "The Show."

Stanley Orville Spence was born on March 20, 1915, in South Portsmouth, Kentucky, nestled across the Ohio River from Portsmouth, Ohio. He was the oldest of four boys born to Vernon and Catherine Spence. Vernon worked in a shoe factory, and Stan himself started in the factory making $14 a week. Having established a local reputation as a fine ballplayer, he was recruited by another company in Portsmouth, where he played ball for the industrial team for an additional dollar a week. While playing with the Portsmouth team, he signed in 1935 with the Boston Red Sox through the efforts of scout Newt Hunter.

A left-handed hitting and throwing outfielder, Spence began his professional career with Eau Claire, Wisconsin, of the Northern League, batting .281 with 9 home runs in 121 games. The next year he moved on to the Piedmont League with Rocky Mount, North Carolina, where he hit

Stan Spence captured in 1941.

.315 in 138 games. After this fine season he ascended to the highest rung of the minor leagues, joining the Minneapolis Millers of the American Association.

Spence spent two years in Minnesota as one of the best players in the league. A solid 5-feet-10, 180-pound centerfielder, he hit .321 and .322 with the Millers, hitting 19 home runs in the latter year. His accomplishments were somewhat overlooked in 1938, understandably overshadowed by teammate Ted Williams' Triple Crown season.

Despite his growing résumé, Spence spent 1939 with Louisville, which had replaced Minneapolis as the Red Sox' highest minor league affiliate. The Boston club was filled with outfielders at this time, with Williams, Doc Cramer, and Joe Vosmik manning posts in 1939, and the arrivals of Lou Finney and Dom DiMaggio in 1940. Spence hit .289 with Louisville in 1939 and .256 over the first 11 games in 1940.

In early June, the 25-year-old Spence was finally promoted to the major leagues. He hit .279 in 68 at-bats in a reserve role over the remainder of the 1940 season, and .232 in 203 at-bats the next year. DiMaggio had become a star on both offense and defense, and Spence was the odd man out. After the season, the Red Sox dealt him with pitcher Jack Wilson to the Washington Senators for pitcher Ken Chase and outfielder Johnny Welaj. Spence was an afterthought in this deal, but turned out to be the best player involved. It proved to be the best thing that happened to Spence in his baseball career.

Senators manager Bucky Harris named Spence his starting center fielder. A month into the season, Spence was hitting over .400, and he did not seemed surprised by it. "I was good enough to play regularly in that Boston outfield, but they kept me on the bench," Spence related to *The Sporting News*. "The few times they played me, I was taken out when I started to hit my stride. I think I'm as good a player as Dominic DiMaggio."

Spence stayed in the batting race all season, finishing third behind Ted Williams and Johnny Pesky with his .323 average. He also recorded 203 hits and a league-leading 15 triples. Local observers considered Spence, a fan favorite, the best defensive center fielder in Washington since Sam West a decade earlier.

Stan struggled to start the 1943 season, hovering near .200 over the first two months, and not striking his first home run until July 3. In late July he was benched briefly, but he finished strong—hitting .267 with 12 home runs and 88 RBIs, while continuing to shine in center field. He batted in the middle of the order during all his years with the Senators, usually hitting third, fourth, or fifth. The left-handed hitter was hurt by his home park, hitting just two home runs in Griffith Stadium all year, and only 12 during his five years there.

Stan rebounded in 1944 to hit .316 with 18 home runs and 100 RBIs, leading the league in RBIs for much of the summer before finishing fourth behind Vern Stephens. He also had an astonishing 29 outfield assists. Though the club finished in last place for the first time since 1909, Spence was held blameless. "The only player on the club who has played good ball," wrote Shirley Povich in *The Sporting News*, "aside from some of the pitchers, is Stan Spence." Povich called Spence the best outfielder in the league.

Spence stayed out of the military for most of the war because he was married with two children, and he was nearly 27 when the United States entered the war. Finally reclassified in early 1945, Stan spent the next several months in the Army, mainly playing baseball at a base on Bainbridge Island, near Seattle.

After rebuffing overtures from the outlaw Mexican League in the spring of 1946, Spence returned to the Senators and took right up where he left off in 1946, hitting .292 with 16 home runs and 50 doubles in 152 games. The remarkably consistent center fielder had his usual fine season in 1947, hitting 16 home runs with a .279 batting average.

In December, the Senators traded Spence back to the Red Sox for infielder Al Kozar and outfielder Leon Culberson. The Senators felt they had a surplus of outfielders and needed infield help, and Kozar had hit .316

for Spokane in 1946 and .340 for New Orleans in 1947. The Red Sox were high on Kozar themselves, but Bobby Doerr blocked his path to the big leagues. Bill Veeck was bitter at Spence's trade to the Red Sox. "I have tried to get Spence the last two years, and I offered Griffith a much better deal," complained the Indians' owner. "I can't mention the players' names because I still have them. I'll assure you it was a better proposition than the one son-in-law Cronin gave him."

Spence had had a very productive five years with the Senators, regularly placing in the top ten in numerous offensive categories, and being named to four All-Star teams. He got two hits in the 1944 game, while also gunning out Phil Cavaretta trying to score on a fly ball. He knocked in the winning run in the 1947 game on a pinch-hit single, finishing 3 for 5 in the three games he played. Over his years in the capital, Spence had fine batting averages supplemented by high walk totals and midrange power, a very valuable package of skills for a good defensive center fielder. Washington's Griffith Stadium sapped power from most left-handed hitters, especially Spence— during his five years there he hit 11 home runs at home and 55 on the road, including 16 road homers in 1944 and 14 in 1946. Over the five-year period, Spence was one of the very best players in the league, and it is no wonder the Red Sox regretted their earlier deal and wanted him back.

With center field still well-manned by Dom DiMaggio, new Boston skipper Joe McCarthy worked Spence at first base in the spring. "I know what he can do in the outfield," reasoned McCarthy, "for I recall several bitter moments in Yankee Stadium at the hands of Spence."

The 33-year-old Spence ended up playing 114 games in 1948, mostly in right field, but did not hit nearly as well as he had in Washington. He finished at .235, though with 82 walks and 12 home runs. The powerful Red Sox twice hit three straight home runs that season, the first team to accomplish the feat twice, and both times Spence was involved in the threesome. Spence began the year hitting fourth in the order behind Ted Williams, though he soon fell down the order behind Vern Stephens and Bobby Doerr.

After just seven games in a reserve role in early 1949, in which he was 3 for 20, Spence was dealt along with a reported $100,000 to the St. Louis Browns for Al Zarilla. Spence ended up playing 104 games for the Browns, and hit .245 with 13 home runs.

In February 1950 Spence was sold to the Los Angeles Angels of the Pacific Coast League. He hit just .228 with 22 home runs for the Angels, and was benched briefly in September for failing to hustle. The next April he was sold to Springfield (Massachusetts) of the International League, but his .204 average in 25 games got him sent to Lynchburg of the Piedmont League, where he hit .258 over 87 games. After a brief partial season with the

American Association's Toledo club in 1952 (.297 in 21 games), Spence walked away from the game. In his last contest, on May 8, he hit a two-run home run, but the next day decided to return home.

After his career, Spence retired to Kinston, North Carolina, his wife's hometown. He had married Mildred Harper in 1936 when he was playing at Rocky Mount. The couple had three children: Carol, Jennie, and Stanley, Jr.

Stan was involved with a number of businesses over the years. He had a septic tank business when he retired, and he later opened a boys' camp in the Blue Ridge Mountains with former Red Sox teammate Herb Hash, and worked for the Gardner Construction Co. for many years. Spence loved to hunt and fish, enjoyed dancing, and was a member of the United Methodist Church in Kinston.

A heavy smoker, Spence died of emphysema on January 9, 1983, in Lenoir Memorial Hospital. According to his widow, Stan Spence lived a happy and full life, though he still carried a bit of a chip on his shoulder about his lack of opportunity in his early years with the Red Sox. He was a proud man to the very end. He is buried in Maplewood Cemetery in Kinston.

Sources

In researching this story, the author relied heavily on *The Sporting News* historical archive accessed at paperofrecord.com, and Spence's clipping file at the National Baseball Hall of Fame Library. I obtained his *Kinston Free Press* obituary (January 10, 1983) with help from the Neuse Regional Public Library in Kinston. I spoke with Spence's widow, Mildred Harper Spence, on March 13, 2007.

VERN STEPHENS *by Mark Armour*

G	AB	R	H	2B	3B	HR	RBI	BB	SO	BA	OBP	SLG	SB	HBP
155	635	114	171	25	8	29	137	77	56	.269	.350	.471	1	2

The 1940s witnessed a special group of major league shortstops, including the likes of Lou Boudreau, Phil Rizzuto, Marty Marion, Pee Wee Reese and Johnny Pesky. During his own career, Vern "Junior" Stephens was considered to be as good or better than any of his illustrious peers, yet within a few years after his retirement, he had been largely forgotten, remembered mostly as a plodding one-dimensional slugger. He was much more than that. Yes, he was a three-time RBI champion, but he was also a fine fielding shortstop, an eight-time all star, and a very popular teammate on some of the era's most successful teams. History ought to remember him.

Vernon Decatur Stephens Jr. was born on October 23, 1920 in McAlister, New Mexico, to Vernon Sr. and the former Grace McMullen. Vern Sr. was born in the Oklahoma territory, and was a farmer in Ft. Smith, Arkansas when he met his future wife, Grace, a schoolteacher and devout Southern Baptist. They soon married, and in 1920, with a one-year-old son, Harry, and a second on the way, Vernon and Grace decided to resettle in the west. They had gotten as far as New Mexico when Vern was born prematurely. The Stephens family eventually settled in Long Beach, California.

Vern Sr., or "Pop," landed a job as a supervisor at a local dairy, which got him out of bed at 3:30 a.m. but also gave him ample opportunity to play basketball and

Vern Stephens.

baseball with his sons when he got home. (Later Pop umpired for several years in the minor leagues.) Harry and Vern played baseball passionately as children. Harry, a pitcher, later signed a contract with the Browns, but hurt his arm before reporting to the minor leagues and never pitched again.

Vern entered American Legion baseball at age 13, and played shortstop on the 1936 Southern California champions. One teammate was Bob Lemon, later a star pitcher for the Cleveland Indians, who remained a close friend for the rest of Vern's life. Stephens went to Long Beach Polytechnic High School, while Lemon was across town at Wilson High School. Vern's high school teammates included future major leaguers Chuck Stevens and Bobby Sturgeon. Vern was a natural athlete-he also played basketball and swam-but he was quite small (5'5" and 120 pounds) in high school. In his late teens, he grew to 5'10", and ended up a powerful 185 pounds. Vern attributed his upper body strength to his swimming.

Vern was a very good student in high school-receiving all A's and B's-thanks largely to his mother, the former teacher, who tutored both of her sons after school. After graduating from high school in 1937, Vern attended Long Beach Junior College for a year and hit .522 for their baseball team. There he met Harriet Bernice Hood, who had dated Bob Lemon in high school. Vern and Bernice (she disliked the name Harriet, and never used it) were soon constantly together, and they married in 1940.

After his one junior college season, Stephens signed with the St. Louis Browns for a $500 bonus. The Red Sox and Indians also expressed interest, but Vern's father saw a quicker path to the majors with the lowly Browns. Vern played sparingly at two minor league stops-first Springfield (Illinois) of the Class B Three-I League and then Johnstown (Pennsylvania) of the Class C Middle Atlantic League-in 1938.

The next year he dominated the Kitty League with Mayfield (Kentucky), leading the circuit with 123 RBIs and a .361 batting average while hitting 30 home runs. After another RBI title with San Antonio of the Texas League in 1940, manager Marty McManus, a former big league shortstop himself, called Stephens the "best short-stop prospect I have ever seen." One more excellent minor league season, with Toledo of the American Association (14 home runs, .281), earned him a recall late in 1941 and a shot at a job with the Browns the following spring.

However, predictions for his stardom were hardly unanimous. His Toledo manager, Fred Haney, supposedly told Browns skipper Luke Sewell that "Stephens will never play shortstop in the major leagues as long as he has a hole in his ass." By the middle of spring training, Sewell had come to disagree, saying, "That kid out there is going to be the kingpin of our defense-and if he comes through as a hitter we're going to cause a lot of trouble this summer."

He came through as a hitter. As a rookie Stephens batted .294 with 14 home runs and 92 RBI, as the Browns achieved their best record in 20 years. Stephens finished fourth in the 1942 MVP balloting, one slot behind fellow rookie shortstop Johnny Pesky of Boston. He led the league with 42 errors, but contemporary accounts make no mention of his defense being a problem. He was only 21, and one of the bright young stars in baseball.

A strong man with a powerful upper body, Stephens did not look like a shortstop. If he had less range than some of his slighter contemporaries, he could play deeper because of his great throwing arm. A right-handed hitter, he had a spread stance, slightly open, and stood deep in the batter's box.

In early 1943, Stephens re-aggravated a knee he had hurt in the minor leagues, causing him to flunk his army physical. The injury caused the Browns to consider moving him to the outfield, where they used him eleven times. At the plate he turned in another fine year—22 home runs, 91 RBIs, and a .289 average. The Browns slipped from third to seventh place, but Stephens still finished ninth in the MVP balloting. Later reclassified as 1-A, he failed the exam again in 1944 and became one of the better players to remain in the major leagues through the entire war. During off-seasons he worked at a shipyard in Long Beach.

Although his friends and family had always called him Vern or Vernie, he was often referred to as Junior in baseball circles. To confuse things further, his close friends in baseball called him Steve or Stevie.

In 1944 Stephens led his team to its first and only American League pennant, hitting .293 with 20 home runs and 109 RBIs. He moved up to third in the MVP vote behind Detroit pitchers Hal Newhouser and Dizzy Trout, who combined to win 56 games. In both 1943 and 1944 Stephens played all nine innings and batted fourth for the American League in the All-Star game. He was the best player on the best team, and he was just turning 24.

In William Mead's classic book on wartime baseball, *Even the Browns*, he quotes several Browns teammates who were seemingly in awe of Stephens. Mark Christman, the team's third baseman, considered Stephens to be as good a shortstop as Cardinals' star Marty Marion: "not as good hands, but he covered as much ground, and he had an arm like a shotgun." Christman also marveled at Stephens' strength, noting that although he played at Sportsman's Park, a tough park for a right-handed hitter, Stephens could hit the ball the other way onto the pavilion roof in right-center.

A few of his Browns teammates remember Stephens as a considerable partier. Don Gutteridge, his roommate, marveled at "how he did it-go out like he did and then play as well as he did. He was superman." In 1945 he had another carbon copy season—89 RBIs, a .289 average, and a league-leading 24 home runs. The Browns dropped to third place, but Stephens continued to impress the MVP voters, finishing sixth.

After the 1945 season, the reigning home run champ thought he deserved a decent raise from his struggling ballclub. Stephens asked for $17,500, while the Browns offered only $13,000. Rathering than reporting to spring training, Stephens decided to hold out in Long Beach and learn to play golf. The Red Sox offered to deal Johnny Pesky, who had spent the last three seasons in the Navy, and cash to the Browns for Stephens. Manager Sewell vetoed the deal because "Stephens has a stronger arm. He'll throw out more men from the hole. I guess we'll hold on to him."

In the spring of 1946 baseball was jolted by unexpected competition from south of the border. While operating outside the sphere of organized baseball, the Mexican League had been in operation since 1924, never posing a threat to the major leagues. In 1946 this suddenly changed, as industrialist Jorge Pasquel, who was president of the league and also owned two teams, began offering large contracts to the biggest stars in the game, among them Ted Williams, Bob Feller, and Stan Musial. Several quality players, including Mickey Owen and Max Lanier, jumped to the rebel circuit.

Pasquel called the disgruntled Stephens nearly every

day for two weeks, before Vern finally decided that the Mexican League could offer him some leverage. In late March, commissioner Happy Chandler announced that all players who did not return to the United States within ten days would be banned from organized baseball for five years. When Pasquel called the next day, Stephens asked for a five-year $175,000 contract, with all the money up front. He also insisted that he be allowed to break the contract at any time. Pasquel said yes.

The next day Stephens was in Mexico City living at the Pasquel mansion. Stephens had $5,000 sent home to Bernice in Long Beach, and the balance put in a local bank. "They couldn't do enough for me," Stephens later told writer Al Hirshberg. "From the time I got to Mexico until the time I left, they were wonderful to me." Stephens played two games for the Veracruz Blues, recording one hit in eight at-bats.

Within a few days, Stephens was ready to return to the States. Though he never had a bad word to say of his hosts, he later claimed he never intended to stay long-he was just trying to get more money out of the Browns. His father, who could not watch Vern throw his career away, drove with Browns' scout Jack Fournier to Monterrey (where the Blues were playing), found his son, put him in the car, and drove him back over the border. Stephens returned all of the money to Pasquel.

Stephens promptly returned to the Browns, getting back to the United States within Chandler's ten-day deadline. Best of all, the Browns gave Stephens a contract for $17,500, exactly what he had asked for.

In 1946 all of the stars returned from the war, and many observers assumed that Stephens' star would dim. He missed 39 games with assorted injuries that made his power (14 home runs and 64 RBIs, both league highs for shortstops) seem to have slipped, but he hit a career high .307. In 1947, he had another pretty good year with the bat (15 home runs, 83 RBIs, and a .279 average). He turned 27 that October and was rightly considered one of the best players-offensively and defensively-in baseball.

The Browns, on the other hand, had fallen into dire straits. In 1947 ownership spent two million dollars to

Stephens working on his stroke.

buy and renovate Sportsman's Park in St. Louis and to build a new facility for their San Antonio farm club. After drawing only 320,000 fans and finishing last, the Browns had to sell players to recover their huge losses. The demand for Stephens, their best player, was high. The Cleveland Indians were prepared to trade Lou Boudreau and cash for him, but when the story was leaked, Indians fans picketed Cleveland Stadium. Newspapers printed ballots asking fans to vote on the trade of their beloved player-manager, and the result was a landslide for keeping Boudreau. Owner Bill Veeck had promised to abide by the will of the people, so the trade collapsed. In any event, Boudreau was the league's 1948 MVP and led his team to a World Series title.

The Boston Red Sox had long coveted Stephens. They had missed signing him in 1938, and had been trying to trade for him every year since he reached the major leagues. Taking advantage of the Browns struggles, the Red Sox finally got their man, forking over eight players and $385,000 for Stephens, Ellis Kinder, Jack Kramer, and Billy Hitchcock. The deal, announced in two pieces on consecutive days in November 1947, was one of the largest transactions yet consummated.

The Boston press corps was skeptical. Tom Yawkey had purchased the team in 1933 and had spent millions acquiring name players, such as Lefty Grove and Jimmy Foxx, without contending for a pennant. Only when this strategy was abandoned in favor of investing in young talent, such as Ted Williams, Bobby Doerr and Dom DiMaggio, did Boston begin to see competitive teams every year. Stephens was an acknowledged star, all agreed, but a temperamental one who battled management every year for more money.

Not only that, but the Red Sox already had an All-Star shortstop in the popular Pesky, a lifetime .330 hitter who had surpassed 200 hits in his each of his first three major league seasons. The deal was seen as another example of the Red Sox needlessly throwing money around.

The Red Sox also had a brand new manager, Joe McCarthy, who had won seven World Series titles with the New York Yankees. The most interesting dilemma facing McCarthy in the spring of 1948 was which of his star shortstops he would move to third base. The prevalent thinking was that he would move Stephens, a powerfully built man who looked less like a shortstop than the slight Pesky. McCarthy did not announce his intentions until spring training in Sarasota, when he moved Pesky to the hot corner.

David Halberstam wrote in *Summer of '49* that Pesky went to third because he had better hands and was quicker than Stephens. In *Red Sox Century*, Glenn Stout and Richard Johnson's team history, the authors theorize that McCarthy moved Pesky to spite the reporters, many of whom had written that Stephens would play third. Neither theory is plausible. McCarthy was one of history's most successful managers; it is presumptuous to write that he would have made the move unless he thought Stephens was at least Pesky's equal at shortstop.

In a June 1948 story in *Sport* magazine, Harold Kaese wrote of the great relationship between Stephens and his teammates, and that Stephens had "won the battle" for the position because he was one of the best fielding shortstops in baseball. Stephens' defensive statistics were very good, and McCarthy was undoubtedly aware of Stephens' great range and arm. Vern had led the league in assists in 1947, and would again in 1948 and 1949. In the same article, Bobby Doerr said: "[Stephens is] nice to work with like Pesky. They co-operate on pop flies in the sun, and work with you on other plays. Perhaps the best thing that impresses me about Vern is the speed with which he goes across the bag on double plays." In a story written just after Stephens died in 1968, Johnny Pesky said: "I always believed McCarthy did it because Stevie had such a great arm."

In 1948, playing in a friendlier park for his skills and hitting behind several great table setters, Stephens hit 29 home runs and drove in 137 (second in the league to Joe DiMaggio). Though his batting average fell to a career low .269, he established a new high with 77 walks. He finished fourth in the balloting for MVP, behind Boudreau, DiMaggio, and Ted Williams. After several weeks of experimentation, McCarthy eventually settled on Stephens to hit cleanup behind Williams, and that's where he would hit for the remainder of his years in Boston. The Red Sox improved from 83 to 96 wins, but lost a one-game playoff for the pennant to the Indians.

In 1949 Stephens slugged a career-high 39 home runs, a record for shortstops later broken by Ernie Banks, and drove in 159 runs, a total not surpassed by in the major leagues for 50 years, when Cleveland's Manny Ramirez totaled 165 RBIs in 1999. He also batted .290 and walked a career high 101 times. Despite great years from several other players, the Red Sox lost a great pennant race on the last day of the season to the Yankees.

At about this point the baseball media began to turn its back on Stephens. The reasoning is not hard to discern: Stephens was putting up great statistics every year, but the Red Sox were still finishing second. He received one first place vote in the MVP balloting and finished seventh, surprisingly low considering his historic year. Yankee shortstop Phil Rizzuto, for example, hit .275 with no power—he had 94 fewer RBIs than Stephens—yet finished second to Williams in the voting.

In August 1949, Boston writer Al Hirshberg penned an article in *Sport* magazine suggesting that only Cleveland fans of Lou Boudreau would argue against Stephens as the most valuable shortstop in baseball. He did not even mention Rizzuto. Hirshberg also wrote that Stephens was the most popular player on the Red Sox with his teammates, the press, and the fans, an observation also made by other writers of the time.

In 1950 Stephens hit 30 home runs, led the league with 144 RBIs and hit .295. Nevertheless, he finished 25th in the MVP balloting, behind six of his teammates. It is hard to fathom how a shortstop could lead the league in RBIs and be considered the seventh-best player on his own club.

One of the knocks on Stephens was that he was a good hitter who was lucky to play in Fenway Park. While the ballpark helped his statistics, from 1948 through 1950 he averaged 15 home runs and 67 RBIs…on the road. A shortstop who hits like that in half of his games, walks 80 times a year, plays good defense, gets along with his teammates and manager, and stays healthy-this was basically Stephens for ten years.

Halberstam writes of an encounter that supposedly occurred between Williams and Yankee pitcher Allie Reynolds at an All-Star game. Williams jokingly asked when Reynolds was going to start giving him some good pitches to hit. Reynolds countered with words to the effect "not as long as Stephens is hitting behind you." Vic Raschi told Halberstam that Stephens could be pitched to by throwing fastballs high and away, but that Doerr (who followed Stephens in the batting order) was as good a hitter as the Red Sox had and required extreme care.

These stories are unconvincing. First, Stephens was a fairly patient hitter who walked 101 times in 1949, the base year for Halberstam's book. Second, Stephens drove in 159 runs, leaving one to question whether the pitchers knew what the heck they were doing. Third, from 1948 through 1950, Stephens had 13 home runs against the Yankees—including four off Raschi himself—and drove in 54 runs, totals in line with his great statistics in those years.

When pitchers were interviewed about Stephens when he was playing, they generally provided a glowing description. In an article in the Fall 1951 issue of *Complete Baseball*, Ed Rummill quotes Ed Lopat on Stephens: "He's tough, real tough…if you throw one to the outside corner, he's liable to hit it down the right field line for two or three bases." Ned Garver told the same writer: "That Stephens gives me as much trouble as the rest of the Red Sox combined." Jack Kramer was just as positive: "Stephens is as strong as Foxx ever was. I'm convinced of it."

Following the 1950 season, the Red Sox acquired yet another shortstop, their 1948 nemesis, Lou Boudreau. New manager Steve O'Neill moved Stephens to third and divided the time at shortstop between Pesky and Boudreau. Unfortunately, Stephens aggravated his old knee injury and played only 91 games in the field. In only 377 at-bats, he hit .300 with 17 home runs, and 78 RBIs—production consistent with the previous three seasons.

He declined fairly rapidly thereafter. Following another injury-laden year in Boston, he moved on to the White Sox, the Browns, and the Orioles for three mediocre seasons. After 1950, when he turned 30, he never again played more than 101 games or hit more than eight home runs. In mid-1955, he signed with the Seattle Rainiers of the Pacific Coast League, where he played through the end of the 1956 season.

There are two theories as to his sudden decline. One suggests that he was never able to recover from his knee injury, which disabled him in both 1951 and 1952. Fifty years ago a bad knee could be devastating to an infielder in his early 30s. According to his son, Vernon III, his eyes also started to fail him about this time.

The other theory is that his nightlife finally caught up with him. Although some of his old Browns' teammates marveled at his after-hours activities, Boston roommate Johnny Pesky downplayed his reputation as a partier, suggesting that this was no longer going on while he was in Boston. Before his knee injury in 1951, Stephens was remarkably durable-he did not miss a single game in 1948 or 1949 and missed ten or fewer several other times.

Stephens was just thirty-five when his baseball career ended. His post-career passion was golf, which he had taken up during his holdout in 1946. He was breaking 100 as a beginner, largely because of his long, powerful drives. Within a few years he was regularly scoring in the low 70s-a scratch golfer. He was one of the best amateurs in California for many years after leaving baseball, and played in many Pro-Ams, including the Bing Crosby National at Pebble Beach.

Vern and Bernice had three children: Vernon III, Ronald, and Wendy. Although the couple met many people during his years in the game, many of their closest friends remained the people they had known back in their school days. Chuck Stevens, Bob Lemon, Bobby Sturgeon and their wives all returned to Long Beach during the off-seasons and after their careers ended, and they all socialized regularly.

Stephens was a sales representative for Hillerich & Bradsby for a while, which afforded him free golf equipment. He also worked in sales for Owl, a trucking and construction company, and then for the Bechtel Corporation. On November 3, 1968, at work, he had a heart attack lifting a piece of machinery. He was rushed to the hospital, where he died several hours later. He was just 48, and still golfing several times a week.

An annual all star and MVP candidate, Vern Stephens' star has faded over the years. In 1962, when he was first eligible for the Hall of Fame, he did not receive a single vote from the writers who had loved him in the 1940s. Histories written about the 1940s have tended to marginalize his story. Why?

His son, Vern III, believes that his brief foray with the Mexican League has hurt his reputation. Chuck Stevens, his life-long friend, believes that his reputation as a drinker has been overblown, to the point where it has obscured his great playing career. Some point out that his record is aided by playing during the war while most of his contemporaries were in the military, but he continued to star when they returned. His statistics were also aided by playing in Fenway Park, although even with proper adjustment they are impressive. When a wave of books was written about his teams and his era in the 1980s, Stephens was no longer alive to be a star in those stories.

Had he been able to extend his peak years a few more seasons, his statistics would have been enough to overcome these handicaps. For ten years, Vern Stephens was one of the better players—offensively and defensively—in baseball. His record speaks for itself, and it speaks loudly.

Sources

In preparing this article, I was able to interview Vern Stephens' eldest son, Vernon III, as well as his lifelong friend and teammate, Chuck Stevens, both of whom were delightfully cordial and helpful. David Vincent provided Stephens' record from SABR's Tattersall/McConnell home run log. David Smith sent me Stephens' game-by-game data sheets for the seasons 1948–50. I obtained a copy of Stephens' file from the Hall of Fame library in Cooperstown, NY.

In addition, I made use of the following sources:

Devine, Tommy. *Fugitive from Futility*, in "Baseball Stars of 1950," [Bob Considine ed.], Lion Books, 1950.

Halberstam, David. *Summer of '49*. Morrow, 1989.

Hirshberg, Al. "Vern Stephens-Junior Red Socker". *Sport*. August 1949.

James, Bill. *The Politics of Glory*. Macmillan, 1994.

Kaese, Harold. "A Little Slug for the Red Sox". *Sport*. June 1950.

Kaiser, David. *Epic Season*. University of Massachusetts, 1998.

Mead, William. *Even The Browns*. Contemporary Books, 1978.

Rummill, Ed. "The Man Behind Williams". *Complete Baseball*. Fall 1951.

Stout, Glenn and Richard Johnson. *Red Sox Century: One Hundred Years of Red Sox Baseball*. Houghton Mifflin Company, 2000.

Williams, Ted and John Underwood. *My Turn At Bat*. Simon and Shuster, 1969.

Waldman, Frank. *Famous Athletes of Today, Eleventh Edition*. L.C. Page and Company, 1950.

CHUCK STOBBS *by Bill Nowlin*

G	ERA	W	L	SV	GS	GF	CG	SHO	IP	H	R	ER	BB	SO	HR	HBP	WP	BFP
6	6.43	0	0	0	0	6	0	0	7	9	5	5	7	4	0	0	0	35

G	AB	R	H	2B	3B	HR	RBI	BB	SO	BA	OBP	SLG	SB	HBP
6	1	0	0	0	0	0	0	0	0	.000	.000	.000	0	0

One of baseball's original bonus babies, Chuck Stobbs was signed by the Red Sox at the age of 17 and went on to enjoy a 15-year career in major league baseball. The lefthander posted a record of 107–130 playing for teams which often placed low in the standings.

He came from an athletic lineage. His father, T. William Stobbs, had been an All-American football player who played the 1921 season with the Detroit Tigers football team. Bill Stobbs didn't see much action; he was a blocking back who played in seven games, accumulating 60 yards rushing, 16 yards as a receiver, and 30 yards passing.

After his football career, Bill took a position at Wittenberg College in Springfield, Ohio, teaching history but primarily coaching football, basketball, and baseball. Serving in the Navy during World War II, he was stationed in Norfolk and coached the Naval Training Station basketball team.

Chuck's mother, Elizabeth "Lib" Stobbs, was quite an athlete herself, having played basketball in high school and college. Chuck's brother Dick remembers, "She was a good athlete and they were quite a team. There is no question but that the players knew that Mother was sitting up in the stands observing and watching what was going on, because she knew the game extremely well, as well as any of the college kids did. Mother and Dad would talk about the game afterward.... Back in those days, they only had one coach—they didn't have eight like they do now—and she would be his eyes up in the stands, and she had an awful lot to contribute."

Bill Stobbs went into private business later in life, and did some volunteer coaching on the side. He ran the Old Dominion Peanut Corporation distributorship in Norfolk for many years, until he retired. Lib Stobbs was a homemaker.

Charles Klein Stobbs was born in Wheeling, West Virginia, on July 2, 1929 as the middle of three brothers—Bill Jr., Chuck, and Dick. By the time Chuck reached high school, the family was in Norfolk and he attended Granby High School, where he ranked as an All-State athlete in football, basketball, and baseball for two years running. Dick remembers, "I can't tell you how many.... There

Chuck Stobbs, 1949.

was a tremendous number of schools that wanted him to play football. He was probably a better football player than he was a baseball player. His abilities were probably stronger there. But he chose to go into baseball for whatever reason."

At a very early age, he and some of his young buddies formed their own team and called themselves the Rinky Dinks. Chuck loved the game, but told his daughter Betsy that if he could have he would have chosen basketball over baseball. He was given a scholarship to Duke, but the money he was offered by the Red Sox was too compelling. Chuck says that both parents were very supportive (he remembers his mother shouting, "Get off the dime!" during his basketball games), but that he made his own decision to get into baseball.

And it was in baseball that Chuck attracted the most attention. The June 7, 1947, *Washington Post* had termed Chuck "one of the greatest athletes to be developed in the Virginia high schools during recent years" and noted that he'd averaged more than 15 strikeouts a game.

Though primarily a pitcher, Chuck was a first baseman on the Granby High team that played in the 1945 state All-Star game. In June 1946, he pitched for the Eastern Virginia All-Star team, defeating the Western Virginia team, 7–1. He was named the outstanding player of a 1946 All-Star baseball game held in Chicago.

A curious incident occurred at the 1947 Virginia high school championship game. Chuck was pitching for the Granby Comets against the George Washington Presidents of Alexandria and he set down the first six Presidents in order on four strikeouts and two infield plays. A grounder to second looked like a routine 4–3 play to first, but the first baseman juggled the ball. The runner was ruled safe and that riled Chuck's father, Bill, the Granby coach, who ran out to argue that the first baseman had possession long enough for it to be an out. The plate umpire ejected Bill Stobbs from the game. On the very next pitch, the runner on first broke for second and looked out, but this time the shortstop bobbled the ball. Chuck ran over to argue with the second base umpire that the shortstop was returning the ball to the pitcher when he dropped it. The home plate umpire came out to see what was going on, and Chuck turned and shouted, "I'm arguing with the second base umpire. This is none of your business. Get back behind the plate where you belong." Chuck had to be restrained by his catcher, and was ejected as well.

A few minutes later, George Washington had the bases loaded and the Granby catcher thought he had a shot to pick off the baserunner leading off first base. The runner broke from third, the first baseman fired home, and the ball got away from the catcher. Granby's nine-year-old mascot, Chuck's brother Dick, thought he'd be helpful and threw the ball back to the catcher. The third Stobbs was banned from the bench, and the umpire waved in one more run for GW. All three Stobbses had been ejected in a matter of a few minutes. George Washington won the game 4–3 in 10 innings.

Chuck had caught the eye of Paul Decker, a local American Legion coach and part-time scout and George introduced him to Red Sox scout George "Specs" Toporcer, the man who signed him to a major league contract when Chuck was still 17, in May 1947. After inking the deal for a reported $50,000 bonus, Chuck came to Boston to work out with the Red Sox before being given his first assignment.

A bonus rule at the time provided that anyone signed to a contract for more than $6,000 had to be kept on the 40-man roster for the two seasons following the year he was signed. It was also mandatory that he be kept on the big league ballclub for those two years and not sent out to a minor league farm club. Though he regrets not branching out and playing as many sports as we could, the bonus given to Stobbs was quite a large one at the time.

In his signing year, 1947, Stobbs pitched for the Lynn Red Sox in the New England League, posting a 9–2 record and a 1.72 ERA in 94 innings of work. He appeared in his first major league game on September 15, entering when starter Harry Dorish tired after 7⅓ innings. Stobbs got the second out of the eighth, but walked a batter and gave up a hit. The Red Sox kept the lead, and won. John Klima, who has studied baseball's bonus rule, notes that many pitchers in particular suffered under the rule, inevitably idle most of the time they were on the big league bench. The Red Sox had to keep Stobbs on the big league club in 1948 and 1949, the two years after his signing, but were able to farm him out in 1947, the year of his signing. Referring to Red Sox farm director Johnny Murphy, Klima wrote, "Stobbs was *extremely* lucky that the Red Sox opted to send him to Class-B, where he could compete, build confidence, and actually get competitive innings, knowing full well that he would be rotting in the bullpen when he first came to the big leagues. You look at his career as opposed to Paul Pettit's and the Red Sox made a wise decision that should be credited. It would have been the farm director's call."

Stobbs got his first starting assignment on September

19 and pitched three perfect innings against Washington, and singled his only time up, but the game was called on account of rain after three innings. His first official start came in the first game of a September 23 doubleheader against Philadelphia. He lasted only 1⅔ innings, driven from the game by four hits, two walks, and a wild pitch. He was charged with three runs and the loss. He ended 1947 with an 0–1 major league record and a 6.00 ERA in nine innings of work.

Stobbs threw only seven innings in all of 1948 and recorded no decisions, with a 6.43 ERA. Though he was eligible for the World Series, the Red Sox hopes ended with the one-game playoff defeat at the hands of the Cleveland Indians.

In 1949 he finally hit his stride—despite the bonus rule costing him a year of seasoning he could have had in 1948. Stobbs started 19 games in 1949 and appeared in seven games in relief. He won 11 and lost six, with a 4.03 ERA, but for the third year in a row walked more than he struck out. At times he suffered from a lack of run support, but at other times benefited from big Boston scores. A particularly nice win came on August 17, though one couldn't say it was any gem: Stobbs got the complete game win in 10 innings, limiting the Athletics to one run on six hits, but was pitching out of trouble throughout, thanks to the 10 bases on balls he granted.

He walked more than he struck out again in 1950, but won 12 games while losing seven (5.10 ERA) in the course of 21 starts and 11 relief roles. June was quite a month. In his six starts, the final scores were 17–7, 29–4, 8–1, 2–10, 12–9, and 22–14. He left with the lead in the first game (June 4), but pitched only 4⅔ innings so had a no-decision. He won the second start (June 8), going the distance despite all the time spent on the bench watching the Red Sox set the modern records for runs scored in a ballgame. He also won on June 13, a two-hitter. Next time out, June 18, he took a loss, giving up three runs in the first before retiring a batter; he didn't make it through three. The 12–9 win on the 23rd was good for the team but Stobbs was long gone when the Sox scored six times in the last two innings. His last start of the month saw another record set for runs scored in a game, this time for the two teams combined. The 22 scored by Boston should have given an easy win to Stobbs, who took the ball after the Red Sox built a 6–0 lead in the top of the first. He retired only two players before he was replaced, after giving up two hits and three walks.

Stobbs had his best year at the plate in 1950, batting .246 (14-for-57), with 12 walks to his credit and nine RBIs. He was a more than adequate fielding pitcher, with a .977 fielding average. At the plate, Stobbs was nothing special. He accumulated 102 hits in 578 at-bats (.176), with 15 doubles his only extra-base hits.

There was a time early in 1951 when it looked as though Stobbs was heading into the Army, but he was

Stobbs with Mickey Mantle, 1951.

rejected twice due to asthma. Stobbs pitched better overall but his last four starts wound up in losses. He finished the season 10–9, with a 4.76 ERA, and was dealt in November to the White Sox. Chicago GM Frank "Trader" Lane sent Randy Gumpert and Don Lenhardt to the Red Sox for Stobbs and infielder Mel Hoderlein. Stobbs had four years of major league experience but was still only 22 years old.

Chuck spent just the 1952 season with the White Sox, with an excellent 3.13 earned run average, but suffering double-digit defeats (7–12). After the season, Chicago traded him to the Washington Senators for Mike Fornieles. Washington manager Bucky Harris really wanted a lefthander. Stobbs played eight seasons with the Senators, with an overall record of 64–89 despite fairly good pitching throughout. He suffered two disastrous seasons (1955: 4–14, 5.00 ERA, and 1957: 8–20, 5.36 ERA), not at all helped by a team that finished last in both years (both times finishing exactly 43 games out of first place).

The biggest headlines from the Washington years came early in his first season when Mickey Mantle slammed a home run off Stobbs that went completely out of Washington's Griffith Stadium on April 7 and measured at 565 feet (this figure is often disputed). The storied blast was one the longest home runs ever hit in major league baseball. Connie Marrero was asked in an early 2008 interview what Stobbs said after he returned to the dugout. Recalling earlier days, Chuck reportedly said, "At least I got to pitch in Yankee Stadium." Four years later, Stobbs said the experience had made him a better pitcher, at least against The Mick. In 1956,

Chuck allowed three singles—and not one RBI—in 27 Mantle at-bats. He also won a career high 15 games, but lost 15, too.

Becoming a 20-game loser in 1957 was discouraging. Stobbs lost his first 10 starts, one after the other, and every one of his first 11 decisions. It was June 21 before he won his first game of the year. It wasn't just hard luck; his ERA was 8.90 after the 11th loss. To make matters worse, he'd lost his last five decisions in 1956. With 16 losses in a row, the Senators pulled out all the stops. They gave him a new uniform number, 13, and gave away a free rabbit's foot to the first 1,000 fans who came out to "Charm Night"—the June 21 game at Griffith Stadium to see Stobbs square off against Cleveland. A New York firm donated another 1,200 rabbit's feet and the National Brewing Company distributed 1,000 "lucky coins." Chuck's mail contained horseshoes, four-leaf clovers, and all sorts of other talismans. Stobbs struck out eight, allowed seven hits, and walked four. He won the game, 6–3. He went 7–9 for the rest of the season.

Stobbs always started poorly, due to the asthma, but when he dropped his first three decisions in 1958 and found himself at 2–6 by late June, he may not have been surprised to find himself sold to the St. Louis Cardinals during the All-Star break for the $20,000 waiver wire price.

Now in the National League, and used exclusively in relief, he pitched more effectively but won only one game against three losses. After the season, the 29-year-old Stobbs married Jocelyn Johns and the couple maintained a home in Washington. When the Cardinals placed him on waivers in January, no one bit and he was given his release. He signed with Washington as a free agent—and came back wearing eyeglasses. An eye examination had shown a 35 percent deficiency in one of his eyes. The Washington team optometrist said that "Stobbs should have far better perception of the target area."

Indeed, he threw 90⅔ innings in 1959 and struck out more than twice as many as he walked (50–24), posting the best earned run average of his major league career at 2.98. He won only one game all year, on May 5. He lost eight. Only seven of his 41 appearances were starts. He was credited with seven saves.

From 1957 through 1959, Chuck had won 12 and lost 17. In 1960, he won as many games as all three years combined, posting a 12–7 record (with a 3.32 ERA.) It was a nice last hurrah in Washington. Stobbs (and the entire Washington team) played in 1961 in Minnesota, when the Senators franchise became the Minnesota Twins. A new expansion franchise was placed in Washington; that team became the Texas Rangers in 1972.

For the Twins, Stobbs started three games, relieved in 21, and went out with a whimper. His last appearance came on August 12. The Tigers were beating the Twins 8–3 after seven full innings. Stobbs gave up two singles, threw a wild pitch, and walked two batters, forcing in a run. That was enough. Four batters, all reached base— and all scored. He finished the year 2–3 (7.46 ERA) and was given his release in October.

Looking back on his 15-year career, there were certainly many good moments but there were naturally regrets as well. It was difficult coming up under the bonus role. "When you're 18 in the big leagues, you don't know a hell of a lot," Chuck said. As far as being a bonus baby, "Yes, I was frustrated. I wore the bench out." With a little sardonic humor, he says that he finally had to be steered to the pitching mound and told when you come to the circle with the white rubber in it, stop and pitch. He hated the inaction, sitting around, because he felt he wasn't really contributing to the team, and it was not a good feeling worrying whether his teammates resented him at some level as the bonus baby. After appearing in 459 major league games, with over 100 victories to his credit, it is safe to say that he'd validated the belief the Boston Red Sox had in his talents.

After baseball, he took a position with the Jim Parker Insurance Agency in Silver Spring, Maryland. Chuck broadcast Washington Senators baseball for one year, 1969, the first year Ted Williams managed the team. In May 1970, Chuck took on additional duties when he accepted an appointment as baseball coach at George Washington University. He'd been assistant coach the year before. Early in 1971, he resigned to take a position as pitching coach with the Kansas City Royals baseball academy in Sarasota which he did through 1976. Chuck lost his wife Jocelyn in the early 1970s to a brain tumor and it was a challenge raising four young children—three girls (Betsy, Nancy, and Hasse) and a boy (Charlie Jr.), the oldest of whom (Betsy) was 12 at the time. He later remarried, to Joyce Robinson. Chuck worked with the Indians from 1979 to 1981 and then retired.

Charlie Jr. played some ball in college and currently works for Nike as a product manager traveling the United States and Europe. Betsy's son Evan Stobbs is a right-handed pitcher and infielder who has already attracted interest from major league scouts and began college at the University of Central Florida in the fall of 2007 on a baseball scholarship. Nancy has three children—Ike, Charlie, and Jocelyn. Hasse has two sons, Austin and Brook, both football players at Sarasota High. Charlie Jr. has four children—Chaz (Charlie), Lauren, Chandler, and Lyndsey. Several are active and talented at sports.

Chuck was diagnosed with throat cancer quite a few years ago and it flared up throughout 2006, though by early 2007 he had begun to prevail in the ongoing battle. Even before the illness struck, he typically declined requests for interviews, being by nature a private man. Chuck is very active in his church and finds comfort there, as he does watching his children and grandchildren develop.

Sources

Interview with Dick Stobbs, December 11, 2006.
E-mail communication from John Klima, February 18, 2007.
E-mail communication from Kit Krieger, February 29, 2008.
Interview with Betsy Stobbs on March 17, 2007. Betsy asked several questions of Chuck and his quotations come from her March 17 discussion with him.
Thanks to Chris Anderson, Denise Holman, and Clyde Metcalf.

LOU STRINGER *by Bill Nowlin*

G	AB	R	H	2B	3B	HR	RBI	BB	SO	BA	OBP	SLG	SB	HBP
4	11	1	1	0	0	1	1	0	3	.091	.091	.364	0	0

A ballplayer turned Hollywood actor and a car dealer who once sold a Corvette to Elvis Presley. Lou Stringer was all three.

Louis Bernard Stringer was born in Grand Rapids, Michigan, on May 18, 1917. When Lou was three years old, his father moved the family to East Los Angeles. Robert Stringer had been a wood mechanic, working with buzz saws, band saws, and other equipment that gave him some respiratory problems. He developed a bad cough and was forced to retire, but with a large family (seven boys and one girl), others in the family began to pick up work so he didn't have to. Lou's mother, Josephine, never worked outside the home.

Most of Lou's brothers worked as mechanics. One ran an upholstery business. Lou's brother Al, five years younger, had worked out with the Cubs as early as 1941 but signed as a shortstop in the Yankees system. He played for three or four clubs in the American Association, but never made the majors.

Lou first started playing ball with the St. Bridget's grade school team in Los Angeles, competed in the local C.Y.O. league, and later attended Washington High School where he played shortstop on the high school team, a contemporary of Jerry Priddy. Six players in his high school club made it all the way to big league baseball: Stringer, Priddy, Cliff Dapper, Al Lyons, Roy Partee, and Eddie Morris. Lou played some semipro ball on city sandlots, often coached by a man named Mike Catron, before signing with the Cubs' organization. Credited with the signing were Jigger Statz and Pants Rowland, but Lou recalls, "Pants Rowland, he wasn't no scout. He was the manager for the club."

After signing his contract, Lou was told to report to Ponca City, Oklahoma, the Cubs' affiliate in the Western Association. He played second base for Ponca City, appearing in 138 games both in 1937 and in 1938. He hit .263 the first year, and .286 the second, improving across the board in his power numbers at the same time. Stringer ranked second or third in the league in several offensive categories, and Ponca City won the pennant that year. The 19-year-old was earmarked for a year in Tulsa but got an invite to spring training when another player failed to show. Instead, he played in the Pacific Coast League for the Los Angeles Angels (alongside Statz) for both the 1939 and 1940 seasons. He hit .272 the first year, but cooled off just a bit to .263 the second, playing in 172 games during the 1940 campaign. He more than doubled his Western Association home run totals. However, Ed Burns, writing in the *Chicago Tribune*, noted, "It's Stringer's defensive skill that has the Cub management a-twitter with excitement."

During the offseason, Stringer worked hard—one article reported 12 hours a day, seven days a week—at the North American Aviation Company plant.

In 1941, Stringer had a very successful spring and Cubs manager Jimmy Wilson termed him "the best rookie I ever saw in spring training." Needless to say, Lou made the Cubs, debuting on Opening Day, April 15, 1941. Batting seventh and playing short, Stringer had a 2-for-3 day, with a two-base hit and two runs scored. He also made four errors. The leftfielder was Lou Novikoff, whose career had paralleled Stringer's, all the way from Ponca City to LA to Chicago. Both had their Los Angeles contracts purchased by the Cubs on the same day in August 1940 and, training on Catalina Island in 1941, both made the club. There had been a little controversy beforehand. Both Stringer and Novikoff held out—unusual for minor leaguers who'd never had a taste of major league ball—but Commissioner Landis intervened and the two players more or less capitulated. "It was stupid. We didn't

Lou Stringer with the Cubs.
Courtesy of Tom Stringer.

get anything out of it. I got $5,000 and that was what I got," Stringer said later.

Stringer had played only second base, but Billy Herman was a fixture at the keystone, so Stringer filled in at shortstop. On May 6, though, Herman was traded to the Brooklyn Dodgers. Stringer had effectively beaten out Herman for the job, but it was the Dodgers who went all the way to the World Series while the Cubs finished 30 games behind. Not surprisingly, though, Stringer very much liked skipper Jimmy Wilson. "I liked Jimmy. He was fine. Good dad, good husband. He was a good manager."

Playing in 145 games, Stringer hit .246, very good figures for a shortstop in that era. He was the first one of the Chicago Cubs to sign his 1942 contract, signing in October 1941. He played out the 1942 season, getting into 121 games and hitting .236, playing some at second base and some at third. With the war under way, he enlisted as a private in the Army Air Corps. He graduated from Air Force Mechanics School at Williams Field Advance Flying School in Chandler, Arizona in January 1943. "I went in as a mechanic and I come out as a (physical training) instructor," he recalled. "I handled all the PT for all the cadets who were there. There were three or four hundred cadets there and I had three or four classes every day for them and I headed up their PT. Williams Field, Arizona. That was an air base." He was sent to the Army's Physical Training Instructors School at Miami Beach. He graduated in November.

News reports indicate that Stringer did well in the service. A May 1943 story in the *Los Angeles Times* said that soldiering was his "greatest thrill" and he was named Soldier of the Month at Williams. At the time of the story, Lou had a .425 average playing for the Williams Field Fliers.

Back from the war, Stringer played second, short, and third for the Cubs in 1946, but got only 209 at-bats, hitting .244. Cubs manager Charlie Grimm "never liked me," he says. Stringer was released to the Angels in January 1947 and the team won the Pacific Coast League pennant. Lou batted .293, driving in 72 runs. In February 1948, the

Cubs sold him for the $10,000 waiver price to the New York Giants, who assigned his contract to the Hollywood Stars, also in the Coast League. The club played just 15 minutes from his house. It was another season he very much enjoyed, this time hitting an even .333 and leading the league with 50 doubles, while driving in 99 runs. At season's end, he was named both the team's MVP and the "most popular player." Manager Jimmy Dykes quit on August 28 and Stringer took over as player-manager. But right after Hollywood finished its season, the Red Sox purchased his contract, and he wasted no time getting to Boston. He'd finished up playing a doubleheader against Sacramento on September 19, took a plane that night, and found himself in a ball game in Detroit the evening of September 20. The *Los Angeles Times* story said that the Stars manager had been "fired" but he was fired "upward, like a space rocket. The Boston Red Sox bought him to help in their frantic fight for the American League pennant."

He got into four games, and only had one hit in 11 times at the plate, but it was a home run. The Sox had another second baseman, named Bobby Doerr, and Stringer found himself in a utility role behind Doerr, Vern Stephens, and Johnny Pesky.

He really liked Pesky: "I got along real good with him. I happened to be Catholic and he was Catholic, and we got along real good. Go to church on Sunday and stuff. Dom DiMaggio, he was Catholic. We had quite a few Catholics on the club."

In 1949, Stringer stayed with the Sox and got into 35 games, but mostly defensively (he only had 41 at-bats, batting .268 during his limited opportunities.) Back for another full year in 1950, Lou had even less work, just 17 at-bats in 24 games. He hit .294. In his two-plus seasons with Boston, he only drove in nine runs.

During the off-seasons, starting right after the war, Stringer worked in the automobile business, selling cars in the Los Angeles area for Harry Mann Chevrolet. Mann later became, Stringer says, "the world's largest Corvette dealer."

The Red Sox let him go and he signed on with Hollywood for 1951, playing a full year and hitting .284. He wasn't entirely unhappy to be playing near home once more. "It's great, of course, to be in the majors," he told Al Wolf of the *Los Angeles Times*. "That's the goal of every ballplayer. And coming down again kinda hurts. But I'd rather play every day in the minors—especially here in my home town—than just sit on the bench in the big time. You go nuts doing nothing." He had no gripes about Boston managers McCarthy and O'Neill, recognizing that the talent on those ballclubs was just so deep he wasn't truly needed. "I just couldn't seem to get a chance to show what I could do." He also had a sense of humor. At one point, he explained why he never worried about slumps: "I've been in a slump all my life." That's a little self-effacing for

a reserve middle infielder of the era with a fine .242 batting average.

After the season, he enjoyed a seven-week tour of Japan with Joe DiMaggio and a number of other players. "We played to over a million people. It was a great, great outing. Joe, Dom, and Vince DiMaggio there in the outfield, and I played third. I think we lost one game, and the only reason we lost that was a couple of the guys got so drunk they couldn't play."

Stringer with Jimmy Stewart while filming "The Monty Stratton Story." Courtesy of Tom Stringer.

He began 1952 with Hollywood, but then moved on to San Diego in May. The combined stats for the year show him hitting a solid .275 with 85 RBIs. The next year began with San Diego, but he moved to San Francisco and became player-manager there. The following four seasons saw Stringer move to a new city, as a player-manager each year. He managed and played for Yakima (1954), Boise (1955), Pocatella (1956), and Des Moines (1957). The final season started with the Des Moines Demons, where he lasted but 47 games. "Charley Grimm. He's the one that pushed me there. He was the big shot, a manager in the big leagues. He knew somebody there and that's the reason I went to Des Moines. I didn't know anybody there at all. I was lost when I went there. And we didn't win... so I just stopped and left after the middle of the season. I came back to L.A." A month later, the Hollywood Stars offered him a contract and he played in an even dozen games for Hollywood and San Francisco, but his pro ball career was really done.

Stringer spent a good deal of time appearing in a number of Hollywood films, particularly those with baseball themes such as *The Jackie Robinson Story* and *The Monty Stratton Story*. He did a fair amount of acting work but became tired of all the downtime—standing around on movie sets—and went back to selling cars.

"I came back and went back to the automobile business. I was there for years. I made more money there than I ever did in baseball." Selling the Corvette to Elvis wasn't a hard sell, Stringer told Steve Buckley. "He called and ordered it over the phone. He wanted me to drive it out to this place he was staying at in Hollywood and drop it off.... When we got there, he gave me a check, and that was pretty much it. Turns out he bought the car so he could give it to some girl. He was nice, but I don't think he said 20 words while I was there."

Sounds a little reminiscent of Lou's teammate Ted Williams. "Ted was a loner. We'd all go out and eat dinner, except Ted. He mostly kept to himself, or he went fishing somewhere." Lou shared an early Ted Williams memory with Buckley, of a time that he was coming out of the batting cage and passed Williams. "He didn't know me very

well yet, and he said, 'Hey, you, who's the best hitter in baseball?' And I said, 'You are.' And he said, 'You're god-damn right I am' as he walked away."

Lou married twice. His first wife, Helen, the mother of his two children, died in 1993. They had one daughter, Linda, and one son, Tom. "My son never played ball. He's a college graduate. He runs this place we're living right now." Stringer lives with his second wife Wilma in a retirement community near San Diego owned by his son and four partners.

Sources

Interview with Lou Stringer done March 3, 2006 by Bill Nowlin. Thanks as well to Tom Stringer for assistance in preparing this biography.

Buckley, Steve. *Boston Red Sox: Where Have You Gone?* (Champaign IL: Sports Publishing, 2005)

BIRDIE TEBBETTS *by Tom Simon*

G	AB	R	H	2B	3B	HR	RBI	BB	SO	BA	OBP	SLG	SB	HBP
128	446	54	125	26	2	5	68	62	32	.280	.371	.381	5	2

In a 1973 SABR survey, Birdie Tebbetts narrowly missed being chosen Vermont's greatest baseball player, finishing second to Larry Gardner by a mere handful of votes. In almost every respect, Tebbetts was a solid candidate: a lifetime .270 hitter, Birdie amassed exactly 1,000 hits in a career that spanned 17 years, three of which were lost to military service. Perhaps what was lacking were strong Vermont ties—whereas Gardner spent nearly his entire life in the Green Mountains, Tebbetts left the state when he was only a couple of months old.

But aside from being born there, Tebbetts had several other connections to the Green Mountain State. He nearly accepted a scholarship from Gardner to attend the University of Vermont—until the aspiring pre-med learned that afternoon laboratory sessions would conflict with baseball practice. Instead he chose Providence College at the behest of the scout who signed him to his first professional contract—none other than Vermont-born Jean Dubuc. But his fondest Vermont memory was of a 1948 barnstorming trip to Burlington, during which he met his future wife.

George Robert Tebbetts was born in Burlington on November 10, 1912. He was the third and final child of Charles and Elizabeth Ryan Tebbetts, and his round, freckled face and flaming red hair reflected his mother's Irish heritage. George's most distinguishing characteristic,

George "Birdie" Tebbetts.

though, was his unusually high-pitched voice. As a toddler he acquired the nickname "Birdie" after an aunt observed that his voice sounded like a bird chirping.

The Tebbetts family lived in a brick Federal-style house that still stands on King Street. Birdie's father, Charles Tebbetts, first appeared in the Burlington City Directory in 1911. At the time he worked as a shipping clerk for Swift & Company, a wholesaler of meats and provisions located at the corner of Maple and Battery streets. That's why the family was living in Vermont when Birdie was born, but Charles was originally from New Hampshire, having grown up on a farm near Dover. Within a couple months of Birdie's birth, Swift promoted Charles to salesman and transferred him back to his native state. The family settled in Nashua, but tragedy struck one year later when Charles died, leaving Mary to raise three children on her own. "We were very poor," Tebbetts recalled.

When Birdie was eight he had the fortune of meeting Francis Parnell Murphy, owner of Nashua's biggest industry, the Thom McAn Shoe Company, and later governor of New Hampshire. Murphy sponsored the Nashua Millionaires, an independent baseball team composed of ex-professionals and collegiate All-Americans, and Birdie served as the team's mascot. "Murphy happened to take a liking to me," Tebbetts said. "Having no father of my own, I guess I adopted him in my mind as a father. He helped me in a number of ways, and no man in my life has ever exerted a more powerful influence on me." One obvious perk was that Tebbetts never had to pay for a pair of shoes.

That stint as mascot for the Millionaires was also responsible for Tebbetts becoming a catcher. His idol on the team was Clyde Sukeforth, best-known today as the man whom Branch Rickey assigned to scout Jackie Robinson for the Brooklyn Dodgers. Sukey was also a pretty good backstop who went on to enjoy a ten-year career in the majors with Cincinnati and Brooklyn, and Birdie imitated his moves behind the plate. Tebbetts became so adept, in fact, that it became a standard pregame attraction for the youngster to warm up Nashua's starting pitcher.

Birdie grew up to be a star athlete at Nashua High School, playing football, basketball, and especially baseball. By his senior year of 1930 he'd received scholarship offers from numerous colleges (one was a six-year scholarship from UVM that included medical school) and professional bids from major league clubs. The man who signed Lou Gehrig, in fact—legendary New York Yankees scout Paul Krichell—told Birdie's mother that the Yankees considered her son the best amateur prospect in the country. Imagine the money he could command if he were in that position today!

Tebbetts eventually chose to sign with the Detroit Tigers after being scouted by Dubuc and approved by the team's manager, future Hall of Famer Bucky Harris.

"I got a bonus that was sufficient to wipe out all our family debts," Birdie said. Better yet, the Tigers agreed to pay his way through any college in the country. Birdie narrowed his choice to Holy Cross and Providence, but it took two stars of the deadball era to help make his final decision. "I was actually leaning towards Holy Cross, which was coached by Jack Barry, the old Philadelphia A's shortstop," Tebbetts said. "But Dubuc had offered to pay my way down to New York so I could work out with the Tigers at Yankee Stadium, and when Barry got wind of it he threatened to have my amateur status revoked." The old Tiger righthander mentioned this to Birdie, who became so angry that he chose Providence. "In my first game for Providence I tripled to beat Holy Cross," Tebbetts said. "It was one of the highlights of my baseball career."

Each summer, following the end of the college baseball season, Birdie played for East Douglas in the Blackstone Valley League, a high-level semipro circuit consisting mostly of teams from New England mill towns. Though supposedly amateur, teams spared no expense in attracting the best talent available. It wasn't uncommon for major leaguers who had off-days in Boston to sign on for important games. That's how Tebbetts in the span of one week found himself catching future Hall of Famers Lefty Grove and Carl Hubbell, both in the prime of their careers.

Tebbetts, Parnell, and Vern Stephens, 1951.

Birdie Tebbetts graduated from Providence College with a degree in philosophy in 1934, the year Detroit purchased future Hall of Fame catcher Mickey Cochrane from the Philadelphia A's. With the veteran backstop installed as player-manager, the Tigers ran away with their first American League pennant since 1909. The following year Cochrane led the Tigers to another pennant and a World Series victory over the Chicago Cubs, giving Detroit its first championship ever. With Cochrane a fixture behind the plate, clearly there was no need for Tebbetts in Detroit.

Birdie spent three seasons in the minors before receiving a call-up to the Tigers in September 1936. In 1937 he made the team out of spring training, but the season was in its infancy when he and three others received notice that they were being sent to Toledo following an afternoon game with the Yankees. The others watched the game from the grandstand, but Tebbetts elected to remain in uniform in case he was needed. In the fourteenth inning Birdie was pressed into duty as a pinch hitter. He delivered a game-winning double into the right-field corner, and after that he didn't leave the majors for another 16 years.

On May 25, 1937, an opening in Detroit's starting lineup suddenly appeared when Cochrane's skull was fractured by a pitch from Bump Hadley of the Yankees. Rookie Rudy York was thrown into the catching breach and responded with 68 home runs and 230 RBIs over the next two seasons, but his defense was awful. By 1939 Cochrane's replacement as manager, Del Baker, had seen enough. He installed Tebbetts as Detroit's regular catcher and Birdie batted a respectable .261 in 106 games.

In 1940, Baker shifted Hank Greenberg to left field to open up a regular spot for York at first base. The pair combined to hit 74 home runs as the Tigers finished a whisker ahead of the Indians and Yankees in one of the closest pennant races ever. After batting .294 for the regular season, Tebbetts went hitless in 11 World Series at-bats, even though the Tigers were stealing Cincinnati catcher Jimmie Wilson's signs. "We knew every pitch the Reds were throwing against us," Birdie said. "The screwiest part of it was that it didn't do us a damn bit of good." With solid pitching from Paul Derringer and Bucky Walters, Cincinnati edged out the Tigers in a seven-game series.

Tebbetts caught for the American League in the 1941 and 1942 All-Star Games, but military service during World War II took him out of baseball for the next three seasons. Birdie batted only .243 on his return in 1946 and continued to struggle in 1947, batting .094 as of May 20. On that date the Tigers traded him to the Red Sox for Hal Wagner, a catcher nearing the end of a 12-year career. The swap proved a bargain for Boston. Tebbetts batted .299 for the remainder of 1947, lifting his average for the year to .267. Reminiscent of the vengeance he inflicted on Holy Cross, Birdie managed to hit nearly .400 against Detroit.

He was Boston's regular catcher again in 1948 and made the American League All-Star Team. After 154 games that season, the Red Sox and Cleveland ended up tied at 96–58, necessitating a one-game play-off On October 4, 1948, the Indians beat Denny Galehouse at Fenway Park, preventing the Red Sox from joining the Braves in an all-Boston World Series.

Following the 1948 season Birdie Tebbetts barnstormed throughout New England with a team of his own composition. The Birdie Tebbetts Major League All-Stars featured Snuffy Stirnweiss and Spec Shea of the Yankees, Vic Wertz of the Tigers, Eddie Pellagrini" of the Browns, Carl Sheib and Joe Coleman of the Athletics, Vern Stephens and Jimmy Piersall of the Red Sox, and Chicago White Sox first baseman Tony Lupien, a Massachusetts native who made his home in Springfield, Vermont.

On Columbus Day the team came to Burlington's Centennial Field to play an aggregation managed by Larry Gardner and composed mostly of players from Burlington's amateur Suburban League. The local squad was beefed up by the addition of St. Louis Cardinals infielder Ralph Lapointe of Winooski, and the two teams exchanged pitchers and catchers to make the game more interesting. A crowd of over 4,500 packed Centennial to see the Tebbetts All-Stars cruise to an 8–4 victory. Appropriately, the game's top performances were turned in by players with Vermont connections: Lupien was 4-for-5 with a triple and three RBIs, while Lapointe paced the locals with two singles and a stolen base.

The game was staged for the benefit of a local charity, and afterwards a banquet was, held at the Hotel Vermont. Birdie was chatting with Stephen Hartnett, proprietor of a Burlington restaurant, when he noticed a beautiful brunette about 20 feet away. "Boy, that's a good-looking girl," Tebbetts said to his companion. "I sure would like to meet her." Hartnett called the woman over and said, "Mr. Tebbetts, I'd like you to meet my daughter Mary." At the time, Mary Hartnett was working as a secretary to Vermont Governor Ernest Gibson, who was unable to attend the banquet and sent Mary in his place.

Stephen Hartnett was active in the Burlington Elks Club, and at her father's request Mary wrote to Tebbetts and asked what he'd charge to give a speech to the Elks at their winter sports banquet. Tebbetts replied to Mr. Hartnett that his usual fee was $350, but he'd donate the money back to the Elks if he could get a date with his daughter. Mary wrote back that "the fee is too high and his daughter is not interested" but Birdie persisted. "That winter I drove up from Nashua through those mountains and spoke at that banquet," Tebbetts said. The effort paid off. Birdie married Mary Hartnett on October 28, 1950.

A 37-year-old Tebbetts batted .310 with a career-high eight home runs for the Red Sox in 1950, but despite the increased production he caught just 74 games—only one more than his back-up, 28-year-old Matt Batts. During a postseason banquet, Birdie told reporters that the reason he'd played so little was that one or two "juvenile delinquents and moronic malcontents" on the Boston pitching staff didn't want him catching them. The Red Sox didn't appreciate Birdie's candor. Though weak behind the plate, they sold Tebbetts to Cleveland. Over the next two seasons he spelled perennial all-star Jim Hegan, a superb defensive catcher.

Tebbetts knew he was nearing the end of his playing days, but he wasn't sure what he wanted to do next. Earlier in his career he'd considered farming, even taking post-graduate courses in agriculture at the University of New Hampshire in 1941. The war halted his studies, however, and he switched to selling insurance as an off-season activity, working as an associate for the Paul Sadler Agency in Nashua. But following the 1952 season. he decided to accept an offer from the Indians to manage their Triple-A farm team in Indianapolis. Sports writers predicted that before long he'd be managing in the majors.

Those predictions came true one year later when a strange set of circumstances led to his hiring by the Cincinnati Redlegs (during the McCarthy era the team preferred not to be called the Reds). The Redlegs didn't have a Triple-A affiliate, so Cincinnati's general manager, Gabe Paul, made a deal with his cross-state counterpart in Cleveland, Hank Greenberg. The Redlegs agreed to send prospects to Tebbetts at Indianapolis if the Indians would help stock Cincinnati's Double-A team at Tulsa. Greenberg asked the Redlegs to send reports on his players from Tulsa's manager, Joe Schultz, so Paul requested Tebbetts' reports on the Redlegs prospects. "When I got them, I was amazed," Paul said. "Birdie's reports were the most complete I'd ever seen."

Frustrated by Cincinnati's fourth consecutive sixth-place finish in 1953, Paul decided to fire manager Rogers

Tebbetts with young admirer.

Hornsby. Initially he'd hoped to hire Al Lopez, but when the Cleveland manager announced his decision to remain with the Indians, Paul asked Greenberg for permission to hire Tebbetts. Not wanting to stand in the way of his old teammate, Greenberg acquiesced, and on September 28, 1953, Birdie Tebbetts became Cincinnati's fifth manager in seven years. To this day he is the only Vermonter ever to manage in the major leagues.

The Redlegs experienced slight improvement in their first two seasons under Tebbetts, finishing in fifth place both years. Then in 1956 the Redlegs stayed in the race until the last day of the season, ending up with a 91–63 record, two games behind Brooklyn and one behind Milwaukee. It was the first time Cincinnati had finished in the first division in 11 years. Tebbetts was voted National League Manager of the Year.

Cincinnati finally appeared to be on the verge of a pennant, but the Redlegs finished a disappointing fourth in both of the next two seasons. Paul and Tebbetts fell under heavy criticism. Finally Birdie decided to quit, as Paul confirmed years later.

Nobody believes me when I say Birdie quit. They still think I fired him. Absolutely not. I tried to get him to stay. He was a nervous wreck and he looked bad.

He came to me and said, "Why don't you pay me off and let me go home?" I talked him out of it. Rumors began to fly and I told the reporters that what we needed were new players, not a new manager. And I meant it.

Three weeks later, he came to me again, requesting to leave. This time I thought it would be the best thing for his health, so I accepted his resignation. But he positively was not going to get fired. He could have stayed at Cincinnati as long as he wanted to. The way he looked, I didn't think he'd ever manage again.

In fact, neither did Tebbetts. At the press conference announcing his resignation, he told reporters he was through with managing.

Birdie landed an executive position with the Milwaukee Braves, but he missed the excitement of being in the dugout. When the team fired Chuck Dressen in September 1961, Tebbetts returned to managing for the last month of the season. Despite talented players like Hank Aaron, Eddie Mathews, Joe Adcock, Warren Spahn, and Lew Burdette, the Braves finished fourth. Ironically, they'd won the pennant in 1958 when Tebbetts last managed the Reds, and in 1961 the Reds won when he was managing the Braves.

During the 1962 World Series Birdie accepted an offer to manage the Indians from Gabe Paul, who'd moved on from Cincinnati to become general manager at Cleveland. In his return to the A.L., Birdie guided a young Cleveland team to a fifth-place tie in 1963. By that point he'd been smoking three packs a day for the last 25 years, and his weight had ballooned to 238 pounds.

In Tucson on April 1, 1964, just as spring training was ending, Tebbetts suffered a heart attack. The 52-year-old underwent bypass surgery at the Mayo Clinic, and it was reported that he was probably out for the season. Miraculously, he returned to the Indians on July 4, remaining with the team until he was fired on August 19, 1966. In 10 seasons as a manager, he'd compiled a record of 748–705 (.515).

Though he never again managed in the majors, Tebbetts worked in professional baseball as a scout and minor league manager for the New York Mets, New York Yankees, and Baltimore Orioles until his retirement in 1992. Settling down in Holmes Beach, Florida, in his eighties. Birdie helped out with the Anna Maria Island Little League.

Birdie Tebbetts died on March 25, 1999. "I'd like to be remembered as a good father and a good citizen," he told *The Bradenton Herald* a month before his death, "but I am a baseball guy. That's all I am. That's all I ever was. That's all I ever want to be."

Sources

A version of this biography originally appeared in *Green Mountain Boys of Summer: Vermonters in the Major Leagues 1882–1993*, edited by Tom Simon (New England Press, 2000).

In researching this article, the author made use of the subject's file at the National Baseball Hall of Fame Library, the Tom Shea Collection, the archives at the University of Vermont, and several local newspapers.

TED WILLIAMS *by Bill Nowlin*

G	AB	R	H	2B	3B	HR	RBI	BB	SO	BA	OBP	SLG	SB	HBP
137	509	124	188	44	3	25	127	126	41	.369	.497	.615	4	3

Any argument as to the greatest hitter of all time always involves Ted Williams. It's an argument that can never be definitively answered, but that it always involves Williams says a lot. One could probably count the legitimate contenders on the fingers of one hand. Most would narrow the field to just two players, Babe Ruth being the other. One could make a good case for Lou Gehrig, and a very small handful of others. Ted himself ranked Ruth, Gehrig, Jimmie Foxx, Rogers Hornsby, and Joe DiMaggio as the top five (he elected not to include himself in any such ranking).

If the name of the game is getting on base, no one ranks above Williams. His lifetime on-base average was .482, and think what that means. He reached base safely 48.2% of the time he came up to bat—almost half the time. Ruth comes in second, at .474. One of the reasons Williams ranked first was his self-discipline; he refused to swing at pitches outside the strike zone. In time, he developed such a reputation that more than one catcher complaining about a pitch being called a ball was told by the umpire, "If Mr. Williams didn't swing at it, it wasn't a strike." But The Kid had the strike zone down cold from the first. Even in 1939, his rookie year, Ted walked 107 times, ranking second in the American League (he led the league that first year in total bases—by a big margin). Across his entire career, which touched four decades (1939–1960), Williams had a walks percentage of 20.75. More than one out of every five times, he took a walk.

Even with a pitch in the strike zone, he wouldn't take a cut at it unless he felt it was a pitch he could drive. "Get a good pitch to hit"—the philosophy imparted to Ted in Minneapolis by hitting instructor Rogers Hornsby, meant more than just a pitch in the strike zone. If the pitcher dropped in a good curveball low and away (which he knew was his most vulnerable spot in the zone), he would figuratively tip his cap, take the strike, and wait for a better pitch. Unless there were two strikes on him, he would take his chances that there was a better pitch coming.

Ted had strong opinions about what made for a great hitter, and it involved hitting for a combination of average

A pensive Kid.

and power. Had he been willing to sacrifice power for batting average, one suspects, he could have ranked right at the top instead of just fifth among "modern era" (post-1901) players. Had he been willing to sacrifice average and just swing for the fences, he would have hit more than 521 home runs. As a young man, he knew what he wanted. At age 20, he said, "All I want out of life is that when I walk down the street folks will say, 'There goes the greatest hitter that ever lived.'" In conversation late in life, when someone asked whether he thought he'd accomplished that, he simply said he didn't know but that it was a great honor just to hear his name in the same sentence as a Ruth or a Gehrig.

Becoming a great hitter was a goal Ted set for himself at a very early age. Born in San Diego on August 30, 1918, he was the first-born son of professional photographer (and former U.S. cavalryman) Samuel Williams and his wife, May Venzor Williams, a Mexican-American who dedicated her life to Salvation Army work. It wasn't the happiest of marriages and both parents were frequently out of the home, often leaving Ted and his brother, Danny (two years younger), to fend for themselves. Fortunately, neighbors welcomed Ted in, but he spent endless hours playing ball on the North Park Playground in the Southern California city where the climate allowed one to play pickup ball all year round. A dedicated playground director, Rod Luscomb, saw Ted's drive and took him under his wing. By the time Ted reached high school, he was an exceptional player who attracted the attention and support of coach Wofford "Wos" Caldwell.

It was his bat that first caught coach Caldwell's eye, but Ted excelled as a pitcher for the Hoover High Cardinals. He often struck out a dozen or more batters in a game, but he hit well, too, and found a place in the lineup for every game. Even while still a high school player, Ted signed his first professional contract—with the locally-based San Diego Padres, of the Pacific Coast League. With the Padres, Ted got his feet wet in 1936, hitting a modest .271 but without even one home run in the regular season. Ted completed high school and then played for the Padres again in 1937, upping his average to .291 and showing some power with 23 homers. Boston Red Sox general manager Eddie Collins had spotted Ted while looking over a couple of Padres players and shook hands with owner Bill Lane on an option to sign the young player, which he exercised in time for Ted to go to the big league training camp in Florida in the spring of 1938.

Williams was a brash and cocky young kid who was deemed to need a full year in the minors and he was assigned to the Minneapolis Millers, where he proceeded to win the American Association Triple Crown with a .366 average, 43 home runs, and 142 RBIs. There was no question that he would be with the Red Sox in 1939, and the buildup in Boston's newspapers was unprecedented. The Kid was all that had been promised, and then some. Playing right field, he hit 31 home runs and batted .327. Not only did he lead the league in extra-base hits and total bases, he also led the league in runs batted in in his rookie year with 145, setting a major league rookie record that has never been beaten. His fresh and evident love of the game won the hearts of many Boston fans.

An animated Williams making a point in the clubhouse.

The following year, 1940, Williams switched permanently to left field and improved his average to .344, though he dipped a bit in home runs (23) and RBIs (113). He placed first in both on-base percentage and runs scored. It was the first of 12 seasons that he led the league in on-base percentage; remarkably, he led in OBP every year through 1958 in which he was eligible. From his very first trip across country to spring training in 1938, Ted became known for his relentless questioning of other players about situational baseball—what was Ted Lyons' "out pitch" to a lefthanded hitter late in the game with runners on base? What would Bobo Newsom start you out on first time up? Williams seemed to live and breathe baseball and it rang true when he later acquired the nickname "Teddy Ballgame."

Maybe he seemed just too good to be true. After a brief honeymoon with the press in the highly competitive newspaper town that was Boston, the critical stories began to come out. Taking on Ted sold newspapers, and writers like Dave Egan and Austen Lake could get under Ted's skin, sometimes provoking a story where none had existed before. He was easy to mock, taking imaginary swings out in the field and letting a fly ball drop in. He was so cocksure that he turned off some of the crusty inkstained wretches, and a little sanctimonious—declining an interview with one of the deans of the press corps, columnist Bill Cunningham, because the writer had been drinking. Some of the writers had it in for Ted, and let

him have it. There commenced a feud with the writers that lasted Ted's whole career, and beyond. He enjoyed barring the scribes from the Boston clubhouse, sniffing the air distastefully as one walked by, and more than once spit toward the press box in contempt. He earned some other monikers—"Terrible Ted" and the "Splendid Spitter"—the latter being a reference to his widely-known nickname as a lanky, gangly kid—the Splendid Splinter.

There were fans who enjoyed egging Ted on, too, and during this second season he turned against the fickle fans. He later admitted he had "rabbit's ears" and could hear the one loud detractor over the hundreds of cheering fans, and he let it get to him. He admitted he was "never very coy, never very diplomatic. As a result I would get myself in a wringer....I was impetuous, I was tempestuous. I blew up. Not acting, but *reacting*. I'd get so damned mad, throw bats, kick the columns in the dugout so that sparks flew, tear out the plumbing, knock out the lights, damn near kill myself. *Scream*. I'd scream out my own frustration." He just could not abide the fair-weather fans who'd be for him one day and against him the next. One thing he determined never to do was tip his cap to the fans; even though there were days that he truly wanted to, he just couldn't bring himself to do so. He was a complicated man and yet, despite all the tumult and turmoil, he never showed up an umpire by arguing a call and never got tossed from a game. And, though he preferred to keep to himself, he got along fine with other ballplayers, both on his own team and on opposing teams.

It was in 1941 that The Kid had a season for the ages—batting .406 despite the sacrifice fly counting against the hitter's average. Few players had achieved the .400 mark, and no one has done so since. Ted also set a single-season on-base percentage mark (.553) that was never topped in the 20th century. (Barry Bonds now holds the highest mark.) Williams led the American League in runs and home runs. Two months after the season ended, Japanese warplanes attacked Pearl Harbor.

As sole supporter of his mother (his parents had divorced), Ted was exempt but that didn't prevent some from questioning his courage when he chose to play baseball (and pay off an annuity he'd purchased for his mother) in 1942. He had already achieved national stature as a star baseball player at a time when baseball was unrivaled by any other sport. This made him a convenient target for criticism, but servicemen attending ball games cheered for Williams. Once he'd made his point, he signed up in the Navy's V-5 program to begin training as a naval aviator when the season was over. In his fourth year of major league ball, Ted hit for the Triple Crown in the major leagues, leading both leagues, as it happened, in average (.356, down a full 50 points from the prior year), home runs (36) and RBIs (137). And then it was off to serve. For the second year in a row, Williams came in second in MVP voting.

Ted Williams spent three prime years training and becoming a Navy (and then Marine Corps) pilot—and becoming so good at flight and gunnery that he was made an instructor and served the war training other pilots. The day he received his commission, he married Doris Soule—the first of three marriages. He kept active to some extent, playing a little baseball on base teams but only as time permitted given his primary duties. Lt. T.S. Williams ended his stretch at Pearl Harbor and never saw combat.

After the war, Ted returned to the Red Sox and received his first MVP award from the baseball writers, helping lead Boston into its first World Series since 1918. He led the league in OBP, total bases, and runs, but an injury to his elbow while playing in an exhibition game to keep loose for the upcoming Series hampered his ability to compete effectively in the fall classic. Boston lost to the Cardinals in seven games, and Ted's weak hitting helped cost them the championship.

In 1947, Ted had his second Triple Crown year, leading the A.L. with .343, 32, and 114. The Red Sox didn't come close to the Yankees that year, and in each of the next two years, they lost the pennant on the final day of the

The classic swing as Ted connects with another one.

season. Williams led the league in both average and slugging both seasons, among other categories. In 1949, he earned his second Most Valuable Player award—and only missed an unprecedented third Triple Crown by the narrowest of margins. He led in homers and RBIs, but George Kell edged him by one ten-thousandth of a point in batting average.

The year 1950 might have been his best ever—he had already hit 25 homers and driven in 83 runs when he shattered his elbow crashing into the wall during the All-Star Game. He missed most of the rest of the season, and said he never fully recovered as a hitter—though one would hardly know it to look at the stats he posted. In 1951, he led the league once more in OBP and slugging.

Come 1952, as the war in Korea mounted, the Marines recalled a number of pilots to active duty. Among them was the less-than-pleased T.S. Williams, now a

captain in the Reserve. He was to turn 34 that August, and Doris and he had a young daughter, Barbara Joyce (Bobby-Jo.) When it was clear there was no choice but to comply, Ted determined to do his best. He requested training on jets and was ultimately assigned to Marine Corps squadron VMF-311 which flew dive bombing missions out of base K-3 in South Korea. Capt. Williams flew some 39 combat missions, though he barely escaped with his life on the third one when his Panther jet was hit and had to crash-land. The plane burned to an irretrievable crisp but Williams was up on another mission at 8:08 the next morning. It truly was an elite squadron to which Williams was assigned; on more than half a dozen missions, Williams served as wingman to squadron mate John Glenn.

A series of ear infections consigned him to sick bay for two stretches and when it was obvious the war would be over in a matter of weeks, Williams was sent back Stateside and mustered out—in time to be an honored guest at the 1953 All-Star Game. He threw himself into preparation to play and he got in 91 at-bats before the season was over—batting .407 in the process.

Ted broke his collarbone in spring training in 1954 and missed so many games at the start of the season that come season's end, he fell 14 at-bats short of having the requisite 400 to qualify for the batting crown he would have otherwise won with his .345 average. Ted appeared in only 117 games, but still drew enough walks to lead the league (136). The walks hurt him, though, since the batting title was based on "official" at-bats alone. This seemed so unfair that the criteria were changed in later years to be based on plate appearances. After the 1954 season, he "retired" (the term is placed in quotation marks because it seemed as though retirement was a strategic move in a divorce) and did not make a start in the 1955 season until May 28. He completed the year with 320 at-bats, but hadn't lost his touch as indicated by his .356 average and 83 RBIs in the two-thirds of a season he played. In 1956, he had what by Williams standards seemed like a pedestrian, even somewhat lackluster year, accumulating an even 400 at-bats with 24 homers, but still hit at a .345 clip. A.L. pitchers were no fools; he drew over 100 walks and led the league in on-base percentage.

The year 1957 is what was arguably the year in which

Ted Williams proved what a great hitter he truly was. No longer the Kid who turned 23 while hitting .406 back in 1941, Ted entered his 40th year in that season. He might have been "splendid" but he was no splinter. He'd filled out his physique, gone through war and divorce, suffered broken bones and pneumonia. Despite all the accumulated adversity, Ted hit .388 (just six more hits would have given him .400 again, hits that a younger man might have legged out) and led the league by 23 points over Mickey Mantle. His .526 OBP was the second highest of his career and so was his .731 slugging average. So, too, were the 38 home runs he hit. It was truly a golden year.

His final three seasons saw a decline, though batting .328 as he did in 1958 would for almost any other player be spectacular. In fact, it was enough to win Ted the batting championship even if it was some 16 points below his ultimate .344 lifetime average. The batting title was his seventh, not counting 1954 as per the rules of the day. 1959 was his one really bad year; he developed a very troublesome stiff neck during spring training that saw him wear a neck brace and have a very difficult time trying to overcome it. He never truly got on track and batted a disappointing .254 with only 10 homers and 43 RBIs in 272 at-bats. It was sentiment alone that placed him on the All-Star squad, one of 18 times he was accorded the honor. Everyone expected him to retire; even Red Sox owner Tom Yawkey, with whom Williams had a good if distant relationship, suggested it might be time.

Ted Williams didn't want to leave with a season like 1959 wrapping up his career. He came back for a swan song season, but insisted that he be given a 30 percent pay cut because of his underperformance in 1959. He felt he hadn't earned the money he was being paid, at the time—as it had been for many years—just about the highest salary in all of baseball, understood to be around $125,000. Williams had hard work in 1960 but he produced, batting .316 with 29 home runs—the last of which was hit in what had been announced as his very last at-bat in the major leagues.

In his latter years, Williams had played for a Red Sox team that offered him little support in the lineup, had not much in the way of pitching, and didn't draw many fans. Even Ted's final home game drew just over 10,000 fans to Fenway Park. How much better he would have done had he played in a park with a friendlier right field, like Tiger Stadium or Yankee Stadium, remains unknowable. How much better he might have done had he had a Lou Gehrig hitting behind him in the lineup, or had he not missed five seasons to military service, remains unknowable.

Leaving on such a high note, Williams couldn't resist a final shot at the Boston press corps with whom he had so frequently feuded since his second year with the Red Sox. The "knights of the keyboard" wouldn't have Williams to kick around anymore. And Ted Williams left town, though in lieu of any farewell dinners he quietly,

and without publicity, stopped to pay a visit to a dying child stricken with leukemia. Teddy Ballgame, as he was known, had been the leading spokesman for Boston's "Jimmy Fund" for many years. Ted had appeared on behalf of Dr. Sidney Farber's children's cancer research efforts since the late 1940s, in fact since before Dr. Farber (the "father of chemotherapy") first achieved remission in leukemia. Today, over 85 percent of children with leukemia are cured.

Save for appearances for the Jimmy Fund, Ted took time off and spent the next several years catching up on his fishing while bringing in some endorsement income through a long association with Sears Roebuck, which produced an extensive line of Ted Williams brand sporting equipment—all of which Ted insisted on testing personally, right down to the tents and sleeping bags that would bear his name. Ted married a second time, to Lee Howard of Chicago in September 1961. It was a short-lived marriage, perhaps in part because Ted had already met the woman who was perhaps his soulmate in life, Louise Kaufman. Though they never married, she loved Ted through both his second and third marriages (the third, to Dolores Wettach, occurred in 1968, when she was apparently already pregnant with the son who became John-Henry Williams.) Dolores and Ted later had a daughter, Claudia Franc Williams, born shortly after Ted and Dolores separated a few years into the marriage. Always in the background was Lou Kaufman, who—though six years older than Ted—was a fishing champion in her own right and apparently had enough salt to spar with Ted with the sort of banter he liked to dish out. There were other women, of course. In many ways, Ted Williams was a "man's man" and perhaps didn't have the patience for a relationship. Visiting one afternoon in the late 1990s at Ted's house in Florida, this author was presented with a blunt, candid, and unanswerable remark when—out of the blue—Ted declared, "Yeah, I guess I was a great hitter, but I was a lousy husband and a crummy father."

After the requisite five years following his playing career, Ted Williams was elected to the National Baseball Hall of Fame in his first year of eligibility. When he was inducted in the summer of 1966, Williams wrote out his speech by hand the evening before (the original is in the Hall of Fame) and after thanking those who helped him on his way, he devoted part of the core of his speech to an impassioned plea that the Hall of Fame recognize the many Negro League ballplayers who had not been allowed to play in the segregated major leagues prior to 1947.

He wrote in his autobiography *My Turn At Bat* (published in 1969) of his Mexican-American mother, "If I had had my mother's name, there is no doubt I would have run into problems in those days, the prejudices people had in Southern California." One can speculate that his own awareness of prejudice may have informed his remarks at the Hall of Fame. The first African American

Williams and Doerr talking hitting behind the cage.

in the American League, Larry Doby, says that Williams went out of his way to make him welcome—not grandstanding but with the simplest of private gestures on the field. When the Red Sox finally integrated by adding Pumpsie Green to the big league roster in 1959, Ted chose Pumpsie as his throwing partner before games.

In the same year as his remarkably self-revealing autobiography was published, Williams became manager of Bob Short's Washington Senators ball club. The team showed a fairly dramatic improvement in team batting his very first year and, while on safari in Africa, Ted received word that he had been named Manager of the Year. It was good timing for Ted's second book (written as had been the first with author John Underwood)—*The Science of Hitting*. The book demonstrated the Ted Williams approach to the game and, as with *My Turn At Bat*, has remained in print ever since—no small feat in the world of books. Even in the 21st century, *The Science of Hitting* is often the book of choice for aspiring batters.

Ted had signed on as manager for five years, but he lost interest after the Senators failed to further improve (and some of the ballplayers chafed under his regime to the point of near-insubordination). Ted traveled to Texas with the franchise and served as the first manager of the Texas Rangers in 1972 but he begged out of the fifth and final year of the deal.

Throughout his years as player and as manager, he was always a colorful "larger than life" figure with a booming voice and a presence that defined charisma. He was often a lightning rod of sorts, loved or hated by fans, and a reliable source of controversial copy for sportswriters and reporters. He was loud and boisterous, but as he himself admitted in his autography, he was "never very diplomatic....I did a lot of yakking, partly to hide a rather large inferiority complex."

After leaving full-time employment in baseball for good, Ted served for years and years as a "special assignment instructor" with the Boston Red Sox. Typically, this meant he would show up at spring training for a few weeks and look over the younger hitters, occasionally taking a player aside later in the year as well. When Carl Yastrzemski was struggling in his first year of trying to fill Ted's shoes as Boston's left fielder, the team flew Williams in from where he was fishing in Canada and he spent a few days working with Yaz. Yastrzemski says, "He really didn't say anything; he was just trying to build me up mentally. He says, 'You've got a great swing—just go out and use it.'" Yastrzemski realized he was trying too hard to emulate Williams as a home run hitter, but Ted helped him settle down and helped him become himself. Over time, Yaz says, "I think the big thing that I learned from him, which he talked about, was the strike zone, strike zone, strike zone."[1]

For many years, Ted lived in a small but comfortable cabin on New Brunswick's Miramichi River where he was able to fish for his beloved Atlantic salmon, a fish he so admired that he became a leader of the fight to preserve the species from overfishing and other encroachments on its habitat. An annual "Ted Williams Award" is presented to others who have joined in the cause. Ted enjoyed the companionship of Lou Kaufman in his later years.

Ted Williams was active on the Hall of Fame's Veterans Committee (and sometimes criticized for being too vocal an advocate for players he championed such as Phil Rizzuto and Dominic DiMaggio). As he grew older, many of the hard attitudes toward Ted softened and, in the words of Doris Kearns Goodwin, "It seemed like his stature...his stature was always there—I don't think anyone ever disputed how great he was—but the kind of emotions he generated in the fans got stronger as time went by rather than weaker, which is really nice. I'm glad he's lived to see all that. It seems to have mellowed and made him a happier person, too."[2]

He always engendered strong opinions and harbored many of his own. This was a man of many interests and an intellectual curiosity perhaps surprising in a ballplayer, a man whom his Marine Corps instructor could conceive of as a Shakespearean scholar and whom Tommy Henrich of the New York Yankees could envision as a brain surgeon or nuclear scientist. Biographer David Halberstam once said that Ted "won 33,277 arguments in a row...the undisputed champion of contentiousness"—but then went on to write a book about the friendship between Ted, Bobby Doerr, Dominic DiMaggio, and Johnny Pesky that endured for six decades.

For the last several years of his life, Ted became active in the memorabilia market, attracting very large sums to appear for occasional signings at industry shows. Some took advantage of his natural generosity and in one case Ted pursued a man who had defrauded him, the case becoming an episode on the *America's Most Wanted* television show. Ted's son, John-Henry Williams, took over management of the marketing of his father with mixed success. Many criticized John-Henry for being too zealous in his father's behalf and for some of his business schemes, but there was no doubt that Ted very much loved his son and was prepared to turn a blind eye to any faults. Ted suffered a stroke and a subsequent heart operation sapped his health, and he entered a period of decline that ended with his passing on July 5, 2002. In death, as in life, controversy swirled around Ted Williams as two of his three children had his body cryonically frozen for the possibility of some later revival if science someday learns a way to restore life to those who have been so preserved. Many of Ted's closest friends were aghast but efforts by his eldest daughter to reverse the decision were in vain. An outpouring of more than 20,000 people attended a memorial at Boston's Fenway Park later in July 2002 and the memory of the man they called The Kid lives on.

Notes

1. Interview by Bill Nowlin, August 31, 1997
2. Interview by Bill Nowlin, May 3, 1997

TOM WRIGHT *by Bill Nowlin*

G	AB	R	H	2B	3B	HR	RBI	BB	SO	BA	OBP	SLG	SB	HBP
3	2	1	1	0	1	0	0	0	0	.500	.500	1.500	0	0

Tom Wright, a left-handed hitting outfielder who played major league baseball over nine seasons, still lived in 2007 in the town where he was born: Shelby, North Carolina. Wright was born on September 22, 1923, one of 10 children (five boys and five girls) raised on the family farm run by his father, J.B. Wright. "Cotton is the thing that sold, but with our family and everything and as poor as we were, they grew all kind of vegetables and everything else," he said recently.

Like many families during the Depression, the family faced tough times, but Tom says, "If I look back, it was real rough. They didn't know it, because we grew a lot of our own food. The textile mills didn't pay anything but we had jobs. Back then, you had your company stores and all that stuff. You could go get your food and then pay for it when you got paid. It was just like that week to week was the way we lived. I never went hungry, though I did eat a lot of beans and a lot of bread. And taters and stuff like that, that we grew ourselves. We didn't consider us all that poor, although we were dirt poor."

With 10 children in the family, they had enough for a baseball team, but none of his siblings showed much interest in baseball. The local textile mill had a team and Tom's brothers played some growing up, but never amounted to much. The family house was down the street from the mill's ball field, just about a block away, Tom and some of the kids his own age played endlessly on the field. "That's where I was raised, really—on that ball field. When we were kids, we ate, we went to the ball field. We went back. A lot of times, it wasn't until close to

Tom Wright.
Courtesy of Tom Wright.

dark before we'd ever go back home. Just playing, in summertime when we were out of school."

Tom who grew to 5 feet 11, played high school ball for Shelby High and some American Legion ball, and even some semipro ball in Florence, South Carolina, during the summer of 1941. Tom typically played infield, mostly shortstop, but after he reported to Danville-Schoolfield in the Bi-State League for the 1942 season, he was converted to outfield. "They had infielders and they said, 'You swing like an outfielder'—so I went to the outfield." He even pitched a bit for Danville, though his one start didn't end too well. "I had a good arm. I went in and relieved two or three times, and I got them out. Then they pitched me one ball game. George Ferrell (brother of Wes and Rick, both major league stars in the 1930s) was the manager of Rocky Mount. I done good all day long, beating them, and I let a little curveball slip and get over the base. They had a short left field. He hit it out. He's the one that beat me."

Red Sox scout Eddie Montague signed Wright to the Red Sox in 1941, right out of high school. He'd watched Wright play both high school and American Legion ball and inked a contract before graduating. It didn't cost the Red Sox a penny. "I guess I didn't have enough sense to ask for a bonus," Wright told writer Tommy Fitzgerald of *The Sporting News* (August 24, 1949). "I was just so tickled to get a chance to play professional baseball that it didn't make any difference."

The Red Sox asked him to report to Canton, Ohio, but he was too young and didn't want to travel so far from home so they suggested Florence. Come 1942, he was assigned to Danville and batted .241 in 394 at-bats, driving in 60 runs. After the season, he was picked up by Greensboro under their working agreement with Danville, but World War II intervened.

He had registered for the draft and was finally taken in March 1943, missing the next three seasons. After the war, he wrapped up his high school diploma, getting a lot credit for the life experiences he'd had. Under The GI Bill, he attended Howard Business College, too, until the money ran out. The owner of the college allowed Tom to keep on at his own pace, though, without payment, and he finally finished up that degree, too. That was mixed in with selling automobiles, painting, some carpentry, and work in supply rooms—a little bit of everything, "so I'd have something I could do when I got through with baseball."

Tom served in the Army Air Corps. He trained as an aerial gunner and an armorer, in charge of the weapons. He tore up a foot parachuting during training in Wyoming, and by the time that healed up, he'd already heard from a friend who had put in his missions overseas. His friend urged him to get out of active flight and transfer to ground crew work. He did, giving up his sergeant's stripes and going overseas as a private first class. The 13th Air Force sent him to the South Pacific, assigned to a P-38 outfit. "I looked after loading bombs and looked after the guns. I went up through New Guinea, and then a replacement center and then up through Moreton, Biak, and those islands over there and I wound up on Palawan in the Philippines. They tell me that's a resort place now. There wasn't nothing over there at that time. I was in for three years, and I spent a year overseas. I was a corporal. I was up for sergeant, they said, but I wasn't worried about that. I was worrying about getting home."

After the war, he took spring training with the 1946 Red Sox in South Carolina. "I'd just got back home from the war. Rainy, misty, cold, and I was trying to throw with some little boy they had training in Florida, but the next day I couldn't. I hurt my arm. In most of my professional

Wright was a prime pinch hitter.
Courtesy of Tom Wright.

years, I had an arm that bothered me but I tried not to show it no more than I had to." As it happens, Wright's foot hadn't healed perfectly, either. "It's still got all the fractured bones and all that kind of cracks and everything in it, but it's OK. I was able to do my whole career with a bad foot. Of course, it was taped up a lot. It was wrapped and taped a lot, but I didn't complain about it. I was trying to keep a job."

He was the property of the Scranton club of the Eastern League, and they had so many players coming back from the service and otherwise out for spring training that it was hard for the staff to evaluate what they really had. Wright felt they weren't really looking at him, so along with one or two others, he simply returned home. In postwar America, the law guaranteed returning veterans the right to return to their own jobs and Wright was reminded that he had a secure job, but he told them he was heading home until they decided where they wanted to send him. They gave him a choice between Canton and Durham. Durham was closer, so he picked that, and played under Pat Patterson for the 1946 Carolina League season. He had an excellent year, leading the league in hitting with a .380 average, banging out an even 200 hits, including 61 extra-base hits, and driving in 116 runs. Nine of those RBIs all came in the July 10 game thanks to two doubles and two triples. His 200 hits remained the league record until 1950. He might have had a few more, except for a time he got beaned that cost him a couple of games. "They were always throwing at me. When you get base hits, they throw at you."

The next year, he trained with Triple-A Louisville. He had a terrific spring, but ended up the exhibition season suffering painful shin splints from the "sandy Florida diamonds." (*The Sporting News*, August 24, 1949) The Colonels were well-enough stocked, so Louisville sent him to Memphis in April but he wound up playing 1947 in New Orleans. Playing for the Pelicans in the Southern Association, he batted .325, again homering 14 times, this time driving in 89 runs, despite missing 11 days after a serious July 29 beaning. After the season, Wright was named to the Southern Association all-star team.

L-r: Wright, Billy Goodman, Dom DiMaggio, Ted Williams, Clyde Vollmer. 1951.
Courtesy of Tom Wright.

In 1948, he advanced to Louisville and racked up 563 at-bats in 151 games, with a .307 average. His power and RBI numbers were virtually identical to the year before. In September, he got called up to the Boston ball club. He'd only just arrived and got his uniform when manager Joe McCarthy told him, "Wright, get your stick!" It was the top of the ninth inning in a September 15 game against the White Sox. First time up, the first pitch he saw, he hit for a triple to the right-center field fence. He soon scored and when he got back to the dugout, "McCarthy said, 'Son, you don't take (pitches) much, do you?' I guess that's the only words that man ever said to me when I was with the ball club." And that included 1949. "He never spoke to the ballplayers. They just sit down on one end and managed. Back in those days, they didn't have hitting coaches, they didn't have fielding coaches, they didn't have all that stuff that they have now. They didn't coach. They didn't do nothing." Players had to pretty much make their own way.

Tom had two at-bats with Boston in 1948 and left with a .500 average. He was with the team right though the end of the year and even had a minor role in the playoff game with Cleveland, entering as a pinch runner for Billy Hitchcock in the ninth. Why did McCarthy decide to pitch Denny Galehouse in the final game? "Everybody there questioned that, because he couldn't break a pane of glass. He didn't throw hard. He wasn't a hard ball thrower. You didn't slip in Fenway. If you did, somebody'd hit the green wall. That's what happened to us."

Wright had been a fan favorite in Louisville and was chosen Most Valuable Players on the Colonels by a vote of the fans. After the season, the Red Sox released Wally Moses to make room for Wright in their plans for 1949. Come springtime, though, it was determined that he needed more seasoning. Wright was candid with *Sporting News* writer Tommy Fitzgerald that he'd been disappointed in his springtime experience with the Red Sox:

"Nobody hardly said a word to me. Nobody showed me anything."

Fitzgerald classified Wright as a "natural straightaway hitter who sends the ball to all fields" and wrote the Boston's farm director Johnny Murphy had tried to get him to pull the ball more to right, but the suggestion didn't work. Murphy also suggested he switch to a larger glove, and that did seem to strengthen his fielding.

In 1949, he spent the full year back in Louisville, again appearing in 151 games, this year rapping out 202 hits and leading the American Association in hitting with a .368 average. Late in the year, he came back to Boston and found himself inserted into the final game of the year. If the Red Sox won the game, they won the pennant and Ellis Kinder had held the Yankees to just one run through eight innings. Unfortunately, New York's Vic Raschi denied Boston even one run. Sox manager Joe McCarthy called on the AA batting champion to pinch hit for Kinder in the top of the eighth; Wright worked a walk but was retired when Dom DiMaggio grounded into a double play. Kinder was a very good hitting pitcher, and though Wright had gotten himself on base, Kinder's replacement—Mel Parnell—was hit hard in the bottom of the eighth, and the game was out of reach.

Most of the time that Wright played in the minors, it was center field he patrolled. But in the majors, it was primarily left field, because of his weaker arm. He knew the Red Sox outfield was a hard one to crack, but he made the team in 1950 as a backup. Wright was with the Red Sox for all of 1950, and got most of his playing time in helping out after Ted Williams shattered his elbow during that season's All-Star Game. Billy Goodman largely took over for Ted in left, and Wright fit in 24 games, 19 in right field and five in left. For the most part, though, he pinch-hit for Boston. He did total 107 at-bats, and hit .318, so he got a fair amount of work.

Manager Steve O'Neill had plenty of praise for his pinch-hitting specialist: "You can call on him any time and he's just as likely as not to deliver the hit you need. Lots of players lose that split-second timing when they lay off for a while. But Tom can sit on the bench for three weeks, then get up and hit just as well as if he was in there every day." O'Neill's comments appeared in a November 1, 1950 *Sporting News* article; author Steve O'Leary characterized Wright as a "soft-spoken southerner" with a "fine sense of humor and he's a great guy to have around for morale purposes. That's another point in his favor with O'Neill, who is blessed with plenty of Irish wit."

In 1951, he tailed off sharply, and was sent back to

Louisville after just 63 at-bats. He was only hitting .222. It was a frustrating time. "Nobody was hitting. Williams wasn't hitting. There wasn't nobody hitting. When Cronin (the general manager) called me up and told me I was going back to Louisville, we got in a cuss fight. I told him if he wanted to, just go look up the records of who Williams was hitting against and who I was hitting against, and see who was hitting. We had to separate. I went back out the next day, and I knew there wasn't no more for me to do but just go back to Louisville. But nobody was hitting. Williams wasn't hitting, either." It was indeed an "off year" for Ted Williams; he only hit .318.

After 28 games with the Red Sox, Wright got in 72 games for Louisville, where he hit .282, but he found it "hard to get tuned in," and after the season was over, he requested a trade. "I told them to get rid of me. They'd done moved me up and down so much. They told me all the time Detroit wanted to buy me and they wouldn't do it. They'd just keep holding me in Triple-A ball. I told them, just get rid of me. So they sent me to St. Louis." A late November swap with St. Louis brought Boston Gus Niarhos and Ken Wood and sent Wright and Les Moss to the Browns. In its December 5 issue, *The Sporting News* contained four separate stories about talked-about trades of Ted Williams, and one suggested that acquiring Ken Wood to play left field was the key element in the trade with St. Louis. Ted was never traded, Wood never panned out, but Wright opened the 1952 season hitting cleanup for St. Louis.

"Early Wallflower Wright Blossoms as Brownie Daisy," headlined an early April *Sporting News*, reporting that Wright had been named starting left fielder. Rogers Hornsby called him "the most improved player on the squad." Wright had a hot start, but cooled off considerably, striking out quite a lot and found himself playing only infrequently. On June 15, the Browns swapped him and Leo Thomas to the White Sox for Al Zarilla and Willie Miranda. Ironically, it was Zarilla as much as anyone who had blocked Wright from playing more in Boston, and now St. Louis sent him to Chicago to acquire Zarilla. Wright finished the season hitting .258 for the White Sox, up from the .242 he'd hit for St. Louis.

Manager Paul Richards told *The Sporting News* in August that three of his players, including Wright, would be getting a refresher course in where the strike zone is located come the next spring. "It is my belief that all three of them could be .300 hitters if they laid off the bad pitches," Richards said of Wright, Jim Rivera, and Hector Rodriguez.

He's been told, he says, that he led the league in pinch hits in 1953. "I get a little bit of this stuff from fans, saying they're wanting autographs and this and that and the other. They'll give me all my records and everything. I've never looked them up." He played in 77 games, getting 132 at-bats and hitting an even .250.

Right at the end of 1954 spring training, the White Sox sent him to the Washington Senators for Kite Thomas. He was on the team all year, but it was a very disappointing one. "I never could get anything going with them. I just couldn't get my rhythm. I didn't even feel like part of the team. I never did get going and I was always sorry for that because I wanted to play for Griffith bad." Wright started the season platooning in right field with Jim Lemon, but he wasn't the answer to Washington's problems and wound up largely used as a left-handed pinch hitter. He got 171 at-bats, but it was just too much stop-and-start— and maybe he just wasn't the same player as he'd been now that he'd hit age 30.

At the end of March 1955, Wright was optioned to Chattanooga and played with the Lookouts for the full year, appearing in 142 games and hitting .293 back in the Southern Association. He drove in 72 runs, and was brought back up to Washington in September, where he had seven at-bats in seven appearances, but didn't record even one hit. Come the spring of 1956, Wright lacked just under 30 days of major league playing time in order to qualify for the pension, and Senators owner Griffith ensured that he was brought back long enough to qualify. Washington manager Charlie Dressen kept him on the team, but didn't use him a bit in spring training. "He didn't even let me pinch hit or do nothing all spring. But I was the first pinch hitter against the Yankees on opening day. Them boys down on the bench said, 'Durn, Tom. What's he trying to do to you?' I says, 'I don't care. Give me the stick.' I didn't get a fair run with him, but really I didn't get a fair run, I didn't think, because I never did get to stay in the lineup to get my timing and everything. I was just fighting to stay in the major leagues. I wasn't going to fuss with nobody." Actually, Wright pinch-ran in the season opener, but pinch-hit in the second game of the regular season, grounding out for the pitcher in the seventh inning. He'd appeared in two games and had just the one at-bat. After he'd logged the requisite time for a pension, Wright was sent to Louisville. Thus ended his time in major league baseball.

When he got to Louisville, Tom recorded a .245 average over 159 at-bats, but was bumped down to Birmingham in midyear. There he did well, hitting .344. He returned again for the 1957 season with Birmingham, but hit only .257. Tom began to figure his time was up. He wasn't hitting as well, and he didn't want to travel by air. He asked that he be sent to a club that didn't fly and was sold to Charleston but he found there was no way to make the schedules without flying, so he just left baseball. Perhaps a bit ironic that the man who'd volunteered to fly in the Army Air Force was now overly anxious at the prospect of travel by air. "I just couldn't stand it. It made me nervous. I flew good, but those two or three days when you're waiting before you know you're going to fly, I was nervous as a cat. It was affecting my life. In fact, I lost my errors that lost the game for New York. After the game, Grimes was sure that he would be sent to the minor leagues. According to Grimes, "Instead, McCarthy slapped me on the back and said, 'Oscar, you'll never believe this, but I once had a worse inning than that at Louisville. Now get out there and win this second game for me.' You know, you've got to play your guts out for a man like that."

McCarthy also succeeded in managing Babe Ruth. According to one writer, "No matter what his thoughts might have been, Joe ran the rest of his club and left Babe to his own devices. Ruth never bothered Joe much either. He did just about as he pleased, just showed up for the games and gave McCarthy four pretty good seasons. It was hard to tell what he thought of the manager." There were, however, reports that Ruth's jealousy of McCarthy led to Ruth's release by the Yankees and signing by the Boston Braves in 1935.

Still, in spite of his successes, McCarthy's teams were not up to the same standards during the latter part of World War II. From 1843 to 1945 the Yankees never finished above third place, as many of his star players had retired, left for other teams, or gone into the armed forces. On May 26, 1946, in a telegram from his farm at Tonawanda, New York, to team president Larry MacPhail, McCarthy resigned. "It is with extreme regret," McCarthy wrote, "that I must request that you accept my resignation as manager of the Yankee Baseball Club, effective immediately. My doctor advises that my health would be seriously jeopardized if I continue. This is the sole reason for my decision, which as you know, is entirely voluntary on my part."

The *New York Times* reported that McCarthy had suffered a recurrence of a gall bladder condition that necessitated his retirement and that McCarthy would remain with the team in an advisory capacity. "McCarthy was the most cooperative manager with whom I have ever been associated in baseball," said MacPhail at the time. Long-time Yankee catcher Bill Dickey was named as McCarthy's replacement.

But that explanation had its doubters. One American League club official who chose to remain anonymous said that McCarthy had "so much success that he went to pieces with a losing club." There were also persistent rumors that McCarthy resigned because of a personality conflict with Larry MacPhail, with whom McCarthy did not have as close a relationship as he had with Ed Barrow.

Said one contemporary article: "There is no question that McCarthy is a sick man, but the prime reason that he is not returning to the Yankees is not his ailments but Larry MacPhail, new president of the club.... Now apparently the more he cogitates on MacPhail's blast about the Yankees not hustling, the more determined he becomes to stay in Buffalo and terminate his connection to the club." MacPhail had also publicly scorned McCarthy for

a confrontation with Joe Page during a flight from Cleveland to Detroit five days earlier.

After two years out of baseball, McCarthy was hired by the Boston Red Sox. Boston had finished 14 games behind the Yankees in 1947, and McCarthy's hiring was part of a larger shakeup that included shifting then-manager Joe Cronin into a front-office position. Cronin sounded impressed also: "Joe's going to have more power than probably any manager since McGraw. He will have complete charge of the team and will have the power to make any deal he wants."

Boston sportswriter Harold Kaese wrote, "McCarthy is more highly rated than Cronin, having won nine pennants to Cronin's two.... When McCarthy signed, Boston fans were confident that another pennant was on the way."

Lou Stringer with McCarthy. Courtesy of Tom Stringer.

Even though McCarthy's Boston teams finished in second place in each of his two full seasons with the Red Sox, it was not enough to satisfy Boston fans who were eager for him to duplicate the World Series-winning success he had in New York. Boston lost a one-game playoff for the American League pennant to Cleveland in 1948 and finished second to the Yankees in 1949, losing the pennant on the last weekend of the season.

In 1969, McCarthy got together with Ted Williams and recalled that Williams had been the last player to leave the locker room after Boston's loss in the 1948 one-game playoff. As recounted by Buffalo sportswriter Cy Kritzer:

'Do you remember what I said to you that day?' Joe inquired.

'How could I ever forget those kind words?' Williams replied. 'They were the kindest words ever spoken to me in baseball.'

Marse Joe had told his star slugger, 'We did get along,

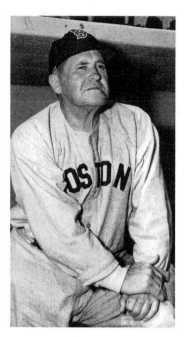

Keeping a watchful eye.

didn't we? And we surprised a lot of people who said we couldn't.'

According to Kritzer, Williams also appreciated how McCarthy never criticized his players in the press.

Still, said Ed Fitzgerald in *Sport* magazine: "The sportswriters of the town, who greeted [McCarthy] with open arms when he took over the job, have been beating him over the head ever since. Not all of them, but most of them.... They criticize his handling of his players, his relations with the press, his every positive or negative act."

And when McCarthy resigned from Boston's managerial position on July 22, 1950, again citing ill health, his critics were ready to pounce. But an admirer, Arthur Daley, wrote in *the New York Times*, "Marse Joe failed at Boston. It's unfortunate that his departure had to come on such a sour note because the small-minded men who don't know any better will definitely remark that he could never manage a ball club anyway and add that it's good riddance. They'll even add that the records are false in proclaiming that the square-jawed Irishman from Buffalo won more pennants than John McGraw and Connie Mack."

Retiring to his farm home in Tonawanda, New York, McCarthy was done with professional baseball for good. He liked, as one UPI report said, "to putter around the garden." In retirement, he was busy: "I don't have time to do any fishing now, either," he said in 1970 when he was 83. "This place is big enough to take care of, so I never get out. I do a few things around the house. A little gardening. Not much. I plant tomatoes and beans and stuff like that." He called his home "Yankee Farm." Joe's wife, Elizabeth McCarthy, died in October 1971 at the couple's 61-acre farm.

McCarthy was elected to the Hall of Fame by the Veterans Committee in 1957 along with former Detroit Tigers star outfielder Sam Crawford.

Joe McCarthy died of pneumonia at the age of 90 on October 13, 1979, at Millard Fillmore Hospital, near his home in Tonawanda. He had been hospitalized twice in 1977, once for a fall and later for pneumonia. He was buried in Mount Olivet Cemetery in Tonawanda.

Sources

McCarthy's biography and World Series statistics on baseball-reference.com.

Clippings from McCarthy's file at the Hall of Fame:

"Cubs Saying Nothing, Sawing Wood and Keeping Stiff Lip." September 6, 1928.

Daley, Arthur, "Delayed Tribute," *New York* Times, September 2, 1951.

Daley, Arthur, "Exit for Marse Joe, *New York Times*, June 25, 1950.

Dawson, James P., "McCarthy Resigns: Dickey Yank Pilot," *New York Times*, May 1946.

Drebinger, John, "Marse Joe Coming Home," *New York Times*. Undated.

Durso, Joseph, "Joe McCarthy, Yanks' Ex-Manager Dies at 90." *New York Times*, January 14, 1978.

Durso, "Whether they liked it or not, McCarthy did things his way." *New York Times*, November 15, 1978.

Enright, James, "Will Luck of the Irish Revive Faded Cubs?' *The Sporting News*, March 23, 1963.

Fitzgerald, Ed, "Nobody's Neutral About McCarthy," *Sport*, August 1950.

"Good for Joe," July 25, 1929.

Grayson, Harry, "McCarthy Recalls Pine St. Baseball Parade That Turned Him from Cricket to Diamond."

"He Welcomed the Honor but Not at Players' Expense."

Kritzer, Cy, "Glory Days Come Alive: Ted Visits McCarthy," September 8, 1969.

Kritzer, Cy, "Marse Joe's Biggest World Series Thrill? Sweep Over Cubs Who Fired Him." May 2, 1956.

Lanigan, Ernest J. "For Any Day"

"Marse Joe Has 88th," UPI, April 22, 1975.

"'Marse Joe' McCarthy, led Yankees to 7 Series," UPI, January 14, 1978.

"Marse Joe McCarthy, at 83, Has Scant Time for Baseball," UPI, April 26, 1970.

"McCarthy Admits Yankees' Hurling Must Stiffen Much," *Philadelphia Record*, February 23, 1931.

"McCarthy Through at Chicago, Hornsby In Line As Successor," September 25, 1930.

McKenney, Joe, "Hub Prospects Rejuvenate McCarthy, *The Sporting News*, October 29, 1947.

"Mrs. Joe McCarthy," Obituaries, *New York Times*, October 20, 1971.

"No Kick on Cubs in Chicago This Time: Joe McCarthy's Debut Year All That Could be Asked." 1926.

Ogle, Jim, "Joe McCarthy: A Tribute." *My Yankee Scrapbook*, 1978.

Porter. David L., "McCarthy, Joseph Vincent," *Biographical Dictionary of American Sports*.

Segar, Charles, "M'Carthy to Quit Yank Post," July 31, 1945.

Vaughan, Irving, "McCarthy Signs to Pilot Cubs for Two Years: Louisville Manager Closes with Veeck."

"Yankees Owe Flag Largely to Marse Joe: McCarthy Shows His Ability in Solving Pitching Problems," *New York Times*, September 24, 1937.

"Yankees To Sign Joe M'Carthy When Series Moves Off Stage," October 9, 1930.

Wedge, Will, "That 'Marse Joe' Nickname." 1931.

Williams, Joe, "Busher Joe McCarthy." *The Saturday Evening Post*, April 15, 1939.

Complete Minor League Playing Record and partial minor league salary record in his Hall of Fame player file.

base..." Star pitcher Grover Cleveland Alexander lit a cigarette and retorted: "You don't have to worry about that, Mr. McCarthy. This club will never get a man that far." A month later, McCarthy sold Alexander to the St. Louis Cardinals. Shortly thereafter, Wrigley told McCarthy: "Congratulations. I've been looking for a manager who had the nerve to do that."

In McCarthy's first season with the Cubs, the team showed marked improvement. A sportswriter wrote, "There has been more interest in the Cubs in Chicago this year than ever before. Their unexpected showing also stimulated business on the road and it is a fair bet when the team holds its annual meeting President William Veeck will be able to tell the few stockholders that a juicy melon is in the safe ready for cutting."

McCarthy's success, the writer said, was even more remarkable considering that Alexander and Wilbur Cooper were both gone from the pitching staff. "Naturally much credit is being cast in the direction of McCarthy and he seems entitled to every nice thing that is said,"

The Cubs finished in fourth place in both 1926 and 1927 behind the strong hitting of Gabby Hartnett, Riggs Stephenson, and Hack Wilson. While the pitching was solid if not spectacular, the Cubs struggled to win on the road—on the road, the Cubs "have fallen down woefully," a newspaper article said. Even in 1928, when the Cubs finished with 91 wins, it was the team's struggles to win away from Chicago that kept it from being more competitive.

McCarthy's managerial decisions paid more dividends in 1929. According to one newspaper account, "It is generally agreed now that McCarthy made a move for improvement when he broke away from the batting layout he had established for himself early in the Spring. This involved only the heavy caliber members of the attack. [Kiki] Cuyler had been third, [Rogers] Hornsby fourth, Wilson fifth, and Stephenson sixth. Now Cuyler has been shunted in fifth place and Hornsby and Wilson have been elevated to third and fourth, respectively."

Although McCarthy was never a particular favorite of the media, his managerial style was appreciated early in his career. Said one account in 1929: "[McCarthy] has one quality which endears him to those who know what a manager has to face in the way of heckling. He stands by his players.... Tell him the team his team is weak here, or weak there, and he will not fly off the handle. On the contrary, he will tell you where it is strong and going along to suit him."

While with the Cubs, McCarthy became known by the nickname Marse Joe, a name that followed him throughout his life. Writer Will Wedge contended: "It is suspected that Marse Joe was hung on Joseph Vincent by a Windy City scribe after he had risen from a rather Little Joe, not so very seriously considered at first, to a veritable Master Joe by his forcing the Cubs up from the ruck into a championship in the space of five years...When you come to think of it that Marse Joe label has a quiet sound, a safe sound. It isn't the name you'd hang on a person who goes off half cocked. It's the title of an overseer who's sane and balanced. And McCarthy is just that."

McCarthy's finest moment with the Cubs ultimately resulted in his undoing there. He led the Cubs to a 95-win season in 1929 and to the World Series. The Cubs, however, lost the Series in five games to Connie Mack's Philadelphia Athletics. Not only did McCarthy's team lose the first game when Mack surprisingly started aging Howard Ehmke, who won, 3–1, and struck out a then-record 13 batters, but the team also allowed the Athletics to overcome an eight-run deficit in Game Four by allowing 10 runs in the seventh inning, keyed by Hack Wilson's losing Mule Haas' fly ball in the sun.

Even with a second-place finish in 1930 supported by Hack Wilson's National League record 56 home runs, McCarthy was not offered a contract by the Cubs at the end of that season and was replaced by Rogers Hornsby. The 1930 Cubs endured an injury to pitcher Charlie Root in September as well as a particularly weak showing on a late-season East Coast trip.

Still, the loss in the 1929 World Series was never truly forgotten. As Joseph Durso later wrote, "neither the Chicago fans nor Mr. Wrigley ever quite forgave Mr. McCarthy for that." Wrigley, in fact, was quoted as saying, "I have always wanted a world's championship, and I am not sure that Joe McCarthy is the man to give me that kind of team." Hornsby also reportedly had "openly censured" McCarthy for using pitcher Art Nehf during that miserable seventh inning in Game Four of the 1929 World Series.

For whatever lack of enthusiasm followed McCarthy out of Chicago, he was eagerly pursued by the New York Yankees to replace Bob Shawkey. Still, McCarthy's arrival in New York was held up since he had promised first to talk to the Red Sox about their managerial vacancy. An unattributed newspaper clipping in McCarthy's Hall of Fame file reports, "The offer [the Red Sox] made was not attractive to him, however, and he felt free to talk to Col. Jacob Ruppert and Edward G. Barrow, which he did last Friday night."

The exact reasons behind McCarthy's refusal of the Red Sox' offer are unclear, but team president Bob Quinn reportedly held nothing back in trying to get the former Chicago manager. "I will pay you more salary than Col. Ruppert of the Yankees is willing to offer," Quinn reportedly said. "You can sign with my club for as many years as you wish. If you come with us, you'll be your own boss. There will be no interference on the playing end or the trading end. You can get your own assistants. If you want me to get you a player, I'll get him." Yet, in the end, McCarthy turned the Red Sox down for a two-year contract with the Yankees.

Even before McCarthy's hiring was officially announced by New York, one reviewer thought well of it. Another Hall of Fame clipping reads: "The coming of McCarthy to the Yankees is regarded in New York as a ten-strike for the Yankees and the American League, as well it should be. After all, here is a man who built up a winning team in Chicago and managed it intelligently— so well did he manage the torn and battered Cubs this year that he came within an ace of winning the pennant again. What he will do with the Yankees is, of course, problematical, but the chances that he will be as successful in New York as he was in Chicago are tremendously in his favor. Managerial ability isn't a matter of geography and a manager who does well in one town should do well in another, provided he isn't hampered by his new surroundings." Yet there were initial jitters: after McCarthy flubbed Colonel Ruppert's name during an early meeting with the press, Ruppert replied: "Maybe McCarthy will stay around long enough to learn my name."

Babe Ruth, who was said to have been disappointed not to get the New York managerial job himself, reportedly praised McCarthy when the latter was hired and said that the two would get along well. One paper in October 1930 even went so far as to say that "the coming of McCarthy to New York is one of the biggest achievements of the American League since Colonel Ruppert engaged the late lamented Miller Huggins 12 years ago. McCarthy is a figure of national importance. He is enjoying the friendship and sympathy of millions of fans who want to see him vindicated."

"I have no illusions about the task ahead of me with the Yankees," McCarthy wrote in a piece published in the *Philadelphia Record* in February 1931 (the Yankees had finished third in 1930). "The pitching staff showed signs of crumbling under Miller Huggins (who last managed in 1929)." He cited the arrival of Joe Sewell, which he felt could help form "an efficient infield combination." McCarthy also placed a lot of stock in rookie players, saying, "This ought to be a pretty good year for the rookie, as I am an American League rookie myself and stand willing to be convinced."

So began one of the most impressive managerial tenures in major-league history. In McCarthy's first 13 seasons with the Yankees, his teams finished in first or second place in every season but one. From 1932 to 1943, his teams won eight American League titles and seven World Series. His teams won more than 100 games in a 154-game season six times, and the Yankees won 90 games or more 11 times during that span.

Speaking in 1956, McCarthy listed his team's 1932 World Series victory over the Cubs as his greatest thrill. "Perhaps you understand why," he said. "First it was my first World Series winner. Secondly, it was against the Cubs."

McCarthy's skill was often praised even while he never was particularly warm or introspective with the media. A representative review appeared in the *New York Times* of September 24, 1937, after the Yankees had again won the pennant: "McCarthy deserves much credit for this year's Yankee success, having turned in the best of all his managerial jobs. He won despite a series of injuries to prominent hitters and an epidemic of lame arms which threw the pitching staff out of kilter. As he went along, Marse Joe proved himself to be an excellent handler of pitchers. He manipulated the staff adroitly, especially through the many weeks in which it was not up to full strength."

Still, his troubles with the press limited his appeal. Writing in 1950, Arthur Daley remarked, "Marse Joe was never easy to know. He was a suspicious man with the press and it was only on the rarest occasions that he'd let down his guard and talk expansively. Yet even then he'd suddenly whip up his guard and start sparring cautiously."

Managing perhaps the broadest collection of stars in major-league history with New York—including Bill Dickey, Lou Gehrig, Joe DiMaggio, Babe Ruth, Tony Lazzeri, and Lefty Gomez, among others—McCarthy was an understated presence, a teacher who insisted on consistent effort and outstanding performance. As Arthur Daley said in the *New York Times*: "Few men in baseball were ever as single-minded as he. That was to be both his strength and his weakness. Baseball was his entire life and it never was lightened by laughter because he was a grim, humorless man with a brooding introspection which ate his heart out."

At the time of his death, Durso remarked: that McCarthy "was a stocky 5-foot-8-inch Philadelphian with a strong Irish face, an inexpressive manner, a conservative outlook—the master of the noncommittal reply and the devotee of the 'set' lineup. He had neither the quiet desperation of Miller Huggins who preceded him as the Yankee empire builder, nor the loud flamboyance of Casey Stengel." As Durso recalled, Joe DiMaggio said, "Never a day went by that you didn't learn something from McCarthy."

With the Yankees, McCarthy maintained strict standards. Shortly after Jake Powell joined the team, for instance, Powell tried to give a teammate a hotfoot while the Yankees were waiting for a train. According to sportswriter Jim Ogle, McCarthy quickly said to Powell: "You're a Yankee now, we don't do that."

As Joe McKenney recounted in the *Buffalo Post*, McCarthy insisted that "his ball players play the part of champions at all times. Their dress and deportment in hotels and on trains was always McCarthy's concern and so successful were his methods that it was always easy to pick out a Yankee in a crowded lobby, even in Boston."

McCarthy, as John Drebinger recounted, had "an extraordinary ability in judging young players." Oscar Grimes, a utility infielder, committed three ninth-inning major league contract over it. I couldn't help it. It was making me so nervous I had to do something."

He returned to Shelby, and has been there ever since. During the off-seasons, Wright had had a strategy: "I sold automobiles and I painted. I carpentered and I worked in supply rooms and all that kind of stuff. I was trying to do a little of everything so I'd have something I could do when I got through with baseball." His first job after retiring as a ballplayer was running the credit department for a local clothing company, but he said he "didn't like messing with other people's money" and so signed up to make polyester and yarn for Celanese. He worked at their textile plant for just over 21 years, ending up as a supervisor and retiring in 1982.

Tom has one son, who's retired as well. Tom Wright Jr. played infield for the University of North Carolina and led the team in hits one year. He was offered a chance to go to spring training with Cincinnati, but he'd gotten married as soon as he got out of school and both he and his wife worked as schoolteachers. Tom and his son own a small farm together, raising some cattle and keeping busy.

Source

Interview done by Bill Nowlin. March 6, 2006

JOE MCCARTHY *by John McMurray*

Self-effacing and relentlessly confident, Joe McCarthy was a relatively silent yet authoritative force behind the success of the New York Yankees during 1930s and most of the 1940s. McCarthy's Yankee teams regularly dominated the American League and, in many seasons, New York faced little competition for the pennant. Although he was once famously scorned by Jimmy Dykes as a "push-button manager" who won largely because of his teams' superior talent, McCarthy's former players regarded him as indispensable to the success of seven World Series-winning teams in New York. "I hated his guts," said former Yankee pitcher Joe Page, "but there never was a better manager."

The first manager to win pennants in both leagues, McCarthy also managed the Chicago Cubs to the World Series in 1929. Overall, McCarthy's teams won seven World Series in nine appearances, and his career winning percentages of .615 in the regular season and .698 in the post-season remain major league records. At the end of his career, McCarthy also managed the Boston Red Sox. Although McCarthy's Red Sox teams won 96 games in both 1948 and 1949, he was never able to manage Boston to the World Series, leading many Red Sox fans to view him as aloof and gruff rather than the taciturn managerial genius that so many Yankee fans embraced.

McCarthy was born in Philadelphia on April 21, 1887. When he was only three years old, his father was killed in a cave-in while working as a contractor. McCarthy's impoverished upbringing forced him to do everything from carrying ice to shoveling dirt. Still, his prowess playing

Manager Joe McCarthy.

baseball in the Germantown section of Philadelphia soon earned him attention. He was a member of his grammar school team as well as a local team in Germantown.

He broke his kneecap as a youth while playing in Germantown, which likely limited his chance to one day be a major-league player. "It left me with a loose cartilage which cut down on my speed," said McCarthy. "But I didn't do so good against a curved ball, either." Even so, McCarthy was productive enough to be offered a scholarship to Niagara University to play baseball starting in the fall of 1905, in spite of never attending high school. McCarthy lasted at college for two years, but the strain of not making any money was too great and he left school to play minor-league baseball.

The 5-foot-8½-inch, 190-pound, right-handed-batting McCarthy signed with Wilmington of the Tri-State League to start the 1907 season. His first game was on April 24, against Trenton, and he got one of his team's four hits and stole a base while playing shortstop in a 9–3 road loss. In 12 games with Wilmington, McCarthy had seven hits in 40 at-bats without getting an extra-base hit or more than one hit in a game. McCarthy was never much of a hitter, and during his entire minor-league career, he batted better than .300 in a full season only once, when he hit .325 for Wilkes-Barre in 1913.

When manager Pete Cassidy was fired and McCarthy's job was given to another player, McCarthy jumped to Franklin of the Inter-State League, where he batted a more impressive .314 with two home runs for the rest of the season while making $80 a month. Three and a half years of minor league ball with Toledo under Bill Armour followed before McCarthy went to Indianapolis of the American Association for the final half of the 1911 season in a trade for Fred Carisch. It wasn't always smooth in Indianapolis: In a game on April 26, 1911, McCarthy made four errors in seven chances at third base.

In 1912 and 1913, McCarthy played for Wilkes-Barre of the New York State League, where Bill Clymer was the team's president and manager. Eventually his salary rose to $350 a month. In 1914 and 1915, McCarthy played for Buffalo of the International League, along with Joe Judge and Charley Jamieson.

McCarthy jumped his contract to sign with Brooklyn of the Federal League in 1916, but the league collapsed and McCarthy never got to play for Brooklyn. That period was particularly confusing for McCarthy, as he received a call from the New York Yankees for a tryout around the same time, but he instead received what author Harry Grayson called "the runaround" when the team refused to commit to McCarthy, saying it might be sold. Instead, McCarthy spent the final six years of his minor-league career with Louisville of the American Association from 1916 through 1921 after being awarded to the team in the dispersal of players from the Federal League.

In spite of his long minor-league playing career, McCarthy was never able to get to the major leagues as a player. As Joe Williams wrote in *The Sporting News* in 1939 when McCarthy was in his 14th season as a major-league manager, "More than half of McCarthy's baseball life was spent in the brambles of mediocrity. He was the confirmed and perpetual busher [in the minor leagues]. He played the tank towns, rode the day coaches, had a gustatory acquaintance with all the greasy-spoon restaurants. He played second base and was an adroit fielder. He hit well enough, especially in the clutches, with men on base. But he was slow. The broken kneecap had left an enduring mark. 'If it wasn't for that knee, we'd recommend you,' the scouts always said."

McCarthy was a versatile player during his minor-league career. He began as a shortstop, moved to third base, later became an outfielder, and ultimately found his greatest success at second base. When Bill Clymer left his job as Wilkes-Barre's manager after the 1912 season, McCarthy received his first managerial job, at the age of 25. He did quite well as the youngest manager in professional baseball, leading his team to a second-place finish only 1½ games behind Binghamton.

McCarthy got the chance to manage again in Louisville. "In those early years in Louisville, I became convinced that I never would set the woods on fire as a player," McCarthy later recalled. "My mind began to work along managerial lines. I studied the systems of successful managers of the period. My chance came midway through the 1919 season when Patsy Flaherty resigned." McCarthy took over as manager of Louisville on July 22,

1919, and won his first game, 6–2. His pitcher that day was Bill Stewart, later a National League umpire.

An insult from a teammate precipitated McCarthy's retirement as a player. During a game against St. Paul in September 1920, McCarthy was playing second base when St. Paul's Bert Ellison was caught in a rundown. When Louisville first baseman Jay Kirke made a throw that was too late, the ball hit McCarthy in the chest and went into center field.

"What made you do a thing like that?' said McCarthy. "Why didn't you give me the ball sooner?"

Kirke, according to Williams, "looked the manager of the Colonels in the eye and imperiously said, 'What right have you got trying to tell a .380 hitter how to play ball?'"

That incident affected McCarthy. According to Williams, "McCarthy was hitting only .220 at the time, so instead of becoming outraged, he bowed to the logic of Mr. Kirke's criticism, and that night he announced his retirement from baseball as an active player. From that point on, he would sit on the bench and tell the players what to do."

After retiring as a player, McCarthy went on to manage Louisville to its first American Association pennant in 1921 (he did play in 11 games that year). The Colonels defeated the Baltimore Orioles in the Little World Series, five games to three. In every year but one after that, McCarthy's teams finished in the top four in the league. He managed the Colonels for four more seasons, leading the team to a second pennant in 1925. This time the Colonels lost the Little World Series to the Orioles, by an identical five games to three, then played a series with San Francisco of the Pacific Coast League, losing five games to four.

After that season William Wrigley, Jr., the Cubs' owner, offered the managerial position with the Cubs to McCarthy. The Cubs in 1925 had, in the words of James Enright, "flopped into the coal hole" employing three managers and finishing in eighth place in the National League with a 68–86 record. McCarthy had hoped to keep word of his new contract with the Cubs out of the press until after the Colonels' post-season series with the San Francisco Seals, but word that he had signed a two-year contract with Chicago soon leaked out.

Before McCarthy began with the Cubs, writer Irving Vaughn noted: "For several years in the American Association, they have regarded [McCarthy] as sort of a miracle worker, but the new graduate into the big leagues can't explain his success. He has no pet theories about managing a team. He says he merely studies each individual player under him and then studies the opposition."

As Joseph Durso recounted, McCarthy was quickly introduced to the star system when he joined the Cubs. Discussing a strategic scenario in the clubhouse, McCarthy reportedly said, "Now, suppose we get a man on second

L-r: Wright, Billy Goodman, Dom DiMaggio, Ted Williams, Clyde Vollmer. 1951.
Courtesy of Tom Wright.

In 1948, he advanced to Louisville and racked up 563 at-bats in 151 games, with a .307 average. His power and RBI numbers were virtually identical to the year before. In September, he got called up to the Boston ball club. He'd only just arrived and got his uniform when manager Joe McCarthy told him, "Wright, get your stick!" It was the top of the ninth inning in a September 15 game against the White Sox. First time up, the first pitch he saw, he hit for a triple to the right-center field fence. He soon scored and when he got back to the dugout, "McCarthy said, 'Son, you don't take (pitches) much, do you?' I guess that's the only words that man ever said to me when I was with the ball club." And that included 1949. "He never spoke to the ballplayers. They just sit down on one end and managed. Back in those days, they didn't have hitting coaches, they didn't have fielding coaches, they didn't have all that stuff that they have now. They didn't coach. They didn't do nothing." Players had to pretty much make their own way.

Tom had two at-bats with Boston in 1948 and left with a .500 average. He was with the team right though the end of the year and even had a minor role in the playoff game with Cleveland, entering as a pinch runner for Billy Hitchcock in the ninth. Why did McCarthy decide to pitch Denny Galehouse in the final game? "Everybody there questioned that, because he couldn't break a pane of glass. He didn't throw hard. He wasn't a hard ball thrower. You didn't slip in Fenway. If you did, somebody'd hit the green wall. That's what happened to us."

Wright had been a fan favorite in Louisville and was chosen Most Valuable Players on the Colonels by a vote of the fans. After the season, the Red Sox released Wally Moses to make room for Wright in their plans for 1949. Come springtime, though, it was determined that he needed more seasoning. Wright was candid with *Sporting News* writer Tommy Fitzgerald that he'd been disappointed in his springtime experience with the Red Sox:

"Nobody hardly said a word to me. Nobody showed me anything."

Fitzgerald classified Wright as a "natural straightaway hitter who sends the ball to all fields" and wrote the Boston's farm director Johnny Murphy had tried to get him to pull the ball more to right, but the suggestion didn't work. Murphy also suggested he switch to a larger glove, and that did seem to strengthen his fielding.

In 1949, he spent the full year back in Louisville, again appearing in 151 games, this year rapping out 202 hits and leading the American Association in hitting with a .368 average. Late in the year, he came back to Boston and found himself inserted into the final game of the year. If the Red Sox won the game, they won the pennant and Ellis Kinder had held the Yankees to just one run through eight innings. Unfortunately, New York's Vic Raschi denied Boston even one run. Sox manager Joe McCarthy called on the AA batting champion to pinch hit for Kinder in the top of the eighth; Wright worked a walk but was retired when Dom DiMaggio grounded into a double play. Kinder was a very good hitting pitcher, and though Wright had gotten himself on base, Kinder's replacement—Mel Parnell—was hit hard in the bottom of the eighth, and the game was out of reach.

Most of the time that Wright played in the minors, it was center field he patrolled. But in the majors, it was primarily left field, because of his weaker arm. He knew the Red Sox outfield was a hard one to crack, but he made the team in 1950 as a backup. Wright was with the Red Sox for all of 1950, and got most of his playing time in helping out after Ted Williams shattered his elbow during that season's All-Star Game. Billy Goodman largely took over for Ted in left, and Wright fit in 24 games, 19 in right field and five in left. For the most part, though, he pinch-hit for Boston. He did total 107 at-bats, and hit .318, so he got a fair amount of work.

Manager Steve O'Neill had plenty of praise for his pinch-hitting specialist: "You can call on him any time and he's just as likely as not to deliver the hit you need. Lots of players lose that split-second timing when they lay off for a while. But Tom can sit on the bench for three weeks, then get up and hit just as well as if he was in there every day." O'Neill's comments appeared in a November 1, 1950 *Sporting News* article; author Steve O'Leary characterized Wright as a "soft-spoken southerner" with a "fine sense of humor and he's a great guy to have around for morale purposes. That's another point in his favor with O'Neill, who is blessed with plenty of Irish wit."

In 1951, he tailed off sharply, and was sent back to

Louisville after just 63 at-bats. He was only hitting .222. It was a frustrating time. "Nobody was hitting. Williams wasn't hitting. There wasn't nobody hitting. When Cronin (the general manager) called me up and told me I was going back to Louisville, we got in a cuss fight. I told him if he wanted to, just go look up the records of who Williams was hitting against and who I was hitting against, and see who was hitting. We had to separate. I went back out the next day, and I knew there wasn't no more for me to do but just go back to Louisville. But nobody was hitting. Williams wasn't hitting, either." It was indeed an "off year" for Ted Williams; he only hit .318.

After 28 games with the Red Sox, Wright got in 72 games for Louisville, where he hit .282, but he found it "hard to get tuned in," and after the season was over, he requested a trade. "I told them to get rid of me. They'd done moved me up and down so much. They told me all the time Detroit wanted to buy me and they wouldn't do it. They'd just keep holding me in Triple-A ball. I told them, just get rid of me. So they sent me to St. Louis." A late November swap with St. Louis brought Boston Gus Niarhos and Ken Wood and sent Wright and Les Moss to the Browns. In its December 5 issue, *The Sporting News* contained four separate stories about talked-about trades of Ted Williams, and one suggested that acquiring Ken Wood to play left field was the key element in the trade with St. Louis. Ted was never traded, Wood never panned out, but Wright opened the 1952 season hitting cleanup for St. Louis.

"Early Wallflower Wright Blossoms as Brownie Daisy," headlined an early April *Sporting News*, reporting that Wright had been named starting left fielder. Rogers Hornsby called him "the most improved player on the squad." Wright had a hot start, but cooled off considerably, striking out quite a lot and found himself playing only infrequently. On June 15, the Browns swapped him and Leo Thomas to the White Sox for Al Zarilla and Willie Miranda. Ironically, it was Zarilla as much as anyone who had blocked Wright from playing more in Boston, and now St. Louis sent him to Chicago to acquire Zarilla. Wright finished the season hitting .258 for the White Sox, up from the .242 he'd hit for St. Louis.

Manager Paul Richards told *The Sporting News* in August that three of his players, including Wright, would be getting a refresher course in where the strike zone is located come the next spring. "It is my belief that all three of them could be .300 hitters if they laid off the bad pitches," Richards said of Wright, Jim Rivera, and Hector Rodriguez.

He's been told, he says, that he led the league in pinch hits in 1953. "I get a little bit of this stuff from fans, saying they're wanting autographs and this and that and the other. They'll give me all my records and everything. I've never looked them up." He played in 77 games, getting 132 at-bats and hitting an even .250.

Right at the end of 1954 spring training, the White Sox sent him to the Washington Senators for Kite Thomas. He was on the team all year, but it was a very disappointing one. "I never could get anything going with them. I just couldn't get my rhythm. I didn't even feel like part of the team. I never did get going and I was always sorry for that because I wanted to play for Griffith bad." Wright started the season platooning in right field with Jim Lemon, but he wasn't the answer to Washington's problems and wound up largely used as a left-handed pinch hitter. He got 171 at-bats, but it was just too much stop-and-start—and maybe he just wasn't the same player as he'd been now that he'd hit age 30.

At the end of March 1955, Wright was optioned to Chattanooga and played with the Lookouts for the full year, appearing in 142 games and hitting .293 back in the Southern Association. He drove in 72 runs, and was brought back up to Washington in September, where he had seven at-bats in seven appearances, but didn't record even one hit. Come the spring of 1956, Wright lacked just under 30 days of major league playing time in order to qualify for the pension, and Senators owner Griffith ensured that he was brought back long enough to qualify. Washington manager Charlie Dressen kept him on the team, but didn't use him a bit in spring training. "He didn't even let me pinch hit or do nothing all spring. But I was the first pinch hitter against the Yankees on opening day. Them boys down on the bench said, 'Durn, Tom. What's he trying to do to you?' I says, 'I don't care. Give me the stick.' I didn't get a fair run with him, but really I didn't get a fair run, I didn't think, because I never did get to stay in the lineup to get my timing and everything. I was just fighting to stay in the major leagues. I wasn't going to fuss with nobody." Actually, Wright pinch-ran in the season opener, but pinch-hit in the second game of the regular season, grounding out for the pitcher in the seventh inning. He'd appeared in two games and had just the one at-bat. After he'd logged the requisite time for a pension, Wright was sent to Louisville. Thus ended his time in major league baseball.

When he got to Louisville, Tom recorded a .245 average over 159 at-bats, but was bumped down to Birmingham in midyear. There he did well, hitting .344. He returned again for the 1957 season with Birmingham, but hit only .257. Tom began to figure his time was up. He wasn't hitting as well, and he didn't want to travel by air. He asked that he be sent to a club that didn't fly and was sold to Charleston but he found there was no way to make the schedules without flying, so he just left baseball. Perhaps a bit ironic that the man who'd volunteered to fly in the Army Air Force was now overly anxious at the prospect of travel by air. "I just couldn't stand it. It made me nervous. I flew good, but those two or three days when you're waiting before you know you're going to fly, I was nervous as a cat. It was affecting my life. In fact, I lost my errors that lost the game for New York. After the game, Grimes was sure that he would be sent to the minor leagues. According to Grimes, "Instead, McCarthy slapped me on the back and said, 'Oscar, you'll never believe this, but I once had a worse inning than that at Louisville. Now get out there and win this second game for me.' You know, you've got to play your guts out for a man like that."

McCarthy also succeeded in managing Babe Ruth. According to one writer, "No matter what his thoughts might have been, Joe ran the rest of his club and left Babe to his own devices. Ruth never bothered Joe much either. He did just about as he pleased, just showed up for the games and gave McCarthy four pretty good seasons. It was hard to tell what he thought of the manager." There were, however, reports that Ruth's jealousy of McCarthy led to Ruth's release by the Yankees and signing by the Boston Braves in 1935.

Still, in spite of his successes, McCarthy's teams were not up to the same standards during the latter part of World War II. From 1843 to 1945 the Yankees never finished above third place, as many of his star players had retired, left for other teams, or gone into the armed forces. On May 26, 1946, in a telegram from his farm at Tonawanda, New York, to team president Larry MacPhail, McCarthy resigned. "It is with extreme regret," McCarthy wrote, "that I must request that you accept my resignation as manager of the Yankee Baseball Club, effective immediately. My doctor advises that my health would be seriously jeopardized if I continue. This is the sole reason for my decision, which as you know, is entirely voluntary on my part."

The *New York Times* reported that McCarthy had suffered a recurrence of a gall bladder condition that necessitated his retirement and that McCarthy would remain with the team in an advisory capacity. "McCarthy was the most cooperative manager with whom I have ever been associated in baseball," said MacPhail at the time. Longtime Yankee catcher Bill Dickey was named as McCarthy's replacement.

But that explanation had its doubters. One American League club official who chose to remain anonymous said that McCarthy had "so much success that he went to pieces with a losing club." There were also persistent rumors that McCarthy resigned because of a personality conflict with Larry MacPhail, with whom McCarthy did not have as close a relationship as he had with Ed Barrow.

Said one contemporary article: "There is no question that McCarthy is a sick man, but the prime reason that he is not returning to the Yankees is not his ailments but Larry MacPhail, new president of the club.... Now apparently the more he cogitates on MacPhail's blast about the Yankees not hustling, the more determined he becomes to stay in Buffalo and terminate his connection to the club." MacPhail had also publicly scorned McCarthy for

a confrontation with Joe Page during a flight from Cleveland to Detroit five days earlier.

After two years out of baseball, McCarthy was hired by the Boston Red Sox. Boston had finished 14 games behind the Yankees in 1947, and McCarthy's hiring was part of a larger shakeup that included shifting then-manager Joe Cronin into a front-office position. Cronin sounded impressed also: "Joe's going to have more power than probably any manager since McGraw. He will have complete charge of the team and will have the power to make any deal he wants."

Boston sportswriter Harold Kaese wrote, "McCarthy is more highly rated than Cronin, having won nine pennants to Cronin's two.... When McCarthy signed, Boston fans were confident that another pennant was on the way."

Lou Stringer with McCarthy. Courtesy of Tom Stringer.

Even though McCarthy's Boston teams finished in second place in each of his two full seasons with the Red Sox, it was not enough to satisfy Boston fans who were eager for him to duplicate the World Series-winning success he had in New York. Boston lost a one-game playoff for the American League pennant to Cleveland in 1948 and finished second to the Yankees in 1949, losing the pennant on the last weekend of the season.

In 1969, McCarthy got together with Ted Williams and recalled that Williams had been the last player to leave the locker room after Boston's loss in the 1948 one-game playoff. As recounted by Buffalo sportswriter Cy Kritzer:

'Do you remember what I said to you that day?' Joe inquired.

'How could I ever forget those kind words?' Williams replied. 'They were the kindest words ever spoken to me in baseball.'

Marse Joe had told his star slugger, 'We did get along,

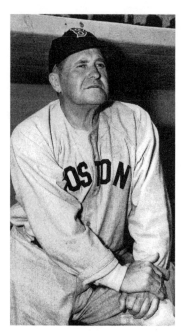

Keeping a watchful eye.

didn't we? And we surprised a lot of people who said we couldn't.'

According to Kritzer, Williams also appreciated how McCarthy never criticized his players in the press.

Still, said Ed Fitzgerald in *Sport* magazine: "The sportswriters of the town, who greeted [McCarthy] with open arms when he took over the job, have been beating him over the head ever since. Not all of them, but most of them.... They criticize his handling of his players, his relations with the press, his every positive or negative act."

And when McCarthy resigned from Boston's managerial position on July 22, 1950, again citing ill health, his critics were ready to pounce. But an admirer, Arthur Daley, wrote in *the New York Times*, "Marse Joe failed at Boston. It's unfortunate that his departure had to come on such a sour note because the small-minded men who don't know any better will definitely remark that he could never manage a ball club anyway and add that it's good riddance. They'll even add that the records are false in proclaiming that the square-jawed Irishman from Buffalo won more pennants than John McGraw and Connie Mack."

Retiring to his farm home in Tonawanda, New York, McCarthy was done with professional baseball for good. He liked, as one UPI report said, "to putter around the garden." In retirement, he was busy: "I don't have time to do any fishing now, either," he said in 1970 when he was 83. "This place is big enough to take care of, so I never get out. I do a few things around the house. A little gardening. Not much. I plant tomatoes and beans and stuff like that." He called his home "Yankee Farm." Joe's wife, Elizabeth McCarthy, died in October 1971 at the couple's 61-acre farm.

McCarthy was elected to the Hall of Fame by the Veterans Committee in 1957 along with former Detroit Tigers star outfielder Sam Crawford.

Joe McCarthy died of pneumonia at the age of 90 on October 13, 1979, at Millard Fillmore Hospital, near his home in Tonawanda. He had been hospitalized twice in 1977, once for a fall and later for pneumonia. He was buried in Mount Olivet Cemetery in Tonawanda.

Sources

McCarthy's biography and World Series statistics on baseball-reference.com.

Clippings from McCarthy's file at the Hall of Fame:

"Cubs Saying Nothing, Sawing Wood and Keeping Stiff Lip." September 6, 1928.

Daley, Arthur, "Delayed Tribute," *New York* Times, September 2, 1951.

Daley, Arthur, "Exit for Marse Joe, *New York Times*, June 25, 1950.

Dawson, James P., "McCarthy Resigns: Dickey Yank Pilot," *New York Times*, May 1946.

Drebinger, John, "Marse Joe Coming Home," *New York Times*. Undated.

Durso, Joseph, "Joe McCarthy, Yanks' Ex-Manager Dies at 90." *New York Times*, January 14, 1978.

Durso, "Whether they liked it or not, McCarthy did things his way." *New York Times*, November 15, 1978.

Enright, James, "Will Luck of the Irish Revive Faded Cubs?' *The Sporting News*, March 23, 1963.

Fitzgerald, Ed, "Nobody's Neutral About McCarthy," *Sport*, August 1950.

"Good for Joe," July 25, 1929.

Grayson, Harry, "McCarthy Recalls Pine St. Baseball Parade That Turned Him from Cricket to Diamond."

"He Welcomed the Honor but Not at Players' Expense."

Kritzer, Cy, "Glory Days Come Alive: Ted Visits McCarthy," September 8, 1969.

Kritzer, Cy, "Marse Joe's Biggest World Series Thrill? Sweep Over Cubs Who Fired Him." May 2, 1956.

Lanigan, Ernest J. "For Any Day"

"Marse Joe Has 88th," UPI, April 22, 1975.

"'Marse Joe' McCarthy, led Yankees to 7 Series," UPI, January 14, 1978.

"Marse Joe McCarthy, at 83, Has Scant Time for Baseball," UPI, April 26, 1970.

"McCarthy Admits Yankees' Hurling Must Stiffen Much," *Philadelphia Record*, February 23, 1931.

"McCarthy Through at Chicago, Hornsby In Line As Successor," September 25, 1930.

McKenney, Joe, "Hub Prospects Rejuvenate McCarthy, *The Sporting News*, October 29, 1947.

"Mrs. Joe McCarthy," Obituaries, *New York Times*, October 20, 1971.

"No Kick on Cubs in Chicago This Time: Joe McCarthy's Debut Year All That Could be Asked." 1926.

Ogle, Jim, "Joe McCarthy: A Tribute." *My Yankee Scrapbook*, 1978.

Porter. David L., "McCarthy, Joseph Vincent," *Biographical Dictionary of American Sports*.

Segar, Charles, "M'Carthy to Quit Yank Post," July 31, 1945.

Vaughan, Irving, "McCarthy Signs to Pilot Cubs for Two Years: Louisville Manager Closes with Veeck."

"Yankees Owe Flag Largely to Marse Joe: McCarthy Shows His Ability in Solving Pitching Problems," *New York Times*, September 24, 1937.

"Yankees To Sign Joe M'Carthy When Series Moves Off Stage," October 9, 1930.

Wedge, Will, "That 'Marse Joe' Nickname." 1931.

Williams, Joe, "Busher Joe McCarthy." *The Saturday Evening* Post, April 15, 1939.

Complete Minor League Playing Record and partial minor league salary record in his Hall of Fame player file.

BROADCASTER JIM BRITT *by Mort Bloomberg*

Jim Britt was the radio and television voice of both the Boston Braves and the Boston Red Sox in 1948—an enviable position he held from 1939 until the Red Sox began to broadcast road games as well as home games and therefore required a full-time broadcaster of their own.

In an era when several of the major radio stations in Boston competed nightly for the attention of sports fans, the most listened-to program on the air was "Jim Britt's Sports Roundup" from 6:15 to 6:30 on WNAC. It consisted of a mix of straight reporting, commentary, and in-studio interviews with newsmakers, and finished up with Jim's signature expression at the end of his program, "Remember, if you can't take part in a sport, be one anyway, will ya." From today's vantage point, that tagline sounds cornball but in the pre-television era it helped accelerate him into Boston's No. 1 sports personality on the air in the 1940s.

Jim Britt, detail from a Narragansett advertisement in a Boston Braves program.

Jim Britt was born in San Francisco in 1911. The well-to-do family (his father was chairman of the board of the Burroughs Corporation) moved to Detroit when Jim was 11. Jim received a bachelor of arts degree from the University of Detroit (where his brother, a priest, would later become president), majoring in English and philosophy with a co-minor in speech and history. After graduation, he earned a law degree at the University of Southern California but chose not to take the bar exam. Always interested in speech, singing, and sports, he returned to Detroit to teach public speaking and debating in local high schools.

His entry into radio was accidental, not in one of the many ways open to those interested in media jobs today. He accepted a dare from the university's football coach to become better behind the mike than the current announcer, who Britt thought was horrendous and had declared emphatically as much to the coach.

Full-time radio work began in 1935 with Notre Dame football and basketball games. Then came two years of Buffalo Bisons baseball doing home games live and road games via telegraphic recreation with Leo Egan. A native Buffalonian, Egan came to Boston after the 1938 hurricane. He wrote for the *Boston Herald* and broadcast baseball and football for 30 years (many pigskin clashes being from atop Harvard Stadium). Ironically, Leo was the person who persuaded Jim to audition for an opening as sports director with WNAC and its Yankee Network. This network was a federation of radio stations from Maine to Connecticut and had nothing to do with the Bronx Bombers.

Britt got the job on November 10, 1939, and became Frankie Frisch's replacement as the voice of New England baseball. During his one year at the mike, Frisch had proven unable to fill the shoes of immensely popular local broadcast legend Fred Hoey and eagerly accepted the chance to return to the diamond as manager of the Pittsburgh Pirates.

Britt began to broadcast home games of the Braves and Red Sox in 1940 with Tom Hussey as his sidekick. Few other baseball announcers have covered two teams at the same time. Their partnership continued until the 1942 All-Star break when Britt received his induction notice from the Navy. He served as an intelligence officer in the Pacific for the next 3½ years, an assignment not without risk. At one point, the bomber in which he was flying suffered a mid-air collision with another American aircraft. Britt was one of eight survivors.

Britt's return to civilian life allowed him to go back to cover Boston baseball games, now available on WHDH. Listeners welcomed the intelligent, smooth, and fluent sound of his voice again because play-by-play announcers assigned by the station in his absence were just not in his league. Reflecting back to when he was 13 years old, *Sporting News* columnist Wells Twombly reminisced, "Jim Britt... makes baseball sound better than red-haired girls with freckles." Ken Coleman, who broadcast for Boston in later years, recalls it as a treat when Britt returned to the booth. "There's no doubt in my mind that of all the broadcasters I've ever heard, and this includes network newspeople, no one had more of a command of the English language than Jim."

Both Twombly and Coleman succeed in putting into words exactly what my own sentiments were. Jim Britt represented Braves baseball for me in the late '40s and early '50s. Thanks to him, I became such a devoted fan of the team that their move to Milwaukee in 1953 was like a death in the family. I still have vivid memories of hiding my portable radio underneath the covers at night listening to him describe yet another heroic comeback staged by the Braves during their victorious pennant chase of 1948. The losses piled up progressively from 1949–52, but the drama in his voice always gave me fresh hope that the outcome of tomorrow's contest would be better.

Just a few months before what would become the final

season of National League baseball in Boston, I wrote to Britt asking how best to pursue my lifelong dream. He took time from what must have been a busy schedule to offer me this advice during my sophomore year in high school: "Most important for either a sports broadcasting or sports writing career—get a good, well-rounded education. Go to college, if you can. There's no possible substitute. Then make the rounds of the various small radio stations and/or newspapers to get a job. It may be hard to break in. But the job is interesting and well worth all the time and trouble to get started. Good luck in whatever you do, wherever you go."

Boston's first baseball telecast occurred on June 15, 1948, with Britt and Hussey calling a contest between the Braves and the Cubs on Massachusetts' pioneer television station, WBZ-TV. Channel 4, as it was known then, had transmitted its inaugural program—a 15-minute newscast—a scant week before this historic event from Braves Field.

As the new medium grew, more games on the Braves (and soon the Red Sox) schedule were carried via television. The original broadcasting tandem remained intact through 1950, although Leo Egan and Bump Hadley also appeared from time to time. Hadley came from Lynn, Massachusetts and capped a 16-year pitching career with three World Series appearances for the New York Yankees in the late 1930s. His legacy forever will be tied to fracturing Mickey Cochrane's skull with an errant pitch that ended the future Hall of Famer's career. Years after this incident, Bump's trademark closing to his popular sports show on WBZ was "heads up and keep pitching."

When Tom Yawkey announced that his ball club planned to air road games in 1951, Britt could no longer broadcast for both the Braves and the Red Sox. He was given his option as to which team to broadcast. His decision to go with the Braves was criticized by many. Even Britt second-guessed himself. However, in hindsight it arguably was not a bad choice given the remarkable success the Braves would enjoy later in the '50s and the hard times the Red Sox had during the same period.

Did Jim evaluate the young talent in the Braves farm system in 1950 (Mathews, Logan, Buhl, Bruton, Conley) and foresee that they would benefit the team in Boston over the next decade while the Red Sox had stars who were aging (Williams, DiMaggio, Doerr, Pesky, Stephens), making the American League outfit more likely to suffer decline? I think he did and, more important, there were upcoming threats to Britt's physical and psychological well-being that renders the Braves vs. Red Sox dilemma inconsequential.

The counter view is that the poor judgment he exercised might have been somewhat attributable to erosion in his health, making the issue vital and far from inconsequential. Without knowing either Britt's rationale to stick with Boston's National League entry or what the aftermath would have been had he chosen the Red Sox, there is no way to tell for sure.

The Red Sox hired Curt Gowdy, who at the time was Mel Allen's junior partner with the Yankees, and retained Tom Hussey. With Narragansett Brewery as their chief sponsor ("Hi neighbor, have a 'Gansett"), they continued to carry their games on WHDH, where they stayed until 1975.

As for the Braves, their 154-game schedule moved to WNAC and was sponsored by Ballantine (remember the three rings?). Britt's backup during the Tribe's final two seasons in the Hub was Les Smith, a journeyman news and special features host at the station. Their sister station, Channel 7, showed home games periodically. The Braves broadcast duo was joined there by an always unintentionally amusing and sometimes seemingly-inebriated Bump Hadley. Bump was that generation's answer to Ralph Kiner with gaffes like "that ball is going, going…and caught by Sam Jethroe in short center field." This is not to say that Britt was without his own shortcomings. Leo Egan saw Britt as "sort of a Felix Unger type—quirksome, picky." He remembers one time when three times in the same game Britt miscalled fly balls as home runs. Egan characterized Britt as "very professional, very difficult. But, God, he was articulate."

Britt was the first broadcaster associated with a local children's cancer charity adopted by the Braves known as the Jimmy Fund, benefiting the Children's Cancer Research Foundation (now Dana-Farber Cancer Institute). His tireless work to help eliminate childhood cancer established a tradition among Boston broadcasters that is followed to this day. Britt's future broadcasting colleague in Cleveland, Ken Coleman, became an especially avid advocate for the Jimmy Fund upon his return to Boston. Ken later served as executive director of the Jimmy Fund from 1978 to 1984. Current Sox play-by-play man Joe Castiglione has carried on in the tradition as a spokesman for the Jimmy Fund since first partnering with Coleman in the mid-1980s, as has Joe's former protégé Uri Berenguer-Ramos, the Spanish radio voice of the club. A cancer survivor and former Dana-Farber patient, Uri knows the importance of the Sox-Jimmy Fund partnership better than anyone.

The size of Britt's audience increased in scope as he did the 1946, 1948, and 1950 World Series on radio, the 1949, 1950, and 1951 Series on television, the first nationally televised football game in 1949, seven All-Star baseball games, and several major college football bowl games during this time span. But his stardom fell as quickly as it rose, mirroring the fortunes of the team with which he was affiliated most closely during the postwar era before its abrupt shift to Milwaukee.

There were four years of Indians telecasts with Ken Coleman and then back to Boston as a news anchor and bowling program host prior to being fired by WHDH-TV.

Drinking problems that led to arrest more than once, and a divorce took their toll, especially when these incidents were splashed across the front page of the *Boston Daily Record* tabloid. Most telling was an eye injury that ended his sportscasting career.

Progressively longer periods of unemployment ensued. He drifted from Boston to Detroit to St. Petersburg to Sarasota and finally to Monterey, California, where he was found dead in his apartment by the police on December 28, 1980, at the age of 70, with no known next of kin. His brother had predeceased him about two months earlier.

In Curt Smith's latest opus, *Voices of Summer*, the author ranks Britt 78th among the 101 all-time best baseball announcers. That placement is just ahead of Joe Angel (San Francisco Giants and Orioles) and right behind Bob Starr (Angels and Red Sox). Joe Morgan and Russ Hodges represent more famous benchmarks, listed 60th and 51st respectively by Smith.

Shortly after Britt's death, Ray Fitzgerald of the *Boston Globe* wrote that "life had turned its back on him a long time ago." And maybe some of his detractors who called him arrogant, uncompromising, perfectionistic, thin-skinned, or unwilling to admit mistakes were secretly tickled that it had.

In his prime, Jim Britt was the king of New England sports radio and early television. He was bright, knowledgeable, and very articulate, took pride in his professionalism, and had a dry sense of humor. He once told radio/TV sports director and announcer Ted Patterson that his credo was "report the game, don't play it." And that he did so objectively, although there was a hard-to-pinpoint pro-Braves and pro-Red Sox quality to his voice that hometowners could sense.

Even during his off-peak years in Cleveland, he never let serious alcohol and marital problems color his description of the game.

A mostly forgotten figure today, the final truth of the matter is that there was an admirable strength of character that defined Jim Britt's work, although not his life.

Sources

Bloomberg, Mort, "The Voice of the Braves" in *Society for American Baseball Research* (Paducah KY: Turner Publications, 2000).

Britt, Jim. Letter to Mort Bloomberg, January 1952.

Buchanan, William, "Jim Britt, 70, broadcast Boston baseball games." *Boston Globe*, January 1981.

Fitzgerald, Ray, "Voice from Hub's past is stilled," *Boston Globe*, January 1981.

Patterson, Ted, *The Golden Voices of Baseball* (Champaign IL: Sports Publishing, 2002)

Patterson, Ted, *The Golden Voices of Football* (Champaign IL: Sports Publishing, 2004)

Redmount, Robert, *The Red Sox Encyclopedia*, 2nd edition (Champaign IL: Sports Publishing, 2002)

Smith, Curt, *Voices of the Game* (Lanham MD: Diamond Communications, 1987)

Smith, Curt, *Voices of Summer* (NY: Carroll & Graf, 2005)

Twombly, Wells, "Those '48 Braves Were the Greatest", *The Sporting News*, July 11, 1970.

Boston streetcar trolley scroll.

Take Me Out to the Wigwam: 1948 and 2008

by Bob Brady

1948

Built on the heels of the Miracle Braves' 1914 world championship, Braves Field celebrated its 33rd birthday in grand style in 1948. For the first time in its history, the ballpark's tenant had captured a pennant, attracting a never-to-be-equaled 1,455,439 fans through its turnstiles.[1]

Affectionately dubbed "The Wigwam,"[2] Braves Field was situated in an amphitheater-like depression in what was once the site of a former golf course in the Allston section of Boston, about a mile to the west of the Fenway Park home of the rival American League Red Sox. Braves Field had a 10-acre footprint. As constructed, its right-field foul line paralleled Commonwealth Avenue while the left-field borderline aligned with Babcock Street. Right and center fields backed up to Gaffney Street (now Harry Agganis Way) and the outfield tract on the port side had the Boston and Albany Railroad yard and the Charles River as neighbors. Built in five months and christened on August 18, 1915, Braves Field with its accommodations for 43,500 spectators, was boastfully billed as the "Largest Ball Ground in the World" on a contemporary postcard. Its erection reflected the movement of the National Pastime from bucolic but inflammable timber structures to "modern" concrete and steel stadiums. The club's prior home, the chummy 11,000 seat South End Grounds, was an ornate but dilapidated double-decked wooden edifice which had been quickly assembled during the 1894 season after its original, larger version burned to the ground on May 15. Boston sportswriter Harold Kaese once described the relocation as comparable to moving from a three room apartment to a grand mansion.

The Wigwam in 1948 continued to exhibit the imprint of its builder, former team owner James E. Gaffney.[3] A New York Tammany Hall-connected contractor, he commissioned Osborn Engineering Company to design his field of dreams to capitalize upon the era's "dead ball" style of play. Its cavernous confines failed to anticipate ominous changes in the sport that would emerge virtually in its very backyard and be led by Red Sox slugging pitcher George Herman Ruth, who was in the beginning stages of transitioning into an outfielder. At its opening, the ballpark's distant outfield dimensions reflected the owner's traditionalist desire to keep the baseball in play inside the park. Fandom's nascent love affair with the home run clout was not intended to be serviced here. Kaese recorded Ty Cobb's prophetic first impression of the Wigwam's confines as the future Hall of Famer stood at home plate for the first time and looked toward the

outfield, "shad[ing] his eyes with his hand like an Indian scout looking over the prairie. 'One thing is sure. Nobody is ever going to hit a ball over those fences.'"[4] The Georgia Peach further reflected, "This is the only field in the country on which you can play an absolutely fair game of ball without interference of fences."

Over the course of intervening years, a series of succeeding club owners recognized the adverse consequences of this unanticipated structural obsolescence on the team's competitiveness and attendance and undertook a variety of measures to correct the serious design flaw. At one time, bleacher seating was constructed in left and in center field. In another instance, the movement of foul lines required the blasting out of a section of the right field corner wall. Home plate was relocated and the distance to the Wigwam's outfield boundaries was in a constant state of flux. By the time of the 1948 season, for a baseball to fly fairly out of Braves Field, it had to travel some 337 feet to left, 370 feet to dead center or 319 feet to right. In contrast, the stadium's inaugural dimensions saw left field extending over 400 feet from home plate and the deepest part of center field was a gargantuan 550 feet away.

There were a number of options for folks coming to the Wigwam in 1948. As an inner-city diamond, the field could be reached on foot or via Boston's famed Metropolitan Transit Authority. From the suburbs, patrons tended to come by train, chartered bus or automobile. A spur off of the MTA's Commonwealth Avenue streetcar line deposited and picked up fans inside the ballpark's perimeter. As attendance swelled, the cream and "traction" orange-colored electrified trolleys lived up to the "cattle car" billing bestowed upon them by riders of the day.

Afternoon games commenced at 2 P.M. sharp with the exception of doubleheaders that began a half hour earlier. Night games started at 8:30 P.M.

Upon arrival, one would immediately be confronted by an imposing 10-foot cement wall surrounding the park and by the first of the Wigwam's many distinctive features—its administration building/ticket office with a terra cotta roof and multi-arched main entranceways.

Box seats ($2.40) and reserved grandstand seating ($1.80) could be purchased in advance at the Jordan Marsh Men's Store in downtown Boston. In addition, at the park, one could buy a spot in the unreserved grandstand for $1.20 or choose between the left- or right-field pavilions (95 cents) or bleachers (60 cents). A "Boy's Grandstand" seat was available for 60 cents for those under 12 years of age. Knothole Gang season membership, a program launched during the old Fuchs regime,

A large crowd gathered on Gaffney Street in front of the main entrance to Braves Field eagerly awaiting the opening of the gates for a World Series contest against the Cleveland Indians.

would also permit entry for youthful Braves fans into the left-field pavilion. Ladies' Days would be announced before the start of a home stand and tickets had to be purchased at the gate prior to the game. For 50 cents, the fairer sex could secure an unreserved grandstand seat.

For the well-heeled, the Braves offered a variety of season ticket packages that today wouldn't cover a day's outing at Fenway Park. A 1948 full season grandstand seat or box seat package set a purchaser back $100 and $150, respectively. A 30-night game reserved grandstand seat package listed at $54.

Just beyond the 24 ticket booths at the entrance were 28 concrete stalls, each with a turnstile that, once rotated, permitted patrons to access passageways leading to various sections of the grandstands and bleachers. Seldom would there be a need to man all of the outposts. Some ticket-takers would "employ" local youths to assist them by turning the revolving gate. As payment, the youngster would be allowed free entry into the ballpark.

An ingenious design prevented ticket-sellers from having to handle large sums of money. Built into the ceilings of each ticket booth were trap doors from which baskets would be used to draw up the proceeds to the offices above. In addition to being a security feature, this device also permitted the treasurer to have the day's receipts counted by the fifth inning.

On the back wall of the administration building was an external set of stairs leading to the Braves' management's offices. Johnny Sain called it the "Golden Staircase" as players in those pre-agent, pre-union, and pre-free agency days were left to their own means in ascending the stairs to bargain for their salaries. Warren Spahn remarked that his pitching "Pray for Rain" cohort was so successful in his negotiations that others climbing these figuratively gilded steps found management's cupboard relatively bare.

Once inside the ballpark, patrons would be confronted with Harry M. Stevens' pitchmen hawking for a dime a booklet-sized, two-toned (red and blue ink), 16-page combined official program and scorecard. Others would be stationed at concession booths above the grandstand, under the pavilions and bleachers and in the stands, offering such food and drink as Hood's Ice Cream, Handschumacher Frankfurts with Gulden's Mustard, orange drink, "tonic," peanuts, beer, and a unique ballpark treat—fried clams. Mini-bats, caps, and pennants numbered among the souvenirs. J-A Cigars and various brands of cigarettes would also be included with items offered for sale in baskets carried into the stands by white-jacketed vendors wearing caps with large cards announcing their wares. Stevens' minions were unsalaried, working solely for a 10% sales commission. Telephone booths were provided at the rear of the Grandstand and by the entrance. Women's "retiring rooms" were also located at the back of the grandstand, "always with a matron in attendance."

Fans would reach their seats via ramps rather than stairs, reflecting the lessened climb required since the playing field was 17 feet below street level. An initial glance revealed the three major sections of Braves Field—the single-decked grandstand that extended from home well beyond first and third bases, large uncovered pavilions along the left- and right-field lines and a small right-field bleacher section, known to all as the "Jury Box." The latter section received its moniker based upon a sportswriter's observation of its courtroom-like population during one of the park's many sparsely attended games prior to the era of the Three Little Steam Shovels. Its size was also a reflection of a decision by James E. Gaffney to mitigate construction costs by temporarily reducing the planned size of the bleachers. Subsequent attendance never justified the completion of original plans for a more extensive facility.[5]

Two recent additions to the Wigwam immediately attracted the attention of 1948 attendees. Atop the roof of the grandstand were new Skyview Box Seats, "the perfect view for those who want the best." Designed to also serve as a post-season press box annex to the regular 200-seat, four-row journalist area should the Braves win the National League pennant, these seats were offered on a season ticket basis for a hefty $200. Not everyone appreciated the steep ascent to the grandstand roof required to access the new seating. Famed sports cartoonist Gene Mack satirized the site in a sketch showing fans laboring to climb to their chairs, along with the following caption set to the tune of *Take Me Out To The Ballgame*:

Take me up to the Sky View.
Take me up in the clouds.
Buy me a spy-glass and let me look.
Down at Johnny Sain's wonderful hook.

Today's massive stadium message boards can trace their roots back to 1948 when the Braves ushered in the modern era by unveiling this 68-foot electric scoreboard.

Braves Field's 2,000 seat right field bleachers section was nicknamed "The Jury Box" as the result of a sportswriter's observation as to the comparability of the population of both.

Let me root, root, root for the home team.
If they don't win I'll feel blue.
For it's huff, puff,
the journey is rough,
to the old Sky View!

During the preseason months, the Braves' ownership also created a left-field attraction that rivaled Fenway Park's trademark barrier. The Wigwam now boasted one of the first electric scoreboards in the majors. The huge $70,000 C.I. Brink-installed monument was capped by a digital clock, 68 feet above the ground. At the time, there was even speculation that it might one day include a television screen. The new tally board complemented the old manual scoreboard that had resided at the back of the Jury Box since 1928. The latter provided an inning-by-inning report on all National League contests as well as for the neighboring Red Sox. Wigwam spectators soon discovered one significant flaw in the electrified scoreboard. The areas that communicated information electrically were nearly impossible to decipher on sunny days from some spots in the ballpark.

Unlike Fenway Park, where owner Tom Yawkey banished the prominent in-park advertisements from the left-field wall in 1947, Braves Field's 1948 outfield barriers were awash in commercials. It seemed that every available spot was covered—from the double-sectioned 25-foot high wall running from left to right center all the way around to the Jury Box's 10-foot high barrier. The ads ran the gamut from alcoholic beverages to clothing, cars, cigars, cigarettes, razor blades, gasoline, Coca Cola, and Lifebuoy Soap—guaranteed to "stop B.O." In addition to carrying its well-known local refrain, "Hi Neighbor, Have a 'Gansett,'" the Narragansett Brewery's bull's-eyed advertisement below the scoreboard challenged batters to "Hit The Spot." However, unlike the famous "Abe Stark" outfield target at Ebbets Field that provided a new suit as a reward, no prize was publicly offered for the Wigwam accomplishment.

Braves Field was ringed by eight soaring light towers that had brought night baseball to Boston on May 11, 1946, a season ahead of the Red Sox. Installed by the Crouse-Hinds Company of Syracuse, New York, these artificial suns were publicized as illuminating the diamond with the equivalent of four times the light of the then-average living room. As a further field enhancement, foul poles were neon lit. During night contests, the Braves donned special reflective "sateen" uniforms.

The three tiers of field boxes in front of the grandstand provided one of the better views of game action at the park due to enhancements made by the ownership during the course of the previous season. With the club on the road, the Three Little Steam Shovels brought their heavy duty construction equipment to the Wigwam and lowered the infield some 18 inches, removing 1,500 tons of dirt in the process. 100,000 square feet of new sod was laid in place, awaiting the Tribe's return. The owners were reacting to suggestions from box-holders who complained about the how the level of their seats in comparison to the infield's "turtle-back" appearance adversely affected the ability to follow the game.

In the grandstand, some views were obstructed by the sixteen posts supporting the roof. Forty-six rows rose from in back of the home plate area and increased to 76 rows in the farthest corner of its first-base section. To traverse the entire outer edge of the grandstand, one would have to walk the equivalent of a quarter mile. The grandstand's gentle slope posed visibility problems especially when a spectator in the preceding row wore a large hat. The pavilions, designed for the possibility of eventually being decked, provided a mixed quality of game viewing, with the uppermost seats distant from the action on the field. Before games, youngsters would congregate by the home dugout area on the third base side to seek autographs from their heroes. Hardcore Tommy Holmes fans populated the Jury Box and were rough on any substitutes for their beloved "Kelly" that manager Billy Southworth might dare to assign to patrol right field.

Despite strong notices that betting and gambling were prohibited in the stadium and that offenders would be ejected and barred from the park, such ne'er-do-wells would routinely congregate and conduct their business openly in the right-field pavilion.

The environment played a significant role in the

Braves Field experience. When the cool wind blew in from the Charles River toward home plate, many would-be home runs became long outs and hitting was noticeably dampened. The adjacent railroad yard beyond left field posed further issues. Smoke from coal-fueled locomotives would waft across the field in dark clouds, depositing soot and cinders on players and patrons alike. Fir trees, planted outside the park to provide a natural barrier, proved ineffective. Even directives from the rail yard superintendent to engineers and firemen to curtail the noxious emissions when the Wigwam was in use, brought little relief.

Braves Field's public address system was adequate at best and was often augmented with musical interludes. John Kiley, the legendary organist at Fenway Park for 31 years, began performing at Braves Field in 1941. His rapid renditions of the National Anthem (once timed at 52 seconds) were said to be heard all the way back to Kenmore Square. When Tom Yawkey hired him in 1958, Kiley became a resource for trivia buffs as the answer to the question of who was only man to "play" for the Red Sox, Bruins, and Celtics during the same season.

Having been booted out of the more staid Fenway Park, the Troubadours, a three-piece jazz band version of Brooklyn's "Sym-phony" took up residence at Braves Field. Also known as the "Three Little Earaches," the trio, comprised in 1948 of Sparky Tomasetti, Sid Barbato, and Hi Brenner, roamed the stadium, playing songs linked to the home team, opponents, and umpires. When Tommy Holmes approached the plate, the Troubadours would break into a rendition of *Has Anybody Here Seen Kelly?* or *"Holmes" on the Range.* Shower-bound enemy hurlers were provided funeral dirges to hasten their exits. Eddie Stanky was notorious for his ability to draw walks, hence their musical tribute of *I Walk Alone.* They were once told to cease and desist performing *Three Blind Mice* when the umpires entered the field. Enemy players such as Mickey Owen and Max Lanier who had returned to the senior circuit after having jumped to the ill-fated Mexican League were serenaded with *South of the Border.* In addition to the musical accompaniment, the Troubadours had a dress code for Tribe opponents. They would appear attired as Bolsheviks when the Reds came to town and as Quakers for the Phillies. For their efforts, the Troubadours received $15 each per game, $25 for doubleheaders and, on occasional road trips, $100 a week plus expenses.

The ballpark also had its fair share of colorful fans, the most notable of which was Lolly Hopkins. Hopkins' loyalty to both of Boston's teams won her complimentary season passes from the clubs. Traveling from Providence, RI, Hopkins would join up with her female entourage and, megaphone in hand, direct her opinions toward players, umpires, official scorers and fellow attendees. She would be included in team promotions such as drawing prizes on fan appreciation days and would participate in the pennant-clinching celebration, dancing on a table with owner Lou Perini.

For some long-time loyal fans, the success of the Tribe in 1948 came at a steep price. Newly minted fans and front runners crowded into Braves Field, competing for choice seating with core rooters. A denizen of the Jury Box, Elmer Foote, remarked in frustration, "We were better off when we were in the second division." Similarly, the father of Boston Braves Historical Association business manager George Altison was irritated when his loyalty wasn't recognized. The elder Altison was a "juror" in the right field bleachers since the early '30s. Owning a tavern in Allston and working nights permitted him to attend most games since day baseball was the standard through the late Forties. He resided amongst a tight-knit group of sun worshippers and Tommy Holmes followers. When he failed to obtain World Series seats through a ticket lottery, Altison stormed the Braves administration office and loudly explained the unfairness of his situation to a clerk. Upon hearing the ruckus, general manager John Quinn left his office and instructed his secretary to provide this fan with two tickets to each home contest. Happiness turned to sadness when Altison later had to return to the same building to redeem his unused Game Seven grandstand tickets for a $10 refund.

Braves Field began 1948 by opening its doors to the public on April 16, 1948, kicking off a three-game preseason Braves-Red Sox City Series. It would not complete its baseball-hosting duties until October 11 when Tommy Holmes flied to left for the final out in Game Six of the World Series.

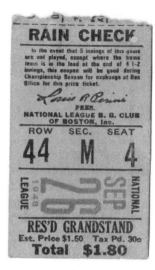

Braves Field ticket stub, 1948.

2008

Today one can still reach what remains of Braves Field by trolley on what is now the MBTA's "Green Line." The ballpark spur no longer exists but from time to time portions of the old tracks resurface due to wear and tear on Babcock Street's asphalt base. Gaffney's old street was renamed Harry Agganis Way in 1995, after the Boston University sports immortal and former Red Sox first baseman whose life was tragically cut short. A bronze statue of the "Golden Greek" in a football rather than baseball pose welcomes pedestrians as they exit the streetcar.

Unlike most of its former green cathedral contemporaries that now only exist in photographs, Braves Field still hosts athletic events within confines that house relics from Gaffney's original ball park. After the Braves' defection to Milwaukee in the spring of 1953, the abandoned field caught the eye of the neighboring and ever-expanding Boston University, which eventually acquired the property.

Almost immediately, the Wigwam's transformation into a college gridiron and athletic field commenced. These alterations were not entirely alien to Braves Field, which served as the site for football contests for both Boston College and the NFL Boston Braves (today's Washington Redskins).

Gradually, however, the university irretrievably altered this baseball diamond to better accommodate its Terriers football team and its followers. By 1955, the left- and center-field walls had been demolished and the huge electric scoreboard shipped off to Kansas City's Municipal Stadium. The demise of the Jury Box and the left-field pavilion quickly followed. Boston University re-christened the hallowed grounds "Nickerson Field." Near the end of the decade, the field was realigned to run parallel to the remaining portion of the right-field pavilion, the last extant piece of the old Wigwam, save the Braves administration building where Babe Ruth signed his last active player contract. Dormitories and other university facilities now encroach upon the sites of that portion of the grandstand that extended from home to left field.

Professional sports persisted over the years on what had been Braves Field turf. Both the AFL Boston Patriots and the USFL Boston Breakers at one time called this historic site their home. Although Boston University has since dropped its collegiate football program, Braves Field continues to be actively used for men's and women's intramural and collegiate sporting events. Its celebrated link to professional sports also remains intact. During 2002–03, the artificially-turfed grounds hosted the now-defunct Boston Breakers of the Women's United Soccer Association. They were succeeded in 2004 by the Boston Cannons, a professional men's lacrosse team.

The Tribe's former administration building retains most of its original external appearance although the distinctive archways have been squared off. The building has been used as a university police station and as a day care facility. In its back courtyard on a pedestal stands a brass plaque, dedicated in 1988, honoring the site of Braves Field. In 2002, the Boston Braves Historical Association successfully petitioned the City of Boston to further memorialize the grounds through the naming of the alley running between Babcock Street and Harry Agganis Way as "Braves Field Way." Unfortunately, the commemorative street signs on both ends of the alley have become the targets of souvenir hunters and are often missing despite the city's best efforts to keep them in place.

The right-field pavilion, the Wigwam's largest remnant, has been modified by the school over the years. A new portion was added in 1959 to square off the stands and the chunk that was removed to shift the right-field foul line in 1937 has been restored. A press box has been grafted onto the top of this section. The 1915 structure can be distinguished from the modern addition by looking for two things. First, a diagonal seam can be detected running from field level to the upper right-hand corner of the stands. Second, the older portion is ringed with capstones on the back wall while the newer part is not. By identifying the original section, one can take a seat there and legitimately claim to have sat in an area of Braves Field where fans once watched three games of the 1948 World Series. In doing so, however, your orientation may be a bit off as the current field is now parallel with the pavilion while in a baseball configuration, the stands were angled toward home plate.

As time passes, memories fade. Few who now attend events at Nickerson Field recall that Boston once had a National League entry, or the exploits of such stalwarts as Spahn, Sain, Elliott, Holmes, Dark, Stanky, Torgeson, Sisti, and Masi, who roamed that great expanse then known as Braves Field during the Braves' Last Hurrah in 1948.

Notes

1. Braves Field had hosted two World Series previously. The Tribe loaned their larger facility to the Red Sox in 1915 and 1916.
2. From 1936–40, the "Wigwam" appellation was replaced by the "Beehive" nickname reflecting the lamentable and temporary shift in the team name from Braves to Bees.
3. Through the Commonwealth Realty Trust, Gaffney's widow Essie and other parties leased the stadium to the team over the years until the Three Little Steam Shovels purchased the facility for an estimated three quarters of a million dollars in 1949.
4. Cobb's prediction held true until May 26, 1917 when Cardinals outfielder Walton Cruise's shot landed in the right field "Jury Box" bleachers. Cruise also claimed Braves Field's second out-of-the-park clout, on August 16, 1921, this time performing for the Braves. He again reached the Jury Box.
5. In March of 1949, owner Lou Perini announced plans to remove the Jury Box and extend the right field pavilion all the way to center field, but with an ominous caveat: "only if conditions warrant it."

Sources

Kaese, Harold, *The Boston Braves*
Miller, Ray, *A Tour of Braves Field*
Brady, Bob, *Diamond Signs* (unpublished manuscript)
Reminiscences from Boston Braves fans George Altison, Mort Bloomberg, Ralph Evans, and various members of the Boston Braves Historical Association

One town, two teams, divided loyalties

by Bill Nowlin and Saul Wisnia

With two Boston baseball teams in town, there was inevitably competition for both fan loyalty and revenue. There were also opportunities for friendship between the ballplayers and occasional jealousies. And there were economic realities, at a time when most ballplayers didn't make that much money during their short careers. After the Braves had it wrapped up and realized they'd be playing either the Red Sox or the Indians in the World Series, several Braves players went on the record as saying they'd rather face the Indians, because a World Series in cavernous Cleveland Stadium would draw far larger crowds than Fenway and thus the players would have more gate receipts to share. The logic was unassailable, and in fact the three games at Cleveland Stadium drew 238,491—an average of 79,497, more than twice as many paying customers than Fenway Park could accommodate.

As Clif Keane pointed out, it wasn't because the Braves disliked any of the Red Sox. Alvin Dark expressed it soberly: "So far as baseball rivalry is concerned, I would like to play the Red Sox. But for business reasons, I naturally would want to see Cleveland win the pennant."

One Braves player had an additional reason for desiring a Cleveland-Boston Series. Braves outfielder Jeff Heath had been a star on the Indians for a decade but had often feuded with management over his salary and other matters. He had also been the reputed leader of the "Cry Baby Revolt" in 1940 when players appealed for the ousting of manager Oscar Vitt, and taunting fans questioned his effort and attitude. When his statistics slipped, management saw its chance and traded Heath to the lowly Washington Senators after the 1945 season, so he was naturally chomping at the bit to show the Cleveland team and fans his full worth. When he broke his ankle days before the '48 season ended, thus sidelining him for the World Series, it cost Heath his shot at redemption—and may have cost the Braves the title.

Needless to say, the remarks didn't play well with Red Sox players or amongst Red Sox fans. When Heath went down with injury, some responded with a lack of sympathy, almost muttering that he got what he deserved. "I hope he broken his leg up to his neck," one of them said. "Too bad, ain't it?," said another. "He wanted to play Cleveland. T'Hell with Heath!" It wasn't the kind of sentiment that would have added luster to the notion of an (almost) perfect summer. Saul Wisnia and Richard Johnson explore the vagaries over the years of Boston as a two-team town in their forthcoming book, *From Yawkey to Milwaukee*, and we urge those interested in learning more to consult that work for more on the subject.

An Alternative Possibility
The Red Sox Meet the Braves in a Simulated 1948 World Series

by Bill Nowlin

Only one loss prevented Boston's (almost) perfect baseball summer from becoming fully realized. Had the Red Sox lost just 58 games instead of 59, they would have been the team facing the Braves in an all-Boston World Series. Had the Indians lost 59 games instead of 58, the result would have been the same. Before the single game playoff that was needed to break the dead-even 96–58 record both the Indians and Red Sox held at the end of the 154-game schedule, the two teams had squared off against each other and held an 11–11 record in face-to-face competition. Both held 6–5 records at home and, obviously, 5–6 records in the other team's ballpark. But winning one more game against any of the other American League teams would have done the trick, too.

It didn't work out that way; Cleveland and Boston were tied and needed the single-game playoff. It might have been a best-of-three matchup, as it had been in the National League just three years earlier, but playing out those games while the AL winner (the Red Sox, as it happened) stood idle didn't seem like the way to go and so a single-game playoff was agreed upon.

Like many fans, Mark Armour wondered what might have happened had the Sox and Braves faced each other in the World Series. Mark had an idea how to find out. Through SABR, he knew of Diamond Mind Baseball, a company that produced a game providing the possibility for simulating matchups on home computers or via the Internet. Would-be managers could strategize, creating their own lineups and playing a simulated game. In 2005, Diamond Mind Baseball was named *PC Magazine* Editor's Choice for PC-based baseball games: "As far as baseball simulations are concerned, Diamond Mind Baseball is the MVP." The company's products allow gamers to play current season games or those from a considerable number of past seasons—or to create fantasy teams that would, for instance, pit Josh Gibson against Walter Johnson. As their website says, "You call all the shots because you are owner, manager and coach!" Over 50 million fantasy games have been played using their software.

Mark suggested that we approach Diamond Mind to see if they'd be willing to run a simulation of a Braves-Red Sox World Series, based on actual 1948 statistics. We approached Luke Kraemer of DMB and he consulted CEO Dayne Myers of parent company Simnasium (now Imagine Sports). They gave us the thumbs-up.

Of course, to get to an all-Boston World Series, we had to arrange for the Indians to lose to the Red Sox in the playoff game. We asked Luke to create a simulation and run the game as many times as it took until the Red Sox won. We figured the answer to how many times that might take would itself be of interest. It was.

Luke asked his associate Jim Wheeler to run the game, and our simulated Red Sox manager even had Denny Galehouse start the game for Boston. The Indians scored five runs in the top of the second, but Sox skipper Joe McCarthy stuck with the veteran pitcher for five full innings and the Red Sox chipped away at the lead, finally tying it and then winning it in the bottom of the ninth when Vern Stephens singled in Ted Williams for a thrilling 6–5 victory that propelled the Red Sox into the World Series for the second time in three years. That was the result on the very first try. We'd had visions of having to run the game many times to achieve the desired result but, after all, these were very evenly matched teams and it's not surprising that the Sox won with the first simulation.

That set up the all-Boston World Series. Bob Brady managed the Boston Braves throughout the simulated Series, and Mark Armour managed the Red Sox. They selected the starting lineups and the starting pitchers, and Diamond Mind did the rest, though there were some instructions. Armour, for example, wanted to preserve Ellis Kinder as a possible starter after Game One, so asked DMB not to use him in relief. After each game, Billy Southworth (Brady) and Joe McCarthy (Armour) selected the starter for the following day's game and made such adjustments to the lineup as they deemed wise. Bill Nowlin became a fantasy newspaperman and wrote up the post-game accounts, interviewing Southworth/Brady and McCarthy/Armour for their reactions. We hope readers enjoy following the '48 Series that might have been.

Diamond Mind Baseball was designed and developed by long-time SABR member and award winner Tom Tippett. The game was first commercially available in 1987, marketed by Pursue the Pennant, and sold under the name Pursue the Pennant PC Baseball. In 1995 Tom ended the marketing relationship with Pursue the Pennant and began marketing the game himself under the name Diamond Mind Baseball (DMB). In 2006 Tom sold the game to Imagine Sports (formally Simnasium) but is still active in the design and development of the PC and now also Internet-based baseball games. DMB is regarded as the most sophisticated baseball simulation with its unique and accurate pitch-by-pitch model. To learn more about Diamond Mind Baseball, visit their website at www.imaginesports.com.

The Single Game Playoff for the 1948 American League Pennant

Simulation run by Jim Wheeler for Diamond Mind

Stephens, Sox win pennant in dramatic fashion

```
October 5, 1948 at Fenway Park, Red Sox 6, Indians 5
Cleveland    050 000 000 – 5 14 1
Boston (A)   010 130 001 – 6 13 0
```

Cleveland	AB	R	H	BI
Mitchell lf	4	0	0	0
Clark 1b	4	1	2	3
Robinson 1b	1	0	1	0
Boudreau ss	5	0	2	0
Gordon 2b	5	0	1	0
Keltner 3b	5	0	1	0
Doby cf	4	1	2	0
Kennedy rf	4	1	1	0
Christopher p	0	0	0	0
Hegan c	4	1	2	1
Bearden p	2	1	2	1
Klieman p	0	0	0	0
Judnich ph	1	0	0	0
Gromek p	0	0	0	0
Tucker ph	1	0	0	0
Totals	**40**	**5**	**14**	**5**

Boston (A)	AB	R	H	BI
DiMaggio cf	4	1	0	0
Pesky 3b	4	1	2	0
Williams lf	5	1	1	0
Stephens ss	5	1	4	3
Doerr 2b	3	0	2	0
Spence rf	3	0	0	0
Goodman 1b	4	1	2	1
Tebbetts c	4	0	1	1
Galehouse p	1	0	0	0
Hitchcock ph	1	1	1	0
Kinder p	2	0	0	0
Totals	**36**	**6**	**13**	**5**

Cle: Judnich batted for Klieman in the 6th; Robinson inserted at 1b in the 7th; Tucker batted for Gromek in the 8th; Doby moved to rf in the 8th; Tucker moved to cf in the 8th. **BoA:** Hitchcock batted for Galehouse in the 5th. **E**—Gordon. **LOB**—Cleveland 10, Boston 8. **2B**—Doby, Bearden, Stephens, Goodman. **HR**—Clark(1). **K**—Boudreau, Gordon, Doby, Williams, Galehouse. **BB**—Mitchell, Doby, DiMaggio, Pesky, Doerr, Spence. **PB**—Hegan, Tebbetts. **GWRBI**—Stephens. **DP**—Cleveland 3, Boston 1.

Cleveland	INN	H	R	ER	BB	K
Bearden	4⅓	8	5	4	4	2
Klieman	⅔	0	0	0	0	0
Gromek	2	2	0	0	0	0
Christopher (L 0–1)	1⅔	3	1	0	0	0
Totals	**8⅔**	**13**	**6**	**4**	**4**	

Boston (A)	INN	H	R	ER	BB	K
Galehouse	5	9	5	5	2	1
Kinder (W 1–0)	4	5	0	0	0	0
Totals	**9**	**14**	**5**	**5**	**2**	**3**

Temperature: 56, Sky: clear, Wind: out to right at 16 MPH.

It took 155 games to win a pennant, and the final game—the first playoff game in American League history—went into the bottom of the ninth inning before Junior Stephens and the Red Sox captured the flag in dramatic fashion, capping a game in which they overcame the 5–0 lead the Indians established in the top of the second inning.

Joe McCarthy's choice of the veteran Denny Galehouse to start the single-game playoff stunned fans and—truth be told—didn't sit well with some of the players, either. Galehouse (8–7 before the game) was matched against Cleveland's star rookie southpaw Gene Bearden (19–7, and the lowest ERA in the league.) It seemed like a mismatch, with both Mel Parnell and Ellis Kinder available, but Galehouse had pitched a good game against the Indians earlier in the year and McCarthy decided to go with experience. In postgame remarks, the Sox skipper seemed to acknowledge that his choice of starting pitcher surprised many: "Well, I went with my gut with Galehouse, and I wasn't looking too smart in the second inning. But I thought Denny settled down well, and our bats finally came around, as they often do. The crowd really helped us today. They stayed with us when we fell behind, and were a big part of the rally in the fifth."

In the end, it was Stephens' day, though, going 4-for-5 at the plate with three runs batted in, including the single that drove in Ted Williams with the game-winner in the final frame. Not since pinch-hitter Del Gainer won Game Two of the 1916 World Series in the bottom of the 14th inning with a single have the Red Sox had such an dramatic final at-bat. "Junior really came through for us today," McCarthy added. "We brought him here to drive in runs, and he drove in a bunch today, didn't he? Like I said, I thought Denny had the stuff to shut down the bats today, He had the one bad inning, but fortunately we came back from it. Ellis saved our bacon today, like he has been doing most of the year. He's got some pitching left in him this year." Stephens ends the season with an even 140 RBIs.

The game began with Dale Mitchell flying out to right in the top of the first, a ball that carried through Monday's cool (56 degrees) afternoon air toward the Red Sox bullpen by the 16-mph winds blowing to right. Stan Spence ran back, set himself, and camped under it for the catch. Allie Clark singled between Johnny Pesky playing third and Stephens at short, but then Lou Boudreau flied out to left and Joe Gordon to center. The Red Sox only got one ball out of the infield, a surprise slap to the left-field side that squirted between short and third, even after the re-positioned fielders had settled into the Williams Shift.

Galehouse got Ken Keltner to weakly ground to second; Bobby Doerr (with only six errors all season) handled it routinely. Larry Doby walked on five pitches, then ran first to third on Bob Kennedy's hard-hit seeing-eye single through the right side of the infield. After three straight balls to Jim Hegan nearly loaded the bases, Galehouse seemed to settle down with a called strike that caught the outside corner against the big right-hander. Hegan dropped in a single to short right field, well in front of the charging Spence. Doby scored easily and Kennedy pulled into second. The pitcher, Gene Bearden, missed two attempts to bunt the runners up, then singled through the hole to the left side. Kennedy was off with the pitch, and Williams was playing deep, so the Indians scored their second run and saw men on first and second. Stephens scooped up a low grounder off Dale Mitchell's bat and threw to Billy Goodman at first; both runners moved up. Clark then boomed a big home run on a 2-0 count to left-center field, for his second hit of the game and three more Indians runs. It was 5-0, Indians, and when Boudreau singled back through the box, Joe McCarthy waved Ellis Kinder up in the Red Sox bullpen. When Gordon lined out to Dom DiMaggio in straightaway center, Kinder took his seat again.

Doerr singled to right field to start off the second for the Sox, but Spence grounded into a tailor-made 6-4-3 double play. Goodman doubled deep to right-center field, the ball one-hopping the bullpen wall but fielded smoothly by Doby. Catcher Birdie Tebbetts singled on a 3-2 pitch and Goodman scored to make it 5-1, but Galehouse struck out on three pitches.

In the third, neither team scored, Keltner's leadoff single followed by three quick outs. DiMag, Pesky, and Ted were put down 1-2-3. Bearden collected his second hit of the game, with a long double to the wall in left-center, and when Mitchell walked, there was stirring again in the Boston bullpen, but Clark grounded into a double play, and Boudreau grounded out, Doerr to Goodman.

The Red Sox picked up another run—but only one, despite a golden opportunity—after Stephens lined a soft single to left field to lead off the bottom of the fourth, and it was men on first and second after Doerr's roller down the third-base line. Spence walked on four straight pitches, loading the bases with nobody out. Goodman lofted a fly ball to center field, deep enough to drive in Stephens on the sacrifice fly, while Bobby took third, but Tebbets hit into a 4-6-3 twin killing and Bearden escaped further damage.

Though Doby doubled down the line in right field, Spence played it cleanly and Galehouse had what was otherwise his best inning with three easy outs bunched around Doby's drive, and was then cheered when the Red Sox plated three runs to tie the game 5-5. But his day was done. McCarthy, hoping to kick-start the offense, put in Billy Hitchcock to hit for Galehouse and Hitch hit the first pitch for a single to left field. Bearden got two quick strikes on The Little Professor, but then Dom took four balls in a row and so did Pesky. The bases were loaded for the Big Guy, but Teddy struck out. Stephens doubled by Keltner into the left field corner, driving in two runs, and Boudreau made a pitching change as well, calling on Ed Klieman for some right-handed relief. Doerr was walked intentionally, but Hegan couldn't handle a ball in the dirt and the passed ball allowed Johnny Pesky to score from third, and both runners to move up. Spence grounded out to short, though, and the runners had to hold, and Goodman reprised the ground out to end the inning.

Both starting pitchers were gone and it was a fresh game, tied 5-5. It stayed that way through the sixth, seventh, and eighth as Kinder set down the Tribe 1-2-3 on three grounders in the top of the sixth. Wally Judnich had pinch hit for Klieman, and Steve Gromek took over for Cleveland. He, too, kept the ball in the infield. In the seventh, Kinder kept the ball down again. Boudreau pushed a single through the left side of the infield, but was forced at second by Gordon's grounder, and once again three ground balls led to easy outs. Eddie Robinson came in to play first for the Indians, but most of the action seemed to be at second base. Pesky lined a single well over Gordon's glove to lead off, but was forced at second on Williams' one-hopper to Boudreau. Stephens' single just eluded Gordon, putting Williams on second. Doerr hit the ball hard, but Gromek stabbed it on the first bounce and threw Williams out at third base. Spence grounded out to Gordon, who stepped on the bag to force Doerr for the third out.

The Indians singled twice in the top of the eighth, around Kennedy's 6-4 play that forced Doby at second. Thurman Tucker hit for Gromek but popped up to Pesky. Although the first pitch to Mitchell scooted past Tebbetts, putting runners on second and third, Mitchell swung at the second pitch of the at-bat and grounded out 4-3.

Russ Christopher allowed a single to Goodman, but Billy was erased by Birdie's double-play grounder to Gordon. McCarthy stuck with his reliable reliever, Kinder, despite his .097 average at the plate. Old Folks got some good wood, but it was a routine fly ball to Tucker, who'd taken over in center, with Doby moving to right field.

Robinson singled to left, Boudreau struck out. Gordon singled up the middle, but Dom played the ball well as usual, and Robinson didn't dare take third. Keltner flied to Ted in left and Doby struck out.

DiMaggio flied out to center. Johnny Pesky looked to get things started when he slapped a single down the left-field line, but Mitchell charged over quickly to field the ball and Johnny had to hold at first. Hitting out of an 0-2 hole, Williams seemed to hit into a sure double play to send the game into extra innings. Boudreau's throw forced Pesky at second, but Gordon lost the handle on the ball and bounced it into the dirt on the relay to first base, and the Red Sox were still alive. Williams took second—and then scored the winning run when Stephens lined a hard single to center field on an 0-1 pitch. The Red Sox mobbed Ted at the plate, and then Junior at first base, and the Fenway faithful cheered into the night as they won the American League pennant for the second time in three years, and the right to battle the Braves in an all-Beantown World Series.

Kinder took home the win, bringing him to 11-7 on the season, and the Red Sox finished up 87-58 on the year.

1948 World Series

Game One

October 6, 1948 at Braves Field, Red Sox 5, Braves 1

Boston (A)	000 001 301 –	5	6	0
Boston (N)	000 010 000 –	1	4	0

Boston (A)	AB	R	H	BI
DiMaggio cf	2	0	0	1
Pesky 3b	4	0	0	0
Williams lf	4	1	1	0
Stephens ss	4	1	1	0
Doerr 2b	4	1	1	1
Spence rf	4	1	1	3
Goodman 1b	3	0	0	0
Tebbetts c	3	1	1	0
Parnell p	3	0	1	0
Totals	**31**	**5**	**6**	**5**

Boston (N)	AB	R	H	BI
Holmes rf	3	0	2	0
Dark ss	4	0	0	0
McCormick,M lf	4	0	1	0
Elliott,B 3b	3	0	0	0
McCormick,F 1b	4	0	0	0
Conatser cf	2	1	0	0
Masi c	2	0	0	0
Stanky 2b	2	0	0	0
Sain p	2	0	1	1
Sisti ph	1	0	0	0
Hogue p	0	0	0	0
Totals	**27**	**1**	**4**	**1**

BoN: Sisti batted for Sain in the 8th. **LOB**—Red Sox 1, Braves 4. **2B**—Tebbetts. **HR**—Doerr(1), Spence(1). **CS**—Holmes. **K**—Spence, Tebbetts, Holmes. **BB**—DiMaggio, Holmes, Elliott, B, Stanky. **SH**—Masi. **SF**—DiMaggio. **HBP**—Conatser. **HB**—Parnell. **GWRBI**—Spence. **DP**—Red Sox 1, Braves 1.

Boston (A)	INN	H	R	ER	BB	K
Parnell (W 1–0)	9	4	1	1	3	1
Totals	**9**	**4**	**1**	**1**	**3**	**1**
Boston (N)	INN	H	R	ER	BB	K
Sain (L 0–1)	8	5	4	4	1	2
Hogue	1	1	1	1	0	0
Totals	**9**	**6**	**5**	**5**	**1**	**2**

Temperature: 57, Sky: clear, Wind: out to center at 11 MPH.

Mel Parnell pitched a four-hit gem at Braves Field, nearly matched by Johnny Sain—but for one pitch Sain wished he could call back, the three-run homer hit by Stan Spence in the top of the seventh that shattered a 1–1 tie.

It was Sain who put the Braves on the board first. After four-and-a-half innings of scoreless ball, the Red Sox had but one hit through the first five—a harmless two-out single in the top of the third by Parnell, the only Sox batter to reach base.

In the home half of the fifth, Parnell hit Braves center fielder Clint Conatser with a 1–1 inside fastball. The Braves had seen Tommy Holmes cut down stealing in the first, saw Eddie Stanky doubled off first in the third, and had seen two walks go for naught in the bottom of the fourth.

Hoping to put a run on board, Phil Masi laid down a bunt to third base and advanced Conatser into scoring position. Stanky flied out to straightaway center. Sain singled to left field and Conatser, off on contact, challenged Williams' arm and scored with ease as Junior Stephens

cut off the throw to hold Sain on first. Holmes singled for the second time in the game, but Ted's throw to Johnny Pesky cut down Sain at third.

The Red Sox promptly replied with a run of their own when Birdie Tebbetts doubled between Holmes and Conatser in right center. Parnell flied out to left field deep enough that Tebbetts tagged and took third. Birdie tagged up again, and scored, on Dom DiMaggio's sacrifice fly to center field. Pesky rolled a dribbler back to Sain, who scooped it easily and threw to Frank McCormick at first.

With his first hit of the World Series, Ted Williams singled hard up the middle despite a full shift. Stephens swung at the first pitch, and singled through the hole between first and second. Bobby Doerr grounded out productively with a weak grounder that left shortstop Alvin Dark no choice but to throw to McCormick as both runners advanced. On a 2–2 count, Stan Spence hit a high curve ball and homered deep down the right-field line into the gap between the Jury Box and the first-base pavilion.

The crowd in the Wigwam was fairly evenly split, about 60/40 in favor of the "home team" Braves, but Spence's drive seemed to suck the air out of the afternoon. It was 4–1 Red Sox.

Mel Parnell held the Braves to one run on four hits and won the first game of the Trolley Series.

Sain got Goodman and Tebbetts with ease but the damage was done. Parnell retired the Braves 1–2–3 in both the seventh and the eighth. Sibbi Sisti pinch-hit for Sain in the eighth, but he grounded out to Pesky at third.

Bobby Hogue came on in relief to pitch the top of the ninth and only in his 11th pitch did he retire The Kid on a grounder to short. Stephens hit a carbon copy grounder on Hogue's first pitch. Doerr got his first World Series hit since 1946, and it was a long home run to straightaway left field over the 25-foot wooden fence installed just before the season began.

Parnell was in command all afternoon and the ninth was no exception. He allowed only his fourth hit of the game, an inoffensive mistake hit off the "other" McCormick—left-fielder Mike McCormick just off to the right out the mound. Parnell smothered the ball but had no play and wisely held the ball.

The only Elliott in the game, third baseman Bob, flied

out to the fleet DiMaggio who ran the ball down in center, and Frank McCormick lined out sharply to Williams in left.

Parnell, who was 15–8 in the regular season, added a World Series win to his resume in just his second year of play. The young southpaw from New Orleans looks to have a brilliant future in Boston. He walked three and struck out just one.

McCarthy plans to start 18–5 righthander Jack Kramer in Game Two before the Series moves to Fenway Park, while Southworth counters with 15–12 southpaw Warren Spahn.

Post-game wrapup

In comments after the game, McCarthy was gracious: "Sain's got that great curve ball, and he doesn't make too many mistakes with it. But he got one up to Stan, and paid for it. He's a great pitcher, and we feel fortunate to come away with a win." It was just one of those pitches that missed its spot, and Spence took advantage, explained Southworth. "Johnny had pretty good luck with Spence the first couple of at-bats so there was no reason to change our pitching strategy. Unfortunately, Spence jumped on one of Johnny's curve balls that broke a bit too high and sent it into the stands."

Reporters asked Billy if it surprised him that it was the fifth and sixth batters in the order that did in the Braves. "The Red Sox have a solid line-up and you can't let your guard down once you get past Williams and Stephens," he said. "Doerr is always dangerous and Spence has some pop in his bat. That kid Goodman looks like he's gonna be a star and ol' Birdie seems to get better with the bat with age." McCarthy added, "We've got a lot of good hitters, and Sain kept most of them down. Like I said, he made a mistake to Stan, and his fastball to Bobby got too much of the plate. It happens to great pitchers too."

What about Parnell? McCarthy swelled up a bit with evident pride. "Mel really came into his own this year, and you saw today why he pitched the first game. He gave up a few long flies today, but thankfully this is a big park." Southworth's take was complimentary: That young fella has a great career ahead of him. He pitched to my guys like a veteran. He kinda reminds me of another lefty from New Orleans—Howie Pollet, who pitched for me with the Cardinals. Parnell showed me a good fast ball and slider and kept jamming righties."

Chuckling a bit at being asked how it felt to take the first game on the road, Marse Joe said, "It's nice that everyone can just go back to their own beds, I'm sure. There were quite a few Red Sox fans in the crowd today, and I hope they show up again tomorrow. I don't expect we'll change anything. We've got Kramer going tomorrow, and he had a nice year for us. They've got a tough lefty, but hopefully we'll score a few runs somehow."

Southworth's strategy for Game Two? "We're gonna stick with what got us here. We weren't as sharp as I'd have liked. The momentum of the close pennant race and the playoff game helped the Red Sox. I expect my guys to rise to the occasion as they've done all season."

Game Two

October 7, 1948 at Braves Field, Red Sox 2, Braves 0				
Boston (A)	100 000 010	– 2	7	2
Boston (N)	000 000 000	– 0	5	0

Boston (A)	AB	R	H	BI
DiMaggio cf	4	0	0	0
Pesky 3b	3	1	2	0
Williams lf	4	1	1	1
Stephens ss	3	0	0	0
Doerr 2b	4	0	1	1
Spence rf	4	0	1	0
Goodman 1b	4	0	2	0
Tebbetts c	3	0	0	0
Kramer p	3	0	0	0
Totals	32	2	7	2

Boston (N)	AB	R	H	BI
Holmes rf	4	0	1	0
Dark ss	4	0	1	0
Torgeson 1b	3	0	0	0
Elliott,B 3b	3	0	1	0
Rickert lf	4	0	0	0
Salkeld c	4	0	1	0
McCormick,M cf	4	0	0	0
Stanky 2b	3	0	0	0
Spahn p	3	0	1	0
Sisti ph	1	0	0	0
Totals	33	0	5	0

BoN: Sisti batted for Spahn in the 9th. **LOB**—Red Sox 5, Braves 9. **E**—DiMaggio, Spence. **2B**—Pesky, Dark. **HR**—Williams(1). **K**—Spence, Kramer 2, Torgeson, Stanky, Spahn. **BB**—Pesky, Stephens, Torgeson, Elliott,B, Stanky. **GWRBI**—Doerr. **DP**—Braves 2.

Boston (A)	INN	H	R	ER	BB	K
Kramer (W 1–0)	9	5	0	0	3	3
Totals	9	5	0	0	3	3
Boston (N)	**INN**	**H**	**R**	**ER**	**BB**	**K**
Spahn (L 0–1)	9	7	2	2	2	3
Totals	9	7	2	2	2	3

Temperature: 56, Sky: clear, Wind: right to left at 7 MPH.

Jack Kramer was the star in the second game of this year's all-Beantown World Series, shutting out the Braves in their own Wigwam with a 2–0 five-hitter. The Braves' Warren Spahn allowed just one first-inning run and a solo homer to Ted Williams in the eighth inning, going the distance but going down to defeat.

"You've gotta drive in runs to win," lamented Braves manager Billy Southworth after the game. "We had a couple of good shots in the fourth and fifth but couldn't catch a break." Red Sox manager McCarthy saw the big play as the one rightfielder Stan Spence made in the fifth inning. "Bases loaded, and their guy hit it on the screws. My heart skipped a beat, but Spence went over and got it. The Braves had a few rallies early, but after that Jack settled down and was lights out. But if that ball lands in the fifth, who knows where this ballgame ends up."

The first couple of batters hit Spahn hard. DiMaggio led off the game with an arcing fly ball to right field and Pesky lined the second pitch he saw for a double to right-center field. Holmes prevented the ball from getting between him and Mike McCormick or Pesky might have reached third. Williams lifted an easy fly to McCormick. Stephens walked. Bobby Doerr hit a soft single to shallow center field and by the time McCormick got to the ball, Pesky was already halfway home. Spence popped up to Dark at shortstop, and the Red Sox held a 1–0 lead.

Kramer set down the Braves 1–2–3, the ball never leaving the infield. Spahn, too, kept the ball in the infield during the top of the second.

Playing his first season at third base, Johnny Pesky led the American League in errors, but Bob Elliott's squibber down the line was a mistake hit that no third sacker would have handled and Elliott reached on a single. Rickert flied out to DiMaggio in straightaway center. Salkeld slapped a liner to Pesky at third, who ranged to his left, fell down and then fired to Doerr at second just in time to retire Elliott, but Salkeld was safe on first. McCormick flied out to center.

Keeping the ball low, Spahn got three groundball outs in the top of the third with only Pesky reaching on a walk. Stanky walked to lead off the third and Spahn bunted safely. With runners at first and second, Holmes tried to advance the runners but popped up to Pesky at third base. Southworth shouldered the blame on that one: "I took a chance at trying to catch them by surprise and get both runners into scoring position, so I flashed Tommy the bunt sign. We'd have had a good chance at getting them both in with Blackie and Torgy coming up." Dark skittered one to Doerr at second, but the only play was to force Spahn, leaving runners on first and third. Torgeson grounded out, Stephens to Doerr.

Billy Goodman hit a single between Pesky and Stephens, but Spahn induced two more grounders and struck out Spence in the top of the fourth. Again, the Braves mounted a bit of a one-out threat when DiMaggio dropped Rickert's one-out looper. Salked singled and Rickert took second. McCormick grounded out, Pesky to Goodman, and both runners advanced, but Stanky hit an easy one-bounder to Stephens who stepped on the bag for the third out.

Kramer struck out for the second time, retired when Salkeld threw the dropped third strike to Torgy at first. Pesky pulled a single through the hole but it was sandwiched between routine fly outs from The Little Professor and The Kid.

After fouling off four straight 1–2 pitches, Spahn struck out. Holmes popped up to Tebbetts, who circled and snared the ball about four feet into fair territory. Dark doubled to deep right field, and then reached third base when Spence let his fingers slip and had to pick the ball up twice. Torgeson walked on the 10th pitch he saw, and then Bob Elliott walked, loading the bases. Rickert hit the ball hard, but Spence reeled it in after a long run. McCarthy saw that as the big play of the game.

Spahn saw three batters in the sixth and three in the seventh; the only hit was Billy Goodman's leadoff single in the seventh, but Kramer hit into a 6-4–3 double play. Kramer mowed down the Braves in both innings, giving up just an uneventful single. With two outs in the top of the eighth, Williams hit his homer, a long arcing fly ball to the deepest part of right-center field. The Braves went down in order in the bottom of the eighth. Spence singled in the top of the ninth, but the Sox hit into another double play.

Kramer was efficient in the bottom of the ninth, getting McCormick to fly out to Ted in left and striking out Stanky—again, Tebbetts dropped the third strike and had to throw to Goodman. Sibbi Sisti came in to pinch-hit for Spahn, but flied out to center field and the game was over.

After the game, McCarthy was asked if he felt good now that the Red Sox were up two games to none in his first year as Red Sox manager. "Sure I do," the skipper replied, but cautioned, "This is a long series, and the Braves have more than just two pitchers. We didn't hit Spahn very much, did we?" Just enough. Asked about Kramer, who'd thrown only two shutouts during the regular season, was McCarthy surprised? "He won a lot of ballgames this year, so we weren't surprised by his performance. He mixed his hard one and curve all day, and it seemed they were always looking for the wrong pitch. Plus, we made all the plays in the field."

Billy Southworth said, "Johnny and Warren both pitched good enough to win but our batting let us down, though Spahnie probably would like to have the pitch back that he threw to Williams in the eighth! I'm confident that our hitting is going to pick up and we'll give the Red Sox a run for their money at Fenway." What about Kramer? How did he keep the Braves off balance all game? "Sometimes you have a hard time adjusting to a quality pitcher when you haven't seen him throw all season. I remember Jack from his time with the Brownies. When I was managing the Cardinals in '44, he beat us in the third game of the World Series. We were only able to get a couple of unearned runs off of him. Our scouting reports told us that he's had a great season and that he'd be tough to get to. He really rose to the occasion today."

And what did Billy think about needing to win at least a couple at Fenway Park? "At least my guys won't be worn down from a long train ride! The Red Sox are built for their ballpark and are very dangerous at home. Fortunately, unlike other National League clubs, we're familiar with that park since we play there every spring. Its dimensions might even help get our hitters going. The left-field wall will be an inviting target to the boys."

McCarthy downplayed the idea the Sox would have an advantage playing at home. "Nah, both teams are familiar with each other's parks. Everyone thought they had the advantage in the first two games, but it didn't make any difference to us. They haven't got their bats going, and we need to keep them from finding their range. We'll go with Dobson tomorrow. He is well rested, and has pitched big games before. We hope he does as well as he did in '46, of course."

The Braves plan to throw rookie starter Vern Bickford (11–5) against the Red Sox tomorrow afternoon. "I'm sticking with our rotation and going with Bickford," said Billy the Kid. "While he hasn't gotten the headlines that Johnny and Warren have grabbed, Vern's had a heckuva rookie season on the mound for us. He won the pennant clincher against Brooklyn and showed that he can pitch under pressure."

Game Three

The Braves finally broke out their bats in a big way. After scoring just one run in the first two games of the Beantown Series, the Braves scored eight runs and beat the Red Sox with room to spare in Game Three, the first played at Fenway Park.

With the Red Sox starting Joe Dobson (16–10, 3.56 ERA), and back in their home park, they hoped to extend their dominance in the still-young Series. The Braves hoped Vern Bickford could stem the tide that Sain and Spahn had not, losing 5–1 and 2–0 respectively. Bickford (11–5, 3.27) pitched a game consistent with his record and a bit better, a complete game eight-hitter with four walks and four strikeouts. The story was more that neither Dobson, nor Earl Johnson in relief, could hold back the rampaging Braves attack.

Though the big Red Sox right-hander got Tommy Holmes to ground out to Stephens for the first out, Al Dark—as likely a candidate as any for Rookie of the Year when the awards are announced later this year—singled sharply down the right-field line. Stan Spence hustled over and grabbed the ball before it got down into the corner or Dark would have had two bases. When Earl Torgeson singled in front of Spence, though, Dark was on second and Torgy on first. Coming to the plate was the Braves' leading RBI man, Bob Elliott, with 100 regular season runs batted in to his credit. Swinging at the very first pitch he saw, Elliott doubled and drove in his first two runs of the World Series. With two outs, Salkeld singled through the middle but DiMaggio came in so quickly to gather the ball up that Elliott stuck at third. There he stayed while Mike McCormick walked to load the bases, but Eddie Stanky grounded out on a 3–1 count back to Dobson, who took the easy throw to first and no doubt felt relieved the Braves had scored but twice.

Dobson likely felt even better when the Red Sox rallied immediately to re-tie the score at 2–2. DiMaggio dropped a single into center. Pesky struck out but, after fouling off several pitches, Ted Williams hit a long home run into the right-field bleachers to tie it up. Two pitches later,

October 8, 1948 at Fenway Park, Braves 8, Red Sox 3

Boston (N)	210	001	301 – 8	13	0
Boston (A)	200	001	000 – 3	8	0

Boston (N)	AB	R	H	BI
Holmes rf	5	0	2	1
Dark ss	5	1	2	0
Torgeson 1b	3	2	2	1
Elliott,B 3b	4	1	2	3
Rickert lf	5	2	2	1
Salkeld c	2	0	1	0
Masi ph	0	0	0	1
McCormick,M cf	4	0	0	0
Stanky 2b	5	1	1	1
Bickford p	4	1	1	0
Totals	**37**	**8**	**13**	**8**

Boston (A)	AB	R	H	BI
DiMaggio cf	5	1	2	0
Pesky 3b	5	0	0	0
Williams lf	5	1	1	2
Stephens ss	4	1	3	0
Doerr 2b	4	0	1	1
Spence rf	2	0	0	0
Goodman 1b	3	0	0	0
Tebbetts c	3	0	1	0
Wright pr	0	0	0	0
Dobson p	2	0	0	0
Moses ph	1	0	0	0
Johnson p	0	0	0	0
Hughson p	0	0	0	0
Batts ph	1	0	0	0
Totals	**35**	**3**	**8**	**3**

BoN: Masi batted for Salkeld in the 7th; Masi moved to c in the 7th. **BoA:** Moses batted for Dobson in the 6th; Wright ran for Tebbetts in the 9th; Batts batted for Hughson in the 9th. **LOB**—Braves 10, Red Sox 9. **2B**—Holmes, Elliott,B. **3B**—Rickert 2, Stephens 2. **HR**—Williams(2). **SB**-Salkeld(1). K—Elliott,B 2, Salkeld, Bickford, DiMaggio, Pesky, Doerr, Spence. **BB**—Torgeson, Elliott,B, Salkeld, McCormick,M, Masi, Spence 2, Goodman, Tebbetts. **SH**—Bickford. **SF**—Torgeson, Masi. **WP**—Johnson. **GWRBI**—Torgeson.

Boston (N)	INN	H	R	ER	BB	K
Bickford (W 1–0)	9	8	3	3	4	4
Totals	**9**	**8**	**3**	**3**	**4**	**4**
Boston (A)	INN	H	R	ER	BB	K
Dobson (L 0–1)	6	8	4	4	3	2
Johnson	0	2	3	3	1	0
Hughson	3	3	1	1	1	2
Totals	**9**	**13**	**8**	**8**	**5**	**4**

Temperature: 56, Sky: cloudy, Wind: right to left at 15 MPH.

Vern Stephens tripled to right-center but was stranded as Doerr struck out and Goodman grounded out. Spence's walk only meant that the Sox had left two men on. For Williams, it was his second homer in as many days. He was putting the lie to the notion that he couldn't come through in big games.

Bickford himself singled to lead off the Braves second. Holmes hit a hard shot to Goodman at first, but Bickford got back to the bag easily enough. Southworth then signaled a hit-and-run and Dark came through, hitting a shallow ball to right, but far enough down the line that Bickford made it to third. Spence threw in to Doerr, who looked at Bickford and then brought the ball to the mound for a word with Dobson. Torgeson's sacrifice fly to center scored Bickford with ease. Even with just one man on, Dobson seemed to pitch too carefully to Elliott and walked him on four straight pitches. Marv Rickert lined out to Doerr, who only had to move a couple of steps to his right to snare the drive.

The Red Sox went down 1–2–3 in the second and in the third. All the Braves did is see Salkeld walk once, and steal second, but otherwise they were quiet, too, both of their next two times up. The Red Sox walked twice in the bottom of the fourth but when Birdie Tebbetts curiously tried to bunt (despite Dobson being up behind him), it backfired when Bickford fielded it cleanly and threw out the lead runner, Spence, who seemed as surprised as anyone at Tebbetts' move. Perhaps the Sox got their signals crossed.

Dobson was showing signs of settling down and retired the Braves in order in the fifth, for the second inning in a row. The Sox hit the ball hard three times but had nothing to show for it in the bottom of the fifth.

With one out in the sixth, Stanky grounded a seeing-eye single between first and second. Bickford went by the book and laid down a perfect sacrifice, moving Stanky into scoring position. Tommy Holmes made his fourth hit of the Series, and drove in his first run, doubling off Dobson with a deep drive to right field. That was all the Braves did, and they saw their two-run margin shrink back to one as the Red Sox once again matched them with a run when Stephens tripled—his second three-bagger of the game—down into the right-field corner. He scored when Bobby Doerr dropped a single into left. After Goodman flied out, Tebbetts walked. With two men on and Dobson due up, McCarthy had Wally Moses pinch hit but Moses skipped the ball to second base and Stanky just stepped on the bag to retire Tebbetts.

The Braves blew the game open in the top of the seventh. Earl Johnson was on in relief and the tall southpaw couldn't get anyone out. It was Earl against Earl but Johnson walked Torgeson on just five pitches, then threw a wild pitch to Elliott and saw Torgy take second. Elliott singled in front of DiMaggio, who was playing deep and couldn't get to the ball in time to risk a throw to the plate. Torgy scored standing up. Rickert then joined the hit parade with a triple into the triangle in right-center field. It was 6–2, Braves. Southworth sent up Phil Masi to bat in place of Salkeld, and McCarthy countered by bringing in Tex Hughson. Masi hit a high fly to the busy DiMaggio in center and Rickert scored, the run charged to Johnson. Hughson got the next two men.

Stephens singled to lead off the eighth, but the next two batters couldn't move him up a base, and Goodman grounded to Dark at short, who threw to second forcing Stephens at the bag for the third out.

In the top of the ninth, the Braves ran the score to 8–3 when Rickert tripled—almost a carbon copy of the

Bob Elliott's three RBIs helped power the Braves to an 8–3 triumph over the Red Sox.

three-base hit he'd had in the seventh. He scored on a fielder's choice three batters later. Though Tebbetts collected his first hit, singling to lead off the bottom of the ninth, and DiMaggio singled after pinch-hitter Matt Batts had flied out, Pesky hit one back to Rickert and Williams flied out to straightaway right to end the game.

McCarthy didn't seem too concerned with the turn of events. Speaking of his starter, Joe said, "I thought he settled down after the first couple of innings, but we never got out of the hole. Joe's a good pitcher, and he will be back this series." Earl Johnson was another matter: "He couldn't throw strikes today. He walked the big fellow, threw a wild one, almost walked Elliott, then had to start laying the ball in there. I thought we were still in the game when he went in there, but that was a tough inning for us."

Ted Williams was up with two on in the ninth, but even a home run then wouldn't have been enough. Southworth praised Bickford's work: "Except for the homer to Ted in the first, he pitched a decent game, though he was often pitching out of trouble. His slider, curve, and change-up were really working for him today. And he spotted his fastball pretty effectively. The rook pitched like a vet under pressure. He's able to keep throwing his good stuff even when he gets a little tired. We've finally been able to put good pitching and good hitting together in the Series."

It seemed like the Braves were hitting almost everything to right field, including Rickert's two triples. Southworth was asked about Fenway's fabled left-field wall. "While it's a tempting target, the wall can also be a trap for hitters who overcompensate and throw off their batting rhythm. Cooney and I told our guys to stick to their normal batting style—and it paid off."

The Red Sox left nine men on base, but it was the disappointment of the "Earl of Emergency" who couldn't get a Braves batter out in the seventh and was tagged for three runs that broke the game open.

Despite the win, Mike McCormick was down in the dumps with an 0-for-12 Series so far. Southworth scuttled thoughts of bringing in Russell or Conatser. "I think Mike is about due and I want to keep his right-handed bat in the lineup at Fenway Park." The Braves batters left 10 men on base. "Yeah, we did," admitted Billy. "But it's hard to complain about that when eight of my guys crossed home plate. I think that just by getting on base, we put a lot of pressure on their pitchers and the runs followed."

It felt good to get a win under his belt. "It sure does.

Especially getting it in the other fella's ballpark. We really needed this one and the boys came through just as they have all season."

McCarthy shrugged off a final question or two. "I guess the Braves are going to try and make a Series of it?" he was asked. "No one is surprised by that," Marse Joe answered back. "They had a great year, and beating them four times is not going to be easy." Who are you pitching tomorrow, Kinder or Galehouse?" asked a reporter. "I will sleep on that a bit and decide tomorrow. Could be Parnell again, too."

Southworth didn't demur when asked about his starter. Was Voiselle going to get the ball? "Yes. Big Bill is ready to go. He's been a mainstay of our rotation and will allow us to come back with Johnny Sain better rested for the next game. Maybe he has a point to make since he was with them in the minors for a while." Voiselle was a Red Sox prospect from 1938 through 1941.

Milder weather was expected for Game Four, which would either see the Braves even the Series at two games apiece or see the Red Sox take a 3–1 lead.

Game Four

Pounding out a record 11 runs in the bottom of the third inning, the Red Sox blew apart the Braves today to take a 3–1 lead in the all-Boston World Series with a 15–6 win that saw every member of the Sox's starting nine drive in one or more runs. Homers by Johnny Pesky, Dom DiMaggio, and Birdie Tebbetts paced the way, battering three Braves pitchers before the situation stabilized. Ellis Kinder threw a complete game that was no gem, but Old Folks could cruise in comfort once the Sox offense dug him out of a bit of a hole. When it was all over, Braves manager Billy Southworth was still upbeat but the Braves were staring elimination in the face.

It was the Braves who took an early lead. Even though both teams put two men on base in the first inning, neither team scored—though only because Ted Williams was thrown out at home plate after Bobby Doerr's single.

In the top of the second, Bill Salkeld drew a leadoff walk off Kinder and took third when Mike McCormick doubled to left. Eddie Stanky grounded to Vern Stephens at short. Salkeld tried to score, but was thrown out at the plate with a couple of steps to spare. McCormick took third on the throw home. Bill Voiselle grounded out to Pesky at third, who held Salkeld on the bag and had time to force Stanky at second base. With two outs, Tommy Holmes collected his second hit of the young game with a sharp single right up the middle, scoring McCormick. Alvin Dark grounded out to third, Pesky taking the ball on one hop and stepping on the bag to force Voiselle.

Voiselle seemed to settle down in the second. He'd walked both Williams and Stephens in the first, but this

October 9, 1948 at Fenway Park, Red Sox 15, Braves 6

Boston (N)	012	300	000 –	6	12	1
Boston (A)	011	220	00x –	15	18	0

Boston (N)	AB	R	H	BI
Holmes rf	5	1	4	1
Dark ss	5	1	1	0
Torgeson 1b	3	1	0	0
Elliott, B 3b	4	1	1	1
Rickert lf	5	1	3	2
Salkeld c	4	0	0	0
McCormick, M cf	2	1	2	2
Barrett p	0	0	0	0
McCormick, F ph	1	0	1	0
Potter p	1	0	0	0
Stanky 2b	4	0	0	0
Voiselle p	1	0	0	0
Shoun p	0	0	0	0
Conatser cf	3	0	0	0
Totals	**38**	**6**	**12**	**6**

Boston (A)	AB	R	H	BI
DiMaggio cf	5	2	1	2
Pesky 3b	5	2	2	3
Williams lf	4	3	3	1
Stephens ss	4	2	3	1
Doerr 2b	5	1	2	1
Spence rf	4	1	1	2
Goodman 1b	5	1	3	2
Tebbetts c	5	1	1	2
Kinder p	3	2	2	1
Totals	**40**	**15**	**18**	**15**

BoN: Conatser inserted at cf in the 3rd; McCormick, F batted for Barrett in the 5th **E**—Dark. **LOB**—Braves 9, Red Sox 7. **2B**—Dark, McCormick, M, Williams 2, Stephens, Doerr. **3B**—Rickert. **HR**—DiMaggio(1), Pesky(1), Tebbetts(1). **K**—Torgeson, Salkeld, Stanky, Potter, DiMaggio 2, Doerr 2, Tebbetts. **BB**—Torgeson 2, Elliott, B, Salkeld, DiMaggio, Williams, Stephens, Spence, Kinder 2. **GWRBI**—Doerr. **DP**—Braves 1, Red Sox 1.

Boston (N)	INN	H	R	ER	BB	K
Voiselle (L 0–1)	2	5	6	6	4	0
Shoun	2	5	4	4	0	0
Barrett	1	3	3	2	0	2
Potter	4	5	2	2	2	3
Totals	**8**	**18**	**15**	**14**	**6**	**5**

Boston (A)	INN	H	R	ER	BB	K
Kinder (W 1–0)	9	12	6	6	4	4
Totals	**9**	**12**	**6**	**6**	**4**	**4**

Temperature: 62, Sky: clear, Wind: out to center at 7 MPH.

time retired the Sox 1-2-3, each batter hitting an infield grounder.

The Braves gave Bill a bigger lead with two more runs in the top of the third. Earl Torgeson walked to lead off. Marv Rickert hit a one-out single to shallow center field, Torgy having to hold at second. Salkeld's ground ball allowed both baserunners to move into scoring position. Then Mike McCormick banged out his second hit, a single right up the middle, driving in two runs and giving the Braves a solid 3–0 lead.

Then Voiselle collapsed and couldn't get another out. In what proved a classic understatement, Southworth said after it was all over, "Bill was struggling with his control the whole game." The Braves righthander walked both Kinder and DiMaggio, the first two batters of the Red Sox third. Johnny Pesky, whose three home runs during the regular season was his career high, hit a home run into the Red Sox bullpen in right-center field and—just like that—the score was tied. The bases were cleared,

Johnny Pesky reads about his Game Four heroics.

but Williams doubled into left-center field and Stephens punched a Texas Leaguer into left. Ted took third. Doerr doubled for his second hit of the game and this time Ted scored with ease. Southworth had seen enough and waved in the southpaw Hardrock Shoun. The first two batters Shoun faced also reached safely, Stan Spence's single driving in both Stephens and Doerr, and Goodman's single putting runners on first and second with no one out. Eight men in a row had come to the plate and none had made an out. Birdie Tebbetts hit into a 6-4-3 double play, though. The inning might have been over, but Kinder's slow roller eluded Shoun and by the time Stanky grabbed the ball, he had no play. DiMaggio homered, driving in two more. After Pesky singled, Shoun was shown the way to the showers and Red Barrett became the third pitcher of the inning. Mike McCormick looked to have pulled a muscle diving to stop Pesky's single because when Barrett was brought in, Southworth called on Clint Conatser to play center. Williams doubled, driving in Pesky, and Stephens doubled, driving in Williams. Finally, after 11 runs had scored, Doerr struck out on three pitches. The score stood 11–3, Red Sox.

The 11 runs scored were the most scored in a single inning in World Series history, one more than the 10 runs scored by the Athletics in 1929's 10–8 Game Four defeat of the Cubs. Southworth was philosophical: "Mike [McCormick] saved him with a strong throw to the plate to get Williams in the first. He settled down a bit in the second inning but had trouble finding the plate in the third when he began the inning by walking Kinder and DiMaggio. After that, he seemed to abandon his usual motion just trying to get the ball over. You can't afford to do that with the heart of the Red Sox order. Maybe

we've drained all of the hits out of their bats today."

It was pointed out that Shoun and Barrett got tagged, too. "I guess when it rains, it pours. Both of those fellas have gotten us out of jams all season. It's just too bad that they both had off days in the same game."

Joe McCarthy shrugged, "Sometimes a team like ours gets on a role, and no one wants to be the guy that makes the out. We have a lot of great hitters, and they don't let you make any mistakes." Of Pesky poling one out to deep right-center, McCarthy said, "He doesn't hit many, but that one seemed to fire everyone up—things were dull in the dugout before that pitch. He came back to the dugout saying he should hit cleanup tomorrow."

The Braves did the best they could to come back. Kinder was still struggling. Clint Conatser was batting in the nine hole (when Barrett had been brought in, he took Mike McCormick's place in the Braves lineup—despite McCormick being involved in all three Braves runs). He grounded out, Doerr to Billy Goodman. But Tommy Holmes got his third hit of the game, a single close to the line in left. Williams fielded it cleanly and quickly. Alvin Dark doubled between Williams and DiMaggio in left-center. Torgeson struck out but Bob Elliott reached on an infield single to the shortstop and Holmes scored. Then Rickert tripled to the wall in left-center, driving in two more runs. The score stood 11–6.

The Sox struck back quickly. Spence popped out to Stanky, and Goodman only reached first when Dark muffed the ball at short. But after fouling off the first pitch into the third-base seats, Tebbetts got ahold of Barrett's second offering and homered into the netting over the National League scoreboard in left.

The other McCormick, Frank, led off, batting for Barrett—the second McCormick to bat seventh for the Braves in the ballgame. He singled in front of DiMaggio, but Stanky hit into a double play and Conatser grounded out.

And the Red Sox added two more runs, facing Nels Potter, when Billy Goodman's single scored both Williams and Stephens in the bottom of the fifth. It was 15–6.

The scoring was over. Neither team managed another run. Holmes got his fourth hit of the game in the eighth, and Kinder almost drove in his second run on a single in the bottom of the eighth when Goodman was thrown out at home on a string throw from Conatser to Salkeld. Kinder allowed 12 hits and walked four, but held on to get the win.

After the drubbing the Braves gave the Sox in Game Three, McCarthy was asked a softball question: "You've got to feel better today, don't you, Joe?" "Sure do, but we still need one more win. That's a good team over there."

The reporter asked, "Rickert hit his third triple in two

days. And Holmes sure had himself a good day. He's batting over .500 through the first four games. . . . what do you do to stop those guys?"

"I am not sure we stopped them much—we just outscored them. They can hit, we need to try to keep them down tomorrow."

Southworth was asked about Rickert, too, asked what he was eating for breakfast. He'd only hit four triples in his whole career. Now he'd hit three in back-to-back World Series games. "I'm gonna ask him and make sure that all the guys have it before tomorrow's game," joked Southworth, but then added, "I'm not as surprised as you about the three-baggers. At Milwaukee this season, he had 13 of 'em before we brought him up and he and Waitkus had those back-to-back inside the park homers with the Cubs in '46. 'Twitch' seems to have a good Fenway Park swing that tends to put the ball into those nooks and crannies of Mr. Yawkey's ballpark."

Did he feel the Braves still had a shot when Rickert made it 11–6 in the fourth? "While it's hard to come back from that deep of a hole, my guys weren't ready to throw in the towel." Of Holmes, now batting over .500, the manager added, "He's having a heckuva Series! I'm sure that all of his pals in the Jury Box will give him a hearty 'welcome back' in Game Six." Southworth was confident that Johnny Sain could salvage the Series for the Braves and bring it back to Braves Field. "Johnny's delivered for us in critical situations all season. He'll keep us in the game. We've just got to get some runs across the plate for him."

McCarthy was proud of the work Stephens had done, 3-for-4 on the day and now batting .467 in the Series. "Junior is one of the best hitters in this game. This doesn't surprise me at all." He admitted that he'd left Kinder in a long time, throwing 139 pitches. "I almost took him out in the fourth, but he settled down. Ellis can throw more pitches than that." After a chuckle, he added a postscript: "We might need him again tomorrow."

What about Sain, the scribes asked, "You think you can beat Johnny Sain twice in one week?" "We're going to try."

"You think you can win yourself another World Series tomorrow?"

"Talk to the players, a lot of these guys out there have never won one. They deserve it. You wouldn't be here talking to me if it wasn't for those guys."

McCarthy was expected to start Mel Parnell, gunning for his second win, while the Braves would start Sain, hoping to even his record at 1–1 and send the Series back to the Wigwam.

Game Five

October 10, 1948 at Fenway Park, Red Sox 3, Braves 1

Boston (N)	000 001 000	–	1	7	0	
Boston (A)	300 000 00x	–	3	7	0	

Boston (N)	AB	R	H	BI
Holmes rf	4	1	3	0
Dark ss	4	0	0	0
McCormick,M lf	4	0	1	1
Elliott,B 3b	3	0	1	0
McCormick,F 1b	4	0	1	0
Conatser cf	4	0	1	0
Masi c	4	0	0	0
Sisti 2b	3	0	0	0
Sain p	2	0	0	0
Ryan ph	1	0	0	0
Shoun p	0	0	0	0
Totals	33	1	7	1

Boston (A)	AB	R	H	B
DiMaggio cf	4	1	1	0
Pesky 3b	4	0	0	0
Williams lf	4	1	1	0
Stephens ss	3	0	1	0
Doerr 2b	3	1	2	3
Spence rf	3	0	1	0
Goodman 1b	3	0	0	0
Tebbetts c	3	0	0	0
Parnell p	3	0	1	0
Totals	30	3	7	3

BoN: Ryan batted for Sain in the 7th. **LOB**—Braves 6, Red Sox 3. **2B**—Holmes, Stephens, Parnell. **HR**—Doerr(2). **K**—Ryan, Williams, Spence 2, Goodman. **BB**—Elliott,B. **GWRBI**—Doerr. **DP**—Braves 1, Red Sox 1.

Boston (N)	INN	H	R	ER	BB	K
Sain (L 0–2)	6	7	3	3	0	3
Shoun	2	0	0	0	0	1
Totals	8	7	3	3	0	4

Boston (A)	INN	H	R	ER	BB	K
Parnell (W 2–0)	9	7	1	1	1	1
Totals	9	7	1	1	1	1

Temperature: 60, Sky: clear, Wind: in from center at 18 MPH.

Before the game, Joe McCarthy had only a few words for the reporters: "We have to win one more, and I hope we get it today. It's a good day for a ballgame, don't you think?" Billy Southworth of the Braves was optimistic. "The boys are in high spirits and are looking forward to Game Five. We've been able to come back before, after having been written off."

The fifth batter in the bottom of the first gave the Red Sox all the runs they needed to win Game Five and the World Series, as Mel Parnell held the Braves at bay for nine innings, allowing just seven hits and one run. Bobby Doerr's three-run homer scored Dom DiMaggio and Ted Williams in the 3–1 win. The hopes of Braves fans had been on Johnny Sain, who'd led the National League in wins with 24 and compiled an excellent 24–15 record with a strong 2.60 ERA. Having lost Game One, even Red Sox fans confessed they didn't expect to beat Sain twice even with their own Mel Parnell on the mound.

Parnell gave DiMaggio a bit of a workout in the top of the first, as The Little Professor hauled in three Braves drives for outs—fly balls by Tommy Holmes and Mike McCormick bracketing a line drive right to DiMaggio off Alvin Dark's bat. The stiff wind coming in from center may have kept a ball or two from scraping the wall or going out.

Dominic singled to short to lead off the Red Sox half. Pesky grounded to the shortstop for a 6–3 play. Williams' single up the middle was played well by Conatser, who held DiMag at third, but Doerr rendered that academic with a home run into the wind and into the center-field bleacher seats. "It was a curveball that I'd like to have back," Sain said after the game. "As soon as I released it, I could tell that it wasn't going where I wanted it to. When I saw Bobby connect, I knew it was gonna go a long way." Braves manager Billy Southworth added, "When you get all of the ball like Doerr did, wind doesn't matter that much." Asked if he felt the whole season had really come down to one bad pitch, he denied it. "Nah! You can't say that. Especially since we had eight more innings to recover and Johnny was back in command after a rocky first. Our run production was off for most of the Series and the Red Sox kept their momentum going after beating the Indians in the playoff game."

Bobby Doerr's first-inning homer off Sain set the stage for the Sox to take baseball's first all-Boston World Series in five games.

The Braves singled twice, but stranded both, in the second. Though Marvelous Mel doubled into the right-field corner, his was the only hit off Sain in the second. Stephens doubled in the third, also right down the line in right, and also with two outs. Holmes had doubled in the top of the third. Both pitchers seemed to settle down in the middle inning, though Parnell faltered in the top of the sixth. The left-hander was tagged with the one run on singles by—naturally—Holmes (who hit .571 in the World Series) and Mike McCormick, who drove in Holmes from second. He'd advanced on a ground ball out which Alvin Dark fielded, his only play to Billy Goodman at first. That brought the score to 3–1. With two outs, Frank McCormick reached on an infield single that pushed Mike McCormick to second, but Parnell got Conatser on a routine fly ball lifted to center field.

After Connie Ryan pinch-hit for Sain in the bottom of the sixth. Clyde Shoun took over pitching for the Braves and retired all six Sox he faced. It was too late. Parnell had tightened up and only allowed a single—to Tommy Holmes—in the top of the eighth. He got Dark, Mike

McCormick, and Bob Elliott each to ground out to the right side of the infield. And on just seven pitches in the top of the ninth, he got Frank McCormick to lift an easy fly to center, Conatser to ground out to Goodman unassisted at first, and Phil Masi—hitless in the Series—to swing at the first pitch and fly out to straightaway center. DiMaggio grabbed the ball to end the World Series and Tebbetts ran to the mound and grabbed Parnell in a bear hug, and soon all the Red Sox were hugging each other. They'd won their first World Series in 30 long years.

"It's a credit to the way Parnell has been pitching," Southworth conceded. "Every time we seemed to be on the verge of getting something going, he closed the door."

It was the first world championship for a Boston ballclub since the Red Sox had won it all in 1918—but that was foredestined, given that either the Braves or Red Sox were going to win. It was just a matter of which club would take baseball's ultimate prize.

Offensive honors were shared by many Red Sox. Doerr drove in the most runs, with seven. Williams scored the most, also with seven. And Stephens had the highest average, at .444 (8-for-18, with two doubles and two triples.) The Sox socked out eight home runs in the five games, with Doerr and Williams hitting two apiece and Pesky, DiMaggio, Spence, and Tebbetts each having a homer after their name.

Bob Elliott's four RBIs (he hit .294) were the most among Braves batters; Rickert and Mike McCormick each drove in three. Rickert's three triples stood out, but not one Brave hit a home run. Elliott took five bases on balls as well. The Red Sox had out-homered the Braves 121 to 95 during the regular season. Tommy Holmes led the Braves for average, hitting a lusty .571 (12-for-21) but he couldn't do it all by himself and only scored twice and only drove in a pair. The Braves hit .244 as a team; the Red Sox hit .274. The biggest disappointments were Eddie Stanky, 1-for-14, and Phil Masi, 0-for-6. Clint Conatser was just 1-for-9 and Alvin Dark 4-for-22.

The Braves pitching was better than the Red Sox during the regular season, almost a run better in earned run average, but in the World Series, the only pitchers who fared well were Spahn and Bickford. The Braves ERA for the Series was 5.65 compared to the 3.20 recorded by Red Sox pitchers.

Asked to sum up after the Series, Southworth was asked a few questions by reporters.

Is there one player that you think really stood out on your team?

"What more could I have asked of 'Kelly?' Bickford impressed me with his poise and confidence, especially for a rookie. Spahn and Sain pitched well enough to win but just didn't get the breaks. To their credit, none of the boys threw in the towel."

What was your biggest disappointment here?

"The lack of timely hitting. We weren't able to get past their starters to test their bullpen."

If you'd faced Cleveland instead of the Red Sox, you think you would have had a better shot?

"I dunno. We might have been more evenly matched given the similarities in the size of our ballparks. There would have been more room to recover from mistakes. I know there was some talk about how the World Series shares would benefit from the huge capacity of Municipal Stadium."

How do feel about your club's chances for next year?

"We have the ability to come back but you also need a lot of luck. We'll have a solid club and Jeff and Eddie should be over their injuries. The loss of Heath took a big bat out of our lineup. You remember how he battled Ted for the home run crown in '47. Stanky wasn't at full strength after coming back from his injury. I'm confident that our ownership will continue to look to strengthen the team during the off season. I'm hoping that Boston fans get to enjoy a rematch in '49!"

Red Sox manager McCarthy was much more terse.

Who do you feel was the star of the Series for the Red Sox?

"They are all stars right now. Parnell was great, but we got some great hitting—Ted, Junior, Bobby. All of them."

Now you've won a World Series for the Red Sox and for the Yankees. How does that make you feel, Joe?

"I think I have had some awful good players on my side. I feel fortunate and proud to be managing these guys."

How do feel about your ballclub's chances for next year?

"It's too soon for that kind of talk. It was an awful tough race this year, and I expect the same next year. We'll put up a good fight, you can bet."

Contributors

Bill Akin is professor emeritus of history at Ursinus College, Collegeville, PA. He wrote *West Virginia Baseball: A History*. His earliest baseball memory is rooting for the Red Sox in the 1946 World Series. For the next 58 years he never gave up hope.

Ron Anderson grew up in the Boston area and is a consummate Red Sox and baseball fan. Ron attributes his love for the game to his father who played ball in the Boston City Park League, and who got him started in a life of baseball. He was a contributing writer to SABR biographies: *'75: The Red Sox Team That Saved Baseball*, *The 1967 Impossible Dream Red Sox: Pandemonium on the Field*, and *When Boston Still Had the Babe: The 1918 World Series Champion Red Sox*. He is currently working on a biography of former Red Sox standout George Scott. He is now retired and lives with his wife, Gail, in Plymouth, MA.

Sheldon Appleton has been hooked on baseball since he saw his first game in 1939. He retired in 2005 as Distinguished Professor of Political Science at Oakland University in Michigan. He's been an SABR member for over 20 years and has written biographies for *American National Biography* and the *Biographical Dictionary of American Sports*.

Mark Armour grew up in Connecticut, but now lives and writes in Oregon's Willamette Valley. The director of SABR's Biography Project, co-author of *Paths to Glory*, and editor of *Rain Check*, Mark is currently writing a book on the life of Joe Cronin. He is supported in all he does by Jane, Maya, and Drew.

Eric Aron has been a SABR member since 2002. He holds a B.A. in history from Clark University in Worcester and a M.A. in history from Northeastern in Boston. His previous bios were on Astros manager Cecil Cooper and '67 Sox skipper Dick Williams, who was elected to the National Baseball Hall of Fame class of 2008. Eric can be reached at e_aron@yahoo.com.

Ray Birch lives in North Kingstown, RI. He is a retired school teacher where he co-taught a class on baseball to students. He has been a member of SABR since 2000. He wrote the article about Rick Burleson for the SABR book on the 1975 Red Sox, the article on Everett Scott for the SABR book on the 1918 Red Sox, and the articles about George Thomas and Joe Foy for the SABR book on the 1967 Red Sox. Ray is a life-long Red Sox fan, who attended his first game at Fenway Park in 1961, just missing seeing the great Ted Williams play. He also was at the game at Fenway Park in July, 1967 against the Orioles where the Red Sox turned a triple play, and Game Seven of the 1975 World Series, thanks to Carlton Fisk's homer in Game Six.

Mort Bloomberg has enjoyed a lifelong love affair with baseball and especially any person, place, or thing connected with the Boston Braves. Their move to Milwaukee on March 18, 1953 was like a death in his family. Born and raised on Boston's North Shore, he is a co-founder of the Boston Braves Historical Association, a SABR member since 1976, and years ago earned a BA from Clark and a PhD in psychology from SUNY at Buffalo. Over the past 15 years, he has had a variety of jobs in pro baseball. Now living in Tempe, AZ where he is an adviser to ballplayers, the "ham" in him awakens each spring training when he becomes one of the Milwaukee Brewers Racing Sausages.

Andrew Blume has long been obsessed with all things baseball and Red Sox. A SABR member since 2001 along with his dad Murray and a contributing author to *'75: The Red Sox Team That Saved Baseball* and *The 1967 Impossible Dream Red Sox: Pandemonium on the Field*, he lives in Natick, MA with his wife Nancy, daughters Emily, and Abigail, and felines Velvet, Holly, and Brady. In his spare time, he practices law.

Bob Brady grew up in Dorchester, MA as a fan of the Boston Braves and the Boston Red Sox and remains true to both to this day. He is the long-standing newsletter editor of the Boston Braves Historical Association. Through that group, Bob has been privileged to meet several of the '48 Braves profiled in this book and once spent a memorable day at Fenway Park reminiscing with Ed Wright, the subject of his player biography submission. Bob has been a SABR member since 1991.

Ryan Brodeur grew up a Red Sox fan in the hotly-contested Connecticut River Valley. He holds a B.A. in French Language and Literature from Trinity College, Hartford and has been teaching high school French since 2005. Ryan moonlights as a baseball writer on his blog, TheHotCorner.org, and has been a SABR member since 2006. He currently lives in Newton, MA with his wife, Kathleen DiSanto.

John Contois grew up in the Boston area and currently lives in Portland, ME, where he serves as Laboratory Director for a non-profit medical research organization. He is a life-long Red Sox fan, long-time SABR member, and proud father of Stephanie and Samantha.

Jon Daly is a life-long resident of the Greater Hartford area. His father introduced him to baseball and the Red Sox during the 1975 season. Because he was a young lad at the time, he expected the Red Sox to play in the World Series every year. Boy, was he wrong! In his free time, he works in the financial service industry. Jon has been a SABR member since 2001.

Sid Davis spent his early teens watching the Braves and Red Sox play Sunday doubleheaders. A lifelong fan of the game he remembers standing next to Earl Torgeson when he picked up a new Studebaker at Dorchester's Seavey Motors. A member of SABR, 2008 will mark the 50th anniversary of his graduation from Boston University where he majored in journalism. He is the Group Publisher of Symphony Publishing LLC, a multi-media company with several trade magazines and websites.

Pat Doyle grew up in Rochester, NY as a fan of the local Red Wings. Learning early that breaking pitches were never meant to be hit, he turned his love of the game to the statistical side and eventually became the author of The Professional Baseball Player Database. He, his wife, and two of their three grown children live in Kansas, and he spends his semi-retirement researching minor league players and teaching Scripture for the Archdiocese of Kansas City.

Alex Edelman is a native of Brookline, MA and has been working in sports since the age of 12. He researched and wrote his contributions for this book from Israel where he was attending Yeshivat Shvilei Hatorah in Jerusalem. He is a recent graduate of Maimonides School. Alex's essay, "Paradise Found," about the 2004 American League Championship Series, won a Will McDonough Writing Award from the New England Sports Museum and the *Boston Globe*, and his biography of Billy Rohr for the book *The 1967 Impossible Dream Red Sox: "Pandemonium on the Field"* was the recipient of a Jack Kavanaugh Award from the Society for American Baseball Research.

A retired English professor, **Jan Finkel** lives with his wife on Deep Creek Lake in western Maryland. Besides great books and baseball, which he sometimes confuses, he enjoys country music and jazz. His son and daughter and their spouses are wonderful people—and, coincidentally, live in Nashville and New Orleans.

John Fuqua has been a National League and St. Louis Cardinal fan all of his life. A late bloomer, he has seen the light and adopted the Red Sox as his American League team. On his last visit to Boston, John and his son Ben visited Fenway Park and Cooperstown in the same week. A SABR member since 2006. John and his wife Beth live in Franklin, TN along with his three children, Ben, Rachel, and Rebecca.

Jim Gormley--SABR member with A.B. and MA from Boston College. He is a retired high school principal, teacher and coach. A lifelong Red Sox fan, he saw his first game with his father in 1949 and watched Joe DiMaggio homer to beat the Sox. He has shared season tickets in the bleachers for the past 20 years.

Gene Gumbs lives in Middletown, CT and is a lifelong Red Sox fan. He is an assistant athletic director at Sacred Heart University and works for Major League Baseball as a stringer at Fenway Park in Boston during the season. He is a 1982 graduate of Franklin Pierce University in New Hampshire where he earned a degree in english. He is the proud father of two daughters, Emily and Hannah.

Tom Harkins is a retired school librarian who lives in Needham, MA. His first major league game was on his seventh birthday in 1952, the Braves played a doubleheader against the Cardinals. He has no personal memories of the 1948 seasons but 1948 was a momentous year for him as he was adopted from NYC into a Boston baseball family. 1948 was also momentous for him because his wife Barbara was born that year.

Jay Hurd is the Preservation Review Librarian for Widener Library, Harvard University. A graduate of the Simmons College Library and Information Science program, he studies baseball history and baseball literature for children and young adults. Jay is a resident of Medford, MA, a long time Red Sox fan, and a member of SABR.

Jim Kaplan grew up in Cambridge and saw his first major-league game at Braves Field. The Dodgers beat the Braves on a cold, dark afternoon, making it a generally miserable experience, but he did get to see Jackie Robinson. Kaplan later covered baseball for *Sports Illustrated* and wrote a biography of Lefty Grove for SABR. In addition to writing baseball books, he turns out a weekly bridge column and a weekly newsletter, Bridge in the 21st Century. Kaplan and his wife Brooks Robards divide their time between Northampton, MA, and Martha's Vineyard.

David Laurila is a lifelong Red Sox fan who grew up in Michigan's Upper Peninsula and now writes about baseball from his home in Cambridge, MA. He authors the weekly Prospectus Q&A column at Baseball Prospectus and is a frequent contributor to *Baseball America* and *Red Sox Magazine*. His first book, *Interviews from Red Sox Nation*, was published by Maple Street Press in 2006.

A member of the Society of American Baseball Research, **Diane MacLennan** is a truly passionate baseball fan, Her fascination with the sport goes beyond obsession. Instead of planning a wedding, she and her husband cancelled the ceremony and spent the money they saved on Baltimore Orioles season tickets. They still enjoy season tickets to Baltimore to see their other favorite team (thank you, Brian Roberts!), as well as spending a lot of time at Fenway Park. Di has a B.M. from Berklee College of Music, an M.S from Boston University, and a Certificate in Paralegal Studies from Boston University. She is currently working at 38 Studios, a media and entertainment company founded in 2006 by Curt Schilling—yes, the pitcher.

Les Masterson is a managing editor at HCPro, a healthcare communications company in Marblehead, MA, where he covers the managed care market. Before covering the healthcare beat, he was an award-winning journalist at *The Arlington Advocate* in Arlington, MA. He lives in Malden, MA, with his wife, Danielle, and black Lab, Jake.

John McMurray is Chair of the Society for American Baseball Research's Deadball Era Committee. Previously, he had overseen the SABR subcommittee that presents the Ritter Award, which is given to the best book on Deadball Era baseball written annually. John has interviewed many current and former major leaguers for profiles published in *Baseball Digest*, including former Red Sox first baseman George Scott.

John Morrison, a lifelong baseball fan, grew up in Minnesota routing for the Twins at Met Stadium, and adopted the Red Sox as his second home team upon settling in Acton, MA. He is a regular of bleacher section 41 with his wife Carolyn and children Megan, Matthew, and Katie. John holds degrees from Middlebury College and Dartmouth and is proud of his seven-game postseason winning streak from the championship seasons of 1991, 2004, and 2007 thanks to Kirby, Black Jack, Big Papi, Bellhorn, Manny, and Beckett.

Dan Mullen is an editor for ESPN MVP/Mobile. A second generation SABR member and baseball fan, Dan credits his father for teaching him to appreciate baseball beginning with taking him to his first Major League Baseball game when he was just three months old. Dan's work has appeared in *The Sporting News*, the *Denver Post*, and Rivals.com among other places.

Bill Nowlin is author or editor of 25 books, mostly on his hometown Boston Red Sox, and national Vice President of the Society for American Baseball Research. A co-founder of Rounder Records of Massachusetts, he's traveled to more than 100 countries, but says there's no place like Fenway Park.

Paul A. Pereira is a lifelong Red Sox fan and season ticket holder dating back to the Kevin Millar era. Paul works in professional services and, when he is not busy providing analytic consulting to his clients, he reads books on baseball while attending as many home and away games as possible. He has been a member of SABR since 2002 and this represents his first contributing effort in support of a SABR publication. Paul grew up in Cumberland, RI and has made Boston his home since 1994.

Mike Richard is a lifetime Red Sox fan who was not born when the Braves played in Boston. He is a high school guidance counselor at Gardner (MA) High School and also writes a weekly sports column for The Gardner News. He has authored the books *Glory To Gardner: 100 Years of Football in the Chair City* and *Super Saturdays: The Complete History of the Massachusetts High School Super Bowl 1972–2002*, and is co-authoring a book on *Baseball Markers, Monuments, Gravestones and Ballparks of New England* that is due out this spring. He lives in Gardner with his wife Peggy and they are the parents of a son Casey and daughter Lindsey.

Paul Rogers is president of the Hall-Ruggles (Dallas-Ft. Worth) SABR Chapter and the co-author of three baseball books, including *The Whiz Kids and the 1950 Pennant* (1996), written with boyhood hero Robin Roberts, and *Memories of a Ballplayer: Bill Werber and Baseball in the 1930s* (2001), with Bill Werber. The 1948 baseball season was his first on the planet since he was born in April of that year. His real job is as a law professor at Southern Methodist University in Dallas, Texas, where he served as dean of the law school for nine years.

The founder of SABR's Deadball Era Committee and Gardner-Waterman (Vermont) Chapter, **Tom Simon** is a lawyer who lives with his wife, Carolyn, four-year-old son, Nolan, one-year-old daughter, Calista, and 15-year-old dog, Kensey, just up the hill from Birdie Tebbetts' birthplace in Burlington, VT. In his limited spare time, he leads historical walking tours of Burlington and works on a book he is writing about the O'Connell-Dolan Scandal.

Doug Skipper is a marketing research, customer satisfaction, and public opinion consultant from Apple Valley, MN, who reads and writes about baseball, and engages in father-daughter dancing. A SABR member since 1982, he researched and wrote four biographies for *Deadball Stars of the American League*, contributed to *The 1967 Impossible Dream Red Sox: Pandemonium on the Field*, and to *When Boston Still Had The Babe*. Doug and his wife Kathy have two daughters, MacKenzie and Shannon. He has followed the Red Sox from afar since his grandfather escorted him and his two brothers to see their first major league game, on Thursday, August 3, 1967 at Fenway Park (a 5–3 win).

Glenn Stout's most recent book is *The Cubs: The Complete Story of Chicago Cubs Baseball*. A native of Ohio, he grew up watching the Pittsburgh Pirates Triple-A farm team, the Columbus Jets in the International League. After graduating from Bard College in 1981 he moved to Boston and for the next 12 years lived within walking distance of Fenway Park. A full-time writer since 1993, Stout lives with his family in Alburgh, VT.

Dick Thompson is the author of numerous articles on baseball history as well as one book, *The Ferrell Brothers of Baseball* (McFarland 2005). He lived in Dartmouth, Massachusetts, and joined SABR in 1979. He was the recipient of the McFarland-SABR Research Award in 2000 and 2001, and the 2004 winner of SABR's highest honor, the Bob Davids Award. At the time of his unexpected death early in 2008, he was working on a biography of Cannonball Bill Jackman, the legendary African-American pitcher who barnstormed throughout New England for nearly 30 years.

Glen Vasey grew up rooting for the incredible Oriole teams of the sixties through the early eighties, became fascinated with the history and personalities in the game, and is currently working on an alternative history novel that examines a different road to the integration of baseball than the one Robinson and Rickey took. By day he is a mild mannered parking meter technician and town friendly guy in Lancaster, PA.

John Vorperian spent his boyhood summers at Fenway Park and Plum Island, MA. The Red Sox Nation member hosts *Beyond the Game*, a sports history show on White Plains Cable TV. When not teaching Sports Law at Concordia College (NY) or Sports Marketing at Manhattanville College, John daydreams about surfcasting with Ted Williams, Yaz, Reggie Smith, and Elston Howard.

Dave Williams was caught in baseball's web as a six year old watching the Amazin' Mets of 1969 magical ride to a World Series title. He has been entangled ever since. He has contributed to *'75: The Red Sox Team That Saved Baseball* with a bio of Tim McCarver and to *The 1967 Impossible Dream Red Sox: Pandemonium on the Field* with a Mike Ryan biography. He resides in Glastonbury, CT with his wife Julia and daughter Clara.

Although **Saul Wisnia** was born in Boston 15 years after the Braves last called it home, he is a passionate fan and historian of both the city's major league clubs. He is a founding member of the Boston Braves Historical Association and emcees (with Joe Morgan) each BBHA fall reunion. As senior publications editor at Dana-Farber Cancer Institute, he chronicles the important role the Red Sox play in the Institute's Jimmy Fund charitable arm, which the Braves helped start in 1948. A former sports correspondent for the *Washington Post*, Wisnia has authored and contributed to numerous books on baseball and other subjects, and his look at Boston's years as a two-team town—*From Yawkey to Milwaukee* (written with Richard Johnson)—will be published by Rounder Books in 2009. Although he now lives in Newton with his wife Michelle, son Jason, and daughter Rachel, he previously resided on streets leading directly to Braves Field and Fenway Park.